COMMERCIAL LAW AND PRACTICE

COMMERCIAL LAW AND PRACTICE

Michael Tookey LLB, Barrister

CLP

Published by

College of Law Publishing,
Braboeuf Manor, Portsmouth Road, St Catherines, Guildford GU3 1HA

British Library Cataloguing-in-Publication Data

A catalogue record for this book is available from the British Library.

ISBN 978 1 905391 84 4

Typeset by Style Photosetting Ltd, Mayfield, East Sussex

Printed in Great Britain by Ashford Colour Press Ltd, Gosport, Hampshire

Preface

All parts of the work are being substantially rewritten, on an ongoing basis, to reflect the changes in modern vocational training practice. It is hoped that the level of detail and analysis of the cases and statutes will be suited to both vocational study and to the early years of practice. Clearly, with such a diverse range of discrete topics, many limitations are imposed upon such a work, but it is intended that the reader should be assisted in gaining a firm grasp of the general principles and a flavour of the current state of legislation and case law.

MICHAEL TOOKEY
The College of Law

Further Study

The following books may be of interest to readers wishing to pursue a particular topic further. In addition, there are some references to Internet sources in the text, as well as the obvious ones such as the European Commission sites and the UK legislation ones.

Sale of Goods

Atiyah, Adams and MacQueen, *The Sale of Goods* (11th edn, Longman, 2005)

Ellinger, *Benjamin's Sale of Goods* (7th edn, Sweet & Maxwell, 2006)

Encyclopedia of Forms and Precedents (5th edn, Butterworths), vol 34 on Sale of Goods (2002 Reissue)

Rosenberg, *Practical Commercial Precedents* (Sweet & Maxwell), section on Sale of Goods: Precedent L1.

(The above works have useful sections on exclusion of liability.)

Drafting

Beale, *Chitty on Contracts* (30th edn, Sweet & Maxwell, 2009)

Christou, *Drafting Commercial Agreements* (4th edn, Sweet & Maxwell, 2009)

Christou, *Boilerplate: Practical Clauses* (4th edn, Sweet & Maxwell, 2005)

Marketing Agreements

Practical Commercial Precedents and the *Encyclopedia of Forms and Precedents* have useful sections on agency distribution and other types of marketing agreement. See also:

Christou, *International Agency, Distribution and Licensing Agreements* (Longmans, 2003)

Goyder, *EU Distribution Law* (4th edn, Hart Publishing, 2005)

Commercial Law

Bradgate, *Commercial Law* (3rd edn, Butterworths, 2000)

Byles on Bills of Exchange and Cheques (28th edn, Sweet & Maxwell, 2007)

Christou, *Drafting Commercial Agreements* (4th edn, Sweet & Maxwell, 2009)

Goode, *Commercial Law* (3rd edn, Butterworths, 2004)

International Chambers of Commerce, *Incoterms 2000* (ICC Publishing, 2000)

Jack, Malek and Quest, *Documentary Credits* (3rd edn, Butterworths, 2001)

Murray, *Schmitthoff's Export Trade* (11th edn, Sweet & Maxwell, 2007)

Sealey and Hooly, *Commercial Law* (4th edn, Butterworths, 2008)

Wilson, *Carriage of Goods by Sea* (6th edn, Pearson Longman, 2008)

Competition Law

Lindrup, *Butterworths Competition Law Handbook* (15th edn, Butterworths, 2009)

Whish, *Competition Law* (6th edn, Butterworths, 2008)

Goyder, *EC Competition Law* (4th edn, Oxford University Press, 2003)

Bellamy and Child, *EC Law of Competition* (6th edn, Sweet & Maxwell, 2009)

A number of works have been written specifically on the Competition Act 1998, including:

Coleman and Grenfell, *The Competition Act 1998: Law and Practice* (Oxford University Press, 1999)

Frazer and Hornsby, *The Competition Act 1998: A Practical Guide* (Jordans, 1999)

Intellectual Property

Cornish and Llewelyn, *Intellectual Property* (6th edn, Sweet & Maxwell, 2007)

CIPA Guide to the Patents Acts (Sweet & Maxwell, 1996)

Phillips and Firth, *Introduction to Intellectual Property Law* (4th edn, Butterworths, 2001)

(For works which consider the relationship of competition law and intellectual property, in particular in relation to licensing, see the list under 'Marketing Agreements' above.)

Consumer Credit

Goode, *Consumer Credit Law and Practice* (3rd edn, Butterworths, 2008)

Guest and Lloyd, *Encyclopaedia of Consumer Credit Law* (Sweet & Maxwell, 2008)

Information Technology

Reed and Angel, *Computer Law* (5th edn, Oxford University Press, 2003)

Susskind, *Transforming the Law* (Oxford University Press, 2000)

Todd, *E-Commerce Law* (Cavendish Publishing, 2005)

Contents

PREFACE			v
FURTHER STUDY			vii
TABLE OF CASES			xv
TABLE OF STATUTES			xxv
TABLE OF STATUTORY INSTRUMENTS			xxxi
TABLE OF EUROPEAN AND INTERNATIONAL LEGISLATION			xxxiii
TABLE OF ABBREVIATIONS			xxxv
Part I	**COMMERCIAL AGREEMENTS**		**1**
Chapter 1	INTRODUCTION TO COMMERCIAL CONTRACTS		3
	1.1	Introduction	3
	1.2	The principles of commercial law	3
	1.3	Drafting and content of a commercial contract	4
	1.4	Introduction to boiler-plate clauses	5
	1.5	Limitation of liability in contracts	8
Chapter 2	THE SALE OF GOODS		9
	2.1	Introduction	9
	2.2	Formation of the contract	9
	2.3	Basics of the law of contract	10
	2.4	Relevant legislation	12
	2.5	What are 'goods'?	13
	2.6	What is 'sale of goods'?	13
	2.7	The price	13
	2.8	Delivery	14
	2.9	Duties of the seller	16
	2.10	Duties of the buyer	20
	2.11	Rights of the seller	22
	2.12	Rights of the buyer	24
	2.13	Effects of a sale of goods contract	26
	2.14	Introduction to retention of title	28
	2.15	Drafting a retention of title clause: a basic checklist	29
	2.16	Retention of title clauses and the creation of charges	32
	2.17	'Backing up' a retention of title clause	32
	2.18	Unfair terms in consumer contracts	34
	2.19	Sale of goods to consumers	34
Chapter 3	EFFECTIVE DRAFTING OF EXCLUSION CLAUSES		35
	3.1	Introduction	35
	3.2	Basic rules for successful drafting of exclusion clauses	35
	3.3	Preparing to draft	36
	3.4	Three stages for effectiveness	37
	3.5	Incorporation	38
	3.6	Construction	39
	3.7	The Unfair Contract Terms Act 1977	40
	3.8	The Unfair Terms in Consumer Contracts Regulations 1999	42

	3.9	Drafting for reasonableness: general principles	43
	3.10	Drafting for reasonableness: relevant factors	44
	3.11	Drafting for severance	50
	3.12	Drafting to litigate or to negotiate?	50
	3.13	Trying to exclude everything	51
	3.14	Drafting specific clauses in a commercial contract	51
Chapter 4	OTHER CONTRACTS UNDER WHICH GOODS PASS		57
	4.1	Introduction	57
	4.2	Types of contract under which goods may pass (other than straightforward sale of goods contracts)	57
	4.3	The provision of services	59
	4.4	Hire purchase and conditional sale	63
	4.5	Leases of goods	67
	4.6	Financing the sale of goods	70
Chapter 5	MARKETING AGREEMENTS		73
	5.1	Introduction	73
	5.2	Agency agreements	74
	5.3	Drafting an agency agreement	75
	5.4	Distribution agreements	88
	5.5	Drafting a distribution agreement	89
	5.6	Structure of the agreements at a glance	94
	5.7	Other types of marketing agreement	94
	5.8	Conclusion	95
Chapter 6	CONSUMER CREDIT ACT 1974		97
	6.1	Introduction	97
	6.2	The Consumer Credit Act 1974 and commercial work	97
	6.3	An outline guide to the CCA 1974	98
	6.4	Consumer credit agreements	99
	6.5	Common forms of consumer credit agreements	103
	6.6	Terminology and examples	104
	6.7	Further reading	106
PART I SUMMARY – COMMERCIAL AGREEMENTS			107
Part II	**INTERNATIONAL SALE AGREEMENTS**		**109**
Chapter 7	INTRODUCTION TO INTERNATIONAL SALE AGREEMENTS		111
Chapter 8	CHOICE OF JURISDICTION AND LAW		113
	8.1	Introduction	113
	8.2	Brussels II – Regulation 44/2001	113
	8.3	Rome Convention	116
	8.4	Rome I – Regulation 593/2008	118
Chapter 9	INTERNATIONAL SALE OF GOODS		121
	9.1	Introduction	121
	9.2	Matters for particular consideration in international sales	124
	9.3	The documents involved	125
	9.4	Multimodal and container transport	128
	9.5	Arranging transportation of the goods – Incoterms	128
	9.6	Developments in international trade	135
Chapter 10	FINANCING AND SECURITY ARRANGEMENTS IN INTERNATIONAL SALE OF GOODS		137
	10.1	Introduction	137
	10.2	Collection arrangements and payment methods	138

	10.3	Negotiable instruments	140
	10.4	Bills of exchange	141
	10.5	Documentary credits ('letters of credit')	144
	10.6	Functions, responsibilities and liabilities of banks in international sales	151
PART II SUMMARY – INTERNATIONAL SALE AGREEMENTS			155
Part III	**INTELLECTUAL PROPERTY**		**159**
Chapter 11	INTRODUCTION TO INTELLECTUAL PROPERTY		161
	11.1	What is intellectual property?	161
	11.2	Types of intellectual property	162
	11.3	Summary of IP rights	165
Chapter 12	PASSING OFF		167
	12.1	Introduction	167
	12.2	The three elements of passing off	168
	12.3	Defences to passing off	172
	12.4	Remedies for passing off	172
	12.5	International aspects	172
Chapter 13	TRADE MARKS		173
	13.1	Functions and purposes of trade marks	173
	13.2	Advantages and consequences of registration	173
	13.3	The registration system, its problems and recent changes	174
	13.4	Can the trade mark meet the definition within s 1(1) of the TMA 1994?	175
	13.5	Absolute grounds for refusal: s 3	176
	13.6	Evidence of use to overcome absolute grounds (the proviso to s 3(1))	182
	13.7	Relative grounds for refusing an application (s 5)	183
	13.8	Protecting the mark, once registered	187
	13.9	Infringement of a registered trade mark	188
	13.10	'Well-known' foreign trade marks (s 56)	193
	13.11	Defences to infringement (ss 11, 12, 48)	193
	13.12	Remedies for infringement (ss 14–19)	194
	13.13	International trade marks	194
	13.14	Classes used in the Register of Trade Marks (Trade Mark Rules 2000, Sch 4)	195
Chapter 14	COPYRIGHT		203
	14.1	What is copyright? An introduction	203
	14.2	Literary, dramatic, musical and artistic (LDMA) works	204
	14.3	Entrepreneurial copyrights	211
	14.4	Infringement of copyright	214
	14.5	Remedies	221
	14.6	Databases	221
	14.7	Copyright and information technology	222
	14.8	Public performances – the collecting societies	223
	14.9	Developments in the law of copyright	224
	14.10	International copyright protection	224
Chapter 15	THE DATABASE RIGHT		227
	15.1	Background and introduction	227
	15.2	Definition of a database	227
	15.3	Qualifications for the database right	228
	15.4	Ownership of the database right	228
	15.5	Duration of database protection	228
	15.6	Infringement of the database right	228
	15.7	Exceptions from the database right	229
	15.8	Application of the database right	229

Chapter 16	DESIGN RIGHTS		231
	16.1	Introduction to design protection	231
	16.2	Registered design right	234
	16.3	Unregistered design right	239
	16.4	Semiconductor topography design right	244
	16.5	Registered and unregistered designs	245
Chapter 17	PATENTS		247
	17.1	Introduction	247
	17.2	Obtaining a patent	247
	17.3	Patentability	248
	17.4	The patent specification	254
	17.5	Who is entitled to grant of a patent?	256
	17.6	Infringement	257
	17.7	Infringers	260
	17.8	Defences	260
	17.9	Remedies	261
Chapter 18	BASICS OF THE LAW OF CONFIDENTIAL INFORMATION		263
	18.1	Introduction to the law of confidential information	263
	18.2	The elements of confidentiality	264
	18.3	Remedies and their availability	266
	18.4	A right of privacy and the Human Rights Act 1998?	268
Chapter 19	INFORMATION TECHNOLOGY		271
	19.1	Introduction	271
	19.2	Information technology and intellectual property rights	271
	19.3	Semiconductor chip protection	272
	19.4	Hardware contracts	273
	19.5	Software	277
	19.6	The Internet	283
	19.7	Computer crime	285
	19.8	Data protection	287
	19.9	The database right	287
Chapter 20	E-COMMERCE		291
	20.1	Introduction	291
	20.2	The legal framework	291
	20.3	Formation and proof of contract	292
	20.4	Law and jurisdiction, choices and application	293
	20.5	The application of intellectual property law to e-commerce	294
	20.6	Business to business e-commerce	296
	20.7	Business to consumer e-commerce	296
	20.8	Payment aspects of e-commerce transactions	301
	20.9	Liabilities of ISSPs and others	302
	20.10	Conclusion	303
Chapter 21	DATA PROTECTION AND FREEDOM OF INFORMATION		305
	21.1	Introduction	305
	21.2	Overview and scope of DPA 1998	306
	21.3	The rights of the data subject and other persons under DPA 1998	311
	21.4	The obligations of the data controller and disclosure restrictions	313
	21.5	Exemptions	314
	21.6	Requests from outside the EC	316
	21.7	Enforcement, offences and civil damages	316
	21.8	Conclusion on data protection	317
	21.9	Freedom of information	318

PART III SUMMARY – INTELLECTUAL PROPERTY 325

Part IV COMPETITION LAW 329

Chapter 22 COMPETITION LAW AND COMMERCIAL AGREEMENTS 331
22.1 Introduction 331
22.2 English competition law 333
22.3 EC competition law 336
22.4 Selective distribution 346

Chapter 23 EC LAW AND INTELLECTUAL PROPERTY RIGHTS 347
23.1 Introduction 347
23.2 Attempting to resolve the conflict 348
23.3 Article 81 EC and the exploitation of intellectual property rights 348
23.4 Licensing agreements and competition law 349
23.5 Article 82 EC and intellectual property rights 351
23.6 Articles 28–30 EC and intellectual property rights 352
23.7 Article 28 EC and Articles 81–82 EC: relationship 354
23.8 EC competition law and franchising agreements 354

PART IV SUMMARY – COMPETITION LAW 355

Appendix LEGISLATION 357

Registered Designs Act 1949 357
Patents Act 1977 367
Copyright, Designs and Patents Act 1988 380
Trade Marks Act 1994 404
Competition Act 1998 415
Enterprise Act 2002 418
Commercial Agents (Council Directive) Regulations 1993 420
Copyright and Rights in Databases Regulations 1997 427
Consumer Protection (Distance Selling) Regulations 2000 431
Electronic Commerce (EC Directive) Regulations 2002 440
Privacy and Electronic Communications (EC Directive) Regulations 2003 445
EC Treaty 448

INDEX 449

Table of Cases

Numerics

800 Flowers, Trade Mark Application; 1-800 Flowers Incorporated v Phonenames Ltd [2001] EWCA Civ 721, [2002] FSR 288 192

A

A & M Records v Video Collection [1995] EMLR 25 214
A Fulton Co Ltd v Grant Burnett & Co Ltd [2001] RPC 16 242
A v B (A Company) and Another [2002] EWCA Civ 337, [2002] 2 All ER 545 269
Actavis Ltd v Merck & Co Inc [2008] EWCA Civ 444 249
Adidas-Salomon AG v Fitnessworld Trading Ltd (Case C-408/01) [2004] 1 CMLR 14, [2004] Ch 120 185, 190
Adonis Construction v O'Keefe Soil Remediation [2009] EWHC 2047 (TCC) 10
Aerotel Ltd v Telco Holdings Ltd; Macrossan's Patent Application (No 0314464.9) [2006] EWCA Civ 1371 253
Ailsa Craig Fishing Co Ltd v Malvern Fishing Co Ltd [1983] 1 WLR 964 49
Aktiebolaget Volvo v Heritage (Leicester) Ltd [2000] FSR 253 194
Alticor Inc v Nutrigreen Health Products Ltd (Trade Mark Registry 09/11/07) [2007] WL 4368242 185
Aluminium Industrie Vaassen BV v Romalpa Aluminium [1976] 1 WLR 676 24, 28, 30
American Motor Insurance Co v Cellstar Corporation and Another [2003] EWCA Civ 206 117
Amersham Pharmacia Biotech AB v Amicon Ltd and Others [2001] EWCA Civ 1042, [2001] WL 720281 251
Amiri Flight Authority v BAE Systems plc [2002] EWHC 2481 (Comm) 40, 49
Amos and Wood Ltd v Kaprow (1948) 64 TLR 110 20
Amp Inc v Utilux Pty Ltd [1971] RPC 397 236
Anders & Kern UK Ltd v CGU Insurance plc [2007] EWHC 377 (Comm) 47
Andersen Consulting v CHP Consulting Ltd (ChD, 26 July 1991) 283
Andrabell Ltd (In Liquidation); Airborne Accessories Ltd v Goodman, Re [1984] 3 All ER 407 28
Annabel's (Berkeley Square) Ltd v Schock (t/a Annabel's Escort Agency) [1972] RPC 838 171
Anthony Snookes v Jani King (GB) Ltd [2006] EWHC 289 (QB) 115
Application No 713,406 by Otto Seligmann for the Registration of a Trade Mark, In the matter of (1954) 71 RPC 52 182
Archibald Kenrick & Sons Ltd v Laird Security Hardware Ltd [2006] EWHC 1675 (Ch) 258
Armour v Thyssen Edelstahlwerke AG [1991] 2 AC 339 28, 29
Arsenal Football Club plc v Reed [2001] RPC 922 171
Arsenal Football Club plc v Reed (Case C-206/01) [2002] All ER (EC) 1 189
Arsenal Football Club plc v Reed [2003] EWCA Civ 696 189
Associated Newspapers Group plc v News Group Newspapers Ltd [1986] RPC 515 218
Associated Newspapers Limited and Another v Express Newspapers [2003] EWHC 1322 (Ch) 175
AT Poeton (Gloucester Plating) Ltd v Horton [2001] FSR 169, CA 268

B

Baby Dan v Brevi [1999] FSR 377 240
Baigent v Random House Group Ltd [2006] EWHC 719 (Ch) 205, 215
Bailey v Haynes, PCC (Judge Fysh QC) LTL 20/10/2006, [2007] FSR 10 241
Baird Textile Holdings Ltd v Marks & Spencer plc [2001] EWCA Civ 274 57
Balfour Beatty Northern Ltd v Modus Corovest (Blackpool) Ltd [2008] EWHC 3029 (TCC) 14
Banham Marshalls Services Unlimited v Lincolnshire CC [2007] EWHC 402 (QB) 33
Bank of England v Vagliano Bros [1891] AC 107, HL 143
Barrett McKenzie v Escada (UK) Ltd (1 February 2001) 86
Bayerische Motorenwerke AG (BMW) and Another v Deenik (Case 63/97) [1999] All ER (EC) 235 193
BBC v Sugar [2008] EWCA Civ 191 319
Beale v Taylor [1967] 1 WLR 1193 18
Benetton Group SpA v G-Star International BV (Case C-371/06) [2008] ETMR 5, ECJ 181
Beta Computers (Europe) Ltd v Adobe Systems (Europe) Ltd [1996] FSR 367 282
Betts v Wilmott (1871) 6 Ch App 239 261
Biogen v Medeva [1997] RPC 1 252
Blackpool Ladder Centre Ltd v BWB Partnership [2000] WL 1791447 63
Blair v Alan S Tomkins and Frank Osborne (t/a Osborne & Tomkins (A Firm)) and Another [1971] 1 All ER 468 208

Blau v BBC [2002] ECDR 34 207
Bloomsbury Publishing Group Ltd and Another v News Group Newspapers Ltd and Others [2003] EWHC 1205 (Ch), [2003] 3 All ER 736 217
Bluck v Information Commissioner, Information Tribunal (2007) 98 BMLR 321
Boehringer Ingelheim KG v Swingward Ltd [2008] EWCA Civ 83 172
Bolam v Friern Hospital Management Committee [1957] 2 All ER 118 60
Bond Worth, In re [1980] Ch 228 29
Bonnier Media Ltd v Greg Lloyd Smith [2002] ETMR 86 192, 284
Booth v Cargo Fleet Iron Co Ltd [1916] 2 KB 570 23
Borden (UK) Ltd v Scottish Timber Products Ltd [1981] Ch 25 28
Bostik Ltd v Henkel KGAA (Trade Mark Registry 3/09/07) [2007] WL 2573891 178
Bostik Ltd v Sellotape GB Ltd [1994] RPC 556 170
BP Amoco plc v John Kelly Ltd [2002] FSR 5 183
British Broadcasting Corporation v British Satellite Broadcasting Ltd [1991] 3 WLR 174 218
British Gas Trading Ltd v Data Protection Registrar [1998] Info TLR 393 (Data Protection Tribunal) 313
British Horseracing Board v William Hill Organisation Ltd [2002] ECC 24 229
British Imex Industries Ltd v Midland Bank Ltd [1958] 1 QB 542 147
British Sky Broadcasting Group plc v Sky Home Services Ltd [2006] EWHC 3165 167
British Sugar plc v James Robertson & Sons Ltd [1996] RPC 281 284
British Telecommunications plc and Others v One in a Million Ltd and Others [1999] 1 WLR 903 192, 284
Britvic Soft Drinks Ltd v Messer UK Ltd [2002] EWCA Civ 548, [2002] 1 Lloyd's Rep 20 19, 44, 45
Brown & Davis Ltd v Galbraith [1972] 3 All ER 31 62
BSC v Cleveland Bridge and Engineering Co Ltd [1984] 1 All ER 504 10
Budejovicki Budvar Narodni Podnik v Anheuser-Busch Inc [2008] EWHC 263 (Ch) 194
Byford v Oliver and Another [2003] EWHC 295 (Ch), [2003] All ER (D) 345 (Feb) 182

C

Cable & Wireless plc v IBM United Kingdom Ltd [2002] EWHC 2059 (Comm) 14
Campbell v MGN Ltd [2002] EWCA Civ 1373, [2003] QB 633, [2004] 2 All ER 995 269, 317
Cantor Fitzgerald International v Tradition (UK) Ltd [2000] RPC 95 221
Cantor Gaming Ltd v Gameaccount Global Ltd [2007] EWHC 1914 (Ch) 229
Cardbase Technologies Ltd v Valucard Nigeria [2002] EWHC 991 (Ch) 281
Catnic Components Ltd and Another v Hill & Smith Ltd [1982] RPC 183 258
Centrafarm BV and Adrian de Peijper v Sterling Drug Inc (Case 15/74) [1974] ECR 1147 261, 353
Centrafarm BV and Adrian de Peijper v Winthrop BV (Case 16/74) [1974] ECR 1183 353
Charge Card Services Ltd, Re [1988] 3 All ER 702 20
Charles Rickards Ltd v Oppenheim [1950] 1 KB 616 17
Charnock v Liverpool Corporation [1968] 3 All ER 472 62
Chaudry v Prabakhar [1988] 3 All ER 718 60
Christopher Tasker's Design Right References; Re Patent Office [2001] RPC 3 241
Cintec International v Parkes [2003] EWHC 2328 262
Citibank NA v Comptroller-General of Patents (ChD, 9 June 2006) 253
Clark (Alan Kenneth McKenzie) v Associated Newspapers [1998] RPC 261 169, 211
Clegg v Olle Andersson (t/a Nordic Marine) [2003] EWCA Civ 320 24
Clough Mill Ltd v Martin [1985] 1 WLR 111 28, 31
Coco v AN Clark (Engineers) Ltd [1969] RPC 41 264
Color Drack Gmbh v Lexx International Vertriebs Gmbh (Case C-386/08) [2008] 1 All ER (Comm) 168 114
Compaq Computer Ltd v Abercorn Group Ltd (t/a Osiris) and Others [1991] BCC 484 31
Competition Authority v Beef Industry Development Society Ltd (Case C-209/107) [2009] All ER 367 (EC), ECJ 332
Confetti Records and Others v Warner Music UK Ltd [2003] EWHC 1274 (Ch) 211
Conroy v SmithKline Beecham plc (Trade Marks Registry 0-085-03, 3 April 2003) 189
Consorzio del Prosciutto di Parma v Asda Stores Ltd (Case C-108/01) [2001] UKHL 7 179
Consorzio del Prosciutto di Parma v Marks & Spencer plc [1991] RPC 351 168
Cooper v Pure Fishing (UK) Ltd [2004] 2 Lloyd's Rep 518 87
Copland v United Kingdom, Application No 62617/00, (2007) 45 EHRR 37 285
Corporate Officer of the House of Commons v Information Commissioner [2008] EWHC 1084 (Admin) 320, 323
Cory v Thames Ironworks and Shipbuilding Co Ltd (1868) LR 3 QB 181 55
Courtney & Fairbairn Ltd v Tolaini Bros (Hotels) Ltd [1975] 1 WLR 297 14
Crane v Sky In-Home Service Ltd [2007] EWHC 66 (Ch) 78, 87
Cray Valley Ltd v Deltech Europe Ltd and Others [2003] EWHC 728 (Ch) 266
Credit Industriel et Commercial v China Merchants Bank [2002] EWHC 973 (Comm), [2002] 2 All ER (Comm) 427 148

Cundy v Lindsay 3 App Cas 459 65
Cureton v Mark Insulations Ltd [2006] EWHC 2279 230
Cyprotex Discovery Ltd v University of Sheffield [2004] EWCA Civ 380 282
Czarnikow-Rionda Sugar Trading v Standard Bank London Ltd [1999] 1 All ER (Comm) 890 148

D

Davis Contractors v Fareham Urban DC [1956] AC 696 52
De Maudsley v Palumbo and Others [1996] FSR 447 264
Decon Laboratories Ltd v Fred Baker Scientific Ltd [2001] RPC 293 184
Designer's Guild Ltd v Russell Williams (Textiles) Ltd [2001] FSR 803 215
Diamond v Chakrabarty 65 Law Ed (2d) 144 (1980) 254
DKV Deutsche Krankenversicherung AG v Office for Harmonisation in the Internal Market [2002] ECR I-7561 178
Douglas and Others v Hello! Ltd and Others [2003] EWHC 786 (Ch), [2003] All ER (D) 209 (Apr); [2005] EWCA Civ 595 268, 317
Douglas and Others v Hello! Ltd and Others (No 3) [2007] 2 WLR 920 264
DPP v Lennon [2006] EWHC 1201 (Admin) 286
Duckett v Patent Office [2005] EWHC 3140 (Pat) 252
Duncan Moore v Piretta PTA [1999] 1 All ER 174 86
Durant v Financial Services Authority [2003] EWCA Civ 1746 308
Dyson Appliances Ltd v Hoover [2001] EWCA Civ 1440, [2002] RPC 42 259
Dyson Ltd v Qualtex (UK) Ltd [2004] EWHC 2981 (Ch) 241
Dyson Ltd v Qualtex (UK) Ltd [2006] EWCA Civ 166 240, 241
Dyson Ltd v Registrar of Trade Marks (Case C-321/03) [2003] EWHC 1062 181

E

Easynet Group plc v Easygroup IP Licensing Ltd [2006] EWHC 1872 177, 178
Edwards Lifesciences AG v Cook Biotech Incorporated [2009] EWHC 1304 (Pat), [2009] EWHC 1443, [2008] All ER (D) 368 (Jul) 260
El Du Pont de Nemours & Co v ST Dupont [2004] FSR 15 177
Ellis v Director of Public Prosecutions [2001] EWHC 362 (Admin) 285
Emaco Ltd and Another v Dyson Appliances Ltd [1999] ETMR 903 190
Enterprise Rent-a-car Co v Eurodrive Car Rental Ltd [2005] Lawtel 2/3/2005 186
Entores Ltd v Miles Far East Corporation [1955] 2 QB 327 293
Equitable Trust Company of New York v Dawson Partners Ltd (1927) 27 Ll L Rep 49 148
ERG Raffinerie Mediterranee SpA v Chevron USA Inc [2007] EWCA Civ 494 17
Esure Insurance Ltd v Direct Line Insurance plc [2008] EWCA Civ 842 187
Euromarket Designs Inc v Peters and Trade & Barrel Ltd [2001] FSR 288 192
European Central Bank v Document Security Systems Inc [2008] EWCA Civ 192 252, 255, 260
Evans v Kosmar Villa Holiday plc [2007] EWCA Civ 1003 61
Exxon Corpn and Others v Exxon Insurance Consultants International Ltd [1981] 3 All ER 241 206

F

Faccenda Chicken Ltd v Fowler [1986] 1 All ER 617 229
Fairfax Gerrard Holdings Ltd v Capital Bank plc [2007] EWCA Civ 1226 28, 31
Farmers Build Ltd v Carrier Bulk Materials Handling Ltd [1999] RPC 461 240
Fearns v Anglo-Dutch Paint and Chemical Co Ltd [2007] EWHC 955; [2008] EWCA Civ 99 168
Filobake Ltd v Rondo Ltd [2004] EWHC 695 (TCC) 24
First Conference Services Ltd v Bracchi [2009] EWHC 2176 (Ch), [2009] All ER (D) 56 (Oct) 169, 267
Fisher v Brooker [2006] All ER (D) 306 (Dec) 210
Fisher v Brooker [2006] EWHC 3239 (Ch), [2008] EWCA Civ 287 205
Fisher v Brooker [2009] UKHL 41, [2009] All ER (D) 338 (Jul) 220
FKI Engineering Ltd v DE Wind Holdings Ltd [2008] EWCA Civ 316 115
Flamar Interocean Ltd v Denmac Ltd (formerly Denholm Maclay Co Ltd) (The 'Flamar Pride' and 'Flamar Progress') [1990] 1 Lloyd's Rep 434 43
Flashing Badge Co Ltd v Groves [2007] EWHC 1372 (Ch) 243
Foley v Classique Coaches Ltd [1934] 2 KB 1 14
Football Association Premier League Ltd v QC Leisure [2008] EWHC 1411 (Ch), [2008] All ER (D) 313 (Jun) 224
Forthright Finance Ltd v Carlyle Finance Ltd [1997] 4 All ER 90 64
Fraser and Others v Thames Television Ltd and Others [1984] 1 QB 44 265
Fraser-Woodward v British Broadcasting Corporation [2005] EWHC 472 (Ch) 219
French Connection Ltd's Trade Mark Application (No 81862) [2005] WL 3734085 182

Friarwood Ltd v Champagne Chatier SA [2006] EWCA Civ 1105 19
FT Everard & Sons Ltd v BP Marine Ltd [2005] EWHC 3142 (Comm) 19
Fulton (A) Co Ltd v Grant Barnett & Co Ltd [2001] RPC 16 240, 242

G

Gabrin v Universal Music Operations Ltd [2003] EWHC 1335 (Ch) 209
Garrison's Patent [1997] CIPA 297 256
GE Capital Bank Ltd v Rushton [2005] EWCA Civ 1556 41
GE Capital Commercial Finance v Sutton [2004] EWCA Civ 315 33
Generics (UK) Ltd v Lundbeck A/S [2008] EWCA Civ 311 251
George Mitchell (Chesterhall) Ltd v Finney Lock Seeds Ltd [1983] 2 AC 803 47
Ghazilian's Trade Mark Application [2002] RPC 23 182
Gian Singh & Co Ltd v Banque de l'Indochine [1974] 1 WLR 1234, [1974] 2 All ER 754 148, 152
Glaxo Group v Dowelhurst Ltd [2004] EWCA Civ 290, [2004] WL 412961, CA 192
Glencore Grain Rotterdam BV v Lebanese Organisation for International Commerce [1997] 4 All ER 514, CA 153
Glencore International AG v Exeter Shipping Ltd and Others [2002] EWCA Civ 528 31
Glencore International AG v Metro Trading International Inc (No 2) [2001] 1 Lloyd's Rep 284, [2001] 1 All ER (Comm) 103 29, 31
Global Projects Management Ltd v Citigroup Inc [2005] EWHC 2663 171
Glyn Mills Currie & Co v East and West India Dock Co (1882) 7 App Cas 591 126
Godley v Perry [1960] 1 WLR 9 20
Goldcorp Exchange Ltd (in receivership), Re [1994] 2 All ER 806, PC 26, 27
Google Inc v Copiepresse SCRL [2007] ECDR 5 228
Gordon v Strange (1847) 1 Exch 477 20
Graham Page v Combined Shipping and Trading Co Ltd [1997] 3 All ER 656 86
Greater Glasgow Health Board's Application [1996] RPC 207 256
Green (RW) Ltd v Cade Brothers Farm [1987] Lloyd's Rep 602 46, 47
Green Lane Products Ltd v PMS International Group Ltd [2007] EWHC 1712 (Pat), [2008] EWCA Civ 358 234
Green v Broadcasting Corporation of New Zealand [1989] 2 All ER 1086 265
Groupement d'Achat Edouard Leclerc (Galec) v Commission of the European Communities (Case T-19/92) [1996] ECR II-1851 346
Guild v Eskandar Ltd [2001] FSR 38 207, 240

H

Hadley v Baxendale (1854) 9 Exch 341 12, 25
Harrods Ltd v Harrodian School Ltd [1996] RPC 697 168
Hartley v Hymans [1920] 3 KB 475 17
Hedley Byrne v Heller [1964] AC 465 62
Helby v Matthews [1895] AC 471 64
Helmet Integrated Systems Ltd v Mitchell Tunnard, PCC 10/2/2006, LTL 15/12/2006, [2006] FSR 41 242
Henderson v Merrett Syndicates Ltd [1995] 2 AC 145 62
Hendy Lennox (Industrial Engines) Ltd v Graham Puttick Ltd [1984] 1 WLR 485 28, 32
Henry Bros (Magherafelt) Ltd v Ministry of Defence [1999] RPC 442 256
Hensher (George) Ltd v Restawile Upholstery (Lancs) [1976] AC 64 207
HFC Bank plc v Midland Bank plc [2000] FSR 176 170
Hickman v Andrews and Others [1983] RPC 174 251
HM Stationery Office v Green Amps Ltd [2007] EWHC 2755 (Ch) 217
Honda Motor Co Ltd v Neesam [2008] EWHC 338 (Ch) 194
Honyvem Informazioni Commerciali Srl v Mariella de Zotti (Case C-465/04) [2006] ECR I-2879 87
Horace Holman Group Ltd v Sherwood International Group Ltd [2000] WL 491372 13
HRH Prince of Wales v Associated Newspapers Ltd [2007] EWHC 1685 (Ch) 269
HRH the Prince of Wales v Associated Newspapers Ltd [2006] EWHC 522 (Ch) 218
Hudson v Shogun [2004] 1 AC 919 65
Hyde Park Residence Ltd v Yelland and Others [1999] RPC 655, [2001] Ch 143 219
Hyde Park Residence Ltd v Yelland and Others [2000] RPC 604 217
Hyperion Records Ltd v Sawkins [2005] EWCA Civ 565 205

I

Ian Stach Ltd v Baker Bosley Ltd [1958] 2 QB 130, CA 132, 152
IBA v BICC Construction Ltd (1980) 14 BLR 9 61
IBM/Computer Programs (Case T-1173/97) [1999] EPOR 219 253

IBM/Computer Programs (Case T-935/97) [1999] EPOR 301 253
IDA Ltd v Southampton University [2006] EWCA Civ 145 252, 256
Improver Corporation and Others v Remington Consumer Products Ltd and Others [1990] FSR 181 258
IMS Health GmbH and Co OHG v NDC Health GmbH and Co KG (Case C-418/01) [2004] ECR I-5039 352
In the Matter of Registered Design No 2044802 in the Name of Household Articles Ltd, Ch D (Patents Ct) 22/1/98, [1998] FSR 676 235
Independiente Ltd and Others v Music Trading On-line (HK) Ltd and Others [2003] EWHC 470 (Ch) 216
Industrial Furnaces Ltd v Reaves and Another [1970] RPC 605 266
Ineos Vinyls Ltd v Huntsman Petrochemicals (UK) Ltd [2006] EWHC 1241 (Ch) 91
Inntrepreneur Pub Co (CPC) Ltd v Sweeney [2002] EWHC 1060 (Ch) 6
Intel Corporation v CPM United Kingdom Ltd [2006] EWHC 1878 (Ch) 186
Intel Corporation v Sihra [2003] EWHC 17 (Ch), [2003] All ER (D) 212 (Jan) 186
Interactive Intelligence Inc's Registration No 873858 WL 1180 176
International Finance Corp v DSNL Offshore Ltd [2005] EWHC 1844 (Comm) 26
Internet Broadcasting Corporation v MAR LLC [2009] EWHC 844 (Ch) 51
Investors Compensation Scheme Ltd v West Bromwich Building Society [1998] 1 WLR 898 11
IPC Media v News Group Newspapers Ltd [2005] EWHC 317 (Ch) 219
Iran Continental Shelf Oil Co v Iri International Corp [2002] EWCA Civ 1024 116
Irvine and Others v Talksport Ltd [2003] EWCA Civ 423, [2003] 2 All ER 881 171
Isaac Oren v Red Box Toy Factory Ltd, Ch D (Patents Ct) 1/2/1999, [1999] FSR 785 237

J

J Choo (Jersey) Ltd v Towerstone Ltd [2008] EWHC 346 (Ch) 235, 238
Jeancharm Ltd v Barnet Football Club Ltd [2003] EWCA Civ 58 21
Jewson v Kelly [2003] EWCA Civ 1030 19
JHP Ltd v BBC Worldwide Ltd [2008] EWHC 757 (Ch) 219
Johnson v Medical Defence Union Ltd [2007] EWCA Civ 262 308, 310, 313
Jones v Gallagher [2004] EWCA Civ 10 18, 25
Jo-Y-Jo Ltd v Matalan Retail Ltd [1999] EIPR 627 240
JP Morgan Europe Limited v Primacom AG and others [2005] EWHC 508 116
Jules Rimet Cup Ltd v Football Association Ltd [2007] EWHC 2376 (Ch) 182, 184
Julius Sämaan v Tetrosyl Ltd [2006] EWHC 529 188

K

Kapur v Comptroller General of Patents Designs and Trade Marks [2008] EWHC 649 (Pat) 254
Kean v McGivan [1982] FSR 119 167
Kestos Ltd v Kempat Ltd [1936] RPC 139 240
KG Bominflot Bunkersgesellschaft für Mineralöle mbh & Co KG v Petroplus Marketing AG [2009] EWHC 1088 (Comm) 18, 125, 132
King v T Tunnock [2000] IRLR 570 86
Kirin-Amgen Inc v Hoechst Marion Roussel Ltd [2002] EWCA Civ 1096, [2003] RPC 3; [2004] UKHL 46 252, 258
Knight v Beyond Properties Pty Ltd [2007] EWHC 1251 169
Koninklijke Philips Electronics v Remington Consumer Products Ltd (Case C-299/99) [2002] 2 CMLR 52, [2003] Ch 159 177

L

L v L [2007] EWHC 140 (QB) 316, 323
L'Oréal SA v Bellure NV (Case C-487/07) [2009] All ER (D) 225 (Jun) 190
L'Oreal SA v Bellure NV [2006] EWHC 2355; [2007] EWCA Civ 968 169, 176
L'Oréal SA v eBay International AG [2009] EWHC 1094 (Ch) 295, 298, 299, 300
Lacroix Duarib SA v Kwikform (UK) Ltd [1998] FSR 493 257
Lambretta Clothing Company Ltd v Teddy Smith (UK) Ltd & Next Retail plc [2003] EWHC (Ch) 240
Landor & Hawa International Ltd v Azure Designs Ltd [2006] EWCA Civ 1285 240, 244
Lenin's Monument, Re [1992] ECC 202 210
LG International (UK) Ltd v GB International Ltd [2005] EWHC 801 (QB) 14
Libertel Group BV v Benelux-Merkenbureau (Case C-104/01) [2004] 2 WLR 1081 183
Light v Ty Europe Ltd [2003] EWCA Civ 1238 78
Lindquist v Kammaraklagaren (Case C-101/01) (ECJ, 6 November 2003) 309
Lombard plc v Butterworth [1987] QB 527 70
London Regional Transport v Mayor of London [2001] EWCA Civ 1491 323
Lonsdale v Howard & Hallam Ltd [2007] UKHL 32 87
LRC International Ltd and Another v Lilla Edets Sales Co Ltd [1973] RPC 560 171

M

Mackenzie Patten & Co v British Olivetti Ltd (1984) 1 CL&P 92 273
Mahonia Ltd v JP Morgan Chase Bank (No 1) [2003] EWHC 1927 (Comm) 149
Mamidoil-Jetoil Greek Petroleum Co SA v Okta Crude Oil Refinery AC (No 3) [2003] EWCA Civ 1031 7
Mastercigars Direct Ltd v Withers LLP [2007] EWHC 2733 (Ch) 63
Masterman's Design, Re [1991] RPC 89 182
McEntire v Crossley Brothers Ltd [1895] AC 457 64
Mehta v J Pereira Fernandes SA [2006] EWHC 813 (Ch) 293
Mercantile International Group plc v Chuan Soon Huant Industrial Group Ltd [2002] EWCA Civ 288 77
Meridian International Services Ltd v Richardson [2007] EWHC 2539 (Ch) 220
Merlet and Another v Mothercare plc [1986] RPC 115 207
Michael Stone v South East Coast Strategic Health Authority and Others [2006] EWHC 1668 (Admin) 323
Micron Computer Systems Ltd v Wang (UK) Ltd (HC, 9 May 1990) 19, 278
Microsoft Corp v Ling [2006] EWHC 1619 169
Midland Bank Trust Ltd v Hett Stubbs and Kemp [1978] 3 All ER 571 60
Moore v Landauer & Co, Re [1921] 2 KB 519 18
Morgans v DPP [2001] 1 AC 315, HL 285
Morning Star v Express Newspapers [1979] FSR 113 171
Morrison Leahy Music Ltd v Lightbond Ltd [1993] EMLR 144 210
Motis Exports Ltd v Dampskibsselskabet AF 1912 (No 1), A/S and Another [2000] 1 All ER (Comm) 91 128
M-Systems Flash Disk Pioneers Ltd v Trek 2000 International Ltd [2008] EWHC 102 (Pat) 259
Mülhens GmbH & Co KG v OHIM and Zirh International Corp (Case C-206/04P) [2006] ETMR 57 195
Multiplex Constructions (UK) Ltd v Cleveland Bridge UK Ltd [2006] EWHC 1341 (TCC), affirmed [2007] All ER (D) 264 (Apr), CA 6
Murphy & Sons Ltd v Johnston Precast Ltd [2008] EWHC 3024 (TCC) 10

N

Neutrogena Corporation and Another v Golden Ltd and Another [1996] RPC 473 168
Newspaper Licensing Agency Ltd v Marks & Spencer plc [1999] RPC 536; [2001] Ch 257; [2001] UKHL 38, [2003] 1 AC 551 215, 218
Nichols plc v The Registrar of Trade Marks (Case C-404/02) [2004] All ER (D) 114 177
Noah v Shuba and Another [1991] FSR 14 208
Norbrook Laboratories (GB) Ltd v Adair [2008] EWHC 978 (QB) 263
Norowzian v Arks Ltd and Others (No 2) [2000] FSR 363 211
Northern Rock plc v Financial Times Ltd [2007] EWHC 2677 (QB) 265
Nouveau Fabrics Ltd v Voyage Decoration Ltd [2004] EWHC 895 (Ch) 217
Nova Productions Ltd v Mazooma Games Ltd [2007] EWCA Civ 219 215
Novartis AG v Ivax Pharmaceuticals UK Ltd [2007] EWCA Civ 971 257
Nungesser (LC) AG and Kurt Eisle v Commission for the European Communities (Case 258/78) [1982] ECR 2015 349, 354

O

O2 Holdings Ltd v Hutchinson 3G Ltd [2006] ETMR 55 190
Oakley Inc v Animal Ltd [2005] EWHC 210 (Ch) 235
Ocular Sciences Ltd and Another v Aspect Vision Care Ltd and Others; Galley v Ocular Sciences Ltd (No 2) [1997] RPC 289 240, 241
Office of Fair Trading v Lloyds TSB Bank plc (1) Tesco Personal Finance Ltd (2) and American Express Services Europe Ltd (3) [2004] EWHC 2600 (Comm) 101
Office of Fair Trading v Lloyds TSB Bank plc and Others [2006] EWCA Civ 268, [2007] QB 1 101, 302
Office of Government Commerce v Information Commissioner [2008] EWHC 737 (Admin) 321
OHIM (Doublemint) v Wrigley (Case C-191/01) (ECJ, 23 October 2003) 179
Oliver v Dubai Bank Kenya Ltd [2007] EWHC 2165 (Comm) 148
Oricon Waren-Handels Gmbh v Intergraan NV [1967] 2 Lloyd's Rep 82 20
Overseas Medical Supplies Ltd v Orient Transport Services Ltd [1999] 2 Lloyd's Rep 273 43, 44
Owusu v Jackson (Case C-281/02) (2005) 114

P

Parker v Tidball [1997] FSR 680 241
PCR Ltd v Dow Jones Telerate Ltd [1998] FSR 170 219
Peachdart Ltd, In re [1984] Ch 131 31

Peek & Cloppenburg v OHIM [2006] ETMR 35 179
Peter Pan Manufacturing Corporation v Corsets Silhouette Ltd [1964] 1 WLR 96 266
Pharmacia Corporation and Others v Merck & Co Inc and Another [2001] EWCA Civ 1610 258
Philips Electronics NV v Remington Consumer Products Ltd (No 2) [1999] RPC 809 180
Phones 4u Ltd and Another v Phone4u.co.uk Internet Ltd [2006] EWCA Civ 244 182, 188, 294
Phonographic Performance Ltd v Candy Rock Recording Ltd [2000] EMLR 618, CA 223
Photo Production Ltd v Securicor Transport Ltd [1980] 1 All ER 556 46, 47
Pitman Training Ltd v Nominet UK [1997] FSR 797 294
PJ Pipe & Valve Co Ltd v Audco India Ltd [2005] EWHC 1904 (QB) 78, 87
Pocket Kings Ltd v Safenames Ltd [2009] EWHC 2529, [2009] All ER (D) 205 (Oct) 294
Postmaster-General v WH Jones & Co [1957] NZLR 829 23
Pozzoli SpA v BDMO SA [2007] EWCA Civ 588 252
Premier Brands UK Ltd v Typhoon Europe Ltd [2000] FSR 767 190
Prince Albert v Strange (1849) 1 Mac & G 25 263
Pro Sieben Media AG v Carlton UK Television Ltd and Another [1999] 1 WLR 605 218
Procter & Gamble Co v Office for Harmonisation in the Internal Market (Trade Marks and Designs) [2002] RPC 17 178
Procter & Gamble Co v Reckitt Benckiser (UK) Ltd [2007] EWCA Civ 936 235
PT Pan Indonesia Bank Ltd TBK v Marconi Communications International Ltd [2005] EWCA Civ 422 116
Pyrene Co Ltd v Scindia Steam Navigation Co Ltd [1954] 2 All ER 158 132

Q

Quantel Ltd v Spaceward Microsystems Ltd [1990] RPC 83 250
Quantum Corp Ltd v Plane Trucking Ltd [2002] EWCA Civ 350 128

R

R & B Customs Brokers Co Ltd v United Dominions Trust Ltd [1988] 1 All ER 847 41
R Griggs Group Ltd v Evans [2005] EWCA Civ 11 209
R v Bow Street Metropolitan Stipendiary Magistrate, ex p United States (No 2); R v Governor of Brixton Prison, ex p Allison [2000] 2 AC 216 285
R v Delamere [2003] EWCA Crim 424 286
R v Gold [1988] 2 WLR 984 286
R v Johnstone [2003] UKHL 28, [2003] 3 All ER 884 189
R v Lindesay [2001] EWCA Crim 1720, [2002] 1 Cr App R (S) 86 286
R v Maxwell-King [2000] 2 Cr App R (S) 136 286
R v Parr-Moore and Crumblehulme [2003] 1 Cr App R (S) 286
R v Registered Designs Appeal Tribunal, ex p Ford Motor Co [1995] 1 WLR 18 236
Radio Telefis Eireann and Another v Commission of the European Communities and Another (Cases C-241/91P and C-242/91P) [1995] ECR 1-801 352
Ray v Classic FM plc [1998] FSR 622 206
Reardon Smith Line v Yngvar Hansen-Tangen [1976] 1 WLR 989 18
Reckitt & Colman Products Ltd v Borden Inc and Others [1990] 1 WLR 491 167
Reddaway and Frank Reddaway & Co Ltd v Banham and George Banham & Co Ltd [1896] AC 199 167
Reed Executive and Reed Solutions v Reed Business Information and Elsevier [2004] EWCA Civ 159, [2004] RPC 40 189, 193
Regus (UK) Ltd v Epcot Solutions Ltd [2008] EWCA Civ 361 39, 43, 44, 45, 55
Rex v Arkwright (1785) 1 WPC 64 252
Rhone-Poulenc Rorer International Holdings Inc v Yeda Research and Development Co Ltd [2007] UKHL 43 256
Riddle v United Service Organisation Ltd [2004] LTL AC9100218 169
Rimeco Riggleson & Metal Co v Queenborough Rolling Mill Co Ltd [1995] CLY 798 10
Roche Products Ltd v Kent Pharmaceuticals Ltd [2006] EWHC 335 194
Rockwater v Technip France SA [2004] EWCA 381 259
Roger Bullivant v Ellis [1987] FSR 172 266
Rolls Royce Power Engineering Ltd v Ricardo Consulting Engineers Ltd [2003] EWHC 2871 60
Ronastone Ltd v Indigo International Holdings Ltd [2003] All ER (D) 332 (Dec) 26
Rowlawn Ltd v Turfmech Machinery Ltd [2008] EWHC 989 (Pat) 238
Rubicon Computer Systems Ltd v United Paints Ltd [2000] 2 TCLR 453 16
Ruttle Plant Hire v Secretary of State for the Environment, Food and Rural Affairs [2009] EWCA Civ 97 34
RV Ward v Bignall [1967] 2 All ER 449, CA 23

S

Sabel BV v Puma AG, Rudolf Dassler Sport (Case C-251/95) [1998] ETMR 1 185
Sagal (t/a Bunz UK) v Atelier Bunz GmbH [2008] EWHC 789 (Comm) 77
SAM Business Systems Ltd v Hedley & Co [2002] EWHC 2733 (TCC) 280
Samuels v Davis [1943] KB 526 59
Saphena Computing Ltd v Allied Collection Agencies Ltd [1995] FSR 616 279, 280, 283
Sauter Automation Ltd v Goodman (Mechanical Services) Ltd (in liquidation) (1986) 34 Build LR 81 10
Sayers v Smithkline Beecham Plc [2007] EWHC 1346 315, 316
Scanvaegt International AS v Pelcombe Ltd [1998] FSR 786 259
Schenkers Ltd v Overland Shoes Ltd [1998] EWCA Civ 234 47
Schering-Plough Ltd v Norbrook Laboratories Ltd [2005] EWHC 2532 (Pat) 255
Scottish & Newcastle International Ltd v Othon Ghalanos Ltd [2008] UKHL 11; [2008] 2 All ER (Comm) 369 17, 114, 132
Seager v Copydex Ltd [1967] 2 All ER 415 266
Secretary of State for the Home Office v British Union for the Abolition of Vivisection [2008] EWHC 892 (QB) 321
Shaw v API Group plc (QBD District Registry (Manchester)), 10 April 2008, WL 265
Shetland Times Ltd v Wills and Another [1997] FSR 604 222, 284
Shield Mark BV v Kist (Case 283/01) [2003] ETMR 822 176
Shogun Finance Ltd v Hudson [2004] 1 AC 919 26
SHV Gas Supply and Trading SAS v Naftomar Shipping and Trading Co Ltd Inc, The Azur Gaz [2005] EWHC 2528 (Comm) 8
Silhouette International Schmied GmbH and Co KG v Hartlauer Handelsgesellschaft mbH (Case C-355/96) [1999] Ch 77, [2000] All ER (EC) 769 194, 353
Sir Robert McAlpine Ltd v Alfred McAlpine plc [2004] EWHC 630, [2004] RPC 36 170
Sir Terence Orby Conran v Mean Fiddler Holdings Ltd [1997] FSR 856 185
Sirdar Rubber v Wallington, Weston & Co (1907) 24 RPC 539 261
Smith Kline & French Laboratories Ltd v Sterling-Winthrop Group Ltd [1975] 2 All ER 578 183
Smith v Bush (Eric S) (a firm); Harris v Wyre Forest District Council [1989] 2 All ER 514 45
Societa Esplosivi Industriali Spa v Ordnance Technologies (UK) Ltd [2007] EWHC 2875 (Ch) 242
Société des Produits Nestlé SA v Mars UK Ltd [2002] EWHC 2533 (Ch), [2002] All ER (D) 05 (Dec); [2004] EWCA Civ 1008 181
Société des Produits Nestlé SA v Mars UK Ltd (Case C-353/03) [2005] 3 CMLR 12, [2006] All ER (EC) 348 183
Société des Produits Nestlé SA v Unilever plc [2002] EWHC 2709 (Ch), [2003] RPC 35 181
Sony Music Entertainment (UK) Ltd and Others v Easyinternetcafé Ltd [2003] EWHC 62 (Ch), [2003] FSR 48 216, 223
South West Water Services Ltd v International Computers Ltd [1999] BLR 420 276
Speed Seal Products Ltd v Paddington and Another [1986] 1 All ER 91 266
St Albans City and District Council v ICL [1996] 4 All ER 481 13, 49, 61, 276, 278
Stag Line v Tyne Ship Repair Group (The Zinnia) [1984] 2 Lloyd's Rep 211 48
Stena Rederi Aktiebolag and Another v Irish Ferries Ltd [2002] EWHC 737 (Ch), [2002] RPC 990; [2003] EWCA Civ 66, [2003] RPC 36 260
Stevenson v Nationwide Building Society (1984) 272 EG 663 45
Stocznia Gdanska SA v Latvian Shipping Co [1998] 1 WLR 574, HL 23
Stringfellow and Another v McCain Foods GB Ltd and Another [1984] RPC 501 171
Stroud Architectural Systems Ltd v John Laing Construction Ltd [1994] BCC 18 30
Suisse Atlantique Société d'Armament v Rotterdamsche Kolen Centrale NV [1966] 2 All ER 61 51
Super Chem Products Ltd v American Life and General Insurance Co Ltd [2004] UKPC 2 53
Sutcliffe v Lloyd [2007] EWCA Civ 153 6
Svenborg v Far East Trading Côte d'Ivoire [2004] EWHC 2929 126
Symbian Ltd v Comptroller General of Patents [2008] EWHC 518 (Pat) 254
Synthon BV v Smithklein Beecham plc [2006] 1 All ER 685 250
System 3R International AB v Erowa AG and Erowa Nordic AB [2003] ETMR 916 185

T

Terrapin Ltd v Builders' Supply Co (Hayes) Ltd [1967] RPC 375 266
Tesco Stores Ltd v Elogicom Ltd [2006] EWHC 403 (Ch) 192
Thain v Anniesland Trade Centre [1997] SCLR 991 19
Thames Valley Power Ltd v Total Gas and Power Ltd [2005] EWHC 2208 (Comm) 26
Thomas v Ladkarn Holdings Limited [1997] Lawtel 16/5/97 63
Thomas Witter v TBP Industries Ltd [1996] 2 All ER 573 6
Thunder Air Ltd v Hilmarsson [2008] EWHC 355 (Ch) 13
Tigana Ltd v Decoro Ltd [2003] EWHC 23 (QB) 85

Timken Co's Application No 2418442 (Trade Mark Registry 18/09/07) [2007] WL 2817814 178
Toprak Mahsulleri Ofisi v Finagrain Compagnie Commerciale Agricole et Financière SA [1979] 2 Lloyd's Rep 98 17
Totalise plc v Motley Fool Ltd [2001] EWCA Civ 1897 314
Totsa Total Oil Trading SA v Bharat Petroleum Corp Ltd [2005] EWHC 1641 (Comm) 18
Trade Electronix Ltd v Best Buy Today (Wholesale) Ltd (in administration) [2009] EWCA Civ 828 16
Trentham v Archital Luxfer Ltd [1993] 1 Lloyd's Rep 25 10
Trident Turboprop (Dublin) Ltd v First Flight Couriers Ltd [2009] EWCA Civ 290 40
Tyco Fire & Integrated Solutions (UK) Ltd v Rolls Royce Motor Cars Ltd [2008] EWCA Civ 286 52

U

Ultraframe (UK) Ltd v Clayton and Others; Ultraframe (UK) Ltd v Fielding and Others [2002] EWHC 1964 (Ch) 242
United Biscuits (UK) Ltd v Asda Stores Ltd [1997] RPC 513 169
University of London Press v University Tutorial Press [1916] 2 Ch 601 206

V

Van der Lely (C) NV v Bamfords Ltd [1963] RPC 61 250
Vector Corp v Glatt Air Techniques Ltd [2007] EWCA Civ 805 260
Vericore Ltd v Vetrepharm Ltd and Another [2003] EWHC 111 (Ch) 250
Vestergaard Frandsen A/S v Bestnet Europe Ltd [2009] EWHC 1456 (Ch), [2009] All ER (D) 57 (Oct) 267
Vicom's Application [1987] OJ EPO 14 253
Victoria Laundry (Windsor) Ltd v Newman Industries Ltd [1949] 2 KB 528 55
Vitof Ltd v Altoft [2006] EWHC 1678 (Ch) 209, 265
von Hanover v Germany, Application No 59320/00 269

W

Wadsworth v Lydall [1981] 1 WLR 598 21
Walker v Boyle [1982] 1 All ER 634 45
Wardars (Import & Export) Co Ltd v W Norwood & Sons Ltd [1968] 2 QB 663, CA 27
Warren v Truprint [1986] BTLC 344 46
Waterford Wedgwood plc v David Nagli Ltd [1998] FSR 92 189
Watford Electronics Ltd v Sanderson CFL Ltd [2001] EWCA Civ 317, [2001] 1 All ER (Comm) 696 6, 44, 45, 46, 49, 55, 276
Welex AG v Rosa Maritime Ltd (The 'Epsilon Rosa') (No 2) [2002] EWHC 2035 (Comm), [2002] 2 Lloyd's Rep 701 117
Wheatley v Drillsafe Ltd [2001] RPC 133 258
Whirlpool Corporation Ltd v Kenwood Ltd [2009] EWCA Civ 753 180, 190
Whitecap Leisure Ltd v John H Rundle Ltd [2008] EWCA Civ 429 20, 22, 25
Williams v Nye (1890) 7 RPC 62, CA 251
Wilson v Best Travel Ltd [1993] 1 All ER 353 61
Wilson v First County Trust Ltd [2001] All ER (D) 28; [2003] UKHL 40, [2003] All ER (D) 187 (Jul) 100
Wilson v Yahoo! UK Ltd [2008] EWHC 361 (Ch) 192, 284
Windsurfing Chiemsee Produktions und Vertriebs GmbH v Boots und Segelzubehör Walter Huber and Another [2000] Ch 523 179
Windsurfing International Inc v Tabur Marine [1985] RPC 59 250, 251
Wombles Ltd v Wombles Skips Ltd [1977] RPC 99 171
Woodhouse UK plc v Architectural Lighting Systems [2006] ECDR 11, [2006] RPC 1 237
Woodman v Photo Trade Processing (CC, 3 April 1981) 46, 47
Worldwide Dryers Ltd v Warner Howard Ltd and Others (1982) The Times, 9 December 26
Wrenn v Landamore [2007] All ER (D) 361 (Jul), aff'd [2008] All ER (D) 134 (Apr), CA 209

Z

Zakritoe Aktsionernoe Obchtechestvo Torgovy Dom Potomkov Postavechtchika Dvora Ego Imperatorskago Velitschestva PA Smirnova v Diageo North America Inc [2003] All ER (D) 99 (Apr) 182
Zenziper Grains and Feed Stuffs v Bulk Trading Corp Ltd [2001] 1 Lloyd's Rep 357 17
Zezev, Yarimaka v the Governor of HM Prison Brixton, the Government of the United States of America [2002] EWHC 589 (Admin), [2002] Crim LR 648 286
Zino Davidoff SA v A & G Imports Ltd; Levi Strauss & Co and Another v Tesco Stores Ltd and Another; Levi Strauss & Co and Another v Costco Wholesale UK (Joined Cases C-414/99, C-415/99 and C-416/99) [2002] All ER (EC) 55 192, 353

Table of Statutes

Bills of Exchange Act 1882 140, 143
s 3(1) 141
s 29(1) 143
s 73 141

Carriage of Goods by Road Act 1965 128
Carriage of Goods by Sea Act 1971 127
Carriage of Goods by Sea Act 1992 127
s 2 127
Companies Act 1985
ss 395–396 30
Competition Act 1980 333
Competition Act 1998 75, 332, 335, 336, 339, 355, 415–17
s 2 333
s 2(1) 333, 334
s 2(2) 333
s 2(4) 334
s 6(1)–(3) 336
s 9 336
s 10 335
s 10(2) 335
s 18 333, 334
s 18(2) 334
ss 25–35 334
s 36 334, 335
ss 37–38 334
s 39 334, 335
s 39(1)(a)–(b) 335
s 39(3)–(4) 335
s 39(9) 335
s 40 334, 335
s 40(2) 335
s 40(3)–(4) 336
s 60 333
Computer Misuse Act 1990 285, 287
s 1 285, 287, 316
s 1(1) 285
s 2 285, 286, 287
s 2(1)(b) 286
s 3 286, 287
Consumer Credit Act 1974 58, 64, 66, 97–108
s 8 98, 99
s 9 99
s 12(b) 102
s 15 98, 99
s 16 99, 104
s 16A 99
s 16B 99
s 19 99
s 21(1) 98
ss 22–41 98
s 56 100, 105
ss 57–58 100
ss 60–61 100
s 61(1)(a) 100
Consumer Credit Act 1974 – *continued*
ss 62–65 100
ss 67–73 101, 102
s 75 101, 102, 105, 302
ss 77–79 101
s 83 302
s 84 302
s 87 102
s 90 63
s 92 102
s 127 100
s 127(3) 100, 101
ss 137–140 102
s 140B 103
s 145 106
s 189 99
Consumer Credit Act 2006 97, 98, 99, 101, 102, 106, 108
ss 3–4 99
ss 19–22 102
Consumer Protection Act 1987
s 7 281
Contracts (Applicable Law) Act 1990 113
Contracts (Rights of Third Parties) Act 1999 11, 61, 282
Copyright (Computer Software) Amendment Act 1985 278
Copyright, Designs and Patents Act 1988 203, 204, 207, 210, 212, 216, 222, 224, 225, 227, 232, 233, 239, 243, 244, 245, 287, 380–403
s 1 204
s 1(1) 204
s 1(1)(a) 205
s 1(3) 204
s 3(1) 205, 222, 272, 278
s 3(2) 207
s 3A 227
s 3A(1)–(2) 288
s 4 206
s 4(1) 205
s 4(1)(a) 206
s 4(1)(b) 207
s 4(1)(c) 206
s 4(2) 205
s 5A 212
s 5A(1) 212
s 5A(2) 211, 212
s 5B 212
s 5B(1)–(2) 212
s 5B(4) 211, 212
s 6 212
s 6(1) 212
s 6(1A) 212
s 6(2) 212
s 6(3) 213
s 6(4) 213
s 6(4A) 213

Copyright, Designs and Patents Act 1988 – *continued*
s 6(5) 213
s 6(5A) 213
s 6(6) 211, 213
s 7 222
s 8 215
s 8(1) 213
s 8(2) 211, 213
s 9 213
s 11 209
s 11(1)–(2) 208
s 12 207
s 13A 214
s 13B 214
s 14 214
s 16 214, 216
s 17 214, 216
s 17(2) 278
s 17(3) 214
s 17(6) 216
ss 18–19 216
s 20 216, 284
s 21 215, 216
ss 22–27 217
s 28A 224, 295
s 29 217
s 30(1)–(2) 218
s 50A 216
s 51 243, 244
s 51(1) 243, 244
s 51(3) 244
s 52 208, 243
s 62 219
s 77 210
s 80 210
s 84 211
s 85 209, 211
s 86(1)–(2) 211
s 94 211
s 96(2) 221
s 97(1)–(2) 221
s 99 221
s 101 221
s 101A 221
s 102 221
s 107 221
s 108 221
s 111 221
s 114 221
s 114A 221
s 213 273
s 213(1) 239
s 213(2) 239, 240
s 213(3) 240, 241
s 213(3)(a) 240, 241
s 213(3)(b)(i)–(ii) 241
s 213(3)(c) 242
s 213(4) 239
s 213(6) 239
s 215 242
s 215(4) 242
s 216 242

Copyright, Designs and Patents Act 1988 – *continued*
s 217 239
s 226(1) 242
s 226(3) 243
s 227 243
s 229(1) 243
s 230 243
s 231 243
s 233 243
s 236 243
s 237 244
s 253 243
s 296 295
ss 296ZA–296ZG 295

Data Protection Act 1984 287, 305, 306, 313
Data Protection Act 1998 285, 287, 301, 305, 306, 307, 308, 309, 311, 313, 314, 315, 316, 317, 318, 321, 323
Part II 311
Part III 317
Part IV 314
Part V 317
Sch 6 301
Sch 9 301
s 1(1) 307, 308, 311
s 2 311
s 3 312
s 4(4) 309
s 7 312
ss 9–11 312
s 12 312
s 12(6)–(7) 312
s 13 312
s 13(3) 312
s 14 313
s 17 310, 311
s 21 317
s 21(1) 310
ss 27–28 314
s 29 314
s 29(3) 315
ss 30–34 314
s 35 314
s 35(2) 315, 316
ss 36–39 314
s 42 313
s 47 313, 317
s 51(3) 310
s 54 316
s 55 317
s 55(6) 317
s 59 317
s 68 308
Sch 1 309
Sch 2 310, 311, 313, 314
paras 1–4 312
Sch 3 311, 313, 314
Schs 7–8 314
Drug Trafficking Act 1994 315

Electronic Communications Act 2000 135

Electronic Communications Act 2000 – *continued*
Part II 293
Enterprise Act 2002 334, 336, 418–19
s 188 336
s 190(4) 336
Estate Agents Act 1979 59

Factors Act 1889 64
Financial Services and Markets Act 2000 59, 117
Freedom of Information Act 2000 306, 308, 318, 319, 320, 321, 322
s 1 319
s 1(1) 319
s 1(4) 319
s 2 320
s 3(1) 318
s 5 318
s 7 319
s 18 322
s 19 319
s 21 318, 320
ss 22–24 321
ss 26–35 321
s 36 321, 322
s 36(2)(b) 322
s 37 321
s 38 321, 322
s 40 321
s 40(1)–(4) 318
ss 41–44 321
s 45 320
s 46 320
s 50 322
s 54 322
s 57 322

Hire Purchase Act 1964 66
Human Rights Act 1998 101, 263, 264, 268, 285, 322
s 6 322
s 12 322
Sch 1, Pt 1, Art 8 268, 269

Insolvency Act 1986
s 107 281
s 127 281
s 178 281
s 239 281

Late Payment of Commercial Debts (Interest) Act 1998 21, 33, 34
Law Reform (Frustrated Contracts) Act 1943 52
s 1(2)–(3) 52
s 2(5) 52
Law Reform (Miscellaneous Provisions) Act 1934 21

Misrepresentation Act 1967 6, 11, 26, 40, 275
s 1 26
s 3 6, 7, 276

Official Secrets Act 318

Partnership Act 1890
s 1 8
Patents Act 1949 258
Patents Act 1977 247, 253, 254, 367–79
s 1(1) 259, 261
s 1(1)(a) 248
s 1(1)(b)–(c) 249
s 1(2) 249, 252, 254, 272
s 1(2)(a) 249, 253
s 1(2)(b)–(c) 253
s 1(2)(d) 254
s 1(3) 252
ss 2–4 259
s 7 259
s 7(2) 256
s 15 255
s 36 261
s 39(1) 256
s 39(1)(b) 256
s 40 256
s 41 257
s 41(3) 257
s 42 256
s 42(3) 256
s 58 259
s 60 257, 260
s 60(1)(a)–(c) 257
s 60(2) 257
s 60(5) 261
s 60(5)(d) 260
s 61 261
s 62 261
s 62(1) 261
s 64 261
s 70 261
s 72 261
s 72(1) 259
s 72(1)(c)–(d) 252
s 73 259
s 74(1)–(3) 259
s 75 260, 261
s 76 259
s 76(3) 260
s 125(1) 258
Plant Varieties Act 1997 254

Registered Designs Act 1787 163
Registered Designs Act 1949 180, 232, 235, 238, 245, 357–66
s 1(2)–(3) 234
s 1B(1)–(2) 234
s 1B(3) 234, 235
s 1B(4) 235
s 1B(5)–(6) 234, 236
s 1B(6)(a) 234
s 1B(7) 234
s 1B(8)–(9) 236
s 1C 236
s 1C(1)–(3) 236
s 2 237
s 2(1) 237
s 2(1A) 237
s 2(1B) 237

Registered Designs Act 1949 – *continued*
s 7(1) 237, 238
s 7(2) 238
s 7A 238
s 7A(2)–(4) 238
s 7A(5) 237
s 7A(6) 236, 238
s 8 237
s 24B 238
s 26 239
Sch 1 237
Regulation of Investigatory Powers Act 2000 284, 315
Resale Prices Act 1976 333
Restrictive Trade Practices Act 1976 333
Restrictive Trade Practices Act 1977 333

Sale of Goods Act 1979 9, 12, 15, 16, 18, 19, 22, 25, 28, 53, 58, 60, 63, 64, 66, 107, 108, 111, 275, 280
Part IV 15
s 2(1) 13
s 2(4) 13
s 5(1) 13
s 6 13
s 8 11, 13, 14
s 9 14
s 10 16, 20
s 10(1) 16, 21, 275
s 10(2) 16
s 11(2) 276
s 11(3) 275
s 12 9, 16, 41, 58, 275
s 12(1)–(2) 16, 280
s 12(2)(b) 16
s 13 16, 18, 24, 28, 41, 58, 275, 276
s 13(1) 280
s 14 18, 24, 25, 28, 41, 55, 58, 61, 93, 275, 276, 278
s 14(1) 16
s 14(2) 16, 18, 19, 43, 275, 280
s 14(2A)–(2C) 16, 18
s 14(2D)–(2E) 16
s 14(3) 16, 19, 43, 275, 280
s 14(4) 16, 20
s 15 16, 18, 20, 24, 28, 41, 58
s 15A 24, 25
s 16 275
s 17 24, 26, 28, 124, 275
s 18 9, 26, 27, 124, 275
s 19 22, 24, 28, 124, 275
s 20 27, 30, 133, 275
s 20(1) 15, 27, 125, 275
s 20(2) 17, 125
s 20A 32
s 25 23, 29, 31, 64, 66
s 25(1) 64, 66
s 27 16, 20, 21, 22, 27
s 28 15, 16, 20, 21, 22
s 29 15, 16, 17
s 29(1) 124
s 29(2) 17, 22
s 29(3) 17

Sale of Goods Act 1979 – *continued*
s 29(5)–(6) 17
s 30 16, 18
s 30(1)–(2) 18
s 30(2A) 18
s 30(3) 18
s 31 16, 18
s 31(1) 18
s 32(1) 15, 17
s 32(3) 134
s 34 24
s 35 24, 276
s 35(1) 22
s 35(2) 21
s 35(4) 22, 24
s 36 24, 25, 54
s 37 17, 24
s 38 22
s 38(1) 22
s 38(1)(c) 22
s 39 22
s 39(1) 22
s 41 22, 23, 24
s 42 22, 24
ss 43–45 22, 23, 24
s 46 22, 23, 24
s 46(1) 23
s 47 22, 24
s 48 22, 23, 24
s 48(2) 23
s 48(3) 21, 23
s 48(4) 21
s 48A 28
s 48A(2)–(3) 28
ss 48B–48F 28
s 49 21, 23
s 50 18, 23
s 50(2) 276
s 50(3) 23
s 51 25
s 51(3) 25
s 52 25, 26
s 53 25
s 54 24, 25
s 55 12, 16
s 61 13, 25, 61, 278
s 61(1) 14
s 62(2) 121
Sale of Goods (Implied Terms) Act 1973 63
s 10(2) 64
s 10(2B) 64
s 10(3) 64
Sale and Supply of Goods Act 1994 24, 25, 26
Solicitors Act 1974 59
Statute of Anne 1709 163, 203
Statute of Frauds 1677
s 4 293
Supply of Goods (Implied Terms) Act 1973 53, 58, 108
ss 8–11 41
Supply of Goods and Services Act 1982 12, 58, 59, 60, 62, 63, 273, 280, 283
s 1 59

Supply of Goods and Services Act 1982 – *continued*
s 1(2) 60
s 4(2) 63
s 4(4) 63
s 6 58
s 7 58
s 7(1)–(2) 280
s 8 58, 280
s 9 58, 61, 63, 278, 280
s 9(2) 63
s 9(5) 63
ss 10–11 58
s 12(3) 59
s 13 59, 60, 61, 278
s 14 59, 62
s 14(2) 62
s 15 59, 63
s 18 61, 278

Trade Marks Act 1938 183, 190
Trade Marks Act 1994 162, 167, 173, 175, 180, 187, 189, 195, 284, 404–14
s 1(1) 173, 174, 175, 176, 177, 188
s 3 174, 176, 193
s 3(1) 176, 177, 180, 182
s 3(1)(a) 176
s 3(1)(b) 176, 177
s 3(1)(c) 176, 177, 178, 179
s 3(1)(d) 176, 177, 188
s 3(2) 177, 180
s 3(3) 177, 181
s 3(3)(a)–(b) 181
s 3(6) 181
s 5 174, 183, 186, 187
s 5(1) 183, 185, 186, 187
s 5(2) 184, 185, 186, 187
s 5(2)(a) 187
s 5(2)(b) 186, 187
s 5(3) 184, 186, 187, 190
s 5(4) 184, 186
s 6A 187
s 9 188
s 9(1) 174, 188
s 10 174, 184, 186, 188, 193
s 10(1) 175, 189
s 10(2) 189
s 10(3) 189, 190
s 10(4) 193
s 10(6) 190, 193
s 11 174, 193, 194
s 11(2) 177
s 11(2)(a)–(b) 193
s 12 193, 194

Trade Marks Act 1994 – *continued*
s 14 188, 194
s 14(2) 194
ss 15–19 194
s 21 194
s 46 188
s 46(1)(a) 187
s 46(1)(d) 188
s 47 193
s 48 193, 194
s 49 179
s 50 179
s 56 193, 195, 284
s 92 189, 194
ss 93–94 194
s 95 188, 194
ss 96–98 194
Sch 1 179
Sch 2 179
Trade Union and Labour Relations (Consolidation) Act 1992 311

Unfair Contract Terms Act 1977 7, 8, 11, 13, 16, 25, 28, 36, 37, 38, 40, 41, 42, 43, 50, 51, 53, 54, 55, 56, 62, 66, 107, 108, 111, 117, 275, 276, 280, 281, 303
s 2 11, 40, 62, 281, 283
s 2(1) 41
s 3 11, 40, 41, 43, 53, 54, 56
s 3(1) 276
s 3(2)(a) 54
s 3(2)(b)(ii) 53
ss 4–5 40
s 6 11, 40, 41, 51, 54, 276, 280
s 6(1) 41
s 6(2) 41, 42
s 6(3) 42, 43, 56
s 7 13, 40, 41, 70, 280
s 7(3) 43
s 11(1) 43
s 11(4) 50
s 11(4)(a) 50
s 11(4)(b) 47
s 11(5) 43
s 12 41
s 12(2) 12
s 13 36, 40
ss 16–21 40
s 26 40, 111
s 26(2) 40
s 27 40
Sch 1 40, 280

Value Added Tax Act 1983
s 10(2) 14

Table of Statutory Instruments

Artist's Resale Rights Regulations 2006 (SI 2006/346) 224
reg 3 224
reg 9 224
reg 16 224

Business Protection from Misleading Marketing Regulations 2008 (SI 2008/1276) 193, 194

Civil Procedure Rules 1998 (SI 1998/3132) 315
Commercial Agents (Council Directive) Regulations 1993 (SI 1993/3053) 77, 78, 82, 84, 85, 86, 88, 93, 108, 117, 420–6
reg 1(1) 77
reg 1(3) 77
reg 2(1) 77, 78
reg 2(2)–(5) 78
reg 3 81
reg 3(1)–(2) 81
reg 3(2)(b) 82
reg 4 83
reg 4(1) 83
reg 4(2) 82, 83
reg 4(2)(b) 84
reg 4(3) 82, 83
regs 6–9 84
reg 8 85
regs 10–12 84, 85
reg 15 80, 84
reg 16 87
reg 17 78, 84, 86, 87
reg 17(1)–(4) 86
reg 17(5) 86, 87
reg 17(6)–(7) 86
reg 18 84, 87
reg 18(a) 87
reg 19 87
reg 23(1) 78
Competition Act 1998 (Determination of Turnover for Penalties) (Amendment) Order 2004 (SI 2004/1259) 334
Competition Act 1998 (Determination of Turnover for Penalties) Order 2000 (SI 2000/309) 334
Competition Act (Small Agreements and Conduct of Minor Significance) Regulations 2000 (SI 2000/262) 335
Consumer Credit (Advertisement) Regulations 2004 (SI 2004/1484) 98
Consumer Credit (Agreements) Regulations 1983 (SI 1983/1555) 100
Consumer Credit (Disclosure of Information) Regulations 2004 (SI 2004/1481) 100
Consumer Credit (Exempt Agreements) Order 1989 (SI 1989/869) 99, 104
Consumer Credit (Exempt Agreements) Order 2007 (SI 2007/1168) 99
Consumer Protection (Distance Selling) Regulations 2000 (SI 2000/2334) 12, 299, 431–9
reg 3 299
reg 5 299
reg 6 299
reg 6(2) 299
reg 6(2)(a)–(b) 299
reg 7 299
reg 8 299
reg 8(2) 299, 300
reg 9 299
reg 10 299
reg 10(1)–(2) 299
reg 10(4)–(5) 300
regs 11–14 299, 300
reg 16 299
reg 17 299, 300
reg 18 299
reg 19(1) 299, 300
reg 19(5) 300
reg 21 302
reg 21(3) 302
reg 24 300
reg 25(1) 300
reg 27 300
Sch 1 299
Consumer Transactions (Restrictions on Statements) Order 1976 (SI 1976/1813) 51, 282
Copyright (Computer Programs) Regulations 1992 (SI 1992/3233) 222, 278
Copyright (Industrial Process and Excluded Articles) (No 2) Order 1989 (SI 1989/1070) 208
Copyright and Related Rights Regulations 2003 (SI 2003/2498) 224, 295
reg 3 224
Copyright and Rights in Databases Regulations 1997 (SI 1997/3032) 206, 221, 227, 287, 427–30
reg 13 228
reg 14 228, 230, 288
reg 15 228, 288
reg 16 228, 288
reg 16(2) 227, 229, 288
reg 17 228, 288
reg 17(3) 228
reg 18 228, 288
regs 19–20 229, 288

Data Protection (Processing of Sensitive Personal Data) Order 2000 (SI 2000/417) 314, 315
Design Right (Semiconductor Topographies) Regulations 1989 (SI 1989/1100) 244, 273
reg 2(1) 273

Electronic Commerce (EC Directive) Regulations 2002 (SI 2002/2013) 12, 291, 292, 296, 298, 299, 303, 440–4
reg 2 296, 297
reg 6 297
reg 6(1) 297
reg 6(1)(g) 297
reg 6(2) 297
reg 7 297
reg 9 297
reg 9(1)(a) 292
reg 9(3) 297, 299
reg 11 297
reg 11(1) 297
reg 11(1)(a) 297
reg 11(1)(b) 297, 299
reg 11(2) 297
reg 11(2)(a) 292
reg 12 292
regs 13–15 299
reg 17 297, 298
reg 17(1)–(2) 298
reg 18 297, 298
reg 18(b) 298
reg 19 297, 298
reg 20 297
Electronic Signatures Regulations 2002 (SI 2002/318) 293
Environmental Information Regulations 2004 (SI 2004/3391) 322

Money Laundering Regulations 2003 (SI 2003/3075) 315

Package Travel, Package Holidays and Package Tours Regulations 1992 (SI 1992/3288) 61–2
Patent Regulations 2000 (SI 2000/2037) 254
Privacy and Electronic Communications (EC Directive) Regulations 2003 (SI 2003/2426) 301, 310, 445–7
regs 4–8 301
reg 8(4) 301
reg 22 301
reg 22(3) 301

Privacy and Electronic Communications (EC Directive) Regulations 2003– *continued*
reg 23 301
regs 30–32 301

Registered Designs Regulations 2001 (SI 2001/3949) 232, 235, 245

Sale and Supply of Goods to Consumers Regulations 2002 (SI 2002/3045) 12

Telecommunications (Lawful Business Practice) (Interception of Communications) Regulations 2000 (SI 2000/ 2699) 285
Trade Mark Rules 2000 (SI 2000/136) 175
r 11A 175
Sch 4 195–201
Trade Marks (Earlier Trade Marks) Regulations 2008 (SI 2008/1067) 187, 193
Trade Marks (Proof of Use) Etc Regulations 2004 (SI 2004/946) 190

Unfair Terms in Consumer Contracts Regulations 1994 (SI 1994/3159) 42
Unfair Terms in Consumer Contracts Regulations 1999 (SI 1999/2083) 12, 34, 42, 117, 282
regs 1–3 42
reg 5(1) 42
reg 6 42
reg 7 42, 43
reg 8 42
regs 10–15 42
Sch 1 42
Sch 2 42, 44, 46, 48, 50

Codes

Banking Code of Practice 59
British Code of Advertising Sales Promotion and Direct Marketing 310
Employment Practices Data Protection Code 310
Solicitors' Costs Information and Client Care Code 63

Table of European and International Legislation

Commission Notices

Notice on Agreements of Minor Importance (OJ 2001 C368/07) 90, 335, 340, 341, 349, 350
Point 4 340
Point 7 340
Point 8 340
Point 10 340
Point 11(2) 340
Notice of May 2000 74, 82
paras 12–15 75, 76, 339
paras 16–17 75, 76, 82, 339
para 18 75, 76, 339
paras 19–20 339, 75
Notice (NAAT) 341
Notice (OJ 2004 C101/06) 339
Notice (OJ 2004 C101/07) 341

Directives

Directive 84/450/EEC 191, 193
Art 3a(1) 191
Art 3a(1)(h) 191
Directive 86/653/EEC (Self-Employed Commercial Agents) 77
Directive 87/54/EEC 273
Directive 87/102/EEC (Consumer Credit) 97
Directive 89/104/EC (Trade Marks)
Art 5(2) 190–1
Art 7 353
Directive 89/104/EEC (Approximation of the Laws of Member States about Trade Marks) 173, 180
Directive 91/250/EEC 225, 278
Directive 92/100/EEC 225
Directive 93/13/EEC 42
Directive 93/98/EC (Copyright Duration) 208
Directive 95/46/EC (Data Protection) 305, 308
Art 18 310
Directive 96/9/EC (Database Directive) 221, 225, 227, 287
Directive 97/7/EC (Distance Selling Directive) 299
Directive 97/55/EC 193
Directive 98/44/EC 254
Directive 98/71/EC (Design Directive) 163, 232
Directive 99/44/EC (Consumer Goods and Associated Guarantees) 12, 28
Directive 99/93/EC (Electronic Signatures) 293
Directive 2000/31/EC (Electronic Commerce in the Internal Market) 135, 291, 292, 296, 298
Art 9(1) 292
Art 14 298
Directive 2000/35/EC (Combating Late Payment in Commercial Transactions) 33
Directive 2001/29/EC (Copyright Directive) 217, 224
Art 6–7 224
Directive 2001/84/EC (Resale Right for the Benefit of the Author of an Original Work of Art) 224
reg 3 224
reg 9 224
reg 16 224
Directive 2002/58/EC (Privacy and Electronic Communications) 301

Regulations

Brussels II *see* Regulation 44/2001
Rome I *see* Regulation 539/2008
Regulation 4087/88 354
Regulation 1768/92 (life or pharmaceutical patent) 256
Regulation 240/96 350
Regulation 1610/96 (life or plant protection product patent) 256
Regulation 2790/99 (block exemptions) 90, 91, 335, 342, 343, 344, 345, 346, 350, 351, 354
Recital 8 343
Recital 9 343
Art 1 343, 344
Art 2 343
Art 2(1) 343, 345
Art 2(2) 345, 344
Art 2(3) 344
Art 2(4) 344, 345
Art 2(5) 344
Art 3 343, 344, 345
Art 3(1) 344
Art 4 343, 345
Art 4(a)–(e) 344
Art 5 343, 344, 345, 351
Art 5(a) 344
Arts 6–8 345
Art 9 344, 345
Art 9(1)–(2) 345
Arts 10–13 345
Regulation 44/2001 7, 113, 114, 115, 116, 155, 156, 293
Art 2 114
Art 4 148
Art 5 114, 148
Art 5(1)(a)–(b) 114
Art 5(3) 114
Art 5(5) 114
Art 6(1) 115
Art 14 150
Art 15 115, 293
Arts 16–18 115
Art 21 115

Regulation 44/2001 – *continued*
- Art 22 114, 115
- Art 23 115
- Arts 27–28 116
- Art 34 148
- Art 38 150
- Art 38(a) 150
- Art 38(d) 150
- Art 39 150

Regulation 6/2002 232, 239, 244
Regulation 1400/2002 342
Regulation 1/2003 338, 339, 342
- Art 10 335, 338

Regulation 772/2004 342, 344, 350, 351, 356
- Preamble 350
- Art 1 351
  - para 1(b) 350
- Arts 2–3 351
- Art 4 351
- Art 4(1) 351
- Art 4(1)(a) 351
- Art 4(2) 351
- Art 4(2)(a) 351
- Arts 5–8 351

Regulation 593/2008 116, 293
- Art 1 118
- Art 1(4) 118
- Art 3 118
- Art 3(4) 118
- Art 4 118
- Art 4(1)–(4) 118
- Art 6(1)(b) 293
- Art 7 118
- Art 9 119
- Art 9(2) 119
- Art 19 119
- Art 19(1)–(3) 119

European treaties and conventions

Constitutional Treaty 337
EC Treaty 331, 332, 348
- Art 3(1)(g) 336, 337
- Art 28 337, 347, 348, 352, 354, 356
- Arts 29–30 337, 347, 348, 352, 356
- Art 81 74, 75, 80, 82, 83, 91, 92, 93, 296, 332, 333, 334, 335, 336, 337, 338, 339, 340, 341, 345, 346, 348, 349, 352, 354, 355, 356, 448
- Art 81(1) 75, 76, 90, 91, 332, 333, 337, 338, 339, 340, 341, 342, 343, 346, 348, 349, 350, 354
- Art 81(2) 338
- Art 81(3) 336, 338, 341, 342, 349, 351, 355
- Art 82 332, 333, 334, 337, 339, 345, 348, 351, 352, 354, 355, 356, 448
- Art 87 355
- Art 295 348, 356

EEA Agreement
- Art 53–54 332

European Patent Convention 248, 249
- Art 52(4) 249
- Art 54(2) 249
- Art 69 258

Lugano Convention 113
Reform Treaty (Treaty of Lisbon) 332, 337
Treaty of Amsterdam
- Art 28 261
- Art 30 261

Treaty of Lisbon 332, 337

International conventions

Berne Convention 204, 225
Convention on the Contract for the International Carriage of Goods by Road (CMR) 1978 128
European Convention on Human Rights 100, 263, 322
- Art 6 100
- Art 8 263, 268, 314, 316
- Art 10 263, 269
- Protocol 1
  - Art 1 100

Hague Convention on Private International Law 113
Hague-Visby Rules 127
Madrid Protocol 195
Paris Convention for the Protection of Intellectual Property 193, 195
Patent Co-operation Treaty 1970 248
Rome Convention 1980 7, 113, 116, 293
- Art 1(2) 116
- Art 3(1) 116
- Art 3(3) 117
- Art 4(1)–(2) 116, 117
- Art 4(3)–(5) 117
- Art 5 117
- Art 6 117
- Art 6(2) 18, 117
- Art 7 119, 117

TRIPS 195
UNCITRAL Model Law on Electronic Commerce (1998) 135
Uniform Customs and Practice for Documentary Credits 147, 149, 152, 158
- Art 2 147
- Art 3 147, 148
- Art 6 149
- Art 6(d)–(e) 153
- Art 14 152
- Art 15 152
- Art 16 152
- Art 16(1) 153
- Art 34 152
- Art 35 153
- Part D 152

Universal Copyright Convention (UNESCO) 225
Warsaw Convention on International Carriage by Air 1929 128

Table of Abbreviations

ADR	alternative dispute resolution
ALCS	Authors' Licensing and Collecting Society
BEA 1882	Bills of Exchange Act 1882
CA 1957	Cheques Act 1957
CA 1998	Competition Act 1998
CCA 1974	Consumer Credit Act 1974
CCA 2006	Consumer Credit Act 2006
CDPA 1988	Copyright, Designs and Patents Act 1988
CFR	Cost and Freight
CIF	Cost, Insurance and Freight
CIP	Carriage and Insurance Paid To
CJJA 1982	Civil Jurisdiction and Judgments Act 1982
CLA	Copyright Licensing Agency Ltd
CPT	Carriage Paid To
CTM	Community Trade Mark
DAF	Delivered at Frontier
DBERR	Department for Business, Enterprise and Regulatory Reform
DC	debtor-creditor
DCS	debtor-creditor-supplier
DDP	Delivered Duty Paid
DDU	Delivered Duty Unpaid
DEQ	Delivered Ex Quay Duty Paid
DES	Delivered Ex Ship
DTI	Department of Trade and Industry
ECB	extortionate credit bargain
ECJ	European Court of Justice
EDI	Electronic Data Interchange
EEA	European Economic Area
EFTA	European Free Trade Area
EPC 1973	European Patent Convention 1973
EPO	European Patents Office
EXW	Ex Works
FAS	Free Alongside
FCA	Free Carrier
FOB	Free On Board
FSR	*Fleet Street Reports*
ICANN	Internet Corporation for Assigned Names and Numbers
ICC	International Chamber of Commerce
IP	intellectual property
IT	information technology
MCPS	Mechanical Copyright Protection Society
NLA	Newspaper Licensing Agency Ltd
OFT	Office of Fair Trading
PA 1977	Patents Act 1977
PCP	Rosenberg, *Practical Commercial Precedents* (Sweet & Maxwell)
PCT	Patent Co-operation Treaty
PLS	Publishers Licensing Society
PPL	Phonographic Performance Ltd

RDA 1949	Registered Designs Act 1949
RPA 1976	Resale Prices Act 1976
RPC	*Reports of Patent, Design and Trade Mark Cases*
RTPA 1976	Restrictive Trade Practices Act 1976
RUC	restricted-use credit
SGA 1979	Sale of Goods Act 1979
SGSA 1982	Supply of Goods and Services Act 1982
UCP	Uniform Customs and Practice for Documentary Credits
UCTA 1977	Unfair Contract Terms Act 1977
ULIS	Uniform Law on the International Sale of Goods
UNCITRAL	UN Commission on International Trade Law
URDG	Uniform Rules for Demand Guarantees (ICC)
UUC	unrestricted-use credit
VPL	Video Performance Ltd
WIPO	World Intellectual Property Organisation

Part I

COMMERCIAL AGREEMENTS

Chapter 1

Introduction to Commercial Contracts

1.1	Introduction	3
1.2	The principles of commercial law	3
1.3	Drafting and content of a commercial contract	4
1.4	Introduction to boiler-plate clauses	5
1.5	Limitation of liability in contracts	8

1.1 Introduction

The word 'commercial' can be given a wide range of meanings, from the very general one of having profit for a primary aim, to the much more specific meaning of the large-scale buying and selling of merchandise in the form of goods ('mercantile activity'). In this work, the word is used to link together the very large number of interconnecting areas of law and practice, within which legal practitioners must work to be able to assist the functioning and needs of a modern world. Such a world must necessarily depend upon the reasonable availability of goods, transport, money, credit, etc to function at all, and there are very close links between these essentials.

The common factor, in making such essentials available, is the use of the commercial contract. Part I of this work is designed to bring together most of the basic considerations that must be addressed in order to understand the nature of contracts under which goods and money are intended to pass from hand to hand. Part II will go on to deal with the extra considerations required where such contracts involve international aspects.

In Part I, the focus is on the content and drafting of contracts for the sale of goods and of other contracts under which goods may pass, such as hire purchase and leasing, with particular emphasis on the position and protection of the commercial supplier, as most of such sales take effect on the seller's standard terms, or variations of them. There is also discussion of contracts for marketing arrangements, as most growers or manufacturers do not, themselves, sell their production directly to end users. The general emphasis in Part I will be on business-to-business contracts rather than on consumer arrangements.

Chapter 6 deals with consumer credit. Although this work is not primarily about consumer law, it is important to realise that the world runs on credit at all levels, and credit availability to the end user is the lifeblood of most of the mercantile and manufacturing communities. It is a massive industry to the suppliers of such credit, and some basic knowledge of it is important.

1.2 The principles of commercial law

Professor Roy Goode has long been an internationally renowned authority on commercial law. In 'The codification of commercial law' [1988] 14 Mon LR 135, he describes eight principles of commercial law:

(a) party autonomy (freedom to contract as the parties wish);

(b) predictability;

(c) flexibility to accommodate new practices;

(d) good faith (although English law is ambivalent);

(e) the encouragement of self-help;

(f) the facilitation of security (over assets);

(g) the protection of vested rights; and
(h) the protection of innocent third parties.

Businesses need certainty in order to flourish. This is particularly important in mercantile activity because of its international nature; predictable outcomes are important. However, a recurrent problem for lawyers is that the law always lags behind new developments. In recent years, for example, e-commerce has sprung up without specific legislation to solve its problems, though the legislation is now appearing (see further **Chapter 20**). Judges often have to deal with commercial disputes where the statute law is inadequate and the behaviour of the parties is framed by the practices of the trade in which they are engaged. They have to produce a decision that fits with commercial practice, and they may have to adapt the law or interpret it in a new way to do so.

Professor Goode also suggests five operative principles of commercial law:

(a) the concept of the market (often, the international market);
(b) the importance of customs or usage of a trade or locality (as a court will recognise them and give effect to them);
(c) the importance of a consistent course of dealing (as not all terms are spelled out in a written contract);
(d) the concept of negotiability (as a holder of a negotiable instrument gets good title); and
(e) the enforceability of abstract payment undertakings (even without consideration, eg in the case of a documentary credit).

These five principles indicate the importance of trade practice and the need to give legal effect to commercial arrangements even if they do not always sit comfortably with some legal concepts. It would be a brave, or foolhardy, judge who sought to construe a written contract in the absence of these factors. Principles (d) and (e) are discussed in **Chapter 10**.

Where do you look to find the legal principles on which commercial law is based? The sources of commercial law which are typically quoted are:

(a) the law of contract;
(b) established custom and usage of the trade;
(c) national legislation;
(d) European Community law; and
(e) international Conventions.

If you are dealing with a commercial contract matter in practice, the sources which are likely to cause you trouble are custom and usage of the trade, and international Conventions. Legal databases are great for legislation, but the 'soft' material can be harder to track down. Indeed, half the problem is knowing that it exists in the first place. As regards the custom and usage of the trade, you will be often be reliant on your client for information on this aspect.

1.3 Drafting and content of a commercial contract

The basic principles of the structure of agreements are set out in ***Skills for Lawyers***. You may also wish to look at Christou, *Drafting Commercial Agreements* (4th edn, Sweet & Maxwell, 2009).

The key factor in drafting a commercial agreement is not to lose sight of your client's commercial aims. In other words, adapt precedents to fit your client's deal, do not adapt your client's deal to fit the precedents. It is easier to say this than to do it in practice.

Commercial agreements have a fairly typical running order:

(a) the parties;

(b) the recitals, if any;
(c) definitions;
(d) conditions precedent, if any;
(e) agreements (eg to sell the goods, or to pay the price);
(f) representations and warranties;
(g) 'boiler-plate' clauses;
(h) execution clause and signature; and
(i) schedules.

Schedules are a way of removing unnecessary detail from the body of an agreement and thereby improving its readability. In a large agreement, representations and warranties would also be removed to the schedules.

1.3.1 The parties

It is not as easy to get this right as you might think. For example, is the seller Longshaw Holdings plc, or Longshaw (Chemicals) Ltd? In other words, which company in the group is the relevant one?

1.3.2 Definitions clause

All defined terms start with a capital letter. If the same word or phrase is used in the agreement without being capitalised then the inference is that something different from the defined term is intended.

It is important that the definitions meet the requirements of the agreement. For example, should the definition of 'Vegetables' include tomatoes? It is important to keep an eye on the definitions as the agreement progresses through a number of drafts and negotiation with the other side (ie, do the definitions still work satisfactorily?). It is equally important that the definitions clause does no more than give a clear meaning to a defined term. It should not stray into operative effects, otherwise it may lead to ambiguity.

Defined terms should be used only where they are recurrent in the body of the agreement or where there is a danger of ambiguity if no clear definition is given. Likewise, all defined terms in the agreement should be defined in the definitions section. (In some complex agreements, the entry in the definitions section will merely be a cross reference, possibly to an appendix or other part of the agreement.)

Care should be taken in defining things which might be subject to change during the contract, such as 'The contract goods'. This definition would need to cover different goods at different periods under the contract, and would need to be expressed accordingly.

1.3.3 Interpretation clause

This section should be non-controversial. It covers the basics of interpretation, for example by providing that the headings do not form part of the agreement (as if they did, lawyers would feel the need to draft them more comprehensively, which would detract from their usefulness).

We shall look later at some key operative provisions, especially in the context of the sale of goods. For now, we shall look at so-called 'boiler-plate' clauses. These are clauses which are standard to most commercial contracts and upon which the parties depend for the certainty and predictability of their arrangements.

1.4 Introduction to boiler-plate clauses

In all commercial contracts there are run-of-the-mill clauses that will occur in most contractual agreements to a greater or lesser extent. They are commonly called 'boiler-plate' clauses (or simply referred to as 'the boiler-plate'). They often remain as drafted in the precedent which is being used. They are not usually individually negotiated, as they are relatively uncontroversial. Nevertheless, you must of course check that they are not contrary to your client's interests when negotiating an agreement. It can be a bad mistake to assume that boiler-plate clauses can just be copied out of a precedent. For general information, see Christou, *Boilerplate: Practical Clauses* (4th edn, Sweet & Maxwell, 2005).

There is no precise definition of 'boiler-plate clauses', nor do they have to appear at a given point in the agreement. However, it is common to have a group of boiler-plate clauses at or towards the end of an agreement. Typical boiler-plate clauses are as follows.

1.4.1 The 'prevail' clause

This clause provides in effect that if there is a battle of the forms (ie both parties seek to impose their own terms on the other) then the seller's terms will prevail. Legally, this clause is ineffective – it is the 'offer and counter-offer' point. However, the prevail clause is often included for bluff value.

1.4.2 The 'entire agreement' clause

The parties to an agreement will normally want to ensure that, for convenience, all of their obligations are recorded in one document. They will also seek to avoid the evidential difficulties associated with oral representations and discussions.

The parol evidence rule supports this, as it provides that outside evidence should not be adduced to vary the written contract. This clause avoids an exception to the rule, which states that a contract can be partly written and partly oral if the parties intend it to be. The clause will not operate to avoid the battle of the forms, however. It can also be seen as an exclusion clause if it attempts to exclude liability for misrepresentation.

The danger of an entire agreement clause is that it might exclude other documents which the parties do wish to have taken into account, for example a price list.

Another danger of an entire agreement clause occurred in *Thomas Witter v TBP Industries Ltd* [1996] 2 All ER 573, where such a clause was held to have excluded liability for fraudulent misrepresentation. It therefore ran foul of the Misrepresentation Act 1967, s 3 and was void. The *Thomas Witter* case has been further explained in *Watford Electronics Ltd v Sanderson CFL Ltd* [2001] EWCA Civ 317. There, it was made clear that an entire agreement clause, if the parties have obviously considered it, often prevents a party claiming that he has relied upon other representations. Consequently, no misrepresentation arises in the first place, and the Misrepresentation Act 1967 has no relevance, in the absence of fraud, which does not require reliance to be shown.

In *Inntrepreneur Pub Co (CPC) Ltd v Sweeney* [2002] EWHC 1060 (Ch), the court held that an entire agreement clause prevented a pre-contractual statement becoming a collateral contract or warranty. The court also held that there had been no misrepresentation. See also *Multiplex Constructions (UK) Ltd v Cleveland Bridge UK Ltd* [2006] EWHC 1341 (TCC), affirmed [2007] All ER (D) 264 (Apr), CA, where such a clause was applied; cf *Sutcliffe v Lloyd* [2007] EWCA Civ 153, where the clause was not effective.

1.4.3 The 'no authority' clause

This is an attempt by the seller:

(a) to put a limit on the extent to which its sales representatives, or other employees, are permitted to negotiate individual terms with the buyer; and

(b) to exclude any extravagant claims made by the sales representatives to induce the buyer to enter the contract.

To some extent, there is overlap with the whole agreement clause, and it is subject to the same difficulties, in that the parties might be seen to have ignored it or waived it.

Sometimes, a seller will want to give the sales representatives limited discretion (eg, to agree discounts) and, if so, the clause will need to be amended appropriately.

1.4.4 Buyer becoming insolvent

This is a standard provision relating to the operation of the agreement. You will recognise the various events described from the insolvency law chapters in ***Business Law and Practice***. This clause is often linked to the retention of title clause in a sale of goods agreement, as the typical use for a retention of title clause is when the buyer is going insolvent (see **2.14**).

1.4.5 Law and jurisdiction

This would normally be the law of England and Wales and the jurisdiction of the English courts. If for any reason this clause had been omitted then the Rome Convention on the Law Applicable to Contracts and Regulation 44/2001 ('Brussels II') would be applied (see **Chapter 8**). If the contract were expressed to be subject to any law other than the law of England and Wales, you would not be qualified to advise on it!

1.4.6 Service of notices

A notice clause has to provide for the places where notice is to be served, the method of service and the time at which the notice is deemed to be served. Such clauses have become more complex with the increase in the number of ways in which notice could be given (eg, fax and e-mail). Most notice clauses will not permit oral notice but rather will require it to be in writing.

The notice clause will specify the address(es) to which notice is to be sent. If one party is located overseas then it may be best to specify an address for service in the UK (eg, the party's solicitors or accountants).

Notice clauses will typically require notice to be served during business hours if served in person. If notice is permitted to be sent by fax or e-mail then it could be deemed served when received. If sent by post then it could be deemed served two days after posting. It will all depend on the wording agreed by the parties.

The person to whom notice is sent may also be specified (eg, the company secretary for a corporate party to the contract).

1.4.7 Force majeure

A force majeure clause is intended to suspend or terminate the contractual obligations in the event of an occurrence outside the control of the parties (eg, bad weather). A force majeure clause is usually for the benefit of the seller or deliverer of the goods, as it is the party obliged to supply and/or deliver the goods.

If one or more of the specified events occurs then contractual performance will be suspended for a specified period. If the event is still continuing at the end of that period then the contract will be considered to be terminated.

The list of events can cause some discussion. The usual ones are so-called acts of God, adverse weather such as floods or snow, war, riot, government action, and embargoes or strikes by third parties. Problems may arise where the list of events includes matters that might be, at least in part, within the control of the seller. This may then cause the Unfair Contract Terms Act (UCTA) 1977 to become relevant (see s 3). In *Mamidoil-Jetoil Greek Petroleum Co SA v Okta Crude Oil Refinery AC (No 3)* [2003] EWCA Civ 1031, the Court of Appeal confirmed a judge's finding that the defendant had initiated a process which ended in a Macedonian

Government request to the defendant not to perform the contract. The clause could not be relied upon.

Force majeure clauses are usually strictly construed because they are designed to defend a party from the consequences of a breach; they cannot be used, in offence, to alter terms which are ordinarily implied into delivery or shipment: see *SHV Gas Supply and Trading SAS v Naftomar Shipping and Trading Co Ltd Inc, The Azur Gaz* [2005] EWHC 2528 (Comm).

1.4.8 The 'no partnership' clause

This type of clause seeks to ensure that the agreement cannot be construed as a partnership between the parties to the agreement. There are obvious disadvantages to partnership law, such as being liable for a partner's debts. However, the factor that determines whether or not a partnership is in existence is the definition of 'partnership' in the Partnership Act 1890, s 1, not the wording of a 'no partnership' clause.

1.4.9 The 'no assignment, no subcontracting' clause

If a buyer has selected a specific supplier, it will not want that supplier to subcontract the work to an unknown third party. Similarly, the buyer may not want the contract to be assigned to another supplier. Thus, a clause to cover both these possibilities is often included in commercial contracts.

1.5 Limitation of liability in contracts

This is an important area of commercial contracts and is dealt with in **Chapter 3**. An important aspect of limitation, exclusion and transfer of liability clauses in commercial contracts is the question whether the clause is liable to come within the scope and effect of UCTA 1977, and this is also dealt with in **Chapter 3**.

Chapter 2
The Sale of Goods

2.1	Introduction	9
2.2	Formation of the contract	9
2.3	Basics of the law of contract	10
2.4	Relevant legislation	12
2.5	What are 'goods'?	13
2.6	What is 'sale of goods'?	13
2.7	The price	13
2.8	Delivery	14
2.9	Duties of the seller	16
2.10	Duties of the buyer	20
2.11	Rights of the seller	22
2.12	Rights of the buyer	24
2.13	Effects of a sale of goods contract	26
2.14	Introduction to retention of title	28
2.15	Drafting a retention of title clause: a basic checklist	29
2.16	Retention of title clauses and the creation of charges	32
2.17	'Backing up' a retention of title clause	32
2.18	Unfair terms in consumer contracts	34
2.19	Sale of goods to consumers	34

2.1 Introduction

In this chapter, we examine various aspects of the sale of goods contract. This is probably the most commonly occurring contract type of all, with countless numbers of contracts being entered into every day. This is a vast area of law and the purpose of this chapter is to introduce you to the legal framework within which such contracts are created, and to draw attention to their most important and contentious features. Like many other types of contract, it is open to the parties to exhibit a great deal of freedom of choice in deciding the terms upon which they contract, but a significant feature of English sale of goods law is the presence of a large body of legislation (backed up by a huge body of case law) which may have two major effects upon contractual freedom. The first effect is that some contractual provisions may be rendered statutorily void (see, eg, Sale of Goods Act 1979 (SGA 1979), s 12 and **2.9.1**). The second effect is that the SGA 1979 acts, in some circumstances, to fill in voids and omissions, to which the parties have not turned their minds, or where they have simply relied upon the Act (see, eg, SGA 1979, s 18, as to time of passing of property in goods). The question of the interplay between express contractual provision and the underlying statute law is not at all easy to simplify but, with experience and careful drafting, it is possible to bypass or modify many of the legislative provisions.

How this chapter deals with the topic is by revisiting the way in which a sales contract comes into being and some general contract law principles. It then goes on to consider some of the main provisions of the SGA 1979 and the incidents, rights and obligations of the parties under the contract and under the general law. Lastly, consideration is given to preserving a final fall-back position for the seller, by retaining ownership and the right to recover the goods, against the buyer's default in payment or insolvency.

2.2 Formation of the contract

It is important not to lose sight of the basics of contract law. You need to differentiate between an invitation to treat on the one hand, and an offer on the other hand. In a well-publicised problem in the recent past, Argos had an incorrect price on their Internet website. The price for one model of television was £3 when it should have been £300. A number of customers 'bought' televisions online at £3. However, Argos declined to supply them, stating that the advertisement on their website was only an invitation to treat. Any response from a customer was therefore an offer which Argos could reject. The aggrieved customers argued that the advertisement was an offer which they were accepting, and that Argos was therefore bound as a party to a contract for the sale of goods. What do you think?

Other aspects of contract law which should be kept in mind are:

(a) whose standard terms apply? – the 'battle of the forms' (eg, *Rimeco Riggleson & Metal Co v Queenborough Rolling Mill Co Ltd* [1995] CLY 798, *Sauter Automation Ltd v Goodman (Mechanical Services) Ltd (in liquidation)* (1986) 34 Build LR 81; see also *Murphy & Sons Ltd v Johnston Precast Ltd* [2008] EWHC 3024 (TCC));

(b) 'prevail' clauses (where one set of terms proclaim that they prevail over any other set of terms) are generally considered not to work;

(c) timing and incorporation of terms– were the terms brought to the other party's attention at the time the contract was made?

(d) signing a document is usually acceptance of its terms; and

(e) a collateral contract could be construed to exist between the parties, so include an 'entire agreement' clause in the terms to attempt to exclude this possibility (see **1.4.2**).

2.3 Basics of the law of contract

The essence of a contract is that it is an agreement between two or more parties. In order for it to be a valid agreement, all parties must have been agreeing to the same thing, and not talking at cross-purposes. Let us consider the steps in the formation of a valid contract.

2.3.1 An agreement: accepting an offer and consideration

The first step is to work out whether the parties have reached an agreement. The key points are as follows:

(a) The existence, or otherwise, of an agreement is judged objectively.

(b) Did the parties intend to create legal relations, or was it merely a 'social' arrangement?

(c) There has to be consideration for the contract (or it has to be drafted as a deed).

(d) The value of the consideration, usually money, will not be looked at by the courts. However, some types of act or promise are not regarded by the law as being good consideration, for example past consideration or performance of an existing legal duty.

(e) Was there an offer, or merely an invitation to treat (ie a preliminary discussion)?

(f) Usually there has to be an identifiable offer and acceptance for there to be a valid contract, but a contract can be held to come into existence by means of performance (see *Trentham v Archital Luxfer Ltd* [1993] 1 Lloyd's Rep 25). Nevertheless, it will still be necessary to identify, from the exchanges between the parties, what the terms were in order for them to have been accepted by performance: see *Adonis Construction v O'Keefe Soil Remediation* [2009] EWHC 2047 (TCC). See also *BSC v Cleveland Bridge and Engineering Co Ltd* [1984] 1 All ER 504 for discussion of 'if' contracts, under which a letter of intent can be treated as a standing offer which could result in a binding contract if acted upon before it lapsed or was validly withdrawn.

(g) Acceptance is the unqualified consent of the buyer to the terms of the offer made by the seller.

(h) Offer and acceptance must be communicated and, generally, actual communication is needed.

(i) An offer can be ended by rejection, counter-offer, lapse of time, death of the other party, or by revocation before it has been accepted.

(j) The limitation period for a simple contract is six years; for a deed it is 12 years.

2.3.2 Problem areas: failure to agree

One of the key concepts in the law of contract is that there must be contractual certainty, that is the parties must all be specific about the conditions of the contract. Mistakes can also intervene to create this problem. The key areas are as follows:

(a) A contract cannot generally impose an obligation on a third party, with the proviso that the Contracts (Rights of Third Parties) Act 1999 allows the contract parties to grant rights to a third party.

(b) It is for the parties to make their agreement, and if they do so incompetently then that is their problem. However, the courts can fix a badly drafted contract if there is other evidence of the intent of the parties which can be used to plug the gaps.

(c) An irrelevant or badly drafted clause might be severed by the court, provided the rest of the contract still makes sense.

(d) Agreements which fail to address a key area, eg price, will be void for uncertainty unless otherwise saved, eg by s 8 of the SGA 1979 (see **2.7.1**).

(e) If the supposed contract is uncertain and therefore void, there could still be a claim for part performance, otherwise one party would be unjustly enriched, ie a quantum meruit claim (*BSC v Cleveland Bridge and Engineering Co Ltd* [1984] 1 All ER 504).

(f) The doctrine of mistake is quite narrow, not least because of the effect on third parties of finding that an agreement is void.

(g) Some contracts must be in writing, eg contracts for the sale of land, or consumer credit agreements.

(h) Misrepresentation, ie an untrue statement which induces one party to enter the contract, could lead to rescission of the contract, and can give rise to liability for damages under the Misrepresentation Act 1967.

2.3.3 Interpretation of contracts

You need to identify the terms of the contract before the contract can be interpreted. The key areas are as follows:

(a) Have any statements made before the contract was concluded been included as terms of the contract, or could they be misrepresentations inducing entry into the contract, or perhaps as a 'last shot' under the 'battle of the forms' (see **2.2(a)** above)?

(b) Is the contract only in writing, or is it both written and oral?

(c) Have the terms been incorporated into the contract, eg by notice or by signature?

(d) Are any terms implied into the contract by custom of that trade, or by statute, eg ss 12–15 of the SGA 1979, or by the common law?

(e) Are any terms, especially those excluding or limiting liability, rendered void by statute, eg ss 2, 3 or 6 of the Unfair Contract Terms Act (UCTA) 1977 (see **Chapter 3**)?

(f) How are contracts to be interpreted – literally or purposively? Lord Hoffman, in *Investors Compensation Scheme Ltd v West Bromwich Building Society* [1998] 1 WLR 898, held that it was appropriate to consider the wider context and to interpret contracts with business common sense, ie purposively.

2.3.4 Discharge of contracts

A contract comes to an end when it has been discharged by:

(a) performance of the contract (which will be the usual situation);

(b) agreement between the parties;
(c) breach, if it is a repudiatory breach, ie breach of a condition not of a warranty, and that repudiation is accepted by the innocent party;
(d) frustration, that is the contract can no longer be performed in manner intended by the parties; or
(e) mistake, but this is very rarely allowed by the courts due to the potentially harmful effect on third parties.

2.3.5 Remedies for breach of contract

The key issues are as follows:

(a) Specific performance can be ordered by a court.
(b) An injunction could be granted.
(c) Damages are the 'usual' remedy and are compensatory, not punitive.
(d) The aim of damages is to put the claimant in the position he would have been in, if the contract had been performed as intended.
(e) Non-pecuniary loss is not generally recoverable.
(f) Consequential loss is recoverable only in limited circumstances (see *Hadley v Baxendale* (1854) 9 Exch 341) and most sellers will want to exclude it if they can.
(g) The claimant is under a duty to mitigate his loss.
(h) Clauses that provide a realistic estimate of the likely damages are enforceable, but penalty clauses are not.
(i) In contracts for the sale of goods, the seller may provide a contractual remedy in the goods themselves (see **2.14**).

2.4 Relevant legislation

The sale of goods is governed by the SGA 1979. Where goods are supplied along with services, eg a contract to decorate a house, the Supply of Goods and Services Act 1982 applies (SGSA 1982).

The UCTA 1977 deals with exclusion clauses, including exclusion of the implied terms under the SGA 1979.

There are also various pieces of legislation aimed at protecting consumers and which we do not consider here, for example the Electronic Commerce (EC Directive) Regulations 2002 (SI 2002/2013), the Consumer Protection (Distance Selling) Regulations 2000 (SI 2000/2334), and the Unfair Terms in Consumer Contracts Regulations 1999 (SI 1999/2083). The Directive on Consumer Goods and Associated Guarantees 1999/44/EC has now been implemented as the Sale and Supply of Goods to Consumers Regulations 2002 (SI 2002/3045). There is a minor amendment to UCTA 1977, s 12(2) concerning auction sales which does affect non-consumer contracts.

2.4.1 Excluding the provisions of the SGA 1979

The SGA 1979, s 55 provides that some of the terms implied into a contract for the sale of goods by the 1979 Act can be excluded by the agreement of the parties, subject to UCTA 1977 (see **3.7**). In many non-consumer contracts therefore, the provisions implied into a sale of goods contract by the SGA 1979 are fallback provisions. They would often be unsuitable for a commercial contract. It may be perfectly valid and desirable to exclude them; the problem usually is, to what extent UCTA 1977 permits this.

2.5 What are 'goods'?

Usually it is perfectly obvious whether the subject matter of the contract is goods (eg buying a chocolate bar in a shop). The SGA 1979, s 61 defines goods as including 'all personal chattels other than things in action and money'. An example of a thing in action is a cheque, which is in effect a promise to pay money.

Section 5(1) differentiates between present and future goods:

> The goods which form the subject of a contract of sale may be either existing goods, owned or possessed by the seller, or goods to be manufactured or acquired by him after the making of the contract of sale, in this Act called future goods.

Thus, the contract can relate to goods which do not yet exist, or which the seller does not yet own.

Section 6 provides that where specific goods have perished, the contract is void.

One area where there has been uncertainty is computer programs. Are they goods or services? (The point is that the implied terms in the contract would be different for goods and for services.) In *St Albans City and District Council v International Computers Ltd* [1996] 4 All ER 481, it was held *obiter* that programs were goods when they were supplied on a disk. More recently, in the case of *Horace Holman Group Ltd v Sherwood International Group Ltd* [2000] WL 491372, there was a dispute as to whether software was goods, and *St Albans* was cited as the authority. The program itself was found not to comprise a sale of goods for the purposes of UCTA 1977, although s 7 of UCTA 1977 was held to be applicable to the contract under which the program was supplied. A similar approach, that documents stored in electronic form do not constitute goods for the purposes of the 1977 Act, was followed in *Thunder Air Ltd v Hilmarsson* [2008] EWHC 355 (Ch).

2.6 What is 'sale of goods'?

The SGA 1979, s 2(1) defines a contract for the sale of goods as:

> ... a contract by which the seller transfers or agrees to transfer the property in goods to the buyer for a money consideration, called the price.

Section 2(4) defines a sale as follows:

> Where under a contract of sale the property in the goods is transferred from the seller to the buyer the contract is called a sale.

These subsections indicate how a sale of goods differs, for example, from a contract for hire of goods because the property in the goods (the title to the goods) changes hands. It differs from a gift of the goods because the buyer pays the seller money for the goods in a sale contract. It also differs from a contract of barter, in which goods are exchanged for goods or a combination of goods and money.

2.7 The price

2.7.1 Definition of 'price' in the SGA 1979, s 8

Section 8 provides that:

> (1) The price in a contract of sale may be fixed by the contract, or may be left to be fixed in a manner agreed by the contract, or may be determined by the course of dealing between the parties.
>
> (2) Where the price is not determined as mentioned in subsection (1) above the buyer must pay a reasonable price.
>
> (3) What is a reasonable price is a question of fact dependent on the circumstances of each particular case.

The basic position is that the parties are free to fix their own price. The fallback position is that if they fail to do so, the price will be a reasonable one. One problem with s 8 is that it is debatable whether or not the parties have concluded a contract at all, if they have not agreed such a basic term of the contract as the price of the goods. If they have not agreed the price then the price has not been fixed by the contract. Alternatively, the parties may conclude the contract but agree that the price will be fixed at some point in the future. This is an 'agreement to agree', which is usually taken to be unenforceable in English law (see, eg, *Courtney & Fairbairn Ltd v Tolaini Bros (Hotels) Ltd* [1975] 1 WLR 297; cf the older case of *Foley v Classique Coaches Ltd* [1934] 2 KB 1, where there was an arbitration clause if the parties could not agree on the price and the contract was upheld).

In *Cable & Wireless plc v IBM United Kingdom Ltd* [2002] EWHC 2059 (Comm), it was held that although the law did not generally recognise agreements to agree, the situation here was different. The fact that the agreement prescribed the means by which dispute negotiation should take place, by the identification of a specific recognised procedure, meant that the requirement for contractual certainty was fulfilled and the agreement was thus enforceable. In *Balfour Beatty Northern Ltd v Modus Corovest (Blackpool) Ltd* [2008] EWHC 3029 (TCC), a mediation agreement was held to be a simple 'agreement to agree' and was too uncertain to be enforced.

2.7.2 Agreeing the price: ss 8, 9

In most circumstances, the parties will agree the price (or, if they do not, then s 8 applies). It could be by use of a price list, or it could be by quotation or by negotiation. The contract should provide that the price is fixed, or, if not, how price changes between signing and delivery are to be dealt with. See *LG International (UK) Ltd v GB International Ltd* [2005] EWHC 801 (QB) for an illustration of the problems arising from failure to deal with this in the contract.

If the parties leave the price to be fixed by the valuation of a third party and he does not do so, the contract is void (s 9). The price may also be determined by a consistent course of dealing between those parties.

2.7.3 Value added tax

A price in a contract is taken as including value added tax (VAT) unless otherwise specified (Value Added Tax Act 1983, s 10(2)). If the prices are to be exclusive of VAT, that must be expressly stated. Failure to do this will result in the seller having to bear the VAT itself and not being able to pass it on to the buyer.

2.8 Delivery

In this section of the chapter we look at two aspects of delivery, namely:

(a) definition of the word 'delivery'; and
(b) methods of delivery.

Other aspects that are dealt with in **2.9** below are:

(a) time of delivery;
(b) quantity and quality of goods to be delivered;
(c) place of delivery; and
(d) allocation of the costs.

2.8.1 What is 'delivery'?

'Delivery' is defined in SGA 1979, s 61(1) as the 'voluntary transfer of possession from one person to another'. It is, if you like, handing over the goods. However, it is not confined to transfer of physical possession of the goods, as there are various ways in which goods can be 'delivered' (see **2.8.2**). Also, 'delivery' in the sense used in sale of goods does not mean the physical transportation of the goods from the seller's premises to another location, eg the buyer's premises. ('Physical transportation' is usually referred to as 'carriage of goods'.) It really means the point in time and space at which the parties can be seen to have agreed that the legal right to possession of the goods passes from the seller to the buyer (note that it is not necessarily the same point that ownership passes – see **2.13.1**).

The contract between the seller and buyer should deal with the issue of when and where delivery is to occur. If it does not, the matter is decided under the rules in s 29 (see **2.9.4**). A clear distinction must be made between 'delivery' (ie the transfer of possession) and the passing of title (ie ownership).

Prima facie, the risk of loss or damage to the goods passes with the property in the goods, that is with the title to the goods (s 20(1)). It does not automatically pass with delivery, ie with possession of the goods. So, it is feasible for the goods to be in the buyer's possession but still be at the seller's risk, if the seller still has title to them. The seller would therefore have the trouble and expense of insuring goods that are no longer in his possession. If this situation is likely to occur in a particular deal, the seller would usually want the contract to be drafted so that the risk of the goods passes to the buyer with possession of the goods. Thus, the buyer would have both control of the goods and the obligation to insure them. This is particularly important in retention of title sales (see **2.14**).

Under s 28, delivery of the goods and payment of the price are concurrent conditions, ie delivery and payment should happen at the same time, unless the contract provides otherwise:

> Unless otherwise agreed, delivery of the goods and payment of the price are concurrent conditions, that is to say, the seller must be ready and willing to give possession of the goods to the buyer in exchange for the price, and the buyer must be ready and willing to pay the price in exchange for possession of the goods.

This is the situation with a normal retail sale, where the customer pays for the goods in the shop and the goods are handed over then and there. However, in a normal business to business sale of goods, the buyer will often be given a credit period of perhaps 30 days after receiving the goods, and an invoice, before they have to be paid for.

2.8.2 How to deliver

There are various methods of delivery, and certain prima facie rules are provided by Part IV of the SGA 1979, but all of these rules can be varied by the parties' express terms. The most obvious is actual delivery, ie physically handing over the goods, as would happen when a consumer is buying goods in a shop. Other methods of delivery include:

(a) transfer of a document (eg, a bill of lading: see **9.2.1**);

(b) delivery of an object giving control (eg, giving the keys to premises where the goods are stored, or even the keys to a motor car);

(c) the buyer's continuance of possession (eg, where the buyer already holds the goods as bailee of the seller, and then on the sale there is a notional delivery of the goods to the buyer);

(d) 'attornment', where a seller or a third party acknowledges that goods which were held by the seller, or on his behalf, are now held on behalf of the buyer; and

(e) delivery to a carrier. Section 32(1) of the SGA 1979 provides that transfer of possession to a carrier who will take the goods to the buyer prima facie constitutes delivery to the buyer. This means that the goods are at the buyer's risk from the point at which they are in the carrier's possession. The buyer should insure them against damage or loss from that point. This arrangement is often varied by express provision in the contract.

2.9 Duties of the seller

The 1979 Act implies various duties into a contract for the sale of goods, subject to agreement to the contrary. The following paragraphs deal with the statutorily implied duties in the order set out below:

(a) passing a good title to the goods (s 12);
(b) handing over ('deliver') the goods to the buyer (ss 27–29);
(c) delivery at an agreed time (s 10);
(d) place of delivery (s 29);
(e) costs of delivery (s 29);
(f) the right quantity of goods (ss 30–31);
(g) the right quality of goods in terms of–
    (i) sale by description (s 13),
    (ii) 'satisfactory quality' (s 14(1), (2), (2A)–(2E)),
    (iii) 'fitness for purpose' (s 14(3)),
    (iv) sale by sample (s 15); and
(h) trade usage (s 14(4)).

Remember that, under s 55, various implied terms can be excluded, especially in non-consumer contracts, subject to UCTA 1977.

2.9.1 Seller must pass good title to the goods: s 12

Section 12(1) implies into the contract a term that the seller has the right to sell the goods. In other words, he has good title to the goods. Section 12(2) provides that there is an implied term:

(a) that the goods are free from any charge or encumbrance not already known to the buyer; and
(b) that the buyer will enjoy quiet possession of the goods.

For example, in *Rubicon Computer Systems Ltd v United Paints Ltd* [2000] 2 TCLR 453, it was held that the seller attaching a time lock to a computer system in order to deny access to the buyer was in breach of the 'quiet possession' term under s 12(2)(b). In *Iran v Barakat Galleries Ltd* [2007] EWCA Civ 1374, the claimant State was able to bring a claim to recover antiquities from an antiquities trader, by virtue of the superior title of the State as against the purely possessory title of the trader. In *Trade Electronix Ltd v Best Buy Today (Wholesale) Ltd (in administration)* [2009] EWCA Civ 828, a claimant failed to show that it had obtained title to goods where the defendant had made a valid sale of goods to another. No valid contract of sale had been entered into between the parties at the date of the sale to the third party.

2.9.2 Seller must deliver the goods: ss 27–29

The SGA 1979, s 27 requires that it is the duty of the seller to deliver, in the legal sense, the goods, and the duty of the buyer to accept and pay for them, in accordance with the terms of the contract of sale.

Section 28 states that delivery of the goods and payment should happen at the same time, subject to contrary agreement (see **2.8.1**).

There is no general duty to transport the goods to the buyer (s 29, see **2.8.2**).

2.9.3 Time of delivery: s 10

The basic position under the SGA 1979 is that time of payment is not of the essence in a sale of goods contract (s 10(1)) unless the terms indicate otherwise. However, s 10(2) provides that the parties can agree whether or not time is of the essence with regard to any other term of the contract. If the obligation under the contract is for the seller to deliver, and there is no time fixed for this, then he must do so within a reasonable time, (s 29(3)). In practice, the tendency is to draft the contract so as to make the time of delivery of the essence. See *ERG Raffinerie Mediterranee SpA v Chevron USA Inc* [2007] EWCA Civ 494 for a case on contractual fixing of delivery time and, in default, resort to delivery within a reasonable time that was contemplated by the contract terms. This case involved delivery under a modified 'Incoterms' standard contract (see **9.5** and **9.5.2** for 'FOB' terms).

The courts have ruled on various aspects on time of delivery. In *Hartley v Hymans* [1920] 3 KB 475, it was held that in ordinary commercial contracts for the sale of goods the rule is that time is prima facie of the essence with respect to delivery. In such a contract, a delivery date will usually have been specifically agreed. This has the effect of making the clause a condition, breach of which has serious consequences. This prima facie rule may be rebutted by the facts in a particular case.

If the buyer waives the delivery date before the goods are delivered, the buyer is entitled to give the seller reasonable notice that he will not accept the goods after a certain date. See the case of *Charles Rickards Ltd v Oppenheim* [1950] 1 KB 616, where the buyer waived the original delivery date but then gave the seller reasonable notice of a revised date. The seller failed to meet even the revised date and the buyer was held to be entitled to refuse to accept the goods. See also *Toprak Mahsulleri Ofisi v Finagrain Compagnie Commerciale Agricole et Financière SA* [1979] 2 Lloyd's Rep 98, where the Court of Appeal applied *Rickards* to extensions of time in the context of shipping.

Even if there is an agreed delivery date, the duty could be suspended or extinguished. This is typically dealt with in a force majeure clause in the contract, which concerns events beyond the control of the parties (see **1.4.7**). Section 29(3) provides for delivery within a reasonable time if no time has been agreed in advance.

2.9.4 Where to deliver: s 29

The place of delivery depends on the contract. It would commonly be the seller's premises, or it could be at the buyer's premises on being transported there by the seller. The SGA 1979, s 29 provides for rules on deciding where delivery takes place, if the contract is silent on the matter. The fallback position is that the goods are delivered at the seller's place of business (s 29(2)). In *Zenziper Grains and Feed Stuffs v Bulk Trading Corp Ltd* [2001] 1 Lloyd's Rep 357, a serious problem arose concerning the nomination of a delivery location. The seller's failure to notify the location was held to be a repudiatory breach.

Delivery must be made at a 'reasonable hour' (s 29(5)).

Delivery to carriers, for onward carriage to the buyer, may constitute delivery (see s 32(1)), and the place of delivery may also be determined by the use of Incoterm contracts (see **9.5**). See also *Scottish & Newcastle International Ltd v Othon Ghalanos Ltd* [2008] UKHL 11, [2008] 2 All ER (Comm) 369.

2.9.5 Who pays for delivery?

The expenses of delivery, ie handing over the goods, will be borne by the seller (s 29(6)), and the expenses of taking delivery by the buyer, unless the contract provides otherwise.

Under s 37, a buyer who refuses to take delivery of the goods is liable to the seller for the seller's loss and also the storage costs. If there is a delay in delivery then the goods are at the risk of whichever party to the contract caused the delay, as regards the loss caused by the delay (see s 20(2)).

Where the buyer has wrongfully refused to accept and pay for the goods, the seller can sue the buyer for damages (s 50).

2.9.6 Delivery of the right quantity: ss 30–31

The seller is required to deliver goods of the right quantity. Under s 30(1), the buyer may reject the goods if the quantity is less than the contract quantity. However, if he accepts them, he must pay for them at the contract rate.

If the seller delivers a greater than contracted quantity, the buyer may accept the contract quantity and reject the rest, or may reject the whole (s 30(2)). If the buyer accepts the whole quantity, he must pay for the excess quantity at the contract rate (s 30(3)). An interesting case on quantity is *Totsa Total Oil Trading SA v Bharat Petroleum Corp Ltd* [2005] EWHC 1641 (Comm), where a quantity of oil, to which water has been unintentionally added, was in dispute. On a strict reading of the contract, the buyer ended up paying for water (allegedly).

If the variation from the contract quantity is slight then the buyer may not reject the goods, unless he is a consumer (s 30(2A)).

Section 31(1) provides that the buyer is not obliged to accept delivery in instalments.

2.9.7 The right quality – sale by description: s 13

Section 13 implies a term that the goods sold should comply with their description. This could apply to goods bought from a catalogue, for example. In *Beale v Taylor* [1967] 1 WLR 1193, the sale was held to be a sale by description even though the buyer inspected the car after having seen the advertisement for it in the local paper. The main point is that the words used must be words of description rather than simply words identifying the goods.

In *Re Moore v Landauer & Co* [1921] 2 KB 519, the goods were not packed as had been described in the contract, which was held to be breach of description entitling the buyer to reject the entire shipment. It is important to note that ss 13, 14 and 15 of the SGA 1979 are all implied as strict conditions in England, Wales and Northern Ireland.

In *Jones v Gallagher* [2004] EWCA Civ 10, an agreement to supply and fit a pine kitchen to match existing units was held to be a sale by description (within the Supply of Goods and Services Act 1982, see **4.3.6** below). For analysis of whether wording comprises a contractual description, sufficient to comprise a sale by description, see *Reardon Smith Line v Yngvar Hansen-Tangen* [1976] 1 WLR 989 (stated location of building dock of ship did not comprise contractual description of ship; buyer's rejection of ship built at different site for breach of condition of compliance with description held to be wrongful).

2.9.8 The right quality – 'satisfactory quality': s 14(2)

Section 14(2) of the SGA 1979 implies a term that, in a sale in the course of a business, the goods are to be, objectively, of satisfactory quality. This includes fitness for the common purposes of the goods, appearance and finish, freedom from minor defects, safety and durability (s 14(2B)). It does not extend to matters specifically drawn to the buyer's attention before the contract is made, or that should have been obvious on examination of the goods (s 14(2C)). It does have to take account of price and description of the goods (s 14(2A)).

Durability of goods can cause particular difficulty. The question of how long a cargo of gas oil (diesel) should remain of satisfactory quality, during what might be a substantial sea voyage, was examined in *KG Bominflot Bunkergesellschaft für Mineralöle mbH & Co KG v Petroplus Marketing AG* [2009] EWHC 1088 (Comm). It was held that the oil needed to be of satisfactory quality (meeting a particular specification) when delivered to the ship (remember that risk passes on delivery in many circumstances, including this particular case) and for a reasonable time after that; there was no implied term that the oil would be capable of enduring a normal voyage and still be of satisfactory quality at the end of the voyage.

In *Friarwood Ltd v Champagne Chatier SA* [2006] EWCA Civ 1105, a retrial was ordered after the court disapproved a judge's approach in deciding satisfactory quality of champagne, allegedly prematurely aged. The judge wrongly rejected expert evidence which should have been taken into account.

In *Britvic Soft Drinks v Messer UK Ltd* [2002] EWCA Civ 548, it was held that contamination of carbon dioxide gas, supplied for making soft drinks, would make the gas of unsatisfactory quality for drinks manufacturing. (The contaminating substance, benzene, was not present in high enough quantity to be a danger to human health but would have damaged the saleability of the drinks.)

In *Thain v Anniesland Trade Centre* [1997] SCLR 991, a six-year-old car, sold for £2,995, was held to be of satisfactory quality, even though the gearbox failed two weeks after purchase of the car.

2.9.9 The right quality – 'fitness for purpose': ss 14(2), 14(3)

As well as fitness for the common purposes of the goods under s 14(2) (see **2.9.8**), s 14(3) implies a term that the goods are fit for any particular purpose which the buyer makes known to the seller, either expressly or by implication. (See *Micron Computer Systems Ltd v Wang (UK) Ltd* (HC, 9 May 1990), where the buyer of a computer system failed to tell the seller of the particular purpose in question and was therefore unsuccessful in its claim.) This term does not apply where the circumstances show that the buyer does not rely upon, or it is unreasonable to rely upon, the skill or judgement of the seller.

FT Everard & Sons Ltd v BP Marine Ltd [2005] EWHC 3142 (Comm) illustrates the difficulty for a claimant in discharging the burden of proving a lack of fitness for purpose in matters requiring (usually disputed) expert technical evidence.

In *Jewson v Kelly* [2003] EWCA Civ 1030, the seller was held by the Court of Appeal not to be liable for breach of the SGA 1979 in the supply of electrical heating equipment. The buyers alleged that the sale was in breach of s 14(2) and (3), as the equipment had reduced the energy efficiency ratings of the flat conversions in question. The Court held that:

> Although there was considerable overlap between s 14(2) and s 14(3), the function of s 14(2) was to establish a general standard, and the function of s 14(3) was to impose a particular standard tailored to the individual circumstances of the case.

The equipment did work as heating equipment, so s 14(2) was held not to be applicable. As regards s 14(3), the buyer was held not to have relied on the sellers as regards the question of the 'particular' fitness for purpose, which was the effect of the heating equipment on the flats' energy efficiency ratings.

In the *KG Bominflot* case discussed at **2.9.8** above, fitness for purpose (the dispute was about sedimentary content of fuel oil) required the oil to remain within its contractual specification for a reasonable time after delivery to the tanker; what was a reasonable time was a question to be decided on the particular facts (this was a trial of preliminary issues). There was no greater implication than this, relating to the duration of the voyage or anything else. Since the sellers had not known the destination of the oil, there was no greater obligation on them than to provide for the oil to remain within its contractual specification for a reasonable time after delivery aboard.

2.9.10 The right quality – sale by sample: s 15

The SGA 1979, s 15 implies a term that where the sale is by sample then the bulk of the goods will correspond with the sample in quality. The goods are also to be free of any defect, not apparent on reasonable examination, which would render the quality unsatisfactory.

In *Godley v Perry* [1960] 1 WLR 9, a retailer bought plastic catapults from a wholesaler. He tested one sample catapult and it worked satisfactorily, so he bought a consignment of them. However, a catapult sold to a customer broke and injured the child using it. The goods were held not to comply with the sample, in breach of s 15. There had been reasonable examination of the sample which had not shown up any defects.

2.9.11 Trade usage: s 14(4)

The SGA 1979, s 14(4) states that an implied condition or warranty about quality or fitness for a particular purpose may be annexed to a contract of sale by usage in the course of a particular trade. The requirements are that the usage or custom must be reasonable, universally accepted by the particular trade or profession, be certain, be lawful, and be consistent with the express or implied terms of the contract (see *Oricon Waren-Handels Gmbh v Intergraan NV* [1967] 2 Lloyd's Rep 82).

2.10 Duties of the buyer

This section deals with the buyer's duties, which are to:

(a) pay the price for the goods; and

(b) take delivery of the goods.

2.10.1 Duty to pay the price: ss 27–28

It is the buyer's duty to pay the price (SGA 1979, s 27). The time for payment is prima facie when the goods are delivered, but the parties may agree otherwise (s 28). The seller is not bound to accept anything but cash, subject to contrary agreement between the parties (see, eg, *Gordon v Strange* (1847) 1 Exch 477).

This would be the normal scenario of buying goods in a shop. The customer gives the shopkeeper the money, and the customer takes the goods away.

Only payment in full will discharge the buyer's liability, unless a discount has been agreed. If the discount is only available for prompt payment within a stated time, failure to do so will leave the buyer liable to pay the full price (see *Amos and Wood Ltd v Kaprow* (1948) 64 TLR 110). Nevertheless, where the buyer has paid sums on account of the price, but eventually successfully rejects the goods, it will be entitled to recover the sums paid on account: *Whitecap Leisure Ltd v John H Rundle Ltd* [2008] EWCA Civ 429. See **2.12.1** below for the right to reject goods.

In any event, if a seller accepts a cheque or other negotiable instrument, this is treated as a conditional payment. If the cheque is not honoured, the seller may sue for the price either as breach of the sale of goods contract, or on the cheque as being a contract in itself. Payment by credit card will usually be treated as an absolute payment. Therefore, failure by the credit card company to pay the retailer does not allow the retailer to sue the customer (see *Re Charge Card Services Ltd* [1988] 3 All ER 702). The customer's only liability is to pay the credit card company when the bill from the company arrives in the post.

2.10.1.1 Time for payment: s 10

If no time for payment is mentioned in the contract, the price is due on the completion of the contract (ie, on delivery), if the seller is willing to deliver the goods.

Section 10(1) provides that:

> Unless a different intention appears from the terms of the contract, stipulations as to time of payment are not of the essence of a contract of sale.

This has been interpreted as meaning that failure to pay is not a breach of condition entitling the seller to treat the contract as repudiated and to sell the goods elsewhere. Rather, it limits the seller's right to the price, and to damages, if any, for late payment.

If the seller is anxious about time for payment, he can of course provide that the contract does make time for payment of the essence. It would also be sensible to provide for interest on late payments (see **2.10.1.2**).

The seller may have reserved the right of resale in the contract in the event of undue delay in payment by the buyer (see s 48(4)). Also, s 48(3) provides that:

> Where the goods are of a perishable nature, or where the unpaid seller gives notice to the buyer of his intention to re-sell, and the buyer does not within a reasonable time pay or tender the price, the unpaid seller may re-sell the goods and recover from the original buyer damages for any loss occasioned by his breach of contract.

So, the unpaid seller can serve a notice on the buyer and then resell the goods if the buyer does not pay within a reasonable time. If the goods are perishable, he does not even need to serve a notice.

2.10.1.2 Late payment

Damages for late payment may be awarded by the court for additional costs caused to the seller (see, eg, *Wadsworth v Lydall* [1981] 1 WLR 598). Interest can be awarded under the Law Reform (Miscellaneous Provisions) Act 1934 and, more particularly, the Late Payment of Commercial Debts (Interest) Act 1998. The 1998 Act restricts the parties' freedom to contract somewhat, in that it provides that the parties may provide another substantial contractual remedy beyond the right to statutory interest but may not provide that late payment will not carry any remedy at all (see **2.17.4**). It would obviously be sensible to provide in the contract for interest for late payment, as this avoids having to rely on these statutory provisions.

Any contractual arrangement to recover, by way of damages or interest, for late payment must not 'amount to a penalty', but must be based upon a genuine pre-estimate of loss. In *Jeancharm Ltd v Barnet Football Club Ltd* [2003] EWCA Civ 58, a clause requiring interest of 5% per week was struck out as penal.

Section 49 of the SGA 1979 provides that the unpaid seller has a right to sue for the price of the goods, even when the title to the goods has not passed, where the price is payable 'on a day certain', regardless of delivery.

The unpaid seller has other statutory rights (see **2.11.2**).

2.10.2 Duty to take delivery: ss 27, 28

The SGA 1979 distinguishes between taking delivery of the goods and acceptance of the goods. For example, s 35(2) provides that:

> Where goods are delivered to the buyer, and he has not previously examined them, he is not deemed to have accepted them under subsection (1) above until he has had a reasonable opportunity of examining them for the purpose—
>
> (a) of ascertaining whether they are in conformity with the contract, and
>
> (b) in the case of a contract for sale by sample, of comparing the bulk with the sample.

So, delivery of the goods to the buyer does not mean that the buyer has agreed that the goods comply with the contract, ie he has not yet accepted them.

Acceptance by the buyer is dealt with in s 35(1):

> The buyer is deemed to have accepted the goods subject to subsection (2) below—
>
> (a) when he intimates to the seller that he has accepted them, or
>
> (b) when the goods have been delivered to him and he does any act in relation to them which is inconsistent with the ownership of the seller.

and s 35(4):

> The buyer is also deemed to have accepted the goods when after the lapse of a reasonable time he retains the goods without intimating to the seller that he has rejected them.

See also **2.12.1** on the rights of the buyer to reject the goods. For a recent case on acceptance/ rejection, see *Whitecap Leisure Ltd v John H Rundle Ltd* [2008] EWCA Civ 429.

Under ss 27 and 28, it is the duty of the buyer to accept and pay for the goods. The prima facie rule is that delivery, acceptance and payment generally take place at the seller's premises (s 29(2)). See **2.9.5** as regards the costs of refusing to take delivery.

A buyer's failure to accept the goods does not by itself allow the seller to sell the goods to someone else; but see s 39(1)(c), which does allow sale to another buyer, subject to the conditions in s 48 (see **2.11.2.3**).

2.11 Rights of the seller

This section deals with the rights of the unpaid seller, which are:

(a) a lien on the goods, ie a right to hang onto the goods;

(b) a right to stop the goods in transit;

(c) a right of re-sale;

(d) an action for the price of the goods; and

(e) a right to retain title to the goods until paid.

2.11.1 Definition of an 'unpaid seller': s 38

Section 38(1) of the 1979 Act defines an unpaid seller in the following manner:

> The seller of goods is an unpaid seller within the meaning of this Act—
>
> (a) when the whole of the price has not been paid or tendered;
>
> (b) when a bill of exchange or other negotiable instrument has been received as conditional payment, and the condition on which it was received has not been fulfilled by reason of the dishonour of the instrument or otherwise.

The rights of an unpaid seller in ss 41–48 (see **2.11.2.1** to **2.11.2.3**) assume that the seller still has physical control over the goods. If this is not the case then the only possibility is the prior inclusion in the contract of a retention of title clause under s 19 (see **2.11.5**).

2.11.2 Rights of the unpaid seller under SGA 1979: s 39

An unpaid seller does, of course, have the right to sue the buyer for the price. However, in addition to this, s 39(1) gives the unpaid seller the following rights:

> Subject to this and any other Act, notwithstanding that the property in the goods may have passed to the buyer, the unpaid seller of goods, as such, has by implication of law—
>
> (a) a lien on the goods or right to retain them for the price while he is in possession of them;
>
> (b) in case of the insolvency of the buyer, a right of stopping the goods in transit after he has parted with the possession of them;
>
> (c) a right of re-sale as limited by this Act.

We shall look at these rights in turn below. For these rights to be relevant, the seller has to have possession, or at least control, over the goods.

There may, of course, be contractual remedies for non-payment, and these can be very imaginatively drafted but sometimes difficult to apply. In *Stocznia Gdanska SA v Latvian Shipping Co* [1998] 1 WLR 574, HL, there was a contract to build six identical ships. Having built parts of two hulls and not having received 'keel stage' payments, the builders then attempted to reallocate those two keels to the remaining four unbuilt hulls, to trigger stage payments on those ships also. The House of Lords rejected that reading of the contractual remedy.

2.11.2.1 Seller's lien: ss 41, 43

Section 41 states that an unpaid seller who is in possession of the goods is entitled to retain possession of them until paid, where any credit period has expired, or the buyer has become insolvent.

The lien is lost when the goods are consigned to a carrier without reserving the right to dispose of the goods, or when the buyer has possession of the goods, or by waiver by the seller (s 43).

2.11.2.2 Stoppage in transit: ss 44–46

Sections 44 to 46 state that the seller may stop the goods in transit where the buyer has become insolvent, and retain them until paid. This has been upheld in a shipping context, eg in *Booth v Cargo Fleet Iron Co Ltd* [1916] 2 KB 570. However, there is no right to interfere with the postal system (*Postmaster-General v WH Jones & Co* [1957] NZLR 829), so goods sent by post cannot be stopped.

The stopping could be either by taking actual possession of the goods, or by giving notice of the seller's claim to the carrier (s 46(1)).

2.11.2.3 Re-sale by seller: s 48

The unpaid seller who re-sells the goods to another buyer (ie, a third party) passes good title to the goods, even where the goods were subject to the unpaid seller's lien or were stopped in transit (s 48(2), (3), and s 25).

The right of re-sale is limited by s 48(3) to goods of a perishable nature, or to the unpaid seller giving notice to the buyer of intention to re-sell and not receiving the price within a reasonable time.

Where the unpaid seller remains in possession of the goods and re-sells them, the original contract of sale is rescinded and the buyer is discharged from further liability to pay the price. The seller is entitled to keep the proceeds of the re-sale and to sue the original buyer for damages for non-acceptance if he makes any loss on the re-sale (including the expense of re-selling) as against the original price (see *RV Ward v Bignall* [1967] 2 All ER 449, CA).

2.11.3 Action for the price: s 49

The unpaid seller can sue the buyer for the price of the goods where the buyer has the property in the goods, ie possession of the goods, but has not paid for them, or where the price is due on 'a day certain' (s 49). This does not help if the buyer is insolvent or likely to become so.

2.11.4 Non-acceptance of the goods – assessment of damages: s 50

Where the buyer has wrongfully refused to accept and pay for the goods, the seller can sue the buyer for damages (s 50). The basis for assessment of damages is laid down in s 50(3):

> Where there is an available market for the goods in question the measure of damages is prima facie to be ascertained by the difference between the contract price and the market or current

> price at the time or times when the goods ought to have been accepted or (if no time was fixed for acceptance) at the time of the refusal to accept.

Presumably, where there is no available market the measure of damages is the contract value of the goods plus any additional direct expenses caused to the seller. Beyond the prima facie measure provided by s 50(3), 'special damages' (ie those losses recoverable under the second limb of *Hadley v Baxendale*) are recoverable (s 54).

A buyer is liable for costs incurred by the seller due to the buyer's neglect or refusal to take delivery (s 37: see **2.9.5**).

2.11.5 The seller who is not in possession of the goods: ss 17 and 19

The rights in ss 41 to 48 (see **2.11.2.1** to **2.11.2.3**) apply where the seller still has possession, or at least physical control, of the goods. A more difficult situation is where the goods are in the possession or control of the buyer but the seller has still not been paid. This is a major concern for the seller, especially where the buyer is going insolvent. The danger is that the goods will be sold by a liquidator. The seller would be only an unsecured creditor and would be unlikely to be paid much, if anything, by the liquidator.

There is a right under SGA 1979, ss 17 and 19 to reserve title to the goods. This can be done in a contract of sale by inserting a retention of title clause (also called a *Romalpa* clause after *Aluminium Industrie Vaassen BV v Romalpa Aluminium* [1976] 1 WLR 676: see **2.14**). The idea behind this is to allow the seller to recover the goods, still being the property of the seller.

2.12 Rights of the buyer

The rights of the buyer are:

(a) to reject the goods and repudiate the contract in certain circumstances;
(b) an action for damages;
(c) specific performance; and
(d) rescission for misrepresentation.

2.12.1 Right to reject the goods: ss 15A, 34–36

A buyer's primary right for breach of a strict condition of a contract by the seller is to reject the goods and repudiate the contract of sale. The seller's breach would have to go to the root of the contract to justify repudiation. Remember that terms implied by ss 13, 14 and 15 are strict conditions in England, Wales and Northern Ireland. The Sale and Supply of Goods Act 1994 made changes to this area of law, including by introducing the new s 15A into the SGA 1979.

Section 15A limits the right to reject the goods for breach of SGA 1979, ss 13–15. It provides that the right to reject is lost where the sale is not a consumer sale and the breach is so slight that it would be unreasonable for the buyer to reject the goods. Section 15A applies only to breach of ss 13–15 and not, for example, to breach of a stipulation concerning time of delivery. *Filobake Ltd v Rondo Ltd* [2004] EWHC 695 (TCC) shows s 15A in application, where a minor breach of s 14 was held to be too slight to justify rejection of an entire bakery production line.

Section 34 of the 1979 Act states that the buyer has a right to have a reasonable opportunity, on request, to examine the goods.

Section 35 deals with the loss of the right to reject. So, for example, the buyer loses the right where he tells the seller that he has accepted the goods, or does something inconsistent with the seller's ownership after the goods have been delivered to him. He also loses the right to reject if he retains the goods beyond a reasonable period of time (s 35(4)). In *Clegg v Olle Andersson (t/a Nordic Marine)* [2003] EWCA Civ 320, the Court of Appeal held that the Sale and Supply of Goods Act 1994 allowed the buyer to have time to ascertain the actions needed to modify or repair the goods. (The 1994 Act amended the SGA 1979.) The case concerned an ocean-going yacht. The buyer took three weeks to assess the situation before rejecting the goods. This was in fact many months after delivery, as the seller was slow to respond to requests for information. The buyer's rejection was upheld.

See also *Whitecap Leisure Ltd v John H Rundle Ltd* [2008] EWCA Civ 429, where the defendant in a complex dispute was held, on appeal, to have effectively rejected a water ski cable tow system, but then refused the seller access to remove it. The buyer was no longer liable for the price, but, because the tow had re-vested in the seller, on rejection the buyer became liable for conversion of the seller's property.

In *Jones v Gallagher* [2004] EWCA Civ 10, the Court of Appeal held that the buyer's right to reject a new fitted kitchen had been lost through delay, not least as the main complaint was that the colour was incorrect. This would have been evident on delivery of the components. It was also said that *Clegg* did not go so far as to suggest that it was generally impossible to lose the right to reject whilst the buyer was still seeking information.

Section 36 of the SGA 1979 states that where the goods have been delivered to the buyer and the buyer rightfully rejects them, he is not obliged to return them to the seller. The seller must therefore arrange for collection of the goods.

Section 61 states that a term which is a warranty does not give the buyer the right to reject the goods and treat the contract as repudiated, only a right to damages (see **2.12.2**). The problem for the buyer is that there are situations where the term breached may be unclear as to whether it is a strict condition or not. Section 15A means that careful judgement is needed before rejection – might a breach of, say, s 14 be so slight as to preclude rejection?

2.12.2 Action for damages: s 53

The buyer can sue for damages for breach of a contract term, either express or implied (s 53). This is either where the term in question is classified as a warranty, or where it is a condition but the buyer has elected not to reject the goods.

Section 51 lays down the principles for calculating damages for non-delivery of the goods, and in particular s 51(3) states:

> Where there is an available market for the goods in question the measure of damages is prima facie to be ascertained by the difference between the contract price and the market or current price of the goods at the time or times when they ought to have been delivered or (if no time was fixed) at the time of the refusal to deliver.

In other words, the buyer's loss is any increase in the price of equivalent goods obtained from another source.

A problem area is consequential loss. This is dealt with on the principles in *Hadley v Baxendale* (1854) 9 Exch 341. That is, that the damages allowed are those that are considered either as arising naturally from the breach of the contract itself, or such as may reasonably be supposed to have been in the contemplation of the parties at the time they made the contract. Such loss recovery is contemplated as 'special damages' by s 54.

Limitation and/or exclusion clauses in sale of goods contracts are often aimed at limiting or excluding consequential loss, subject to being disallowed under the UCTA 1977. The seller does not want to take on liabilities that might far exceed his profit on the sale.

2.12.3 Specific performance: s 52

The buyer's right to apply for specific performance is regulated by s 52. The right is only for specific or ascertained goods, that is goods identified and agreed upon at the time the contract is made. The right applies whether or not the property in the goods (title to the goods) has already passed to the buyer. Whether or not specific performance is ordered is a matter within the discretion of the court.

The right under s 52 does not extend to unascertained goods. These are goods which are not identified and agreed upon at the time a contract of sale is made. They may be divided into the following categories:

(a) a quantity of a type of goods in general, eg 5 kilos of potatoes;

(b) future goods, goods which are not yet in existence, eg next year's potatoes; or

(c) part of a larger quantity of ascertained goods, eg 5 kilos of potatoes out of the 2 tonnes in the Tesco shop in Chester.

In each case, the identity of the particular batch of potatoes contracted for is not knowable until ascertainment. See also *Re Goldcorp Exchange Ltd (in receivership)* [1994] 2 All ER 806, PC, where it was held that no title to goods arose from unascertained shares in bulk bullion.

However, there are some cases where an order for unascertained goods has been granted, albeit in exceptional circumstances. For example, in *Worldwide Dryers Ltd v Warner Howard Ltd and Others* (1982) *The Times*, 9 December, the buyer's business would have collapsed pending the full trial if the seller had cut off supplies of the goods which were imported from the United States. These would be 'future goods' under the classification above. In *Thames Valley Power Ltd v Total Gas and Power Ltd* [2005] EWHC 2208 (Comm) specific performance was ordered of a contract to supply gas.

It seems that an equitable lien may arise where the buyer (in a work and materials contract which results in an overall contract within the SGA 1979) has paid for some of the goods involved. Such a lien would justify the court in restraining disposal of the resulting assembled equipment to a third party (see *International Finance Corp v DSNL Offshore Ltd* [2005] EWHC 1844 (Comm)).

2.12.4 Rescission for misrepresentation

This is now controlled by the Misrepresentation Act 1967. If a pre-contractual misrepresentation has become a term of the contract, or the contract has been performed, then the buyer may still rescind the contract (s 1). Rescission is possible for innocent misrepresentation. The buyer does not have to rely on an allegation of fraud or negligence, although recission is also available in those circumstances. See *Shogun Finance Ltd v Hudson* [2004] 1 AC 919.

Rescission for misrepresentation is barred by affirmation, lapse of time, inability to restore the parties to their original position, or the goods being acquired by an innocent third party.

Damages for misrepresentation are also a possibility, but there can be no double recovery. See the discussion of reliance upon the misrepresentation in *Ronastone Ltd v Indigo International Holdings Ltd* [2003] All ER (D) 332 (Dec).

2.13 Effects of a sale of goods contract

The effects of a sale of goods contract are that:

(a) ownership of the goods is transferred to the buyer;

(b) the risk in the goods passes to the buyer; and

(c) the seller is paid.

2.13.1 Transfer of ownership: ss 17–18

The property in the goods, ie the title to the goods, passes when the parties intend it to pass (s 17). Section 18 of the 1979 Act contains rules for ascertaining the intention of the parties, subject to their contrary intention. It is important to consider dealing with this as an express provision, if there is any danger of unintended effects arising out of the application of the s 18 rules. The question of express retention of title clauses is dealt with at **2.14 et seq** below. You will also see that the use of Incoterms in contracts does not help with the question of ascertaining when property passes (see **9.2.3**).

A particular danger of unpredictability as to when property passes, arises out of the operation of s 18, Rule 5. Here, in contracts for unascertained or future goods, where 'goods of that description and in a deliverable state are unconditionally appropriated to the contract, either by the seller with the assent of the buyer or by the buyer with the assent of the seller, the property in the goods then passes to the buyer; and the assent may be express or implied, and may be given either before or after the appropriation is made'. The obvious danger here, unless express contrary provision is shown in the contract, is that the property might pass to the buyer long before the seller wishes that to happen. Another serious consequence is that the risk of the goods will pass over to the buyer (under s 20(1), see **2.13.2**) at a time when they could easily still be in the possession of the seller. Again, this may not be the desired result at all; see *Wardars (Import & Export) Co Ltd v W Norwood & Sons Ltd* [1968] 2 QB 663, CA.

Contracts for unascertained goods present serious problems for the buyer if the seller becomes insolvent. This is because the authorities show that no buyer can acquire title under such contracts simply by virtue of the sale; the goods must be ascertained for the title to pass to the buyer. Until then, the buyer has only contractual rights, which are often worthless in insolvency. See *Re Goldcorp Exchange Ltd (in receivership)* [1994] 2 All ER 806.

2.13.2 Passing of risk: s 20

The SGA 1979, s 20(1) provides that the goods remain at the seller's risk until the property in them, ie title, is transferred to the buyer. This is the case whether or not delivery has been made, unless the parties agree otherwise. In other words, the risk prima facie only passes with the title to the goods, whether or not the goods are in the possession of the seller or the buyer. This can be altered by the intentions of the parties (see **2.15.4**).

This can be an important issue, for example, in the installation of a new computer system. The buyer will not want to pay the whole price until the system is running properly, yet the goods are on the buyer's premises and under his control while they are being installed. In such circumstances, the contract should provide that the risk in the goods passes to the buyer when the goods arrive at the buyer's premises (that is, they are delivered in the legal sense). It is then for the buyer to insure the goods, for example against theft or fire (see also **Chapter 9** on 'International Sale of Goods'). This is also a problem for the seller who supplies goods under retention of title clauses – see **2.15.4**.

2.13.3 Payment of the seller: s 27

At the completion of the contract, the seller will have been paid, as otherwise the whole transaction is rather pointless. It is the buyer's duty to pay the price (SGA 1979, s 27).

2.13.4 Force majeure clause

A force majeure clause is included in a contract to deal with circumstances beyond the reasonable control of the parties, as well as those that would frustrate the contract at common law. The terms of the clause are a matter of negotiation between the parties, but would typically include the effects of government action and extreme adverse weather. The idea is that the operation of the contract is:

(a) suspended for a defined period of time; and then

(b) terminated if the continuing circumstances in question render operation of the contract impossible.

A force majeure clause may go well beyond the range of events that would cause a contract to be frustrated at common law, eg it could deal with shortage of raw materials, etc. The wider the range of matters included, the more likely it is that the clause may come within the scope of UCTA 1977.

2.13.5 Additional rights under the SGA 1979 in consumer cases

Sections 48A to 48F were introduced into the SGA 1979 by Directive 1999/44/EC on Certain Aspects of the Sale of Consumer Goods and Associated Guarantees. These rights apply only to sales to consumers.

The buyer may require the seller to repair or replace goods if the goods do not comply with the implied terms under ss 13 to 15. The buyer has the right to require the seller to replace or repair the goods (s 48B), or to reduce the purchase price or to rescind the contract (s 48A(2)). These rights apply if the goods do not meet the implied terms within six months of the goods being delivered to the buyer (s 48A(3)).

2.14 Introduction to retention of title

There is a right under SGA 1979, ss 17 and 19 to reserve title to the goods. This can be done in a contract of sale by inserting a retention of title clause (also called a *Romalpa* clause after *Aluminium Industrie Vaassen BV v Romalpa Aluminium* [1976] 1 WLR 676). The idea of retaining title to the goods until they are paid for, or until they are sold on or used up (as with components/ingredients, etc), is that, in the last resort, the seller can recover his own goods and prevent a liquidator or trustee in bankruptcy of the buyer disposing of the goods.

The advantage for the buyer is that, up until such time as the seller might need to rely upon its retention of title clause, the buyer is free to sell or deal with the goods as it wishes. See *Fairfax Gerrard Holdings Ltd v Capital Bank plc* [2007] EWCA Civ 1226, where it was held that there is no inconsistency between the presence of a retention of title clause and an implied or even express right to sell the goods.

The validity of retention of title clauses has been upheld where the goods remain identifiable (see, eg, *Clough Mill Ltd v Martin* [1985] 1 WLR 111). This case concerned the yarn which had been sold to a manufacturer of fabrics. The seller was held to have title to the unused yarn.

Retention of title clauses are generally not registrable as they are considered to operate by preventing the property in the goods from passing to the buyer in the first place (see *Clough Mill Ltd v Martin* and also *Armour v Thyssen Edelstahlwerke AG* [1991] 2 AC 339). You cannot and would not take a charge over your own property by way of security. You would only grant such a charge to someone else to secure the debt owed by you to him.

There are a number of potential complications which could occur, for example, where:

(a) the original goods have been used in a manufacturing process and have lost their original identity (*Borden (UK) Ltd v Scottish Timber Products Ltd* [1981] Ch 25);

(b) the goods have been mixed with other goods and are no longer identifiable (*Re Andrabell Ltd (In Liquidation); Airborne Accessories Ltd v Goodman* [1984] 3 All ER 407);

(c) the goods have been attached to other goods (*Hendy Lennox (Industrial Engines) Ltd v Graham Puttick Ltd* [1984] 1 WLR 485); and

(d) the goods have been sold on to an innocent third party.

A problem area is where the goods have been incorporated into other products. Generally, the original goods are considered to have been subsumed into the new products and the seller has no right to the new products. In *Borden (UK) Ltd v Scottish Timber Products Ltd*, the sellers sold resin to manufacturers of chipboard. It was held that they did not have title to the chipboard, or to the proceeds of its sale (see **2.15.5**).

In *Re Andrabell Ltd*, the seller sold travel bags in a number of consignments. The contracts did not have an 'all moneys' clause (see **2.15.1**) so any rights attached only to the consignment for which the seller had not been paid. The seller was not able to identify those bags from all the other bags, so could not recover any bags. It was also not allowed to trace the proceeds of sale through the buyer's general bank account.

However, where the goods are readily detachable then it is appropriate to have a clause reserving the right of the seller to detach his goods and remove them. For example, in *Hendy Lennox (Industrial Engines) Ltd v Graham Puttick Ltd*, it was held that the sellers were entitled to detach their diesel engines from electrical generating sets.

There is no particular problem if the seller's goods are of a type that can be stored, typically in bulk, along with the goods of other suppliers or even of the buyer, eg diesel oil or grain, provided the goods are all of the same type and specification. In such a 'commingled' mass, it may be possible to hold that title has not passed to the buyer but, instead, that all contributors become owners in common, in proportion to their contributions to the bulk (*Glencore International AG v Metro Trading International Inc (No 2)* [2001] 1 Lloyd's Rep 284). See **2.15.6**. If the goods from the different sources are of different types or specifications, then mixing them together will constitute 'blending', and the individual sellers will have no title to the blended bulk or any part of it.

Under SGA 1979, s 25, an innocent third party will get good title to the goods (see **2.15.5**), so if a buyer of your goods sells them on, the sub-buyer will get good title to your goods.

2.15 Drafting a retention of title clause: a basic checklist

You should appreciate by this stage that no clause can always be guaranteed to be appropriate in all situations. You must always remember to check when using a precedent that it fits in with your client's needs and instructions. The following suggested provisions aim to cover the basic situation of retaining title to the goods, but also to go further and cover some of the problems mentioned above.

2.15.1 Reserving title

The seller should make it clear that he will remain the owner of the goods, and that (legal) ownership will not pass to the buyer until one of the two events described takes place. These events are:

(a) the buyer has paid all amounts owing to the seller in respect of all goods which the seller has supplied to the buyer (ie, paid for not just this consignment of goods, but any others which the buyer has bought previously); or

(b) the buyer sells the goods on in accordance with the agreement.

Point (a) is called an 'all moneys' clause. It aims to retain ownership of the goods until all outstanding sums have been paid. Many precedents are likely to include an 'all moneys' provision. It is not necessary for a retention of title clause to include this provision, but it is potentially a very useful protection for the seller (see *Re Andrabell*, at **2.14**). Such clauses have been upheld at the highest level – see *Armour v Thyssen Edelstahlwerke AG* [1991] 2 AC 339.

Point (b) acknowledges SGA 1979, s 25, which states that an innocent third party gets good title to the goods when the goods are sold on to him by the original buyer.

To be effective a retention of title clause must retain legal title to the goods. It is not sufficient to retain 'equitable and beneficial ownership' (see *In re Bond Worth* [1980] Ch 228). In this case the seller was held to have passed title to the goods, and then the buyer created an equitable charge which was then void for lack of registration under Companies Act 1985, ss 395 and 396. Although this explanation has been criticised, it has been followed in *Stroud Architectural Systems Ltd v John Laing Construction Ltd* [1994] BCC 18.

2.15.2 Rights of entry, seizure and sale

The seller must make sure that the clause specifically provides for the right to go on to the buyer's premises (or the seller will commit trespass in doing so) to recover the goods (which would otherwise be conversion) and also to re-sell them. This right would often be expressed as arising when the buyer is overdue in paying for the goods (ie, the consignment actually sold under *this* agreement, or any other goods which the seller has supplied to the buyer). This could be linked through to a clause in the agreement making the price become due immediately on the buyer becoming insolvent.

2.15.3 Storage of the seller's goods while in the buyer's possession

The seller needs to decide whether anything can or should be done to maximise the chances of being able to recover the goods (or at least getting some money back if something happens to them while in the buyer's possession).

So, a clause could be included to provide for separate storage in order to maximise the chances that the seller can identify its own goods when trying to recover them. This could raise a problem with bulk materials such as oils, etc.

Likewise, if the goods were destroyed, the seller would want recompense. So, a clause should be included to require the buyer to insure the seller's goods and to hold the proceeds on trust for the seller.

A further possibility for protection of the goods is the seller marking its goods to make them easily identifiable. Obviously this will not always work – for example, 100 tons of gravel is impossible to mark! Where practicable, this can be a useful back-up to a separate storage clause (which the buyer may disobey). Note that the seller will sometimes reserve the right to inspect the buyer's premises to check if separate storage provisions are being complied with. Although this may be a useful power to have, the reality is often that separate storage provisions are impossible to police. If the buyer does disobey it will obviously be in breach of contract, but this may be of no use to the seller (eg, if the buyer has become insolvent).

2.15.4 Passing of risk

It is important for sale of goods agreements to provide expressly for the passing of the risk of accidental loss of, or damage to, the goods. This may be done in a separate clause, but is often found in a retention of title clause.

Under SGA 1979, s 20, goods remain at the seller's risk until the property in them (ie, ownership) is transferred to the buyer, unless the parties agree otherwise. This is not the desired situation in a contract with a retention of title, so a clause is added which displaces s 20 by contrary agreement. The seller will usually stipulate that risk passes on delivery. This will often be linked to a requirement that the buyer insures the goods and holds any proceeds of the policy on trust for the seller.

2.15.5 Tracing into the proceeds of sale, separation of proceeds and assignment of debts

Tracing has been done successfully only once, in *Aluminium Industrie Vaassen BV v Romalpa Aluminium* [1976] 1 WLR 676. The sellers there tried to claim the proceeds of sale of the goods once the goods themselves had been sold on. The Court of Appeal allowed this on the grounds that there was an express fiduciary relationship between the sellers and the buyers (with the buyers selling the goods on to a third party as agents for the sellers rather than in their own right). Subsequently, the courts have been unwilling to recognise this fiduciary relationship, which seems to have been based, in *Romalpa*, upon concessions made by one party, probably unnecessarily.

Over the years, there have been many attempts to draft retention of title clauses to permit the seller to claim sale proceeds. Very simple clauses entitling the seller to the proceeds are almost certain to be construed as charges over the proceeds (see **2.15.1**). It seems from the cases that the courts will take exactly the same view of more complex attempts (eg, elaborate clauses describing the existence of a fiduciary relationship between the parties).

In *Compaq Computer Ltd v Abercorn Group Ltd (t/a Osiris) and Others* [1991] BCC 484, Abercorn was appointed as an authorised dealer of Compaq's computers. The agreement contained a clause that the goods were held by Abercorn as 'bailee and agent' and proceeds of sub-sales were to be accounted for to Compaq. The arrangement was held to be a charge over the proceeds of the sub-sales which was void for want of registration. It seems that even a very carefully worded clause will create only a charge. This does not stop such clauses being included, if only in the hope that they might serve to exert commercial pressure, but enforcement is unlikely to succeed.

A typical clause would also require the buyer to pay the proceeds into a separate bank account, where the buyer will hold them on trust for the seller. The idea is to stop the money generated by the sale of the seller's goods from becoming mixed up with other money the buyer may have which is nothing to do with the seller. Such a clause would facilitate tracing if it were to be allowed by the court. (Do not forget that under SGA 1979, s 25, an innocent third party will get good title to the goods. So, once the goods have been sold on, the original seller's title to the goods themselves no longer exists.) The difficulty with all such clauses is that the relationship between a seller and a buyer of goods is rarely of a fiduciary nature. Such clauses are usually seen as creating charges only, usually void for non-registration.

It is quite common to find that a clause requires the buyer to assign the debts arising from any credit sub-sales that it makes to the seller. The problem with such a clause is that if the sub-buyer fails to comply with this or does it when it is insolvent, the seller will not usually recover the money. The rights are merely contractual and of little use in insolvency. See *Fairfax Gerrard Holdings Ltd v Capital Bank plc* [2007] EWCA Civ 1226.

2.15.6 Claiming ownership of 'mixed' goods

The typical commercial situation where a retention of title clause is used is in manufacturing, or construction or reselling. In manufacturing and construction, it is likely that the goods supplied will have been incorporated into other products (see, eg, *In re Peachdart Ltd* [1984] Ch 131, where the leather hides had been made into handbags). The resulting goods are referred to variously as 'mixed', or 'manufactured' or 'altered' goods. The consequence is usually that, because the goods have lost their identity, they no longer exist in the ownership of the seller.

The seller may try to extend a retention of title clause to cover these 'mixed' goods. In *Clough Mill Ltd v Martin* [1985] 1 WLR 111, the seller supplied yarn to a manufacturer of fabrics. It was held not to have title to the finished fabric, only to the unused yarn.

A different situation arose in the cases of *Glencore International AG v Metro Trading International Inc and Others* [1999] 2 All ER (Comm) 899, HC; *Glencore International AG v Metro Trading International Inc (No 2)* [2001] 1 All ER (Comm) 103; *Glencore International AG v Exeter Shipping Ltd and Others* [2002] EWCA Civ 528, where the subject matter was oil from different suppliers, but of the same type and grade, which the buyer stored co-mingled in bulk containers. It was held that the onus of proof as to which unpaid supplier was entitled to a specific quantity of oil was on the defendant as it had caused the problem in the first place. It was also held that upon commingling in storage oil owned by Glencore with oil owned by MTI or other persons, Glencore would become an owner of the whole of the commingled bulk in common with MTI and any other persons whose oil had contributed to the bulk. This would be in proportion to the quantity of oil contributed by each of them. This illustrates the problems that such cases throw up. This rule is similar to the statutory rule for buyers of an unascertained part of a bulk quantity, set out in SGA 1979, s 20A. The big difference is, as between these cases and the earlier 'mixed goods' cases, that in the bulk storage cases, it can be seen that the goods have not lost their identifiable nature and title does not pass to the buyer. Nevertheless, slight differences in grade or specification between the separate quantities supplied would easily cause a mixing or blending into a bulk, in which the separate sellers had lost their titles and property.

Mixed goods clauses are usually interpreted as charges over the buyer company's assets, which are usually void for want of registration. (The charge will still be valid against the buyer, but the typical situation we are concerned about here is an insolvency.) However, you will still see mixed goods clauses included in a retention of title clause, usually more in hope than in expectation.

2.15.7 Detachable goods

If the goods supplied to the buyer are readily detachable without damage to the buyer's products, the seller's goods can be recovered. We have already mentioned *Hendy Lennox (Industrial Engines) Ltd v Graham Puttick Ltd* [1984] 1 WLR 485 (see **2.14**), where the seller had sold diesel engines to the buyer. The buyer had bolted the engines to electrical generators. It was therefore feasible to detach the engines without damaging the generators.

A clause allowing the seller to separate and remove detachable goods is likely to be upheld by the court.

2.16 Retention of title clauses and the creation of charges

Some of the tactics used by sellers are not going to work in court because they create a charge which is void for want of registration. Is it feasible to register a charge in such circumstances? In practice, it is not going to be practical. A new charge would come into existence each time the buyer resold the goods, in the case of a proceeds of sale clause, or mixed them with others, in the case of a mixed/manufactured goods clause. The seller would find it very hard to police this. It would also be onerous to complete the necessary Form 395 each time, identifying the property over which the charge had been created. Registering all these charges could also lead to adverse credit ratings for the buyer if it is a company, because the buyer's file at Companies House would show numerous charges registered against it. This would discourage anyone thinking of lending money to the buyer. The effect of such actions by the seller would be to put off the buyer from contracting with the seller in the first place. In practice, therefore, the seller will not usually attempt to register any charge which a retention of title clause might create.

2.17 'Backing up' a retention of title clause

It is worth encouraging a seller to back up any retention of title clause by taking practical steps either to minimise the chances of dealing with buyers who may not pay, or to provide an incentive for the buyer to pay up, or both. The possibilities include the following.

2.17.1 Checks on the buyer/controlling the credit the buyer is given

This is likely to be a useful practical back-up to retention of title. In an ideal world, it would include the following measures:

(a) Encourage the seller to run a tight system of credit control, with frequent checks on buyers' creditworthiness. The seller should take steps to ensure that buyers always pay by the due date, send out invoices on time and chase debts before they start to become a problem. Ensure that all relevant staff know precisely the limit of the credit that the buyer is allowed.

(b) If buyers start to fall behind in paying for the goods, the seller may want to consider reducing any credit period allowed, or even move on to demanding cash on delivery or 'up front'. Obviously, whether this is a practical solution will vary from case to case (eg, will the buyer agree to the new terms?).

(c) If the contract permits, the seller should consider removing its goods from the buyer's premises at the first hint of trouble rather than waiting for a receiver or liquidator to be appointed. Once creditors become twitchy, things can happen very quickly indeed.

(d) If a buyer persistently pays late, consider not dealing with him in future!

2.17.2 Debt factoring

Factoring is where the debts are sold to someone else who will then collect them. This is an alternative to retention of title rather than a supplement to it. Obviously, the debts cannot be sold for 100% of their value, as the factor has to make a profit. The discount can vary considerably, according to the credit period and/or the creditworthiness of the debtor.

Debt factoring arrangements can also create problems where information and documents are disclosed or obtained (see *GE Capital Commercial Finance v Sutton* [2004] EWCA Civ 315), particularly if legal professional privilege or other protections attach to the disclosed material.

2.17.3 Credit risk insurance

A seller may also be able to insure against the risk of the buyer not paying. Credit risk insurance may sometimes be too expensive to be worthwhile, but in the last few years it has become cheaper and more widely available. Sellers are able to obtain policies tailored to their precise needs rather than on an 'all debts' basis, which would be very expensive for the seller.

2.17.4 Providing for interest

The seller may charge interest on sums which become overdue. This may act as an incentive to the buyer to pay on time, and will give the seller some recompense if the payment is late. Normally, the best way to deal with interest is to provide for it expressly in the contract. The seller must not go over the top when providing for the amount of interest, as a provision which claimed excessive interest could be struck down as a penalty (see **2.10.1.2**).

The Late Payment of Commercial Debts (Interest) Act 1998 provides specifically for the payment of interest in certain commercial situations. It is now fully implemented, so that all businesses and the public sector can claim interest on late payments. The Directive on Combating Late Payment in Commercial Transactions (2000/35/EC) required Member States to deal with combating late payments in commercial transactions.

The 1998 Act works in the following way:

(a) it implies into applicable contracts a term relating to interest (basically commercial contracts for the supply of goods or services);

(b) the term is to the effect that any 'qualifying debt' created by the contract carries simple interest in accordance with the Act, known as 'statutory interest'; and

(c) in certain circumstances, this right to interest can be ousted by contract terms if there is another 'substantial contractual remedy' for late payment, but the contract may not provide that late payment carries no remedy at all.

Many businesses which might benefit under the Act are becoming aware of its existence and there is some evidence that it is beginning to have some impact.

In *Banham Marshalls Services Unlimited v Lincolnshire CC* [2007] EWHC 402 (QB), the Act was even applied to payments which were being withheld because of a genuine legal dispute, where one party had delayed the commencement of proceedings. See also the detailed analysis of entitlement to statutory interest and the interplay between the 1998 Act and the Supreme Court Act 1981 in *Ruttle Plant Hire v Secretary of State for the Environment, Food and Rural Affairs* [2009] EWCA Civ 97.

Even if there is no express provision in the contract and the Act does not apply, there are statutory provisions for claiming interest in both the High Court and county court. This has the disadvantage that technically any award of interest is in the discretion of the court (although this is rarely a problem). Also, to be certain of its entitlement to interest, the seller must incur the cost of proceedings and wait for judgment. Debtors routinely rely on this loophole and refuse to pay interest unless proceedings are commenced.

2.18 Unfair terms in consumer contracts

See **Chapter 3** for a brief account of the Unfair Terms in Consumer Contracts Regulations 1999 (SI 1999/2083).

2.19 Sale of goods to consumers

Consumer contracts are largely beyond the scope of this book, although you may well come across the issues outlined at **3.7** and **3.8** when you are in practice. Many commercial clients will have dealings with consumers, and will need to consider the particular issues raised by the dealings with this type of buyer. There is, however, one type of contract which this book deals with in some detail, that is contracts for consumer credit (see **Chapter 6**).

Chapter 3
Effective Drafting of Exclusion Clauses

3.1	Introduction	35
3.2	Basic rules for successful drafting of exclusion clauses	35
3.3	Preparing to draft	36
3.4	Three stages for effectiveness	37
3.5	Incorporation	38
3.6	Construction	39
3.7	The Unfair Contract Terms Act 1977	40
3.8	The Unfair Terms in Consumer Contracts Regulations 1999	42
3.9	Drafting for reasonableness: general principles	43
3.10	Drafting for reasonableness: relevant factors	44
3.11	Drafting for severance	50
3.12	Drafting to litigate or to negotiate?	50
3.13	Trying to exclude everything	51
3.14	Drafting specific clauses in a commercial contract	51

3.1 Introduction

Commercial clients will always be concerned about the liability which they may incur in performing their contracts, and in most cases their instinct will be to try to reduce their exposure as much as possible. The solicitor is likely to be approached for advice in two respects:

(a) drafting an agreement to minimise the client's liability if things should go wrong;

(b) advising on the protection given by exclusions in an agreement once problems have arisen.

Most of this chapter deals with the first point; it looks at the various matters which the solicitor should bear in mind when drafting (or reviewing) an agreement. The use of exclusion and limitation clauses, particularly in commercial contracts, is part of the process by which the parties agree to allocate risk, liability and responsibility for performance as between themselves. Much like other clauses in the contract, the exclusions will usually reflect the nature and context of the contract, as well as the relative needs and bargaining power of the parties.

This chapter considers exclusion of liability mainly from the point of view of a solicitor drafting on behalf of a commercial client which is entering into agreements with other commercial parties.

3.2 Basic rules for successful drafting of exclusion clauses

Three points are particularly important:

(a) know the commercial background;

(b) know the law;

(c) know the drafting principles.

3.2.1 Know the commercial background

Although this may at first seem obvious, the solicitor needs to know how a client's business operates before it is possible to draft effectively for exclusion of liability on behalf of the client. Exclusion clauses in commercial contracts are in many cases subject to the reasonableness test under the Unfair Contract Terms Act 1977 (UCTA 1977), and many of the factors which are relevant in deciding whether or not a clause passes the reasonableness test are specific to the circumstances of each contract. The solicitor should, therefore, obtain full instructions before drafting, learning as much as possible about the circumstances in which a client makes its commercial contracts, as well as about the client's business methods generally and with whom the client is likely to enter contracts. Although it will not be possible to cover every eventuality, the likely effectiveness of an exclusion clause can be greatly enhanced if the person drafting it is familiar with the commercial background against which it will operate.

3.2.2 Know the law

Three areas are relevant:

(a) the principles relating to incorporation and construction;

(b) the rules in UCTA 1977; and

(c) the factors which determine whether a clause will pass the reasonableness test or not.

All these points, and (c) in particular, are considered in more detail at **3.4** to **3.10**.

3.2.3 Know the drafting principles

The way in which an exclusion clause has been drafted may have a profound influence on its effectiveness. Although the client's instructions, or the circumstances in which the clause is to operate may in practice limit how a clause can be put together, the solicitor should always bear in mind the principles of good commercial drafting. This topic is not, however, considered further in detail in this chapter; for a full discussion of the principles of drafting, see the relevant chapter in ***Skills for Lawyers***.

3.3 Preparing to draft

Before beginning to draft, there are several general considerations which the solicitor should have in mind, as they will relate to the likely effectiveness of the finished clauses.

3.3.1 What is an 'exclusion clause'?

There is no really comprehensive definition of what constitutes an 'exclusion' or 'exemption' clause. The closest approach to a full definition is probably s 13 of UCTA 1977, which defines very widely the type of clause to which the 1977 Act applies. In addition, all the relevant sections of UCTA 1977 refer to 'exclusion or restriction of liability', so the Act clearly covers limitation clauses as well as strict exclusion clauses. However, bear in mind that UCTA 1977 does not cover every case of exclusion or limitation of liability (see **3.7.1**). For the sake of simplicity, this chapter uses the expression 'exclusion clause' to cover all the possibilities, unless the context requires otherwise.

3.3.2 Ways of eliminating liability

Although it may be tempting to draft the 'exclusions' after the 'substantive' parts of the contract (so that, broadly speaking, the contract takes away something which it has already given), this may not always be the right approach. A 'duty-defining' clause may sometimes work better. For example, instead of one party agreeing to do something under the contract, and then excluding or limiting its liability should things go wrong, it may be more appropriate to draft the contract so that the party never agrees to do that thing in the first place. This type of clause is still, however, likely to fall within the scope of UCTA 1977, and care needs to be taken that the 'contract' does not become a mere declaration of intent because, if any dispute gets to court, the language used will be construed by the court to ascertain what the parties must be taken to have meant by it, regardless of what the draftsman might have thought he was achieving.

3.3.3 Background knowledge

An exclusion clause will be of little use to a client unless it has been drafted to suit the client's business. For example, a long, elaborate clause may look impressive on paper, but turn out to be unworkable in practice because it does not fit the way in which the client operates. When drafting, therefore, the solicitor must be realistic, and, as previously noted, this involves finding out as much as possible about how the client's business works (in particular, how the client actually makes contracts with customers). Basic questions to ask would include:

(a) With what sort of customers does the client normally deal?

(b) Which of the client's employees actually make the contracts (and therefore 'operate' the exclusion clauses)?

(c) How, if at all, are any exclusions introduced to the customers?

(d) Are certain exclusions/limitations or standard form contracts likely to be familiar to both your client and and/or other prospective parties as part of their normal dealings (see the significance of this at **3.10.7** and **3.10.8.1**)?

This background knowledge is particularly important in the light of the reasonableness test under UCTA 1977 (see **3.10**).

3.3.4 Instructions and advice

A particular problem arises when drafting exclusion clauses, since there are frequently several different and conflicting factors governing the effectiveness of the clause (see generally **3.10**). Although the solicitor must try to achieve what the client has requested, the client must also be advised (as constructively as possible) that no exclusion clause can be guaranteed to work in all circumstances.

3.3.5 Precedents

Because the effectiveness of an exclusion clause will depend to a large extent on its own individual context, precedents for exclusion clauses need to be used with some caution. The solicitor should always consider how a clause might work in a particular business context, and think carefully before simply copying a precedent which appears to be suitable on paper. Having said that, precedents can be very useful in this context as a source of inspiration, or as a guide to how the layout of the exclusions within the contract might be organised (see **3.10.7.2**).

3.3.6 Testing the clause

Although this chapter deals almost entirely with the drafting of exclusion clauses, rather than the more general contractual background against which they will operate, it is often helpful at the drafting stage to consider that contractual background; this can be an extremely useful way of assessing a draft clause's potential strength. The solicitor should try to anticipate what problems may arise, and consider:

(a) identifying the terms of the contract which are likely to be relevant, ie those terms which may lead to liability if breached – some terms may not have this effect;

(b) deciding whether those terms have actually been breached by what has happened;

(c) anticipating what remedy the injured party will be seeking.

These points will form an integral part of the process of applying the clause if problems occur, and will often provide important information at the drafting stage as to how well the clause is likely to work in those circumstances.

3.4 Three stages for effectiveness

A party who wishes to claim the protection of an exclusion clause must prove three things:

(a) incorporation: that the clause forms part of the contract;

(b) construction: that the wording of the clause is wide enough that, on its true construction, it covers the breach which has occurred;

(c) UCTA 1977: that the clause is not invalidated by UCTA 1977 (if applicable).

This 'exclusion clause checklist' can be used just as much in drafting clauses as in assessing their validity once problems have arisen.

3.5 Incorporation

3.5.1 Clause must be incorporated

To be effective, a clause must form part of the contract. Whether it does or not is assessed by reference to the normal contractual principles of incorporation. It is, therefore, important to consider exclusion of liability when starting to draft, rather than when the rest of the contract is finished. The solicitor must consider what practical problems of incorporation may arise in relation to the contract, and whether anything can be done about them.

3.5.2 Signed or unsigned documents?

If a clause is contained in a contractual document which the client's customers will sign, the chances of incorporation are very good (the normal contractual rules on signature will apply). If, however, the clause is in an unsigned document, it will form part of the contract only if reasonable steps are taken to bring it to the customer's attention before the contract is made. Putting the clause into a document which is to be signed should, therefore, be less risky as far as incorporation is concerned. However, this may not be the best solution if it does not fit in with the client's normal business practices. There may also be problems over signature itself. What if the clause is in a document which should be signed but which the customer does not sign? What if a regular customer normally signs a contractual document but fails to sign on one or more occasions? Is it possible to draft and locate the clause so that it will be incorporated even if the document is not signed? There can be no general answers to these questions; in each case, the solicitor must obtain full instructions and then draft to meet the needs of the client's particular business.

3.5.3 Timing

If the clause is contained in a document which is not intended to be signed, problems may arise if there is normally an interval between drawing the buyer's attention to the clause and the contract being made. Again, it will help to find out how the client's business operates, but the solicitor may in practice be unable to resolve this problem. There may be problems if it is intended to incorporate exclusion clauses by reference to other documents (see **3.10.7.5** below).

3.5.4 Course of dealings

If the clause is in an unsigned document, it may be incorporated into the contract by way of regular and consistent course of dealings. Once again, the solicitor needs to know how the client's business works in order to decide whether this is likely. Does the client do a lot of business with regular customers, is it involved mainly in 'one-off' transactions or (perhaps most likely) is there a variety of different dealings? Note that incorporation by course of dealings is far more likely to happen with contracts made between commercial parties than with contracts between a commercial party and a consumer, but it may be unwise to depend too much upon a course of dealing as a reliable method of incorporation because exclusion clauses and, particularly, limitation clauses do tend to vary over time.

3.5.5 Preventing incorporation problems

If the solicitor has acquired a background knowledge of how the client actually makes contracts, it should be possible to spot potential incorporation problems and take action before they arise. This could, for example, take the form of advice to the client (eg, about staff training in relation to how contracts should be entered into), or building in safeguards when drafting (eg, paying particular attention to the layout of the contract and the location of the clause). Whatever method is chosen, the client should always be made aware of the dangers; in particular, that its employees' actions when making contracts on the client's behalf could actually prevent exclusions in the contract from working.

3.6 Construction

3.6.1 Does the clause cover the breach?

Even if the clause is incorporated into the contract, it will be effective only if, on its true construction by the court, it is worded so as to cover the breach which actually occurs. As with incorporation, this poses problems when drafting: how far can the solicitor foresee the circumstances in which the clause will eventually operate, or the breaches which might occur? Once again, knowing the client's business as thoroughly as possible and taking full instructions will help; an awareness of the basic contractual principles of construction is also important, particularly in trading contexts where disputes and litigation arise with some frequency, such as freight and insurance contracts.

3.6.2 *Contra proferentem*

An exclusion clause will be construed strictly *contra proferentem* (ie, against the person attempting to rely on it). One important aspect of this principle relates to exclusion of liability for negligence, for which clear and unambiguous words are required. From this point of view, it is therefore desirable for a clause excluding liability for negligence to refer clearly to 'negligence' (or an appropriate synonym). However, a client may be extremely reluctant to state in the contract that it is excluding liability for negligence. The solicitor may use expressions such as 'howsoever caused', but whether this (or similar wording) will be effective is uncertain; it will depend on the circumstances. Whether or not to take the risk is a matter which the solicitor must discuss fully with the client.

It should be borne in mind that the particular provision will be construed against the background of the wording within which it is set. For example, a restricted construction was given to the words 'in any circumstances' by the court in *Regus (UK) Ltd v Epcot Solutions Ltd* [2008] EWCA Civ 361. The phrase was construed in the light of its neighbouring sub-clause so as to apply only to damage caused without fraud, recklessness or malice (but on the facts of the case this did not operate *contra proferentem*).

3.6.3 Other principles of construction

In construing an exclusion clause, the court may apply various other principles to decide whether or not the clause covers the breach, for example:

(a) *Expressio unius est exclusio alterius*: by this principle, if a contract expressly mentions one or more matters, those not mentioned are automatically excluded. For example, if a clause lists claims which are to be barred, it will not apply to claims not mentioned.

(b) *Ejusdem generis*: this is a general aid to construction, which is sometimes seen as being more appropriate to property documents than to commercial contracts. The principle is that general words which follow two or more specific words are restricted to the same type of item or situation as the preceding specific words. (Note that this principle does not apply to a force majeure clause; see further **3.14.1.1**.)

3.6.4 Avoiding loose terminology

If words or phrases are used inappropriately, this may mean that a clause does not cover the breach which it was intended to cover. In particular, jargon may be misused (even by lawyers). For example, the words 'rescission', 'condition' and 'warranty' are all often used in commercial contracts in ways which pervert their strict legal meaning. A similar problem arises from the use of words which may mean different things to different readers of the contract (eg, 'consequential loss'). When drafting, therefore, the solicitor should either try to avoid expressions which may cause problems, or define clearly what a particular expression means in context (for further discussion of this point in relation to the expression 'consequential loss', see **3.10.8.2**). Note that even if loose terminology does not prevent the clause from covering the breach, it may make the clause less likely to pass the reasonableness test if, for example, the effect is to make it difficult to understand (see further **3.10.7** and the discussion of *Regus (UK) Ltd v Epcot Solutions* at **3.6.2** above)).

3.7 The Unfair Contract Terms Act 1977

The solicitor will obviously need to be aware of statutory controls on the drafting of exclusion clauses. By far the most important of these is UCTA 1977.

Note: In December 2004, the Law Commission published a detailed review of the law on unfair contract terms, with proposals for major reform of the 1977 Act. The Commission's report contains an extensive summary of its recommendations for reform and a draft Unfair Contract Terms Bill showing how the Commission recommends that these should be put into practice. However, at the time of writing (September 2009) it remains unclear when (or whether) the Government might decide to pursue reform of this area. It is not thought to be a priority at the moment.

3.7.1 Scope of UCTA 1977

Section 13 of UCTA 1977 gives the Act a wide scope, but it will by no means apply in every case.

3.7.1.1 Contracts to which UCTA 1977 does not apply

The most important examples of this are:

(a) contracts listed in UCTA 1977, Sch 1. By this Schedule, ss 2–4 and 7 do not apply to certain types of contract, including contracts relating to land and contracts relating to intellectual property rights;

(b) international supply contracts (UCTA 1977, s 26). By s 26(2), the reasonableness test under ss 3 and 4 of UCTA 1977 does not apply to an international supply contract.

For an explanation of why international supply contracts are generally excluded from the provisions of UCTA 1977 as well as the Misrepresentation Act 1967, and for examples of the problems in deciding whether these Acts apply to the particular contract, see *Trident Turboprop (Dublin) Ltd v First Flight Couriers Ltd* [2009] EWCA Civ 290 and *Amiri Flight Authority v BAE Systems plc* [2002] EWHC 2481 (Comm).

Note also that, by s 27 of UCTA 1977, if the applicable law of the contract is that of some part of the UK only because of the choice of parties (and would, apart from that choice, be the law of a country outside the UK), then ss 2–7 and 16–21 of UCTA 1977 do not operate as part of the law applicable to the contract.

3.7.1.2 Clauses to which UCTA 1977 does not apply

Even if UCTA 1977 can apply generally to a particular type of contract, it may not apply to certain individual clauses within that contract. For example, assume that two businesses are entering into a tailor-made (ie, not standard-form) contract for the sale of goods. The seller inserts a clause into the contract excluding liability for late delivery of the goods. UCTA 1977, s 3 will not apply to this clause because the buyer deals neither as consumer nor on the other party's written standard terms of business: no other section of UCTA 1977 is relevant to the clause either.

3.7.2 Continuing relevance of common law principles

Where UCTA 1977 does not apply, it is worth remembering that certain common law principles may still be relevant. Before the advent of UCTA 1977, the courts developed numerous principles to control the use of exclusion clauses, which have survived the Act. Discussion of the principles is outside the scope of this chapter, and admittedly they have lost much of their importance as a result of UCTA 1977, but the solicitor should be aware that even if UCTA 1977 does not apply, he may not have a completely free hand in drafting.

3.7.3 A reminder of the effect of UCTA 1977 on contractual terms

The following is a brief reminder of the main points.

3.7.3.1 Void clauses

Note that although the word 'void' is used here to describe the effect of the relevant sections of UCTA 1977 on exclusion clauses, and is a convenient shorthand description, none of the sections of the Act actually uses this word. Instead, each section provides that the relevant liability cannot be excluded or restricted.

Section 2(1)

By s 2(1) of UCTA 1977, a person cannot, by reference either to a contract term or a notice, exclude or restrict his liability for personal injury or death resulting from negligence.

Section 6(1)

By s 6(1) of UCTA 1977, liability for breach of the implied condition of title under either s 12 of SGA 1979 or s 8 of the Supply of Goods (Implied Terms) Act 1973 cannot be excluded or restricted by reference to any contract term.

Section 6(2)

By s 6(2) of UCTA 1977, as against a person who deals as consumer, liability for breach of the implied conditions in ss 13–15 of SGA 1979 or ss 9–11 of the Supply of Goods (Implied Terms) Act 1973 cannot be excluded or restricted by reference to any contract term. The expression 'deals as consumer' is defined in s 12 of UCTA 1977; perhaps surprisingly, the Court of Appeal has held that, in certain circumstances, a company can deal as consumer (for example, in *R & B Customs Brokers Co Ltd v United Dominions Trust Ltd* [1988] 1 All ER 847). Broadly speaking, the point arises when a company does not make the contract 'in the course of a business' and the goods are of a type ordinarily supplied for private use or consumption. (Note that s 7 of UCTA 1977, which applies to miscellaneous contracts under which goods pass (eg, work and materials contracts), contains provisions similar to those in s 6.) For further analysis of 'dealing as a consumer', see *GE Capital Bank Ltd v Rushton* [2005] EWCA Civ 1556.

3.7.3.2 Clauses subject to the reasonableness test

The two ways in which the contractual reasonableness test (see **3.9.1**) is most likely to apply are as follows.

Section 3

Section 3 of UCTA 1977 applies either where one party deals as consumer, or, significantly for commercial contracts, where one party deals on the other party's written standard terms of business. It imposes the reasonableness test on a wide variety of clauses.

Section 6(3)

An attempt to exclude the liability mentioned in UCTA 1977, s 6(2) (see **3.7.3.1**) against a person who does not deal as consumer is subject to the reasonableness test.

3.8 The Unfair Terms in Consumer Contracts Regulations 1999

These Regulations provide (in certain circumstances) a further important statutory control on drafting exclusion clauses.

3.8.1 Introduction

The original version of these Regulations (the Unfair Terms in Consumer Contracts Regulations 1994, SI 1994/3159) came into force on 1 July 1995, and implemented Directive 93/13/EEC on unfair terms in consumer contracts. However, it subsequently proved necessary to make a number of changes to the Regulations in order to achieve full and correct implementation of the Directive, and as a result, the 1994 Regulations were revoked and replaced (with effect from 1 October 1999) by the Unfair Terms in Consumer Contracts Regulations 1999, SI 1999/2083.

Note that the Regulations do not apply to a contract between two commercial parties; however, for the commercial client which enters into standard-form contracts for the supply of goods and/or services to consumers, their impact is likely to be significant.

3.8.2 The Regulations in outline

Regulations 1 and 2 deal with commencement of the 1999 Regulations and revocation of the 1994 Regulations; the definitions are found in reg 3. The definitions of 'consumer' and 'seller or supplier' require that a consumer must be a natural person who is not acting for business purposes, and that a seller or supplier must be acting for business purposes. Regulation 4 provides that the Regulations apply 'in relation to unfair terms in contracts concluded between a seller or supplier and a consumer', and also indicates a number of terms to which the Regulations do not apply.

'Unfair term' is then defined by reg 5(1):

> a contractual term which has not been individually negotiated shall be regarded as unfair if, contrary to the requirement of good faith, it causes a significant imbalance in the parties' rights and obligations arising under the contract to the detriment of the consumer.

An 'illustrative and non-exhaustive list of terms which may be regarded as unfair' can be found in Sch 2. Regulation 6 describes how unfair terms are to be assessed. The effect of an unfair term (found in reg 8) is that it 'shall not be binding on the consumer'.

Regulations 10–15 give power to the Office of Fair Trading (OFT) and 'qualifying bodies' (specified in Sch 1; they include bodies such as the Consumers' Association) to consider complaints that contract terms drawn up for general use are unfair, and to take action.

3.8.3 Relationship with UCTA 1977

The Regulations apply in addition to rather than instead of UCTA 1977. Thus, a solicitor will have to advise on situations where a term is subject not only to the UCTA 1977 reasonableness test, but also to the test of fairness under the Regulations.

3.8.4 The requirement of 'plain, intelligible language'

By reg 7, a seller or supplier 'shall ensure that any written term of a contract [to which the Regulations apply] is expressed in plain, intelligible language'. This concept is not further defined in the Regulations, neither is it clear from the Regulations what will happen if a term is not expressed in plain, intelligible language. Perhaps the most appropriate conclusion is that it is one of the factors which may render a term unfair (compare the relationship of UCTA 1977 and 'plain English'; see **3.10.7**). Regulation 7 also provides that 'if there is doubt about the meaning of a written term, the interpretation most favourable to the consumer shall prevail'; compare the normal *contra proferentem* rule (see **3.6.2**).

3.9 Drafting for reasonableness: general principles

3.9.1 The contractual reasonableness test

In practice, when UCTA 1977 applies to a commercial agreement, most (if not all) of the agreement's exclusion clauses will be subject to the reasonableness test, so it is usually against this test that the solicitor will need to assess a clause.

Section 11(1) of UCTA 1977 states that:

> In relation to a contract term, the requirement of reasonableness ... is that the term shall have been a fair and reasonable one to be included having regard to the circumstances which were, or ought reasonably to have been, known to or in the contemplation of the parties when the contract was made.

It is, therefore, a test of reasonableness of incorporation, not reasonableness of reliance. If (in the light of the actual and constructive knowledge of the parties at the time) it is reasonable to include a particular clause when the contract is made, it should pass the reasonableness test: the court should not look at whether it was reasonable for the 'guilty' party to rely on the clause in the light of the events which actually happened (although it has to be said that it is not uncommon in practice for courts to do this). It is for the party claiming that a term satisfies the reasonableness test to show that it does (s 11(5)).

3.9.2 The Sch 2 guidelines

The guidelines include: the relative bargaining power of the parties; whether the buyer was offered any inducement to accept the clause; whether any choice was available (eg, could the buyer have acquired the goods elsewhere without the clause?); and the extent of the parties' knowledge of the existence and effect of the terms. The list is not intended to be exhaustive and, strictly speaking, applies only when the court is assessing reasonableness under s 6(3) and s 7(3) of UCTA 1977. However, the courts often apply the guidelines when considering the reasonableness test in relation to other sections, notably s 3: see, eg, *Flamar Interocean Ltd v Denmac Ltd (formerly Denholm Maclay Co Ltd) (The 'Flamar Pride' and 'Flamar Progress')* [1990] 1 Lloyd's Rep 434. This approach was confirmed as appropriate by the Court of Appeal in *Overseas Medical Supplies Ltd v Orient Transport Services Ltd* [1999] 2 Lloyd's Rep 273 and, more recently, in *Regus (UK) Ltd v Epcot Solutions Ltd* [2008] EWCA Civ 361. The former case also contains a useful discussion and summary of the factors which are generally relevant to assessing the reasonableness of a clause.

3.9.3 Is it a consumer contract or a commercial contract?

In determining whether a clause will survive the application of UCTA 1977, the crucial factor is often whether the contract is a consumer contract or a commercial contract. For example, a clause which excludes liability for breach of s 14(2) or (3) of SGA 1979 is subject to the reasonableness test only against a commercial buyer; it is void against a buyer who deals as consumer. Even if a clause is subject to the reasonableness test whatever the status of the 'victim' (eg, under s 3), the courts are often prepared to be stricter in applying the test where that person is a consumer. The clause may in fact be less likely to pass the test for that reason alone. If the client deals with both commercial and consumer buyers, it is important for the solicitor to recognise this when drafting. There may be several different ways of dealing with the problem, depending on how the client does business and the other relevant circumstances. For example, the solicitor may decide to draft two different forms of contract, with the 'consumer' version either omitting certain exclusion clauses, or containing only modified versions. However, this may be risky; it would then be necessary to ensure that those operating the contract are able to distinguish between the two versions (perhaps by printing them on different coloured paper). A simpler solution, where possible, may be to have one contract for all customers, but to draft any exclusion so that it will apply only to commercial customers.

3.9.4 No guarantee of success

Because of the way in which the contractual reasonableness test is worded, the factors which are relevant when drafting for reasonableness (see **3.10**) are often specific to the circumstances of each individual contract. The solicitor must therefore advise the client that even the best-drafted clause cannot be guaranteed to work in all circumstances. However, careful drafting can often significantly increase the likelihood of the clause passing the reasonableness test.

3.10 Drafting for reasonableness: relevant factors

3.10.1 Introduction

Looking at the cases in which the courts have applied the contractual reasonableness test, it is possible to identify a number of factors which have been held to have a bearing on reasonableness. These must be treated with some caution when used as an aid to drafting – each contract and the exclusions it contains must be considered in its own particular context. Even if a clause has been interpreted in a particular way or held to be reasonable on one occasion, this is no guarantee that a court will react in the same way when faced with the same clause in a different case. As a result, it is not possible to produce an exhaustive list of relevant factors on reasonableness. In addition, it is unusual for one factor alone to be conclusive on reasonableness; in drafting, the solicitor must take into account all the factors (often conflicting) which could apply, and try to assess on balance whether the clause is likely to be held reasonable. However, if all this is taken into account, the following list should provide a useful guide when drafting. The Court of Appeal's decision in *Overseas Medical Supplies Ltd v Orient Transport Services Ltd* [1999] 2 Lloyd's Rep 273 (noted at **3.9.2**) provides a good summary of the relevant factors. Other interesting and illuminating cases on the application of the reasonableness test in a commercial situation include *Watford Electronics Ltd v Sanderson CFL Ltd* [2001] EWCA Civ 317, *Britvic Soft Drinks Ltd v Messer UK Ltd* [2002] EWCA Civ 548 and *Regus (UK) Ltd v Epcot Solutions Ltd* [2008] EWCA Civ 361.

3.10.2 Relationship between the parties

In deciding whether a clause is reasonable, the courts will often be influenced by the relationship between the parties and the strength of their bargaining positions (this is of course a Sch 2 guideline: see **3.9.2**). For example, in a consumer case, the fact that bargaining power is normally on the side of the supplier may be a vital factor in the court's decision; the court may be more likely for this reason alone to declare the supplier's attempts at exclusion to be unreasonable. Relevant factors connected with the relationship between the parties may include those set out below.

3.10.2.1 Negotiated or standard-form contract?

If the contract was individually negotiated, so that both sides were able to influence its contents, the courts may be more likely to decide that exclusions are reasonable than they would if one party had simply imposed terms on the other (as in a standard-form contract). Note, however, that a contract may not necessarily fall neatly into one particular category. An example of this is where the original 'framework' of the contract is negotiated between the trade associations of the parties, but by the time it goes into operation, the contract is in effect standard-form.

3.10.2.2 Market in which the parties operate

This raises a number of issues on reasonableness and bargaining power. The courts tend to hold that commercial parties which are operating in the same market may be taken to know exactly how that market works: if they have provided for this accordingly in their contracts, the courts are likely to assume that those provisions are reasonable. This conclusion may be reinforced where both parties are known to have used the same or similar clauses in their own standard form contracts. See, for example, *Watford Electronics Ltd v Sanderson CFL Ltd* and *Regus (UK) Ltd v Epcot Solutions Ltd*, discussed at **3.10.2.5** and **3.10.2.8** below. This may relate to the previous point; in some cases, the courts have suggested that a distinction can be drawn between types of standard-form contract which have been settled over the years to reflect the realities of a particular business operation, such as bills of lading and charterparties, and standard-form contracts which are simply imposed by the strong on the weak. However, if there is a very considerable imbalance of bargaining power, the courts may still be prepared to hold that a clause imposed by the stronger party is unreasonable, even if both parties operate in the same market.

3.10.2.3 Nature of the goods

In *Watford Electronics Ltd v Sanderson CFL Ltd* [2001] EWCA Civ 317 (a case which is discussed in more detail at **3.10.8**), the Court, in finding the exclusion clauses in issue to be reasonable, was clearly influenced by the nature of the product (computer software) as being liable to give rise to predictable problems (and, potentially, to extreme liability). In *Britvic Soft Drinks Ltd v Messer UK Ltd*, the court found the exclusions unreasonable and noted that the goods in question (carbon dioxide for use in manufacturing soft drinks) were not ones where the end-user of the goods would reasonably expect to have to test them for compliance with the contract.

3.10.2.4 Financial pressure

One party may have been forced to accept an exclusion because its financial situation at the time of the contract means that it cannot afford to turn down the deal which the other side is offering, despite the presence of an exclusion. This may make the exclusion unreasonable.

3.10.2.5 Age and experience of the buyer

The courts may hold that an experienced buyer (whether individual or commercial) should know what it is doing when it enters into contracts, and, therefore, be more likely to decide that an exclusion clause against such a buyer is reasonable (see **3.10.2.8** below). Compare, for example, two cases on property surveys: in *Stevenson v Nationwide Building Society* (1984) 272 EG 663, the buyer was an estate agent, and an exclusion in the contract relating to the negligent performance of a survey was held to be reasonable. In *Smith v Bush (Eric S) (a firm); Harris v Wyre Forest District Council* [1989] 2 All ER 514, however, the buyer was inexperienced in buying property, and a similar exclusion was held to be unreasonable against him. In *Regus (UK) Ltd v Epcot Solutions Ltd* [2008] EWCA Civ 361 the attempt by the 'buyer' (an experienced commercial tenant in this case) to renegotiate other terms of the contract, but not the exclusion clause, was seen by the court as a significant indication of the reasonableness of the clause.

3.10.2.6 Effect of legal advice

If the 'victim' of the clause received legal advice, any exclusion stands a better chance of being held reasonable. However, in *Walker v Boyle* [1982] 1 All ER 634, the 'victim', the buyer in a conveyancing transaction, was legally advised (as was the seller) and the clause was a standard term in the then edition of the National Conditions of Sale. Nevertheless, it was still held to be unreasonable.

3.10.2.7 Drafting techniques

In a tailor-made (ie, fully negotiated) contract, it may be useful to include a preamble to the exclusion, referring to as many of the above factors as are relevant, and stating whether and, if so, how those factors have been taken into account in drafting the exclusion. If the court appreciates the background, it may be more likely to hold that the exclusion is reasonable.

3.10.2.8 Attitude of the courts

To sum up, as a general proposition, it seems that if the buyer is a consumer, any exclusion clause is more likely to fail the reasonableness test; if the contract is between commercial parties, it is more likely to pass. In a commercial contract where there is no great inequality of bargaining power, and particularly where the parties have had the opportunity to identify the risks under the contract and cover them by insurance (see **3.10.5**), the courts have often taken the view that they should not interfere with what the parties have done (see, eg, the remarks of Lord Wilberforce in *Photo Production Ltd v Securicor Transport Ltd* [1980] 1 All ER 556 and, more recently, the views of the Court of Appeal in *Watford Electronics Ltd v Sanderson CFL Ltd* [2001] EWCA Civ 317, a case which is discussed in more detail at **3.10.8**). However, it must be stressed that there is no guarantee that a court will always take this view; each case must turn on its own facts. A factor that clearly influenced the Court of Appeal in both *Watford Electronics Ltd v Sanderson CFL Ltd* and *Regus (UK) Ltd v Epcot Solutions Ltd* was that both parties in each case had used the same terms before in their respective standard form contracts.

3.10.3 Choice

3.10.3.1 Do other suppliers use the clause?

Could the buyer have obtained the goods or services from another supplier which does not impose the exclusion clause in question? This factor (a Sch 2 guideline) may point in either direction. If the buyer could have gone elsewhere without having the clause imposed, and yet chose to make this particular contract, this may mean that the clause is more likely to be reasonable. Note that the buyer's knowledge of the existence and extent of the clause (see **3.10.7**) is likely to be relevant. On the other hand, if the supplier is the only one in a particular line of business using a particular exclusion clause, and is, therefore, out of step with its competitors, this may be evidence that it is unreasonable to use the clause at all.

3.10.3.2 Two-tier pricing

In a clause of this type, the supplier of the goods or services charges a lower price if the buyer accepts the exclusion clause, and a higher price if the contract contains either a modified version of the clause or no clause at all. Using two-tier pricing can help the clause to pass the reasonableness test. For example, in *Woodman v Photo Trade Processing* (CC, 3 April 1981) it was held that a clause limiting the liability of a film processor to the cost of the film was unreasonable because (amongst other things) the processor had failed to use a two-tier pricing system recommended by its own trade association. However, the use of two-tier pricing is not an automatic guarantee of success. In *Warren v Truprint* [1986] BTLC 344, it was held that an exclusion clause based on two-tier pricing was unreasonable because its wording was too vague.

Note that two-tier pricing can work in both consumer and commercial cases. For example, in *RW Green Ltd v Cade Brothers Farm* [1987] Lloyd's Rep 602, the seller in a commercial sale of goods contract used an exclusion with two-tier pricing, and the clause passed the reasonableness test.

3.10.4 Price

If the loss which may result from breach of contract is wholly disproportionate to the contract price, it may be reasonable for the contract to contain an exclusion (or limitation) clause. If both parties are aware of this from the outset, the chances of the clause being reasonable may be enhanced. In a tailor-made contract, a preamble can be used to set out the basis on which the parties are contracting.

3.10.5 Allocation of risk and insurance

The parties to a commercial contract will usually be in the best position to decide what the risks under the contract are, and how to deal with them. If they decide to use an exclusion or limitation clause which has the effect of passing the risk of loss or damage from one party to the other, and the contract then clearly requires the party with the risk to take out appropriate insurance, this should improve the chances that the clause will be held reasonable. Even where there is no specific obligation to insure, the court may attach considerable significance to how the parties have identified and dealt with the risks under the contract (eg, by reflecting them in the contract price, then backing this up with a limitation clause). For the significance attached by the court to the availability of insurance to the parties respectively, see *Photo Production Ltd v Securicor Transport Ltd* [1980] 1 All ER 556 and *Anders & Kern UK Ltd v CGU Insurance plc* [2007] EWHC 377 (Comm).

It may be worthwhile obtaining expert evidence on insurance before drafting the contract and its exclusions. Without such evidence, the parties may be left at the mercy of judicial assumptions about which party should have insured, and against what. For example, in *George Mitchell (Chesterhall) Ltd v Finney Lock Seeds Ltd* [1983] 2 AC 803, the contract provided that the seller's liability for supplying defective seed was limited to the price of the seed. The House of Lords accepted that a supplier of seed could insure against liability for delivering the wrong seed, without significantly increasing its prices, and assumed that this would be more appropriate than for a farmer buying the seed to insure against loss of crop. The clause failed the reasonableness test for a number of reasons, but the House of Lords was obviously impressed by evidence that it would have been easy and inexpensive for the supplier to cover itself by insurance against extra loss caused. However, the courts will not always be in the best position to assess what the risks and the most suitable insurance arrangements are, and may, therefore, in the absence of suitable evidence, make an inappropriate decision on the reasonableness of any exclusion.

If the circumstances allow (eg, in a tailor-made contract), it may be useful to preface an insurance clause with a preamble explaining how the insurance arrangements and the exclusions have been arrived at. There will, of course, be many different arrangements which can be made, and ways in which they can be expressed. The main requirement, however, is that the position should be clear. Each party should be fully aware of its rights and responsibilities.

Note that where a limitation clause is concerned, UCTA 1977, s 11(4)(b) specifically mentions the availability of insurance as a factor in assessing reasonableness (see further **3.10.8.1**).

3.10.6 Trade associations

Approval by a trade association (or similar body) may help an exclusion clause to pass the reasonableness test. For example, in *RW Green Ltd v Cade Brothers Farm* (see **3.10.3.2**), the parties used a standard-form contract which had originally been negotiated between the National Farmers' Union and the National Association of Seed Potato Merchants. The exclusion was found to be reasonable. Equally, ignoring a trade association's recommendations may cause problems, as in *Woodman v Photo Trade Processing* (see **3.10.3.2**). See also *Schenkers Ltd v Overland Shoes Ltd* [1998] EWCA Civ 234, where a member of a freight-forwarding association was able to show that the association's standard form clause excluding set-off was reasonable.

3.10.7 Buyer's knowledge and understanding of the clause

This factor (a Sch 2 guideline) is particularly important where the buyer is a consumer, but is by no means confined to that situation. Consider, for example, the following comments of Staughton J in the commercial case of *Stag Line v Tyne Ship Repair Group (The Zinnia)* [1984] 2 Lloyd's Rep 211:

> I would have been tempted to hold that all of the conditions are unfair and unreasonable for two reasons; first, they are in such small print that one can barely read them; secondly, the draftsmanship is so convoluted and prolix that one almost needs an LLB to understand them.

See also the discussion of the *Watford Electronic Ltd* and *Regus (UK) Ltd* cases at **3.10.2.8** above.

3.10.7.1 Short and simple drafting

This can be difficult to achieve, but is worth aiming for. The solicitor should, in particular, consider the likely reading abilities of those involved with the contract. For a more detailed discussion of this topic, see the chapter on writing and drafting in ***Skills for Lawyers***.

3.10.7.2 Size of print, layout and appearance

Wherever possible, the solicitor should advise the client to use easily readable print, and to set documents out in a way which assists reading (if this can be done without wasting space). Devices such as different typefaces, bold type, underlining and boxes are all useful for drawing attention to significant parts of a contract.

The solicitor will also need to consider where and how the exclusion should appear in the contract. There is no single correct way of doing this; it is often helpful to look at several sets of precedents to get a feel for the different methods. For example, some contracts will place each exclusion immediately after the clause to which it relates; some will have a separate section for the exclusions, cross-referring to other relevant clauses where necessary. The main thing to remember is that the way in which the exclusions are presented may have a bearing on the victim's knowledge and understanding of them, and therefore affect their reasonableness.

3.10.7.3 Practical problems

Following these guidelines should increase the chances of a clause being held reasonable, but may also create difficulties. For example, will a clause which is well laid out and clearly expressed fit onto the back of an order form? Sometimes 'wall-to-wall' layout (where the print covers virtually the entire surface of the paper, without margins or adequate space between lines) is essential because space is limited. Nevertheless, it is worth trying to achieve the best of both worlds. For example, consider whether space can be increased by getting rid of redundant clauses, or deleting clauses which cover contingencies so remote that they are not worth providing for (or which would cause few problems if they did occur). It is also possible that a document written in 'plain' English may turn out to be shorter than the same thing expressed in traditional 'legal' English. The solicitor should at least try to see what can be done.

3.10.7.4 Tactics

The solicitor must, however, also be aware of tactical considerations. The client may not want the finished document to be too clear. It may be valid to obscure the meaning of a clause for tactical reasons (and some clients may be uncomfortable with a document which is not written in what they perceive to be 'legal' English). There are no clear-cut solutions to the problems which this raises: solicitor and client must discuss the pros and cons of each approach in each individual case.

3.10.7.5 Incorporation by reference

Incorporation by reference is a common practice in both consumer and business contracts. For example, the supplier under a sale of goods agreement may wish to use standard terms laid down by its trade association as the basis of any contracts it makes. To save space, the agreement can state that the goods are sold subject to the relevant trade association's standard terms, and that the supplier will provide the buyer with a copy of the terms.

Bear in mind, however, that this practice involves some risk. It may be a useful space-saving device, but there can be problems on both incorporation and reasonableness. It may also raise uncertainty about the intended application of the exclusion clauses; see *Amiri Flight Authority v BAE Systems plc* [2002] EWHC 2481 (Comm) (whether an exclusion clause incorporated by reference applied to personnel training services or to a contract to supply aircraft, or to both).

3.10.7.6 Conclusion

Because of its numerous different aspects, this factor will often be difficult to weigh up; solicitor and client will have to decide what the priority is in each particular case. On the one hand, if a contract is drafted and set out clearly, clauses which are subject to the reasonableness test are more likely to pass the test. On the other hand, fitting a contract into a set amount of space (eg, the back of the client's order form) may be seen as more important, even though this may require a compression of drafting and layout which could render a clause unreasonable. However, there may be some room for compromise; just because a contract must fit on to an order form, it does not necessarily also have to be drafted 'wall-to-wall', difficult to read and full of jargon.

3.10.8 Exclusion or limitation?

3.10.8.1 General principle

The House of Lords has held on a number of occasions (eg, *Ailsa Craig Fishing Co Ltd v Malvern Fishing Co Ltd* [1983] 1 WLR 964) that a clause which limits liability is more likely to pass the reasonableness test than one which excludes it altogether. However, this principle should be treated with caution; arguably, what is important is the difference in degree of exclusion, not simply in type of clause. A clause which limits the supplier's liability to the contract price, where the damage likely to be caused is far in excess of this, may be little different in effect from a strict exclusion, especially if the contract price is low.

For a useful discussion of the principles relating to limitation of liability and assessing the reasonableness of limitation clauses, see *St Albans City and District Council v ICL* [1996] 4 All ER 481). In addition, the Court of Appeal considered the reasonableness of a limitation clause in *Watford Electronics Ltd v Sanderson CFL Ltd* [2001] EWCA Civ 317, a case which makes a number of important points about reasonableness in relation to limitation and exclusion in commercial contracts generally.

In this case, the seller had supplied the buyer with computer hardware and software; the supply was on the seller's standard terms, which contained the following provisions:

(a) a clause limiting the seller's liability to the contract price and excluding liability for consequential or indirect losses;

(b) a clause providing that neither party relied on any representation by the other party, in entering the contract; and

(c) an addendum to the contract (the 'side letter') in which the seller agreed to use its best endeavours to allocate appropriate resources to the contract to minimise any losses which might arise from its performance of the contract.

The software did not perform to the buyer's satisfaction, and the buyer sued for damages for breach of contract. The Court of Appeal held that the limitation clause passed the reasonableness test, noting generally that the parties were both experienced commercial parties and of roughly equal bargaining power; this clearly influenced the court's decision. In addition, the parties would (or should) have taken into account the risk of the software failing to perform when settling the contract price. The buyer also appeared to have taken a conscious decision to live with the exclusion clauses in return for various concessions from the seller (in particular the addendum referred to at (c) above, the side letter obliging the seller to use its best endeavours to allocate resources so as to minimise the effect of any failure). As a matter of construction, the limitation clause did not deprive the buyer of the chance to recover damages for breach of contract in all situations, and the seller's ability to rely on it was further qualified by the addendum to the contract.

In the circumstances, and having regard to the Sch 2 guidelines, the clause satisfied the reasonableness test.

3.10.8.2 UCTA 1977 guidelines

Note that UCTA 1977, s 11(4) contains two guidelines which apply only where a term is designed to limit liability to a specified sum of money, rather than to exclude it altogether. By s 11(4)(a), the court should take account of the resources available to the person relying on the limitation to meet liability, should it arise; and, as previously noted at **3.10.5**, by s 11(4)(b), the court should have regard to how far it was open to that person to cover himself by insurance.

3.10.8.3 Drafting techniques

A common drafting technique with limitation clauses is to limit liability to 'direct loss' and exclude liability for 'consequential loss'. However, since neither of these terms has any precise, agreed meaning, the solicitor should either avoid using them, or try to make as clear as possible what they cover in each particular contract.

3.11 Drafting for severance

Instead of drafting one clause to cover all the exclusions under the contract (which carries the risk that the clause may then be struck down in its entirety as unreasonable), it is usually more appropriate to draft a series of clauses or subclauses, so that if one is found to be unreasonable, the others may still survive because the court is able to apply the normal principles of severance. To reinforce the point, the series can end with a statement that each clause or sub-clause is to be treated as separate and independent.

3.12 Drafting to litigate or to negotiate?

3.12.1 Tactics

In most cases, a solicitor will be drafting to negotiate, rather than to litigate, should problems arise with the agreement in the future. It is therefore often valid to draft a clause which a court might hold unreasonable, if litigation is in fact unlikely and the clause achieves the right result for the client (eg, the client's opponent makes no claim, or agrees to settle any claim on suitable terms). Obviously, the client should be informed of what the solicitor is doing (and why) and warned that it is impossible to guarantee that the clause will achieve this result. It is also important when using this technique to distinguish between clauses which are void and clauses which are subject to the reasonableness test.

3.12.2 Void clauses

The solicitor should not use any clause which is void under UCTA 1977. A clause of this nature should be easy to spot, especially if the 'victim' takes legal advice, and so is unlikely to prevent a claim being made anyway. At best, the clause will create a bad impression; at worst, it may not only be ineffective, but its use may be a criminal offence. For example, under the Consumer Transactions (Restrictions on Statements) Order 1976 (SI 1976/1813), a supplier commits a criminal offence if, in a consumer sale of goods contract, he uses a clause which is void under s 6 of UCTA 1977 (see **3.7.3.1**).

3.12.3 Clauses subject to the reasonableness test

Where a clause is subject to the reasonableness test, the position is quite different. It may be possible to achieve good results for the client by using a clause which might be of doubtful reasonableness if it were ever litigated, as long as the client understands and approves of the tactic.

3.12.4 Drafting for good public relations

In some circumstances, it is worth drafting positively rather than (as is traditional with exclusion clauses) negatively. This could be worthwhile, for example, in a contract for the performance of services, where the supplier promises to exercise reasonable care and skill in carrying out the work under the contract, and to accept full liability for any personal injury or death caused by breach of his promise. This gives the other party no more than its legal rights, but creates the impression that the supplier is being generous.

3.13 Trying to exclude everything

Sometimes, the client may want the solicitor to exclude all liability which could arise from breach of any contractual obligation. This cannot be done. Obviously, some liability is non-excludable because of UCTA 1977 (see **3.7.3**). In addition, a contract which purports to exclude one party's liability for breach in respect of all its contractual obligations would not be a contract at all. That party would not be binding itself to do anything, and the 'contract' would be no more than a declaration of intent. A court faced with this situation would probably assume that the parties had made a mistake, and attempt to construe the contract in such a way that it does not exclude liability for everything. The solicitor will have to judge carefully how far it is possible to go if the client requests as much exclusion as possible.

A problem that may arise is where a client seeks to insert an exclusion clause that contemplates the situation where the client is, itself, in fundamental, repudiatory breach of contract. This is not impossible to achieve, but the scope for excluding liability in such circumstances is very narrow and will turn upon the construction of the exclusion (see *Suisse Atlantique Société d'Armament v Rotterdamsche Kolen Centrale NV* [1966] 2 All ER 61 and *Internet Broadcasting Corporation v MAR LLC* [2009] EWHC 844 (Ch)).

3.14 Drafting specific clauses in a commercial contract

This chapter ends with a closer look at three types of exclusion clause commonly found in commercial contracts: force majeure, non-rejection and time bar clauses. It considers their use and their relationship with UCTA 1977. For suggestions as to how the clauses could be drafted, see for example the appropriate sections of *Practical Commercial Precedents* or the *Encyclopaedia of Forms and Precedents* (for references, see the section on 'Further Study' at p vii).

3.14.1 Force majeure clauses

A force majeure clause is designed to apply where contractual performance has become impossible because of circumstances unforeseen by the parties and outside their control. In a sale of goods contract, it will normally seek to excuse the seller for failure to deliver the goods on time (or even at all) in these circumstances. A force majeure clause is normally classified as part of the boiler-plate of an agreement (see **1.4.7**).

3.14.1.1 Meaning of 'force majeure'

The expression 'force majeure' has been interpreted by the courts to cover a range of events, including act of God, war, strikes, embargoes, Government refusal to grant licences and abnormal weather conditions. The common factor in each case is that the event is outside the contracting parties' control. However, it is usual for a force majeure clause to do more than simply state that the supplier will not be liable for non-performance caused by 'force majeure'. Instead, it will normally set out a (non-exhaustive) list of specific events which the clause is intended to cover and the consequences of any of those events arising, so that both parties know exactly where they stand. (As noted at **3.6.3**, the *ejusdem generis* rule does not apply to force majeure clauses; specifying events does not cut down the meaning of any general words which follow.)

In force majeure clauses that contain no-fault events, as well as matters which can arise by fault of the parties or others, the application of the wording which describes the trigger event can be problematic (see *Tyco Fire & Integrated Solutions (UK) Ltd v Rolls Royce Motor Cars Ltd* [2008] EWCA Civ 286).

3.14.1.2 Frustration of the contract

Before considering further how the contract can best provide for the situation where performance has become impossible due to events beyond the parties' control, it is worth briefly looking at what will happen if nothing is mentioned in the contract: namely, frustration of the contract.

Frustration defined

A contract will be frustrated when a supervening event unforeseen by the parties and not due to their fault renders performance of the contract either impossible or radically different from that envisaged (*Davis Contractors v Fareham Urban DC* [1956] AC 696). Thus, for example, a contract for supply of goods will be frustrated if it becomes clear that any delivery of the goods will be so late that performance of the contract will be radically different from that envisaged by the parties.

Effect of frustration

If the contract is frustrated, the provisions of the Law Reform (Frustrated Contracts) Act 1943 will come into operation. Prima facie, the buyer can recover any payments he made before frustration (s 1(2)) and any sums which are due before the frustration date will cease to be payable. The court, however, has the discretion to allow the seller to keep all or some of any advance payment if it considers that this will be just, having regard to any expenses which the seller may have incurred in preparing to perform the contract. If one party has conferred a valuable benefit on the other, the court may allow the first party to claim a just sum in respect of that benefit (s 1(3)), although this is less likely to be relevant in a supply of goods case. It might be more relevant in a services contract, where the supplier has done some of the work but has been unable to finish it due to a frustrating event.

Note that the above discussion assumes that the seller is unable to deliver because of some problem of transporting the goods, such as industrial disputes at the port of shipment or unloading. If the problem is that the goods themselves have perished (eg, if they have been destroyed in an accident) then special rules apply and the Law Reform (Frustrated Contracts) Act 1943 will not generally apply (s 2(5)). For further discussion of these and other rules relating to frustration and its effects, reference should be made to the standard textbooks on contract.

Advantages of a specific provision in the contract

The problem about frustration is that it is rather uncertain (how long must the buyer wait before the performance of the contract will become radically different from that which the parties envisaged?) and its effects are rather arbitrary. Thus, although it will act as a kind of 'safety net' if the parties do not turn their attention to what will happen if unforeseen events occur, it is generally preferable to have a specific provision (ie, a force majeure clause) in the contract dealing with this situation. The parties can then agree that when the disrupting circumstances have been in existence for a specific time, either party may cancel the agreement by giving the other a certain period of written notice. The contract can also make specific provision for the financial consequences of such a cancellation.

3.14.1.3 Application of UCTA 1977

As long as one party deals as consumer, or on the other party's written standard terms of business, a force majeure clause will be subject to the reasonableness test under s 3 of UCTA 1977, as an attempt by the party relying on the clause to render no contractual performance at all (s 3(2)(b)(ii)). Although this may appear to be a rather drastic type of exclusion at first sight, courts often are prepared to treat force majeure clauses favourably (ie, hold that they are reasonable) if care is taken over drafting.

3.14.1.4 Drafting points to consider

If a force majeure event occurs, what should happen to the contract? Possibilities include suspension or cancellation of the contract (or suspension for a certain period followed by cancellation). Which is appropriate will depend on the client's instructions and the circumstances.

If cancellation is chosen, is it more appropriate to have automatic cancellation of the contract if a force majeure event occurs, or should the party relying on the force majeure give notice of cancellation to the other? The latter will usually be preferable. (Note that the party relying on force majeure will have to prove that the event in question has arisen.)

Should the party relying on force majeure refund any payments which the other party has already made to it? If UCTA 1977, s 3 applies (see **3.14.1.3**), the clause will be valid only if it passes the reasonableness test. Providing for a refund should help to ensure that the clause is reasonable. It need not always be a full refund; a partial refund may be appropriate, especially if the supplier has already incurred expense.

3.14.2 Time bar clauses

A client who is involved in the supply of goods or services may wish to reduce the limitation period which would normally apply to claims arising from breach of the contract (the basic contractual limitation period is six years). This may be justifiable: long before the statutory limitation period expires, evidence of a breach of contract may become hard to pin down, and perishable goods will have lost any market value they may have had. In addition, a supplier will probably want to close its books on a particular contract reasonably soon after performance. In a commercial contract, therefore, it may be appropriate to include a 'time bar' clause (eg, in a sale of goods contract, stating that the buyer cannot claim in respect of defects in the goods unless it notifies those defects to the supplier within a certain period of time).

Time bar clauses will usually be effective (and reasonable) if they are included for good commercial reasons, particularly if they result from insurance consequences or requirements (see *Super Chem Products Ltd v American Life and General Insurance Co Ltd* [2004] UKPC 2).

3.14.2.1 Application of UCTA 1977

If (as will usually be the case) the effect of the time bar clause is to exclude liability for breach of the implied conditions under SGA 1979 or the Supply of Goods (Implied Terms) Act 1973 (see **3.7.3**) then UCTA 1977, s 6 will apply, and the clause will either be void or subject to the reasonableness test, depending on whether the buyer deals as consumer or not. Otherwise, UCTA 1977, s 3 will apply (as long as one party deals as consumer, or on the other party's written standard terms of business); the clause is an attempt by one party to exclude or restrict its liability when in breach of contract (s 3(2)(a)).

3.14.2.2 Drafting points to consider

Does the party relying on the clause want to be notified of defects (ie, of the possible existence of a claim) or of the claim itself within a specified period, or to impose a time-limit for bringing proceedings, or all of these? A clause which raises too many barriers or is too complex may fail the reasonableness test.

It is, however, often sensible to distinguish between patent and latent defects, giving a longer time period for notification in respect of defects which are not immediately apparent on delivery. This is more likely to be reasonable than having the same time period for notification of both types of defect.

The clause should state whether it is a particular remedy (eg, rejection, damages) or the claim itself which is to be barred. If only the remedy is barred, the buyer might be able to use the claim as a defence to an action for the price by the seller.

If the contract is between members of the same trade association, a time bar clause probably has a better chance of passing the reasonableness test. Parties operating in the same market should know and accept the problems likely to arise in that market, and it may then be possible to make the clause stricter (eg, cut down the notification period) than if the other contracting party is unfamiliar with the problems of the trade.

3.14.3 Non-rejection clauses

For his own convenience, a seller may want to prevent SGA 1979, s 36 from applying to the contract. Broadly speaking, this provides that if the buyer refuses to accept goods (having the right to do so), it is not obliged to return them; the seller must collect them. This can cause problems if the goods are distant from the seller, both in checking that rejection is justified (eg, that the goods really are defective) and in arranging collection. In addition, a seller may want to stop its buyer from taking advantage of a fall in the price of the contract goods by finding a technical breach of contract, rejecting the goods (with a view to getting its money back from the seller, or not having to pay at all) and then buying replacement goods more cheaply at the new, lower market price. In both cases, the seller should consider using a non-rejection clause.

3.14.3.1 Application of UCTA 1977

Like a time bar clause (see **3.14.2**), a non-rejection clause may, depending on the circumstances, be subject to either s 6 or s 3 of UCTA 1977.

3.14.3.2 Drafting points to consider

As there may be different reasons for including a non-rejection clause (see above), different types of clause will be necessary according to the client's needs. Note that it may be worth using a preamble to explain why the clause has been included.

Sometimes, a simple reversal of s 36 of SGA 1979 will meet the seller's needs (eg, allowing the buyer to reject but making it clear that, following rejection, the buyer must return the goods to the seller).

However, the seller may wish to go further and state that the buyer cannot reject at all. This will also prevent the buyer claiming restitution of the purchase price, but not from suing for damages for breach of contract.

3.14.4 Loss of profits, indirect and consequential loss clauses

Few exemption clauses have caused as much difficulty, for both parties and the courts, as those clauses that purport to relieve liability from these types of loss. There are two main reasons for this: the first lies in the difficulty of construing what is meant by the expressions 'loss of profits', 'indirect' loss and, in particular, 'consequential' loss. The second major difficulty lies in the increasingly common practice of excluding or limiting implied terms, whether statutory or at common law, that imply a certain standard of performance by the seller (eg SGA 1979, s 14) and replacing them with express warranties of performance; typically, any failure by the seller to comply with the contractual warranty is then dealt with by offering some other remedy under the contract (usually a very limited one). Such clauses, including the express contractual remedies, are likely to be viewed as restricting the rights of the buyer and, therefore, within the ambit of UCTA 1977. See, for example, the exclusions and express warranty (to use best endeavours to minimise the buyer's loss) in *Watford Electronics Ltd v Sanderson CFL Ltd* [2001] EWCA Civ 317. A detailed examination of the voluminous case law in this area is beyond the scope of this work, but the following generalisations should help alert you to the pitfalls of such clauses:

(a) *Clauses excluding or limiting liability for 'loss of profits'.* At first glance, this looks plain enough, but the difficulty lies in the fact that 'profits' may apply to a wide variety of different types of gain. Contracts are designed to achieve profits, so some profits are always foreseeable to the parties, but the common law rule in *Hadley v Baxendale* shows, under its second limb, that foreseeability of a particular type of profit (if not its extent) is a vital prereqisite to the recovery of 'special' or 'exceptional' profits (see *Victoria Laundry (Windsor) Ltd v Newman Industries Ltd* [1949] 2 KB 528). One way of dealing with this difficulty could be expressly to enumerate what types of profit are contemplated or, more riskily, to leave the liability to be excluded under 'indirect' or 'consequential' losses – a problem with this approach is that 'ordinary' profits, eg anticipated re-sale profits, might well not then be covered by the clause. Clearly, ordinarily contemplated re-sale profits (as in distribution or wholesale contracts) would naturally fall within loss of profits; it may be more problematic where the goods are likely to be used by the seller in a way not directly linked to profit making, rather than being simply sold on.

(b) *Clauses excluding or limiting liability for 'indirect' or 'consequential' loss.* These expressions can be difficult to construe, in terms of their width, and that is perhaps why they have proved popular with businesspersons who believe that any dispute will be looked at from their side only! About the only thing that can be said with any certainty about such wording is that it appears to extend to (depending on context) those matters that are contemplated by the second limb in *Hadley v Baxendale*. The problem remains, however, of just how wide the wording extends, on the instant facts. If the width of exclusion, contended for by the seller, goes beyond the type of recovery permitted by the rule in the second limb, that will not usually raise a problem because the law will not (in the absence of fraud) usually allow recovery of damages, beyond those matters recoverable under *Hadley v Baxendale* (although, see the rare example in *Cory v Thames Ironworks and Shipbuilding Co Ltd* (1868) LR 3 QB 181). A complication that you should always have in mind is that the clause may be intended also to limit liability in tort, as well as in contract; therefore, the meaning and construction given to the clause is very important. A further generalisation that might be made on the authority of *Regus (UK) Ltd v Epcot Solutions Ltd* [2008] EWCA Civ 361 is that such wording will not naturally be construed so as properly to exclude liability for fraud, malicious or wilful damage by the seller; liability for such matters could probably never be successfully excluded. As to attempted exclusion of liability where the seller is, itself, in fundamental breach of the contract, see **3.13** above.

3.14.4.1 Application of UCTA 1977

Clauses purporting to exclude or limit liability for losses and some clauses purporting to replace common law or statutory remedies with contractual ones will, depending on circumstances, be subject to either s 6(3) or s 3 of UCTA 1977.

3.14.4.2 Drafting points to consider

With clauses concerning loss of profits, close attention should be paid to what types of profit will be in contemplation at the time of entering the contract and, if necessary, the wording to be used should be carefully selected to try to minimise construction problems. Are there likely to be any unusual forms of gain or profit that might need special contractual provision if they are to be successfully excluded or limited? With clauses dealing with indirect or consequential losses, the scale and type of matters within reasonable contemplation should be considered and, if necessary, investigated with the client. Further, are there standard clauses which have proved reasonably acceptable and successful within recent time in this trade context? If so, are there any authoritative and useful judicial authorities in which helpful guidance on construction and UCTA 1977 reasonableness can be found? With words of such considerable width and potential scope, care should be taken in their use and in their setting against neighbouring clauses and against the contractual document(s) read as a whole. The effect of construing clauses in this way may considerably restrict or influence their meaning.

Chapter 4
Other Contracts Under Which Goods Pass

4.1	Introduction	57
4.2	Types of contract under which goods may pass (other than straightforward sale of goods contracts)	57
4.3	The provision of services	59
4.4	Hire purchase and conditional sale	63
4.5	Leases of goods	67
4.6	Financing the sale of goods	70

4.1 Introduction

The key issues we are considering in this chapter are:

(a) contracts for the supply of goods and services;

(b) implied terms for services contracts; and

(c) the various transactions in which title to goods may pass.

We shall look at a wide variety of commercial arrangements. Some of these concern services only, others deal with the provision of goods and services, and others with the provision of goods other than by a conventional sale. From this, it should be obvious that there are innumerable commercial mechanisms which business has developed in this area. The task of commercial lawyers is to rationalise these, make them work, and reduce them to written contracts.

We have already looked at the sale of goods. Now we shall look at contracts for goods and services. As we shall see, many of the legal controls on the 'goods' part are in effect the same as for the sale of goods, but in addition there are controls on the 'services' component.

We shall consider other contracts under which goods may pass, such as conditional sale, hire purchase, leasing, bailment and factoring. Let us start off by looking at an overview of some of the common types of contract under which goods will pass, other than a straightforward sale of goods contract.

4.2 Types of contract under which goods may pass (other than straightforward sale of goods contracts)

Even with sale of goods contracts, matters can be less than totally clear. In *Baird Textile Holdings Ltd v Marks & Spencer plc* [2001] EWCA Civ 274 the parties had never concluded a formal written agreement. The dispute concerned the termination of a multi-million pound contract for the supply of clothing to a well-known chain of retail stores. The claimant was also arguing that the defendant was estopped from terminating their relationship at very short notice. Both claims failed, at least partly because of uncertainty as to the terms of their unwritten contract.

4.2.1 Exchange and barter

Contracts of exchange and barter are found relatively rarely in practice. In the past, they have been most frequently encountered in dealings with businesses in developing countries, where foreign currency may not be available to allow the buyer to pay in cash. There is evidence that they are now also being used in some forms of online trading.

4.2.2 Hire purchase

In a hire purchase agreement, the buyer obtains immediate possession of the goods, in return for making regular payments. However, ownership remains with the other party to the agreement. The buyer has an option to obtain ownership by paying a final instalment. The buyer 'buys' the goods not from the 'seller' but from the finance house, pursuant to the hire purchase agreement.

Hire purchase agreements are regulated under the Consumer Credit Act 1974 (see **Chapter 6** for more details). However, the 1974 Act does not deal with implied terms relating to title to the goods or quality. These are governed by Supply of Goods (Implied Terms) Act 1973, which implies terms similar to those implied into sale of goods agreements by ss 12–15 of the SGA 1979.

4.2.3 Conditional sale

A conditional sale agreement achieves a very similar result to a hire purchase agreement. Again, the buyer obtains immediate possession and makes regular payments in return. Again, ownership remains with the other party, although the buyer can obtain ownership by making a final payment. However, the agreement is structured rather differently in that there is no option to purchase. Instead, it is a sale of goods agreement under which ownership does not pass until the final payment is made.

Conditional sale is often used to finance consumer purchases in exactly the same way as a hire purchase agreement. When used in this way it is regulated by the Consumer Credit Act 1974. Because they are sale of goods agreements, the SGA 1979 applies to conditional sale agreements in the normal way and so, for example, ss 12 to 15 imply terms regarding title to the goods, quality, etc.

4.2.4 Hire agreements

A hire agreement differs from a sale of goods agreement in that ownership of the goods does not pass as the hirer obtains only possession, not title to the goods. In some situations, hire agreements with consumers are regulated by the Consumer Credit Act 1974.

The SGA 1979 does not apply to hire agreements. Instead, terms relating to right to transfer possession and quality are implied by Supply of Goods and Services Act 1982 (SGSA 1982), ss 6–11. The terms are very similar to those implied in sale of goods agreements by SGA 1979, ss 12–15. Exceptions are that s 7 of SGSA 1982 implies a term that the owner, referred to as the 'bailor', has the right to transfer possession rather than a right to sell the goods. In a hire agreement, of course, it is only possession of the goods which is being transferred, not the title to them, so that is the important thing here.

4.2.5 Contracts for services

Contracts for services are governed by the SGSA 1982 (see further at **4.3** below). The main terms implied by this Act are:

(a) the service will be performed with reasonable skill and care;

(b) the work will be carried out within a reasonable time, but only if no time for performance has been fixed by the contract; and

(c) a reasonable charge will be paid, but only if no consideration is fixed by the contract.

4.2.6 Contracts for work and materials

A good example of a contract for work and materials (ie, goods and services) is a contract for repair, where the repairer supplies not only his own labour but also the necessary parts. These contracts are governed by the SGSA 1982. It is important to remember that it is *not* the SGA 1979 itself which applies in such cases (SGSA 1982, s 1).

It can sometimes be difficult to decide whether a contract should be categorised as a sale of goods contract, or a contract for work and materials. Suppose, for example, that a customer engages a designer to design and build a chair. Is this a sale of goods contract (for the sale and purchase of the chair), or is it a work and materials contract? In *Samuels v Davis* [1943] KB 526, the Court of Appeal suggested that it did not matter too much how the agreement was categorised, as long as the correct terms were implied.

4.3 The provision of services

4.3.1 Introduction

The provision of services is a common business activity. There are many different types of transactions which include services. For example, the plumber coming to repair your central heating system charges for his services, but also may supply spare parts for the central heating. This is a sale of goods along with the supply of the services. There are other types of contract which are purely for services, for example the provision of legal or accountancy advice, or leisure services including the provision of holidays and entertainment. One you may also think of is financial services, which is a major industry in itself.

Until the SGSA 1982, there was no statutory regulation of services, the area instead being regulated by common law. The SGSA 1982 applies to all contracts which concern the supply of services, with or without the associated sale of goods. As we will see, the implied terms in the SGSA 1982 in regard to the sale of goods are, in effect, the same as those under the SGA 1979. The terms in regard to services which the SGSA 1982 implies into a contract are that:

(a) the service will be performed with reasonable skill and care (s 13);

(b) the work will be carried out within a reasonable time, but only if no time for performance has been fixed by the contract (s 14); and

(c) a reasonable charge will be paid, but only if no consideration is fixed by the contract (s 15).

The SGSA 1982 was intended to embody in statute the provisions existing at common law. The standard adopted by the three implied 'services' terms is that of reasonableness. This is very flexible and can be made to fit the facts of any particular case. It does, however, focus on the supplier's obligations to his customers. It creates a clear statement of the supplier's essential duties.

The SGSA 1982 does not attempt to control the whole relationship between supplier and customer. So, there would need to be express terms in the contract as well as the terms implied under the SGSA 1982. There could also be terms implied at common law.

In addition to the SGSA 1982, some types of provision of services are subject to additional statutory control. For example, the provision of financial services is controlled by the Financial Services and Markets Act 2000. Under this Act, it is generally forbidden to provide financial services without being appropriately registered. Similarly, the activities of solicitors are regulated by the Solicitors Act 1974. The activities of estate agents are controlled by the Estate Agents Act 1979. There are also instances of self-regulation, such as in the banking industry, where the regulation of banking services is under the Banking Code of Practice.

4.3.2 The Supply of Goods and Services Act 1982

The SGSA 1982 applies to all contracts involving the supply of services. Under s 12(3), it even applies to the bailment of goods (see **4.6.4**). There is also a power to make orders which exempt particular classes of service from one or more of the implied terms. So, for example, the power has been exercised to exclude the 'reasonable skill and care' implied term in relation to advocates, arbitrators and company directors, amongst others.

The SGSA 1982 applies to contracts for the transfer of goods, save for the 'excepted contracts' at s 1(2). The exceptions include contracts for the sale of goods (ie, goods only) and hire purchase. These contracts are controlled by other legislation. We shall deal with hire purchase at **4.4** below.

The terms implied by ss 13–14 are referred to in the 1982 Act as 'terms', not as 'conditions' or 'warranties' (see **4.3.3** and **4.3.4** below). The effect of this is that breach of one of the terms will entitle the innocent party to terminate the contract only if the breach 'goes to the root of the contract', or if it deprives the innocent party of substantially the whole benefit of it.

4.3.3 The implied term of reasonable skill and care: SGSA 1982, s 13

Section 13 implies a term of reasonable care and skill. It only applies to a supplier acting in the course of a business. This is similar to the situation with implied terms of satisfactory quality and fitness for purpose under the SGA 1979 (see **2.9** above).

The common law may imply such a term even into a non-business contract (see *Chaudry v Prabakhar* [1988] 3 All ER 718, which concerned a friend vetting a used car). The standard adopted is that of common law negligence. In general, the supplier is expected to 'exercise the ordinary skill of an ordinary competent man exercising that particular art' (*Bolam v Friern Hospital Management Committee* [1957] 2 All ER 118). The limitation is that the standard would be raised if the supplier of the service had any special skill or expertise, such as professional qualifications. For example, a solicitor who failed to register a land charge would be likely to fall beneath the standard (*Midland Bank Trust Ltd v Hett Stubbs and Kemp* [1978] 3 All ER 571). However, the supplier of services would not usually contract to the effect that the services would achieve a particular result. Thus, Lord Denning held in *Greaves & Co Contractors Ltd v Baynham, Meikle & Partners* [1975] 3 All ER 99:

> The law does not usually imply a warranty that he will achieve the desired result, but only a term that he will use reasonable care and skill. The surgeon does not warrant that he will cure the patient. Nor does the solicitor warrant that he will win the case.

It is possible for the parties to agree to a standard which is higher than reasonable skill and care. Thus, in *Rolls Royce Power Engineering Ltd v Ricardo Consulting Engineers Ltd* [2003] EWHC 2871, it was held that the defendant company had agreed to provide services of 'first class quality'. This was held to be more onerous than the obligation to exercise reasonable skill and care. Clearly, an obligation to use 'best endeavours' to achieve something would, likewise, exceed the implied term.

4.3.3.1 When does 'reasonable skill and care' under s 13 apply?

If the supplier of the services contracts to make a product, it is important to decide whether the contract is one for sale of goods, or a contract for services. If it is a contract for the sale of goods then the implied terms would be those of 'satisfactory quality' and 'fitness for purpose' (see **2.9**). If it is a contract for services then the standard is that the services will be carried out with reasonable skill and care, but the supplier may not achieve the desired end product. This difference has been a key issue in the computer software industry, that is when somebody is contracted to write a computer program. Is that person engaged to produce an end product, ie a computer program that functions properly, or to give his services in an attempt to produce a program, which may or may not work properly?

The problem is whether, legally speaking, software is classified as goods or services, and therefore which implied terms are relevant. This makes it necessary to consider the nature of software. Software consists of many thousands of lines of written instructions, and is usually sold on floppy disks, or CD-ROM disks. The disks themselves are clearly 'goods', but what about the instructions (the program)? In *St Albans City and District Council v ICL* [1996] 4 All ER 481, Glidewell LJ said that

> A computer disk is within the definition of goods contained in s 61 of the Sale of Goods Act 1979 and s 18 of the Supply of Goods and Services Act 1982. A computer program, however, is not. Nevertheless, if a disk onto which a program designed and intended to instruct or enable a computer to achieve particular functions has been encoded is sold or hired but the program is defective, so that it will not instruct or enable the computer to achieve the intended purpose, the seller or hirer of the disk will be in breach of the terms as to quality and fitness for purpose implied by s 14 of the 1979 Act and s 9 of the 1982 Act.

(Remember that both SGA 1979, s 14 and SGSA 1982, s 9 deal with satisfactory quality and reasonable fitness for the buyer's purpose.) On the other hand, if the software was regarded as services, the standard which the provider of the services would have to reach is that of providing those services with reasonable skill and care under SGSA 1982, s 13. To paraphrase the situation, it is the difference between 'having a good attempt' and producing a 'satisfactory end product'. In short, it is in the customer's interests to have the situation construed as being a contract for the sale of a finished item, ie goods, because of the difference in the implied terms.

In a similar case, the House of Lords held that structural engineers who had designed a television mast were responsible for its collapse. This was held to be the case even though they had not been negligent, on the basis that the mast could not have been fit for its purpose (ie, 'reasonable care and skill' was not enough) as they had to produce a functioning, safe mast (*IBA v BICC Construction Ltd* (1980) 14 BLR 9).

In *Wilson v Best Travel Ltd* [1993] 1 All ER 353, the allegation was that the tour operator had breached its duty under s 13 of the 1982 Act, in that it did not ensure that the guest could spend a holiday in reasonable safety. The guest in question had fallen through a glass door, which complied with the local Greek standards but not with British ones. The court held that the operator had complied with its duty under s 13 by checking that the hotel complied with Greek safety regulations. See also *Evans v Kosmar Villa Holiday plc* [2007] EWCA Civ 1003, on the relevance of the application of English common law defences to s 13 claims arising from foreign holidays. This brings us on to the topic of subcontracting.

4.3.3.2 Subcontracting and 'reasonable skill and care'

A party who is contracting to supply services may use a subcontractor to discharge its duties under the contract. A typical example is construction contracts. Specialist subcontractors would be used, for example, for the electrical work, or for the plumbing work on a new building. If the work has not been carried out to an adequate standard then we would need to consider the liability of both the main contractor and the subcontractor. One possible way of looking at the situation is that the main contractor may act as agent when arranging the subcontract. Consequently, there would be a direct contract between the customer and the subcontractor. Also, it might be feasible for the customer to enforce the contract between the main contractor and the subcontractor as one made for his benefit, under the Contracts (Rights of Third Parties) Act 1999. However, he would have had to be intended to have such rights at the outset. If the customer still wishes to press a claim against the main contractor, the question is whether the main contractor was committed to perform the services, or merely to arrange for them to be done. If the main contractor's duty is merely to arrange, its obligation is to exercise reasonable care in the selection of subcontractors (*Wilson v Best Travel Ltd* [1993] 1 All ER 353, see **4.3.3.1** above). On the other hand, if the main contractor's duty was to supply the building services, the requirement is that the building services should be performed with reasonable skill and care. If the subcontractor performs inadequately, the main contractor would be liable for any loss the customer suffers.

Certain areas of the supply of services are specifically regulated, for example package holidays are regulated by the Package Travel, Package Holidays and Package Tours Regulations 1992 (SI

1992/3288). Under these Regulations, the tour organiser is liable to the consumer for the proper performance of the contract, no matter whether the obligations are to be performed by the tour organiser itself, or by subcontractors.

4.3.3.3 Contract and tort, and 'reasonable skill and care'

The same breach by a party could give rise to liability in both contract and tort. The limitation periods are different, as are the methods of calculation of damages.

This choice of suing in contract or tort may be to a customer's advantage, depending upon the circumstances. However, the tendency of the courts is to rely on the terms of the contract. The situation was reviewed by Lord Goff in *Henderson v Merrett Syndicates Ltd* [1995] 2 AC 145. In effect, it was held that there was no bar to pursuing the action under negligence as well as contract, if the component parts for negligent advice (in this case) were present under *Hedley Byrne v Heller* [1964] AC 465 and negligence was not excluded by the contract. The case concerned losses in the Lloyd's insurance market. Investors were suing 'members' agents', both in contract and in tort. The members' agents had agreed to underwrite on behalf of all the investors. They had delegated that task to 'managing agents'. The House of Lords held that this did not alter the implicit promise of the members' agents that reasonable care and skill would be exercised in carrying out that agreement.

4.3.3.4 Exclusion of liability for reasonable skill and care

Liability for a breach of the implied term of 'reasonable care and skill' may be excluded or limited by a term in the contract. This is subject to the restrictions on exclusions or limitations imposed by s 2 of UCTA 1977. Do not forget that any purported exclusion of liability for death or personal injury caused by a breach of this implied term will be ineffective. Liability for other types of damage, for example property damage, can be excluded or limited if the exclusion satisfies the requirements of reasonableness, as defined in the 1977 Act. However, in contracts where the customer is a consumer, the implied terms concerning quality of the goods supplied may not be excluded.

4.3.3.5 Remedies for breach of 'reasonable skill and care'

The implied terms under the SGSA 1982 that concern the quality of the goods supplied are classified as conditions. (Breach of a condition entitles the innocent party to terminate the contract.) However, the implied term of reasonable care and skill is classified as a 'term'. It is therefore an 'innominate' term. The remedies available would depend on the seriousness of a breach of contract and its consequences. Usually, the claimant would only be entitled to damages for breach of such a term. The breach of contract would have to deprive the claimant of substantially the whole of the benefit under the contract before he would be entitled to terminate the contract (as well as claim damages).

4.3.4 Time for performance: SGSA 1982, s 14

Section 14 implies a term that the supplier will carry out the service within a reasonable time. However, this comes into effect only if the time for service is not fixed by the contract. This is, in fact, a restatement of a common law rule. There are two requirements here. The first is that the work should be started within a reasonable time, and the second is that it should be completed within a reasonable time.

A 'reasonable' time is a matter of fact in any particular instance (s 14(2)). The test is objective. In *Brown & Davis Ltd v Galbraith* [1972] 3 All ER 31, it was held that there was an implied term in a repair contract for a car that the repairs would be done 'expeditiously and promptly'. In *Charnock v Liverpool Corporation* [1968] 3 All ER 472, it was held that a garage which took eight weeks to undertake a vehicle repair which should have been done in five weeks had breached the 'reasonable time' term.

4.3.5 A reasonable price: SGSA 1982, s 15

Section 15 implies that a reasonable price will be charged, provided the price is not decided by the contract. It may seem a rather odd to enter a contract without having fixed the price. However, in real life many contracts are indeed made in this way. Solicitors would not normally agree a fixed fee, but would charge an hourly rate for their services. Also, if repairs are required to a central heating system, the cost of the work may well not be known in advance. An estimate can of course be sought, but it is only an estimate of the likely cost of parts and labour, ie goods and services. The customer may prefer to have a quotation. This is usually regarded as a binding statement of the price to be charged. However, there is the practical problem that tradesmen know that as well and are unlikely to agree to a quotation, preferring to give an estimate.

In *Mastercigars Direct Ltd v Withers LLP* [2007] EWHC 2733 (Ch), a dispute over solicitors' costs in litigation, the judge held that the right question to ask, in law, was what, in all the circumstances, the client could expect to have to pay. The judge was not willing to imply a term that 'reasonable remuneration' should be limited or capped by reference to the Solicitors' Costs Information and Client Care Code.

A reasonable charge is an issue of fact. If the customer believes the charge to be excessive, he should dispute it at the time, even if he has to pay it under duress in order to retrieve his goods. In *Thomas v Ladkarn Holdings Limited* [1997] Lawtel 16/5/97, the claimant's assertion that s 15 required that the price charged was a reasonable one was held to be incorrect, as the contract in question already had a consideration clause.

4.3.6 Other terms applying under the 1982 Act

As well as the 'services' part of a contract for the supply of goods and services, the SGSA 1982 also deals with the sale of goods in such a contract. Under a contract for the supply of goods and services, s 4(2) implies 'satisfactory quality' and s 4(4) is the fitness for purpose provision, both fitness for usual purposes and for specifically specified ones. Section 9 deals with the equivalent implied terms when the goods are hired. So, s 9(2) implies satisfactory quality. Section 9(5) implies fitness for purpose, whether the purpose is the common one or not. In *Blackpool Ladder Centre Ltd v BWB Partnership* [2000] WL 1791447, s 9 was the relevant provision as the goods in question, a specially equipped Land Rover, were hired. There was a breach of fitness for the special purpose, inspecting a pier from the beach below. In contrast to the 'services' part of the SGSA 1982, the terms here are expressly stated to be implied 'conditions'.

There are other implied terms under the SGSA 1982 which are equivalent to those under the SGA 1979, but we will not go into those here.

4.4 Hire purchase and conditional sale

4.4.1 Introduction

The basic legal concept of a hire purchase agreement is that the goods are hired by their owner to the hirer. In fact, this is legally a bailment of the goods. The owner is the bailor and the hirer is the bailee. The idea is that the hirer pays a hire fee for the goods and is granted an option to purchase the goods at the end of the hire period. This agreement is, in fact, something of a legal fallacy. The payments which the hirer makes would normally be much more than would be required under a real rental agreement. The object of the agreement is, of course, that the hirer in fact purchases the goods on credit. There also needs to be security for the supplier, in case the hirer defaults on the payments. The supplier can repossess the goods if the hirer defaults, subject now to statutory control (see eg s 90 of the Consumer Credit Act 1974). Hire purchase is *not* 'sale of goods' and so it is outside the SGA 1979. It is governed by the Sale of Goods (Implied Terms) Act 1973. This Act implies similar terms in relation to satisfactory quality and fitness for purpose, respectively in s 10(2) and (2B) for fitness for usual purposes of the goods, and s 10(3) for fitness for special purposes.

In contrast, a conditional sale is where the parties are committed to buy and sell the goods from the moment the contract is formed. However, the seller keeps the title to the goods until the buyer has paid the whole of the price. Payment would, of course, usually be by instalments and interest would be payable on top of the price of the goods themselves. The agreement is structured rather differently in that there is no option to purchase, as there is in a hire purchase sale. Conditional sale *is* 'sale of goods' and so is controlled by the SGA 1979. There is therefore the problem that the buyer could pass good title on to an innocent third party who bought from the buyer before the buyer had paid all the instalments to the seller, under s 25 of the SGA 1979.

A credit sale is where the goods are supplied, title to them passes, but the buyer pays the price only at some point in the future, though usually within a short time period. This would be a common situation in business to business sales, where the buyer expects a credit period of, say, 30 days. It is simply sale of goods, with slightly delayed payment of the entire price in one amount.

4.4.2 Development of hire purchase

Hire purchase was developed because it offered the supplier of the goods a high level of protection against the goods being sold on by the buyer, before the buyer had discharged all his liabilities under the hire purchase contract. A person who has bought or agreed to buy goods can, in some cases, sell them to a third party and pass good title to the third party. In *Helby v Matthews* [1895] AC 471, the House of Lords established that the owner of goods which are supplied under a hire purchase agreement could not lose his title under the Factors Act 1889, or now under s 25(1) of the SGA 1979, because the hirer (who was trying to sell them on) was not a person who had 'agreed to buy' the goods. (Under s 25 of the SGA 1979, an innocent third party will get good title to the goods if bought without notice of the true owner's rights, as happened in *Forthright Finance Ltd,* below.)

A second ruling of the House of Lords in *McEntire v Crossley Brothers Ltd* [1895] AC 457 established that a hire purchase contract was not a disguised transaction for obtaining security (eg a mortgage over the goods). These two cases established that hire purchase was a valid form of contract and would be upheld by the law.

In fact, the distinction between conditional sale and hire purchase is usually of little importance today, as both transactions are 'consumer credit agreements' within the meaning of the Consumer Credit Act 1974. They are therefore both regulated by the 1974 Act, if they are consumer transactions. However, in *Forthright Finance Ltd v Carlyle Finance Ltd* [1997] 4 All ER 90, the contract was between two businesses so that the 1974 Act did not apply. The contract in question did claim to have an option to purchase, but also provided that the option would be deemed to have been exercised when all the instalments had been paid. The Court of Appeal held that it was in reality a conditional sale arrangement because of that, and was not the hire purchase agreement it purported to be.

4.4.3 Hire purchase arrangements

The hire purchase contract is usually between a finance company and the consumer. Thus, the retailer sells the goods to the finance company, and the customer enters into a hire purchase agreement with the finance company. Doubtless, in most instances the customer thinks he is contracting with the retailer for the purchase of the goods, but this is not the case.

In the early part of the 20th century, hire purchase was becoming well established as a means of buying goods on credit. At that time, the agreement was between the seller of the goods and the customer. Thus, the retailer was also providing the finance for the goods. The retailer was not paid, therefore, until the customer had paid the final instalment, along with the optional fee to transfer ownership of the goods. The financing limitations of the retailers were hindering the expansion of this system of selling consumer goods. There was also the disadvantage to the retailers, in that they were not being paid until the final instalment from the customer, perhaps many years after the goods left the shop. Consequently, finance houses, that is specialised banks, grew up in the 1920s and 1930s. There were also finance houses created by manufacturers to promote the sale of their own goods. (This last situation still exists today – the Ford Motor Company was reported in 2004 as having made more profit from its financing operations than from its car manufacturing operations.)

The contractual situation is as follows. The retailer sells the goods to the finance house and is paid at the time the customer receives the goods. The financial relationship is therefore between the finance house and the customer, as we have said already. The diagram below represents a conventional hire purchase arrangement, ie 'direct collection'. Note the lack of a contract between the retailer and the customer.

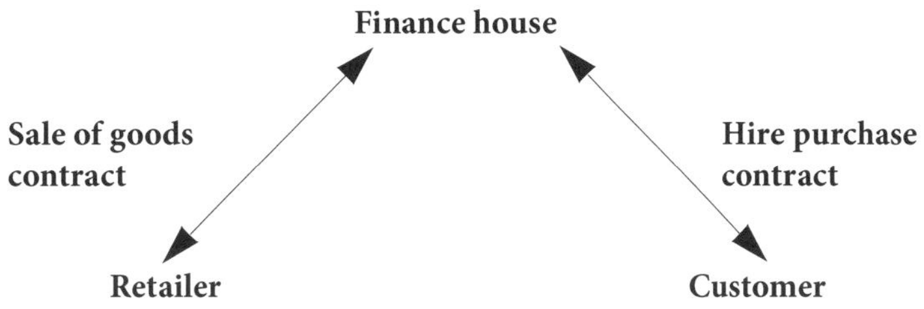

It has been debated whether the retailer is the agent of the finance company. There has been a House of Lords case on such a finance transaction which describes the status of the retailer, in that case in a vehicle financing deal. In *Hudson v Shogun* [2004] 1 AC 919, the status of the dealer is described as follows:

> Nor should the House of Lords find that the existence of the dealer who transmitted the documents from the rogue to the claimant made this a face to face dealing. The dealer, who was not the claimant's agent, was nothing more than a conduit for the rogue, performing the role of the post office in *Cundy v Lindsay* 3 App Cas 459, and did not make this a face to face dealing any more than a motorcycle courier delivering the documents to the claimant would have done.

In other words, the dealer did not have power to form the hire purchase contract between the finance house and the customer. He only passed the paperwork over to the finance house and it was for them to make the decision whether to enter a contract with that particular customer.

An alternative to the conventional 'direct collection' arrangement for hire purchase is 'block discounting'. In this situation, the finance house and the retailer enter into a master contract under which the retailer agrees to offer for sale to the finance house batches of hire purchase agreements. These agreements are in fact made directly between the retailer as the seller, and the customer. The block discounting contract will provide that the finance house will pay the retailer the outstanding balance of the purchased hire purchase agreements, less a sum retained by the finance house in case of default by any customers. This situation differs from direct collection in that the finance house is paying for the right to collect the instalment payments from the customers. (In direct collection arrangements, the finance house is buying the goods themselves from the retailer.) As a matter of basic arithmetic, the finance house is paying the retailer a smaller sum for this right than it hopes to collect from the customers. That is, it aims to make a profit on the transaction. A diagrammatic representation of 'block discounting' appears below.

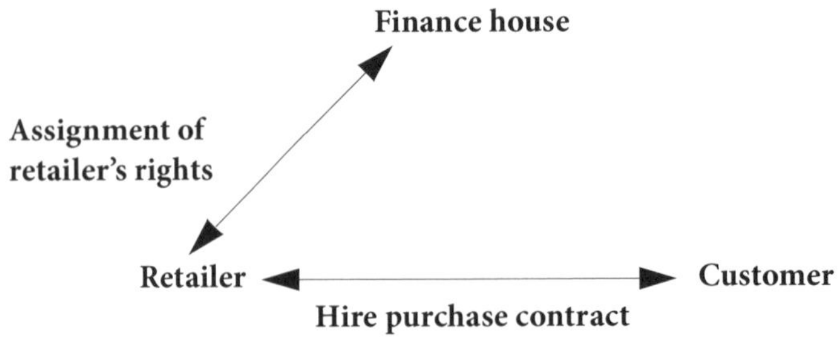

Note that the contract between the retailer and the finance house could include the retailer's title to the goods, which however is academic unless the customer defaults on its payments. There is no direct contract between the finance house and the customer. The customer may be unaware of the existence of the finance house in the whole transaction. However, the finance house may give notice of the assignment contract to the customer, and call upon the customer to pay future instalments directly to it.

4.4.4 Differences between hire purchase and conditional sale

Under a conditional sale agreement, the title to the goods (ownership) remains with the seller until the purchase price has been paid in full. Despite this, the buyer is contractually committed to buying the goods from the outset. Under hire purchase, by contrast, the customer merely has an option to buy the goods, but no obligation to do so. As we have said at **4.4.1** above, the significance of the difference is primarily that a buyer under a conditional sale agreement can pass good title to a third party under s 25(1) of the SGA 1979.

A conditional sale contract will have all requirements of a contract for sale of goods. The SGA 1979 will apply, except where it has been effectively excluded, subject to UCTA 1977. Thus the typical contract would require the customer to pay the instalments punctually, to retain possession of the goods, and to keep the goods in good condition. There would also be obligations not to sell the goods. The customer would also be required to pay the seller for any loss which remains after the goods have been repossessed. Repossession of goods from a consumer is subject to the requirements of the Consumer Credit Act 1974.

Many of the requirements of a conditional sale contract would also appear in a hire purchase contract. However, in a hire purchase contract the customer may terminate the contract at any time. If he does so, he must return the goods to the seller in good condition. He will also have to compensate the seller for any loss resulting from termination.

Under a conditional sale contract, the buyer is committed to paying the full price from the outset. Consequently, a clause in such a contract specifying that the seller will receive the full price of the goods in any event, after taking into account the value of the repossessed goods, is likely to be enforceable as a reasonable estimate of liquidated damages. In contrast, an equivalent clause in a hire purchase contract would impose on the defaulting customer a liability greater than that which he would have otherwise incurred. This could be struck down as a penalty. You will, it is hoped, recall that English law permits a reasonable estimate of loss as 'liquidated damages', but not an excessive sum payable on default, ie a penalty.

We have already mentioned that a customer under a hire purchase agreement cannot pass good title to a third party under s 25 of the SGA 1979. However, if the goods are a motor vehicle then the Hire Purchase Act 1964 applies and provides an exception to this general rule. Under the 1964 Act, the disposal of a motor vehicle by a debtor under a hire purchase or conditional sale agreement transfers to a 'private purchaser' the title to the goods. The private purchaser must buy in good faith and without notice of the original hire purchase or conditional sale contract. The 1964 Act is intended to deal with the problem where an innocent third-party purchaser buys a car, possibly through the small ads in a newspaper. If the 1964 Act did not apply then the third-party purchaser would find himself subject to the original finance agreement between the seller and the original buyer. In other words, the third-party purchaser would have paid the market price for the vehicle, but still be liable on the finance agreement as well.

4.4.5 Which one to choose?

As regards business equipment, there is little to choose between hire purchase and conditional sale. If the finance house is concerned to recover a sum equal to the full price of the goods if the buyer defaults, it could opt for conditional sale. However, if it is concerned about the possibility of losing title on an unauthorised disposal of the goods, the choice should be hire purchase. Of course, most finance agreements are carried through to completion to the mutual satisfaction of the supplier of the goods, the finance house and the customer.

4.4.6 Other varieties

There are various forms of hire purchase agreement. One of these is lease purchase. This gives the customer reduced rental payments during the agreement, with a so-called 'balloon' payment at the end of the lease period, if the customer wishes to keep the goods. (There would usually still be an initial deposit required, like hire purchase.) This can be an advantage in regard to motor vehicles, in that the agreement should be structured so that the market value of the vehicle at the end of the lease period is greater than the balloon payment. This means that the vehicle could be traded in for a further vehicle to be taken on a lease purchase basis. The difference between the market value of the trade-in and the actual value of the balloon payment serves as a down payment for the replacement vehicle.

Other varieties of the same arrangement are personal contract purchase and personal contract hire. These often require no deposit. Some finance arrangements will have the maintenance of the vehicle included in the payments, whereas others will not. We look at some of them below.

4.5 Leases of goods

4.5.1 Introduction

A lease is the contract between a lessor and a lessee for the hire of an asset. Today, this would be an expensive item of equipment, perhaps industrial machinery, a computer system, lorries or other motor vehicles. The lessor need not necessarily be the manufacturer or a seller of the equipment. It could instead be a finance company. The lessor is the owner of the equipment, and keeps the ownership. The lessee has the right to possess and use the equipment during the term of the lease. The lessee pays the lessor rental payments as specified in the lease contract. At the end of the lease, the equipment is returned to the lessor who may lease it out again, or more usually sell it. If the equipment is sold to the lessee, the danger is that the contract may instead be construed as a hire purchase contract and therefore be subject to the legislation on hire purchase.

Leasing of business equipment was used in the 1800s to provide rolling stock for the new railways. It became more prevalent in the later part of the 20th century. Part of the reason was the use of expensive technology, for example computers, which become obsolete relatively quickly. It is even possible to lease major items of equipment, such as aircraft, ships and railway rolling stock. The advantage to the business is that it has the use of the equipment in question without having to pay for the initial cost of it. It may well be that some elements of maintenance are also included in the lease contract. At the end of the lease, the business can return the equipment to the lessor and take out a new lease for new equipment. The fact that the business is paying for the equipment in instalments means that it can finance the equipment out of its monthly income. In the appropriate language, the business is financing the equipment out of its cash flow rather than by capital expenditure.

4.5.2 Types of lease

4.5.2.1 Finance leases

There are two basic categories of lease: finance leases and operating leases. With a finance lease, the equipment is supplied to one user only, who retains possession of it for substantially the whole of its working life. The rental payments are calculated to allow the lessor to recover the capital cost of the equipment over the period of the lease, along with its own costs and a profit. The contract is likely to be phrased so that it could be cancelled only on payment of a specified sum of money. Part of the reason for this is that the equipment in question may be very difficult for the lessor to lease out to another customer, as it may be highly specialised equipment, eg a particular type of computer system. It is possible that the lessee may be able to continue the lease after the initial period has expired. This would, of course, be at a lower cost. However, as we saw at **4.5.1** above, the lessee should not have the option of purchasing the equipment, as that would turn the agreement into a hire purchase contract.

Leases can be arranged to include the maintenance of the equipment, or that may be something which the lessee has to pay for separately.

In a finance lease, the lessor is simply providing the finance. The equipment would usually be selected by the lessee. Any backup or warranty provision would have to come from the supplier or manufacturer, as it would not be feasible, for example, to expect a bank to fix a lorry or a computer. There may therefore have to be some contractual links between the supplier and the customer.

4.5.2.2 Finance leasing of computer systems

With a lease of computer hardware, ie the electrical equipment, the lessee has the right to use the equipment but the lessor remains the owner of it. Most computer leases will be finance leases.

A finance lease of computer equipment basically works as follows. The finance company (lessor) acquires the computer hardware by buying it from a supplier. The finance company pays the supplier for the hardware. It then leases the hardware to the user, and the user pays the finance company a leasing payment, probably monthly. At the end of the lease, the hardware will have little residual value and will be sold off by the lessor. The lessor may credit the user with the sale proceeds (depending on the terms of the lease), but the user must not have the right to acquire title to the hardware, otherwise it will be a hire purchase contract, not a lease. A diagrammatic representation of a finance lease is set out below.

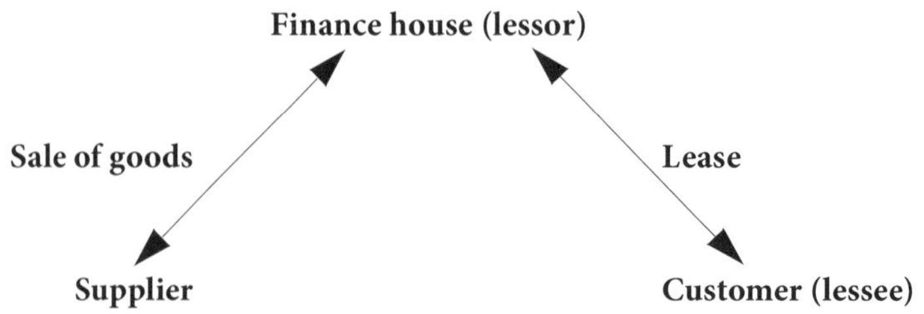

With a finance lease, there is no contractual relationship between the user and the supplier of the hardware. Therefore, it can be difficult for the user to obtain redress against the supplier for defects in, or maintenance of, the equipment. This problem can be solved by:

(a) *assignment of rights* by the finance company to the user, but the user's damages would be limited to those recoverable by the finance company, which could be nothing;

(b) *partial novation,* where the deal is structured as a sale to the user from the supplier, followed by novation, ie a new contract, of the financial terms between the finance company and the supplier, leaving the supplier liable to the user for, for example, the warranties on the system; and

(c) *a direct collateral contract,* where a collateral contract dealing with, for example, the warranties which cover the hardware is created between the user and the supplier.

Note that the lease should provide for the following matters where the user (lessee) breaches the lease:

(a) the lessor to have the right to repossess the equipment (so the lease should include a right of entry onto the premises);

(b) a liquidated damages clause – this is more appropriate than unliquidated damages, which would be difficult to calculate, as the lessor has a duty to mitigate his loss; or

(c) minimum payments, including accelerated payment of all future payments on default.

4.5.2.3 Operating leases

With an operating lease, the equipment is hired out to the user (the lessee) for a short period of time, returned to the lessor and then hired out to another user. This is, for example, how a tool-hire shop would normally operate. With a finance lease, the equipment is supplied to one user only, who retains possession of it for substantially the whole of its working life.

An operating lease would be terminable at short notice without payment of a penalty. The lessor would intend at the outset that the equipment would be leased to a succession of different lessees. The lessor would be responsible for the maintenance of the equipment and for its eventual replacement. The lessor takes the risk that the equipment could become obsolete before the end of its working life. As a result of all these factors, the rental payments will be higher than for the typical finance lease.

4.5.3 Other aspects of leasing

One of the advantages of leasing, at least in the past, was that lease contracts did not have to be disclosed in any business's balance sheet. The balance sheet is part of the annual accounts of a business, listing its assets and liabilities. For companies, the annual accounts are published and are a key indicator of the financial health of those companies. They are especially significant for companies which are quoted on the stock exchange. Thus, if such liabilities could be left off the balance sheet, the company would seem to be in better financial health than might be the case in reality. For example, in 1974 Court Line Ltd became insolvent. The annual accounts had not revealed leasing obligations of £38m. As a result of problems of this kind, the reporting requirements for lease obligations have been changed under statements of standard accounting practice – see SSAP 21 (1984) *Accounting for Leases and Hire Purchase Contracts.* Amongst other matters, SSAP 21 requires lessees to capitalise 'material' finance leases as a liability on the balance sheet, ie to record as a capital liability the money owing on major finance leases. The transaction is considered to be the economic equivalent of borrowing to acquire an asset.

Under the system for allowing expenses against tax liabilities for income tax, or corporation tax for companies, it is possible to obtain relief for relevant business assets, primarily plant and machinery. These are known as capital allowances. However, in a leasing situation it is the lessor which owns the assets and therefore the lessor which can claim the capital allowances. If the lessor does this, the rentals paid by the lessee should be decreased appropriately.

4.5.4 Terms of the contracts

4.5.4.1 The lease contract

The basic position is that there is freedom of contract between the lessor and the lessee. Leasing agreements often have a number of events of default. Any one of these would entitle the lessor to terminate the agreement, subject to any right against forfeiture that the lessee might have.

There are two types of clause in a leasing agreement which may cause particular difficulty. The first is a clause whereby the lessor ensures that he will not suffer a loss if he has to terminate the contract because of the lessee's default. Any such minimum payment clause which is intended to provide the lessor with the value of the remains of the contract, may be struck down as a penalty. In *Lombard plc v Butterworth* [1987] QB 527, it was felt that the minimum payment specified in the contract would have been a penalty, if the breach had not been a repudiatory one under the terms of the contract. Most finance leases commit the lessee to pay the rental instalments without the power to terminate the agreement. So a minimum payment clause simply provides for the payment of those rentals which would have been paid anyway if lessee had not breached the contract. Such a clause is therefore less of a problem than it would be in a hire purchase agreement, where it is likely to be struck down as a penalty under English law. A hire purchase contract is, at least in theory, a contract for hire which should therefore only give the lessor a right to hire payments pending rehiring of the goods by a new lessee. A major difficulty in the calculation is to know the discount which should properly be allowed for accelerated receipt of the lessee's payments.

The other type of clause which causes problems is where the lessor seeks to exclude liability for defects in the equipment. If the lessee were a consumer then, under s 7 of UCTA 1977, it would not be possible to exclude the implied terms in regard to quality of the goods. If the lessee is not a consumer, the test is one of reasonableness. If the effect of the clause is to remove the lessee's remedies, the court may well take an unfavourable view of such an exclusion clause. Thus, a lessor may assign his rights as a buyer to the lessee, or undertake to enforce them on the lessee's behalf (see **4.5.2.2**).

4.5.4.2 The sale of goods contract between the supplier and the lessor

The relationship between the supplier and the lessor is usually that of the seller and buyer of the goods. However, this is not always the case. If the lessor authorises the lessee to purchase the equipment in the lessee's own name, the supplier may treat the lessee as the other contracting party. On the other hand, the supplier may treat the lessor as the other contracting party, thus making the lessor liable on the sale contract. This is an example of the law of agency. In any event, the supplier would often know at the outset that the lessor is buying the equipment to supply to the lessee on a lease. Thus, failure by the supplier to provide the equipment in accordance with the sale of goods contract would cause loss to the lessor under the leasing contract. The supplier would be liable for all such loss as would normally flow from the breach. If the lessor had managed to conclude a leasing contract on unusually favourable terms for the lessor, the supplier would not be liable for the additional loss caused by those unusually favourable terms.

4.6 Financing the sale of goods

4.6.1 Introduction

The situation we considered in **Chapter 2** was that of the buyer simply paying the seller for the price of the goods. Now we look at methods of financing sales of goods. The typical situation is that of a business which requires financial support from a lender, possibly to be able to buy stock, or to raise money against the prospect of being paid by its customers. We shall look first at financing against stock.

4.6.2 Financing against stock

This is sometimes referred to as 'wholesale finance'. This is because the financing is required by a retailer, rather than by the customer. The typical situation is that of a motor dealer. Such a business must maintain a stock of cars to attract customers. The dealer would have to buy second-hand cars and also pay for new ones from the manufacturer (although in practice the dealer is allowed a period of time before the manufacturer requires to be paid). A dealer of even moderate size could have a stock of cars on its premises which is worth several hundred thousand pounds. Few dealers could afford to finance that themselves. So, the lender tides the dealer over during the period after he has paid the manufacturer for the cars but before he has sold them on to his own customers.

One of the aims of lenders is to be in a close enough relationship with the dealer that the dealer's own customers will buy their cars on hire purchase from that particular lender. Retail customers will accept higher interest rates than would business customers. This can be seen from the huge increase in consumer credit in recent years. The lender can thus make more money out of the retail customer. The finance houses are often in keen competition for business from the dealers. Inducements which they may offer include a reduced rate of interest for financing stock and the payment of commission on retail hire purchase contracts. This last aspect may, perversely, lead to the customers being offered a better deal if they buy on hire purchase rather than buying their new cars with cash. The dealer may be prepared to use some of his commission, which he receives from the hire purchase aspect, to enhance the car purchase deal for the customer.

4.6.3 Security over the stock

The concept we are dealing with here is that of the finance house having some control over of the legal ownership of the goods in question, here the cars. In practice this is difficult, not least because the dealer will be buying and selling cars on a weekly basis, so the identity of the vehicles will change frequently. This will usually limit the security charge to a floating charge, with all the difficulties of priority that attach to such charges. As a matter of practice, the identity of the specific second-hand cars held by a dealer is recorded with an organisation that alerts buyers to potential problems with cars. Thus, any attempt by the dealer to sell the car without notifying the lender, and having the details of that car removed from the register, would be futile if the proper searches with that organisation are conducted by, or on behalf of, the purchaser. The market-leading organisation in the UK is HPI: see http://www.hpicheck.com. An alternative mechanism, which has never caught on in the UK but is used in the US, is field warehousing. Here, the vehicles are controlled by a warehouseman employed by the finance house. He releases a vehicle to the dealer only on the instructions of the finance house.

4.6.4 Bailment

There are various types of bailment financing plan for retailers. A common feature is that the dealer does not buy the goods from a supplier and then finance the arrangement through a finance house. Instead, the dealer will act through the finance house itself, ie the sale of goods contract is between the manufacturer and the finance house. The arrangement could be a conditional sale, hire purchase, or consignment to the finance house from the manufacturer. The retailer then holds the goods as a bailee, that is he has possession of the goods but never gets title to them.

4.6.5 Financing against receivables

This is where finance is provided to the retailer by a finance house on the basis of the money which will be received by the retailer from its customers in due course. Perhaps the most common illustration of this is factoring.

Receivables financing involves lending money to a business now, in the expectation that the business will repay the loan in instalments from the income it makes by selling goods or services to its own customers. A key element is that 'book debts', ie money owed to the business by its customers, are something that can be bought and sold. In effect, book debts are valuable, as they can be turned into cash by pressing the customers for payment and, if need be, suing them to recover the money.

In factoring, the business 'sells' the book debts, ie the sums owed to it by its customers, to the factor. Obviously, this is not for the full face value but for perhaps 90% of the value. The business thus gets its money very quickly, or at least 90% of it, and the factor makes a 10% profit when it extracts the money from the debtor.

Chapter 5
Marketing Agreements

5.1	Introduction	73
5.2	Agency agreements	74
5.3	Drafting an agency agreement	75
5.4	Distribution agreements	88
5.5	Drafting a distribution agreement	89
5.6	Structure of the agreements at a glance	94
5.7	Other types of marketing agreement	94
5.8	Conclusion	95

5.1 Introduction

The topic of agreements for the marketing of goods and services is introduced in **Chapters 34** and **35** of ***Business Law and Practice***. Like those chapters, this chapter concentrates on two of the most commonly encountered marketing agreements: agency and distribution. It begins with a brief reminder of the nature of each type of agreement, and its advantages and disadvantages as a marketing vehicle, and then goes on to consider how each type of agreement might be put together. There is a short concluding section on other types of marketing agreement (including franchising and licensing; note that licensing, insofar as its EC competition law implications are concerned, will be covered in more detail in Chapter 22).

5.1.1 Agency

The term 'agency' is often used very loosely in relation to commercial activities to cover a number of different types of business relationship, and it is extremely important not to take at face value the label which the parties have put on their arrangement; always check carefully the actual nature of the relationship. A true sales agency agreement is one where the agent makes contracts with customers on behalf of its principal; in other words, the agent binds the principal, so there is a contract between the principal and the customer (but none between the agent and the customer).

Other types of agency agreement are possible; for example marketing or 'introducing' agency. This term normally covers the situation where the agent simply finds customers and introduces them to the principal, which then negotiates and makes the contract for itself; however, it is also used where the agent finds customers and negotiates terms on the principal's behalf but without having the authority to make the contract on the principal's behalf. Again, it is important not to be influenced by the terminology but always to check the true nature of the relationship between the parties.

In any dispute, the court is likely to attach little weight to the labelling of an agreement; substance and effect will determine the matter.

5.1.2 Distribution

In a distribution (also known as distributorship) agreement, the supplier sells goods to the distributor, which buys them in order to re-sell on its own behalf (a common example of a distribution agreement is where a manufacturer sells its products to a wholesaler, which buys them to sell to its own customers, to retail onwards; the relationship between manufacturer and wholesaler is a distribution agreement). The supplier has no contractual relationship with the distributor's customers.

5.1.3 Advantages and disadvantages of each type of agreement

An agency agreement (particularly a sales agency) may require close supervision by the principal and may, therefore, not be suitable as a marketing vehicle if agent and principal are based in different countries, or the principal cannot spare the time to supervise the agent's activities. On the other hand, an agency agreement may be essential if the principal needs to maintain close contact with the ultimate buyers of its products (eg, because the products are tailor-made for each buyer). In addition, agency agreements normally cause few competition law problems. Genuine agency agreements are likely to be unaffected by English competition law, and are also unlikely to infringe EC competition law (see **5.3.1.1**). Note that an agency agreement can also be used as a vehicle for marketing services, unlike a standard distribution agreement, which is really only appropriate for marketing goods.

A normal distribution agreement requires little supervision by the supplier; once the supplier has sold the goods to the distributor, it is the distributor's responsibility to decide how best to market them. If problems arise in relation to the goods which the distributor supplies, the distributor's customers have a contractual claim against the distributor and not against the supplier, with whom they have no contract. (Note, however, that this does not mean that the ultimate customer can never have a claim against the original supplier. Where, for example, the supplier is a manufacturer, claims in tort or for product liability may arise.) It may, therefore, be easier and cheaper for a supplier to operate a distribution agreement. However, a distribution agreement (in particular an agreement which gives the distributor some form of territorial protection; see **5.5.1.2**) is more likely than an agency agreement to be at risk from competition law problems. Unless care is taken with drafting, a distribution agreement can infringe EC competition law, in particular Article 81 EC (ex Article 85). This aspect of distribution agreements is covered in more detail at **21.3**.

5.2 Agency agreements

5.2.1 Introduction

To help in considering how to approach an agency agreement, this section will refer to an expanded version of the agency example described in ***Business Law and Practice*** at **35.6**.

Example

Wood Magic Ltd is a medium-sized company in Chester. It has been established for about 20 years, and has built up a thriving business making custom-designed furniture in luxury woods such as yew and cherry. Its sales have been largely confined to the North of England, where it has built up an excellent reputation. However, following a recent change of management and an injection of new capital, the directors plan to expand the business. In particular, they want to target London and the South-East, but have not yet decided how best to do this. Up to now, Wood Magic has carried out its own marketing, and there are no plans to change the set-up for the existing Northern operations. However, the directors feel that Wood Magic needs to find a 'trading partner' with a presence in the target market to help the furniture become established in that market. They are prepared to commit at least one director to be permanently engaged on developing this side of the business and establishing good relations with the trading partner. This commitment will be a long-term one and, despite having the trading partner to find customers for it, Wood Magic needs to maintain customer contact itself to ensure that customers get the products they need. The directors would like to know how the involvement of a trading partner might affect Wood Magic's liability to customers, but see no problem in being liable to customers if things go wrong, as they are proud of the company's reputation.

5.2.2 Initial advice

At this stage of the proposed transaction, the solicitor is likely to be asked to advise in two related areas:

(a) What sort of marketing arrangement is most suitable for Wood Magic?

(b) What factors should it take into account when looking for a trading partner?

The facts indicate that some form of agency agreement would be most appropriate:

(a) Wood Magic needs to be able to supervise its trading partner quite closely, and is prepared to commit resources to this supervision.

(b) Wood Magic needs to have some sort of contact with the buyers of its furniture to give them the products they need.

(c) Wood Magic is not concerned about being liable to its ultimate customers.

(d) The target market is in the UK, so supervision of the trading partner should be easier.

In addition, it is unlikely that Wood Magic would need to be concerned about competition law problems if it chose to enter into an agency agreement: see **5.3.1.1**.

Either marketing or sales agency may be suitable, depending on whether the directors simply want the agent to find customers, or whether they want to give the agent authority to make contracts on Wood Magic's behalf. In both cases (but particularly the second), Wood Magic should be looking for a reliable, well-organised and creditworthy business, preferably with an established reputation.

5.3 Drafting an agency agreement

5.3.1 Preliminary considerations

Assume now that Wood Magic's directors have found a suitable trading partner, a company called Lynwood Ltd, which is based in Kingston-upon-Thames. They have checked Lynwood's business credentials and are satisfied that it will make a suitable trading partner. In particular, Wood Magic is satisfied that using Lynwood will give Wood Magic an appropriate level of customer contact. The prospective parties are now negotiating the agency agreement, and have provisionally agreed certain terms, including the following:

(a) Lynwood will have authority to find customers and make contracts on Wood Magic's behalf.

(b) Wood Magic will deliver the finished furniture direct to customers.

(c) Wood Magic will pay Lynwood a monthly commission.

(d) Wood Magic will set the prices for the furniture (as it is custom-made, Wood Magic will supply Lynwood with a detailed 'pricing menu' which will allow Lynwood to work out the price for each order).

(e) Lynwood will keep certain display items of Wood Magic's furniture at its premises to show potential customers what can be achieved. Wood Magic will supply Lynwood with these items free of charge and will remain the owner of the items.

The solicitor is ready to begin drafting the agreement: what preliminary considerations should be taken into account?

5.3.1.1 How far will the agreement be affected by competition law?

If the proper law of the contract is to be English law (for choice of law, see **Chapter 8**), English competition law is potentially applicable.

The Competition Act 1998 contains a basic prohibition (the *Chapter I Prohibition)* on anti-competitive agreements which is almost identical to Article 81(1) EC; as Article 81(1) EC generally does not apply to genuine agency agreements (see next paragraph) the position will be the same in English law.

In practice, genuine agency agreements will fall outside the scope of Article 81 EC as a result of paras 12–20 of the Commission Notice of May 2000 which sets out guidelines on vertical restraints (see **21.3.7** for further explanation of this Notice and the block exemption to which it relates).

Paragraph 12 of the Notice defines an agency agreement for this purpose; broadly speaking, it is an agreement where one person (the agent) is 'vested with the power to negotiate and/or conclude contracts on behalf of another person (the principal)' for the sale or purchase of goods or services by the principal. Paragraph 13 states that in the case of 'genuine agency agreements, the obligations imposed on the agent as to the contracts negotiated and/or concluded on behalf of the principal do not fall within the scope of application of Article 81(1)'. It goes on to state that the determining factor in assessing whether Article 81(1) EC is applicable to an agency agreement is the 'financial or commercial risk borne by the agent in relation to the activities for which he has been appointed as an agent by the principal'. The paragraph concludes by stating that 'non-genuine' agency agreements may be caught by Article 81(1) EC.

Paragraphs 14–17 then indicate the types of financial or commercial risk which are material to assessing whether an agency agreement is 'genuine' or not (note that para 16 indicates that this assessment must be made on a case-by-case basis, and with regard to the economic reality of the situation rather than the legal form of the agreement). Paragraph 14 states that two types of risk are material: risks related directly to the contracts which the agent negotiates and/or concludes for the principal (eg, the financing of stocks of goods), and risks related to 'market-specific investments' (investments specifically required to enable the agent to negotiate and/or conclude the contracts). The implication is that acceptance of such risks by the agent to a significant degree will stop the agreement being a genuine agency agreement.

In para 16, the Commission states that it considers that Article 81(1) EC will not generally be applicable where the property in (ie, ownership of) the contract goods does not vest in the agent, or where the agent does not itself supply the contract services; it goes on to give a non-exhaustive list of indications that an agent is not accepting significant financial or commercial risks (including that the agent does not contribute to the supply of goods or services, that the agent is not required to invest in sales promotion, does not maintain at its own cost or risk stocks of the contract goods, and does not create and/or operate after-sales, repair or warranty services unless it is fully reimbursed by the principal).

Paragraph 18 indicates that if an agency agreement falls outside the scope of Article 81(1) EC, all the obligations imposed on the agent in relation to contracts made fall outside Article 81(1) EC. The following obligations are specifically identified as forming an 'inherent part' of an agency agreement:

(a) limitations on the territory in which the agent may sell the goods/services;
(b) limitations on the customers to whom the agent may sell these goods/services;
(c) the prices and conditions at which the agent must sell or purchase these goods or services.

On the basis of the terms agreed in principle, will Wood Magic and Lynwood have the benefit of the Notice? There seems a good chance that their agreement will be a 'genuine' agency agreement, as Lynwood does not appear to be accepting financial or commercial risks that would make the agreement 'non-genuine'. In particular, there is no evidence that Lynwood will ever be the owner of the contract goods, and although Lynwood keeps display items of furniture at its premises, these are not 'stocks' in the normal sense (Lynwood has not paid for them and does not own them); there is also no evidence of Lynwood providing promotional or after-sales services. On the basis that their agreement is 'genuine', neither the Competition Act 1998 nor Article 81 EC (which would, of course, only be applicable anyway if the agreement were capable of affecting trade between Member States) would apply.

5.3.1.2 How far should the agreement expressly refer to the basic principles of agency law?

Again, this discussion assumes that the proper law of the agreement is to be English law. Should the agreement, for example, refer expressly to the agent's fiduciary duties (such as acting in all good faith towards the principal)? Should it set out the other duties which will be implied into the contract in the absence of agreement between the parties? These are difficult points to resolve. Ultimately, the answer must depend upon the relationship of the parties and how familiar they are with the principles of agency law generally. If they are new to one another and have little experience of agency agreements (this would seem to apply to Wood Magic and Lynwood), setting out the principles could be beneficial; both parties will know exactly where they stand. If, however, the parties are both experienced and already have a long-standing relationship, express inclusion of basic agency principles may only offend both sides.

In general terms, if the agency falls within the ambit of the Commercial Agents (Council Directive) Regulations 1993 (SI 1993/3053), wide fiduciary duties are imposed upon the parties (see **5.3.1.3** and **5.3.3.1** below). Where the agreement does not fall within the Regulations, a lesser but still considerable fiduciary duty is implied by the common law.

5.3.1.3 Statutory restrictions on drafting

For many years, there was comparatively little statutory provision in English law which could affect the contents of an agency agreement. However, many agency agreements are now subject to the Commercial Agents (Council Directive) Regulations 1993, which came into force on 1 January 1994 and enacted into English law the requirements of the EC Directive on the Co-ordination of Laws of Member States relating to Self-Employed Commercial Agents (Directive 86/653/EEC). The Regulations 'govern the relations between commercial agents and their principals ... in relation to the activities of commercial agents in Great Britain' (reg 1(1)). Provision is made in reg 1(3) (as amended) for agreements which are to be governed by the law of another Member State.

'Commercial agent' is defined in reg 2(1) as:

> a self-employed intermediary who has continuing authority to negotiate the sale or purchase of goods on behalf of another person (the 'principal') or to negotiate and conclude the sale or purchase of goods on behalf of and in the name of that principal ...

This definition means that the type of 'marketing' agent which only has authority to find customers and is not authorised to 'negotiate' on the principal's behalf will not be a 'commercial agent'. Obviously, it will be very important for the parties to agree the extent of the agent's authority to act on the principal's behalf.

For an interesting case on what constitutes a 'commercial agent' and on the application of the Regulations, see the Court of Appeal's decision in *Mercantile International Group plc v Chuan Soon Huant Industrial Group Ltd* [2002] EWCA Civ 288. Here, the arrangement between the parties was described as an 'agency agreement', and contracts which the claimant made with customers stated that the claimant was acting as agent for the defendant. However, the claimant was not paid by commission but (like a distributor) was remunerated by mark-up; it charged customers for the goods and paid a smaller sum to the 'principal'. On the other hand, the claimant clearly had authority to negotiate in the principal's name; the principal delivered direct to customers and the claimant never held any stock.

The Court of Appeal decided that, in the light of all the above factors, the agreement was an agency agreement: although the way in which remuneration was paid might appear to point against agency, this was outweighed by the other factors and did not determine the question in this case. The agreement was also consistent with the agent being a 'commercial agent', and the Regulations therefore applied.

See, by contrast, *Sagal (t/a Bunz UK) v Atelier Bunz GmbH* [2008] EWHC 789 (Comm) where, in a complex contractual relationship, the claimant was held not be a commercial agent. Despite all other appearances, the claimant did not negotiate the sale of jewellery as an intermediary; he negotiated the sale on his own behalf.

In *PJ Pipe & Valve Co Ltd v Audco India Ltd* [2005] EWHC 1904 (QB), the High Court made an interesting ruling on the meaning of 'to negotiate' in reg 2(1). In this case, the defendant engaged the claimant to promote the defendant as an approved supplier of certain goods to construction projects. Once the claimant had achieved this, its role largely ceased, and the defendant and the customer negotiated the terms of their relationship themselves. The claimant's role therefore consisted of identifying opportunities for the defendant, advising it of those opportunities and promoting it to potential customers, rather than negotiating specific terms on the defendant's behalf.

The High Court ruled that, on the facts, the claimant was a commercial agent within the meaning of reg 2(1), and was therefore entitled to compensation under reg 17 as a result of a repudiatory breach of contract which the defendant had committed. In particular, the court gave the words 'to negotiate' a broad meaning, ruling that if the agent spent time and resources on developing the principal's goodwill, and it was in the principal's commercial interest for the agent to do this, this could amount to 'negotiation', just as much as negotiating specific terms of the contract between principal and customer.

Note the situations in which the Regulations will *not* apply:

(a) where the agent does not come within the definition of 'commercial agent' (reg 2(1));

(b) where the agent is an agent of a type listed in reg 2(2);

(c) where the agent's activities as a commercial agent are to be considered secondary (regs 2(3), 2(4) and the Schedule). For discussion of when an agent's activities are considered 'secondary', see *Light v Ty Europe Ltd* [2003] EWCA Civ 1238 at para 26, and, more recently, *Crane v Sky In-Home Service Ltd* [2007] EWHC 66 (Ch).

From *Light v Ty Europe Ltd* (see (c) above) it seems that sub-agents who do not have a contractual relationship with the principal to a sales agency agreement are unable to assert rights under the Regulations against that principal. That would be to give the Regulations a meaning they cannot bear.

In addition, the Regulations do not extend to Northern Ireland (reg 2(5)).

The Regulations lay down rules with which the parties must comply in relation to a number of important areas of an agency agreement, in particular:

(a) the rights and obligations of both parties (see **5.3.3** and **5.3.4**);

(b) the agent's remuneration (see **5.3.5**); and

(c) the conclusion and termination of the agency contract (see **5.3.6**).

Note that, by reg 23(1), the Regulations apply not only to agency agreements which have been entered into on or after 1 January 1994, but also to those which were already in existence on that date.

Assuming that Lynwood falls within the definition of 'commercial agent' (which it will, as long as it has in practice 'continuing authority to negotiate and conclude the sale … of goods on behalf of another person'), the Regulations will apply to its agreement with Wood Magic.

5.3.1.4 Precedents

Obviously, no single agreement or set of clauses can ever claim to be a comprehensive guide to drafting a particular agreement; the commercial draftsman should always be ready to consult a wide range of precedents and other sources. For the sake of convenience, however, **5.3.2–5.3.7** refer to just one of the standard agency precedents available: Precedent K1 (Sales Agency Agreement), in Rosenberg, *Practical Commercial Precedents* (Sweet & Maxwell) (PCP).

5.3.1.5 Planning, form and content of agreement

The rest of this section describes the likely structure and contents of a typical sales agency agreement such as might be suitable for Wood Magic and Lynwood, and falls into six distinct parts: **5.3.2** (introduction to a sales agency agreement); **5.3.3** (agent's rights and duties); **5.3.4** (principal's rights and duties); **5.3.5** (financial provisions); **5.3.6** (termination), **5.3.7** (miscellaneous clauses) and **5.3.8** (drafting).

5.3.2 Introduction to the agreement

This section of the agreement is likely to cover the following areas:

(a) a preliminary clause setting out the date of the agreement, the parties and any recitals which are felt to be necessary;

(b) a definitions and interpretation clause; and

(c) a clause dealing with the appointment of the agent.

5.3.2.1 Date, parties, recitals (PCP K1-021)

The date of the agreement should cause few problems, but the description of the parties may need some thought. The principal will often be a manufacturer (as with Wood Magic), but as agency can be created at any stage of the marketing chain, it could be, for example, a wholesaler. Recitals may be useful for setting out the basis on which the parties are making their agreement. For example, Wood Magic and Lynwood might use a recital to show that their relationship is such that the agent (Lynwood) is not accepting significant financial or commercial risk, and to indicate therefore that the parties believe that the agreement will not be affected by competition law.

5.3.2.2 Definitions and interpretation

Two definitions which are likely to require some thought are 'Products' and 'Territory'.

'Products'

It is useful for the agreement to contain a comprehensive definition of the products which the agent is marketing on the principal's behalf. In the case of the agreement under consideration, this is clearly Wood Magic's furniture, but a more precise definition is likely to be needed. For example, will the agent handle the principal's whole product range, or only some of the principal's products? Will it handle all products of a particular type which the principal manufactures? This is often best dealt with by listing the relevant products in a schedule to the agreement. Often the main problem in a continuing relationship is how to handle changes which may occur (eg, what will happen if the principal ceases to manufacture a particular product or begins to manufacture a new one?). To cover this, should the agreement include provision for a mutually agreed variation? Will the principal want to force the agent to take up a new product (either with or without notice), or should any changes to the product range be made only with the agent's consent? The answers will obviously depend upon the relationship between the parties, their relative needs and their bargaining strengths.

'Territory'

Where will the agent market the goods? In Lynwood's case, the relevant area is to be London and the South-East of England. In many cases, defining 'territory' will be straightforward, but it should be expressed as precisely as possible. If this is not made clear, it may lead to disputes over territorial rights between different agents and between agent and principal. This may also involve disputes over exclusivity of the agency (see **5.3.2.3**, 'Agent's authority', below).

5.3.2.3 Appointment of the agent (PCP K1-023, clause 2)

The appointment clause defines the agent's role in the agreement, and is perhaps the single most important clause in an agency agreement. In particular, it defines the extent of the agent's authority to bind the principal, which in turn will determine a number of other matters. It is likely to cover the following areas.

Agent's authority

In a sales agency agreement, the agent is given authority to enter contracts on the principal's behalf for the sale of the products. As the agent binds the principal, the principal must honour any contracts which the agent has made on its behalf. As noted previously, a marketing agent's authority will be more restricted; it will either be limited to finding customers and introducing them to the principal, or to finding customers and conducting some negotiation on the principal's behalf without, however, binding the principal. Whatever the parties decide is best for them, the appointment clause should always make clear the extent of the agent's authority.

Agent's operations

In attempting to define the geographical limits of the agent's operations and the extent to which the agent will be protected from competition by others within this territory, the clause should be as clear as possible. A particular problem arises with the use of the expressions 'sole' agency and 'exclusive' agency. Strictly speaking, 'sole' agency means that the principal will not appoint any other agents within the defined territory, but that the principal can still sell its products there itself. 'Exclusive' agency means that the principal itself cannot sell the products within the territory, or appoint any other agents in the territory. However, the legal and commercial meanings of both terms have become confused, and may even mean different things in different product markets. It is, therefore, unsafe to define the scope of the agent's protection from competition in the territory simply by using the words 'sole' or 'exclusive' in the agreement. It is better to state clearly whether the principal can appoint other agents or market the products in the territory itself (and in what circumstances). It is also sensible to make clear how far (if at all) the agent can extend its operations beyond the territory. On this last point, note that forbidding the agent to accept unsolicited orders from outside the territory can cause real problems if Article 81 EC does apply to the agreement.

Duration and termination

The appointment clause often also deals with duration and termination of the agreement (compare the PCP precedent, which has a combined Duration and Termination clause at clause 10).

The parties may consider entering into a fixed-term agreement. It may be desirable to grant the agent a reasonably long initial fixed term, in order to give it an incentive to build up the business. However, there are, of course, other possibilities. If the parties want an indefinite term, or a fixed term followed by an indefinite term, a suitable notice provision should be included. (Note that under reg 15 of the Commercial Agents (Council Directive) Regulations 1993, the agent is entitled to certain minimum periods of notice.)

Del credere agency

If the agency is to be a del credere agency (ie, where the agent agrees to guarantee the customer's performance of the contract in return for an additional commission), this is likely to be an appropriate part of the agreement to include the del credere provision.

In the proposed agreement between Wood Magic and Lynwood, the solicitor will need to take instructions on most of the preceding matters, as there is no evidence that the parties have yet considered any of them (except the matter of Lynwood's authority).

5.3.3 The agent's rights and duties (PCP K1-024, clause 3)

5.3.3.1 Introduction

The principal needs to have an appropriate amount of control over its sales agent's activities, so the section on agent's duties is likely to be the longest of the agreement. Broadly speaking, the principal will want to ensure (as far as possible) that the agent observes certain limitations (eg, in a sales agency, that the agent does not make unsuitable contracts on the principal's behalf), while still encouraging the agent to exploit the agency to its full potential. It may be appropriate when drafting the agreement to have a clause relating to general duties, followed by individual clauses covering particular duties (such as advertising and promotion). Note the provisions of reg 3 of the Commercial Agents (Council Directive) Regulations 1993 on the agent's duties. By reg 3(1), a commercial agent must look after the interests of his principal and act dutifully and in good faith; reg 3(2) deals with a number of specific developments of these general duties.

5.3.3.2 General duties

The principal may want to provide that the agent uses its 'best endeavours' in promoting and marketing the products. 'Best endeavours' does, however, put a considerable burden upon the agent (it means that the agent must make every effort possible to find customers and make contracts), and the agent may consider this duty too strict.

5.3.3.3 Specific duties

Licences and permits

It may sometimes be necessary to obtain a licence for the sale of the products in the territory, or to comply with local regulations. Clearly, this is unlikely to be a problem for Wood Magic and Lynwood. However, if this is the case, the agreement should allocate responsibility for doing so. The solicitor should consider which party is best placed to obtain any licence or comply with any regulations, and draft accordingly. It is often sensible to make the agent responsible for getting permits and licences for the sale of the products and in respect of its own performance. It is also customary to provide that the agent must comply with laws and regulations concerning the sale of the products, but not those concerning the nature of the products or their packaging; this will normally be for the principal to do (see **5.3.4**).

Promotion and marketing

The principal will want the agent to promote the principal's business and to keep up good relations with customers. It is clear, for example, in the agreement under consideration, that Wood Magic and its products already enjoy an excellent reputation, and Wood Magic will obviously want this to continue. The principal may want to make this duty more specific, for example by requiring the agent's staff to be available when needed for meetings with the principal or potential customers, or for attending trade fairs and other relevant marketing events. The principal may also require the agent to provide premises which the principal considers suitable (it may also want the right to inspect these premises from time to time), and to set up proper office facilities and a suitable organisation for the efficient operation of the agency.

The parties need to agree which of them will have the responsibility and expense of advertising. It is common to find a clause which requires the agent to pay for the advertising, but to use only material which has either been supplied or approved by the principal, thus allowing the principal to keep considerable control of the agent's activities. For example, Wood Magic may want Lynwood to use advertising and promotional tactics which Wood Magic knows to be effective from its own marketing experience.

Note that paras 16–17 of the Notice of May 2000 indicate that if the agent is 'directly or indirectly obliged to invest in sales promotion' (eg, by contributing to the principal's advertising budget), this may amount to incurring a 'risk' which would bring the agreement within the ambit of Article 81 EC. Caution may therefore be required.

Stock

Principal and agent may agree that the agent will itself keep stocks of the principal's products in order to fulfil the contracts it makes on the principal's behalf. If the parties have agreed, however, that the principal will supply customers direct, the stock clause could be much simpler, or perhaps omitted altogether. If the agent is to keep stocks of the products, the agreement should deal with the level of stock which the agent is to carry and what is to happen to stock while it is on the agent's premises. The principal will not want the stock to be counted as part of the agent's assets, and therefore claimable by the agent's creditors if the agent becomes insolvent, so it is desirable to provide, for example, that the stock is clearly marked as being the principal's, and is stored separately from other goods while on the agent's premises. The principal may want to add the right to inspect the agent's premises from time to time to ensure that the agent is complying with this. Note that if it is clear that the agent bears the risk of loss while the stock is on its premises, the Notice of May 2000 would probably cease to apply, and Article 81 EC problems might arise. Similarly, if there is any requirement for the agency to provide specialised premises or handling facilities, etc, these could be treated as 'market-specific investments' which could comprise 'risk' for these purposes. However, Wood Magic and Lynwood will not have problems in this respect: Wood Magic will deliver direct to customers.

Duty to supply information

It may be useful (eg, in order to plan future products, or to improve existing ones) for the principal to receive feedback from the agent on how customers are reacting to the products. How much information the principal wants from the agent, and on what matters, will obviously vary from case to case; for example, some principals may be satisfied with a clause which requires the agent to report 'from time to time', others may want the agent to report on a regular basis and at definite times. The principal may also wish to restrict the agent's right to get involved in disputes or proceedings concerning the products without the principal's written consent. If the agency falls within the Commercial Agents (Council Directive) Regulations 1993, there are very specific and non-derogatable duties on both parties to supply each other with information, particularly so with regard to the principal's duties (see regs 3(2)(b) and 4(2) and (3)).

Confidentiality

An agency agreement will not always require highly sophisticated confidentiality provisions; if the agent is simply finding customers and making contracts, it may not be privy to any information or process which could be described as confidential. If, however, the agent will be handling confidential material, the principal will need to consider how best to protect its interests. This is usually done by making clear what information is confidential, and what the agent is and is not entitled to do in relation to confidential information. In the agreement under consideration, Wood Magic will need to decide if Lynwood needs any confidential information (eg, about how the furniture is made) to be able to fulfil its role as sales agent. For more on the law of confidence (and, in particular, the implied duty of confidentiality), see **Chapter 18**.

Intellectual property

This section of the agreement is likely to vary considerably and will not be necessary at all if the agent does not 'handle' any intellectual property rights under the agreement. If such a clause is necessary, its specific nature and extent will vary according to the circumstances and the type of intellectual property involved. Generally speaking, however, the clause will be designed to protect the principal's rights in the intellectual property and prevent the agent from getting any interest in it. It may be necessary to include clauses which:

(a) require the agent to inform the principal of any infringement of the principal's rights in the territory, or any claim by a third party that the principal has infringed its rights;

(b) require the agent to act on the principal's instructions and at the principal's request to institute or defend proceedings, or to do whatever else is necessary to maintain the validity and enforceability of the principal's rights;

(c) state that the agent is not to have, or seek to gain, any interest in the principal's rights (eg, trade marks on products, goodwill);

(d) require the agent not to damage the principal's goodwill by using confusingly similar trade names or trade marks, or behaving in any way that would invalidate the principal's rights or be inconsistent with them. A clause of this type would in most agreements need to be made subject to the rights of the agent and any third party to challenge the validity of the principal's intellectual property, or Article 81 EC problems could arise (see **Chapter 23** for a fuller discussion of the relationship of intellectual property and competition law, and how this may affect the drafting of commercial agreements).

The solicitor would need to take full instructions from Wood Magic about intellectual property rights which may be involved in the marketing (eg, any trade mark which Wood Magic uses, and any registered or unregistered design rights relevant to the furniture).

Miscellaneous clauses relating to the agent's duties

It is quite common to find a clause in the 'Agent's Duties' section which gathers together clauses which do not fall under any other heading. Obviously, the solicitor will need to decide whether this is appropriate or necessary in the light of Wood Magic's instructions, but a 'Miscellaneous Provisions' clause could include the following terms:

(a) that the agent will meet targets set by the principal: depending on the nature of the agency, these might be for numbers of customers found and introduced, or numbers of contracts made on the principal's behalf;

(b) that the agent will not pledge the principal's credit;

(c) that the agent will not become involved in or try to settle any dispute about the products without first getting the principal's permission to do so;

(d) that the agent will not do anything which might prejudice the principal's business or the marketing of its products;

(e) that where the agent makes contracts on the principal's behalf, the contracts will be made on the principal's standard terms;

(f) that the agent will not become involved in any way with goods which compete with the products which are the subject of the agency agreement.

5.3.4 The principal's rights and duties

These are often less onerous than the agent's duties to the principal. However, note the provisions of reg 4 of the Commercial Agents (Council Directive) Regulations 1993. By reg 4(1), a principal must act dutifully and in good faith in his relations with his commercial agent; reg 4(2) and (3) deal with specific aspects of these general duties.

Again, the solicitor would need to take instructions from Wood Magic as to what it intends its rights and duties as principal to be. However, the following provisions are commonly encountered (note how many of them complement duties which have already been imposed on the agent):

(a) the right for the principal to amend the listed products which are the subject of the agreement (see PCP K1-027, clause 6.2);

(b) the duty for the principal to pay commission to the agent (see PCP K1-028, clause 7.1). It is customary for an agent to be remunerated by commission; the duty to pay it may be stated as part of the principal's rights and duties, or it may be included as part of a complete financial provisions clause (see **5.3.5);**

(c) the duty of the principal to comply with all relevant laws relating to the composition, packaging and labelling of the goods (see PCP K1-027, clause 6.3.7); this is likely to make sense, as these matters will be under the principal's control;

(d) the duty for the principal to supply advertising and promotional material (see PCP K1-027, clause 6.3.1);

(e) the duty for the principal to pass on to the agent any information which might assist the agent in marketing the goods (see generally PCP K1-027, clauses 6.3.2 and 6.3.9);

(f) if the agreement requires the agent to hold stock, the duty for the principal to supply stock (this should also encompass how and when stock is to be supplied, ordering procedure, returns and so on);

(g) the duty for the principal to provide an after-sales service for the products;

(h) the duty for the principal to indemnify the agent against any liability which the agent incurs as a result of being held out as the principal's agent (eg, costs and expenses which the agent may incur in relation to claims arising out of the agency);

(i) in contracts within the ambit of the Regulations, the duty to notify the agent within a reasonable period once he anticipates that the value of commercial transactions will be significantly lower than normal expectations (see reg 4(2)(b));

(j) in contracts within the Regulations, the duty to give minimum periods of notice, except where immediate termination would be justified by conduct or other exceptional circumstances (eg repudiatory breach or frustration etc) (see reg 15). Note that this provision applies to either party.

5.3.5 Financial provisions (PCP K1-028, clause 7)

This section of the agreement is likely to vary considerably in content and layout. The parties are obviously free to choose the form of agreement which suits them best, and could combine the financial provisions with the principal's and the agent's duties respectively, if appropriate. However (especially where the financial provisions in the agreement are elaborate), it will often make sense to deal with them in a separate section relating to both parties. Note that where the Commercial Agents Regulations 1993 apply, the solicitor must be aware of their impact on the financial provisions of the agreement; the Regulations have provisions relating to agent's remuneration generally (regs 6–12) and compensation or remuneration on termination of the agreement (regs 17 and 18, see **5.3.6**).

5.3.5.1 Commission

Most genuine agency agreements deal expressly with matters such as how the commission is to be calculated, and when it is to be paid. All Wood Magic and Lynwood have agreed so far is that Wood Magic will pay Lynwood a monthly commission, so the solicitor will clearly need to take full instructions on the precise requirements. In practice, there may be considerable variation in the way commission can be dealt with (for a good standard precedent, see PCP K1-028, clause 7, or the remuneration clause in the sales agency agreement of the *Encyclopaedia of Forms and Precedents* (Butterworths, 1994)), but it is important to note that the parties may not always be completely free to make their own arrangements. In particular, where the Commercial Agents Regulations 1993 apply, the principal must ensure that the remuneration provisions are consistent with the Regulations (this is something which Wood Magic must bear in mind). Briefly, reg 7 provides for the agent's right to commission on transactions which are concluded during the agency agreement, and reg 8 gives the agent certain rights to commission even after the agency agreement has ended (note that the agent's right to commission can be extinguished only in the circumstances described in reg 11; broadly, that the contract arranged by the agent will not be carried out, but that this is not the principal's fault). For an interesting case on the application of reg 8 and, in particular, the circumstances in which transactions concluded after the termination of the agency contract will still be 'mainly attributable' to the agent's efforts during the agency, see *Tigana Ltd v Decoro Ltd* [2003] EWHC 23 (QB), in which the agent was awarded the equivalent of nine months' commission in relation to such transactions. In addition, reg 10 controls when commission becomes due and when it must be paid.

5.3.5.2 Accounting arrangements for commission

The agreement should also deal with how the agent is to get the commission. A number of possibilities arise. For example, the agent may collect payment for the goods from customers, and then account to the principal after deducting its commission. If the agent collects money, the parties may prefer the agent to pay the gross sum to the principal, which then pays commission over to the agent. Alternatively, the principal may collect payment from customers, and then pay the agent a regular amount of commission. If the parties are based in different countries, it is also particularly important that the agreement should state the currency in which the commission is to be paid.

5.3.5.3 Deductions

If the agent does collect money from customers on behalf of the principal, it may sometimes be obliged to deduct certain sums (eg, in respect of local taxes) before handing over the balance. If this is the case, the parties should deal with the deductions expressly in the agreement.

5.3.5.4 General accounting arrangements

The parties may wish to provide, where appropriate, for the payment of interest on any sums outstanding if either side fails to account to the other (the agent in respect of money collected from customers, the principal in respect of commission). The agreement should also provide for the keeping of accounts and other financial records. This should cover not only which records each party is to keep, but also whether either party has the right to inspect or ask for copies of the other side's records. Note that where the Commercial Agents (Council Directive) Regulations 1993 apply, reg 12 obliges the principal to supply the agent with a statement of commission, and entitles the agent to demand the information he needs (including 'an extract from the books' to check the amount of commission due to him).

5.3.6 Termination (PCP K1-031, clause 10)

5.3.6.1 What circumstances will allow either party to terminate?

Circumstances in which either side may want the right to terminate the agreement would normally include:

(a) either side getting into financial difficulties, such as receivership, winding up or making a voluntary arrangement;

(b) breach of the agreement (consider drafting a notice procedure under which the party in breach can be required to remedy the breach where possible); and

(c) change in control of the agent if the agent is a company.

It is normally desirable to set out the circumstances expressly in the agreement. See also **5.3.4(j)** on notice requirements in cases within the Commercial Agents (Council Directive) Regulations 1993.

5.3.6.2 What will the effects of termination be? (PCP K1-032, clause 11)

The agreement should state how termination will affect the following:

(a) Any stocks of the product, samples and advertising material held by the agent.

(b) Sales which the agent has already negotiated, but in respect of which no moneys have been paid over.

(c) The agent's authority to negotiate on behalf of the principal.

(d) The agent's duty of confidentiality.

(e) The agent's right to compensation on termination.

5.3.6.3 Does the principal need to pay anything to the agent on termination?

This would normally be a matter for agreement between the parties. However, where the Commercial Agents Regulations 1993 apply, solicitor and principal must be aware that, in many cases, reg 17 obliges the principal to give the agent a 'pay-off' on termination of the agreement.

The position under reg 17 may be briefly summarised as follows. Broadly speaking, reg 17(1) provides that, on termination of the agency contract, the agent is entitled either to be 'indemnified' in accordance with reg 17(3)–(5), or to be 'compensated for damage' in accordance with reg 17(6)–(7). Regulation 17(2) states that except where the agreement provides otherwise, the agent is entitled to be compensated rather than indemnified.

The indemnity option is based on German law (it is sometimes referred to as the 'German model'), and may seem attractive to principals because it provides a limit on the payment the agent can get; ie no more than one year's commission, based on the agent's actual annual remuneration over the past five years (see reg 17(4)). There is also some evidence in practice that the actual payment will often be less than this.

The 1993 Regulations are considerably less clear about what 'compensation for damage' is. 'Compensation' in this context is based on French agency law (sometimes referred to as the 'French model'), and often, in practice, French law allows the agent on termination a sum equivalent to two years' commission (see below for the possible significance of this in the UK).

Regulation 17 is one of the most difficult areas of the 1993 Regulations. The first Court of Appeal case to consider reg 17 was *Graham Page v Combined Shipping and Trading Co Ltd* [1997] 3 All ER 656; however, this was in fact a case about the grant of a *Mareva* injunction (now known as a freezing injunction), and so the discussion of reg 17 was very limited. The Court did emphasise, however, that because the Regulations are implementing legislation, courts must adopt a purposive approach to their interpretation. The Court was in no doubt that the main purpose of the Commercial Agents Directive was to protect the agent.

In a number of cases (eg, *Duncan Moore v Piretta PTA* [1999] 1 All ER 174) the courts have awarded an indemnity in accordance with reg 17(3)–(5) (in the *Duncan Moore* case, which is still considered to be the leading case on indemnity, the judge expressly stated that his calculation was based upon the 'German model'). Authority on the meaning of 'compensation for damage' has built up gradually, but until recently was somewhat scarce and contradictory. For example, in the Scottish case of *King v T Tunnock* [2000] IRLR 570, the Inner House of the Court of Session indicated that it was appropriate to refer to the relevant principles of French law in assessing compensation for damage. However, the High Court in *Barrett McKenzie v Escada (UK) Ltd* (1 February 2001) held that the French tariff system of calculating compensation on termination of an agency agreement was not applicable when calculating compensation for damage under the Regulations.

In *Tigana v Decoro Ltd* (see **5.3.5.1** above) the High Court considered the previous authorities, and the judge set out an extensive (although not exhaustive) list of factors which had assisted him in arriving at his decision on compensation for damage. However, since July 2007, there has been House of Lords' authority on the calculation of compensation for damage: *Lonsdale v Howard & Hallam Ltd* [2007] UKHL 32. The House of Lords confirmed the approach previously taken by the Court of Appeal:

(a) It was inappropriate in the UK to apply the French law which exists in this area; in particular, there was no reason why courts in the UK should use two years' commission as a basis for calculating compensation for damage. French and English practices on damages differed, not because their respective courts were applying different rules of law but because they were operating in different markets. The House of Lords noted that the ECJ had made it clear that the method of calculation of the damage which the agent suffers as a result of termination is, as long as this is done consistently with the Directive, a matter for the law of each Member State (*Honyvem Informazioni Commerciali Srl v Mariella de Zotti* (Case C-465/04) [2006] ECR I-2879).

(b) The purpose of reg 17 was to compensate for damage to the agent's business as a result of the termination.

(c) Compensation should be calculated on the value of the agency business to the agent (including goodwill) at the date of termination of the agency. In giving the leading opinion in the House of Lords' judgment, Lord Hoffmann noted that this should be assessed on the basis of what a buyer would be prepared to pay to 'stand in the shoes' of the agent.

Even now, commentators are still somewhat divided on the likely impact of the ruling in the long term. Most agree that it confirms the clarity the Court of Appeal sought to bring to this area in its judgment, but there is some concern that the decision favours principals at the expense of agents, especially where (as in *Lonsdale* itself) the agency business is declining.

Note that reg 17(5) expressly provides that the grant of an indemnity 'shall not prevent the commercial agent from seeking damages'. It is generally assumed here that 'damages' refers to normal contractual damages, and that this provision would be relevant where, for example, the agreement has been unjustifiably terminated with no or insufficient notice. There is no express equivalent of this provision in relation to compensation for damage. In *Tigana Ltd v Decoro Ltd*, it was held that damages which would otherwise be payable on termination of an agency are subsumed into compensation under reg 17; loss caused by breach of contract can be taken into account when calculating compensation. Nevertheless, there will be cases where the claimant may have concurrent claims, both as a commercial agent and also in a different capacity, arising out of the same circumstances. The latter claims would not be subsumed. See *PJ Pipe & Valve Co Ltd v Audco India Ltd* [2005] EWHC 1904 (QB).

There is still considerable debate in practice as to whether an agreement should go for indemnity or compensation, how far the agreement should deal expressly with the point (in many cases, the agent will be entitled to a pay-off regardless of what the agreement says: see next paragraph) and how any termination payment clause should be worded: for one way of approaching the problem, see PCP K1-032, clause 11.

Whatever the parties decide, the principal should be aware that there are only very limited grounds for excluding the agent's right to either indemnity or compensation. These are contained in reg 18, and include default by the agent justifying immediate termination under reg 16. For a helpful discussion of reg 18 by the Court of Appeal, see *Cooper v Pure Fishing (UK) Ltd* [2004] 2 Lloyd's Rep 518.

In *Crane v Sky In-Home Service Ltd* [2007] EWHC 66 (Ch) there was further interesting discussion of reg 16 (and reg 18(a) which refers to it). The judge held that reg 16 applied when the principal has the right to terminate immediately by the acceptance of a repudiatory breach. In addition, reg 19 provides that the parties may not derogate from regs 17 and 18 to the detriment of the agent before the agency contract expires. This appears to mean that any provision in the agreement which removes or cuts down the agent's right to a pay-off will be of no effect.

5.3.7 Miscellaneous

An agency agreement will usually have a 'boiler-plate', containing a number of miscellaneous clauses (eg, arbitration, choice of law and jurisdiction). For the 'boiler-plate' of the PCP agreement, see K1-030–K1-035.

5.3.8 Particular points to consider when drafting a marketing agency agreement

A standard marketing agency agreement will be substantially similar in content and layout to a sales agency agreement; the main differences will result from the fact that a marketing agent has no authority to conclude contracts on the principal's behalf. A complete precedent for a marketing agency agreement can be found in PCP section K2.

5.3.8.1 Appointment

The agreement should define the nature of the agent's operations, with a clear statement that the agent is not authorised to enter into contracts on the principal's behalf. Normally, the agent also agrees not to describe itself as a sales agent.

Care needs to be taken about defining the exact limits of the agent's authority: is it to have authority only to find potential customers and pass them on to the principal; or is it to have authority to do at least some negotiating on the principal's behalf (without actually making any contract)? Although the terms 'marketing' and 'introducing' agency are widely used, they have no legally exact meaning, and so should not be used without additional explanation to make the extent of the agent's authority clear. Note that an agent which does not have 'continuing authority' to negotiate on the principal's behalf is not a 'commercial agent' within the meaning of the Commercial Agents (Council Directive) Regulations 1993 (see **5.3.1.3**).

5.3.8.2 Introducing potential customers

The agreement should provide that the agent is to pass on all orders and enquiries promptly to the principal.

5.3.8.3 Principal's response to potential customers

Is it desirable or possible to provide that the principal should comply with all orders generated by the agent's efforts? A marketing agent does not bind its principal. If the principal refuses to accept an order from a particular customer introduced by the agent, however, this could damage the agent's reputation, and possibly make it more difficult for the agent to earn commission in future. The parties may be able to agree some sort of compromise, for example that the principal will comply with orders from all customers, as long as it is satisfied that they are good credit risks. (Note how this point is dealt with in the PCP agreement at K2-027, clause 6.1.1; the principal is in fact entitled to reject any order for any reason.)

5.3.8.4 Agent's duties

A marketing agent is very unlikely to carry stock, or collect payments on the principal's behalf.

5.4 Distribution agreements

5.4.1 Introduction

This section continues with the Wood Magic example (see **5.2.1**), but in relation to a different aspect of Wood Magic's business.

Note that a distribution agreement is sometimes referred to as a 'distributorship agreement' (or simply 'distributorship'). Some commentators prefer this term, on the ground that, in practice, 'distribution agreement' is sometimes used loosely to refer to an agreement for the carriage of goods.

> **Example**
>
> Assume that Wood Magic has, for the past five years, carried on a small sideline business of manufacturing ready-made furniture (such as coffee tables, dining tables and chairs). The directors feel that this side of the business is now ready to be developed much further. Wood Magic recently rented a stand at a trade fair in Paris to show this furniture. The response was such that the directors believe that there is an important market in France, consisting of wealthy customers who admire 'le style anglais' and want English furniture for their country homes. In the short term, the directors believe that Wood Magic can spare the time and commitment needed to establish relations with a 'trading partner' in France; the directors who attended the trade fair made some promising contacts and believe that one company in particular, Bois Massif SA, could be the partner Wood Magic is looking for. However, assuming that they do establish relations with a partner they can trust, the directors would, in the long term, seek to market Wood Magic's goods in France in a way which does not require close day-to-day supervision. They believe that if they give the right training to the French partner at the outset, it will be easy for the partner to sell the ready-made furniture, without major involvement from Wood Magic. One particular reason why the directors are keen to involve a trading partner in this part of Wood Magic's expansion is that they have little experience in the export trade, and they admit that their collective knowledge of the French language and of French business practices is negligible.

5.4.2 Initial advice

At this stage (as with an agency agreement) the solicitor is likely to be asked to advise in two related areas:

(a) What sort of marketing arrangement is most suitable for Wood Magic?

(b) What factors should it take into account when looking for a trading partner?

This time, the facts indicate that a distribution agreement would be appropriate:

(a) The goods can be marketed in France in the same form in which Wood Magic sells them (eg, no customising is necessary).

(b) Wood Magic needs the help of a trading partner based in the target territory, because it is not familiar with that territory's language or business practices.

(c) The marketing of the goods does not require much supervision by Wood Magic (after initial training has been given).

(d) Wood Magic will not be liable in contract to the ultimate customers.

Note that whereas some of these factors would not necessarily make an agency agreement unsuitable, they indicate that the main advantages of that type of agreement (eg, supervision of agent, contact with customers: see **5.1.3**) are not really needed here. A distribution agreement is likely to be the cheapest and most efficient way to market these goods.

Wood Magic will need to be aware, however, that, depending on the terms which are included in the agreement with Bois Massif and the circumstances in which the agreement operates, competition law problems may arise (see **5.5.1.2** and **Chapter 22**).

As with the agency agreement, Wood Magic should check out any potential trading partner very carefully; for example, creditworthiness is even more important here than in the agency agreement, as the distributor will actually be buying the goods from Wood Magic, and therefore Wood Magic is directly at risk of non-payment by its trading partner.

5.5 Drafting a distribution agreement

5.5.1 Preliminary

Assume now that Wood Magic's directors are satisfied that Bois Massif is the right trading partner for them in France, and have begun detailed negotiations over the terms of the distribution agreement which the parties will enter. They have still to decide how to deal with many areas of the agreement, but have agreed the following in principle:

(a) Wood Magic has agreed that (to give Bois Massif the best possible chance of getting the distributorship established) it will not appoint any other distributors (or agents) for the sale of its goods in France, and that it will not sell any of its own goods in France.

(b) In return, Bois Massif has agreed to concentrate on the French market only: it will not actively seek customers from outside France (although it will be free to fulfil unsolicited orders).

What considerations arise for the solicitor in drafting the agreement?

5.5.1.1 Agency and distribution agreements: similarities and differences

It is important to note that the relationship of distributor and supplier is created and defined by the distribution agreement. Many of the clauses already discussed in relation to agency agreements are equally relevant to distribution agreements: these include interpretation, appointment, duration and many of the 'duties' clauses (allowing for some necessary modifications: see below). However, a distribution agreement is essentially an agreement for the sale of goods from the supplier to the distributor, and so matters relevant to drafting a sale of goods agreement must be considered (see **Chapter 2**). A complete precedent for a distribution agreement can be found in PCP section K3.

5.5.1.2 Distribution agreements and competition law

This topic is discussed in more detail in **Chapter 22**. Briefly, however, a distribution agreement is more likely than an agency agreement to infringe Article 81(1) EC as, depending on the terms which the parties include and the circumstances in which the agreement operates, its potential for affecting trade and competition is greater. However, there are several ways of avoiding the impact of Article 81(1) EC. For example, the agreement may be ignored by the Commission if it falls within the Notice on Agreements of Minor Importance (to advise on this, it would be necessary to know the parties' market shares; see **22.3.5.4**). Even if this does not apply, it may be possible to draft the agreement to comply with a relevant block exemption.

In the agreement under consideration, Wood Magic is offering Bois Massif 'exclusive territory' (see **5.5.2** below) and Bois Massif will agree not to sell actively outside that territory. Both parties are therefore limiting their commercial freedom, and (in theory at least) doing so in a way which may affect trade and competition (eg, French buyers will have only one authorised source of supply within France) and infringe Article 81(1) EC. However, if in practice the agreement contained only these two restrictions, the block exemption contained in Regulation 2790/99 would apply to the agreement, and therefore Article 81(1) EC would not. This block exemption is discussed in more detail at **22.3.7**.

5.5.2 Introduction

5.5.2.1 Date, parties, recitals, interpretation

This part of the agreement is likely to be very similar to the corresponding section of a sales agency agreement (see **5.3.2**). In particular, similar points are likely to arise in relation to 'Products' (see PCP K3-051, Sch 1) and 'Territory'.

5.5.2.2 Appointment

The appointment clause will be vitally important; in particular, the question of exclusivity. How much protection will the distributor get against competition from others in its territory? The distributor may want such protection (eg, against the supplier appointing other distributors or agents, or against the supplier selling within the territory) in order to benefit as much as possible from its investment in the distributorship. Businesses often regard territorial exclusivity as a fundamental term in a distribution agreement, without which a potential distributor might not agree to take on the distributorship at all. To some extent, even under competition law, protection from competition in this respect is permitted (see **22.3.7** for a discussion of block exemption).

It is always desirable to define the extent of the distributor's protection from competition as clearly as possible, rather than relying on the words 'sole' or 'exclusive' territory or distribution, which raise problems in the same way as they do in an agency agreement (see **5.3.2.3**). Strictly speaking, a 'sole' distribution agreement is one in which the supplier agrees not to appoint any other distributors in the territory but reserves the right to sell in the territory itself. An 'exclusive' distribution agreement is one in which the supplier agrees not to appoint any other distributors in the territory, nor to sell there itself (as with Wood Magic and Bois Massif). However, the legal and commercial meanings of these words have become too confused in practice to make it safe to rely on them alone when drafting (see how PCP K3-023, clause 2.2 deals with this point). The agreement should also define the limits of the distributor's freedom to operate outside the defined territory. Note that if Article 81 EC applies, the agreement must not forbid the distributor to export the goods from the territory, as this is likely to infringe Article 81(1) EC (and will not get the benefit of Regulation 2790/99: see **22.3.7**). It is, however, possible to provide that the distributor must not actively solicit orders from outside the territory, as Wood Magic and Bois Massif have in mind.

The appointment clause may also deal with the duration of the agreement, although this can be done elsewhere in the agreement (see PCP K1-032, clause 11). Whichever method is chosen, note that an initial fixed term may be even more appropriate here than in an agency agreement, as it will give the distributor (which may have taken risks by making a large investment in the distributorship) both security and an incentive to build up the business. If this is what the parties require, the agreement must state when the fixed term is to commence. If the parties require an indefinite term, the agreement must include suitably drafted notice provisions.

5.5.3 The distributor's duties

Some of the distributor's duties will be similar to those in an agency agreement (eg, in relation to confidentiality, transmission of information, training and availability of the distributor's representatives). However, other duties are likely to be significantly different because of the different nature of the agreement.

5.5.3.1 Minimum target obligations

The supplier will normally want to impose some form of minimum target obligation on the distributor to ensure that the distributor exploits the relevant market to the full. The supplier will often see this as justifiable in return for giving the distributor an initial fixed term. A minimum target obligation can be either for a minimum level of sales by the distributor to its customers, or for a minimum level of purchases by the distributor from the supplier. It is sometimes suggested that the latter may be more commercially flexible. For example, with a minimum purchase target, the distributor can buy extra goods from the supplier to meet the targets, and so perhaps cover a temporary bad patch more easily; purchase targets are also easier for the supplier to monitor. Note that although target obligations are often acceptable from a competition law point of view, care may be needed if the target is so exacting that it effectively limits the distributor's commercial freedom. Where minimum target obligations can, potentially, cause competition problems, such problems are likely to be complex and expensive to resolve (see *Ineos Vinyls Ltd v Huntsman Petrochemicals (UK) Ltd* [2006] EWHC 1241 (Ch)). The supplier should consider carefully the implications for both parties before deciding on such provisions. (For more on the potential competition law implications of distribution agreements, see **Chapter 22**.)

If targets of either sort are imposed, the supplier must decide what is to happen if the distributor does not comply with them. The supplier may want either to end the distributor's freedom from competition in the territory, or to terminate the agreement itself. The former may appear to be less drastic from the distributor's point of view, but could be as devastating as termination of the entire agreement in the long run. Note that ending territorial protection for failure to meet targets is not always seen as being commercially sensible; if the distributor is finding it hard to succeed with the help of sole or exclusive territory, presumably its task will be even more difficult without it, and the supplier may not benefit in any way. The supplier should therefore consider doing this only if it is certain that matters will improve if the distributor's protection from competition is ended (eg, it will encourage the distributor to make greater efforts, or the supplier will benefit by being able to appoint another distributor or market the goods itself).

5.5.3.2 Advertising and promotion

The distributor is normally made responsible for advertising and promotion. It will often be better placed than the supplier to know what sort of advertising and promotional campaigns will succeed in the territory. Wood Magic may see this as a valuable contribution which Bois Massif can make to the success of Wood Magic's furniture in France. However, the supplier may wish to reserve the right to vet the distributor's activities, especially if it wants to keep a reasonably uniform brand image over several different territories. The supplier may also wish to provide that the distributor spends a minimum sum each year (or quarter, or month as the case may be) on advertising and promotion.

5.5.3.3 Stock

The distributor will inevitably hold stock – it has actually bought the products from the supplier. The agreement will therefore need to provide for numerous matters relating to stock, including the following:

(a) How much stock should the distributor carry?

(b) What procedure should the distributor follow when it orders and pays for the goods?

(c) What procedure should the distributor follow for returning unsatisfactory goods?

(d) When are title and risk in the goods to pass to the distributor?

(e) Is it necessary to insure the products (eg, while they are in transit from supplier to distributor)? If so, who should do this?

(f) What is to happen to stock if the agreement is terminated? The supplier often faces a dilemma here, especially when Article 81 EC could apply to the agreement. If the distributor is still holding stock after termination, it may deal with it in ways which could damage the brand's reputation (eg, sell it cut-price in markets or through discount shops). However, because the stock is the distributor's own property, to deal with as it sees fit, any clause in the agreement which obliges the distributor to sell the stock back to the supplier on termination potentially restricts competition, and could infringe Article 81 EC. In most cases, the supplier will have to decide whether the risk of competition law problems is greater than that of harm to the supplier's reputation. However, note that a clause which gives the distributor the option of selling the stock back to the supplier (rather than forcing the distributor to do this) should not cause competition law problems, as the distributor is not then obliged to deal with its own property in a particular way. Subject to these points, any clause dealing with the fate of stock on termination is more likely to be an aid to negotiation than anything else.

(g) What is to happen to any advertising or promotional material on termination?

(h) What is to happen to obsolete stock? If the agreement requires the distributor to sell it back to the supplier, competition law problems may arise (in the same way as in (f) above). The parties should try to come to a workable compromise which will prevent obsolete stock affecting the market for new stock.

5.5.3.4 Confidentiality and intellectual property

The areas of confidentiality and intellectual property may be more relevant in a distribution agreement than in an agency agreement. As the distributor is actually buying the products and then selling them on, it may be necessary to supply the distributor with confidential information relating to the products, or to allow the distributor to use the supplier's intellectual property. PCP K3-029, clause 8 gives a standard precedent for a confidentiality clause; PCP K3-028, clause 7 covers intellectual property.

5.5.3.5 Competing products

The supplier may want the distributor to agree not to handle products which could compete with the products being supplied under the agreement. However, this may cause problems if the agreement could be subject to Article 81 EC, as being potentially restrictive of competition. For more detail on how this might be handled, see **Chapter 22** and PCP K3-023, clause 2.8.

5.5.4 The supplier's duties

If dealt with separately (the PCP agreement, for example, does not do this), the list of supplier's duties is likely to be comparatively small. It may be appropriate to deal with the following:

(a) Will the supplier need to supply any promotional literature, models or samples of the goods to allow the distributor to market them properly?

(b) Should the supplier be obliged to supply the distributor with information which may help the distributor to market the goods?

(c) Is the supplier prepared to offer the distributor an indemnity against defects in the products? If so, what liabilities will it cover? In addition, does the supplier wish to give limited warranties to the distributor (eg, to cut down the protection given by s 14 of SGA 1979 if English law applies)? PCP K3-030, clause 9 illustrates how this may be done.

5.5.5 Sale of goods terms

Because the supplier will be selling goods to the distributor, it will be necessary to include in the agreement suitable terms to cover this sale of goods. For discussion of the basic terms in a sale of goods agreement, see ***Business Law and Practice*** and **Chapter 2** of this book. Consider particularly in relation to a distribution agreement:

(a) Are the supplier's sales to the distributor to be on the supplier's standard terms (see PCP K3-024, clause 3.9)? If so, the agreement should make clear what these are. Perhaps the best way of doing this is to set them out in a schedule to the agreement, so that both parties are certain which terms apply.

(b) Which basic sale of goods terms (such as price, payment, delivery, description and quality) need to be included in the distribution agreement? Note that the term relating to price will be of particular importance to the distributor; it will make its money from the difference between the price at which it buys the goods from the supplier and the price at which it can sell them to its customers.

5.5.6 Termination

The termination of the agreement and the consequences of termination may be handled in a number of ways (see, eg, PCP K3-032, clause 11 on termination and K3-033, clause 12 on consequences of termination). One matter which will require particular care (for the reasons outlined in **5.5.3.3**) is disposal of stock on termination, which the solicitor may feel is better dealt with here than in the 'stock' clause. Note that it is relatively rare for distributors to be entitled by law to compensation on termination (compare the position of agents under the Commercial Agents Regulations 1993; see **5.3.6.3**), but this may be relevant in certain jurisdictions (not the UK). The supplier, may, however, be prepared to agree to include a term in the agreement providing for compensation.

5.5.7 Miscellaneous

Like an agency agreement, a distribution agreement usually has a 'boiler-plate'. Many of the miscellaneous clauses will be the same as those arising in an agency agreement (see, eg, PCP K3, clause 10 on force majeure, clause 14 on arbitration and proper law, and clause 15 on notices and service).

5.6 Structure of the agreements at a glance

The following lists summarise the likely structure of the two agreements previously considered.

Agency

(a) Date, parties, recitals.
(b) Interpretation clause.
(c) Appointment of the agent.
(d) Agent's rights and duties.
(e) Principal's rights and duties.
(f) Financial provisions.
(g) Termination (if not dealt with elsewhere).
(h) Boiler-plate clauses.
(i) Signatures.
(j) Schedules.

Distribution

(a) Date, parties, recitals.
(b) Interpretation clause.
(c) Appointment of the distributor.
(d) Standard terms of sale (may be reserved to a schedule).
(e) Distributor's rights and duties.
(f) Supplier's rights and duties.
(g) Termination (if not dealt with elsewhere).
(h) Boiler-plate clauses.
(i) Signatures.
(j) Schedules.

5.7 Other types of marketing agreement

Given the nature of Wood Magic's business operations, it is unlikely for the moment to need to consider anything other than agency and distribution. However, if it continues to be successful and the business develops, other marketing situations may arise.

5.7.1 Licensing

Assume that Wood Magic comes up with a very popular new product (eg, a new design of chair), but that it does not have the resources to manufacture and distribute enough of the new product to satisfy customer demand. It therefore grants a licence to a much larger furniture manufacturing business, allowing that business to use Wood Magic's designs to make and sell the chair. Very broadly, the licence agreement will permit the licensee to do this in return for payment to Wood Magic (possibly a one-off licence fee, but more likely continuing payments of royalties on chairs manufactured and sold).

Licensing agreements (or simply 'licences') will usually involve the licensing of intellectual property rights. For example, Wood Magic may own design rights (see **Chapter 16**) in relation to the chair, which it will license to the furniture manufacturer. They may also involve competition law considerations. Intellectual property rights generally are dealt with in **Chapters 11** to **19** and the competition law aspects of licensing in **Chapter 23**.

5.7.2 Franchising

In the example given at **5.2.1**, Wood Magic decided to extend its custom-made furniture business by opting for an agency agreement. Another way of extending this business format would be to franchise the Wood Magic 'concept' of furniture making. This would mean that Wood Magic (the franchisor) would establish a 'Wood Magic' uniform business format, which it would then authorise other businesses (the franchisees) to use in return for payment. In the franchise agreement, Wood Magic would lay down conditions and specifications for the franchisees to meet (eg, what their premises should look like, how they should offer the furniture-making service to customers). This would allow Wood Magic to extend this part of its business without having to raise capital to do so, while still retaining considerable control over what the franchisee does with the business.

A franchise agreement often involves the franchisor giving the franchisee the right to use the franchisor's intellectual property rights (eg, the 'Wood Magic' name may be a registered trade mark, and intellectual property rights and trade secrets may be involved in the design and manufacture of the furniture). There may also be competition law considerations (see **Chapter 23**).

5.7.3 Joint venture

The nature of joint ventures and their likely advantages and disadvantages are dealt with in **Appendix 1** of ***Business Law and Practice***. A joint venture may become relevant if Wood Magic's directors come up with a project which requires input from another business with different but complementary skills. For example, assume that the directors decide to develop a range of upholstered furniture: they may seek to set up a joint venture with a company specialising in furnishing fabrics. If they did so, the two businesses would normally pool their resources to set up a separate joint venture company to carry out the project.

5.8 Conclusion

This chapter can do no more than give an outline introduction to two important types of commercial agreement. Further exploration of other agency and distribution precedents (and, indeed, of precedents for other types of marketing agreement, such as franchising) is therefore recommended. The book already mentioned in this chapter (Rosenberg, *Practical Commercial Precedents* (Sweet & Maxwell)) provides a wide range of precedents for commercial agreements generally.

Chapter 6
Consumer Credit Act 1974

6.1	Introduction	97
6.2	The Consumer Credit Act 1974 and commercial work	97
6.3	An outline guide to the CCA 1974	98
6.4	Consumer credit agreements	99
6.5	Common forms of consumer credit agreements	103
6.6	Terminology and examples	104
6.7	Further reading	106

6.1 Introduction

This chapter provides a brief guide to the Consumer Credit Act 1974 (CCA 1974) by summarising its main provisions and indicating how it may be relevant to commercial practice. The points it makes are particularly relevant to the financing of agreements; for more on this, see **6.2.1** and **6.2.2** below.

The law on consumer credit in the UK has changed over the past few years in a number of respects as a result of the Consumer Credit Act 2006 (CCA 2006).

For the most part, the CCA 2006 amends the CCA 1974 (and a number of other statutes) rather than containing 'free-standing' provisions. The DTI's explanatory notes relating to the CCA 2006 indicate that the purpose of the CCA 2006 was to reform the CCA 1974 in the following ways:

(a) to provide for the regulation of all consumer credit and consumer hire agreements subject to certain exemptions;

(b) to make provision in relation to the licensing of providers of consumer credit, consumer hire and ancillary credit services, and the functions and powers of the OFT in relation to licensing (this is rather misleading, in that the CCA 1974 and secondary legislation already make provision in all these areas; it would be more accurate to say that the CCA 2006 makes further, and potentially more effective, provision in these areas);

(c) to enable debtors to challenge unfair relationships with creditors;

(d) to provide for an Ombudsman scheme to hear complaints in relation to businesses licensed under the CCA 1974 (as amended).

These were all areas in relation to which the CCA 1974 was perceived to have significant weaknesses.

In addition, there is a European Commission proposal for a directive to update the Consumer Credit Directive (Directive 87/102/EEC). This draft directive was originally adopted in 2002, but is still undergoing consultation and revision. At the time of writing (September 2009), it is still unclear when the directive is likely to be adopted.

6.2 The Consumer Credit Act 1974 and commercial work

Despite the reference to 'Consumer' in its title, the CCA 1974 is frequently relevant to commercial practice, and it is important for the commercial solicitor to have at least an outline knowledge of its provisions. The main points to be aware of are discussed below.

6.2.1 The Act may be relevant when advising commercial clients who are finance providers ('creditors')

This point makes it very important for the commercial solicitor to be aware of the scope and effect of the CCA 1974. As explained in more detail at **6.4**, the Act (and secondary legislation made under it) lays down many rules which creditors must observe in relation to credit agreements, and the consequences of infringement of these rules can be severe (eg, inability to enforce any agreement against the debtor, which in practice may make it impossible for a creditor to recover money lent under the agreement or enforce the payment of interest). It is therefore vital for the solicitor to know when the Act will apply and to be able to advise on the detail of how to comply with the Act: all sorts of finance-providing clients, such as banks, finance houses and credit card companies, are potentially within its scope.

6.2.2 The Act may be relevant when advising certain commercial clients who wish to obtain finance for their business activities

As explained in more detail at **6.3**, the CCA 1974 applies to credit transactions between a business ('the creditor') and an individual ('the debtor') where the creditor provides credit to the debtor. Thus, some commercial clients (eg, sole traders) can benefit from the Act's protection when entering into credit agreements (eg, bank loans) because, as individuals, they will qualify as debtors under the Act.

6.3 An outline guide to the CCA 1974

It is very important to remember that the main objective of the CCA 1974 is the protection of the debtor. It seeks to achieve this objective in two ways:

(a) the regulation of the consumer credit 'industry' (this is done by way of a licensing system and the provision of detailed rules covering how creditors can advertise and seek business generally); and

(b) the control of individual agreements between creditors and debtors.

6.3.1 Regulation

6.3.1.1 Licensing (CCA 1974, ss 21–41)

A creditor who wishes to carry on a consumer credit or consumer hire business (see **6.3.2**), must obtain a licence from the Office of Fair Trading (OFT) (s 21(1)). Licences can be revoked, suspended or varied if, for example, the OFT believes that the licence-holder is acting improperly. Any agreement made by an unlicensed trader is unenforceable without a validating order from the OFT (s 40). In practice, this means that the creditor will, for example, be unable to demand payments of interest or repayment of the credit without the OFT's sanction. Schedule 1 to the Act also makes unlicensed trading a criminal offence.

Note that although the CCA 2006 makes numerous detailed amendments to the licensing regime, the general scheme summarised above remains in place.

6.3.1.2 Restrictions on advertising and seeking business

The CCA 1974 itself contains a general prohibition on false or misleading advertising. However, the detailed rules on this point can be found in the Consumer Credit (Advertisement) Regulations 2004 (SI 2004/1484).

6.3.2 Control of individual agreements

The CCA 1974 covers:

(a) consumer credit agreements (s 8);

(b) consumer hire agreements (s 15);

(c) certain 'linked transactions' (s 19).

In practice, the Act is capable of covering virtually all forms of consumer credit, including hire purchase, conditional sale and credit sale agreements, loans and most credit cards. Certain mortgages are also covered. There is a summary at the end of this chapter of how the main forms of credit work.

The following summary concentrates on the consumer credit agreement. Note, however, that by s 15, the Act will apply when an individual, eg, a sole trader, enters into certain agreements to hire goods; this could cover, for example, commercial clients who hire business equipment.

6.4 Consumer credit agreements

Section 8 of the CCA 1974 defines a consumer credit agreement as a personal credit agreement (ie, an agreement under which the person receiving credit is an individual; the creditor can be 'any other person') whereby 'the creditor provides the debtor with credit of any amount'.

'Individual' was, until recently, defined by s 189 of the CCA 1974 as including a partnership. However, as a result of the changes made to s 189 by the CCA 2006, a partnership only qualifies as an 'individual' for the purposes of the CCA 1974 if it consists of two or three partners, not all of whom are bodies corporate.

As a result of changes made by the CCA 2006, all consumer credit agreements are regulated by the CCA 1974 unless specifically exempted (a similar change has been made to the definition of 'consumer hire agreement' under s 15 of the CCA 1974).

By s 9, 'credit' includes a cash loan, or any other form of financial accommodation; this is wide enough to cover any circumstances in which a customer is allowed time to pay.

Such an agreement is 'regulated' by the Act unless it is exempt. Exempt agreements are defined by s 16 of the Act and the Consumer Credit (Exempt Agreements) Order 1989 (SI 1989/869, as amended). They include, for example, agreements for normal trade credit, and credit card agreements where all the debtor's indebtedness must be discharged by a single payment (eg, the type of agreement sometimes known as a 'charge card' agreement; see further **6.5.5**). Many agreements for land mortgages are also exempt.

The CCA 2006 added two new exemptions to this list:

(a) Section 3 of the CCA 2006 inserts a new s 16A into the CCA 1974, allowing the Secretary of State to make an order exempting agreements with 'high net worth' debtors or hirers from regulation by the CCA 1974. What constitutes a 'high net worth' individual for this purpose is fixed by statutory instrument, the Consumer Credit (Exempt Agreements) Order 2007 (SI 2007/1168).

(b) Section 4 of the CCA 2006 inserts a new s 16B into the CCA 1974, which exempts agreements from regulation by the CCA 1974 where they are wholly or predominantly for the purposes of the debtor's or hirer's business, and the credit or hire payment exceeds £25,000.

However, the new provisions on unfair relationships (see **6.4.1.5** below) still apply in both of these situations.

6.4.1 The Act's protection for individual agreements

The CCA 1974 aims to provide protection for the debtor at every stage of an agreement's 'lifetime'.

6.4.1.1 Prior to making the agreement

Both parties need to be aware that the potential debtor has certain important rights even before the agreement has been concluded:

(a) the right to withdraw (s 57): this makes it clear that the debtor can withdraw from a transaction before it has become binding and, in particular, makes communication of withdrawal easier;

(b) a special right, in land mortgage cases, for the potential debtor to reflect on the wisdom of entering into the transaction before becoming bound by it (s 58). In practice, the CCA 1974 applies to comparatively few land mortgages; as noted at **6.4** above, many are exempt;

(c) by s 56, antecedent (ie, pre-contract) negotiations conducted by a supplier or credit-broker (a credit-broker is someone who puts potential debtors in touch with sources of credit) are deemed to be conducted by that person as agent for the creditor as well as in the supplier's or broker's own capacity.

An example of this last point may assist:

Example

Assume that a sole trader wishes to buy a van on hire purchase (HP). This sort of agreement works in such a way that, although there will be a contract (the hire purchase agreement) between the sole trader and the finance company and also between the garage and the finance company (in HP, the credit-broker literally sells the HP goods to the creditor, who is the person who actually supplies them to the debtor), there is no direct contract between the sole trader and the garage. This could cause a problem for the sole trader if the garage makes false or misleading statements about the van during pre-contract negotiations. Section 56 improves the debtor's position by deeming that such negotiations are conducted by the credit-broker as agent for the creditor, thus giving the debtor a right of action against the creditor in relation to the garage's false or misleading statements.

In addition, under the Consumer Credit (Disclosure of Information) Regulations 2004 (SI 2004/1481), the prospective debtor in most types of agreement has the right to be given a certain amount of pre-contract information, and to be given it in a prescribed manner.

6.4.1.2 On making the agreement

Sections 60–64 of the Act and the Consumer Credit (Agreements) Regulations 1983 (SI 1983/1555), as amended, lay down numerous formalities which an agreement must satisfy. The formalities relate to, for example:

(a) the size and legibility of print used;

(b) the contents of the agreement;

(c) the prominence of certain information;

(d) the way in which the agreement must be signed.

It is vital for creditors to comply with these formalities. If they do not, by s 65, the agreement is 'improperly executed' and unenforceable by the creditor without a court order under s 127. In the case of *Wilson v First County Trust Ltd* [2001] All ER (D) 28, the Court of Appeal held that s 127(3) of the CCA 1974 was incompatible with Article 6 of the European Convention for the Protection of Human Rights and Article 1 of the First Protocol to that Convention, on the grounds that the absolute bar on enforceability by the creditor contained in s 127(3) disproportionately infringed the creditor's Convention rights in relation to the policy aim of the section (essentially, s 127(3) provides that a court shall not make an enforcement order in certain circumstances where there has been a failure to comply with s 61(1)(a) on signature of the agreement). The Court made a declaration of incompatibility under the Human Rights Act 1998. However, on appeal to the House of Lords (*Wilson v First County Trust Ltd* [2003] UKHL 40), their Lordships ruled that the Court of Appeal had been wrong to make the declaration of incompatibility in relation to s 127(3). This was primarily because the cause of action in the case arose before the Human Rights Act came into force. However, the House of Lords was also of the opinion that even if s 127(3) did have the effect of interfering with rights under the Convention, the interference was justified.

There are also detailed rules on how many copies of the agreement the debtor must receive and when they must be provided; the sanction for non-compliance by the creditor is, again, unenforceability without a court order.

Both parties to a regulated agreement must also be aware that, in certain circumstances, the debtor has the right to cancel (without penalty) an agreement which has become binding upon him. The detailed rules on cancellation are outside the scope of this chapter, but the relevant provisions can be found in ss 67–73.

6.4.1.3 During the agreement

The debtor has the following rights:

(a) to receive certain information about the agreement (ss 77–79);

(b) in certain cases, to take action against the creditor for breach of contract or misrepresentation committed by the supplier (s 75).

The CCA 2006 makes certain amendments to ss 77–79 (as from 6 April 2008), but the basic ethos of the provisions (that debtors should be able to receive information during the course of the agreement) remains untouched.

It is very important to be aware that s 75 only applies to the kind of agreement where the creditor and supplier are different people. In consumer credit jargon, this type of agreement may be referred to as a 'three-party debtor-creditor-supplier agreement', or 'three-party DCS' agreement. This includes most credit cards and certain types of loan agreement, but not hire purchase (which is a 'two-party DCS' agreement), or ordinary bank loans where the debtor is actually given cash or a cheque (this is a 'debtor-creditor' or 'DC' agreement; for a fuller explanation of DC and DCS agreements, see **6.6.2**).

Example

Assume that a sole trader uses a credit card to buy goods from a retailer which cost £5,000. The goods turn out to be defective.

Obviously, the sole trader has a contract with the retailer, and could sue the retailer in relation to the defective goods in the usual way. However, s 75 provides that the credit card company is jointly and severally liable for breaches of contract committed by the retailer. This means that the sole trader could sue the credit card company in addition to, or even instead of, the retailer. This is often particularly useful if the retailer has gone out of business.

Note that:

(a) the same rule applies to misrepresentations made by the retailer;

(b) the goods bought must have a cash price of more than £100 but less than £30,000.

For many years, it was disputed whether s 75 applied to transactions entered into overseas. In 2004 the Office of Fair Trading (OFT) brought a test case to seek clarification (*Office of Fair Trading v Lloyds TSB Bank plc (1) Tesco Personal Finance Ltd (2) and American Express Services Europe Ltd (3)* [2004] EWHC 2600 (Comm)). The High Court held that where the contract was made entirely outside the UK, was governed by law other than that of a part of the UK, and the goods or services paid for by the credit card were supplied outside the UK, s 75 did not apply.

However, the OFT appealed against this decision and, in March 2006, the Court of Appeal allowed the appeal (*Office of Fair Trading v Lloyds TSB Bank plc and Others* [2006] EWCA Civ 268, [2007] QB 1).

The Court of Appeal held that, under s 75, the existence of the transaction, wherever it was entered into, was sufficient to provide a basis for the connected lender liability imposed by s 75 as long as it was financed by a DCS agreement falling within s 12(b) of the Consumer Credit Act 1974. In October 2007, the House of Lords upheld the Court of Appeal's judgment, noting that there was nothing in the language of s 75 to exclude foreign transactions ([2007] 3 WLR 733).

6.4.1.4 Ending the agreement

The CCA 1974 also gives protection to a debtor on the ending of the agreement. This is a difficult topic to summarise briefly, because the protection given may vary according to what type of agreement it is, and why it is being brought to an end. A solicitor advising either of the parties must always check these two points very carefully. In particular, a debtor under a DC agreement (eg, an ordinary bank loan) receives less protection than a debtor under a DCS agreement. The following main points are, however, worth noting:

(a) in many cases, the debtor is entitled to a warning in the form of a 'default notice' from the creditor (s 87) if the creditor wishes to do more than simply sue for arrears under the agreement (eg, terminate the agreement or repossess goods). The CCA 2006 makes some alterations to these default notice provisions to give debtors better protection;

(b) debtors who are in possession of goods which they do not own (under HP or conditional sale agreements) have special protection against repossession under ss 90 and 92;

(c) the debtor may be able to cancel the agreement under ss 67–73 without penalty (see **6.4.1.2**);

(d) the Act provides that, in many situations associated with the ending of agreements (eg, service of a default notice, creditor attempting to repossess goods), the debtor will have the right to apply to the county court, which has wide powers to look at the situation and make orders to sort it out (eg, a 'time order', which allows the debtor extra time to pay what he owes).

6.4.1.5 Extortionate credit bargains and unfair relationships

Sections 19–22 of the CCA 2006 repealed and replaced the extortionate credit bargain (ECB) provisions in ss 137–140 of the CCA 1974. These gave the court powers to deal with agreements which required the debtor to make 'grossly exorbitant payments' or otherwise 'grossly contravene the ordinary principles of fair dealing', and had attracted much criticism over the years. The ECB provisions were widely perceived to be ineffective in practice in controlling disadvantageous credit deals (eg, those with very high rates of interest, inordinately high repayments or unfair terms), and were regarded as failing to protect debtors adequately. The little case law which developed on ECBs showed that courts were reluctant to find that an agreement was an extortionate credit bargain.

The test which is now to be applied is one of 'unfair relationships' rather than 'extortionate credit bargains'. The intention is to allow the court to take into account a much wider range of matters in deciding whether there is an unfair credit relationship than it was able to do in deciding whether a credit bargain was extortionate. Broadly, the court must decide whether the relationship between debtor and creditor arising out of an agreement is unfair because of:

(a) the terms of the agreement; or

(b) the way in which the creditor operates the agreement; or

(c) any other thing done or not done by or on behalf of the creditor before the agreement is made.

This has been deliberately made very wide; in addition, the court can take into account all matters relating to debtor and creditor which it thinks relevant.

Under the new s 140B, which is inserted into the CCA 1974, the court is given the power to make a much wider range of specific orders to sort out the unfairness, including repayment of money or return of property to the debtor.

6.5 Common forms of consumer credit agreements

6.5.1 Hire purchase

A hire purchase (HP) agreement is a contract for the bailment of goods (ie, the debtor gets possession but not ownership of the goods) in return for periodical payments by the debtor (the HP instalment payments). Ownership of the goods does not pass to the debtor unless and until the contract terms are fulfilled, and one or more of the following occurs:

(a) the exercise of an option to purchase by the debtor;

(b) the doing of any other specified act;

(c) the happening of any other specified event.

The most common of these in practice is probably (a): in effect, the debtor notifies the creditor on payment of the last instalment that he now wishes to 'buy' the goods from the creditor and become their owner.

Example

Billy, a sole trader, wants to buy a van on HP for making deliveries. He selects the van from stock at Ace Motors, which puts him in touch with Mammoth Credit, a finance house. Mammoth Credit is prepared to give Billy credit by entering into an HP agreement with him. The arrangement which now results is often called the 'HP triangle'. In Consumer Credit Act terms, Billy is the debtor, Mammoth Credit the creditor, and Ace Motors the credit broker. Note that Mammoth is legally also the supplier of the goods under the agreement. Ace Motors will actually sell the van to Mammoth, and Mammoth will then bail the van to Billy, who makes instalment ('periodical') payments to Mammoth (ie, the finance house). Mammoth remains the owner of the van until one of the events noted above takes place.

6.5.2 Conditional sale

A conditional sale is an agreement for the sale of goods (or land) with the price payable by instalments, and under which ownership does not pass to the buyer until certain conditions are satisfied (eg, payment of the last instalment). Consequently, conditional sales are similar to HP agreements, and because ownership of the goods is retained by the creditor until the relevant condition is satisfied, extra protection for debtors under these agreements is incorporated into the CCA 1974.

6.5.3 Credit sale

A credit sale is similar to a conditional sale, except that ownership of the goods passes immediately to the buyer at the time of the contract, without any preconditions. The creditor allows credit to the buyer, who is allowed to pay the price by instalments.

6.5.4 Loan

The term 'loan' is generally used to denote a fixed-term loan by a bank or finance company, repayable by instalments. Loans may be secured or unsecured. They are often secured so that if the borrower defaults with payment, the lender can realise the security to recoup the money lent. A loan is often given to finance a particular transaction, for example the purchase of a car, as an alternative to buying the car under a HP or credit sale agreement. In a business context, however, the debtor may simply be obtaining the money for general business purposes (eg, a sole trader or partnership may borrow money from a bank to improve the business's general cash flow).

> **Example**
>
> Alma, a sole trader, arranges a loan of £10,000 from Midwest Bank to help improve her cash flow position. Midwest opens a loan account for her and puts the £10,000 into it. In Consumer Credit Act terms, Midwest Bank is the creditor and Alma the debtor, and the agreement is a DC agreement. Note that there is a variation on this situation called the 'connected loan', where the creditor does not provide the credit directly to the debtor, but instead provides it to a supplier of goods or services to assist the debtor with the purchase of those goods or services. For example, Ethel wants to buy a carpet from Floorworld; she arranges a loan from Tonto Credit, which pays the loan money directly to Floorworld. Ethel can now get her carpet (Floorworld has been paid), and she will make repayments of the loan to Tonto Credit. A connected loan is a DCS rather than DC agreement (see **6.6.2.2**).

6.5.5 Credit card

A credit card can be used to obtain cash, goods or services up to a stipulated credit limit. The supplier is subsequently paid by the credit card company (eg, Barclaycard), which, in due course, is reimbursed by the credit card holder, who will be charged interest at the end of the credit period if any money is still owing. Some card agreements demand payment in full at the end of a specified period (eg, Diner's Club and certain types of American Express card). These are commonly known as charge card agreements, and are exempt under CCA 1974, s 16 and the Consumer Credit (Exempt Agreements) Order 1989.

Care must be taken to distinguish between a genuine credit card (eg Barclaycard) and a card which does not, on closer investigation, involve the provision of credit. Examples of the latter include:

(a) a cash card used to obtain cash from an automated teller machine (ATM) or cash machine;

(b) a debit card used in conjunction with a current account. These cards dispense with the need for cheques. The card-holder's bank account is debited when the card is presented to pay for a transaction and there is no pre-set transaction limit. The only limit on the card's use is the amount of funds available to the card-holder under his current account. The most common examples of debit cards are Maestro and Delta cards;

(c) a cheque guarantee card issued by a bank or building society for use in connection with a cheque. The bank or building society guarantees payment of individual cheques in the amount shown on the card (often £50, but sometimes up to £200 or more);

(d) a pre-payment card issued in respect of a certain sum against the pre-payment of that sum. Examples include phone cards for use in connection with pay phones and cards to pay for photocopying.

The CCA 1974 will not apply to any card being used to perform these functions, as there is no 'credit' involved.

Note that many cards combine the functions (a), (b) and (c) ('multi-function' cards). Some multi-function cards also operate as credit cards; thus, with a multi-function card, if problems arise concerning its use, it is important to check exactly what function the card was being used to perform.

6.5.6 Bank overdraft

A bank overdraft occurs when a bank allows a customer to overdraw against his current account. The customer is regarded as owing money on the account, and this may be seen as the equivalent of a bank loan (the finance is simply being provided in a slightly different way).

6.6 Terminology and examples

Consumer credit is a topic with its own particular jargon. This section aims to define and explain some of the terms which you are most likely to come across, either in the Act or in relation to consumer credit generally.

6.6.1 Types of credit

6.6.1.1 Fixed-sum and running-account credit

Fixed-sum credit

As its name suggests, this is where the credit which the creditor provides to the debtor is a fixed sum (eg, loans, HP, conditional and credit sales).

Running-account credit

In this sort of agreement, the amount of credit advanced will fluctuate from time to time, the amount available depending upon what transactions and what repayments have been made. Credit card and overdraft agreements fall into this category: both are, of course, normally subject to 'credit limits'.

6.6.1.2 Restricted- and unrestricted-use credit

The Act defines unrestricted-use credit (UUC); everything else is restricted-use credit (RUC).

Unrestricted-use credit

In this case, the credit is provided in such a way that the debtor is free to use it as he sees fit (ie, he gets his hands on money or the equivalent of money, as with a bank loan provided in the form of a cheque payable to the debtor, or money paid into an account in the debtor's name; overdrafts also fall into this category).

Restricted-use credit

In this case, the credit is provided in such a way that the debtor is not free to use it as he sees fit, chiefly because he does not get his hands on money or the equivalent of money. Examples include HP, conditional sale and credit cards being used to buy goods. In this last case, the credit is restricted in the sense that the card can only be used at outlets which accept that card.

Note that it is irrelevant for the purpose of deciding if credit is RUC or UUC whether the agreement stipulates how the credit is to be used (eg, a bank loan advanced on condition that the debtor buys a car). If the debtor puts the credit to a different use, this will be breach of contract, but it does not stop the credit being RUC.

6.6.2 Classification of agreements

The CCA 1974 makes a number of important distinctions between DC and DCS agreements. For example, it is crucial to know whether an agreement is DC or DCS when considering whether it is regulated or exempt. In addition, many important provisions of the Act (notably ss 56 and 75) apply only to DCS agreements.

The key factor is the relationship between the supplier of the credit and the supplier of the goods, land or services.

6.6.2.1 Where they are the same person

In this case, the agreement is a DCS agreement (often known as a 'two-party DCS' agreement, although the Act does not in fact use this term). Examples include credit sale agreements (eg, where a shop sells goods and allows the buyer to pay for them in instalments) and HP agreements (where the finance company provides credit and supplies the goods to the debtor, having previously bought them from the retailer).

6.6.2.2 Where they are not the same person, but have business arrangements between themselves

This type of agreement is often known as a 'three-party' DCS agreement. Most credit card agreements work in this way: the credit card company has contractual arrangements with a wide variety of outlets (shops, garages, theatres, etc) under which the outlet is authorised to accept the card. Note that a three-party DCS situation contains two other contracts: the credit card agreement between the card company and the debtor; and the contract between the debtor and the supplier, known as a 'linked transaction' in Consumer Credit Act terms. Both of these contracts will normally be regulated by the 1974 Act.

6.6.2.3 Where they are not the same person and have no business arrangements

This is a DC agreement. Many loan agreements work in this way; eg, a sole trader gets a bank loan and then uses the money to buy a car from a garage. There will be no 'business arrangements' between the bank (creditor) and the garage (supplier). Although the matter is not entirely free from doubt, it is normally assumed that when a credit card is used to obtain cash, this is a DC agreement.

6.6.2.4 Types of credit activity

The CCA 1974 applies to all types of credit transactions, and also to certain 'ancillary credit businesses'. By s 145, this is defined as any business which comprises or relates to:

(a) credit brokerage;

(b) debt-adjusting (renegotiation of debts on debtors' behalf);

(c) debt-counselling (advising debtors on the payment of debts);

(d) debt-collecting;

(e) the operation of a credit reference agency (ie, the kind of business that collects financial information on debts for the purpose of providing it to others, eg potential creditors).

This list is expanded by the CCA 2006 to include debt administration and credit information services, but this expansion has, at the time of writing, yet to come into force.

6.6.2.5 Working out what 'credit' is

As the amount of credit is one of the factors which determines whether or not an agreement is regulated, it is important to be able to identify the various sums which are likely to be involved in a credit transaction, and to appreciate which of these sums constitute the 'credit'. This is best done by way of example:

Example

Tom wishes to buy a new car with a cash price of £15,000, but cannot afford to pay for it all out of his own resources. The garage therefore arranges for him to enter a HP agreement with a finance company on the following terms:

(a) he will pay a cash deposit of £2,000;

(b) he will receive a part-exchange allowance of £7,000 for his existing car;

(c) he will pay 40 monthly instalments of £200 each; and

(d) he will pay an administration fee of £50.

The total payable is £17,050 (ie, the aggregate of everything he has to pay to the finance house). This figure is also known as the total price.

The total charge for credit is £2,050 (ie, the total price less the cash price of the car (£17,050 – £15,000).

The credit advanced under the agreement is £6,000 (ie, the total price, less the total charge for credit and less any sums which Tom himself is providing (ie, £17,050 – (£2,050 + £2,000 + £7,000)).

6.7 Further reading

Goode, *Consumer Credit Law and Practice* (Butterworths, 2000)

Part I Summary
Commercial Agreements

Topic	*Summary*
Definition	There is no single definition of what constitutes a 'commercial agreement' or 'commercial contract', although a basic starting point would normally be 'a deal made between two (or more) parties, both or all of whom are in business'.
Scope	A variety of elements might be relevant in a commercial agreement: the principles of commercial drafting, contracts for the sale of goods, exclusion and restriction of liability, other types of contract under which goods pass, agency and distribution agreements and the principles of consumer credit.
Contracts for the sale of goods	These are, broadly speaking, contracts between a buyer and seller, under which the ownership of goods changes hands in return for the payment of a money consideration known as the price, and where the buyer is not intending to resell the goods (cf 'Distribution agreements' below).
Sale of Goods Act 1979 (as amended)	Although normal principles of freedom of contract apply to commercial agreements, the Sale of Goods Act 1979 provides a type of regulatory framework for sale of goods agreements.
Implied terms	The Sale of Goods Act 1979 implies a variety of terms into contracts for the sale of goods; which terms will be implied depend on the circumstances of the contract (for example, some implied terms, such as those relating to price, are implied only where the parties have not expressly or impliedly decided the matter for themselves).
Duties of the parties	The Sale of Goods Act 1979 outlines the duties of the buyer and seller under a sale of goods agreement; however, virtually all these duties can be modified or excluded by agreement between the parties.
Rights of the parties	The Act also sets out the rights of the parties (eg, the buyer's right to reject the goods; the seller's rights if the buyer fails to pay for the goods).
Remedies	The Act also outlines the remedies which are available if either party breaches the contract.
Retention of title	This is a particularly important device in a commercial agreement for the sale of goods: the right of the seller to retain ownership of the goods until the buyer has paid for them.
Exclusion and restriction of liability	This is another important device: the ability of either party to exclude or restrict liability for breach of contract. Normal contractual principles of incorporation and construction apply to exemption clauses in commercial contracts; so does the Unfair Contract Terms Act 1977.

Topic	*Summary*
UCTA 1977	UCTA 1977 generally allows parties to commercial contracts more freedom to use exemption clauses than it allows for consumer contracts. With a very few exceptions (eg, purported exclusion of the implied condition relating to title, which is always void) liability can generally be excluded in a commercial agreement in so far as it is reasonable.
Other contracts under which goods pass	These include contracts of exchange, barter, hire purchase, conditional sale, work and materials and contracts of hire. They are governed by a variety of statutory provisions, all of which are closely modelled on the Sale of Goods Act 1979, so the points made above concerning implied terms are also relevant here.
Contracts for services	These are governed by the Supply of Goods (Implied Terms) Act 1982; the Act implies a small number of terms into contracts for the supply of services, including a term that the services will be provided with reasonable skill and care.
Marketing agreements	Some agreements involving goods concentrate on getting the goods to a wider market. Examples include agency agreements and distribution agreements.
Agency agreements	Although agency agreements come in a number of different types, the classic sales agency agreement involves one party (the principal) giving authority to the other party (the agent) to take actions on the principal's behalf to find customers for the principal's goods or services.
Commercial Agents Regulations 1993	Agency agreements are to a large extent governed by the normal law of contract and law of agency. However, a substantial number of agency agreements are also subject to the Commercial Agents Regulations 1993, which lay down a framework of rules concerning the rights and duties of each party (notably the agent's right to a payment on termination of the agency agreement).
Distribution agreements	A distribution agreement is fundamentally based on a sale of goods agreement. However, in a distribution agreement the parties specifically agree that the buyer of the goods (the distributor) is buying them for the purpose of re-selling them, rather than for end-use in its own business. Distribution agreements are chiefly subject to the ordinary law of contract (and sale of goods), but may have competition law implications.
Consumer credit	In spite of its name, the law on consumer credit can be relevant to deals between two business parties, where one is granting credit to another. This is because the definition of agreements which are regulated by the Consumer Credit Act 1974 will cover some sole traders and partnerships.
Consumer Credit Act 1974 (as amended by the Consumer Credit Act 2006)	The 1974 Act, as amended, seeks to regulate all stages of the credit cycle (pre-contract negotiations, the granting of the credit, the lifetime of the credit agreement, its termination and consequences of termination). Very broadly, its aim is to protect the users of credit; it seeks to do this in a variety of ways (eg, presenting the contents of credit agreements so that potential debtors know what they are getting into and are, as far as possible, protected against unfair terms).

Part II

INTERNATIONAL SALE AGREEMENTS

Chapter 7
Introduction to International Sale Agreements

An international sale of goods contract will need to cover the same type of issues as a domestic agreement (eg, price, payment, delivery). However, there are added complications. Generally, UCTA 1977 does not apply (see s 26), although there are anomalous situations where it can be relevant. On the other hand, if the contract is subject to English law, the SGA 1979 will apply to an international contract.

There are various additional, or increased, risks. For example:

(a) physical risks to the goods associated with sea or air transport and the associated extra handling;

(b) the increased costs of long-distance freight carriage;

(c) the increased delivery period because of long journeys;

(d) financial risks, for example due to changes in currency exchange rates;

(e) increased risks of not being paid, or being paid late, possibly by reason of buyer insolvency;

(f) political risks, possibly even of war, or terrorist attack or blockades;

(g) legal risks if the contract is subject to foreign law (are you qualified to advise on foreign law?); and

(h) the difficulty of applying remedies attaching to the possession of goods and asserting the seller's title, as the goods leave the seller's jurisdiction.

Some issues can be covered by insurance, if it is economically viable for the seller to purchase it. Other issues can be covered by care in drafting the contract. Many problems can be solved by the parties using a standard contract drawn up by a trade association, or by an international body. For example, there are the GAFTA contract forms of the Grain and Feed Trade Association, or those of the London Metal Exchange. The ones which we shall look at in this Part are the Incoterms, produced by the International Chamber of Commerce. These are a set of standard form rules which can be used in various commercial situations. It is for the parties to choose which one is best for them. They are produced in a variety of languages, so the use of Incoterms can avoid misunderstandings due to language problems.

Because of these additional factors and complications, international sale of goods contracts commonly include terms dealing with international carriage arrangements, insurance provision, complex financing and credit provision, and closely related payment provisions. Any of these matters may require the parties to enter contractual arrangements with third parties, in order to fulfil their obligations under the principal sale of goods contract.

Some familiarity with the terminology and commercial concepts used in international sales is indispensable to the student of commercial law; after all, the 'law merchant' is probably the earliest identifiable form of internationally recognised law. The English courts of the Middle Ages were very familiar with the mercantile customs and practices of both North Europe and the Mediterranean lands, and were prepared to apply laws which had their roots in Roman times. Part II of this work is designed to give a flavour of these very large bodies of law, but an in-depth analysis is beyond its scope.

Chapter 8
Choice of Jurisdiction and Law

8.1	Introduction	113
8.2	Brussels II – Regulation 44/2001	113
8.3	Rome Convention	116
8.4	Rome I – Regulation 593/2008	118

8.1 Introduction

The whole area of jurisdiction, and of law, has been given a boost in the minds of commercial lawyers by the advent of e-commerce. Today, international contracts can be concluded with a mouse-click. The collision of opposing jurisdictions is therefore an increasingly important issue.

Jurisdiction determines which courts could have power to resolve the dispute. Normally, any contracts you deal with in practice would be subject to the jurisdiction of the English courts. Choice of law obviously means choosing which law would apply to the contract. Normally, both law and jurisdiction would be decided by a clause in the contract. If that has not been done then the Convention and EU Regulation 44/2001 discussed below will apply.

The basic principle is that if the parties choose the law and jurisdiction which they wish to cover the contract then that choice prevails. In practice, any competently drafted written contract should have a clause covering law and jurisdiction. However, there will be circumstances where the issues need to be resolved. The 1980 Rome Convention deals with choice of law. It is implemented by the Contracts (Applicable Law) Act 1990, but see **8.4** below, which deals with changes to Community law which will affect this from 17 December 2009.

Choice of jurisdiction is now dealt with by EU Regulation 44/2001, also known as Brussels II; this extends to 'civil and commercial' matters. The main change from its predecessor is that it gives greater protection to the consumer, including when the consumer contracts with a business on the Internet. (There is also a draft convention on jurisdiction and foreign judgments under the Hague Conference on Private International Law, but it is unclear how it will relate to Brussels II if the Hague Convention does come into existence.)

For the record, the Lugano Convention still determines jurisdiction between EU Member States and the European Free Trade Agreement (EFTA) States (of which there are now very few). We will not consider it further.

However, there are circumstances where the outcome of the Conventions would be different for law and for jurisdiction, so it is feasible to have an English court hearing a dispute under German law, for example. In such circumstances, the English court will be advised by experts in the law in question, here that of Germany. (For an example of an English court deciding a case under foreign law, see the *Glencore* litigation at **2.15.6**, where the court considered the law of *Fujairah,* as well as English law.) The English court will treat the expert evidence as a type of fact evidence and draw conclusions accordingly.

8.2 Brussels II – Regulation 44/2001

This deals with jurisdiction. It applies, generally, where defendants are domiciled in Member States. (Strictly speaking, Brussels II does not apply to Denmark which is still bound by Brussels I.) Domicile is decided without regard to nationality in this context. The general scheme of the Regulation is that jurisdiction should usually be available to the defendant in the Member State of his domicile, except in a few, well defined circumstances.

8.2.1 The basic position under Brussels II – general jurisdiction

The basic rule is that a defendant, domiciled in a Member State, is sued in the courts of his home country, subject to the other provisions of the Regulation (Article 2). This rule is said to give 'general jurisdiction' to those courts. There are exceptions to the rule. The major ones are contracts, torts, situations where the defendant has a local branch office, real property, companies, IP, insurance, consumer contracts, and employment matters, see **8.2.2–8.2.4**. In *Owusu v Jackson* (Case C-281/02) (2005), the ECJ held that Article 2 is a mandatory provision, and therefore an English court could not decline jurisdiction in favour of a court of a non-Member State (Jamaica). (See **8.2.5** for contracting out of Article 2.)

8.2.2 Special jurisdiction – contract, tort and local branch offices

If the dispute is a contract matter then there is the option of suing the defendant in the Member State where the contract should have been performed (Article 5(1)(a)). If more than one obligation is in question, the Brussels II Regulation gives jurisdiction to the courts of the place of performance of the principal obligation.

In the case of a sale of goods contract, it is presumed that the 'place of performance of the obligation in question' is the Member State where the goods were delivered, or should have been delivered (Article 5(1)(b)). Thus, for sale of goods contracts, there is only one 'place of performance of the obligation in question' for the whole of the contract. See *Scottish & Newcastle International Ltd v Othon Ghalanos Ltd* [2008] UKHL 11; [2008] 2 All ER (Comm) 369, where a seller of goods had arranged an international contract which, on its proper analysis, could be seen to be of a type which created a delivery within the UK. That was enough to give the English court jurisdiction to hear the seller's claim for non-payment. See **9.5.2.3** for discussion of 'FOB with services' contracts.

This type of rule can still give rise to difficulties where there are multiple delivery points (see *Color Drack Gmbh v Lexx International Vertriebs Gmbh* (Case C-386/08) [2008] 1 All ER (Comm) 168).

In matters relating to tort, the defendant may be sued in the courts of the Member State where the harmful event occurred, or may occur (Article 5(3)).

If the defendant has a branch or office in another Member State then he may also be sued there (Article 5(5)) if the dispute arises out of the operations of that branch or office.

The special jurisdiction in Article 5 arises in addition to the general jurisdiction in Article 2, so that, in some cases, there will be a choice of forum (see **8.2.5** and **8.2.6**).

8.2.3 Exclusive jurisdiction

Under Article 22 of Regulation 44/2001, there are situations in which certain courts are regarded as having particular expertise and so are given exclusive jurisdiction. This overrides the normal rules on general and special jurisdiction. The main instances are:

(a) proceedings concerning rights in rem in immovable property, or tenancies of immovable property: the Regulation normally gives exclusive jurisdiction to the courts of the Member State in which the property is situated;

(b) proceedings concerning the constitution or dissolution of companies: the Regulation gives exclusive jurisdiction the courts of the Member State in which the company has its 'seat' (in the UK this will usually be the registered office); and

(c) proceedings concerning the registration or validity of registered intellectual property rights: the Regulation gives exclusive jurisdiction to the courts of the Member State in which the right is registered, or in which registration has been applied for. This will not automatically extend to infringement proceedings if registration or validity are not in question.

8.2.4 Special rules for insurance, consumer contracts and employment contracts

These are situations in which one party is considered to have greater economic power than the other. In order to redress the balance, the rules on jurisdiction are shifted in favour of the 'weaker' party. Generally he can be sued only in his own courts, but is given the choice as to whether he sues the other party in his own courts or in the other party's courts. There are limits to the extent to which the parties can contract out of these rules.

The rules on consumer contracts are contained in Articles 15–17. They apply in various situations set out in Article 15. The most usual of these is where the consumer concludes a contract with a person 'who pursues commercial or professional activities in the Member State of the consumer's domicile'. This provision should be fairly self-explanatory. However, Article 15 also applies where the other party 'by any means, directs [his commercial or professional] activities' to the Member State in which the consumer is domiciled. This is taken to include Internet selling (ie, e-commerce: see **19.10**). So, Articles 15–18 will protect the Internet consumer by requiring that he be sued only in his own courts, whilst giving him a choice as to where he sues the seller.

This can mean that an Internet business could be sued in any jurisdiction in which its website happens to be accessible to potential customers. It might be worthwhile considering which jurisdictions the business is prepared to deal with. Most businesses that sell goods can control this by refusing orders from countries to which they are not prepared to sell, and by not sending the goods. It would be harder to exercise such control in a business involving the sale of on-line products such as plane tickets, or the downloading of software.

8.2.5 Contracting out – express choice of jurisdiction clauses

Article 23 allows the parties to override the rules on general and special jurisdiction by agreeing that the courts of a specified Member State are to have jurisdiction. The Article lays down the formal requirements for such an agreement. Generally, it must be in writing, or at least evidenced in writing.

However, it is not possible to contract out of the rules on exclusive jurisdiction (in Article 22 – see **8.2.3**). There are also limits to the extent to which the parties can contract out of the rules on insurance, consumer and employment contracts. Generally, any contracting out of the effects of the Regulation in these three areas is only possible after the occasion for dispute has arisen.

8.2.6 First to file

The court which is first involved in the proceedings will generally have jurisdiction (Article 21). Any other court may decline jurisdiction, or stay proceedings if the actions are related (Article 22). It is possible to designate a particular court within a jurisdiction under Article 23; see *Anthony Snookes v Jani King (GB) Ltd* [2006] EWHC 289 (QB). This case also shows that the Regulation applies even where both parties are domiciled within one Member State.

A different problem arises with multiple defendants, some of which are domiciled in different Member States. In *FKI Engineering Ltd v DE Wind Holdings Ltd* [2008] EWCA Civ 316, the Court of Appeal held that Article 6(1) applied to give the English court jurisdiction to hear a claim against a German-domiciled defendant. The claim was contingent upon the outcome of proceedings already under way in the German courts. As the English courts were to hear claims against other defendants, arising out of the same factual situation and which raised the same issues, it was expedient to hear the claims against all the defendants together, to avoid the risk of irreconcilable judgments resulting from separate proceedings (in England and Germany).

In England, the principle of *forum non conveniens* means that the court could stay proceedings in the English court that have also been brought in another jurisdiction.

Judgments obtained in contracting States must be recognised and enforced, but with some exceptions (Articles 27 and 28). Thus, under Articles 27 and 28, any court of a Member State must stay the action before it, if another court within the EC has previously agreed to hear the case. In *JP Morgan Europe Limited v Primacom AG and others* [2005] EWHC 508, the defendant got in first and issued proceedings for a declaration in Germany that no interest was owed by it under the loan agreement. The English High Court subsequently held that it did not have jurisdiction to hear the matter until such time as the German courts decided whether or not they had jurisdiction. This decision was valid even though the commercial agreement in question had an express jurisdiction clause giving jurisdiction to the English courts.

For another decision involving Brussels I, see the *Bonnier* case at **19.10.3**.

8.3 Rome Convention

This applies, at the time of writing, to the Member States of the EU, and it contains the rules ascertaining the 'applicable law' of a contract. That is to say, the system of law which is properly applicable (either by the express choice of the parties, or, absent a choice, by the rules of the Convention) to contractual obligations in any situation involving a choice between the laws of different countries. This will change for the United Kingdom and the other Member States (excluding Denmark), which will, as regards contracts entered into after 17 December 2009, come under a different regime created by Regulation (EC) 593/2008, which is broadly aimed at facilitating the mutual recognition of judgments. There are some significant differences from the Rome Convention; these differences and Regulation 593/2008 are discussed at **8.4** below.

8.3.1 The basic position under the Rome Convention

Article 1(2) specifies the matters to which the Convention does not apply, for example wills and probate, and matters governed by company law.

Article 3(1) allows the parties to choose the law of the contract, either expressly or impliedly. If they have done so, then that is the applicable law that governs the contract.

If no such choice has been made then the contract will be governed by the law of the country with which it is most closely connected (Article 4(1)). Article 4(2) provides that the relevant country is the one where the party who is to effect 'characteristic performance' of the contract has its habitual residence. In the case of a company, this is the place where it has its central administration. 'Characteristic performance' is the performance for which money is due (ie, delivery of the goods, or the provision of a service). In *PT Pan Indonesia Bank Ltd TBK v Marconi Communications International Ltd* [2005] EWCA Civ 422, the Court of Appeal held that the contract in question was most closely connected with Indonesia, as that was where the goods and services were to be provided. However, the Court then used its discretion to decide that English law was the more appropriate, not least as the payment by documentary credit was to be made in England (see **10.4** for more on documentary credits).

In *Iran Continental Shelf Oil Co v Iri International Corp* [2002] EWCA Civ 1024, it was held that the Article 4(2) presumption that the US administration centre of the supplier required US law to apply was displaced by the contractual requirements that the UK office dealt with the performance of the contract. The applicable law was therefore that of England and Wales.

For some other examples of the Rome Convention in practice, see *American Motor Insurance Co v Cellstar Corporation and Another* [2003] EWCA Civ 206 and *Welex AG v Rosa Maritime Ltd (The 'Epsilon Rosa') (No 2)* [2002] EWHC 2035 (Comm), [2002] 2 Lloyd's Rep 701.

8.3.2 The exceptions to the 'characteristic performance' presumption

There are exceptions to Article 4(2), in Article 4(3), (4) and (5). These provisions create rebuttable presumptions as to the meaning of 'most closely connected', so that 'characteristic performance' is no longer the predominant factor.

Article 4(3) deals with a right in 'immovable property'. The presumption here is that the contract is most closely connected with the country where the immovable property is situated. This does not apply to contracts for repair or construction of immovable property.

Article 4(4) provides that the presumption in Article 4(1) does not apply to a contract for the carriage of goods (not *sale* of goods). In that case, it is the country where the carrier has its place of business if that is also the country of loading or discharging the goods, or if it is also the country where the consignor has its principal place of business.

Article 4(5) provides that the court may disregard the presumption in Article 4(2) if it appears that the contract is more closely connected with another country. In practice, it is likely that a court will endeavour to use this provision.

8.3.3 Local 'mandatory rules'

There are limitations on the use of the applicable law. If any provisions of the applicable law conflict with local laws of the jurisdiction where the dispute is heard, relating to the contract, those conflicting provisions of the applicable law cannot validly be used. These local law provisions are the 'mandatory rules' which are referred to in Article 7 of the Convention. These are 'rules' which cannot be derogated from (eg, in the case of the UK, the Financial Services and Markets Act 2000, the Unfair Terms in Consumer Contracts Regulations 1999, etc). Article 3(3) provides that the choice of foreign law by the parties will not prejudice the application of the mandatory rules of the home country to the contract. So, even if the applicable law was held to be, say, Austrian law, the Financial Services and Markets Act 2000 could also apply to a relevant dispute heard by a court in England and Wales, and would override any inconsistent provisions in Austrian law.

There are four particularly important situations in which the mandatory rules will take precedence over the applicable law. The first is where the contract is connected with only one country. In that situation, the parties cannot avoid their country's mandatory rules by choosing the law of another country as the applicable law. The second situation is where the applicable law conflicts with the mandatory rules of the country whose courts are hearing the dispute. So, for example, a commercial agency contract for UK activities could not prevent the application of the Commercial Agents (Council Directive) Regulations 1993 (SI 1993/3053) to the contract. These Regulations have long been recognised as mandatory rules. The other situations relate to consumer and employment contracts and are dealt with below.

8.3.4 Exceptions for consumer and for employment contracts

Article 5 concerns the supply to a consumer of goods or services, or credit for their supply. The choice of law shall not operate so as to deprive the consumer of his protection under the mandatory rules of his country of residence. So, a consumer in England and Wales could not be deprived of the protection of UCTA 1977, for example. Many consumer protection rules and regulations would, likewise, be treated as mandatory rules.

Article 6 deals with individual contracts of employment. Where there is no choice of law in the contract then the presumption is that contained in Article 6(2). This is basically that the law is that of the country where the work takes place, or where the business is situated if the work takes place in a different country. However, a contractual choice of law cannot operate so as to deprive the employee of the protection of the mandatory rules which would apply under Article 6(2).

8.4 Rome I – Regulation 593/2008

Where contracts are entered into after 17 December 2009, this Regulation will apply within all Member States of the EU except Denmark. This Regulation will form the basis on which those other courts will determine questions of conflict of laws. Whatever happens, the effects of Articles 3(4) (mandatory rules overriding express choice of law) and 7 (insurance contracts) are expressed to apply to all Member States of the EU, regardless of whether the Regulation itself applies to them (Article 1(4)).

8.4.1 Scope of the Regulation and exclusions (Article 1)

In many respects, the scope of the Regulation and the exclusions are very similar to the corresponding matters in the Rome Convention (see **8.3**). The main thrust of the Regulation is to deal with questions of conflict of laws in contractual and commercial obligations, but it does not apply to revenue, customs or administrative matters.

8.4.2 Primacy of express or implied choice of law by the parties (Article 3)

Article 3 of the Regulation is very close to the corresponding Article 3 of the Rome Convention (see **8.3.1**): the same overall result obtains, in that the parties can choose a particular system of law to apply to all or part of the contract; they can, within limits, change the chosen law by agreement during the contract; and they cannot, by express choice of law, avoid mandatory rules of law, ie those which cannot be derogated from by contract (see **8.3.3**).

8.4.3 Applicable law in the absence of express or implied choice (Article 4)

There are some very considerable changes to what results would have followed under the Rome Convention. Article 4(1) of the Regulation provides the following prima facie rules:

(a) in contracts for the sale of goods or for provision of services, the contract is governed by the law of the country where the seller or provider of services, respectively, has its 'habitual residence';

(b) in rights *in rem* in land, including tenancies, the contract is governed by the law of the land where the property is situated;

(c) in private tenancies up to six months' duration, the contract is governed by the law of the country where the landlord has his habitual residence, provided that the tenant is a natural person and has his habitual residence in the same country;

(d) in franchises, the law is that of the place where the franchisee has its habitual residence;

(e) in distribution contracts, the law is that of the country where the distributor has its habitual residence.

In matters which are not covered by Article 4(1), the first fallback position is determined by providing that the governing law is that of the country where the party effecting characteristic performance has its habitual residence (Article 4(2)).

If it is manifestly clear that the contract is most closely connected with a country other than that indicated by Article 4(1) or 4(2), the law of that other country will be applied (Article 4(3)) as an overriding matter. If the question is simply that, after applying Article 4(1) and 4(2), there is no clear determination and there is no manifestation sufficient for Article 4(3), Article 4(4) provides that the law applicable should be that of the place with which the contract is most closely connected.

8.4.4 Overriding effect of mandatory rules of law (Article 9)

This is not so very different from the effects of Article 7 of the Rome Convention (see **8.3.3**), and the overriding principle is that the mandatory rules of the forum cannot be displaced by the law applicable to the contract (Article 9(2)).

8.4.5 Meaning of 'habitual residence' (Article 19)

So much turns on this, under the Regulation, that a careful eye should be applied to the definitions of 'habitual residence' set out below:

(a) regarding companies and other incorporated or unincorporated bodies, 'habitual residence' means in the place of central administration; regarding natural persons, 'habitual residence' means at their principal place of business (Article 19(1));

(b) as regards branches or agencies, where the contract is entered into or there is responsibility for performance at such branch or agency, habitual residence is the place where the branch or agency is situated (Article 19(2)).

The point in time for the determination of habitual residence is when the contract is concluded (Article 19(3)).

Chapter 9
International Sale of Goods

9.1	Introduction	121
9.2	Matters for particular consideration in international sales	124
9.3	The documents involved	125
9.4	Multimodal and container transport	128
9.5	Arranging transportation of the goods – Incoterms	128
9.6	Developments in international trade	135

9.1 Introduction

Of all the areas covered by this book, the international sale of goods transaction has probably the longest history in a form which is still recognisable today. Many of the types of contract which are now in everyday use around the world would have been recognisable to the mercantile community of Europe and the Mediterranean, in mediaeval times or earlier, as part of the 'law merchant', some parts of which are preserved by our present law (see SGA 1979, s 62(2)). This internationally known, customary law system was eventually, in part, absorbed into the English common law system, but the commercially recognised nature of many of its long-established principles explains much of the difference in emphasis when comparing international sales with what you already know about domestic sales law. It also explains the wide international recognition of many types of standard transport and financing contracts that are discussed below and in **Chapter 10**.

It helps to start by examining those extra considerations that attach to an international sale, as against one within a single State. Modes of transportation are likely to be different: within the United Kingdom, road or rail are likely to be the predominant method; whereas international sales are likely to involve some combination of road, water (inland or sea) and/or air carriage. The timescales for the carriage of the goods may be much longer. The time periods between the contract being entered into (and the need for the seller to start to spend money) and the date at which the buyer actually gets possession of the goods will be commensurately greater.

Financing the sale and securing the seller's position become ever more critical as the chance of the seller exercising any rights over the goods themselves (such as retention of title) when those goods sail away from these shores and into different jurisdictions becomes increasingly remote. The need to consider choice of jurisdiction of the contract and the choice of law (or choices, if different laws are chosen for different parts of the contract) becomes of major importance. The questions of passing of property and of risk become more complicated by reason of the different modes of handling and transporting the goods. Most significantly, the cost and complexity of arranging transport, loading arrangements etc (and/or insurance) can be much greater and also subject to uncertainty (particularly sea transport), so that whichever of the parties incurs such expense must build this into its calculations.

The mechanism that evolved, long ago, to deal with many of these points is to give far greater contractual significance to the transfer of documents, of types and in appropriate forms as required by the contract, in association with a delivery of the goods themselves to a certain place and at a certain time. The legal significance of this type of arrangement is that the seller and the buyer agree that the seller completes its contractual delivery (for example, in an FAS contract – see **9.5.2.2**) by the physical placing of the goods, in a particular type of contract, alongside a named ship at a named location by a certain time and date. If the seller does this and then takes the documentation required by the contract, without undue delay, to a person authorised by the buyer to check and to accept the documents for onward transmission to the buyer (who will need them to take possession of and to deal with the goods), the seller has done all that it can do under the contract. If the ship sinks or the documents are destroyed, whatever occurs, the seller will not be concerned as it is entitled to be paid (there may, of course, be quality disputes, etc once the buyer gets the goods, but those are dealt with by the normal contractual remedies available and are not relevant for present purposes).

The additional advantage, for all concerned, in this method of performing the contract is that those best suited to the close scrutiny, acceptance and forwarding of such documents are organisations of high probity, financial standing and expertise, such as banks. Banks are central to most business arrangements, and are particularly vital to the facilitation and financing of international trade because of their close knowledge of and connections with other banks, nationally and internationally. See **10.6** below on the role of the banks.

In practice, you will soon come to recognise the close and mutually advantageous relationships between the various mercantile and financial bodies that come into play in international sales of goods. A simple example may help to explain the stages in the process – see **Figure 9.1** below.

Figure 9.1 Stages involved in an international sale of goods

Scenario

A supplier of goods based in England ('S') begins contractual negotiations with a potential buyer in the USA ('B'). B would like to contract at a price that includes all costs and expense, land and sea transport, insurance etc, to a port in the USA, from which it can collect the goods on its own transport (that preference is so that B knows exactly what price it would have to pay to get the goods onto USA soil, without having to risk any variations in the price).

S is unwilling to become involved in any expense or risk beyond such outlay as is involved in getting the goods to a UK port and on board a ship, inclusive of the necessary loading costs. The expense, risk and arrangements for the sea voyage outwards from the UK, and all subsequent costs, would have to be borne by B, if S is to agree to enter the contract.

↓

Stage 1 – entering the contract

B agrees to accept S's preferred arrangement (in reality, this would be decided on the basis of the relative bargaining powers of the parties). The parties agree to incorporate into the contract certain well-known international sale of goods terms, known as 'Incoterms 2000 FOB' ('free on board') contract terms (this type of arrangement is explained in more detail at **9.5.2.3** below).

(*Note*: the parties also agree to use a documentary method to provide for:

(a) the means by which S would be paid;

(b) a way of providing a credit period for B; and

(c) an arrangement, under which S could be sure to get its money, if B should fail to collect the goods and/or refuse to pay, or become unable to pay.

To facilitate a step-by-step, less complicated explanation of the contracting process, this aspect of the financial working of the contract and use of documents in this scenario is illustrated separately at **10.2** below.)

↓

Stage 2 – making delivery of the goods

B arranges sea transportation of the goods with a sea carrier (the 'affreightment' or 'carriage' contract) and notifies S of the name of the ship, and of the place and time at the UK port when the ship will be ready to accept the goods on board from S ('nomination' of the vessel). (Note that S is *not* a party to this contract.) S sends the goods to the ship at the appointed time on its own transport, and allows the goods to be taken from its vehicle and placed aboard the ship, at S's expense. The contractual place and time of delivery occurs, under FOB, when the goods 'pass the ship's rail'. From this point, provided that the goods were in conformity with the contract at that point, S has done all it needs to do to make delivery, and all expense, risk and responsibility for the goods passes away from S towards B. If the ship sinks or blows up at the dockside immediately thereafter, S is not concerned; it can still proceed to complete the documentary part of its contract.

↓

Stage 3 – provision of documents by S

Although S has made delivery, it still has part of its contract to perform, which is the provision and tender of documents (without these, B will not be able to collect the goods from the ship). Incoterms 2000 FOB requires S to provide very specific documentation to B. In this case, it is likely to comprise, at the least:

(a) an on-board receipt to show that the goods were actually placed on board;

(b) a commercial invoice to describe and identify the goods, to help get them through USA Customs (any duty is assessed on the invoice value), and also to provide B's evidence to take possession of the goods; and

(c) any export licence that might have been required (B will already have the contract documents for the freight and any insurance contract, as it arranged those contracts itself).

Extra documentation of a wide variety may be required to be provided by the terms of the contract.

↓

Stage 4 – tender and forwarding of documents

The likely contractual arrangement would be for S to forward these documents to B through the international banking system. S would initially take the documents required by the contract (these will be the documents required by the FOB terms, as well as any other required documents relating to the method of payment, which you will see in **Chapter 10**) to the commercial department of one of the larger branches of a bank in the UK, perhaps to its own branch for internal forwarding.

The bank would examine the documents carefully to check that they appear to be in strict conformity with what was required by the contract (the precise type, form, content and tender requirements of the documents may well be determined under a parallel documentary credit arrangement, which is part of the overall contractual relationship of the parties: see **10.5** below). The documents, if satisfactory, would be forwarded swiftly, through the secure channels of the banking system, to a USA bank from which B would collect them and then proceed to collect its goods from the USA port.

↓

Stage 5 – payment of S

Once S has tendered the documents and they have been accepted by the bank, S will be paid in accordance with whatever contractual arrangements have been made (unless it had already been paid in advance, which is rare in such contracts). This stage is dealt with in more detail throughout **Chapter 10**, but a continuation of this illustration may be seen at **10.2**.

9.2 Matters for particular consideration in international sales

The points requiring particular examination in this type of contract are:

(a) which party has responsibility for arranging and paying for the various incidents of the arrangement, such as loading/offloading, transportation, insurance, inspection and export/import clearances, etc;

(b) where and when delivery takes place;

(c) the passing of property in the goods;

(d) the passing of risk in the goods; and

(e) responsibility to obtain and to pass on necessary documentation.

9.2.1 Respective responsibilities of the parties

This is clearly a question of commercial convenience, turning upon the facts of the particular contract. There are all sorts of reasons why the seller or the buyer may wish, or be pressed by the other party, to undertake responsibility for a particular part of the arrangement. The principal reason why the buyer may want the seller to undertake to provide and pay for, eg transport, may be that the buyer would then be able to know just what he is contracted to pay for the goods, regardless of price fluctuations or difficulties in arranging shipping. Much will turn upon which party could, most conveniently, arrange certain matters, particularly where those arrangements take place in another country. Many of these matters can conveniently be allocated between the parties by the simple stratagem of incorporating 'Incoterm' arrangements into the contract (see **9.5** below). These standard terms, if left unamended, place responsibilities upon each party as to transport, loading, insurance and documentation, in a very clear way. Ultimately, though, it is for the parties to decide who does what and it is common to modify Incoterms.

9.2.2 Where and when delivery takes place

This is always a matter of importance, but particularly so where the goods are likely to be out of the physical possession of either party for long periods, as with international sales. The general rule in s 29(1) of the SGA 1979, that it is open to the parties to decide the place of delivery, is often overtaken by the use of Incoterms, which have very clear rules as to when and where delivery takes place (see **9.5**). In many types of international sale, the point of delivery is often where risk of damage also passes from the seller to the buyer. Because of the particular hazards involved in transferring goods from one mode of transport on to another, such as in loading goods from a vehicle on to a ship, the precise point and time of delivery and passing of risk must be exactly ascertainable, so the certainty of standard arrangements is valuable.

9.2.3 The passing of property in the goods

This is one important area that is not dealt with by Incoterms; they have no effect upon when property passes. This question remains one of evidence of the parties' intentions or, failing that, using the fallback provisions under ss 17, 18 and 19 of the SGA 1979. In international sales, the factor that is of the greatest significance is that such contracts normally require, in addition to the contractual delivery of the goods, transfer of documentation in such precise form and circumstances as are required by the contract. There are many rules of commercial practice that are taken to show the parties' intentions as to passing of certain types of property (as well as the statutory presumptions mentioned above, in the absence of any express agreement), but the discussion of such rules is not necessary for present purposes, as there are almost infinite variations in different fact circumstances. The most common times for property to pass in international sales are either upon contractual delivery of the goods taking place (see the rules on this in the Incoterms at **9.5** below; and see also *Scottish & Newcastle International Ltd v Othon Ghalanos Ltd* [2008] UKHL 11, [2008] 2 All ER (Comm) 369, where the jurisdiction of the English court to hear a case was established by the fact of delivery having been made in Liverpool under a CFR contract – see **8.2.2** and **9.5.3.2**), or on the transfer of documents, in accordance with the contract. The property issue sometimes arises in association with the question of risk in the goods, but may also arise in connection with disputes about the right of the buyer to sell the goods on or, indeed, about jurisdiction to hear a dispute. See **2.13.1** for further discussion.

9.2.4 The passing of risk in the goods

This is of extreme importance for obvious reasons and, generally, the rule is that risk will pass with property (see SGA 1979, s 20(1), (2)). This is subject to the contrary agreement of the parties, and very often that contrary agreement is shown by the choice of an Incoterm arrangement. The effect of incorporating such Incoterms into the contract, without any further express reference to risk passing, is to fix precisely when risk will pass. It is always possible to use modified versions of the Incoterms, and the needs of the parties may well require special contractual provision. See *KG Bominflot Bunkersgesellschaft für Mineralöle mbh & Co KG v Petroplus Marketing AG* [2009] EWHC 1088 (Comm), where the parties had combined an express delivery specification for oil with an FOB contract. The risk had passed on delivery, and the court was unwilling to imply a term of durability of quality and compliance with specification for any longer than a reasonable time after delivery. The seller had no knowledge of the likely length of the transit.

Another point that must be understood is that it is fairly common for sellers in international sales to be required to include provision of insurance within their contractual obligations, even though the risk of the most hazardous part of the journey may lie with the buyer (see CIF contracts at **9.5.3.1**, below). There is nothing unusual about one party agreeing to pay for arrangements which are provided for the protection of the other party. It usually reflects the needs, convenience and economic circumstances of each party, and the geographical context of the contract.

9.2.5 Responsibility for providing documentation

This is usually an obligation of the seller and the documents typically required will provide the buyer with evidence that the seller has done all that it can do to fulfil its part of the contract. Mercantile practice has created certain requirements for the form and content of such documents so that any departure from those requirements is likely to be spotted by whoever (and it is likely to be a bank) is responsible for accepting the documents from the seller; if the documents are wrongfully accepted by a bank, then that bank will be liable for any loss suffered by the buyer. The place and time of tender should be dealt with in the contract, to avoid doubt. If the seller is, for any reason, unable to provide the necessary documents or, for example, a document was 'claused' where it was required to be 'clean' (for example, a document showing that the goods were received into a ship, which contained a note that the goods, or packaging, were damaged before they were 'delivered' aboard), then the seller is in serious breach of contract in tendering the documents. The buyer would be entitled to treat the contract as repudiated and it would be up to the seller to try to persuade the buyer to accept the documents and the goods, perhaps by negotiating the price or giving undertakings.

9.3 The documents involved

The key documents are:

(a) the shipping/transportation document, which may vary from a simple on-board receipt for the goods (such as are seen in 'F' class Incoterm contracts) to a complex contractual and/or title document (such as a bill of lading or waybill, as described at **9.3.1** and **9.3.2**, below);

(b) the commercial invoice, which shows the buyer's obligation to pay the price;

(c) any policies of air or marine insurance required; and

(d) any other documents required by the contract, such as export/import licences, certificates of origin, packing lists or inspection certificates.

In the remainder of this section, the more appropriate and commonly used terminology of 'shipper' will be applied to the seller (as the party 'shipping' its goods to the buyer) and 'carrier' will be used for the ship operators.

9.3.1 The bill of lading

This document, of considerable antiquity, is only appropriate to transport of goods by water. It is initially raised by the carrier, at the time that the goods are put aboard and given to the shipper. The bill serves three principal purposes (although its effects are somewhat wider in law):

(a) as evidence that the goods have been received from the shipper, and (if a 'clean' bill) that they are in apparently undamaged condition at the time of loading;

(b) to show the contractual terms under which the goods are carried; and

(c) as a document of title to the goods, while the goods are in transit to the buyer, and as evidence of a right to their possession.

If a bill of lading is required by the contract, no other type of transport document will do, because of this unique triple function.

You have already seen how the document is used by the shipper to show its performance of the contract, by tendering all necessary documents to some intermediary, such as a bank. Once accepted, the bill of lading (along with the other documents) is forwarded to the buyer (usually, by air, for speed), which is then in the position of being able to present it at the port of arrival to show its right to the goods. Also, on receipt of the bill of lading, the buyer is in a position to sell or charge the goods, if it chooses. This is an important point, because many types of bulk or commodity goods can change hands several times, during a long sea voyage; with highly volatile market prices, the flexibility of being able to sell, or raise money on goods afloat is vital.

There are two principal disadvantages to the use of bills of lading, which have caused them to become less favoured in recent times, except where bulk cargoes are concerned. The first major problem is that only an original bill of lading will suffice. Photocopies, faxes or electronic versions simply do not have the legal status to pass title or possession to the buyer or anyone else. The consequence of this, particularly for short sea journeys, is that the goods are likely to get to their port of arrival before the original bill of lading gets to the buyer.

Bills of lading are still favoured in the transport of bulk cargoes, eg grain, coal, metal ores. There are attempts to produce an e-commerce equivalent by creating a network of contracts that has the same end effect as a paper bill of lading, eg the system known as BOLERO (Bills of Lading Electronic Registry Organisation). This would seem to be where the future lies for bills of lading. For further information on BOLERO, see www.bolero.net. As matters stand, there is a good deal of optimism about progress, but the increasing technical expertise of electronic fraudsters may hold it back on this front.

An additional complication is that it is common practice to issue bills of lading in sets of three. Only one copy needs to be presented to claim the goods from the carrier. The practice was originally devised to enable the resale of goods whilst at sea in days gone by, even though criticised then (see *Glyn Mills Currie & Co v East and West India Dock Co* (1882) 7 App Cas 591). In *Svenborg v Far East Trading Côte d'Ivoire* [2004] EWHC 2929, a forged bill of lading was used to obtain delivery of the goods from the shipping agent. The defendant was held liable in the tort of deceit.

The second main drawback of shipping goods under a bill of lading, from a UK port, is that, by the combined effects of the Carriage of Goods by Sea Acts of 1971 and 1992, the carriage contract will have rules of construction applied to it – the Hague-Visby Rules. These Rules, in effect, give great advantage to the carrier and its use of contractual exclusion/limitation clauses, in the event of any contractual dispute between the carrier and any other party who can sue under the carriage contract. This will include the buyer, because, even where the shipper has paid for the carriage, it is the buyer who is likely to suffer any delays or damage to the goods. Section 2 of the Carriage of Goods by Sea Act 1992 extends privity to the buyer, among others. The Hague-Visby Rules and disputes under them are beyond the scope of this work, but such considerations will be of importance in a practical mercantile context.

Bills of lading are governed by the Carriage of Goods by Sea Act 1992.

9.3.2 An alternative to bills of lading – waybills

A waybill is an alternative to a bill of lading. A waybill is a receipt for the goods and evidence of the carriage contract, but it does not constitute a document of title to the goods. It also specifies the person to whom delivery should be made. The original does not have to be sent to the buyer for him to be able to collect the goods from the carrier. Its disadvantage is that it does not enable the buyer to sell the goods on before he has possession of them, as he can with a bill of lading.

An advantage of waybills is that they can be sent electronically (or by fax). The transaction can thus by undertaken as e-commerce, with the payment being sent from the buyer to the seller by electronic means (see **19.10**).

Waybills have traditionally been used for air freight. They have been used for sea freight with increasing frequency. This trend is explained by the fact that the Hague-Visby Rules (see **9.3.1**) have no application to waybills.

9.3.3 The commercial invoice

This lists and describes the contract goods (eg, '20 cases of Adams Baked Beans, each comprising 30 tins of 100g size'). It will also usually constitute a demand for payment by the buyer.

9.3.4 The policy of marine (or air) insurance

This should be worded so as to cover the goods specified in the commercial invoice for the journey described in the bill of lading. The policy would be transferred from one party to another along with the bill of lading (and would obviously need to be a transferable policy).

9.3.5 Effect of transfer of the documents

The Carriage of Goods by Sea Act 1992 provides a solution to earlier problems of privity of contract which would occur when the bill of lading is transferred from one holder to another. The Act provides that anyone who holds the bill of lading is entitled to sue the carrier on the contract of carriage. A holder, however, also assumes the contractual burdens imposed by the freight contract. (The Act also applies to other documents such as waybills, which are mentioned at **9.3.2** and **9.3.3**.) The holder also has rights in tort in relation to the goods (eg, for negligent damage, even though such damage might have occurred at a time before the holder had ownership of the goods).

The buyer who is in possession of the shipping documents can enforce his:

(a) contractual rights against the person who sold to him, under the contract of sale;

(b) contractual rights against the carrier under the contract of carriage; and

(c) rights against the insurer under the terms of the policy of which he is the assignee.

All documents must, of course, be genuine and not forgeries. *Motis Exports Ltd v Dampskibsselskabet AF 1912 (No 1), A/S and Another* [2000] 1 All ER (Comm) 91 is an example of the problems of bills of lading. In that case, the defendant carrier delivered goods against a forged bill of lading. The owner of the goods successfully sued the carrier, as the Court of Appeal affirmed that a forged bill of lading was simply a worthless piece of paper.

9.4 Multimodal and container transport

One of the greatest innovations in international sales has been the use of standardised metal containers, easily transferable between road, rail, ship and air modes of transport. The container has become the 'maid of all work' for many types of good (other than bulk goods) and, because of its standard 'building-block' design and dimensions, it has become commonplace to arrange so-called multimodal transport arrangements, which permit a carrier to transport goods, using several different modes of transport to carry the containers (eg road in UK; sea and road in US) within one combined contract. This is increasingly facilitated by the use of huge container facilities, both at seaports and inland. An incidental effect has been the growth in number and size of international businesses that combine road and sea transport with operation of land-based storage and handling facilities. This type of transport operation has rapidly found favour and become familiar to the international mercantile community. The following sections on Incoterms contracts show that standard types of contract for multimodal transport are as well provided for as their lineal ancestors, the traditional shipping carriage contracts.

The use of documents is still a necessary part of the contractual performance by the seller in multimodal contracts, but there is, as yet, no precise legal equivalent to the bill of lading, in its clear acceptance as a document of title, during transit. Nevertheless, there are certain types of receipt given by the carrier to the seller which appear to be able to provide title in particular circumstances, according to some judicial authority. The problem does not seem to have created difficulties in recent times and, probably, a legitimate carrier's receipt, in combination with the seller's invoice and the general law concerning a buyer's right to sell goods on, will be enough to make good title to a sub-buyer.

A problem that does arise in many container transport situations is that the legal framework covering the contract can vary according to which leg or mode of transport is involved. For example, the road leg(s) of the journey may fall within the CMR Convention, an international agreement given force in English law by the Carriage of Goods by Road Act 1965. A leg by air might fall within the Warsaw Convention on International Carriage by Air 1929. These matters govern liability and exclusion, etc. See *Quantum Corp Ltd v Plane Trucking Ltd* [2002] EWCA Civ 350, where such a question arose.

9.5 Arranging transportation of the goods – Incoterms

In an international sale of goods, there will be various stages in the transport chain. For example, if the goods are being exported to Korea from a factory in Manchester, they will first of all have to be taken by road or rail from Manchester to a British port, possibly Liverpool or Hull. They will then need to be loaded on to a ship and be taken by the ship from the British port to a port in Korea. Once they reach there, they will then be taken by road or rail from the Korean port to the premises of the buyer.

There are legal and practical issues to be considered. The major ones are:

(a) who pays for each stage and incidental expense of the journey; and

(b) which party is responsible for the goods at each stage?

So, how do we draft the contract to take care of this? One way is to use a standard form of contract. The mercantile community has a long history of developing trade custom and practice into legally recognised standard contract arrangements, having known obligations and rights for each party. The FOB, FAS, CIF and CFR contracts discussed below are examples of these and in their modern form they are part of the International Chamber of Commerce official rules for interpreting mercantile trade terms, known as Incoterms. The obligations of each party, under particular types of contract, are laid out in simple terms in a standard book, along with guidance, currently issued as Incoterms 2000. These terms are written in non-legal language, aimed at commercial parties rather than at lawyers and, being published in many languages, the aim is to avoid misunderstanding, disputes, expense and litigation within the international mercantile community.

An Incoterm can form part of a sale of goods contract if it is expressly incorporated by reference into it, eg 'This contract is to be FOB Hull and is governed by Incoterms 2000'. If this is not expressly done, a court may well take the view that the parties intended the terms to be incorporated, but this is risky, particularly if the express terms of the contract are at variance with the obligations under the Incoterms. This is not to say that it is impossible to modify Incoterms arrangements; it is, but care is needed if that is the aim. The remainder of this section deals only with unmodified Incoterms.

The effect of incorporating Incoterms, unmodified, into the sale of goods contract is that they provide some, but not all, of the carriage terms of the contract. They deal with, primarily, the respective responsibilities of each party to arrange and pay for each stage of the carriage and handling of the goods; the seller's obligations to deliver the goods and to provide any necessary documents or other formalities; the place and time of contractual delivery; the passing of risk; and the buyer's obligation to pay the price and to take delivery. The main aspects of the sale contract that are beyond the scope of the Incoterms are the questions of passing of property, the time of payment and most of the consequences of breach, although the Incoterms do provide, under division of costs requirements, that certain defaults by either party which cause extra cost to the other party, such as failure to notify a shipping or loading date, or to accept delivery, allow contractual recovery of that cost by the innocent party. Clearly, the appropriate Incoterms arrangement should be incorporated in the first place, because some terms are only applicable to, for example, sea transport at the buyer's expense (FOB or FAS) and will not apply to multimodal arrangements, where the seller is paying for several of the different transport stages.

There is information on the ICC site at www.iccwbo.org/incoterms/id3042/index.htm and at www.export911.com.

The ICC Incoterms are as follows:

(a) ex works (EXW);

(b) free carrier (FCA);

(c) free alongside (a ship) (FAS);

(d) free on board (a ship) (FOB);

(e) cost and freight (CFR);

(f) cost, insurance, freight (CIF);

(g) carriage paid to (CPT);

(h) carriage and insurance paid (CIP);

(i) delivered at frontier (DAF);

(j) delivered ex ship (DES);

(k) delivered ex quay (DEQ);

(l) delivered duty unpaid (DDU);

(m) delivered duty paid (DDP).

The burden of expense and responsibility on the seller increases as one goes down the list. Thus, the lightest burden on the seller is when the goods are delivered to the buyer 'ex works', that is at the seller's premises. The heaviest is when they have to be delivered to the buyer's premises with the relevant duty paid. These burdens on the seller are reflected in the price agreed for the deal. The less the burden, the less the price and the risk of fluctuating rates of carriage and insurance. However, it does mean that the buyer has to arrange and pay for the other parts of the chain of transport. This is usually decided as a matter of convenience, cost and bargaining power by the parties.

Both the 'F' group and the 'C' group of Incoterms are contracts where the seller fulfils its obligations in the country of shipment, ie the country of departure of the goods. The 'D' group is different in nature from the 'F' and 'C' groups, in that the seller is responsible for the arrival of the goods in the country of destination and must bear all the risks and costs of achieving it.

The traditional 'F' and 'C' terms cannot always be adapted for modern shipping practice. For example, the typical situation today is not of the ship lying at the dockside waiting for cargo to be loaded. Rather, the aim is to minimise the time spent in port. The goods are often in shipping containers which are stored in or close to the docks pending arrival of the appropriate ship (as discussed at **9.3** above). It would also be typical today for goods to be put into shipping containers at the sellers' premises, or at a depot run by the carrier. They would stay in the container until they reached either the buyer, or a carrier's depot in the country of destination. FCA, CPT and CIP are designed for use in the container trade.

Almost all of the Incoterms contracts also involve the parties having the obligation to give each other notice of certain matters, time, places, etc. These are vital obligations of such contracts but, for brevity, are not dealt with in the summaries below. Notice is of very great importance in shipping contracts.

9.5.1 Examples of Incoterms – ex works (EXW)

The burden is lightest on the seller and heaviest on the buyer, in that the buyer has to arrange and pay for collection at the seller's premises.

The seller delivers the goods when he places the goods at the disposal of the buyer at the seller's premises (or other named location, eg a warehouse).

The first point is that the place where the 'works' are has to be specified. So, it could be 'ex works Adams Waste Recycling, Pepper Street, Christleton', for example.

The obligations on the two parties are as follows:

(a) Seller is required to:
   (i) supply goods conforming to the contract, measured and packed;
   (ii) supply the invoice and any other documents;
   (iii) deliver the goods (in the legal sense of transfer of possession) by placing them at the buyer's disposal at the named delivery point ('the works');
   (iv) pay for any costs incidental to placing the goods at the buyer's disposal; and
   (v) provide further assistance to the buyer for the buyer to obtain necessary export licences or compliance with other formalities, at the buyer's request and expense.

(b) Buyer is required to:
   (i) accept delivery of the goods and pay for them;
   (ii) obtain appropriate licences and customs clearances; and
   (iii) pay any costs incidental to the export of the goods, such as pre-shipment inspection.

Under EXW, the seller does not arrange for export clearance (which is, of course, only relevant to sales to a buyer located outside the EU). If the buyer were unable to arrange export clearance, then the FCA set of terms should be used instead (see **9.5.2**), providing that the seller is also willing to take on the burden and risk of loading the goods.

The purchase price would always become due on delivery of the goods unless the parties agreed otherwise.

The risk in the goods passes once the seller has placed the goods at the buyer's disposal.

9.5.2 Examples of Incoterms – the 'F' group of terms: main carriage unpaid

These impose more responsibility on the seller than under the ex works terms (see **9.5.1**), but the risk of fluctuating freight or insurance rates rests with the buyer. The 'F' group of terms require the seller to deliver the goods for the main carriage (usually sea or air transportation) as required by the buyer. The buyer will usually arrange and pay for the main carriage and the insurance for that journey. In the 'F' group, risk in the goods passes with legal delivery. There is a variety of 'F' terms. The difference between the 'F' terms is in the hand-over point for the goods (ie, the point of legal delivery of the goods).

9.5.2.1 Free carrier (FCA) (named place)

The seller fulfils his obligations when he delivers the goods to the carrier chosen by the buyer at the named point and time. The risk of loss or damage is transferred at that point. The hand-over point could be the seller's premises, in which case the seller must provide loading onto the carrier's vehicle, or it could be the carrier's depot, especially if the goods are to be sent by container, in which case the buyer must pay for loading into the container. The term is frequently used when goods are shipped by container. It can also be used for air freight. Any export clearance is the responsibility of the seller.

9.5.2.2 Free alongside ship (FAS) (named port of shipment)

Here, the seller fulfils his obligations when he delivers the goods alongside the named ship (ie, on the dockside) at the named port of shipment (ie, the port of departure), within the stipulated time. The buyer will have arranged for the ship, and be paying for the sea carriage and insurance (if any). The costs of loading the goods on to the ship will also be the buyer's expense. Any export clearance is the responsibility of the seller. Risk will pass when the seller delivers alongside, in accordance with the contract.

9.5.2.3 Free on board (FOB) (named port of shipment)

These terms impose higher obligations on the seller than FAS. Here, the seller undertakes to place the goods on board a specified ship in a specified port of shipment, within the stipulated time. All charges up to and including loading the goods on to the ship are the seller's expense. The buyer has to pay the subsequent charges, including sea freight, marine insurance (if any), unloading charges and import duties.

'Free on board' means the seller delivers the goods when the goods 'pass over the ship's rail' at the port of shipment. (If this is not suitable then FCA or FAS should be used.) The buyer therefore has the task of making the shipping arrangements and the insurance arrangements. FOB can only be used for sea or inland waterway transport (but may be adapted for air transport).

The delivery point in FOB is the same as for CFR and CIF (see **9.5.3**). Although consideration was given to changing this for FOB in the revisions to Incoterms, it was decided to keep it as it was for Incoterms 2000. The 'over the ship's rail' provision does not always accord with modern shipping practice, that is containerised transport and roll-on, roll-off ferries. However, it was felt that FOB was adapted in practice by commercial parties to modern loading techniques and to the goods in question. It is also widely understood in the commercial world.

The clarity of the delivery rule in FOB and its utility in resolving commercial disputes are manifest in *Scottish & Newcastle International Ltd v Othon Ghalanos Ltd* [2008] UKHL 11; [2008] 2 All ER (Comm) 369, and also in *KG Bominflot Bunkersgesellschaft für Mineralöle mbh & Co KG v Petroplus Marketing AG* [2009] EWHC 1088 (Comm).

FOB contracts were analysed in *Pyrene Co Ltd v Scindia Steam Navigation Co Ltd* [1954] 2 All ER 158 and *Ian Stach Ltd v Baker Bosley Ltd* [1958] 2 QB 130.

The risk in the goods passes with delivery, that is the goods are at the seller's risk until they cross the ship's rail.

Under FOB, the following are the obligations on the seller and buyer:

(a) Seller is required to:
   (i) supply goods conforming to the sale of goods contract;
   (ii) deliver the goods to the buyer by placing them on board the ship, that is 'over the rail' of the ship;
   (iii) place them on board;
   (iv) pay any costs incidental to delivery of the goods;
   (v) obtain any export licence and arrange any export customs formalities; and
   (vi) provide to the buyer proof of delivery to the ship.
(b) Buyer is required to:
   (i) give sufficient notice to the seller of the time and location of the delivery point (the buyer having contracted with a carrier for the sea journey, and insured the goods from the port of shipment);
   (ii) obtain any appropriate licences;
   (iii) pay costs incidental to the importation of the goods; and
   (iv) pay for the goods.

You should be aware that there are many varieties of FOB contract used in international trade, because it is not uncommon to use so-called 'FOB with services' contracts under which the seller may arrange shipping or insurance, not on its own behalf, but as agent for the buyer. Clarity is vital if expensive litigation is to be avoided (eg, 'Incoterms 2000 FOB Hull' is clear in scope). FOB is one of the two sets of Incoterms that you will come across frequently in practice (the other is CIF), although FOB contracts do seem to be declining in popularity now.

9.5.3 Examples of Incoterms – the 'C' terms: main carriage paid

These sets of terms impose more onerous obligations on the seller than do the 'F' group of terms. In the 'C' group, the seller arranges and pays for the main carriage, usually the sea freight. Therefore, the point up to which the seller is responsible for transport costs needs to be stated after the relevant 'C' term (eg, CIF Sydney). In the CIF and CIP terms, the seller is also responsible for arranging and paying for the insurance. However, the 'C' terms are still contracts where the seller fulfils the contract by delivery in the country of dispatch (ie, usually the seller's own country), like the 'F' terms. Thus, the goods are at the seller's risk under the 'C' terms only until they are handed over to the carrier, that is in CIF and CFR when they pass over the ship's rail. So, under the 'C' terms the passing of risk differs from the place to which the seller arranges transport. Under the 'D' terms, the risk will not pass until the goods reach their destination (see **9.5.4**). It is easy to see that the overall responsibility for the seller is much greater with the 'C' terms than with the 'F' terms. The seller will have to factor the cost of the sea voyage (and potential variations upon that expense) into the price of its goods.

Documentary credits are quite commonly used with 'C' terms, because the seller is now exposed to greater expense from an earlier stage in the contract and the assurance of credit arrangement is an important requirement, if available (see **10.5**).

9.5.3.1 Cost, insurance, freight (CIF) (named port of destination)

This is the typical contract where payment against documents would be used, usually on presentation of a bill of lading. In a CIF contract, the seller is in effect undertaking to arrange for the goods to be supplied and transported to the buyer's country. The CIF contract has been, and remains, a popular and commonly used arrangement. One reason for this is that a CIF contract can be performed, if necessary, by the seller buying goods already afloat to sell on to the buyer.

The seller is required to:

(a) ship goods conforming to the description in the contract;
(b) clear the goods for export;
(c) arrange a contract for sea carriage to the port of destination;
(d) obtain a bill of lading or waybill when the goods are loaded;
(e) arrange and pay for insurance under which the buyer can claim, and provide insurance documents to the buyer;
(f) provide an invoice for the cost of the goods and carriage and insurance;
(g) transmit to the buyer the bill of lading, insurance documents and invoice, and any other documents needed, in accordance with the contract; and
(h) arrange any necessary export clearances.

The buyer is required to:

(a) accept the documents tendered by the seller if they are in order;
(b) pay the contract price;
(c) receive the goods at the port of destination;
(d) pay any ancillary costs of the sea voyage, and costs of unloading and land transport to the buyer's premises;
(e) bear all risks of the goods after their passing over the ship's rail at the port of shipment;
(f) pay all customs dues and taxes; and
(g) obtain any import licences, or formality requirements.

Under CIF, the price quoted to the buyer for the goods includes insurance and freight to the buyer's home port. This increases the certainty of the price for the buyer. Under an FOB contract, the buyer bears the risk of fluctuations in freight and insurance rates. The use of payment against documents means the seller will be paid quickly, and that the goods, if shipped under a bill of lading, can be sold on by the buyer whilst they are still on the high seas.

The property in the goods passes when the documents are transferred to the buyer in accordance with whatever has been agreed in the contract. This is a strict rule, and the required documents may be tendered by the seller and must be accepted by the buyer, even if the goods have been lost or damaged after loading. However, the risk in the goods has already passed to the buyer when the goods were loaded on to the ship in the port of shipment (ie, in the seller's country). Thus, CIF (along with FAS, FOB, CFR and other Incoterms) displaces SGA 1979, s 20, where prima facie risk passes with the property in the goods.

A CIF contract is usually an export contract, and can be used only for sea or inland waterway transport.

As with FOB, there are many variations of CIF used in the commercial world. CIF and FOB are the two most common sets of Incoterms in commercial use.

9.5.3.2 Cost and freight (CFR) (named port of destination)

The seller has to arrange and pay for the carriage of the goods to the foreign port. He is not obliged to take out insurance for the sea voyage, which is the buyer's responsibility both to arrange and to pay for, unlike CIF. If the seller fails to give the buyer enough notice for the buyer to be able to insure the goods, the goods could be regarded as travelling at the seller's risk, under SGA 1979, s 32(3). Otherwise, delivery takes place and risk passes, as with CIF, over the ship's rail.

The CFR terms lead to a rather artificial division between the arrangements for carriage and those for insurance. As such, they are not frequently used. They may be of use where the buyer's country requires its importers to insure at home, possibly for foreign exchange reasons.

9.5.3.3 Carriage and insurance paid to (CIP) (named place of destination)

This is on the borderline between being a CIF contract and one of the 'D' group (see **9.5.4**).

These terms are suitable for any mode of transport, including multimodal transport. The seller pays the freight to the place of destination (which could be a port, as with CIF), but in addition the seller arranges and pays for insurance to that place of destination for the buyer's benefit. As with CIF, the risk in the goods passes when the goods are handed over to the carrier (ie, over the ship's rail if it is sea transport) and, if there are several different carriers involved, on delivery to the first of them.

9.5.3.4 Carriage paid to (CPT) (named place of destination)

This differs from CIP in that the seller is not obliged to obtain insurance cover for the transport. Again, this type of contract is suitable for any mode of transport, including multimodal arrangements. Delivery and risk pass, as with CIP, on handing over goods to the carrier.

CPT should be used (rather than CIF or CFR) if the goods are not intended to be delivered 'over the rail' of the ship.

9.5.4 Examples of Incoterms – the 'D' group of terms: arrival

This group of terms imposes the highest burden on the seller.

In the 'D' group of terms, the passing of risk and delivery of the goods occur at the same time. The goods are delivered, in the legal sense, to the buyer at the point required in the buyer's country, at which point risk passes as well. Technically, this happens when the goods are placed 'at the disposal of the buyer'. This is in contrast to the 'C' group of terms, where (legal) delivery takes place in the port of shipment (see **9.5.3**). In the case of 'D' contracts, payment by the buyer is made, more typically, against the goods arriving, rather than against documents. However, the seller would hand over a bill of lading or a waybill to the buyer to enable the buyer to obtain delivery of the goods from the carrier.

9.5.4.1 Delivered ex ship (DES) (named port of destination)

This set of terms is only suitable for transport of goods by sea or inland waterway. The seller is not under an obligation to the buyer to insure the goods for the sea voyage as they are at the seller's risk. Thus, if the goods are lost at sea, the buyer would have had no insurable interest in the goods.

The goods would normally be described as being delivered on a named ship on a specific day at a specified port. The expense and risk in removing the goods from the ship (eg arranging import licences) falls on the buyer.

9.5.4.2 Delivered ex quay (DEQ) (named port of destination)

This set of terms is only suitable for transport of goods by sea or inland waterway. The seller's obligations are similar to DES, but in addition the seller agrees to pay for unloading charges at the port of destination. The buyer is responsible for onward carriage from the quayside to the ultimate destination. DEQ is not often used in British practice, as it is necessary for the seller to have a local agent in the port of destination.

9.5.4.3 Delivered at frontier (DAF) (named place at frontier)

This set of terms may be used for any mode of transport where goods are delivered, not unloaded, at a land frontier. The terms do not require the seller to obtain insurance for the buyer's benefit. It is for the parties to come to an agreement. The contract would normally specify the border and the place on the border where delivery is to take place, as well as the time/date. This set of terms is suitable for any mode or for multimodal transport, but if the 'frontier' is at a seaport of arrival, DES or DEQ should be used instead.

9.5.4.4 Delivered duty paid (DDP), delivered duty unpaid (DDU) (named place of destination in the buyer's country)

These terms place the highest burden on the seller of all the Incoterms. They would normally be used only for the supply of a small quantity of goods by air.

The goods are at the seller's risk and expense until the buyer takes delivery at the place of destination. Under DDP, the seller pays all charges, including import duties and carriage in the buyer's country. Under DDU, the buyer undertakes the costs of import formalities.

There is no obligation on the seller to insure the goods under either DDU or DDP.

9.6 Developments in international trade

Most of the impetus towards change in this area arises from the increasing speed of transport and handling, on the one hand, and electronic modes of communication, on the other. A great deal of experimentation with paperless communication is proceeding in the mercantile world, which is already reflected in various forms and initiatives. The BOLERO system, for developing internationally acceptable, paperless, communication equivalents of shipping and trade documents, is making steady progress and this general aim, of utilising electronic document transmission and validation, is beginning to shape the mercantile law of most trading nations. Although the matter is beyond the scope of this work, there has been a huge amount of international effort by the United Nations Commission on International Trade Law (UNCITRAL) and the ICC. This has led to such developments as the UNCITRAL Model Law on Electronic Commerce (1998), the Electronic Commerce in the Internal Market Directive 2000/31/EC and the Electronic Communications Act 2000. Generally, the time honoured legal forms of international trade contract are likely to be around for a very long time, simply speeded up by modern technology.

Chapter 10

Financing and Security Arrangements in International Sale of Goods

10.1	Introduction	137
10.2	Collection arrangements and payment methods	138
10.3	Negotiable instruments	140
10.4	Bills of exchange	141
10.5	Documentary credits ('letters of credit')	144
10.6	Functions, responsibilities and liabilities of banks in international sales	151

10.1 Introduction

As was discussed in **Chapter 9**, international sales of goods create their own particular problems of finance and security for the seller. This is because the seller usually has to buy or manufacture the goods with which to perform the contract, often entering into other contracts for this purpose or for transport arrangements, etc, where necessary, before any money is received. On occasions, the seller may be in a strong enough bargaining position to demand payment in advance or, at latest, before the time of shipment of the goods, but this is very much the exceptional situation. In most cases, the seller will be required to allow a credit period to the buyer, to reflect the economic reality that the buyer is unlikely to be able to use the goods or profit from them until they arrive at their ultimate destination.

The problem for the seller is twofold: it needs money at the earliest possible time to meet its own outgoings, and it needs some sort of security that it will actually get paid, because the chances of recovering the goods, on default by the buyer, are extremely remote once they are offshore. Centuries of experience by mercantile traders has provided workable methods to deal with these problems. We saw, in **Chapter 9**, that the exchange of documents provided a very reliable method of performing the contract, where accompanied by the appropriate delivery of the goods to a carrier. Similarly, two types of document provide many of the answers to both financing and security problems: negotiable instruments, such as bills of exchange, and documentary credits. Where the parties agree that either or both of these documents should be used, their provision and use become as much a part of the overall sale contract as any other terms, such as delivery or price.

Financing the sale can be facilitated by the use of negotiable instruments, such as bills of exchange, which are documents designed for the purpose of being freely transferable from hand to hand, in lieu of money, because the document itself is designed to be exchanged, in due course, for a fixed sum of money.

To secure the seller's position, from the earliest time that it begins to incur expense against the contract, it is possible for the buyer to arrange for a third party, such as a bank, to provide documentary credits. These are contractual agreements by which the bank itself will undertake various liabilities towards the seller, particularly payment, additional to and independent of the buyer's obligation to pay for the goods.

You should be very clear about the distinctions in use and function between documentary credits and bills of exchange; they are very different entities in law, and aimed at solving very different problems. A commercial sale of goods, even an international one, does not strictly need either of them; they are there only to satisfy the needs and convenience of the parties. The provision of a documentary credit is required by the contract where the seller is completely unwilling to contract with the buyer without one, and where it is powerful enough to get its own way. Be very clear that the function of the credit is to give a security guarantee to the seller, provided by a third party bank at the considerable expense of the buyer, against the risk of the buyer's default; it is a heavy burden for the buyer. Once the credit is in place (and is an irrevocable credit, see **10.5.5**), its terms will strictly have to be complied with by the seller; but subject to the seller performing its part of the contract properly, the bank will pay up, whatever happens subsequently to the goods or the buyer. The credit arrangement is really at the heart of the contract, and without it the seller will not begin to perform its part. Documentary credits are dealt with in more detail at **10.5**.

The bill of exchange, by sharp contrast, is simply a widely-used and flexible commercial method of dealing with various needs and requirements of the parties to a commercial transaction, domestic or international. The primary function of the bill of exchange is as a means of providing payment to the seller, by the provision and transfer of a legally recognised and easily transferable document rather than by way of a straightforward payment of cash, after receipt of an invoice. The bill may be used, as you will soon realise, in a wide variety of ways: it may be used as a very simple contractual method of transferring money from one person to another, without having to use cash at the point of transfer; it may be used to show an obligation to pay at a fixed future date (ie to give a credit period to a buyer); it provides a simplified, informal means of assigning a debt (sometimes by the simple hand-to-hand transfer of a 'bearer' bill, see **10.3**). There are many other uses to which a bill of exchange can be put, such as providing pledges or security for a charge, but they are beyond the scope of this chapter. Other than as a flexible tool for dealing with the payment obligation, the bill of exchange is not at the heart of the contract in such an important way as a documentary credit. You can see a widely-employed method of using bills of exchange, where the seller has been unable to require the provision of a documentary credit, at **10.4.7** below.

These types of document are discussed in more detail below, but it should be realised that only a broad outline is possible within the scope of this work.

10.2 Collection arrangements and payment methods

We can start by a simple method if we assume that the goods have been sent on a CIF contract (see **9.4.3.1**); the seller will then obtain from the ship operator a bill of lading (or a waybill). It will send this with the insurance documents and the commercial invoice to its own bank (or such other bank as agreed) in the UK, with any other relevant documents (eg an export licence, packing list, etc). That bank could then forward the documents to the buyer's bank in the buyer's country. The buyer's bank then, with extreme care, would check that the documents are exactly of the type and in the condition required by the contract, as any defect in the documents would be a serious breach by the seller and any acceptance of defective documents would make the buyer's bank liable to the buyer for any loss. If the documents are in order, the buyer's bank will then make them available to the buyer once the buyer has put it into funds to transfer the payment for the goods to the seller's bank in the UK (if that is the contractual arrangement and there is no credit period provided). That would be one simple method of collection and payment, but it has the drawback for the buyer of being more or less cash on delivery of the documents, and the disadvantage for the seller that its goods have gone abroad and that it is not guaranteed to be paid.

Where a credit period is stipulated, a more convenient method that has found favour is the use of a bill of exchange (see the discussion of 'term bills' at **10.4.1** and the example at **Figure 10.1** in **10.2.1** below). Using this arrangement, the seller will be able to obtain, quite quickly, the ownership and possession of a bill of exchange, which it will be able to exchange at the end of the credit period for the full contract sum or, if necessary, 'negotiated' before that date, for a lesser sum ('discounting' a bill of exchange). This use of a bill gives considerable flexibility to the seller in its need to raise interim finance, and the mechanisms for raising, accepting and transferring of bills are dealt with at **10.4** below. For the moment, the illustration given in **Figure 9.1** above is continued to show the financial arrangements.

10.2.1 Illustration of transaction

In the transaction outlined in **Figure 10.1** below, the assumption is made that the parties agree to make use of both a bill of exchange and a documentary credit arrangement. You should realise that documentary credits are very expensive for the buyer, and in many cases contracts are entered into without such credit arrangements. The next best arrangement for the seller, from the point of view of security, is to make use of a 'documentary bill'. The nature and use of a documentary bill is discussed at **10.4.7** below, immediately before the section on documentary credits at **10.5**.

Figure 10.1 Financing and security stages in an international sale of goods

Scenario

The same arrangements are contemplated between S and B, but we now become aware that S has not dealt with B before and has reservations about entering the contract with B for two main reasons:

(a) S must buy the components for these goods and pay S's own assembly workers before it is able to deliver the goods and invoice B for them; also, B is demanding a 60-day credit period from the date of shipment of the goods; and

(b) S normally sells its goods on a retention of title basis, so that it can physically recover any unsold goods if a buyer fails to pay or becomes insolvent. Once the goods have left the UK, this ceases to be a practicable option for S.

↓

Stage 1 – entering the contract

S and B agree to enter the contract on the terms already described at **9.1**, but in addition to these terms they have agreed to the following terms for the financing and security arrangements:

(a) Before S will commence putting the goods together, B must pay for an independent bank to put in place a type of financial guarantee to safeguard S, known as a 'letter of credit' or more simply as a documentary credit (a more detailed description is given at **10.5**). This credit is required to operate over the period between the date when S begins production of the goods and the date when, following delivery to the ship, S presents the documents required to the bank specified in the credit. These documents, as well as the time and place of presentation, must comply with the details shown on the face of the documentary credit itself (the credit will have to display an expiry date, but see **10.5.5** on this point). The actual presentation of the documents might not be done by S itself but by S's bank acting as S's agent, although nothing turns on that for present purposes.

(b) As part of this list of documents, S will itself draw up another document in the form of a bill of exchange, which, if all documents (including the bill of exchange) comply with the terms of the documentary credit, will be signed ('acceptance') by the bank and immediately returned to S, the other documents being forwarded to B as explained at **9.1**. The bill of exchange will, effectively, be an order to the bank itself to pay S the contract sum at a future date, in this case 60 days after presentation and acceptance by the bank's signature.

↓

Stage 2 – making delivery of the goods

This all proceeds as described in **9.1** above; the financing arrangements agreed do not alter this.

↓

Stages 3 and 4 – provision and tender of documents by S

The documents described in **9.1** above remain the same, but now there is added to the list the bill of exchange, which will be required to show, on its face, the documentary credit arrangement and number under the terms of which it is presented and under which payment is guaranteed. The documentary credit will be very specific about the manner in which the bill of exchange is to be drawn up and presented for acceptance, as well as the form and content of all the other documents. Strict compliance will be required, otherwise the documents are unlikely to be accepted and the credit will not operate (see **10.5.3** below).

↓

Stage 5 – payment of S

Once the required documents have been accepted by the bank for forwarding to B, and S has had its bill of exchange accepted by the bank's signature, S's options are really quite wide: S could simply wait the 60 days after acceptance and then go back and present the bill for payment at full face value; if S chooses not to wait, it could 'negotiate' the bill for a slightly reduced cash sum now ('discounting' the bill), either to the bank itself or to another buyer (the reduction or 'discounting' is to reflect the 60-day period that the new holder of the bill will have to wait for its money; money can earn money during that period!). A third, very useful option is that S may be able to negotiate the bill to one of S's own creditors; in times of difficult cash flow, that might achieve a better value from the bill for S than a straight sale of it. The sale and negotiation of bills of exchange is a considerable business in itself in the commercial world.

10.3 Negotiable instruments

From ancient times, the mercantile practice has been to use paper as a convenient substitute for dangerous and weighty forms of payment, such as gold or other metal. This practice became possible only because of the mutual recognition, by people of business, of certain types of paper document and, more significantly, of those persons who had put their names to those documents. This led to the mercantile practice of 'negotiation', that is the giving and receiving of documents which evidenced promises to pay and to receive money, in much the same way and to the same effect as handing over the money itself. The document is said to be 'negotiable', and the common law, as well as statute (Bills of Exchange Act 1882 (BEA 1882)), has recognised the lawfulness and value of this practice.

An instrument is a document which evidences the holder's right to enforce a legal right, such as, say, a promise to pay a sum of money (a 'promissory note') or an order to someone else to pay out a sum of money (a bill of exchange). A negotiable instrument is one that is intended to be freely transferable from person to person, either by a simple transfer of the document (as with a banknote or a 'bearer' bill of exchange) or by the transfer of the document along with an 'endorsement', a signature on the document (as with a cheque). The effect is that the legal rights of the transferor pass to the transferee, without further formality; this is one of the main advantages of negotiable instruments. 'Negotiation' simply summarises this transfer of rights by a legally valid method of transfer of the document to a person who becomes a bona fide holder of the bill for value.

Negotiable instruments include:

(a) cheques;
(b) bills of exchange;
(c) bank notes;
(d) banker's drafts; and
(e) promissory notes (in some circumstances).

Sometimes they can be made payable to the person in possession of them (ie, 'to bearer'), as with bank notes or 'bearer bills'. In other cases, they are made out to a specific payee who can endorse the instrument and make it payable to a third party, perhaps a creditor of the original payee named on the bill or of a 'holder in due course', who has become part of a succession of persons to whom the bill has been negotiated (see **10.4.3**). Cheques used to be widely negotiable but, as a fraud prevention measure, most cheques are now printed with crossing lines and 'a/c payee', which prevents them being transferable by endorsement.

Bills of exchange are defined in the BEA 1882, s 3(1) as follows:

> A bill of exchange is an unconditional order in writing, addressed by one person to another, signed by the person giving it, requiring the person to whom it is addressed to pay on demand or at a fixed or determinable future time, a sum certain in money to or to the order of a specified person, or to a bearer.

A cheque is defined as a 'bill of exchange drawn on a banker, payable on demand' (BEA 1882, s 73). A cheque is therefore a sub-species of a bill of exchange.

10.4 Bills of exchange

There are three original parties to a bill of exchange:

(a) drawer;
(b) drawee; and
(c) payee.

Perhaps the analogy of a personal cheque is the easiest one to visualise. Here, you would be the drawer of the cheque, your bank would be the drawee (eg, Barclays Bank) and the payee would be the person you are paying (eg, your landlord). The biggest difference to a personal cheque situation is that the drawee must 'accept' the bill by signing it, in order to become liable to pay out on it (see **10.4.1** and **10.4.2**).

With a bill of exchange one basic position could be:

(a) drawer – the buyer;
(b) drawee – the buyer's bank; and
(c) payee – the seller of the goods.

This arrangement may be varied by the agreement of the parties who have decided to use the bill as a method of payment, usually to suit commercial convenience (see **10.4.2**).

Typical characteristics of a bill of exchange are:

(a) every obligation in the bill must be expressed in writing;
(b) the order to pay must be unconditional;
(c) it is addressed by one person to another (see **10.4.2**);
(d) it is payable on demand or at a fixed time in the future (see **10.4.1**);
(e) it is for a specific sum of money;
(f) the drawer, or his agent, must have signed it;
(g) the obligations, typically payment, can be transferred by 'negotiation', usually at a discount (see **10.4.1**); and
(h) performance of the obligations (eg, payment) can be demanded only by the person holding the bill.

A bill of exchange will specify the place of payment (eg, 'payable in New York City at XY bank').

10.4.1 'Term' bills and 'sight' bills

Bills of exchange must be presented to the drawee, for acceptance, in order to become payable. Most bills of exchange are 'term bills', that is they are expressed to be payable at some date after they have been initially presented to the bank (which is the drawee). This is usually 90 or 180 days from that date, eg, '90 days after sight'. In other words, they must be presented twice to the bank, and payment is due on the second occasion. 'Negotiation' means discounting the bill of exchange, that is, selling it at less than its full value to a third party who will eventually present the bill to the bank for payment. When a bill is negotiated, the original payee will not receive 100% of the face value as it is to his advantage to have payment early rather than wait for 90 or 180 days, as the case may be. (In many cases the bill is in fact negotiated between the original payee and the bank, so the bank pays out immediately but for less than 100% of the face value.)

The other type of bill is a 'sight' bill, which will be paid on the first occasion it is presented to the drawee (the bank), so the payee does not have to wait for payment.

In both cases, payment of the bill depends on the conditions on the bill being met, including, for example, the place of payment; also, where the contract includes a documentary credit, the bill and any other documents specified by the credit must be drawn up and presented in accordance with the credit.

10.4.2 Methods of use of bills of exchange

The simplest way in which a bill could be used would be by the buyer drawing up the bill, drawn on its own bank, and giving it to the seller, who would then present it at the buyer's bank for immediate payment, or for acceptance which would then render the bill fully negotiable. That would work well where seller and buyer are located in the same place, but could be very inconvenient where they are in different countries. In this latter situation, the seller holding a term bill would, if it chose to not negotiate the bill, have to arrange two visits to the offshore buyer's bank: one to present the bill for acceptance, and another for payment.

That would not be sensible and, instead, a commonly agreed practice is for the seller to draw up the bill and to present it to its own bank for acceptance. The seller's bank will be prepared to accept the bill if it has already agreed with the buyer's bank that the buyer's bank will reimburse it in return for the documents required to perform the sale of goods contract. Where a bill of exchange is used in this way it is often referred to as a 'documentary bill' because of its association with the other documents.

Bills of exchange can be used in a great variety of circumstances, and detailed discussion of these is beyond the scope of this work, but in simple terms, almost any type of payment transaction can be facilitated by their use. Probably the simplest use is to carry a single paper banker's draft in preference to a large amount of currency, where it is convenient or requisite to do so. Many commercial and business creditors are happy to take term bills of exchange by discounting them, as discussed at **10.4.1**. At the other end of the scale, complicated loan, instalment and credit arrangements can be achieved by the use of series of bills, presentable for acceptance and/or payment at different stages.

10.4.3 The relationship of the bill of exchange and underlying sales contracts

Because of the unconditional nature of the obligation to pay on a bill of exchange, the bill develops an autonomy of its own, quite divorced from the underlying sale of goods transaction. In effect, the bill is given to be treated as cash, and the general rule is that any question of liability to meet payment on the bill is unaffected by any defect or breach of the underlying sales contract on the part of the seller. The only real exception to this is if there is complete or partial and quantified failure of consideration by the seller and he is the one who is suing for payment; here, the buyer can raise the breach as a defence to an action for refusal to pay the bill. There can be no defence at all to a claim by a transferee of the bill based upon the underlying sales contract. This is the explanation for the so-called 'cheque action', where a buyer of goods who has paid by cheque and subsequently stopped the cheque, because of some complaint about the goods, is usually sued not for breach of the sales contract, but for obligations arising from giving the cheque in lieu of cash; it is an action on a bill of exchange, on a promise that the paper could be turned into cash, which usually succeeds.

10.4.4 Liability on a bill of exchange

In general terms, any person who becomes a party, by signature, to the contractual arrangement contained within a bill of exchange, can become liable to the payee or any 'holder in due course' (see **10.4.5**). This possibility of spreading of liability on a bill by multiple signatures is another of the commercial safeguards and advantages of their use. The primary liability is clearly intended to be that of the drawee, the person 'on' whom it is drawn and who should, normally, accept it. If the drawee refuses to accept, ie 'dishonours' the bill, then the drawer of it normally becomes secondarily liable. Any person (apart from one who signs it as an agent) who endorses the bill can usually be made liable on it, so there could be a 'chain' of endorsers, although a forged endorsement (usually following a theft of the bill) will usually remove the liability of earlier endorsers. Despite this, the bill would remain valid and later endorsers would be liable on it, and it would be able to be presented for payment at its due date. This is a very important point of legal principle, that the inherent negotiability and commercial value of a bill are not destroyed by a dishonest dealing with the bill; it remains solidly negotiable (*Bank of England v Vagliano Bros* [1891] AC 107, HL),

This is a very general statement of the liability situation and reference should be made to other texts for dealing with detailed questions, such as liability and indemnity between different parties.

10.4.5 The 'holder in due course'

There are three different types of holder of a bill, but the most important and favourable status is that of a 'holder in due course'. This is similar to the concept of being 'equity's darling'. Basically, a person who takes a bill, 'complete and regular on the face of it', before it becomes overdue and without notice of dishonour or defect in title of the previous owner, for value and in good faith, will be a holder in due course (BEA 1882, s 29(1)). The strength in such a holder's position comes from the fact that it takes the bill 'free of equities', which means that any defect in title of prior holders, or any defences which might have been available to any of them (eg, total failure of consideration set up against a seller/drawer of the bill), are simply washed away and the bill is perfected for future negotiation and use, even by later transferees who knew of problems relating to earlier holders . This all helps to add to the commercial willingness to use bills of exchange; they can suffer a degree of error and misuse but still be kept commercially valid and useful.

The other types of holder under the 1882 Act are 'holders for value' and mere 'holders', who have reduced rights and are not discussed further.

10.4.6 Claused bills

A bill of exchange is not normally set out as simply as is a personal cheque. It has 'clauses'. There could be provisions, for example, dealing with exchange rates for currencies, or stating that the bill is payable with bankers' charges. If a bill does not stipulate that incidental charges are borne by the drawee (the bank) then they are borne by the drawer (buyer of the goods). An example of a simple draft bill of exchange (without clauses) is set out on page 145.

10.4.7 The use of documentary bills

Using a 'documentary bill' to facilitate an international sale of goods is a common and well-tried technique to give a measure of security to the seller of goods to an overseas buyer. The main use of this method is where the seller wishes to guard against problems in getting paid but is not in a strong enough bargaining position to be able to demand the provision of a documentary credit (see **10.1** above). The next best thing is to make use of the skill and probity of the banking system to safeguard the seller's position. It is usually used where goods are being shipped under a document of title, such as a bill of lading (see **9.3.1**), which would normally allow the buyer, once in possession of the bill, immediately to make good title to another by selling the goods onwards, even if they are still afloat. This creates a serious risk of non-payment for the seller, but it can be reduced somewhat, in the following way:

(a) The seller agrees to contract on the basis that the bill of lading, plus any other documents required by the contract (insurance policy, etc), should be accompanied by a term bill of exchange (the 'documentary bill'). This complete bundle of documents would be taken to the seller's own onshore bank (a 'remitting bank', see **10.6** below), for onward tender to the buyer abroad.

(b) The safeguard for the seller is that a precondition for the onward transmission of the documents is that they do not go directly to the buyer but go first to a bank in the buyer's country, known as the 'collecting bank', from which the buyer can receive the documents only if it accepts the bill of exchange, this accepted bill being then remitted to the seller.

This arrangement may have the consequence that the bill of exchange is accepted by the offshore buyer, allowing him to get the title documents and the immediate right to sell the goods on. Nevertheless, the bill can still become dishonoured by non-payment when it becomes due for payment; that is the main reason why a seller will try to get a documentary credit put in place, whenever possible (see **10.5** below).

10.5 Documentary credits ('letters of credit')

We have just looked at the use of bills of exchange and other ways to facilitate the payment to the seller, but payment may never be made at all if the buyer refuses to or cannot pay for the goods, perhaps because of insolvency, or the bill of exchange is dishonoured for some reason. In international sales and supply contracts, the use of documentary credits is very widespread as a means of ensuring and guaranteeing the performance of the buyer. The buyer, as part of the contract, agrees to arrange and pay for a creditworthy bank (the 'issuing bank') to enter into an agreement under which it provides a written assurance, the documentary credit, that, if the seller properly performs its side of the contract, the bank will pay the seller. In this, the bank acts directly as principal towards the seller, and not simply as a guarantor if the buyer does not pay. The bank, rather than the buyer, is the paymaster to the seller, and the seller's rights are directly enforceable against it.

There are many advantages to this type of arrangement:

(a) Supervening insolvency of the buyer becomes less of a risk for the seller.

(b) It is possible (at additional expense to the buyer) to have the credit confirmed by another bank (the 'confirming bank', typically in the seller's country). That would be known as a 'confirmed credit' – see **10.5.5**.

(c) The seller can use a bank in its own country as an 'advising bank'. Here, the advising bank takes on the responsibility (as agent for the issuing bank) to advise the seller when the credit is opened, to receive and check the shipping documents for the sale, and to pay the seller, or accept and/or pay up on bills of exchange payable to the seller. The advising bank's liability is only to advise; it does not guarantee the credit.

(d) The credit can be arranged to open from whatever date the seller requires to safeguard its position, so, if it is required to buy the goods for resale to the seller or incur expense in their manufacture, it could have the credit period cover those periods of exposure.

(e) Whatever bank is holding the shipping documents will be able to retain the documents, if necessary, to secure its own position if the buyer cannot refund the bank what it has paid to the seller.

BILL OF EXCHANGE
(DRAFT)

No ....

Exchange for .... [AMOUNT] [6].................... [DATE] .... *20* ....
.... [AT SIGHT/90 DAYS AFTER DATE] [5].............. *of this* BILL OF EXCHANGE
pay to the order of [4]................. *[OURSELVES]* .... *the sum of* ....
[AMOUNT IN WORDS] ....

To NORTH EAST BANK plc[2]
COMMERCIAL ROAD, DALEBY,
EAST YORKSHIRE, DN1 72Y

FOR AND ON BEHALF OF
NORTHERN SPINNERS LTD[1,3]

____
DIRECTOR

1. addressed by one person (the drawer)
2. to another (the drawee), here the seller's bank
3. signed by the person giving it (the drawer)
4. requiring the person to whom it is addressed to pay to the order of a specified person or to bearer (the payee)
5. on demand, or at a fixed or determinable future time
6. a certain sum in money.

[Note: acceptance by signature will be required with a 'term bill' (see point 5 in this example and **10.4.1**); it is quite normal to insert words of acceptance on the face of the bill, but this is not essential as signature will suffice without more. With a sight or demand bill, no signature is required.]

(f) The added security for a seller is likely to be reflected in reduced sale prices in many cases.

(g) The involvement of banks and experienced staff, and the potential liability of the banks to the parties to the sale transaction, ensures great particularity in the handling of documents, to the advantage of all concerned.

(h) Much progress is being made towards the electronic handling of documentation connected to letters of credit, using the BOLERO system discussed in **Chapter 9**.

In international (and sometimes in domestic) sales of goods, it is quite common for the seller to require a documentary credit to be opened, as a guarantee that the seller will be paid, once he presents the documents specified in the credit to the bank.

An example of an irrevocable, unconfirmed letter of credit is set out below.

Lloyds TSB
Commercial

an irrevocable letter of credit

Advice for the beneficiary

NAME OF ISSUING BANK
ABC Bank Plc, International Division,
1, Broadway, London EC27

Irrevocable documentary credit — Number 62340

Place and date of issue
London 15th April 1998

Place and date of expiry
at counters of advising bank 31st August 1998

Applicant –
Playtime Toys Limited
Blisset Street
London W36

Beneficiary –
The Orient Toy Company
Cornwall Road North
Hong Kong

Advising Bank – Ref. No. –
Bank XYZ
Duke Road
Hong Kong

Amount –
HK$ 9,000 (Hong Kong Dollars nine thousand)

Availability
☐ by sight payment ☒ by acceptance ☐ by negotiation
☐ by deferred payment at
against the documents detailed herein
☒ and beneficiary's draft at 90 days sight
on Bank XYZ, Duke Road, Hong Kong

Partial Shipments ☐ allowed ☒ not allowed
Transhipment ☐ allowed ☒ not allowed

Shipping/despatch/taking in charge from/at Hong Kong
for transportation to: Heathrow Airport, London

INVOICE IN THREE COPIES ALL ORIGINALLY SIGNED certifying that the goods are in accordance with Playtime Toys Limited Order Number 51 dated 4.2.1998.

AIR CONSIGNMENT NOTE evidencing goods dispatched to Playtime Toys Limited London W36 marked "Freight Paid".

PACKING LIST IN TRIPLICATE

We are informed that insurance is being arranged by our principals.

DESCRIPTION OF GOODS

Plastic toy cars

CFR Heathrow Airport, London.

Specimen

Documents to be presented within 7 days after the date of issuance of the transport document(s) but within the validity of credit.

We hereby issue the Documentary Credit in your favour. It is subject to the Uniform Customs and Practice for Documentary Credits (1993 Revision International Chamber of Commerce, Paris, France, Publication No. 500) and engages us in accordance with the terms thereof. The number and the date of the credit and the name of our bank must be quoted on all drafts required. If the credit is available by negotiation, each presentation must be noted on the reverse of this advice by the bank where the credit is available.

ABC Bank Plc, International Division
1, Broadway, London EC27

This document consists of 1 signed page(s)

The College of Law wishes to thank Lloyds TSB for its kind permission to reproduce this document.

10.5.1 The Uniform Customs and Practice for Documentary Credits

Almost all documentary credits are expressed to be drawn up under the Uniform Customs and Practice for Documentary Credits (UCP) published by the ICC. The current version is UCP 600 (2007 revision), which came into effect on 1 July 2007; a supplement, 'eUCP', deals with electronic documents.

The documentary credit is the issuing bank's guarantee that the beneficiary will be paid and also states the method of payment (the specimen provided shows that payment is by acceptance of a 90-day 'term bill'; this specimen is drawn up in accordance with UCP 600). Once the bill of exchange is accepted, the documentary credit has achieved its purpose and has no further function.

The documentary credit could provide for any one of four methods of payment contemplated by the UCP:

(a) cash on presentation of the documents by the seller – 'payment at sight';

(b) cash at some future time, eg after 90 days – 'deferred payment';

(c) a bill of exchange drawn by the seller, probably a term bill payable at a future date – 'acceptance credit'; or

(d) negotiating a bill of exchange drawn by the seller – 'negotiation credit'.

There are also different types of documentary credit which are beyond the scope of this chapter, but all have the common feature that they are intended to facilitate some underlying contract, typically for a sale or, perhaps, for construction.

The definition of a documentary credit in UCP 600, Article 2 is:

> Any arrangement, however named or described, . . . that is irrevocable and thereby constitutes a definite undertaking of the issuing bank to honour a complying presentation.

To 'honour' means to fulfil the credit arrangement by one or another of the payment methods shown at (a) to (d) above. A 'complying presentation' of documents is one that is in accordance with the terms and conditions of the credit, the applicable provisions of the UCP and with international standard banking practice.

The buyer will be the applicant for the credit. The seller will be 'the beneficiary' under the credit.

There are two fundamental principles of documentary credits. These are:

(a) the autonomy of the documentary credit; and

(b) the doctrine of strict compliance.

10.5.2 The autonomy of the documentary credit

It is of the highest importance that the documentary credit is completely independent of any other contractual arrangements or disputes arising from the underlying sale of goods contract, although the credit comes into being only as a result of that contract. Once in place, the credit contract is autonomous and has a separate life of its own. It is also generally independent of any disputes arising out of the associated use of bills of exchange. The above statements are generalisations and are subject to some caveats in complex circumstances. The seller only needs to fulfil the terms of the documentary credit by presenting the required documents (see the documents required under the specimen credit reproduced above, which also extend to presenting a bill of exchange for acceptance). See also *British Imex Industries Ltd v Midland Bank Ltd* [1958] 1 QB 542 and UCP 600, Article 4.

10.5.3 The doctrine of strict compliance

At common law and under UCP 600, Article 4, 'banks are in no way concerned' with the underlying contracts for sale and are only to concern themselves with the question whether the documents provided by the seller are in accordance with the instructions of the buyer (see UCP 600, Articles 5 and 34). These instructions must be complied with very strictly, and the bank is only entitled to accept or reject documents accordingly. In the case of an advising bank, if it wrongly accepts documents, it will be liable to the issuing bank (as its agent); and if it wrongly rejects documents, it may well be liable to the seller, but also to the buyer and to the issuing bank (see **10.6.1** on this point).

In *Equitable Trust Company of New York v Dawson Partners Ltd* (1927) 27 Ll L Rep 49, which concerned a fraudulent seller and a contract to buy vanilla beans from Indonesia, Sumner LJ held: 'There is no room for documents which are almost the same or which will do just as well.' The House of Lords held that the claimant bank could not recover from the buyer as it had relied on the opinion of one expert, not of two experts as specified in the documents.

An example of the limits of this doctrine is the case of *Gian Singh & Co Ltd v Banque de l'Indochine* [1974] 1 WLR 1234. The Privy Council allowed the defence of a bank that used reasonable care in complying with the prima facie requirements of a documentary credit, notwithstanding that one of the specified documents was in fact a forgery. The point to take from this important case is that the visual appearance of good order and compliance is all that needs to be determined on presentation of the documents.

In *Credit Industriel et Commercial v China Merchants Bank* [2002] EWHC 973 (Comm), [2002] 2 All ER (Comm) 427, the documentary credit did not require the bills of exchange themselves to be in English, only the documents needed to negotiate the bills. The bills of exchange were from a French bank, and were in French. The defendant was held to be unjustified in rejecting the documents.

In *Oliver v Dubai Bank Kenya Ltd* [2007] EWHC 2165 (Comm), the court refused to give a declaration that a document which should have been provided by the beneficiary could be dispensed with. It was a documentary condition of the credit and should have been complied with.

10.5.4 The fraud exception to acceptance of complying documents

As seen at **10.5.3**, the banks must accept documents which are in strict compliance, but a very narrow exception is available to the bank that wishes to reject the documents, or to a buyer who wishes to restrain the bank from paying out on the credit. This exception may be available where either the documents presented by the seller or some aspects of their presentation are tainted by fraud.

Czarnikow-Rionda Sugar Trading v Standard Bank London Ltd [1999] 1 All ER (Comm) 890 is a good illustration of the general reluctance of judges in commercial law cases to interfere with established commercial practices, in this case reliance upon documentary credits (letters of credit). Thus, Rix J held:

> ... even if I assume for the sake of argument that Rionda [the buyer] has otherwise brought itself within the fraud exception, its claim against Standard [the bank] for a pre-trial injunction must fail on the balance of convenience alone. I would seek to put the matter in the following way.
>
> (1) The interest in the integrity of banking contracts is so great that not even fraud can be allowed to intervene unless the fraud comes to the notice of the bank (a) in time, ie in any event before the beneficiary is paid, and (b) in such a way that it can be said that the bank had knowledge of the fraud.
>
> ... Unless the banking commitment can be insulated from disputes between merchants, international trade would become impossible.

(2) … Once, however, a letter of credit arrangement has been set up, the special rule that only the fraud exception permits interference comes into play.

(3) Thus, in the absence of the fraud exception, a buyer can no more seek to prevent his seller from drawing on the letter of credit for which the seller has stipulated, than the buyer can seek to prevent his bank from making the payment under it. The reason is that otherwise the special rule could be subverted, and the integrity and insulation of banking contracts could be overthrown, simply by the device of injuncting the beneficiary rather than the bank.

So, Rix J would not allow an injunction to prevent the bank from paying out on the documentary credit, or an injunction to prevent the seller from drawing on the documentary credit. Instead, he suggested that the claimant could seek a freezing order against the seller's bank accounts, so that the proceeds of the alleged fraud could not be disposed of before the dispute was resolved.

By contrast, in *Mahonia Ltd v JP Morgan Chase Bank (No 1)* [2003] EWHC 1927 (Comm), the court refused to order payment against a documentary credit which had been entered into for the purpose of share swap transactions which were illegal in the US. The illegality had 'tainted' the credit arrangement.

10.5.5 Practical considerations in using documentary credits

The starting point is with the cost to the buyer of using letters of credit. These are very expensive to arrange, and the less creditworthy the buyer, the more expensive the credit, because of the risk to the credit supplier. Clearly, a seller is able to obtain a documentary credit only if it has enough bargaining power, but where a credit is available, the provision of it will become a buyer's obligation in the sale contract.

The next question is what type of credit is required. The normal practice is to use an irrevocable credit, which cannot be revoked by the buyer once it is put into place. You will have seen at **10.5.1** above that UCP 600 applies only to irrevocable credits (the previous version, UCP 500, did extend to revocable credit, but this is no longer the case). If the seller is in a particularly strong position, it may be able to require the provision of a confirmed credit, which will be a completely independently guaranteed credit provided by, typically, an onshore bank in the seller's country. This is to cover the possibility that some problem may arise with the issuing bank or its location – problems such as insolvency, war or political instability can create difficulties in international sales. This may considerably increase the cost of the credit, but if the issuing bank is a substantial organisation, the extra cost in having an onshore confirmation may not be too great; it is a 'belt and braces' arrangement. The confirmed credit will usually be arranged by the issuing bank, but actually provided by the confirming bank.

The next stage is for the buyer to arrange with the issuing bank, possibly in its own country, to open the credit in favour of the seller; the issuing bank will then usually ask a bank in the seller's country to 'advise' the seller of the credit and to act as its agent in that matter. The advising bank will also usually act as the confirming bank, where a confirmed credit is provided, but it is not essential that they be one and the same bank. The advising bank will notify the seller, who will then proceed to the performance of the sale contract.

The period of validity of the credit is important, and the specimen documentary credit shown at **10.4.6** has a clear issue and expiry date. The seller thus knows exactly for how long he is covered by the credit (if no opening date is specified in the sale contract, there will be an implied term that the credit will open and be advised to the seller within a reasonable period before the shipment date). All credits must stipulate an expiry date and a place for presentation of documents (UCP 600, Article 6), and the documents must be presented before the expiry date. The credit should also state a period of time after shipment within which the documents should be tendered by the seller. If no such period is stated, 21 days only is allowed (UCP 600,

Article 14). So, the longstop date for presenting documents is either the expiry date of the credit, or 21 days after shipment, whichever occurs first (see **10.6.2** below).

At this point, the seller having tendered the documents to the bank, the documents are examined for strict compliance. This will often involve two detailed examinations, one by the advising bank and another by the issuing bank upon transfer to it of the documents. This is because either bank may be liable for wrongfully accepting or rejecting documents. If all is well with the documents, the advising bank will pay out the seller in accordance with the payment scheme shown on the credit itself. The specimen credit shown at **10.4.6** has four options shown on it: payment in cash on sight of the documents; by acceptance of a bill of exchange; by negotiating a bill of exchange; and by a deferred cash payment. The acceptance option has been chosen on that specimen.

10.5.6 Transfer and assignment of documentary credits

There is a very limited regime of transfer of documentary credits permitted by Article 38 of UCP 600, to cover the situation where the seller might, itself, need to transfer (typically, in part) its credit to a third party (usually, one of its own suppliers or creditors) where the situation demands it. This could happen, perhaps, in 'string' contracts for commodities, etc. To do this, the credit must be clearly expressed to be 'transferable'; nothing less will do. Even then, it is only a right to request the issuing bank to transfer the credit at its own choice; the bank cannot be required to do so, and it would need to consent expressly to the extent and manner of the transfer (Article 38(a)). Even if the issuing bank agrees, there can be no further transfer thereafter (Article 38(d)).

It is not possible to 'assign' a credit, in the sense that one could assign the right to present shipping documents, etc. That would need to be achieved by transfer, as discussed above. All that can be assigned, in connection with a credit, is the right to money received or receivable under the credit contract (UCP 600, Article 39).

10.5.7 Brief glossary of credit types

A brief guide to the descriptions given to different types of documentary credit may help:

(a) 'straight credit' – here, only the beneficiary (seller) is able to use the credit and to deal directly with the issuing and/or confirming bank;

(b) 'negotiation credit' – here, the intention is that the beneficiary may negotiate a bill of exchange, for early payment, to a bank, and that bank will then be able to stand in the shoes of the original beneficiary as against the issuing bank. These are used only where the credit does not provide for immediate payment;

(c) 'standby credit' – this is quite different to the other credits discussed and is much more like a guarantee, which can be required by either party to an international sale or supply. The credit is called upon, as an 'insurance', only should the other party be in breach of its obligation, and the documents presentable will show breach of obligations rather than performance of them (cf ordinary commercial letters of credit);

(d) 'revolving credit' – this is a bit like a running balance, where the seller can draw up to a certain maximum amount at any time, and is designed to meet the needs of ongoing supply arrangements;

(e) 'back to back credits' – where, in a 'string' of sales, the same goods pass through different hands, a party may need to provide a letter of credit to the person who sells the goods to him and so on back up the string. In this case, the process of transferring credits, which is limited to one transfer only (see **10.5.6**), can be extended without limit; the first credit arrangement, in favour of the 'final' seller in the string, is used as security to arrange credits going back up the string towards the first seller.

10.6 Functions, responsibilities and liabilities of banks in international sales

The terminology used in the commercial practice area of documentary transactions can be very confusing, so a short glossary is given below. The seller and the buyer will often choose to use their local banks to act as trustworthy agents for the purpose of delivering or collecting documents, but it does not follow that those particular banks will fall within the definitions below. The terms below refer to common commercial descriptions of banks, by their function, without having regard to mere agency use:

(a) '*Remitting bank*' and '*collecting bank*' - the remitting bank is the bank in the UK to which the seller takes those documents required to be remitted to the seller; the collecting bank is the overseas bank, from which the buyer will obtain the documents. Both of these banks are treated as collecting banks for the purposes of the Uniform Rules for Collections of the International Chamber of Commerce, which usually govern the relationships involved in dealing with the documents (see **10.6.1**). The terminology of remitting and collecting banks is more appropriate to sales made by using documentary bills (see **10.4.7**), rather than where documentary credits are used.

(b) '*Presenting bank*' - the process of the seller presenting the conforming, stipulated documents in exchange for payment or acceptance/negotiation of a bill of exchange at a particular bank is known as 'presentation' and, not unnaturally, that bank is sometimes referred to as the 'presenting bank'. Here, we shall use the UCP term of 'nominated bank' instead (see (f) below).

(c) '*Issuing bank*' - the bank that provides, as principal, the documentary credit facilities under which the seller ('beneficiary') is to be paid, either directly by the issuing bank or indirectly, by a 'nominated bank' (see (f) below). The issuing bank may be located anywhere, but it will be assumed for present purposes to be in the buyer's country.

(d) '*Confirming bank*' - where the seller is able to demand a confirmed documentary credit, this is the bank that provides the completely independent contractual guarantee to the seller, in case the issuing bank defaults for some reason. The issuing bank instructs the confirming bank to provide the confirmation credit, but the confirming bank, acting as a principal, gives an independent undertaking to the beneficiary/seller. The confirming bank will often also be the 'advising bank' (see (e) below) but need not be.

(e) '*Advising bank*' - this is the bank, usually in S's country, that has been instructed by the issuing bank to advise the seller that the credit is open. In this, it acts as agent to the issuing bank, and its letter to the seller advising of the opening is the actual 'letter of credit'; from the moment of its receipt, the issuing bank is bound by the credit. It could easily be the seller's own bank.

(f) '*Nominated bank*' - any bank that is nominated by the issuing bank to accept or negotiate bills of exchange; it acts as an intermediary and has no privity with the buyer.

(g) '*Acceptor*' - a person undertaking to accept the presentation of a bill of exchange. This will usually be a bank, and it is assumed, for present purposes, that the nominated bank will perform this function.

10.6.1 Responsibilities and liabilities of banks

It will be clear to you that many of the different functions and capacities described in the glossary at **10.6** above can be carried out by a single bank, eg a single bank reasonably convenient for the seller, that can combine the separate functions of remitting bank, advising bank, confirming bank, nominated bank/acceptor, etc. The important thing to realise is that each discrete function may give rise to different responsibilities and liabilities towards different persons, so care is needed to analyse just what function a bank is performing at any particular time. A brief summary of the main points is as follows:

(a) *Remitting and collecting banks* - as their function is in dealing with the process under which the seller tenders documentation to the buyer in a documentary bill arrangement (see **10.4.7**), this will raise duties of good faith and reasonable care as between seller and bank, and between the banks (see Part D of the Uniform Rules for Collections, URC 522, 1995), but this is subject to the Uniform Rules being incorporated into the contract, to rights of disclaimer and to force majeure exclusions. There will also be common law contractual duties involved between seller and remitting bank, and between the banks, but not between seller and collecting bank. Nevertheless, each bank is responsible only for what it has been instructed to do.

(b) *The nominated bank, confirming bank and issuing bank, in respect of documents* - here again, the principal role of these banks is that of examining documents to see whether they constitute a 'complying presentation', but this time it is for the purposes of satisfying the requirements of a documentary credit arrangement. Now the matter will fall within the terms of UCP 600 (2007 revision), Article 14. This Article covers nominated banks, confirming banks and the issuing bank; it provides that the standard of examination on presentation is 'to determine, on the basis of the documents alone, whether or not the documents appear on their face to constitute a complying presentation', and that the banks shall have a maximum of five banking days, following the day of presentation, to determine that matter. That period is not curtailed or otherwise affected by the occurrence on or after the date of presentation of any expiry date or last day for presentation. This confirms the rule that banks need only be concerned that the documents have the appearance of being in good order and strict conformity; the banks need not go behind the appearance (*Gian Singh & Co Ltd v Banque de l'Indochine* [1974] 2 All ER 754). The banks do not assume any liability for the form, sufficiency, accuracy, genuineness, falsification or legal effect of any document (UCP 600, Article 34).

The main liability that can arise out of carelessness of the banks in dealing with the documents, and wrongfully accepting or rejecting them, usually will arise towards the buyer, with whom the issuing bank is in contract (but liability can arise towards the seller too, as the bank undertakes to accept complying documents). In consequence, the buyer would usually be justified in refusing both to accept the documents and to pay the issuing bank; in such circumstances, the bank would be likely to end up saddled with the goods!

(c) *The issuing bank/confirming bank/nominated bank, in respect of providing and facilitating the credit facility itself, as against the seller* - the seller will have contractual rights against these banks, even though the seller did not itself enter contracts with those banks. The bank's undertakings to the seller, under the documentary credit, will involve duties of care and skill (as we have already seen with respect to documents at (b) above). If the credit is not opened by the date agreed between the seller and buyer, the seller's remedy will usually be against the buyer, for breach of the terms of the agreement to provide the credit, rather than against the issuing/confirming bank (*Ian Stach Ltd v Baker Bosley Ltd* [1958] 2 QB 130, CA). If the failure to open the credit is the fault of the issuing/confirming bank then the buyer would still be liable to the seller, but would be able to recover against the defaulting bank.

Under UCP 600 Article 15, the issuing bank, once it has determined that a presentation of documents complies, must honour the credit. Nominated or confirming banks that make such a determination must honour or negotiate under the credit terms and forward the documents to whichever bank has instructed them to act. Ultimately, the issuing bank will get the documents and will make sure of its own position before it lets the buyer have them. If the issuing/confirming/nominated bank decides to refuse to honour the credit arrangement, it has only up to the close of the fifth banking day after presentation of the documents to give notice of rejection to the presenter of the documents(UCP 600, Article 16). The bank must, in that notice, give details of the discrepancies justifying rejection; if the bank fails to comply with these requirements, it is precluded from claiming that there is not a complying presentation (Article 16(f)).

(d) *The issuing bank/confirming bank/nominated bank, in respect of providing and facilitating the credit itself, as against the buyer* - the nominated bank is usually treated as the agent of whichever bank has nominated it to act, and is therefore not considered further in this paragraph. Likewise, the confirming bank, although it gives an independent undertaking, as principal to the seller, need not be separately considered in respect of liability towards the buyer, as it would be liable to the issuing bank, under agency principles, for default. The governing factor, in this situation, is the contractual relationship between buyer and issuing bank, which will normally incorporate the terms of the UCP into a standard form contract provided by the bank itself. Provided that the issuing bank follows carefully the instructions given by the buyer, acts with care in arranging a confirmation undertaking (if any) and in instructing a nominated bank as to precise presentation requirements for documents, payment, acceptance or negotiation, then the buyer will have nothing to complain about. If there is default in respect of any of these matters that causes loss to the buyer, the buyer has remedies under the contract subject to any contractual limitations and any force majeure or frustration circumstances (see UCP 600, Article 35).

10.6.2 Duration and expiry of the documentary credit

10.6.2.1 Opening the credit

The credit arrangement should commence in accordance with the agreement between seller and buyer. If there is a commencement date, this must be strictly complied with, as it is often construed as a condition precedent to the entire sales agreement. If the date is not met, the seller could walk away from the contract or, at its option, waive the breach and/or seek damages (see *Glencore Grain Rotterdam BV v Lebanese Organisation for International Commerce* [1997] 4 All ER 514, CA). If no opening date is agreed, the authorities seem to point towards a prima facie implication that it should be opened by the earliest likely shipping date, at the latest.

10.6.2.2 Expiry of the credit

According to UCP 600, Article 6(d) and (e), a credit must state an expiry date for presentation and that an expiry date for honour or negotiation is to be treated as an expiry date for presentation, a complying presentation having to be made on or before that date. This date may be brought forward by the effect of Article 14(c), which requires that a presentation that includes any original transport documents (eg a bill of lading) must be made not later than 21 days after the shipment date, and in any event not later than the expiry date of the credit.

Part II Summary
International Sale Agreements

Topic	*Summary*
Jursidiction	This term means that a court has the constitutional power to hear and decide a legal matter between parties. These powers extend to geographical limits as well as to the range of persons and issues which fall within the legal competence of any particular court or system of courts. Any attempt by a court to give a legal ruling outside of its jurisdiction will result in a nullity, both in the place for which the court has jurisdiction, as well as elsewhere in the world. Many nations and States recognise the jurisdictions and judgments of other countries as a matter of international convention.
Choice of applicable law	When any court has to decide a civil legal dispute, it also has to decide what national system of law should be applied to decide the issues. In the areas with which this text deals, these are mainly contractual issues and the question is of which national law is applicable to the contract or, if more than one system is applied to different parts of the contract, which systems should be applied. Generally, if the parties have made an express choice in a contract, that choice will be respected and applied by the court.
'Brussels II'	This started as an international agreement between the Member States of the EC (apart from Denmark) and is now Regulation (EC) 44/2001, which provides the rules of jurisdiction under which the courts of those States work. It prevents disputes arising over which courts, within that system, should hear a particular matter: typically, disputes where the parties have their residence or domicile in different Member States, or indeed, if one party is not within the EC at all. An express choice of jurisdiction by the parties to a contract will usually be respected, except in matters in which any particular court has exclusive jurisdiction.
Exclusive jurisdiction	This means that there are issues in the case that extend to legal considerations, which the courts of particular Member States only can hear, to the exclusion of all others. Matters such as land, trusts, company matters and validity of intellectual property rights fall under this heading, where those matters are closely connected to a particular Member State, eg the location of land or the place of incorporation of a company etc.

Topic	*Summary*
General jurisdiction	This is the right of a Member State-domiciled defendant to expect that the courts of his own place of domicile will exercise jurisdiction and hear the case against him. There are other provisions (Special Jurisdiction) in Brussels II which, additionally, give jurisdiction to other Member States to hear the dispute, in addition to the courts having general jurisdiction. The court first applied to by the claimant will usually accept jurisdiction although there are special rules, relating to insurance, consumer and employment claims, that prevent some defendants in those matters being sued elsewhere than in their own national courts. Once the courts of one Member State accept jurisdiction, the courts of other Member States should not accept jurisdiction over the same matter.
Rome Convention	This is an international treaty between the EC Member States which provides a system of prima facie rules to help a court decide which system of law is the applicable law for any particular contract. It only applies to contractual disputes. Primacy is usually given to express contractual choice. In the absence of choice, the court looks for the law of the place with which the contract is most closely connected.
Mandatory rules	These are rules of national law that cannot be displaced by the courts of that Member State, where the court is applying an applicable law to a contract, other than the court's own national law. The mandatory rules displace the applicable law, to the extent that the two systems are incompatible.
Bill of lading	This is a document provided by a carrier of goods over water to the person who is shipping the goods, ie sending them off to somewhere else. Its function is to show that the goods have been received by the carrier, to show their quantity and condition, to show the terms under which the goods are being carried and, if necessary, to act as a document of title to show the right to sell the goods or to take possession of them from the carrier, at the end of the journey.
Multimodal transport	This term refers to the method of transporting goods from one place to another where the goods, typically packed into steel containers, can easily be carried by a succession of different vehicles and vessels. Such a trip might initially involve road transport, then cargo air transport, then further road or inland waterway transport, to its ultimate destination.

Topic	*Summary*
Incoterms	These are a comprehensive set of standard form contracts, drawn up by the International Chamber of Commerce, to allow for international transport of goods. They are based on long-settled mercantile practices and provide contracts, under which the rights and responsibilities of the parties are very clearly laid out and recognised. The terms deal particularly with demarcation of responsibility for timing and place of delivery, responsibility for cost allocation and arrangement of the different stages of the transport process, insurance obligations, etc. They are designed to be incorporated by simple reference within sale of goods contracts, with or without express modification.
Negotiable instrument	This refers to a variety of written documents, which are intended to form the subject matter of contractual promises to exchange money for the written document itself. The paper is treated as being equivalent to a certain amount of money, and the right to the money represented by the paper can be transferred by the transfer of the paper document, from one person to another, by whatever method the particular type of instrument requires, in law. Bills of exchange, cheques, banker's drafts and promissory notes are all negotiable instruments.
Bill of exchange	This is a type of negotiable instrument in which one person instructs someone else to pay money to, or to the order of, a specified person. Although these can be drawn against and addressed to private persons, they are much more commonly drawn against and payable by a person's bank ('the drawee'). Typically, they are used by a buyer of goods, who has arranged to pay the seller by the use of a bill of exchange. They are much used in international commerce. Primary liability to pay out on the bill arises upon 'acceptance', by the signature of the drawee (eg the buyer's bank).
Term bill	This is a bill of exchange which is designed to be paid out, not on the day of acceptance, but at some period later. This is often used to provide a credit period to a buyer, who can get his bill accepted and with it the acceptor's promise to pay up. In the alternative, he could take the accepted bill and attempt to negotiate it on (at a small discount) to someone else who is prepared to wait for the term to expire, in order to cash it at full face value.
Sight bill	This is a bill of exchange which is designed to be paid immediately upon acceptance ('on sight'), at full face value.

Topic	*Summary*
Documentary credit	This is a written contractual promise that the person to whom it is intended to give a benefit will be guaranteed to be paid out, provided that that beneficiary performs his part of a contractual arrangement properly. The idea is to provide a solvent and reliable assurance, independent of the buyer of goods, that the seller will be paid. Usually, the credit will be raised by a bank ('the issuing bank'), instructed and paid by the buyer, at the buyer's expense. Most documentary credits are issued under the Uniform Customs and Practice for Documentary Credits. The contract of credit itself is a separate contract from the sale of goods, so failure or insolvency of the buyer would not affect the seller, once the contract is under way. The credit may, quite independently, be confirmed by another bank, eg an offshore issuing bank and an onshore 'confirming bank'.

Part III

INTELLECTUAL PROPERTY

Chapter 11
Introduction to Intellectual Property

11.1	What is intellectual property?	161
11.2	Types of intellectual property	162
11.3	Summary of IP rights	165

11.1 What is intellectual property?

The basic concept of intellectual property (IP) is that of protecting the products, results and rewards of the exercise of human intellectual and commercial endeavour. The property rights in these matters are a form of intangible property, comprising the legal right to stop others using the owner's property without permission and, in some cases, to give a monopoly right to exploit that property commercially.

A problem with protecting things that originate in a person's mind is that much of the subject matter comprised in IP gets dangerously close to claiming, as private property, some things which, at least in theory, should belong to humanity in common. Matters such as use of words of the language, shapes and forms, colours, ideas, ways of thinking and doing things, methods of manufacture, even geographical locations can form the subject matter of such rights. It follows from this that the legal framework for identifying the existence and scope of a private IP right must be very precise and technically ascertainable, if private rights are not to interfere in the free and normal conduct of a civilised society. This has become an ever-increasing problem as we have moved away from a chattel-based world towards a much more information-based existence, where by making a few electronic connections, a person may use and engage the IP of many different owners, possibly in many different places.

Only a limited treatment of these extensive areas of law is possible in this work and the matters are approached as follows.

The question of protection of business reputation is dealt with in **Chapters 12** and **13**, which deal with passing off and trade marks. Business exists to make profits and the surest way to make a profit is to become known and identified as a reliable and reputable supplier of whatever a market requires. It is this protection of the identity of the mark of an organisation with its own particular reputation and output, particularly through the eyes of customers, that is the binding connection between trademark law and passing off.

The second area of protection is that given to creative expression and the right of a creative person to develop property rights in the tangible results of creative talents, so as to be able to stop other persons from making free use of that property without the permission of the creator, by way of copying or otherwise, whether for gain or not. This is dealt with in **Chapters 14** and **15**, on copyright and database right protection.

A third area of protection, similar to protection of creativity, is that given to designs for shapes (both internal and external shapes) and appearances of objects, which are intended to be created to that design, typically by way of manufacture. This is a vital area for protection and one calling for some very fine distinctions, if freedom of design and manufacture is to be generally available to anyone who wishes to make use of it. **Chapter 16** deals with this area. The general idea, here, is to prevent unauthorised commercial exploitation of the designs, rather than simple copying for non-commercial purposes.

The fourth area of protection is that which allows persons of an inventive nature (in terms of being able to do or make things) to be able to take advantage of a limited time period in which they are able to exploit the commercial possibilities of their invention, in a monopolistic way, by the use of registered patents. Even during this limited time period, the underlying inventive thinking must be available to the public at large, so as to enter the collective body of human knowledge, in exchange for the monopoly right of exploitation. This area is dealt with in **Chapter 17**.

These areas of law, along with other concepts such as the protection of confidential information and 'know-how' protection (dealt with in **Chapter 18**), provide the framework within which individuals, businesses and the general public are able to benefit from a principled, reasonably predictable and equitable sharing of human intellectual output. This framework gives protection to those who create and think; it allows the public to benefit and develop from steps taken by innovators and designers; it encourages and stimulates business growth and entrepreneurial spirit; lastly, it prevents an unseemly and ultimately destructive free-for-all in the unlimited and unscrupulous use and misuse of other people's property, to the common good – the so-called 'springboard' doctrine (see **18.3**).

A consequence of the ownership of IP is that it can come to represent much, if not all, of the real asset value of many businesses. Like most other property it can be dealt in, sold, bought, licensed or charged by way of security. Modern giants, such as the Microsoft organisation, could not have come into existence so quickly, on such a titanic, financial scale, unless they consisted primarily of IP assets. Apart from dealing with the licensing and assignment aspects of IP rights, the asset value aspect of such property is not dealt with further in this work.

11.2 Types of intellectual property

Intellectual property rights are now primarily statutory, supported by considerable case law. Some common law rights come under the heading of IP, mainly passing off and breach of confidence. There is also a number of lesser IP rights, some of which are mentioned at **11.2.7** and **11.2.8**.

11.2.1 Trade marks

A trade mark is a brand name or other mark of trade origin, for example Coca-Cola for soft drinks, BMW for cars and motorcycles, or Levi's for jeans. It is a highly commercial right. Trade marks are best protected by registration (and all well-known trade marks are registered). This gives the owner of the trade mark statutory rights, under the Trade Marks Act 1994 (TMA 1994), to defend its trade mark against infringers who are using the same mark or a similar one.

The registration of a trade mark can be renewed indefinitely, provided the trade mark does not run foul of some restrictions under the TMA 1994. The oldest trade mark in the UK is the Bass red triangle for beer. It was registered in the 1870s and is still valid today.

If a trade mark is not registered then it can be protected only by the law of passing off.

11.2.2 Passing off

This is a common law tort which enables a business to defend itself from someone who is trying to take unfair advantage of the trading reputation of that business, for example by using its name or selling goods in packaging that looks similar. Passing off is less important than trade mark law, and also less certain as regards the outcome. It has also been diminished by the increased scope of registered designs (see **11.2.4**). Nevertheless, there are many situations in which the scope of passing off can reach further than trade mark protection, so the two rights can complement each other as they are not mutually exclusive, often being pleaded in the same action.

11.2.3 Copyright

Copyright is a right to prevent copying of creative expression, such as writing, art, music, architecture, film and even computer software.

The printing of books was a monopoly granted by the Crown up until the 18th century. By this means, the Government could control the printed media. The Statute of Anne in 1709 granted book publishers copyright to protect them against unlicensed copyists, which the common law was unable to do. Thus, authors and their publishers were protected from copying as such. It has to be 'copying'. Copyright does not stop you writing an exciting book about wizards just because JK Rowling has produced many such books. However, it does stop you copying the works and detailed plots of JK Rowling.

Copyright extends to pictorial and photographic creation, industrial plans, sculpture, recorded music and films. These media are 'artistic' but also highly commercial, if you think about the money involved in a major film, such as the James Bond films. It is the principal IP right in computer programmes and therefore of great importance today. Nevertheless, the right is not registrable and comes into existence when the work is first created.

11.2.4 Designs

Designs can be protected by registration. The first Act in 1787 protected the patterns of textiles. Since then, the period of protection has extended and the coverage has been revised. A major revision to the design regime occurred in December 2001, thanks to an EC Directive. Designs are commercial rights.

Designs that relate to the appearance of the object can be registered, but ones that relate solely to its technical function cannot. Registration gives statutory protection for up to 25 years.

There is also statutory unregistered design right protecting features of shape or configuration of articles which are intended to be made available commercially. This protection can extend for between 10 and 15 years, according to circumstances.

11.2.5 Patents

Patents are a commercial IP right. A patent is protection for an invention. The invention could be a better mousetrap, or a wonder drug to treat cancer. A patent is a registered right, administered by the Patents Office.

A patent gives the holder the right to a monopoly for 20 years over the technology revealed in the patent. 'Revealed' is an important concept. 'Patent' is derived from 'letters patent', meaning that the description of the invention is made public in return for the grant by the Crown of the period of protection. Thus, after the 20-year period expires, the invention is then public property. Anybody can use it because the technology is revealed in the patent document, known as a patent specification.

The philosophy is that inventors, and those who employ or sponsor them, should have this 20-year period in which to exploit their monopoly. Were it otherwise, it would never be worth the financial risk of the huge research and testing regimes needed for many modern inventions or patented ideas undertaken by, eg, drug manufacturers. Sometimes, very good ideas are bought up and 'buried' by organisations with a vested interested in keeping the matter out of public knowledge; the inventor is paid for his silence and the matter goes no further.

Another possible means of exploiting a patent is by commercial exploitation of any confidential information concerning the most efficient way to make the patented invention or process work. The registered patent specification will show the world the inventive concept itself and how it broadly works, but that is very different from showing the best and most cost-effective way to make it work. Such additional information is termed 'know-how' and is, itself, highly valuable and exploitable material, as long as it remains confidential. Typically, it is not independently protected as a patent but is often ancillary to the patent, so that a patent licence will be accompanied by a know-how licence, to give the licensee the best chance of using the patent efficiently.

11.2.6 Public registration and administration

It can be seen that much IP is protected by the use of registration of rights in public registers. This is the work of what is now entitled the Intellectual Property Office ('the IPO') (www.ipo.gov.uk), which covers the formerly more separated functions of registration of trade marks, designs and patents and various other matters connected with different types of IP within the UK. Additionally, IP issues which have an EC component are likely to come into contact with the Office for the Harmonisation of the Internal Market ('OHIM'), based in Alicante, Spain. There is an almost seamless joint between the registration process and the way in which courts, both national and EC, deal with IP actions and proceedings, in that harmonisation and approximation of national IP legal frameworks, within the EC, has gone much further than in many other areas of business and property law. This has followed upon a long established international tradition of according reciprocal rights to some IP, in the interests of fostering world trade and development; see **13.13** and **14.10**.

11.2.7 Confidential information

The law of confidence is not an IP right in a pure sense, but is often classified with the mainstream rights as it is sometimes associated with them. For example, maintaining confidentiality before submitting a patent application is vital to avoid destruction of the invention's novelty.

Case law rather than statute governs the law of confidence and, as you would expect, the vast majority of cases relate to circumstances where express obligations of confidence are lacking and implied duties of confidentiality have to be considered. It is, however, important to remember that express obligations can (and often should) be imposed (eg, on key employees or independent contractors). Where confidentiality cannot be protected by contractual means, eg once it gets to third parties, the courts may use trust principles to restrict its use.

11.2.8 What else is there?

There are various other IP rights. For example:

The IP right	**What does it protect against?**
Database right	Copying of information
Semiconductor topography	Copying of computer 'chips'
Plant varieties	Anyone else selling the registered new variety of plant
Moral rights	Inappropriate treatment of an artist's work
Performers rights	Copying of live performances

11.3 Summary of IP rights

11.3.1 Trade marks

What is protected?	a brand name and/or a logo for goods or services (also, in limited circumstances, shapes)
What benefit is there?	exclusive right to the use of the trade mark with statutory protection
How is it obtained?	registration
How long does it last?	indefinitely

11.3.2 Passing off

What is protected?	goodwill (eg, a logo or a name or associated 'get up')
What benefit is there?	gives protection against unfair imitation
How is it obtained?	arises automatically (no registration)
How long does it last?	indefinitely

11.3.3 Copyright

What is protected?	'artistic output'; creative expression
What benefit is there?	preventing copying
How is it obtained?	arises automatically (no registration)
How long does it last?	70 years from death (usually)

11.3.4 Database right

What is protected?	collections of information
What benefit is there?	protects against unauthorised copying
How is it obtained?	arises automatically (no registration)
How long does it last?	15 years from creation or revision of the database

11.3.5 Registered design right

What is protected?	new designs for products
What benefit is there?	monopoly right to use and benefit from the design commercially
How is it obtained?	registration
How long does it last?	25 years from registration (maximum)

11.3.6 Unregistered design right

What is protected?	three-dimensional shapes of articles
What benefit is there?	prevents commercial copying of articles
How is it obtained?	arises automatically (no registration)
How long does it last?	10 years in most cases (maximum of 15)

11.3.7 Patents

What is protected?	new invention or process
What benefit is there?	monopoly right to apply the technology
How is it obtained?	registration
How long does it last?	20 years from application

11.3.8 Confidential information

What is protected?	secret information
What benefit is there?	protects against unauthorised disclosure
How is it obtained?	arises automatically (no registration)
How long does it last?	indefinitely

Chapter 12
Passing Off

12.1	Introduction	167
12.2	The three elements of passing off	168
12.3	Defences to passing off	172
12.4	Remedies for passing off	172
12.5	International aspects	172

12.1 Introduction

Passing off is about stopping the infringer from selling his goods or services by making unfair use of the claimant's reputation. Passing off can happen in a number of different ways. Typically, passing-off cases concern the get-up of goods (ie, their packaging and presentation as seen by the consumer). Passing off is often used as an additional remedy to trade mark infringement claims, and will sometimes succeed where the trade mark claim does not (see the *Phones 4u* case at **13.9** and the *United Biscuits* case at **12.2.2**).

The classic quote is from Lord Halsbury in *Reddaway and Frank Reddaway & Co Ltd v Banham and George Banham & Co Ltd* [1896] AC 199: 'nobody has any right to represent his goods as the goods of somebody else'. Other cases have made clear that passing off also applies to services.

Passing off has to be in relation to a commercial activity. In *Kean v McGivan* [1982] FSR 119, an action concerning the name of a political party (the Social Democratic Party) did not succeed. Usually, something must be happening that is capable of causing people to spend money.

In the classic case of passing off, the defendant adopts some mark, or sign or other distinguishing feature (eg, the appearance of the packaging of the goods) which customers associate with the claimant. He uses this, or something confusingly similar to it, for his own goods/services, with the result that customers are fooled into thinking they are buying the claimant's product. In one of the most famous passing-off cases, *Reckitt & Colman Products Ltd v Borden Inc and Others* [1990] 1 WLR 491, the distinguishing feature of the claimants' goods was that their juice was sold in a plastic lemon. The defendant also started selling lemon juice in a plastic lemon. Reckitt & Colman succeeded in stopping the defendant using this shape of container. Today, the claimants could use trade mark infringement as, under TMA 1994, they have been able to register the shape of their lemon as a registered trade mark (see **Chapter 13**).

There are variations on the classic case, such as where the defendant is passing off someone else's goods as being made by the defendant, or where handouts and inserts are put into newspapers between wholesale delivery by the publisher and sale by the retailer; here, the intention is often to represent that the insert is published by or allowed in by the publisher. Modern marketing methods have created many hugely ingenious ways of free-riding on the business reputations and goodwill created by others. In *British Sky Broadcasting Group plc v Sky Home Services Ltd* [2006] EWHC 3165, various defendants had made use of the SKY word in corporate names, as well as in marketing material and telephone sales methods used for selling extended warranties for maintenance of satellite TV reception equipment. Passing off was established fairly easily in the circumstances of such a widely known organisation as the claimant.

Particular problems can arise in the use of franchising arrangements, under which franchisees can use the marks and marketing/selling format of the franchisor. In *Fearns v Anglo-Dutch Paint and Chemical Co Ltd* [2007] EWHC 955, a franchisor who sold high-quality car paints under his own mark of 'Autopaint' to his franchisees, was able to show passing off by one of the companies that supplied him with paint (with his Autopaint mark on it), which he (as franchisor) sold on to his own franchisees. That defendant had gone further than it should by also supplying the same marked product directly to the franchisees, thus cutting out the franchisor. This amounted to a clear passing off, by the use of the claimant's mark, as was further distribution of the goods to the trade and to the public by other distributors and non-franchisees. This point was not disturbed when the Court of Appeal dealt with an issue of causation ([2008] EWCA Civ 99).

What is protected?	goodwill, eg logo or name, 'get-up'
What benefit is there?	protects against unfair use of, or damage to, business reputation
How is it obtained?	arises automatically (no registration)
How long does it last?	indefinitely

12.2 The three elements of passing off

In *Consorzio del Prosciutto di Parma v Marks & Spencer plc* [1991] RPC 351, the House of Lords judgment of Lord Oliver in *Reckitt & Colman* is quoted as a good exposition of the elements of passing off:

> More specifically, it may be expressed in terms of the elements which the plaintiff in such an action has to prove in order to succeed. These are three in number. First, he must establish a goodwill or reputation attached to the goods or services which he supplies in the mind of the purchasing public by association with the identifying get-up (whether it consists simply of a brand name or a trade description, or the individual features of labelling or packaging) under which his particular goods or services are offered to the public, such that the get-up is recognised by the public as distinctive specifically of the plaintiff's goods or services. Secondly, he must demonstrate a misrepresentation by the defendant to the public (whether or not intentional) leading or likely to lead the public to believe that goods or services offered by him are the goods or services of the plaintiff . . . Thirdly, he must demonstrate that he suffers or . . . that he is likely to suffer damage by reason of the erroneous belief engendered by the defendant's misrepresentation that the source of the defendant's goods or services is the same as the source of those offered by the plaintiff.

12.2.1 First element: goodwill

Goodwill means business reputation. The reputation must be among customers, or prospective customers (ie, buyers, or prospective buyers of lemon juice, for example).

The reputation also needs to be in relation to some distinguishing feature, eg, in the plastic lemon. What the claimant needs to show is not only that customers associate the plastic lemon with the claimant, but also that they understand the plastic lemon as an indication or sign that the lemon juice comes from the claimant. The claimant generally demonstrates his reputation to the court by showing sales figures and expenditure on advertising (using the distinguishing feature in question), by witness evidence and survey evidence.

The distinguishing feature could be:

(a) logos, shape or style of packaging, get up, colour (eg, Heinz beans tin (colour, shape of label, name); the classic Coca-Cola bottle (shape, name); Body Shop bottle (the rounded shape and lettering); Penguin (six-pack wrapper)); or

(b) a name (eg, 'Neutrogena', where the defendant was restrained from using the similar name 'Neutralia' (*Neutrogena Corporation and Another v Golden Ltd and Another* [1996] RPC 473), or 'Harrods' (*Harrods Ltd v Harrodian School Ltd* [1996] RPC 697), although

Harrods were unsuccessful in stopping the school using the same name because they could not show that this would result in damage).

In *Riddle v United Service Organisation Ltd* [2004] LTL AC9100218, the claimant was the son of the late Nelson Riddle, a composer and orchestra leader. Riddle senior and his orchestra had last toured the UK in the 1960s. It was held that there was no goodwill remaining after 40 years, so the son could not maintain a passing-off claim against defendants who ran an orchestra called the Nelson Riddle Orchestra UK. This can also be a problem for new businesses or ventures, where the goodwill has yet to become established.

In *Knight v Beyond Properties Pty Ltd* [2007] EWHC 1251, the court held that the word 'Mythbusters', although descriptive of a series of books, was capable of generating goodwill for the purposes of passing off. Nevertheless, a minor reputation in the title at the end of 1993 had disappeared by late 2003, when the title was used for TV programmes on the Discovery Channel.

The category of things in which the claimant can have reputation is not closed and cannot be conclusively defined or limited. Being common law based, the limits of the tort are potentially very wide. Reputation as a diary writer was able to be protected in *Clark (Alan Kenneth McKenzie) v Associated Newspapers* [1998] RPC 261, where parodied versions of Alan Clark's diaries were held to be passing off. Scents of products can be another tricky area, as seen in *L'Oreal SA v Bellure NV* [2006] EWHC 2355, where the scent of a fine perfume, although important to the customer, was held to be not protected, on the facts of that case, although there were trade mark infringements of other features. The trade mark issues were remitted to the ECJ by the Court of Appeal ([2007] EWCA Civ 968); the ECJ's judgment is discussed at **13.9** below. In other circumstances, different results might follow. Protection of a reputation for probity in certifying one's own products as genuine was seen in *Microsoft Corp v Ling* [2006] EWHC 1619, where summary judgment was granted to the claimants against software systems builders who had installed Microsoft products under licence but had allegedly separated Microsoft compliance certificates from the installed software and were, effectively, trading in them and using them for unauthorised purposes as instruments of deception.

12.2.2 Second element: misrepresentation, leading to confusion

There must be a misrepresentation made by the defendant in the course of trade. In the Jif lemon case (see **12.1**) the misrepresentation was the use of the plastic lemon. In most passing-off cases the misrepresentation is deliberate. In other words, there is a deliberate attempt by the defendant to 'ride on the back' of the claimant's success. For example, consider the 'Penguin and Puffin' case, *United Biscuits (UK) Ltd v Asda Stores Ltd* [1997] RPC 513, which concerned the similarity in packaging for the two brands of chocolate biscuit. Asda produced the Puffin biscuit. They had designed packaging that was very similar to that of the Penguin biscuit. They even ran an advertising campaign with the slogan 'pick up a Puffin'. This rather suggested deliberate reference to Penguin, and did not help Asda's case in court, as passing off was easily established.

However, a misrepresentation could be innocent. The defendant need not even be aware of the claimant's products, but intention to misrepresent is not an essential element.

The misrepresentation must lead to confusion of customers or potential customers, and generally it must be confusion as to trade source. The customers must be fooled into thinking that the defendant's products come from the claimant, or that they are associated with the claimant (eg, that they are made/supplied by a company within the same group, or by a licensee). A classic example of such misrepresentation may be seen in *First Conference Services Ltd v Bracchi* [2009] EWHC 2176 (Ch), [2009] All ER (D) 56 (Oct), where a former employee of the claimant attempted to pass off conferences organised by him as those of his old employer. He did this by stating that the speakers would be 'previous speakers', ie those at conferences organised by the claimant the year before. He also misled the speakers themselves as to the identity of the true organiser of the conference.

The confusion must be at the point of sale, or before it. In *Bostik Ltd v Sellotape GB Ltd* [1994] RPC 556, the makers of Blu-tack failed to obtain an injunction in passing off against a rival manufacturer of a similar looking product. The similarity in the product could be realised only when the packaging was removed. There was no possibility of confusion by the customer at the point of sale. So far, English courts have refused to follow other jurisdictions where post-sale confusion is enough.

It is not enough that there is confusion between the claimant's and the defendant's product. Customers must believe that the defendant's products are associated with the claimant. This was illustrated in the case of *HFC Bank plc v Midland Bank plc* [2000] FSR 176. When Midland was taken over by HSBC and changed its name to HSBC, HFC Bank objected. They argued that customers would confuse HSBC with HFC. However, among other things, HFC were not able to show they had achieved sufficient brand name recognition in relation to the letters HFC. Even if customers did confuse the two acronyms, they would not necessarily think HSBC was a reference to HFC.

The removal of a distinguishing feature can result in unintentional misrepresentation. In *Sir Robert McAlpine Ltd v Alfred McAlpine plc* [2004] EWHC 630, [2004] RPC 36, it was held that the defendant's dropping of the first name 'Alfred', so that it used the name McAlpine alone, did amount to a misrepresentation. In other words, it caused confusion with the claimant's name.

There needs to be overlap between the alleged infringer and the proprietor in that there is a 'common field of activity', in the following respects:

(a) type of goods or services: would someone confuse a bicycle maker with a law firm?

(b) geographical area: a restaurant in Aberdeen is unlikely to take away trade from one in Plymouth; and

(c) time: the overlap must be more or less contemporaneous.

Unless there is a common field of activity, it will be difficult (but not impossible) to show confusion or, indeed, damage to goodwill in many cases. Nevertheless, as large national or multinational organisations, such as Tesco or BP etc, are commonly known to be involved in a hugely diverse range of goods and services, it would be very easy for passing off to take place without a common activity taking place at all, but it would still be open to the claimant to have a good chance of stopping the activity, as can be seen from the case law.

12.2.2.1 Evidence of confusion

A passing-off case will not succeed without evidence of confusion. Customer confusion is a question of fact, and it is always very difficult to predict the outcome of a passing-off claim. It is difficult to generalise about the type of thing that will lead to confusion, but the confusion must be as to trade source.

The usual evidence might be survey evidence or witness evidence, preferably from people employed in the relevant trade. In effect, they become expert witnesses on the question of likely confusion. The burden on the claimant is heavy and is often difficult to discharge. In *Julius Sämaan v Tetrosyl Ltd* (see **13.8.2**), a passing-off claim failed for lack of evidence of confusion, even though there was a clear trade mark infringement; packaging and price were very different.

The courts are sceptical about survey evidence, but nevertheless it is frequently presented. Often what will be conclusive is placing the two products before the judge. Does he think customers are likely to be confused? If he agrees, he is more likely to accept the survey evidence. If he does not, he is likely to reject it.

Although the defendant may use the claimant's distinctive feature in some way, there might not be confusion if either the claimant or the defendant has clearly distinguished their products in some way. In *Arsenal Football Club plc v Reed* [2001] RPC 922, a long-standing trader in club memorabilia was not found to have created any confusion in the minds of customers, merely by using the club's logo and name (not least, because of a clear disclaimer). The passing-off action failed (but see the trade mark case at **13.9**).

If people merely recognise the look-alike as being a cheaper copy of the branded product then this is not going to be enough for passing off. There is then no confusion as to the trade source of the goods or services. Some allowance is made for the circumstances under which the customer will look at and decide about buying the material. A quick selection from a shelf is very different from a considered examination of the matter, perhaps over days. For there to be a likelihood of confusion, it would need to confuse a more alert customer than 'a moron in a hurry' (*Morning Star v Express Newspapers* [1979] FSR 113). Also, the imperfections of ordinary memory recall by a typical customer are taken into account, in assessing likely confusion.

12.2.3 Third element: damage

The claimant must show damage, or the likelihood of damage. Often, because of the likelihood of damage, the claimant will generally be seeking an interim injunction. In the ordinary case, where the claimant and defendant are trading in the same line of business, once goodwill and misrepresentation have been established the court is usually willing to infer damage.

The main types of damage are:

(a) loss of profits – people buy the infringing product instead of the claimant's product; and

(b) loss of reputation – usually because the infringing product is of inferior quality, and customers think the infringing product is made by the claimant.

If the infringer is in a different field of activity, the claimant might not succeed because he cannot show damage. For example, in *Stringfellow and Another v McCain Foods GB Ltd and Another* [1984] RPC 501, the nightclub was not able to stop oven chips being sold under the name 'Stringfellows'. In *Wombles Ltd v Wombles Skips Ltd* [1977] RPC 99, the copyright owners of the Wombles books and television series could not stop rubbish skips being hired out under the name 'Wombles'.

However, in other cases, claimants have been able to establish damage as a result of not being able to expand into a new market. The manufacturer of 'Marigold' rubber gloves was able to stop a toilet tissue being called 'Marigold' (*LRC International Ltd and Another v Lilla Edets Sales Co Ltd* [1973] RPC 560). Also, if the infringer's product is in a field that brings disrepute on the claimant then this can be a ground of damage. In the case of *Annabel's (Berkeley Square) Ltd v Schock (t/a Annabel's Escort Agency)* [1972] RPC 838, the use in question could have created an assumption that a well-known nightclub had started an escort agency. See **12.2.2** on the significance of large organisations and common field of activity problems.

In *Global Projects Management Ltd v Citigroup Inc* [2005] EWHC 2663, the judge, in giving summary judgment for Citigroup, was prepared to accept that a domain owner, in using 'citigroup.co.uk', had created such a risk of e-mails going to unintended recipients that damage was self-evident, even if unquantifiable.

In *Irvine and Others v Talksport Ltd* [2003] EWCA Civ 423, [2003] 2 All ER 881, the matter concerned a well-known racing driver. A photograph of him was altered to add a radio with the words 'Talk Radio' on it, and was then used by the defendants on a promotional leaflet for their activities. The Court of Appeal held that this was passing off, and that the measure of damages for a false product endorsement was the typical fee which the claimant would usually have sought.

Another problem area, involving passing off and damage, is the frequently occurring requirement for the re-labelling and repackaging of goods by parallel importers within the EC, to comply with national regulatory rules. In *Boehringer Ingelheim KG v Swingward Ltd* [2008] EWCA Civ 83, the Court of Appeal held that importers who repackaged and re-applied marks could infringe national IP laws unless they followed ECJ guidelines. The issue of damage, however, was a question of fact for national courts.

12.3 Defences to passing off

There are a number of defences to passing off which have developed through the case law, in a random and somewhat overlapping manner. The principal ones are as follows:

(a) careful and honest use of defendant's own name, mark or get-up;

(b) defendant's or claimant's use otherwise than in trade;

(c) claimant has no goodwill or the goodwill is owned by someone else;

(d) claimant's acquiescence, encouragement or consent to use;

(e) no provable damage or loss to claimant.

12.4 Remedies for passing off

Remedies for passing off can include:

(a) an injunction;

(b) damages (nominal, if innocent passing off);

(c) an account of profits;

(d) an order to cover up marks or repackage;

(e) an order for delivery up or destruction of the offending items;

(f) declarations as to rights.

Note: remedies (b) and (c) are normally mutually exclusive.

12.5 International aspects

Other common law countries, such as Australia and New Zealand, also have laws of passing off, but their case law has developed differently on some points. Civil law countries have the law of unfair competition, which sometimes overlaps with passing off, but it is definitely not the same. Passing off, by use of the Internet, is discussed at **20.5.2** below.

Chapter 13
Trade Marks

13.1	Functions and purposes of trade marks	173
13.2	Advantages and consequences of registration	173
13.3	The registration system, its problems and recent changes	174
13.4	Can the trade mark meet the definition within s 1(1) of the TMA 1994?	175
13.5	Absolute grounds for refusal: s 3	176
13.6	Evidence of use to overcome absolute grounds (the proviso to s 3(1))	182
13.7	Relative grounds for refusing an application (s 5)	183
13.8	Protecting the mark, once registered	187
13.9	Infringement of a registered trade mark	188
13.10	'Well-known' foreign trade marks (s 56)	193
13.11	Defences to infringement (ss 11, 12, 48)	193
13.12	Remedies for infringement (ss 14–19)	194
13.13	International trade marks	194
13.14	Classes used in the Register of Trade Marks (Trade Mark Rules 2000, Sch 4)	195

13.1 Functions and purposes of trade marks

As discussed briefly at **11.2.1**, a trade mark is simply a badge or indication of the trade origin of goods or services from a particular supplier. The legislative framework for registered marks in the United Kingdom is primarily the Trade Marks Act 1994 (TMA 1994), which implements Council Directive 89/104/EEC ([1989] OJ L40/1) so as to harmonise to a large degree the national trade mark laws of Member States with each other. As part of this purpose, the TMA 1994 deals with matters such as the implementation of the Community trade mark (CTM) scheme and other international matters affecting trade marks. Detailed discussion of the CTM is beyond the scope of this work, but the system is dealt with briefly at **13.13.1**.

Unregistered marks are protected, if at all, by the law of passing off, as seen in **Chapter 12**. The modern process of registering trade marks began in English law in 1875 and provided, for the first time, a system that provided a clear public notice that a particular trader was entitled to exclusive use, in trade, of a particular trade mark, subject to keeping the mark registered. This solved many of the earlier problems of showing title to the mark (and any goodwill in it, still a necessary feature of passing-off actions). It can be said that the main functions of a registered trade mark are as follows:

(a) to indicate the trade origin of the goods or services with a particular supplier; see the definition in s 1(1) of the TMA 1994:

> In this Act 'a trade mark' means any sign capable of being represented graphically which is capable of distinguishing goods or services of one undertaking from those of other undertakings;

(b) as a likely indication of the quality of product associated with that supplier;

(c) as a measure of the ongoing and changing value of the particular brand image of particular products, or of the image of the supplier as a whole;

(d) as a useful and commercially exploitable piece of property, in itself.

13.2 Advantages and consequences of registration

The two greatest advantages of registration of trade marks are that the period of protection given by registration is, potentially, unlimited and that the scope of protection is equivalent to an exclusive right to use the mark in trade for most commercial purposes permitted by the particular registration. Almost all other advantages and consequences stem from these two incidents of registration as can be seen from the brief following analysis.

13.2.1 Duration

The period of registration is an initial 10 years, with the option to renew the mark for subsequent 10-year periods, without limit in time. Provided that the mark does not lose its ability to distinguish the particular goods or services in question and is kept in (at least limited) use, it can remain in registration. The Bass red triangle trade mark for beer has been in use for more than 130 years and still retains its validity. An incidental gain from such long use is the possibility to develop wide and immediate recognition for a good brand, possibly at international level, and, additionally, a very strong presumption that the mark was validly registered in the first place (see, however, the discussion of the new system of registration at **13.3**). It is possible for registered trade marks to lose their validity by various means, in due course, but this is discussed at **13.8**.

13.2.2 Exclusive rights

The starting point, here, is s 9(1) of the TMA 1994:

> The proprietor of a registered trade mark has exclusive rights in the trade mark which are infringed by use of the trade mark in the United Kingdom without his consent.

The infringing acts are then set out exhaustively in ss 10 and 11. All the various infringing acts involve use of the trade mark, 'in trade', without consent, in some way or another. This very clear statutory framework has the consequence that the public register of trade marks provides an easily accessible check on any particular trade mark, as regards ownership and current registration status. It is not necessary to develop any particular goodwill in a mark to register it initially (cf passing-off actions), and so it is quite easy to gain the maximum novelty effect and commercial impact from new, well-conceived trade marks, provided that the product bearing the mark becomes fairly quickly available itself after registration. Infringement actions are far easier to bring than typical passing-off claims; provided the elements of the statutory infringement can be evidenced and that the mark is still being used and validly in registration at the time of the infringement, the claimant will succeed.

13.3 The registration system, its problems and recent changes

Very widespread and far-reaching changes have been made to the system of registration and dealing with trade marks in the United Kingdom. For a very long time, the UK Trade Mark Registry ('the Registry') applied three quite different tests in considering whether any trade mark should be registered or not; if the mark failed to comply with any of them, registration was refused. It considered:

(a) whether the mark was capable of being a trade mark within the s 1(1) definition at all;

(b) whether, if it was, it should be refused registration under any of the absolute grounds under s 3 of the TMA 1994 (including the law on passing off); and

(c) whether it should be refused registration for any of the relative grounds in s 5 of the TMA 1994.

These steps are discussed in more detail below and at **13.4–13.6**. This system long had the advantage that trade marks registered here were seen as having a very strong presumption of validity because of the care with which the Registry formerly investigated prior registrations and, indeed, unregistered marks before allowing a mark to be registered.

The difficulty was that this was not the general practice in most of Europe, and what brought the matter into sharp focus was the very large expansion in the CTM system (see **13.13.1**). Under the CTM system, a type of unitary protection is given throughout the EC to trade marks, and the main considerations applied by the UK Registry are also applicable to applications to register a CTM. That means that the UK Registry must have regard to existing CTMs when considering relative grounds for refusing a new application, whereas those CTMs were not subjected to any such examination in the first place. The broad rule for CTMs and trade marks throughout much of the EC (other than in the UK until recently) is that it is for objectors to registration to raise the objection themselves, rather than for the registrars to search. The registrar does, however, retain the discretion to search for prior registrations under the Trade Mark Rules 2000 (SI 2000/136), r 11A.

This created such a problem that the UK Registry has now adopted the technique of relying upon objections being raised by persons adversely affected by an application for a UK trade mark. This may well create great expense and difficulty, especially for the smaller undertaking, in protecting registered trade marks (as well as unregistered matters which might be passed off). The following description deals with the practice followed in registration. The new approach to dealing with relative grounds objections is dealt with at **13.7.3**.

Anyone can apply to register a trade mark in the UK, whether they own the trade mark or not, provided that they are using the mark for goods or services, or intend to do so. It does not matter where the applicant comes from. There is a fairly large number of formalities, which are not extensively reviewed here, but which can fairly easily be ascertained by a visit to the website at www.ipo.gov.uk. The main legal source of these requirements is the TMA 1994 and the Trade Mark Rules 2000 made under the Act. The formal and procedural stages of the registration process are not dealt with further, but they may be seen on the website mentioned above and in the Trade Mark Rules 2000.

A trade mark has to be registered in relation to named goods or services. There will be a 'statement of goods or services' for the trade mark in each of the registration classes in which it is registered, eg one of the registrations for Coca-Cola is in class 32, beers and non-alcoholic drinks. The statement for that registration is 'syrup for use in making a beverage'. Trade marks are registered in one or more of 45 classes (see **13.14**). The main purpose of the classes is to facilitate searching for trade mark registrations. However, the more important issue is the statement of goods or services, as that determines the scope of the registration. It is a central factor when looking at possible infringement. A trade mark will often be registered in more than one class. For example, the trade mark for a beer would be registered in class 32, but the same trade mark could also be registered in class 25 for clothing, as the name might be used on clothing to promote the beer.

The importance of the wording in a statement of goods or services was illustrated in *Associated Newspapers Limited and Another v Express Newspapers* [2003] EWHC 1322 (Ch). The proprietors of the *Daily Mail* and the *Mail on Sunday* newspapers tried to prevent the use of the registered trade marks 'Mail' or 'Mail on Sunday'. The defendants were seeking to launch free newspapers with the titles *London Evening Mail* or *Evening Mail*. The claimants failed under s 10(1) of the TMA 1994 for infringement by use of an identical trade mark on identical goods, as their trade marks were registered for 'newspapers for sale'. It was held that, as the defendants' newspapers would be free newspapers, the proposed use of the trade marks by the defendants did not come within the ambit of the statement of goods and services of the registered trade marks, although the claimant did succeed on other grounds.

13.4 Can the trade mark meet the definition within s 1(1) of the TMA 1994?

There are two distinct questions posed by this. Can the sign be graphically represented? Can it distinguish the goods or services of the applicant from those of other undertakings?

13.4.1 Graphic representation

This is an absolutely crucial requirement, if the limits of the protection given are to be ascertainable and clear. The starting point is the Trade Mark Rules' requirement that the sign be capable of being clearly reproduced in an 8 cm by 8 cm square in the *Trade Mark Journal*, which is the official means by which applications for registration are first published to the world, in order to allow persons to object and, if it becomes registered, to illustrate how the sign will be shown on the register. It follows from this that unless the sign can be be drawn, written in words, numbers or other symbols, or described in very clear words, it is unregistrable. This raises some degree of problem for certain types of distinctive features such as sounds or scents, but even these areas are capable of being utilised for trade mark purposes, in some cases. Clearly separated colours might be able to be specified by their wavelength or by reference to agreed classification systems and there are a (very) few of these (eg BP green, Heinz turquoise etc); mostly, colour registrations involve a combination of colours and other signs such as a word or other logos, etc (known as 'device' marks).

Sounds, other than words, are problematical; about the only reliable means of ascertaining these graphically being by use of wavelength, musical notation and/or duration. Music, jingles, etc are fairly easy to deal with in this way, but other sounds are very difficult to deal with in terms of clear graphical description; see *Shield Mark BV v Kist* (Case 283/01) [2003] ETMR 822. Scent/olfactory mark registrations are almost impossible to achieve, in terms of clear graphic representation, because descriptions or chemical formulae do not evoke the scent itself but, at best, the reader's imagined perception; to achieve certainty and clarity would require a sample of the substance: see *L'Oreal SA v Bellure NV* [2006] EWHC 2355, discussed at **12.2.1**. The use of the chemical formula symbols for a substance is probably not capable of satisfying the graphic representation requirement.

13.4.2 Capable of distinguishing

Many signs and words are so commonplace in everyday use as to be incapable of having a distinctive quality in isolation. There is a strong overlap between the general limitations of the s 1(1) definition and the absolute bars to registration in s 3, so most of the discussion on the distinctiveness requirement follows in **13.5**, but it should be borne in mind that what needs to be distinctive is the mark, as a whole, rather than particular features within it. It is, therefore, quite normal to find imaginative combinations of rather commonplace symbols, words or colours achieving registration as trade marks; all that matters is to find something distinctive about the overall arrangement. A well-known example is the 'Finish' title, combined with the red 'powerball' device mark for dishwasher products. None of the component parts of the mark is particularly distinctive, but in aggregate they become highly distinctive and recognisable.

The word mark 'Deliberately Innovative' was found to lack any distinctive character in *Interactive Intelligence Inc's Registration No 873858* [2007] WL 1180.

13.5 Absolute grounds for refusal: s 3

In s 3 of the TMA 1994, the absolute grounds for refusal to register are laid down. The most common ones are in s 3(1):

> The following shall not be registered—
>
> (a) signs which do not satisfy the requirements of section 1(1),
>
> (b) trade marks that are devoid of distinctive character,
>
> (c) trade marks which consist exclusively of signs or indications which may serve, in trade, to designate the kind, quality, quantity, intended purpose, value, geographical origin, the time of production of goods or of rendering of services, or other characteristics of goods or services,
>
> (d) trade marks that consist exclusively of signs or indications which have become customary in the current language or in the bona fide and established practices of the trade:

> Provided that, a trade mark shall not be refused registration by virtue of paragraph (b), (c) or (d) above if, before the date of application for registration, it has in fact acquired a distinctive character as a result of the use made of it.

Distinctiveness, in the eyes of the customer, is the idea that lies behind all the paragraphs of s 3(1). A helpful analysis of the relationship between distinctiveness and the descriptiveness implied in s 3(1)(c) is given in *Easynet Group plc v Easygroup IP Licensing Ltd* [2006] EWHC 1872, which concerned the attempt to register easy.com. A mark will undoubtedly be distinctive if it is a made-up name. The ones usually quoted are 'Kodak' or 'Exxon'. Beware of words that are merely phonetic spellings of ordinary words so that they look distinctive until pronounced (eg, 'Orlwoola' for all wool (see **13.5.5**), or 'Writs' for a sandwich bar (ie, potential problems with the Ritz restaurant)).

Clearly, the bars to registration in s 3(1)(b) to (d) can largely be bypassed by the proviso that distinctiveness has been acquired by extensive use of the trade mark. That will not, however, cure any objections under paragraph (a), such as that the sign fails the s 1(1) requirement that the mark can be graphically represented; no amount of use can get over that hurdle and that sign will remain unregistrable. Distinctiveness acquired through use is discussed in more depth at **13.6**.

The main s 3(1) problem areas in registration tend to be associated with:

(a) the use of names of individuals or businesses;

(b) aspects of the goods or services on offer; and

(c) geographical origins of the goods or services.

These matters are dealt with at **13.5.1**, **13.5.2** and **13.5.3**. The difficult question of shape marks (s 3(2)) is dealt with at **13.5.4** and public policy objections (s 3(3)) at **13.5.5**.

13.5.1 Use of names as trade marks

Because a registered trade mark gives an effective monopoly for its use in trade, there are great dangers in allowing such registrations. Nevertheless, it is long established that any person is entitled to use his own personal or business name and address, fairly and honestly, without it comprising an infringement; see s 11(2) of the TMA 1994. It does not follow from this that everyone can register their own name, in that way. Many names are so common as to be unable to distinguish goods or services for the purposes of s 3(1)(b), so that the name, standing alone, is unregistrable; combine it with an address or some other distinctive feature, however, and that may solve the problem. Nevertheless, people like short, catchy trade marks. An unusual name is unlikely to create such distinctiveness problems, but common names, even if presented in an eye-catching way, can be difficult to register, although sometimes personal signatures are trade marked (consider the 'Ford' signature mark). Often, the problem is that there are already prior registered marks, using the same name.

The former Registry practice was to use a simple rule of thumb, based on the statistical incidence of the name in the London telephone directory, as a guide. This was held, with reason, to be so arbitrary as to be useless in deciding the question of distinctiveness, in the ECJ decision in *Nichols plc v The Registrar of Trade Marks* (Case C-404/02) [2004] All ER (D) 114. The approach of the ECJ was that an individual assessment needs to be made on the facts of each application, taking into account the likely scope of use of the mark, as to area of use, range of products marked and likely customer group, allowing for a certain level of reasonably informed and aware customers; see *Koninklijke Philips Electronics v Remington Consumer Products Ltd* (Case C-299/99) [2002] 2 CMLR 52, [2003] Ch 159. This approach seems now to have been adopted by the IPO, but it should still be borne in mind that even common names can acquire distinctiveness through use; see *El Du Pont de Nemours & Co v ST Dupont* [2004] FSR 15.

The trade mark use of names, other than that of the provider of the goods or services, raises different considerations such as arise in character merchandising, franchising and IP licensing. Those matters are beyond the scope of this part of the text.

13.5.2 Aspects of the goods or services themselves within s 3(1)(c)

This is a vital protection against unfair monopolisation of descriptive signs or indications by any particular person. The paragraph only strikes at trade marks consisting exclusively of such indications (which are usually terms common in the trade). In *Timken Co's Application No 2418442* (Trade Mark Registry 18/09/07) [2007] WL 2817814, the Registry refused 'friction management solutions' as far too descriptive of the services offered to be registered. If the descriptive aspect is used in combination with more distinctive features, there is usually no problem. Signs only serving to describe the type of good cannot be registered by themselves: orange juice, cornflakes or crisps are obviously unregistrable, but even more imaginative signs may still fail for descriptiveness. 'Tastee-Freez' for ice cream and 'Weldmesh' for reinforcing mesh were too descriptive to register, whereas 'Twiglets' has long been registered for snack-type biscuits for both humans and animals. The obvious difference is that although the snacks look like twigs, they are, in fact, completely different things; the mark is not descriptive of the kind of good, only suggestive of its appearance. This imaginative mark is highly distinctive among biscuits.

Words of quality or value are, likewise, unregistrable, by themselves, particularly 'laudatory' words such as 'magic', 'supreme', etc. Some imagination, though, can change the situation considerably; there are very large numbers of registrations, in all sorts of classes, for variations on 'exel', 'excell', 'XL' etc. Some of the most imaginative trade mark concepts have come from the confectionery world, with imagery such as 'Mars', 'Galaxy', 'Smarties', 'Quality Street', etc. The list is endless but all have the same aspect: they do not directly, or in many cases indirectly, suggest the nature of the good itself, but may, indirectly, suggest qualities and connotations beyond the mundane and mediocre. A case that is very close to the line is *Bostik Ltd v Henkel KGAA* (Trade Mark Registry 3/09/07) [2007] WL 2573891, where the applications to register 'Hyper Glue' and 'Hypaglue' were upheld, because 'hyper' was not found to be synonymous with 'super' (which would not have been registrable). Similarly, with words or signs showing the intended purpose of the good, one needs to go beyond mere descriptiveness to achieve registration: the 'Walkman' personal stereo and 'Workmate' portable work bench illustrate the successful registration and use of such marks.

The case of *Procter & Gamble Co v Office for Harmonisation in the Internal Market (Trade Marks and Designs)* [2002] RPC 17 has widened the scope for businesses that want to use trade marks which could be descriptive. This was a case before the ECJ. The applicant appealed from a decision of the OHIM. The application was for registration as a European trade mark of 'Baby-Dry' for 'disposable diapers made out of paper or cellulose and diapers made out of textile'. The application had been rejected by OHIM as being the combination of two descriptive words, that is 'baby' and 'dry'. However, the ECJ held that while each word on its own was not distinctive, the use of the two words together produced an unusual combination which was not in common English usage.

In contrast, in *DKV Deutsche Krankenversicherung AG v Office for Harmonisation in the Internal Market* [2002] ECR I-7561, the appeal against the refusal of OHIM to allow 'Companyline' to be registered as a Community trade mark for insurance and financial advice was rejected by the ECJ. The judgment of the Court of First Instance, and therefore the refusal to register, was upheld. The ECJ held that coupling together two such general words as 'company' and 'line' created nothing distinctive in the factual circumstance. In *Easynet Group plc v Easygroup IP Licensing Ltd* [2006] EWHC 1872, Mann J confirmed that the correct approach was an overall assessment of the composite expression as to whether it is descriptive or not. If it is not, it is likely to be distinctive and registrable. The registration of 'easy.com' for a range of goods and services was upheld.

In the case of the 'Doublemint' trade mark for chewing gum, the ECJ held that the trade mark was descriptive, ambiguous, and therefore deceptive, and could not be registered. Part of the reason for distinguishing this application from Baby-Dry was that Baby-Dry was an unusual combination of two ordinary words, in the reverse order from any common usage of the terms. This was not the case with 'Doublemint' (*OHIM (Doublemint) v Wrigley* (Case C-191/01) (ECJ, 23 October 2003)). The judgment followed the *Chiemsee* case, in that the ECJ held that this was a trade expression that should be kept free for other businesses to use if they so wish (see **13.5**).

13.5.3 Marks suggesting geographical origin

In the majority of cases, geographical names will not be acceptable as trade marks.

In the leading case of *Windsurfing Chiemsee Produktions und Vertriebs GmbH v Boots und Segelzubehör Walter Huber and Another* [2000] Ch 523, the ECJ refused to allow the geographical name to be registered. It held that a geographical name had to be left available for other traders to use in the future, particularly those actually located at Chiemsee (a holiday lake in Bavaria). A geographical name which did not indicate the origin of the goods would be unregistrable for being deceptive. For example, 'Swiss Miss' was refused as the chocolate was not produced in Switzerland. However, if it is totally fanciful it could succeed, for example 'Sahara' for ice cream. An objection on grounds of deceptiveness could not be overcome by any amount of use of the mark.

There are some indications that a more relaxed attitude is being taken towards geographical marks in Community trade mark applications (see **13.13.1**), particularly so with small geographical locations (see *Peek & Cloppenburg v OHIM* [2006] ETMR 35).

The problem of geographical indications can be cured, for trade marks purposes, by making certain that the mark is not exclusively geographical, eg, 'Grants of St James's', although high-class areas are not easy to use in this way because of the possibility of deceptiveness.

Another possible protection, one that often overlaps with geographical indications, is the use of 'collective marks'. These can be registered under s 49 and Sch 1 of the TMA 1994 and comprise marks which show that the goods or services are provided by a member of a particular trade association, so as to distinguish them from those of other organisations or persons. These can be registered and frequently contain indications of geographical origins (subject to most relevant traders in that product and location being willing to join the association, as with the Melton Mowbray Pork Pie Association, which has 'AUTHENTIC . MELTON MOWBRAY' as its mark); this is permitted by the Schedule, but the collective trade mark cannot be used to prevent other persons (typically, those local traders who do not wish to join up), who would be following normal, honest business practice, from using that geographical indication in their business. In a similar way, 'certification marks' can be registered under s 50 and Sch 2 of the TMA 1994 to show other highly descriptive characteristics of goods or services that would normally be caught by s 3(1)(c); things like the 'Woolmark' for textiles and 'Stilton' for cheese are registered.

There are further levels of protection available to geographical indications at the EC level by way of 'protected designations of origin' ('PDO') and 'protected geographical indications' ('PGI'), as well as at international level, where there are World Intellectual Property Organisation 'appellations of origin'. The general idea of most of this protection is to allow persons to use and register official logos and titles to show that certain products (and only those products) are designated by and linked to particular geographical origins and locations. In *Consorzio del Prosciutto di Parma v Asda Stores Ltd* (Case C-108/01) [2001] UKHL 7, the Parma Ham Association attempted to prevent Asda from further processing Parma ham, protected by a PDO, by way of slicing, labelling and packaging it in the UK. The ECJ, on a reference from the House of Lords, found that this further protection for the ham was justified by its protection under the PDO and was a valid Community right, directly enforceable in Member States (subject to its being properly publicised to the Community). The Melton Mowbray Pork Pie Association has now achieved PGI status for a range of its products. Further discussion of geographical indications is, however, beyond the scope of this book.

13.5.4 Shape marks (s 3(2))

It is now possible to register trade marks for the shape of goods or their packaging, subject to their not consisting exclusively of:

(a) the shape which result from the goods themselves;

(b) the shape of goods which is necessary to achieve a technical result; or

(c) the shape which gives substantial value to the goods.

Again, the key to these exclusions is that what needs to be shown is that the mark is distinctive, eye-catching and memorable in some way and, additionally, raises the association with a particular trade source. The main problem with allowing registration of shape marks is that the potentially unlimited duration of the mark contrasts so vividly with the limited protection period (25 years maximum) of other industrial and commercial designs (see **Chapter 16**). It is very dangerous to allow anyone a monopoly on shapes – that is why they were not capable of trade mark protection until 1994 – and it is still not easy to achieve shape mark registration.

The case law is often quite speculative in its interpretation of s 3(2) and Council Directive 89/104 EEC, to which it gives effect. It is quite clear that there is a substantial overlap between the three excluded cases in s 3(2); it is also clear that the s 3(1) provision for distinctiveness, acquired by use, does not apply to shape marks which are excluded by s 3(2), although it could apply to marks comprising, in part, matters restricted by s 3(2). That explains how the Coca-Cola bottle achieved its registration.

The key to understanding much of the case law on s 3(2) lies in the fact that to exclude a shape mark from registration, that mark must consist 'exclusively' of the proscribed shape. Many marks will consist of other things beyond mere shape. Some indication of the judicial approach is seen as follows.

13.5.4.1 The shape of the goods themselves

The Court of Appeal upheld the Registrar's refusal to register the shape of the shaver heads of the Philishave razor (*Philips Electronics NV v Remington Consumer Products Ltd (No 2)* [1999] RPC 809). On a reference to the ECJ on construction of the Directive on the Approximation of the Laws of Member States about Trade Marks (Directive 89/104/EC) from which TMA 1994 derives, the ECJ held that a shape determined by technical function of the product was not registrable as a trade mark (Case C-299/99). The Court of Appeal ultimately held that the shape of the shaving head was necessary to its technical function and should not have been registered as a shape mark. By contrast, certain 'device' marks showing a schematic version of the shaving surface were properly registered ([2002] EWCA Civ 16). This result is in line with the permitted registration, under the CTM system, of 'fanciful configurations' (see Communication Notice No 2/98 of the President of OHIM, concerning three-dimensional marks). This is discussed in *Whirlpool Corporation Ltd v Kenwood Ltd* [2009] EWCA Civ 753, a dispute about a CTM in the rather fanciful shape of a kitchen mixer.

In effect, the logic behind the s 3(2) exclusion is that the shape of products should be given a lesser protection as a registered design if the shape is new and has individual character (see **16.2.1**). A registered trade mark is not the appropriate right. Since the amendment in December 2001 of the Registered Designs Act 1949 (RDA 1949), the scope of registered designs has been increased to include the possibility of registering as a design even the appearance of the packaging of a product.

In *Dyson Ltd v Registrar of Trade Marks* (Case C-321/03) [2003] EWHC 1062 (Ch) Dyson attempted to achieve a very wide-ranging protection for all conceivable shapes and configurations of the external face of its transparent collecting chamber. This was treated by the High Court, as well as the ECJ on reference, as not being a shape mark application at all, but simply a feature, which had a function and a potentially variable appearance. The ECJ was also asked as to whether public association of such features with Dyson was enough for it to be registrable. The ECJ found that such an infinitely variable shape could not be graphically represented so as to constitute a distinctive trade mark, because it was simply not a 'sign' in the first place. The question of distinctiveness by use did not arise on those facts.

In *Société des Produits Nestlé SA v Unilever plc* [2002] EWHC 2709 (Ch), [2003] RPC 35, it was held that it was arguable that the shape of Vienetta ice cream resulted from the nature of the product itself, which of course would render it unregistrable as a trade mark. It was also held that there was insufficient evidence that the public recognised the shape of Vienetta as a badge of origin of the goods (ie, as emanating from Unilever), which also renders it unregistrable. In *Société des Produits Nestlé SA v Mars UK Ltd* [2004] EWCA Civ 1008, the Court of Appeal confirmed the refusal of an application to register as a trade mark the three-dimensional shape of a 'Polo' mint, which did not have the word 'Polo' embossed on it. The Registrar would have allowed registration if the application had been for mint-flavoured confectionery only, and had been for the colour white and only for the size of a standard 'Polo' mint. The Court upheld his opinion.

13.5.4.2 The shape of the goods which is necessary to achieve a technical result

This was the real basis of the result in the *Philips* case (see **13.5.4.1**); the 3-rotor configuration gave the technical superiority to the shaver in the first place, and the ECJ made it clear that the exclusion was not limited to situations where the shape in question was the only available shape to achieve that particular technical result. As long as the shape is important to the technical outcome, that is likely to prevent its registration. One solid advantage of this is that interesting shapes might be registrable in other applications, where they are not technically necessary, technically, eg, a small pistol as a trade mark for '*femme fatale*' scent.

13.5.4.3 The shape which gives substantial value to the goods

This seems to be a rather difficult exclusion to apply, and it gave difficulties to the High Court and the Court of Appeal in attempting to rationalise its meaning in the *Philips* case (see **13.5.4.1**). It may well be that a shape which makes goods substantially more valuable to the user, but which is protected by way neither of patent nor design, is what is really being aimed at here. In that case, it would be a retrograde step to allow anyone to have a permanent monopoly by way of trade mark over it. Possibly, things like pistol-grip shapes, spout shapes etc, which do not fit easily into the other exclusions but are intensely used and valued by buyers, might be caught here.

In *Benetton Group SpA v G-Star International BV* (Case C-371/06) [2008] ETMR 5, ECJ, the Court held that a jeans manufacturer should not have been given registration of two shape marks for jeans where the public recognition was based upon extensive advertising of the interesting shapes. The rule in the *Philips* case was applicable, and distinctiveness acquired by use could not cure the statutory bar to registration. The marks were annulled.

13.5.5 Public interest objections (s 3(3)) and bad faith applications (s 3(6))

An application will not succeed if the trade mark in question is contrary to public policy or morality (s 3(3)(a)), is likely to deceive (s 3(3)(b)) or is made in bad faith (s 3(6)).

13.5.5.1 Likely to deceive

For example, 'Orlwoola' for clothes would be deceptive if the clothes were not made entirely of wool (and if they were, it would be descriptive). 'Instant dip' for cleaning materials was refused on the basis that some of the materials were not in fact dips (*In the matter of Application No 713,406 by Otto Seligmann for the Registration of a Trade Mark* (1954) 71 RPC 52).

Often, a significant limitation to such objections can arise if a mark has been registered for use in only particular colours. The use of a similar mark in quite different colours may not necessarily be deceptive (see *Phones 4u Ltd and Another v Phone4u.co.uk Internet Ltd* [2006] EWCA Civ 244).

13.5.5.2 Bad faith applications

An example of an existing trade mark registration being struck off as being in bad faith occurred in *Byford v Oliver and Another* [2003] EWHC 295 (Ch), [2003] All ER (D) 345 (Feb). This concerned a number of registrations obtained in 1999 by the defendants for the name 'Saxon', which was a 1980s heavy metal band that is still performing – very loudly. The membership of the band had changed over the years but the claimant had always been a member. The defendants had been members for only part of the period. The defendants were held not to own the name and goodwill of the band 'Saxon' in its various guises. There appear to be other disputes concerning the reformation of earlier successful bands and the use of associated names and marks, so more legislation is likely, shortly.

In *Jules Rimet Cup Ltd v Football Association Ltd* [2007] EWHC 2376 (Ch), the court held that the claimant had acted, both subjectively and objectively, in bad faith, in seeking to register the 'World Cup Willie' logo and words as trade marks. The claimant must have known that there was still valuable residual goodwill in the UK for such a familiar mark.

An application to strike off a mark as being deceptive was made in *Zakritoe Aktsionernoe Obchtechestvo Torgovy Dom Potomkov Postavechtchika Dvora Ego Imperatorskago Velitschestva PA Smirnova v Diageo North America Inc* [2003] All ER (D) 99 (Apr). The (Russian) appellant's argument was that the (American) respondent's 14 registrations of the word 'Smirnoff' implied an unjustified connection with the Russian Federation. Smirnoff vodka has been sold since 1952 and is described as the world's leading brand. The appeal failed, as there was held to be no deception as to the origin of the goods. The registrations for 'Smirnoff' were upheld.

13.5.5.3 Public policy or morality

In *Ghazilian's Trade Mark Application* [2002] RPC 23, the applicant appealed the refusal of the Registrar of Trade Marks to register as a trade mark for clothing the words 'Tiny Penis'. Not surprisingly, the judge agreed with the Registrar and refused registration. The judge held that the hearing officer had to consider objectively how a right-thinking, but open-minded, member of the public would view the mark in question, as in *Re Masterman's Design* [1991] RPC 89. (This concerned a Scottish doll wearing a kilt but nothing under it. Registration of the design was allowed.)

An attempt to have the FCUK registration declared invalid on public policy grounds failed; the mark had been properly registered and any objectionable use of the mark by third parties could not affect its continued validity (see *French Connection Ltd's Trade Mark Application (No 81862)* [2005] WL 3734085). This reasoning can be seen in the successful registration of many highly suggestive marks.

13.6 Evidence of use to overcome absolute grounds (the proviso to s 3(1))

In **13.5** we saw how the criteria for absolute grounds work. However, there are lots of registered trade marks which would offend these criteria. The registration system would therefore unfairly deprive the proprietors of the protection of registration, when in fact the trade marks are already well known in the trade or to the public. Examples of trade marks which prima facie offend the criteria for absolute grounds but yet have been registered include the 'York' trailer trade mark (geographical objections) and 'Premier' luggage (laudatory description). The reason is that lack of distinctiveness can often be overcome by publicly recognised use, that is, by building up goodwill in the mark. If an applicant can show that it has built up a reputation in, say, a descriptive mark by using it, then it may have acquired distinctiveness in fact through use and it can be registered. The Coca-Cola bottle shape was universally associated, by use, with the company, although the bottle shape had some distinctive features anyway. The applicant will establish reputation in the mark by sending a statutory declaration to the Trade Mark Registry giving evidence of advertising spend, turnover in the goods and length of use. (Also it needs to be use as an indicator of origin of the goods or services, sometimes referred to as 'trade mark use'.) An informal minimum number of years' use is five. If you do not have five years of use, it is not generally worth trying. Usually the client does better to choose a mark that is registrable from the outset without use but valuable marks do often arise over time.

Very few colours are registered, but the colour of Heinz tins of baked beans has now been registered on the basis of use. Usually, for colour to be considered it has to be a combination of colours, not just a single shade. See *Smith Kline & French Laboratories Ltd v Sterling-Winthrop Group Ltd* [1975] 2 All ER 578, where a complex of colours for a pharmaceutical capsule was accepted on evidence of wide recognition of the complex as distinguishing the goods. (Be aware that this case was under the old Trade Marks Act 1938.) Nevertheless, in *BP Amoco plc v John Kelly Ltd* [2002] FSR 5, it was held that BP's trade mark registration of a single colour was valid. The trade mark consisted of the shade of green defined in colour charts as Pantone 348C, which BP used as the livery for their petrol filling stations. In *Libertel Group BV v Benelux-Merkenbureau* Case (C-104/01) [2004] 2 WLR 1081, the ECJ held that in order to be capable of being registered as a trade mark, a colour had to be defined by reference to an international identification system. It was not sufficient to lodge a sample with the trade mark office in question. The colour also had to have distinctive character (ie, to have been used in relation to the goods or services in question).

A type of mark that often arises over time is in the recognised use of slogans; these can become very well known indicators of trade origin. But they have their own problems. The long-running attempt to register 'HAVE A BREAK', quite independently of the well-known 'have a break … have a Kit Kat', has produced an ECJ reference by the Court of Appeal that appears to give support for the proposition that long use and recognition of the mark, in association with a registered trade mark, even as part of a more extensive slogan, can give the necessary distinctiveness of trade origin for registration; see *Société des Produits Nestlé SA v Mars UK Ltd* (Case C-353/03) [2005] 3 CMLR 12, [2006] All ER (EC) 348, ECJ. The problem, up to the stage of the reference, was the High Court view, supporting the refusal to register, that 'have a break', standing alone, was a common phrase that had no distinctive quality in itself.

Generally, with slogans, the more curious the expression and the less related to the particular goods or services, the greater the likelihood of registration, the downside being that the promotional value must, necessarily, be very indirect. Established use is very helpful in trying to register slogans as trade marks, in part because it allows a trial period to see whether the slogan is effective, in a commercial sense, before trying to register.

13.7 Relative grounds for refusing an application (s 5)

13.7.1 What does 'relative grounds' mean?

'Relative grounds' means a conflict with an existing registered trade mark, belonging to someone else, which is identical or similar to the one being applied for. In TMA 1994, s 5, the relative grounds for refusal are laid down. The most common ones are as follows:

> (1) A trade mark shall not be registered if it is identical with an earlier trade mark and the goods or services for which the trade mark is applied for are identical with the goods or services for which the earlier trade mark is protected.

> (2) A trade mark shall not be registered if because—
>
> (a) it is identical with an earlier trade mark and is to be registered for goods or services similar to those for which the earlier trade mark is protected, or
>
> (b) it is similar to an earlier trade mark and is to be registered for goods or services identical with or similar to those for which the earlier trade mark is protected,
>
> there exists a likelihood of confusion on the part of the public, which includes the likelihood of association with the earlier trade mark.
>
> (3) A trade mark which—
>
> (a) is identical with or similar to an earlier trade mark, ...
>
> (b) ...
>
> shall not be registered if, or to the extent that, the earlier trade mark has a reputation in the United Kingdom (or, in the case of a Community trade mark, in the European Community) and the use of the later mark without due cause would take unfair advantage of, or be detrimental to, the distinctive character or the repute of the earlier trade mark.

How do you find out whether your client's proposed trade mark is going to run foul of an existing registration? The answer is to do a trade mark search. Most firms have facilities for doing this online; alternatively, you can get one through an agency like Compumark. If you are inexperienced in this kind of work then it is best to go to an agency because they will analyse it for you to some extent. If you really don't know what you are doing, you instruct a trade mark agent. Beware that the results of a trade mark search are never completely up to date. The search facilities available on www.ipo.gov.uk are admirably easy to use.

Because trade marks are registered in relation to specified goods or services, the starting point is to look for trade marks registered for the same types of goods and services, that is, in the relevant classes (see **13.3** and **13.15**).

A trade mark application can also be refused on the grounds that it is likely to be the subject of a passing-off action (TMA 1994, s 5(4) and see **12.1**). To check for earlier rights in passing off, you can do a common law search by looking in telephone directories and journals (eg, in magazines on mountain bikes for marks used in connection with push bikes), etc. This common law search cannot, of course, be comprehensive. Some earlier rights may well be obvious, even without a search. See *Jules Rimet Cup Ltd v Football Association Ltd* (at **13.5.5.2**), concerning an application to register the 'World Cup Willie' logo and words.

The starting point, then, with relative ground objections, is to show an identical or similar pre-existing registration; dissimilar marks usually create few problems. The same concepts and case law come into play when considering infringements under s 10, which are discussed at **13.9**, and the same matters need to be considered. It is very important, therefore, to consider how identity and similarity are assessed in this circumstance and it is not at all easy to summarise the approaches taken. Generally, the test is one for the registration authorities and the courts, according to legal principles, a brief summary of which now follows.

13.7.1.1 Identical marks

The broad approach is for the court to put itself in the position of a reasonable, well-informed and alert customer, seeing the mark and having all the usual imperfections of recall of earlier marks that would be normal in such a person. It follows that tactile, visual and aural perceptions are important and it is probably only going to be clearly an identical mark if, without much modification, the essential elements of the earlier mark, as registered, are reproduced in the later one. Usually, the difficulties come where someone has used only part of an earlier mark, or has used all of an earlier mark and added more to it to create a larger, more complex mark, eg, if someone used the famous 'Smartie' mark in a larger composition. Generally, anyone doing the latter would infringe the earlier mark, because they have reproduced it in its entirety, albeit as part of a mark; that could be done by extending a trade marked word into a longer word or phrase; see *Decon Laboratories Ltd v Fred Baker Scientific*

Ltd [2001] RPC 293 and *System 3R International AB v Erowa AG and Erowa Nordic AB* [2003] ETMR 916. Stylising the word in a different way may still amount to using an identical mark. The advantage of finding an identical mark, as compared with a similar one, is that, if used on identical goods, nothing more needs to be established to prevent registration (compare s 5(1) with s 5(2)).

13.7.1.2 Identical goods or services

This can be a problem area in some respects; it is certainly not enough that the goods or services are within the same registration class. The goods or services need to have a considerable identity in terms of what they are, in themselves, as well as with respect to what the customer is expecting to obtain, as can be seen in the *Associated Newspapers* case, discussed at **13.3**, where free newspapers were held to be similar to retailed newspapers but not identical. There is no requirement for direct identity between the particular appearance or other aspects of the compared matters; a square, red ceramic floor tile is identical, for these purposes, with a round, blue one.

13.7.1.3 Similarity of marks

Here, somewhat different considerations apply, because the point has been visited on many occasions and there is now a fairly well-established approach, as shown by the ECJ in *Sabel BV v Puma AG, Rudolf Dassler Sport* (Case C-251/95) [1998] ETMR 1. A court should take an overall impression of the visual, aural and conceptual similarities of the marks, looking in particular at distinctive and dominant features. To this list, scents and smells must now be added. The whole point about this test is that it concentrates upon similarities, rather than distinctions. One might well add all sorts of fancy differences on top of someone else's registered mark, but if the 'distinctive and dominant' features of the prior registered mark are still discernible enough to lead to the necessary confusion in the mind of the customer, causing him to associate the mark before him with a completely different trade source that he already associates with of those features, it will be a similar mark; see *Sir Terence Orby Conran v Mean Fiddler Holdings Ltd* [1997] FSR 856, where the 'Zinc' mark was successfully protected in opposition proceedings. The question of similarity cannot really be divorced from the question of confusion as to trade source, and similarity, in the absence of confusion or, at least, association with the registered mark, is not a relevant consideration.

In *Alticor Inc v Nutrigreen Health Products Ltd* (Trade Mark Registry 09/11/07) [2007] WL 4368242, an application was upheld to register 'NUTRILIFE' as a trade mark over opposition from the owner of the registration of 'NUTRILITE'. The mark applied for comprised 'NUTRI' and 'LIFE' on different lines, and the words were linked by other graphic imagery. Taking the totality of each mark into consideration, the differences far outweighed the similarities.

13.7.1.4 Similarity of goods and services

Here, much more emphasis is placed upon the fact that, to deny registration, there must be demonstrable confusion and wrong association of the trade source of the goods or services to be marketed under the sign for which registration is sought. Everything, here, is likely to turn upon what, exactly, the likely users of goods or services might expect to find on offer under a particular registered trade mark (bearing in mind the uses for which the trade mark is registered) and where or when those goods or services might be expected to be offered. Clearly, the closer the range and type of goods and/or services to be marketed under the new application, where they are to be marketed, and the marketing techniques used are to those under the existing registration, the more likely it is that there will be found to be similarity; see *Adidas-Salomon AG v Fitnessworld Trading Ltd* (Case C-408/01) [2004] 1 CMLR 14, [2004] Ch 120. The conclusion to be drawn from the many cases in this area seems to be that the greater the reputation and public goodwill in the prior registered trade mark, the emphasis of the comparison by the court tends to shift, noticeably, from the question of similarity of the goods or services offered towards the question of confusion or wrong association of the trade source. It is a subtle point but one that it is necessary to understand the judicial and registration approach.

13.7.2 Relative grounds, registration and specific examples

Someone trying to register 'Coca-Cola' for fizzy drinks would find it impossible on relative grounds because of the existing registrations for the real 'Coca-Cola' (ie 'identical' goods (s 5(1))). However, this could also be the case for someone trying to register 'Coca-Cola' for cars, lavatory brushes or other 'dissimilar' goods. In the case of the use in relation to cars, it would be held as obtaining an unfair advantage from the reputation of the existing trade mark. In the case of goods such as lavatory brushes, it could be held to be detrimental to the existing mark, as well as taking unfair advantage (s 5(3)).

In *Enterprise Rent-a-car Co v Eurodrive Car Rental Ltd* [2005] Lawtel 2/3/2005, the case concerned an application for a trade mark stylised letter 'E' for car rental services. The appellant objected, as it was the proprietor of various trade marks beginning with the letter 'E'. It was held that there was no likelihood of confusion under s 5(2)(b).

In *Intel Corporation v Sihra* [2003] EWHC 17 (Ch), [2003] All ER (D) 212 (Jan), registration of 'Intel-Play' was refused as it was held that it would take unfair advantage of, or be detrimental to the character and repute of the existing registered trade mark 'Intel', under s 5(3). The application was for use on constructional toys, whereas the Intel registration was for computer components. See also the *Associated Newspapers* case at **13.3**.

By contrast, in *Intel Corporation v CPM United Kingdom Ltd* [2006] EWHC 1878 (Ch), it was held that CPM's application to register INTELMARK for marketing and telemarketing services was valid. There would be no material damage to the distinctiveness or reputation of the 'Intel' mark for such services; there was no evidence of any discernible impact on the public's view of the mark. The matter has now been referred to the ECJ by the Court of Appeal; see [2007] EWCA Civ 431.

The situation with relative grounds is very close to that under s 10 for infringement (see **13.9**), and for most purposes ss 5 and 10 can be treated as equivalent provisions.

13.7.3 When might relative grounds show themselves?

The relative grounds are likely in some cases to show themselves at the first stage of application to register, where there is an initial examination and search of the Register to ensure the application complies with the substantive requirements of a trade mark and that there are no absolute or relative grounds of objection, as discussed above at **13.7.1**. The Trade Mark Manual of the IPO shows that, since October 2007, the Registrar has only been able to refuse registration on relative grounds if there is a successful objection by a proprietor of an existing trade mark or sign. If the examiner's preliminary search shows up a potential relevant ground opposition, the result of this is notified to the applicant for the new registration, so that the applicant can withdraw or amend, at this early stage. This initial check is relevant only to objections under s 5(1) and (2). Grounds of objection based upon the other parts of s 5 – s 5(3) and (4) – would not be apparent to the examiner on his initial examination.

If the relative ground difficulty has not been spotted by the examiner, or if the applicant decides to press ahead, notwithstanding potential opposition, the application is then published in the *Trade Marks Journal*, as discussed earlier at **13.4.1**. At the same time as the new application is published, the owners of the prior-registered trade mark(s) that have been identified by the initial examination will be notified of the new application. That triggers a three-month period in which any person objecting on relative grounds, in respect of prior registered marks, can bring opposition proceedings. These commence with a hearing between the parties by a hearing officer at the Registry, with available appeals either to an 'Appointed

Person', appointed by the Lord Chancellor (usually a very senior practitioner), or to the Chancery Division of the High Court.

Under this more modern practice, whereby the Registrar cannot simply, on his own initiative, refuse registration on relative grounds, opposition proceedings are bound to become more frequent.

A useful case to examine the proper approach to opposition proceedings on relative grounds is seen in *Esure Insurance Ltd v Direct Line Insurance plc* [2008] EWCA Civ 842. Here, the owners of the well known 'red telephone on wheels' device trade mark for insurance objected to the application to register a computer mouse on wheels as a device mark for insurance and financial services. The Hearing Officer upheld the objection, on grounds of similarity and likelihood of confusion. On appeal to a judge, the judge disallowed the objection, mainly because of the approach to similarity taken by the Officer. The Court of Appeal, allowing the appeal from the judge below and upholding the objection, gave some useful pointers on s 5(1) and (2). First, confusion was ascertained from the point of view of the average consumer in the light of all factors, and there was no need to apply a strict threshold of similarity, completely independently of confusion. Provided that the Hearing Officer had seen evidence of the marks themselves and the class of registration, that was enough for him to come to his view. It was said, per curiam, that little would be gained by the use of expert evidence in such cases, except where the particular market in question might be one with which the general consumer was unfamiliar.

These changes have necessitated some amendments to the TMA 1994, and these may be seen in the Trade Marks (Earlier Trade Marks) Regulations 2008 (SI 2008/1067). The changes also include giving better protection to 'well-known' trade marks (see **13.10**) as against later registered national trade marks.

13.7.4 Summary

It can be seen, by examining the extract from s 5 shown at **13.7.1**, that all different combinations of identity/similarity of both the marks and the relevant goods/services can now be objected to on relative grounds. This is extended by s 5(3), to deal with the circumstance of identical/similar marks being used even on dissimilar goods. The position is summarised in the table below.

Goods or services	**Trade mark identical**	**Trade mark similar**
Identical	no proof of confusion needed (s 5(1))	likelihood of confusion needed (s 5(2)(b))
Similar	likelihood of confusion needed (s 5(2)(a))	likelihood of confusion needed (s 5(2)(b))
Identical, similar, dissimilar	unfair advantage or detriment needed (s 5(3))	unfair advantage or detriment needed (s 5(3))

13.8 Protecting the mark, once registered

Once the client has the registration, he needs advice on protecting the mark. If it is not protected it can become subject to misuse, including infringement, and ultimately to revocation. The most important grounds of revocation to be aware of are as follows.

13.8.1 Non-use

If the mark has not been used for five years following registration, or any subsequent five-year period, it can be struck off for non-use in that category of goods or services. It is a matter of 'use it or lose it' (ss 46(1)(a) and 6A). This happened in the *United Biscuits* case, discussed at

12.2.2, where the successful claimants nevertheless had four trade mark registrations revoked for non-use.

13.8.2 Has become generic

A trade mark becomes generic if, as a result of action or inaction by the proprietor, it has become a common mark in the trade for a product or service for which it is registered. So, under s 1(1) of the TMA 1994, the trade mark no longer distinguishes the goods or services of one business from those of another business and would not be registrable because of s 3(1)(d). This may lead to a revocation application under s 46 of the TMA 1994; see **13.8.3**.

In *Julius Sämaan v Tetrosyl Ltd* [2006] EWHC 529, owners of fir tree marks for cardboard strip air fresheners were able to show infringement by Tetrosyl, which made similar items for use in cars. A defence that 'tree' marks were now generic was rejected as the only other relevant 'tree' mark in the market showed an oak tree.

Biro, Linoleum, Refrigerator and Launderette have become generic terms. These were once registered trade marks, but they have lost their ability to identify the goods of one business and are now simply part of the language.

How do you avoid your trade mark becoming generic? You should:

(a) use it as an adjective and not as a noun, eg, 'Gordons gin and tonic', not 'Gordons and tonic';

(b) distinguish it from the surrounding writing, eg, by putting it in bold, or in capitals or quotation marks; or

(c) acknowledge it as a trade mark (use ® if registered; but do not use ® if it is not registered because this is a criminal offence – TMA 1994, s 95).

13.8.3 Has become misleading

A trade mark can be revoked if it has become misleading because of the way the proprietor has used it, or allowed it to be used (s 46(1)(d)). One concern here is that if the mark is licensed to others then they may not produce goods of the same quality as the trade mark proprietor, or as each other. For this reason, it is essential to include quality control provisions in any licence to manufacture goods under a trade mark and to make certain that they are applied by the licensee.

13.9 Infringement of a registered trade mark

Under s 14, infringement of a registered trade mark is actionable by the proprietor of the trade mark. This is because s 9(1) says the proprietor has exclusive rights in the mark which are infringed by the use of it in the UK without his consent. It is important to realise that not every use of someone else's mark will be an infringement for these purposes. There must be a use of the mark in the course of trade, as distinct from use for non-trading purposes, eg, painting the Mercedes badge onto your wall at home out of enthusiasm. There must also be use of the mark as a trade mark, as a badge of trade origin, as distinct from serving some other purpose. These matters are discussed in more detail below.

There can only be infringement of the trade mark as actually registered. Any limits on the registration are strictly observed, as in *Phones 4u Ltd and Another v Phone4u.co.uk Internet Ltd* [2006] EWCA Civ 244. There, the registered colours of the mark limited the scope of infringement.

To constitute infringement, use of the offending mark (or 'sign', as it is referred to in s 10, to distinguish it from the mark being infringed) must be 'in the course of trade'. Thus, a painting by Andy Warhol of a can of soup did not infringe Campbells' trade mark as Andy Warhol was not in the business of making soup. The s 9 territorial limit on trade mark use within the UK may sometimes create problems involving importing and exporting trade-marked goods; see *Waterford Wedgwood plc v David Nagli Ltd* [1998] FSR 92 on goods passing through the jurisdiction en route from one country to the other.

The issue of use of the mark as a badge of trade origin came up in the case of *Arsenal Football Club plc v Reed* [2003] EWCA Civ 696. Mr Reed sold football merchandise outside the ground of Arsenal Football Club on match days. He had a notice on his stall to the effect that the goods were not official Arsenal regalia. However, the goods did bear the Arsenal logo. At first instance, there was some doubt as to whether this use was use as a trade mark at all. Was the Arsenal badge being used as a trade mark, or was it just an indication of loyalty to a football team? The ECJ held that the badge was a trade mark (*Arsenal Football Club plc v Reed* (Case C-206/01) [2002] All ER (EC) 1). Professional football clubs such as Arsenal are multi-million pound businesses. They register trade marks to protect their commercial rights. The ECJ held that this was use of an identical mark on identical goods. The Court of Appeal followed the reasoning in the ECJ judgment. Aldous LJ explained that the unauthorised goods sold by Mr Reed affected the ability of the trade marks to guarantee the origin of the goods.

A different problem occurred in *R v Johnstone* [2003] UKHL 28, [2003] 3 All ER 884. In this case, the defendant dealt in bootleg copies of music CDs. Various of the artists concerned had registered their names as trade marks. Was the existence of such an artist's name on a CD merely an indication of the identity of the performer, or was it use of the name in a trade mark sense? The House of Lords held that to come within the criminal offence under s 92 of the TMA 1994, the use of the artist's name had to be use of a trade mark as an indication of trade origin of the CDs. Whilst the use of a trade mark such as 'Sony' or 'EMI' would be such a use, this was not the case with the name of an artist. Consequently, the defendant's actions did not fall within s 92.

13.9.1 The methods of infringement

The TMA 1994 now specifies four types of infringement; here you should consider the points on identical similar signs, goods/services etc at **13.7**:

(a) Use of an identical sign for identical goods or services (as determined by the statement of goods or services with which the mark was registered) (s 10(1)). The question of being 'identical' or not was examined by the Court of Appeal in *Reed Executive and Reed Solutions v Reed Business Information and Elsevier* [2004] EWCA Civ 159, [2004] RPC 40. There, the claimant argued that 'Reed Business Information' was identical under s 10(1) to its registered trade mark 'Reed'. In other words, if the registered trade mark cropped up in only part of another business name, that was use of an identical sign. The Court rejected this argument and held that the words 'Business Information' were part of the defendant's business name. Consequently, 'Reed Business Information' was not identical to 'Reed', so the issue was not use of an identical sign in s 10(1), but rather of a 'similar' sign under s 10(2). In other words, you have to look at the whole of the allegedly infringing sign or mark.

(b) Use of an identical or similar sign for similar goods or services, or a similar sign for identical goods or services, if there is a likelihood of confusion (s 10(2)). This is a higher hurdle for the trademark proprietor to overcome, hence the argument at (a) above in the *Reed* case. Confusion must be as to the trade origin of the goods and services.

(c) Use of an identical or similar sign for goods or services, whether identical, similar or dissimilar, if the use is detrimental to, or takes unfair advantage of, the distinctive character or repute of the mark (s 10(3)). In *Conroy v SmithKline Beecham plc* (Trade Marks Registry 0-085-03, 3 April 2003), the applicant had applied to register 'Nit Nurse' in class 3 for oils and shampoos for the control of head lice. The opponents objected, successfully. They held registrations in class 5 for respiratory decongestants under the trade marks 'Night Nurse'. There were arguments that a consumer could confuse the two products, with unfortunate results. In contrast, see also *Premier Brands UK Ltd v Typhoon Europe Ltd* [2000] FSR 767, where the proprietors of 'Typhoo' for tea, objected unsuccessfully to a registration of 'Typhoon' for kitchen utensils. It should be noted that the tests in ss 5(3) and 10(3) were amended by the Trade Marks (Proof of Use) Etc Regulations 2004 (SI 2004/946). This was to fill a gap in these subsections; originally they did not extend to unfair use of a mark on similar or identical goods, only dissimilar ones. See *Adidas-Salomon AG v Fitnessworld Trading Ltd* (Case C-408/01) [2004] 1 CMLR 14, [2004] Ch 120.

It is not sufficient to show that the alleged infringer has gained an advantage; what must be shown is that the advantage was gained because the registered mark was highly distinctive, and that the reminder of it given to the public by the infringer's use of the sign is strong. The claimant was unable to show this in *Whirlpool Corporation Ltd v Kenwood Ltd* [2009] EWCA Civ 753 (application alleging infringement of a CTM shape mark, in form of a kitchen mixer, causing detriment and taking unfair advantage, was dismissed). See also the important development concerning unfair advantage claims discussed at **13.9.2** below.

(d) Any use of a trade mark which is not in accordance with honest practices in industrial and commercial matters. Honest use is not infringement, so comparative advertising is not infringement (s 10(6) (which it was under the 1938 Act)), provided it does not overstep the boundaries. A case where it did go too far is *Emaco Ltd and Another v Dyson Appliances Ltd* [1999] ETMR 903, where both parties were held to have made unfair comparisons of the goods and thereby infringed each other's trade mark registrations for Electrolux and Dyson. Note that mere advertising puffery does not count as being dishonest, but use of a mark in a manner disparaging to the mark or its owner may take the use outside of honest practice.

An extensive analysis of comparative advertising can be seen in *O2 Holdings Ltd v Hutchinson 3G Ltd* [2006] ETMR 55, where Lewison J upheld the robust, but fair, comparison of products and the validity of different 'bubble' marks used by the parties. Further questions from this case were referred to the ECJ by the Court of Appeal: see [2006] EWCA Civ 1656. The initial opinion given by Advocate-General Mengozzi in Case C-533/06 showed that permissible use of a trade mark in comparative advertising can go some way beyond merely identifying particular goods or services as originating from a competitor, and that such use need not be indispensable to the purposes of the advertiser. The opinion of the ECJ was that, taking the defendant's use of the bubble marks as a whole, it did not give rise to likelihood of confusion, was not misleading and did not suggest any commercial link between the parties. It seems likely, now, that a far more widely applicable source of guidance on the boundary between permissible comparative advertising (which will not infringe trade mark rights) and impermissible comparative advertising (which will do so) is to be seen in the *L'Oréal SA v Bellure NV case*, discussed at **13.9.2** below.

These grounds are much the same as the relative grounds for invalidity (see **13.7**).

The proprietor of a registered trade mark would usually have to produce evidence of confusion, or unfair advantage or detriment, as the case may be. This could be in the form of survey evidence, or expert witnesses from the trade in question, but the nature of the required evidence must be considered now in the light of the ECJ ruling in *L'Oréal SA v Bellure NV*, discussed in **13.9.2** below.

13.9.2 Detrimental or unfairly advantageous use

Very significant guidance has recently been given by the ECJ in *L'Oréal SA v Bellure NV* (Case C-487/07) [2009] All ER (D) 225 (Jun), on the evidential and legal requirements of an infringement claim under s 10(3) (see (c) at **13.9.1** above) and of Article 5(2) of Directive 89/

104. Here, the claimant manufacturer of high-quality beauty products sought remedies, inter alia, for trade mark infringements against 'smell-alike' importers using packaging and comparison lists from which the alleged infringements arose. There were issues concerning the scope of taking unfair advantage of the reputation of a trade mark, both for the purposes of trade mark infringement and for the closely connected question of permissible comparative advertising under EC law on misleading advertisements. The matter went to the Court of Appeal, from which the following questions were referred to the ECJ (summarised here, for simplicity, as the ECJ dealt with them in a slightly different way from that in which the Court of Appeal referred them) for preliminary rulings:

(a) *Whether a third party using a sign, identical to a trade mark with a reputation, in comparative advertising in relation to identical goods, could be held to take unfair advantage where the third party gained a marketing advantage, but without causing confusion to the public as to trade origin, or causing detriment to the mark or its proprietor.* The ECJ ruled that unfair advantage could be taken of the distinctive character or the repute of the mark, without requiring a likelihood of confusion or detriment. The unfairness of the advantage lay in the third party riding 'on the coat-tails' of the trade mark, to exploit the marketing effort and expense needed to maintain the registered mark's image, without paying any compensation for it.

(b) *Whether the proprietor of a well-known registered mark could prevent such a use in comparative advertising as is described in (a) above, by a third party, where such use is not capable of jeopardising the essential function of the trade mark as an indicator of trade origin.* The ECJ ruled that the proprietor of the mark could prevent such use, even in those circumstances, provided that such use was liable to affect some other function of the mark (examples were given, in particular, of the functions of guaranteeing quality, of communication, investment or advertising). It would be for the referring court (in this case, the Court of Appeal) to determine whether the use made of the infringing sign was liable to affect one or more of the functions of the trade mark. The case law showed that the proprietor cannot oppose the use of an identical sign, if that use is not liable to cause detriment to any of the functions of the trade mark. Nevertheless, the ECJ made very clear that an advertiser, in a comparative advertisement that satisfied all the requirements of Article 3a(1) of Directive 84/450 (the Directive covering misleading advertising, which extends to comparative advertising: see further **13.9.4** below) could not be prevented from honest use of the mark by the proprietor of it. (See **13.9.4** on the point of regulation of misleading advertisements.)

(c) *Whether Article 3a(1) of Directive 84/450 means that where an advertiser indicates through a comparison list, without in any way causing confusion or deception, that his product has a major characteristic similar to that of a product marketed under a well-known trade mark, of which the advertiser's product constitutes an imitation, that advertiser takes unfair advantage of the trade mark (for the purposes of Article 3a(1) of Directive 84/50), or presents 'goods or services as imitations or replicas' for the purposes of Article 3a(1)(h).* The ECJ ruled that such an advertiser would be both taking unfair advantage of the reputation of the mark and presenting the goods or services as imitations or replicas within the meaning of Directive 84/450. It appears to follow from this ruling, and the view of the Court of Appeal in the case, that because such a use was impermissible and would be inconsistent with fair competition or honest practice, it was unlawful, and must be regarded as taking unfair advantage of the reputation of the mark, for trade mark infringement purposes, too (this point was not referred to the ECJ as being self-evident).

It seems very likely that this guidance will figure prominently in future cases on comparative advertising, both with respect to trade mark infringements per se and with respect to questions of permissible use of signs and marks in comparative advertising within Directive 84/450, as amended (see **13.9.4**).

13.9.3 Trade marks and the Internet

Trade marks are national rights (but see **13.13** below for the international dimension), so the use has to be within the UK. Thus, on the Internet, pre-emptive registration of a domain name that is similar to a registered trade mark might not necessarily be use in the course of trade within the UK. However, the Court of Appeal held it was so likely to lead to infringement that an injunction was granted (*British Telecommunications plc and Others v One in a Million Ltd and Others* [1999] 1 WLR 903). In that case, someone had registered as Internet domain names the names of various well-known businesses, including BT and Virgin. The aim presumably was to sell the domain name to the rightful owner for large sums of money. See also *Tesco Stores Ltd v Elogicom Ltd* [2006] EWHC 403 (Ch), where use of the 'Tesco' mark, as part of several domain names, constituted serious infringement of the trade mark.

A website can be accessed from anywhere in the world; this does not always mean that for trade mark purposes the trade marks are being used in the course of trade in a particular jurisdiction (see *800 Flowers, Trade Mark Application; 1-800 Flowers Incorporated v Phonenames Ltd* [2001] EWCA Civ 721, [2002] FSR 288 and *Euromarket Designs Inc v Peters and Trade & Barrel Ltd* [2001] FSR 288, where the mere possibility of accessing a site from the UK did not necessarily mean that there was infringement of a UK trade mark). In the *Euromarket* case, Jonathan Parker LJ said:

> So I think that the mere fact that websites can be accessed anywhere in the world does not mean, for trade mark purposes, that the law should regard them as being used everywhere in the world. It all depends upon the circumstances, particularly the intention of the website owner and what the reader will understand if he accesses the site. In other fields of law, publication on a website may well amount to a universal publication, but I am not concerned with that.

In *Wilson v Yahoo! UK Ltd* [2008] EWHC 361 (Ch), the defendant was granted summary judgment to strike out a claim that it had infringed the claimant's trade mark via two sponsored links on its Internet search engine. It was held that the trade mark had not been used by the defendant but only by the browser. This happened when the browser put the word mark in as a search term.

Thus, in *Bonnier Media Ltd v Greg Lloyd Smith* [2002] ETMR 86, the Scottish Court of Session held that the defendants could be sued in Scotland in regard to material accessed on the Internet, even though the originating site was outside the UK. The defendants intended to set up a website with a domain name similar to Bonnier's trade mark. It was held that the defendants' activities were aimed at damaging Bonnier's business, which was based in Scotland. In other words, the defendants' intentions are a key part in deciding whether or not there is trade mark infringement (or passing off).

Another aspect of the international dimension of trade marks is the interface with competition law. A trade mark proprietor could not use national trade mark rights to prevent parallel importation of his goods from another EU Member State. However, he can use trade mark rights to prevent importation of goods he has produced and has sold for resale on to a non-EU market. This was the case in *Zino Davidoff SA v A & G Imports Ltd; Levi Strauss & Co and Another v Tesco Stores Ltd and Another; Levi Strauss & Co and Another v Costco Wholesale UK* (Joined Cases C-414/99, C-415/99 and C-416/99) [2002] All ER (EC) 55. Here, the claimants succeeded in preventing Tesco from continuing to import supplies of the Levi Strauss goods from North America and Mexico. The goods were for resale in the Tesco stores in the UK at lower prices than the goods officially released on to the UK market by Levi Strauss (see also the *Silhouette* case at **13.11**). In the case of *Glaxo Group v Dowelhurst Ltd* [2004] EWCA Civ 290, [2004] WL 412961, CA, pharmaceutical products were sold to the defendant company for sale in Africa but were in fact sold within the UK. An injunction was granted to prevent this activity.

Further discussion of trade mark use in Internet trading can be found at **20.5.3** below.

13.9.4 Honest and fair use of a trade mark

All the infringing acts within s 10 are subject to the proviso within s 10(6) (see (d) at **13.9.1** above), namely that any honest and fair use of another person's registered trade mark for the purpose of identifying any goods or services as being those of the proprietor or a licensee of the mark is to be allowed. This is essential, of course, to the widespread modern practice of comparative advertising, ie comparing a range of competing products on price, performance etc. This is very important, because the infringing acts set out in s 10(4) include use of the mark on business papers or in advertising.

You will have realised from your reading of the *L'Oréal SA v Bellure NV* guidance at **13.9.2** above, that where the use of a trade mark in permissible comparative advertising is concerned, the proprietor of the mark cannot prevent fair and honest use of his mark by a competitor or other advertiser. The overall framework governing what is permissible is found in Directive 84/450 EEC, as amended by Directive 97/55 EC. The object of this Directive is to provide a system of Member State regulation, under which misleading and unfair anti-competitive advertising practices (including comparative advertising) can be controlled by public enforcement authorities. It is only when the unauthorised use of a trade mark fails to comply with the regulatory requirements that the proprietor can take his own private law steps to seek remedies against the persons responsible for any misuse in comparative advertising.

United Kingdom protection for trade marks against comparative advertising has been provided by the Business Protection from Misleading Marketing Regulations 2008 (SI 2008/1276), which are intended to address confusion between, or damage to, trade marks, names or products, although these Regulations have a far wider reach than trade mark use.

13.10 'Well-known' foreign trade marks (s 56)

Section 56 was introduced as part of the UK implementation of the Paris Convention. If a foreign trade mark is well known in the UK, the foreign proprietor will be able to get an injunction to restrain the use of that mark in the UK where the use would cause confusion. This measure is to protect foreign trade marks that are not registered in the UK. The most likely instance is that of a famous shop, or restaurant or hotel which has no branches in the UK. The section limits the remedy available to injuction but, no doubt, a passing-off claim would be available if further remedies are sought.

These marks are now given better protection under the Trade Marks (Earlier Trade Marks) Regulations 2008 (see **13.7.3**).

13.11 Defences to infringement (ss 11, 12, 48)

The first line of defence to a trade mark infringement action is that the trade mark is not validly registered and should be removed from the register under s 47 of the TMA 1994. The basis of the invalidity must be that one or more of the absolute grounds for refusing registration (s 3) can be shown.

The next line of defence to consider is s 11, which limits the scope of a registered trade mark and therefore provides some defences. For example, s 11(2)(a) allows the honest use of a person's own name or address. In *Reed Executive and Reed Solutions v Reed Business Information and Elsevier* [2004] EWCA Civ 159, [2004] RPC 40, the case concerned two businesses with similar names but operating in different fields of activity. It was held that a company could avail itself of the 'own name defence', and that the existence of the word 'Limited' was not relevant. Section 11(2)(b) allows use for the purposes of indicating the nature of the goods or services, so, for example, allowing an independent business to indicate that it supplied parts for BMW cars (*Bayerische Motorenwerke AG (BMW) and Another v Deenik* (Case 63/97) [1999] All ER (EC) 235).

However, in *Aktiebolaget Volvo v Heritage (Leicester) Ltd* [2000] FSR 253, the defendant motor trader had not made it sufficiently clear that it was no longer an authorised Volvo dealer. Consequently, its use of the Volvo trade mark was held not to fall within s 11, and it had infringed the trade mark registration by using an identical mark on identical goods.

Section 12 deals with the exhaustion of rights. Goods put on to the market elsewhere in the EU by the trade mark proprietor can be legitimately sold under that trade mark in the UK. Note that this does not cover goods put on to the market elsewhere in the world (*Silhouette International Schmied GmbH and Co KG v Hartlauer Handelsgesellschaft mbH* (Case C-355/96) [1999] Ch 77 and see the *Zino Davidoff* case at **13.9**). To exhaust the rights, the owner must have actually consented to the product being placed on the market within the EEA, or there must be a strong implication of such consent. The mere fact that packaging was printed in three European languages was not enough to raise that implication in *Roche Products Ltd v Kent Pharmaceuticals Ltd* [2006] EWHC 335.

An interesting case that shows how the implication of consent can arise is *Honda Motor Co Ltd v Neesam* [2008] EWHC 338 (Ch). Here, sales by Honda to its Australian subsidiary, which sold the motor bikes to a dealer who was known to deal in the UK market, were held to show an implied consent, sufficient to exhaust the right.

Section 48 deals with the question of acquiescence. If a proprietor of an earlier mark acquiesces in someone else's use of the registered mark for a continuous period of five years, the right is lost to apply for invalidity of the later mark or to oppose its use. See *Budejovicki Budvar Narodni Podnik v Anheuser-Busch Inc* [2008] EWHC 263 (Ch). In this recent round in the lengthy litigation over the 'Budweiser' and 'Bud' marks (in which both parties have legitimate interests), an acquiescence defence was upheld, in part.

13.12 Remedies for infringement (ss 14–19)

Section 14(2) provides that the usual remedies of 'damages, injunction, accounts or otherwise' are as available as 'in respect of the infringement of any other property right'. To this are added:

(a) orders against an infringer to erase or remove the offending sign or, if that is not possible, to destroy the goods or materials (s 15);

(b) the availability of an order to deliver up infringing goods or materials held in the course of business (s 16);

(c) orders concerning the disposal of matter delivered up under (b) (s 19);

(d) relief, including damages, declaration and injunction, against groundless threats of infringement proceedings (s 21).

There are also criminal law sanctions under ss 92–98, creating offences involving unauthorised use of trade marks, subject to defences of reasonable belief that no infringement was involved. There is also the possibility of forfeiture of counterfeit goods, in connection with such offences, under s 97. Further, there is the possibility of injunction and criminal prosecution at the instance of enforcement authorities under the Business Protection from Misleading Marketing Regulations 2008.

13.13 International trade marks

We have been looking at the law of UK trade marks. If you apply for a UK trade mark, this will give you the right to stop infringements only in the UK. If you want protection in other countries (eg, US, Japan, Hong Kong) then you have to make a separate application there. So if you want to protect your mark world-wide, this will be a very expensive process.

Within Europe, two processes allow the applicant to get wider protection on the basis of a single application.

13.13.1 Community trade mark

The CTM is a single trade mark, effective throughout the European Community. You apply to the OHIM at Alicante. The CTM system is still quite new, but it is proving very popular. Between the start of the system in 1996 and the end of May 2004, there were 378,000 applications made to OHIM. If you can get a CTM then this will give you protection throughout the Community on the basis of one registration. The difficulty is that the registration can be defeated by similar prior marks anywhere in the European Community. Many well-known UK marks would not be able to achieve a Community registration for this reason. However, the CTM system does not carry out extensive investigation of existing marks but rather leaves the proprietors of existing marks to object to published applications. This happened in *Mülhens GmbH & Co KG v OHIM and Zirh International Corp* (Case C-206/04P) [2006] ETMR 57, where the owners of the earlier CTM 'Sir' were able to block the registration of 'ZIRH' for the same class of goods, on grounds of similarity.

If an applicant is unsuccessful, it is then left with the possibility of applying in each of those countries where there is no problem in order to get a bundle of national registered trade marks.

13.13.2 Madrid Protocol

This is a system that allows you to make one application in one country initially. Then an application can be made for registrations in all the other countries listed on the application form, and which are Member States of the Madrid Protocol. The system is run by the World Intellectual Property Organisation (WIPO). The European Community itself has become a member, as opposed to the individual countries. The CTM can thus now be used as a basis for an international application to obtain trade mark protection outside the EC, as well as giving protection inside it.

13.13.3 Other international aspects

International treaties such as the Paris Convention for the Protection of Intellectual Property and TRIPS (part of GATT) ensure that there are certain similarities between the intellectual property laws of many countries in the world (eg, TMA 1994, s 56 arises out of an obligation under the Paris Convention).

In addition, TMA 1994 implements the European Trade Marks Directive, which had as its aim the partial harmonisation of European trade mark laws. However, despite this, there are many important differences between the trade mark laws of different countries, both inside and outside Europe. There are also many technical differences. One should never assume, therefore, that the position is the same in another country. Foreign legal advice is often necessary, and most intellectual property practices have foreign lawyers with whom they deal on a regular basis.

13.14 Classes used in the Register of Trade Marks (Trade Mark Rules 2000, Sch 4)

CLASSIFICATION OF GOODS AND SERVICES

When you apply to register a trade mark you must include a list of all goods and services which you want to use the mark for. You must list the goods or services in the class or classes they fall in.

The following headings give general information about the types of goods and services which belong to each class. The list is not complete. It is there to guide you to the classes that you need. If you click on the class number you will see a full list of goods or services in that class, as provided by WIPO, the international organisation which decides trade mark classification.

Goods are in classes 1–34. Services are in classes 35–45.

If you do not know which class(es) your goods or services are in, please use our Classification search.

Goods

CLASS 1

Chemicals used in industry, science and photography, as well as in agriculture, horticulture and forestry; unprocessed artificial resins, unprocessed plastics; manures; fire extinguishing compositions; tempering and soldering preparations; chemical substances for preserving foodstuffs; tanning substances; adhesives used in industry.

Includes chemicals for the making of products belonging to other classes.

Does not include fungicides, herbicides, insecticides or preparations for destroying vermin which are in Class 5.

CLASS 2

Paints, varnishes, lacquers; preservatives against rust and against deterioration of wood; colorants; mordants; raw natural resins; metals in foil and powder form for painters, decorators, printers and artists.

Does not include paint boxes for children which are in Class 16 or insulating paints and varnishes which are in Class 17.

CLASS 3

Bleaching preparations and other substances for laundry use; cleaning, polishing, scouring and abrasive preparations; soaps; perfumery, essential oils, cosmetics, hair lotions; dentifrices.

Includes deodorants for personal use.

Does not include air deodorising preparations which are in Class 5 or scented candles which are in Class 4.

CLASS 4

Industrial oils and greases; lubricants; dust absorbing, wetting and binding compositions; fuels (including motor spirit) and illuminants; candles and wicks for lighting.

Includes combustible fuels and scented candles.

Does not include fuel for nuclear reactors or electricity which are both in Class 1. CLASS 5

Pharmaceutical and veterinary preparations; sanitary preparations for medical purposes; dietetic substances adapted for medical use, food for babies; plasters, materials for dressings; material for stopping teeth, dental wax; disinfectants; preparations for destroying vermin; fungicides, herbicides.

Includes foods and beverages which are adapted for medical purposes. *Does not include* supportive bandages which are in Class 10.

CLASS 6

Common metals and their alloys; metal building materials; transportable buildings of metal; materials of metal for railway tracks; non-electric cables and wires of common metal; ironmongery, small items of metal hardware; pipes and tubes of metal; safes; goods of common metal not included in other classes; ores.

Includes unwrought and partly wrought common metals as well as simple products made of them; metallic windows and doors and also metallic framed conservatories.

CLASS 7

Machines and machine tools; motors and engines (except for land vehicles); machine coupling and transmission components (except for land vehicles); agricultural implements other than hand-operated; incubators for eggs.

Includes parts of engines and motors; some parts for vehicles (eg exhausts for vehicles); vacuum cleaners.

Does not include engines or motors for land vehicles which are in Class 12 or specialist machines (eg weighing machines are in Class 9).

CLASS 8

Hand tools and implements (hand operated); cutlery; side arms; razors.

Includes electric razors and hair cutters; cutlery made of precious metal.

Does not include surgical cutlery which is in Class 10 or hand held and electrically powered tools (eg electric drills are in Class 7).

CLASS 9

Scientific, nautical, surveying, photographic, cinematographic, optical, weighing, measuring, signalling, checking (supervision), life-saving and teaching apparatus and instruments; apparatus and instruments for conducting, switching, transforming, accumulating, regulating or controlling electricity; apparatus for recording, transmission or reproduction of sound or images; magnetic data carriers, recording discs; automatic vending machines and mechanisms for coin operated apparatus; cash registers; calculating machines, data processing equipment and computers; fire-extinguishing apparatus.

Includes computer hardware and firmware; computer software (including software downloadable from the Internet); compact discs; digital music (downloadable from the Internet); telecommunications apparatus; computer games equipment adapted for use with TV receivers; mouse mats; mobile phone accessories; contact lenses, spectacles and sunglasses; clothing for protection against accident, irradiation or fire.

Does not include printed computer manuals which are in Class 16, self contained computer games equipment which is in Class 28, various electrical items (eg electric screwdrivers are in Class 7 and electric toothbrushes are in Class 21).

CLASS 10

Surgical, medical, dental and veterinary apparatus and instruments, artificial limbs, eyes and teeth; orthopaedic articles; suture materials.

Includes electro-medical or surgical apparatus; massage apparatus.

Does not include contact lenses, spectacles or sunglasses which are in Class 9 or wheelchairs which are in Class 12.

CLASS 11

Apparatus for lighting, heating, steam generating, cooking, refrigerating, drying, ventilating, water supply and sanitary purposes.

Includes air conditioning apparatus; electric kettles; gas and electric cookers; vehicle lights.

CLASS 12

Vehicles; apparatus for locomotion by land, air or water.

Includes motors and engines for land vehicles and certain other parts and fittings (eg vehicle body parts and transmissions).

Does not include certain parts or fittings for vehicles (eg exhausts and starters are in Class 7, lights and air conditioning units are in Class 11) or children's toy bicycles which are in Class 28.

CLASS 13

Firearms; ammunition and projectiles, explosives; fireworks.

Does not include apparatus for use in playing paint ball combat games which are in Class 28.

CLASS 14

Precious metals and their alloys and goods in precious metals or coated therewith, not included in other classes; jewellery, precious stones; horological and chronometric instruments.

Includes clocks and watches; costume jewellery.

Does not include certain precious metal items (eg cutlery is in Class 8, pens are in Class 16).

CLASS 15

Musical instruments.

Includes stands and cases adapted for musical instruments.

CLASS 16

Paper, cardboard and goods made from these materials, not included in other classes; printed matter; book binding material; photographs; stationery; adhesives for stationery or household purposes; artists' materials; paint brushes; typewriters and office requisites (except furniture); instructional and teaching material (except apparatus); plastic materials for packaging (not included in other classes); printers' type; printing blocks.

Includes disposable nappies of paper for babies; printed publications.

Does not include adhesives for industrial purposes which are in Class 1, electronic publications (downloadable) which are in Class 9, providing electronic publications (not downloadable) which are in Class 41 or wallpaper which is in Class 27.

CLASS 17

Rubber, gutta-percha, gum, asbestos, mica and goods made from these materials and not included in other classes; plastics in extruded form for use in manufacture; packing, stopping and insulating materials; flexible pipes, not of metal.

Includes semi-finished plastics materials for use in further manufacture.

Does not include unprocessed plastics in the form of liquids, chips, granules etc which are in Class 1.

CLASS 18

Leather and imitations of leather, and goods made of these materials and not included in other classes; animal skins, hides; trunks and travelling bags; umbrellas, parasols and walking sticks; whips, harness and saddlery.

Includes handbags, rucksacks, purses; clothing for animals.

Does not include leather clothing which is in Class 9 (for protection against injury) or in Class 25 (ordinary apparel); certain specialist leather articles (eg cheque book holders are in Class 16).

CLASS 19

Building materials (non-metallic); non-metallic rigid pipes for building; asphalt, pitch and bitumen; non-metallic transportable buildings; monuments, not of metal.

Includes non-metallic framed conservatories, doors and windows.

CLASS 20

Furniture, mirrors, picture frames; goods (not included in other classes) of wood, cork, reed, cane, wicker, horn, bone, ivory, whalebone, shell, amber, mother-of-pearl, meerschaum and substitutes for all these materials, or of plastics.

Includes both metallic and non-metallic furniture including garden furniture; pillows and cushions.

Does not include duvets or covers for pillows, cushions or duvets which are in Class 24, furniture adapted for medical use which is in Class 10 or furniture adapted for laboratory use which is in Class 9.

CLASS 21

Household or kitchen utensils and containers (not of precious metal or coated therewith); combs and sponges; brushes (except paint brushes); brush-making materials; articles for cleaning purposes; steel wool; un-worked or semi-worked glass (except glass used in building); glassware, porcelain and earthenware not included in other classes.

Includes both electric and non-electric toothbrushes.

Does not include electric kitchen appliances (eg electric food processors are in Class 7, electric kettles are in Class 11) or kitchen and table cutlery which is in Class 8.

CLASS 22

Ropes, string, nets, tents, awnings, tarpaulins, sails, sacks and bags (not included in other classes); padding and stuffing materials (except of rubber or plastics); raw fibrous textile materials.

Includes bags and sacks for transporting bulk materials.

CLASS 23

Yarns and threads, for textile use.

CLASS 24

Textiles and textile goods, not included in other classes; bed and table covers.

Includes textile piece goods; textiles for making articles of clothing.

Does not include table linen of paper which is in Class 16 or electric blankets (not for medical use) which are in Class 11.

CLASS 25

Clothing, footwear, headgear.

Does not include clothing for the prevention of accident and injury which is in Class 9, surgeons' clothing which is in Class 10 or clothing for animals which is in Class 18.

CLASS 26

Lace and embroidery, ribbons and braid; buttons, hooks and eyes, pins and needles; artificial flowers.

Includes dressmakers' articles; badges for wear (other than precious metal badges). CLASS 27

Carpets, rugs, mats and matting, linoleum and other materials for covering existing floors; wall hangings (non-textile).

Includes wallpaper.

Does not include mouse mats which are in Class 9, mats specifically shaped/adapted for vehicles which are in Class 12 or travellers' rugs which are in Class 24.

CLASS 28

Games and playthings; gymnastic and sporting articles not included in other classes; decorations for Christmas trees.

Includes hand-held computer games equipment which is self contained (not adapted for use with TV receivers).

Does not include computer games equipment adapted for use with TV receivers or software for all types of electronic games which are in Class 9.

CLASS 29

Meat, fish, poultry and game; meat extracts; preserved, dried and cooked fruits and vegetables; jellies, jams, fruit sauces; eggs, milk and milk products; edible oils and fats.

Includes prepared meals and snacks whose main ingredients are proper to this class (eg soups and potato crisps).

Does not include sandwiches which are in Class 30 or foodstuffs for animals which are in Class 31.

CLASS 30

Coffee, tea, cocoa, sugar, rice, tapioca, sago, artificial coffee; flour and preparations made from cereals, bread, pastry and confectionery, ices; honey, treacle; yeast, baking-powder; salt, mustard; vinegar, sauces (condiments); spices; ice.

Includes prepared meals and snacks whose main ingredients are proper to this class (eg pizzas, pies and pasta dishes).

Does not include foodstuffs for animals which are in Class 31.

CLASS 31

Agricultural, horticultural and forestry products and grains not included in other classes; live animals; fresh fruits and vegetables, seeds, natural plants and flowers; foodstuffs for animals; malt.

Includes all food and beverages for animals.

CLASS 32

Beers; mineral and aerated waters and other non-alcoholic drinks; fruit drinks and fruit juices; syrups and other preparations for making beverages.

Includes shandy, de-alcoholised drinks, non-alcoholic beers and wines.

Does not include tea, coffee or chocolate-based beverages which are in Class 30.

CLASS 33

Alcoholic beverages (except beers).

Includes wines, spirits and liqueurs; alcopops.

Does not include beers which are in Class 32.

CLASS 34

Tobacco; smokers' articles; matches.

Includes lighters for smokers.

Services

CLASS 35

Advertising; business management; business administration; office functions.

Includes the organisation, operation and supervision of loyalty and incentive schemes; advertising services provided via the Internet; production of television and radio advertisements; accountancy; auctioneering; trade fairs; opinion polling; data processing; provision of business information; certain specific services provided by retailers.

Does not include computer programming which is in Class 42 or raising finance for business which is in Class 36.

CLASS 36

Insurance; financial affairs; monetary affairs; real estate affairs.

Includes building society services; banking (including home banking); stockbroking; financial services provided via the Internet; issuing of tokens of value in relation to bonus and loyalty schemes; provision of financial information.

Does not include accountancy which is in Class 35, lottery services which are in Class 41 or surveying and conveyancing services which are in Class 42.

CLASS 37

Building construction; repair; installation services.

Includes installation, maintenance and repair of computer hardware; painting and decorating.

Does not include installation, maintenance and repair of computer software which is in Class 42.

CLASS 38 Telecommunications.

Includes all telecommunications services, (eg e-mail services and those provided for the Internet); providing user access to the Internet (service providers); operating of search engines.

Does not include creating, maintaining or hosting web sites which are in Class 42. CLASS 39

Transport; packaging and storage of goods; travel arrangement.

Includes distribution of electricity; travel information.

Does not include travel insurance which is in Class 36 or booking holiday accommodation which is in Class 43.

CLASS 40

Treatment of materials.

Includes the development, duplicating and printing of photographs; generation of electricity.

CLASS 41

Education; providing of training; entertainment; sporting and cultural activities.

Includes electronic games services provided by means of the Internet; the provision of on-line electronic publications and digital music (not downloadable) from the Internet.

Does not include downloadable on-line electronic publications or digital music which are in Class 9 or educational materials in printed form which are in Class 16.

CLASS 42

Scientific and technological services and research and design relating thereto; industrial analysis and research services; design and development of computer hardware and software; legal services.

Includes installation, maintenance and repair of computer software; computer consultancy services; the following Internet related services are also proper to this class: design, drawing and commissioned writing for the compilation of web sites; creating, maintaining and hosting the web sites of others; compilation, creation and maintenance of a register of domain names; leasing of access time to a computer database (the last item reflects the leasing of access time to a computer database on a dedicated line and not access provided by Internet Service Providers to databases in general which is in Class 38).

Does not include providing access to the Internet or portal services which are in Class 38.

CLASS 43

Services for providing food and drink; temporary accommodation.

Includes restaurant, bar and catering services; provision of holiday accommodation; booking/reservation services for restaurants and holiday accommodation.

Does not include provision of permanent accommodation which is in Class 36 or the arranging of travel by tourist agencies which is in Class 39.

CLASS 44

Medical services; veterinary services; hygienic and beauty care for human beings or animals; agriculture, horticulture and forestry services.

Includes dentistry services; medical analysis for the diagnosis and treatment of persons (such as x-ray examinations and taking of blood samples); pharmacy advice; garden design services.

Does not include scientific research for medical purposes (such as research into cures for terminal diseases which is in Class 42), ambulance transportation which is in Class 39, health clubs for physical exercise which are in Class 41 or retirement homes which are in Class 43.

CLASS 45

Personal and social services rendered by others to meet the needs of individuals; security services for the protection of property and individuals.

Includes dating services; funeral services and undertaking services; fire-fighting services; detective agency services.

Does not include beauty care services for human beings or animals which are in Class 44 or educational services which are in Class 41.

Chapter 14
Copyright

14.1	What is copyright? An introduction	203
14.2	Literary, dramatic, musical and artistic (LDMA) works	204
14.3	Entrepreneurial copyrights	211
14.4	Infringement of copyright	214
14.5	Remedies	221
14.6	Databases	221
14.7	Copyright and information technology	222
14.8	Public performances – the collecting societies	223
14.9	Developments in the law of copyright	224
14.10	International copyright protection	224

14.1 What is copyright? An introduction

The law of copyright protects the results and expressions of creative ability. No formality is involved; the right comes into existence as the tangible results of that creativity appear. Copyright is said to arise 'before the ink is dry upon the paper'. It is this simple arising of property rights, concurrent with the creation of the protected copyright material, that makes copyright such a valuable protection for the creative person against intentional or unintentional, unauthorised copying. The downside of such informal creation of copyright in a piece of creative work is that it is very easy to use, without realising it, elements of other people's copyright material in creating your own new work. There is no 'registry' of copyright material to guide you on this and, in an age of unlimited electronic access to information and imagery of all sorts (including the computer programs that permit you to access other material), the danger of infringement is ever present. The law has, therefore, to achieve a balance between the protection of creative persons and the freedom of others to create new works.

What is protected?	creative output
What benefit is there?	prevents copying
How is it obtained?	arises automatically (no registration)
How long does it last?	70 years from death of creator (in most cases)

The first statutory copyright in England was the Statute of Anne 1709, although the history of copyright goes back much further. The Statute was passed at the request of book publishers, because they were unable to protect their rights effectively against copyists under the common law. The first items protected were therefore books. Over the years, other artistic items have been added, including music and paintings. In the 20th century, new technology allowed the development of new aspects of artistic works, such as film versions of books and plays, and protection became available to the sort of works that lie behind such creations: music, sounds, visual effects etc. This led, via technological progression, to copyright protection of the computer programs that lie behind most modern inventions.

The main legislation on copyright is the Copyright, Designs and Patents Act 1988 (CDPA 1988). In the period before the CDPA 1988, there were attempts to use copyright for industrial items (eg, *British Leyland Motor Corp Ltd v Armstrong Patents Co Ltd* [1986] 1 AC 577 on spare parts for cars) – see **16.1.1**. The philosophy behind the relevant parts of the CDPA 1988 was to push industrial items in the direction of registered and unregistered design right (which the CDPA respectively strengthened and created), and to restrict copyright to more artistic three-dimensional items. The reason was that copyright would otherwise have given a period of protection of at least 70 years for an industrial item, whereas the duration of a registered design right is 25 years. The copyright period for artistic items which are mass-produced is now restricted to 25 years, to be in parallel with the registered design right period (see **14.2.4**).

The 'classic' copyrights are original literary, dramatic, musical, and artistic (LDMA) works.

The 'entrepreneurial' copyrights are films, sound recordings, published editions, broadcasts and cablecasts.

These copyrights protect the type of creative expression that is necessary if a work is to be made available to the wider public, recognising the effort and investment usually involved in such ventures.

It is important to be able to distinguish between the different categories of copyright, for the following reasons:

(a) If you cannot find a category for the item, copyright will not subsist in it. A good example of this is the position of computer programs, which are now in s 1 of CDPA 1988. Until the Berne Convention (see **14.10**) clarified the position by defining software as a literary work, there was some uncertainty about whether copyright subsisted in it at all, although there had been some cases suggesting it did.

(b) The rules relating to the subsistence, duration, ownership and infringement of the copyright can vary considerably for the different types of work.

(c) If there is more than one type of work in relation to an item, the different copyright works will often be owned by different people. A film or TV production might need to take account of large numbers of copyright owners, usually by licensing or purchase of the various rights.

Let us look at the classic copyrights.

14.2 Literary, dramatic, musical and artistic (LDMA) works

These are the 'classic' copyrights, that is, the authors' and artists' rights that most people associate with copyright. These rights have many things in common, so we are going to deal with them together.

The CDPA 1988 provides as follows:

> **1 Copyright and copyright works**
>
> (1) Copyright is a property right which subsists in accordance with this Part in the following descriptions of work—
>
> (a) original literary, dramatic, musical or artistic works,
>
> (b) sound recordings, films, broadcasts or cable programmes, and
>
> (c) the typographical arrangement of published editions.
>
> ...
>
> **3 Literary, dramatic and musical works**
>
> (1) In this Part—
>
> 'literary work' means any work, other than a dramatic or musical work, which is written, spoken or sung, and accordingly includes—
>
> (a) a table or compilation other than a database,
>
> (b) a computer program,
>
> (c) preparatory design material for a computer program, and (d) a database;
>
> 'dramatic work' includes a work of dance or mime; and
>
> 'musical work' means a work consisting of music, exclusive of any words or action intended to be sung, spoken or performed with the music.

4 Artistic works

(1) In this Part "artistic work" means—

(a) a graphic work, photograph, sculpture or collage, irrespective of artistic quality,

(b) a work of architecture being a building or a model for a building, or

(c) a work of artistic craftsmanship.

(2) In this Part—

'building' includes any fixed structure, and a part of a building or fixed structure;

'graphic work' includes—

(a) any painting, drawing, diagram, map, chart or plan, and

(b) any engraving, etching, lithograph, woodcut or similar work;

'photograph' means a recording of light or other radiation on any medium on which an image is produced or from which an image may by any means be produced, and which is not part of a film;

'sculpture' includes a cast or model made for purposes of sculpture.

The definition of 'literary work' in s 3(1) excludes dramatic or musical works. Thus, a play or script for a film will have dramatic copyright, not literary copyright. Also, words of a song will have literary copyright, but the music will have musical copyright. This means that usually the copyright in the words and music will be separately owned and have separate duration. For example, with many of the songs of Sir Elton John, John wrote the music and Bernie Taupin wrote the words. So, the musical copyright in the music will expire 70 years after the death of Sir Elton John, and the literary copyright will expire 70 years after the death of Bernie Taupin.

A 'dramatic' work could be a play, but it also could be dance or mime. So a ballet is a dramatic work, but the music is a musical work. Again, the usual situation would be that the dramatic and musical copyrights are separately owned.

14.2.1 Originality

For LDMA works, copyright will not subsist unless the work is 'original' (see s 1(1)(a)). 'Originality' here means that the work must be the author's own work, not copied from anything else. It is very difficult to come up with completely novel expressions of creativity without borrowing something from elsewhere. Copyright in an organ solo from 'A Whiter Shade of Pale' was considered in *Fisher v Brooker* [2006] EWHC 3239 (Ch). The claimant's contribution to the musical arrangement arose out of an earlier arrangement by the first defendant (which itself was based on an original theme dating back at least three centuries!). The claimant was held, nevertheless, to have created an original arrangement because of its highly distinctive quality. The finding that the claimant was a co-author of the work was upheld by the Court of Appeal (but see the reference to this case at **14.2.5** on the question of ownership of the copyright) ([2008] EWCA Civ 287). Further declarations by the judge concerning the claimant's right to assert his copyright (after 38 years) were struck down by the Court of Appeal but subsequently restored on an appeal to the House of Lords (see **14.4.5** below).

It is originality of expression and form, not of idea or content, that is required. For example, someone could not legally copy a book by John Grisham without his consent, but he has no monopoly over thrillers based on the exciting lives of lawyers, so you could write your own. The distinction between idea and expression has received much attention in recent times in the context of the 'Da Vinci Code' case, *Baigent v Random House Group Ltd* [2006] EWHC 719 (Ch) (discussed at **14.4**), and, to a lesser degree, in musical arrangements (see *Hyperion Records Ltd v Sawkins* [2005] EWCA Civ 565).

14.2.2 Minimum effort

A work may be an original work, but it may be completely trivial. Does it still enjoy copyright protection? There will be no copyright unless a certain minimum amount of effort has gone into the work. The amount of effort required is generally low. But the exact amount depends on the category of work.

To be a joint author, a significant creative contribution as an author has to be made to the production of the work. A joint author has to do more than merely contribute ideas and has to participate actively in the writing or creation of the work (see *Ray v Classic FM plc* [1998] FSR 622).

14.2.2.1 Literary works

Generally, the level of effort required is very low. Any level of writing might attract copyright. For example, there is literary copyright in a junior school pupil's essay, or in an ordinary business letter. In *University of London Press v University Tutorial Press* [1916] 2 Ch 601, 608 it was suggested by Peterson J that almost any 'work which is expressed in print or writing, irrespective of the question whether the quality or style is high', might have the necessary minimum effort. This is slightly circular but it shows that the threshold of minimum effort and quality is quite low. The subject matter is irrelevant; the work could be highly-polished literature or a mundane memorandum or timetable.

However, the writing has to be substantial enough to constitute a 'work'. Consequently, an advertising jingle or a title will not usually be protected by copyright. The courts have been reluctant to grant copyright in single words. For example, EXXON was refused copyright protection (though it would of course get trade mark protection if validly registered) (*Exxon Corpn and Others v Exxon Insurance Consultants International Ltd* [1981] 3 All ER 241).

'Compilations', ie collections of information, are one aspect of literary copyright. Generally the English courts have been willing in the past to grant copyright in almost any compilation, eg, television listings, a directory of solicitors' names and addresses, and football pool coupons. It is likely, for example, that an ordinary, alphabetical telephone directory would have been protected by copyright under English law. However, following the adoption of the Copyrights and Rights in Database Regulations 1997 (SI 1997/3032), there is now a question mark over whether courts will in the future allow copyright in such commonplace compilations where there is nothing special about the selection or arrangement of the contents (see **15.2**). Commentators seem to think it is likely that the alphabetical telephone directory would now no longer be protected by copyright. This is because it would fall within the definition of a 'database' in the Regulations (databases do not have to be electronic) for which the Regulations impose a slightly higher standard of originality for copyright to apply. It may well be, for example, that the *Yellow Pages* would still be protected by copyright, because of the extra effort involved in dividing and classifying its contents. However, the key point is that the database right will apply and protect such collections of mundane information, and copyright will probably be largely irrelevant (see **14.5**, **15.1**).

14.2.2.2 Artistic

Artistic works divide into:

(a) those that fall under s 4, which are protected 'irrespective of artistic quality', that is, graphic works, photographs, sculptures and collages (s 4(1)(a)); and

(b) those for which a degree of artistic quality is required, that is, architecture and works of artistic craftsmanship (s 4(1)(b) and (c)).

For the first category, the standard of effort required is low. For example, copyright has been found to subsist in a very simple picture of a hand pointing, as used at a polling station to guide people round the corner. A straight line or circle would not normally be protected. In any event, it would not be substantial enough to constitute a 'work', and would be unlikely to be original. The English law approach is quite different to that applied to artistic works in some other legal systems; see *Blau v BBC* [2002] ECDR 34, where the Swiss law provided a result somewhat different to what might have followed in an English court.

Some artistic merit is required for architecture, as the words 'irrespective of artistic quality' do not appear in s 4(1)(b). Cornish and Llewelyn, in *Intellectual Property* (5th edn, Sweet & Maxwell, 2003), suggest that the artistic merit must be 'something more than the common stock'. Perhaps a mass-produced estate of similar mundane houses might not qualify, but a small development of individual 'executive' homes might. Architectural works are limited to buildings themselves, and models for buildings. Architectural drawings would be protected as graphic works, so a different standard would apply to determine copyright in the drawing to that in the building itself.

14.2.2.3 Works of artistic craftsmanship

This is a topic much beloved by academic writers but of negligible practical relevance. A work of artistic craftsmanship is a three-dimensional item which is not a sculpture, but which results from a combination of artistic and craft skills. Examples could be seen in hand-made musical instruments, furniture or wooden boats etc, provided there is evidence of both artistry and craftsmanship. For works of artistic craftsmanship, it seems that a significant degree of artistic merit is required before copyright protection will be given. The policy reason behind this is that most three-dimensional items that are not sculptures tend to be made to industrial designs, and should normally be protected by the law on designs rather than by copyright.

Unfortunately, the cases on works of artistic craftsmanship do not tell us how much artistic merit is needed for something to qualify as a work of artistic craftsmanship. In *Hensher (George) Ltd v Restawile Upholstery (Lancs)* [1976] AC 64, it was held that a mass-produced suite of furniture did not have enough artistic merit. In *Merlet and Another v Mothercare plc* [1986] RPC 115, it was held that a rain cape made by Mrs Merlet to protect her baby from the weather in Scotland did not have enough artistic merit. Most industrially manufactured articles will also lack any craft skills.

A key factor in deciding whether an item is a work of artistic craftsmanship is to ask: did the author consciously intend to create a work of art? In *Guild v Eskandar Ltd* [2001] FSR 38, the claimant alleged breach of copyright in garments which she had designed for mass-production. These were held not to be works of artistic craftsmanship, because of lack of evidence of craft skills used in the manufacture, but were protected by unregistered design right as they were original and not commonplace (see **16.3.1**).

In practice, one should never rely on there being copyright in three-dimensional objects other than sculptures, but instead advise the client to register a design.

14.2.3 Recorded

For literary, dramatic and musical works, copyright will subsist only if the work is recorded (s 3(2)). This can be in writing or otherwise. Recording can be in any medium, so recording on tape, or typing into a word processor is fine.

There is no express requirement as such in CDPA 1988 that an artistic work must be recorded, but of course it is difficult to conceive of an artistic work that is not recorded. How else could you create a drawing or a sculpture, for example, and not record it?

14.2.4 Duration of copyright

14.2.4.1 Literary, dramatic and musical works (CDPA 1988, s 12)

The normal duration is life of the author plus 70 years. The 70 years runs from the end of the year of the author's death. If copyright vests in the employer because the author was an employee, the duration of the employer's copyright is the employee's life plus 70 years. The same situation applies if the rights have been assigned. For example, in the copyright in the songs of Buddy Holly (now owned by Sir Paul McCartney), the period is 70 years from the death of Buddy Holly (ie, it expires in 1959 + 70 = 2029).

The basic term for copyright used to be life plus 50 years. The Directive on Copyright Duration (93/98/EC) increased it to 70 years. This not only extended the life of existing copyright works, but also even revived lapsed copyright if the work was still in copyright anywhere within the EU on 1 July 1995. This would have been so at that date in Germany, where the copyright term then was life plus 70 years.

If the work is of unknown authorship, the period of 70 years runs from the year of creation, or the year of first publication, whichever is the later.

For a computer-generated work, the period is 50 years from creation.

14.2.4.2 Exploited copyright works (CDPA 1988, s 52)

If a copyright work is exploited by making articles industrially then the term of copyright it enjoys is for most purposes cut down to 25 years. The 25 years are measured from the end of the calendar year in which the articles are first marketed. Examples would be a design that is put on wallpaper, or a work of artistic craftsmanship that is exploited by making it industrially (eg, a chair by Charles Rennie Mackintosh). 'Industrial' exploitation means making more than 50 articles, or making things in lengths by an industrial process (eg, wallpaper).

The term is not cut down for all purposes, but only in relation to reproducing articles. So after the 25 years are up, it will not be copyright infringement to use the wallpaper design on wallpaper or on a bread bin, but it would still be copyright infringement to make a copy of, for example, a painting that had first shown the wallpaper design.

There are exceptions to this rule limiting copyright to 25 years, and these are defined by statutory instrument. Exceptions include most sculpture, wall plaques and medals, and printed matter which is primarily of a literary or artistic character (a long list is given in the Copyright (Industrial Process and Excluded Articles) (No 2) Order 1989, SI 1989/1070). So, for example, putting a painting on a postcard will not result in the 25-year term applying. This is an important protection against premature loss of copyright protection by art galleries, artists and owners of valuable artistic copyright.

The policy reason for cutting down the term for industrially exploited copyright is that governments do not consider it appropriate that industrial designs should have long copyright protection. The period of 25 years is the same as the term of protection given to registered designs (see **16.2.7**). See also **16.3.7** for discussion of the overlap between copyright protection and design rights.

14.2.5 Ownership of copyright in LDMA works

As copyright arises 'before the ink is dry on the page', the initial copyright is owned by the author or co-authors (CDPA 1988, s 11(1)). The main exception is if the author is an employee, in which case the copyright is owned by the employer (s 11(2)). The provisos are that the work was done in the course of the employee's employment, and that there was no contrary agreement. In *Noah v Shuba and Another* [1991] FSR 14, it was held that an employed government epidemiologist had not written a document entitled 'A Guide to Hygienic Skin Piercing' in the course of his employment. He therefore owned the copyright, not his employer.

Be aware that if the work has been commissioned then the copyright rests with the author (s 11(1)), not with the person commissioning the work. A properly drafted agreement would include a clause providing for an assignment, or licence, of the copyright to the commissioner. In the absence of such a clause, a licence would usually be implied (*Blair v Alan S Tomkins and*

Frank Osborne (t/a Osborne & Tomkins (A Firm)) and Another [1971] 1 All ER 468), as otherwise the commissioner would be prevented from using the work he had paid for. Thus, the copyright in a photograph of Elvis Costello, taken at a photo shoot where the photographer had not been commissioned, was owned by the photographer (*Gabrin v Universal Music Operations Ltd* [2003] EWHC 1335 (Ch)). Some years before, a similar dispute was settled during litigation about the artwork and photographs for the famous 'Sergeant Pepper' album cover. Where a photograph or a film has been commissioned for private and domestic purposes (eg, a wedding), the person commissioning the material will have the right to prevent publication of the material (s 85).

In *R Griggs Group Ltd v Evans* [2005] EWCA Civ 11, the defendant designer was a freelance engaged by an advertising agency. The agency had been commissioned by the claimants to produce drawings for a new combined logo for their 'Dr Martens' range of footwear. The designer fulfilled the commission, but subsequently also sold the designs to an Australian rival of the claimants. It was held that the claimants were entitled in equity to the beneficial title, as a mere licence would not give them enough rights to stop the work being used by a rival. The judge said of s 11(1) on ownership of copyright works:

> 33. However, it is well established that this refers to the legal title to the copyright. But it is possible for a person to own the legal title to property, not for his own benefit, but for the benefit of another person. That other person is said to be the owner in equity. It is well established that the s. 11 of the Copyright Act does not purport to legislate for equitable ownership, which is left to a well established body of rules that have been built up by the courts over many generations. For example, suppose a freelance designer orally agrees with a company that he shall create a website for use in its business, for payment, and on terms that the copyright shall belong to the company. Because the designer is not an employee of the company the legal title to the copyright belongs to him, because the Copyright Act says so; but the equitable title belongs to the company. This means that the designer can be called upon to assign the legal title to the copyright to the company; and, if he refuses, the law will compel him to do so.
>
> 34. An equitable title is thus stronger than a legal title, with one exception. If the legal owner should sell the copyright to a third party who buys it in good faith, without having had notice of the equitable interest, the buyer acquires full ownership, free of the claims of the equitable owner. For that reason it is always prudent for the equitable owner to insist on a document, signed by the legal owner, transferring the legal title to the copyright to him, and to do so as soon as possible.

On the basis of this, it looks as if the courts are prepared to rectify the situation, save where a bona fide third party acquires title in the interim. See *Vitof Ltd v Altoft* [2006] EWHC 1678 (Ch), where these principles came into play in a four-way dispute between two individuals, the company they incorporated and a further company that they commissioned, concerning the copyright and design in circuit boards. The moral from this complex case is that copyright, which comes into existence by the creation of copyright material, needs to have ownership considerations addressed well in advance, if at all possible.

Vitof Ltd v Altoft illustrates a common cause of copyright disputes, in that there is often a complex interplay of ownership and licence in cases where the author of the copyright material (either in existence or contemplated) enters a contractual agreement, under which some sort of business venture is planned, which will expressly or impliedly cause the ownership or rights to use the material to pass under the agreement. Because the agreement will often contemplate the use of the material by corporate bodies (possibly even incorporating them for the purpose), a further level of complexity is added.

A good example of this type of problem can be seen in *Wrenn v Landamore* [2007] All ER (D) 361 (Jul), aff'd [2008] All ER (D) 134 (Apr), CA. In this case, a dispute arose where the claimant (C, who had formed his own company, ICD) entered a contract with the defendant (D) under which D would produce computer programs for C, for which D would be paid royalties. Later, the parties entered into a second agreement, under which the parties would establish a joint venture company, IMMS, in which the copyright in the programs would vest;

also each party would have half the shares in IMMS and the pair would become its only directors (the resulting eventual deadlock of the company led to the action). The parties later disputed the effect of this second agreement, C claiming that the earlier agreement made ICD the owner of the copyright and that any royalties were owed to D by ICD rather than by C. C further claimed that because ICD was not a party to the second agreement (under which IMMS was created), that the second agreement could not affect ICD's continued ownership of the copyright. C did, however, concede during the trial that if IMMS were held to own the copyright then there could not be any infringement claim against D. D counterclaimed against C, personally, for the royalties.

The judge found that the first agreement (and the second, too) had been entered into by the parties in person, and that neither had contemplated that C would not be personally liable on it. He held that the second agreement should be given its proper and full effect, and as both parties to it were before the court, there was no reason why the court should not make a declaration as to the rights arising under the second contract. The copyright had become vested in IMMS, as the parties had intended should happen; if the parties could not break their deadlock of the company by agreement, the company would have to be wound up and the copyrights realised by the liquidator. This result was affirmed by the Court of Appeal.

Sometimes the ownership disputes in copyright arise because a person may not necessarily realise that he has all, or a share of, the copyright in a work, until considerable time has passed and further contractual and property interests have developed in the work. In such circumstances, the legal issues can become very complex indeed. One of the best examples of this, in recent times, has been the protracted dispute concerning a co-author's share of the copyright interests in the musical arrangement of the cult-status popular song 'A Whiter Shade of Pale'. This litigation – commencing with the judgment of Blackburne J in *Fisher v Brooker* [2006] All ER (D) 306 (Dec), which judgment was subsequently affirmed by the House of Lords at [2009] UKHL 41, [2009] All ER (D) 338 (Jul) (partly reversing the Court of Appeal) – is a highly illuminating case on ownership, assignment and assertion of rights in copyright material. It also illustrates the potential to lose the right to assert copyright ownership by the defences of estoppel, laches or acquiescence. The important point to take from the case, for the purposes of copyright ownership, is to understand how the 'layers' and shares in the copyright in the final recorded version were built up, in succession in time, and by the input of different band members; this temporal progression influenced the question of which particular shares in the copyright could be the subject of assignments, contractual waivers of rights and implied licence arrangements. The case is dealt with in more detail at **14.4.5** below.

A similar situation exists as regards ownership of entreprenurial works (see **14.3.3**).

14.2.6 Moral rights

These are a Continental concept brought into English law by the CDPA 1988. It is the idea that the creative author or artist should retain certain rights in relation to his creation, even after he has sold the copyright to somebody else. In fact, moral rights have slightly wider implications.

The moral rights are as follows:

(a) The right to be identified ('right of paternity') (s 77). This applies only if the right has been asserted by the author. This is usually done in the copyright assignment or licence.

(b) The right to object to derogatory treatment (s 80). For example, a novelist might object if his novel were abridged in a way that compromised its artistic integrity. In *Morrison Leahy Music Ltd v Lightbond Ltd* [1993] EMLR 144, the claimants obtained an injunction to restrain the release of a recording consisting of the claimants' music interspersed with other music, as they felt this altered the character of their music. In the unusual German case of *Re Lenin's Monument* [1992] ECC 202, the son of the sculptor of a statue of Lenin failed in his attempt to assert the moral right akin to s 80.

The City of Berlin was held not to be planning to destroy the statue, which could have been derogatory treatment, but merely 'to preserve it by burying it', following the demise of the former communist State of East Germany. An interesting claim to derogatory treatment of a sound recording by adding a rap line failed in *Confetti Records and Others v Warner Music UK Ltd* [2003] EWHC 1274 (Ch) because there was nothing prejudicial to the honour and reputation of the author of the original work.

(c) The right against false attribution of a work (s 84). A novel use of this right was in *Clark v Associated Newspapers* [1998] RPC 261. This concerned the *London Evening Standard*, which was then running a spoof political column called 'Alan Clark's Secret Election Diary'. Mr Clark succeeded on the basis that some people might believe that the views expressed in the column were his.

(d) The right to privacy in private photographs and films (s 85).

If the author still owns the copyright then he should not normally need to rely on these moral rights as he can control all copying of the work; for example, he can insist on being credited as a condition of allowing the work to be used. The importance of moral rights is in a situation where the author has assigned the copyright to somebody else.

Moral rights are inalienable rights, in that they cannot be assigned (s 94). However, they can be waived. Anyone acting for the assignee of copyright should always consider whether it is appropriate to insist on a waiver. You probably would not expect somebody who has produced a real work of art to waive their moral rights. However, in many commercial situations it will be appropriate (eg, for advertising copy, or designs for use on fabrics or products).

Moral rights apply only to literary, dramatic, musical and artistic works, and also to films (where the director enjoys moral rights). The most important exceptions to be aware of are computer programs and employees. In most situations employees do not enjoy moral rights.

In terms of duration, most of the moral rights will last as long as the copyright itself (s 86(1)). The exception is the paternity right, which lasts for only 20 years after the death of the author (s 86(2)).

14.3 Entrepreneurial copyrights

The descriptions 'classic' and 'entrepreneurial' copyright are not terms of art. However, the distinction is often made between:

(a) the classic LDMA copyrights, that is, the traditional authors' rights which protect creativity (see **14.2**); and

(b) the entrepreneurial copyrights which, broadly, protect people who invest in creativity, that is, production companies, broadcasters, publishers, etc.

The entrepreneurial copyrights serve the same purpose as the classic rights. That is, they give a right to stop copying of the relevant 'work'.

14.3.1 Differences between classic and entrepreneurial copyrights

The rules are slightly different for the entrepreneurial copyrights, in particular:

(a) There is no general requirement of originality and minimum effort (see **14.2.1** and **14.2.2**). Instead there are various detailed rules for each right, which have the broad aim of ensuring that there is no copyright in a mere copy. For example, if I copy somebody else's tape, with or without their permission, I have no copyright in the copy I make. These rules are beyond the scope of this book, but their broad effect can be seen in ss 5A(2), 5B(4), 6(6) and 8(2). (Note that in the case of *Norowzian v Arks Ltd and Others (No 2)* [2000] FSR 363, the claimant failed in his assertion that copyright existed in an editing process for films. The case concerned an advert for Guinness produced by the defendant by a technique devised by the claimant, termed 'jump cutting'.)

(b) Of the entrepreneurial copyrights, only films have moral rights. These vest in the director. The thinking behind this is, of course, that it is the director who has given the artistic input. He is the person who might want to defend his artistic integrity. (The director is the one who sits in the canvas chair behind the camera operator and tells the actors what to do.)

(c) The rules about ownership of the entrepreneurial rights vary (see **14.3.3**).

(d) The duration of the entrepreneurial rights varies (see **14.3.4**).

The rules are designed to give effect to the commercial, artistic and financial realities of creativity in the modern world.

14.3.2 Definitions of some entrepreneurial rights

The following definitions are taken from the CDPA 1988:

5A Sound recordings

(1) In this Part 'sound recording' means—

(a) a recording of sounds, from which the sounds may be reproduced, or

(b) a recording of the whole or any part of a literary, dramatic or musical work, from which sounds reproducing the work or part may be produced,

regardless of the medium on which the recording is made or the method by which the sounds are reproduced or produced.

(2) Copyright does not subsist in a sound recording which is, or to the extent that it is, a copy taken from a previous sound recording.

5B Films

(1) In this Part 'film' means a recording on any medium from which a moving image may by any means be produced.

(2) The sound track accompanying a film shall be treated as part of the film for the purposes of this Part.

...

(4) Copyright does not exist in a film which is, or to the extent that it is, a copy taken from a previous film.

...

6 Broadcasts

(1) In this Part a 'broadcast' means an electronic transmission of visual images, sounds or other information which—

(a) is transmitted for simultaneous reception by members of the public and is capable of being lawfully received by them, or

(b) is transmitted at a time determined solely by the person making the transmission for presentation to members of the public,

and which is not excepted by subsection (1A); and references to broadcasting shall be construed accordingly.

(1A) Excepted from the definition of 'broadcast' is any internet transmission unless it is—

(a) a transmission taking place simultaneously on the internet and by other means,

(b) a concurrent transmission of a live event, or

(c) a transmission of recorded moving images or sounds forming part of a programme service offered by the person responsible for making the transmission, being a service in which programmes are transmitted at scheduled times determined by that person.

(2) An encrypted transmission shall be regarded as capable of being lawfully received by members of the public only if decoding equipment has been made available to members of the public by or with the authority of the person making the transmission or the person providing the contents of the transmission.

(3) References in this Part to the person making a broadcast or a transmission which is a broadcast are—

(a) to the person transmitting the programme, if he has responsibility to any extent for its contents, and

(b) to any person providing the programme who makes with the person transmitting it the arrangements necessary for its transmission;

and references in this Part to a programme, in the context of broadcasting, are to any item included in a broadcast.

(4) For the purposes of this Part, the place from which a wireless broadcast is made is the place where, under the control and responsibility of the person making the broadcast, the programme-carrying signals are introduced into an uninterrupted chain of communication (including, in the case of a satellite transmission, the chain leading to the satellite and down towards the earth).

(4A) Subsections (3) and (4) have effect subject to section 6A (safeguards in case of certain satellite broadcasts).

(5) References in this Part to the reception of a broadcast include reception of a broadcast relayed by means of a telecommunications system.

(5A) The relaying of a broadcast by reception and immediate re-transmission shall be regarded for the purposes of this Part as a separate act of broadcasting from the making of the broadcast which is so re-transmitted.

(6) Copyright does not subsist in a broadcast which infringes, or to the extent that it infringes, the copyright in another broadcast.

8 Published editions

(1) In this Part 'published edition', in the context of copyright in the typographical arrangement of a published edition, means a published edition of the whole or any part of one or more literary, dramatic or musical works.

(2) Copyright does not subsist in the typographical arrangement of a published edition if, or to the extent that, it reproduces the typographical arrangement of a previous edition.

You should be aware of the following points from the above definitions of the entrepreneurial copyrights:

(a) An attempt has been made to make the definitions of 'film', 'sound recording', etc technology neutral so that they will cover future technological developments. So, for example, 'film' includes any recordings on any medium from which a moving image can be produced. It will include, for example, videos, DVDs and many 'multi-media' recordings (like computer games and websites) where you have moving images. These can be 'films' even though they may be interactive.

(b) A 'broadcast' has been redefined to make the definition generic, so as to include not only terrestrial broadcasts (BBC and ITV, etc), but also satellite (Sky) and cable broadcasts (NTL) and some Internet transmissions.

(c) The soundtrack of a film is protected by film copyright unless it is issued as a stand-alone entity, when it would be protected as a sound recording.

14.3.3 Ownership of the entrepreneurial copyrights (s 9)

The first ownership goes to the 'creator' of the copyright work (see the table, 'Ownership of entrepreneurial rights', below). So, for example, the owner of the copyright in a broadcast would be:

(a) the person providing the programme; and

(b) the person transmitting who has responsibility for its content.

This could mean that the independent television company and the broadcasting authority could jointly own the copyright.

Entrepreneurial Right	Ownership
Sound recording	Producer
Film	Producer and principal director
Broadcast	Person making the broadcast
Typographical arrangement	Publisher

Establishing the identity of the 'creator' of the work can become a problem, especially for commissioned works (see also **14.2.5**). Thus, the management company of the skaters Torville and Dean commissioned a recording of music for one of their skating routines. The company was held to be the 'maker' of the sound recording, as it had thought of the idea and taken the financial risk, not the person with whom it had contracted to organise the musicians and the studio (see *A & M Records v Video Collection* [1995] EMLR 25).

14.3.4 Duration of the entrepreneurial copyrights (ss 13A, 13B, 14)

The duration of the entrepreneurial copyrights is a bit more complex than the standard period of life of the creator plus 70 years that applies to the classic copyrights. The duration depends on the type of entrepreneurial right concerned. Thus:

(a) Sound recording – 50 years from making or being released, if later.

(b) Film – 70 years from end of life of last to die of principal director, author of screenplay, author of dialogue, or composer of specially written music.

(c) Broadcast – 50 years from first broadcast.

(d) Typographical arrangement – 25 years from end of year of publication.

14.4 Infringement of copyright

The starting point is s 16, which gives the copyright owner the exclusive right to copy, publish, perform or show in public and/or to adapt the work. If anyone else does any of those things within the UK without permission, it will be likely to infringe.

There are two types of infringement: primary infringement and secondary infringement. The primary infringer is liable regardless of his state of mind, whereas the secondary infringer is liable only if he knew, or had reason to believe, that he was dealing with an infringing copy. It is certainly not the case that the part that is copied would, standing by itself, have necessarily qualified for copyright protection, so a person might be quite unaware of any infringement. The reason for this is explained below.

Copying need not be of the whole work. The copyright is infringed if a 'substantial part' is taken. The question of what is a substantial part is considered qualitatively. So, even if you take only one line of a poem, the copyright will be infringed if it is a significant line. Similarly, a parody of a work will infringe the copyright if it amounts to a substantial copy of it. The dangers for the infringer are thus twofold: first, he may not realise that he is using a copyright work; secondly, he may not realise that he is using a legally 'substantial' part of the work.

Section 17 shows that copying of literary, dramatic, musical or artistic works means reproducing the work in any material form. That would include storing the work in any medium by electronic means. Artistic copyright can be infringed, for example, by turning a two-dimensional image into a three-dimensional solid object, and vice versa (s 17(3)).

Copyright in a literary or dramatic work will be infringed by translating it into another language, by making it into a play (or vice versa), or by making it into a cartoon. Copyright in a musical work will be infringed by making a different arrangement. These are 'adaptations' of works within s 21.

Some guidance on the judicial approach may be seen in the following cases:

(a) *Designer's Guild Ltd v Russell Williams (Textiles) Ltd* [2001] FSR 803

Here, the dispute was about alleged infringement of fabric designs, combining stripes and flowers. The House of Lords, allowing the claimants' appeal, said that the first instance finding, after comparing similarities and differences, that copying had taken place should not have been rejected by the Court of Appeal. That is the first stage of the process. Only after that should the inquiry turn to the question whether what was copied represented a qualitatively substantial part of the claimants' created output. The Court of Appeal's approach had been wrong.

(b) *Baigent v Random House Group Ltd* [2006] EWHC 719 (Ch)

In this case the writers of *The Holy Blood and the Holy Grail* ('HBHG') sued Dan Brown for breach of copyright in *The Da Vinci Code* ('DVC'). The claim was that DVC had used the central theme from HBHG and so breached copyright. The defence was that, although HBHG had been used along with many other sources, only information and general ideas had been used, not detailed copyright expression. The court held that there could be such a concept as a non-literal copying (a concept well known in software copyright claims), but where the purported copyright material largely comprised factual statements and hypotheses, this could only be protected by copyright if there was a discernible 'architecture' in the way it had been used and arranged. In this case, the supposed central theme of HBHG was at too general a level of abstraction to be protected; the claim failed. The Court of Appeal ([2007] EWCA Civ 247) confirmed the broad conclusions of Smith J, but found some faults with his approach. The judgments are very helpful in explaining the judicial approach to qualitatively substantial copying.

(c) *Newspaper Licensing Agency Ltd v Marks & Spencer plc* [2003] 1 AC 551

The House of Lords had to decide whether selective copying of cuttings from parts of newspaper editions breached, substantially, the copyright in the typographical arrangements of the editions. Although the CDPA 1988, s 8 definition extended to 'any part' of a work, what comprised a substantial part had to be decided qualitatively, not simply by reference to quantity and proportion to the whole. As none of the copied cutting sections reproduced anything like the layout of entire pages, it was not a substantial copying and the claim failed.

(d) *Nova Productions Ltd v Mazooma Games Ltd* [2007] EWCA Civ 219

In another case which turns on the distinction between idea and expression, the Court of Appeal dismissed claims that the defendant's computer game about pool infringed the claimant's copyright in its game. There were three substantial issues, all of which are helpful to an understanding of infringement. The first point was the claimant's assertion that a sequence of graphic images showed some similarity in both games. The Court said that the starting point was that each frame comprised a separate graphic; the fact of a sequence of them added nothing to that (ie, the sequence is not a graphic work in itself). There was no substantial copying of the individual graphics. The second issue was that although there was some evidence of the copying and taking of ideas, that did not mean that a substantial part of the defendant's creative form and expression had been copied (similarly with the '*Da Vinci Code*' case, above). The third issue related to the alleged copying of the computer program. The mere creation of a computer code that gave a similar effect to another one, without copying the computer code of that other, was more to do with protecting ideas than expression. The claimant's ideas had inspired the defendant, but at too general a level to constitute substantial copying.

From these cases, it can be seen that it may be possible to imitate a certain style or way of expressing things, without necessarily infringing the original. Much of today's surreal imagery can be seen to be influenced by the works of Salvador Dali, without close copying. Dali's works, in their time, were heavily influenced by the much earlier work of Hieronymus Bosch. The distinction between copying and reflecting an influence is a hard one to draw.

Copyright is not normally infringed simply by using the work. For example, you do not infringe the copyright in a book by reading it. You do not infringe a recording by playing it. This is because using it does not normally involve making copies of it. However, if you read or play it in public you do infringe. The CDPA 1988 specifically provides that performing or showing a work in public will infringe the copyright, and this is primary infringement (s 19). Similarly, including a work in a broadcast or cablecast will normally be primary infringement (s 20). So the permission (ie, the licence) of the copyright owner is necessary in these circumstances.

14.4.1 Special position of computer programs (software) (s 17(6))

Although the normal position is that you do not infringe by using a work, such as by reading it, a computer program is different in this respect. When a program is run in a computer, the computer has to make at least a transient copy of it in order to run it. This transient copying will infringe the copyright without the copyright owner's permission (s 17(6)). It is not possible, therefore, to use a program without a licence. Often this licence is express. For example, you get a licence with any program you buy off the shelf. Sometimes, this licence may be implied by the circumstances. If someone is a lawful licensee then he is also entitled to make one back-up copy of the software (s 50A). There is a special provision to permit transient copying as part of a larger technological process: see **14.9** below.

14.4.2 Primary infringement (ss 16–21)

The most usual act of primary infringement is copying. Copyright is not a monopoly right. As its name implies, it is the right not to be copied. Independently produced items cannot be objected to. It follows that you cannot infringe copyright if you have never had any access to the original. So in a copyright infringement action, if the defendant had no opportunity to copy, he will not be liable. On the other hand, if the defendant did have the opportunity to copy and the defendant's work is so similar to the claimant's that the most likely explanation is that he has copied, then there will be an inference of copying. The defendant will have to prove that he did not copy.

Having said that, copying can be indirect. Copying can occur as a result of seeing not the original work itself but a copy of it, or something derived from it. For example, if a novel has been adapted to make a play, you infringe the copyright in the novel by copying the play. (In that case the separate copyright in the play is also infringed.)

The late George Harrison was sued in the US, as it was alleged that his song 'My Sweet Lord' was a subconscious copy of an earlier work. The song which was the subject of the alleged copying was 'He's So Fine', composed by Ronald Mack and sung by The Chiffons. It was a minor hit in the UK in 1963 and a major one in the US. The Harrison song was held to have infringed the earlier song. Ultimately, George Harrison is reputed to have bought the copyright to the earlier song, so solving the problem.

In *Sony Music Entertainment (UK) Ltd and Others v Easyinternetcafé Ltd* [2003] EWHC 62 (Ch), [2003] FSR 48, the claimants obtained an injunction against the operators of some Internet cafés. They recorded music from the Internet on to CDs for their customers for a fee. This was held to be breach of ss 17 and 18. In *Independiente Ltd and Others v Music Trading On-line (HK) Ltd and Others* [2003] EWHC 470 (Ch), the claimants were seeking to stop the defendants from supplying sound recordings via the Internet to the UK, when those recordings had been licensed for use only outside the EU. (They failed because they did not have the consent of the copyright holders; although the matter was ultimately settled, there has been further litigation about the terms upon which the matter was settled.)

14.4.3 Secondary infringement (ss 22–26)

This is all about dealing with or facilitating the manufacture of 'infringing copies'. These are copies made without the copyright owner's permission. So, the trader who imports copies into the UK may be liable for secondary infringement, as will the trader who sells, distributes or stores such copies. It will extend to persons who provide the means to make the copy, or who provide premises or equipment for infringing public performances. Section 27 defines the wide range of meaning given to 'infringing copy'.

In the typical infringement situation, there will be more than one infringer. However, the main culprit will be the person who manufactures the goods. He will be the primary infringer, because he is actually copying the work in order to make the goods.

Then there will be the dealers who buy or import the goods. Maybe this is a wholesaler who buys from the manufacturer and the retailers who buy from the wholesaler. The wholesaler and retailers will be secondary infringers, but only if they knew or had reason to believe that they were dealing with infringing copies. Usually, the copyright owner is mainly concerned with stopping the manufacture. He will normally write to the retailers and the wholesalers (if known) enclosing evidence of his copyright title and asking them to stop selling the goods. If they then carry on, they will be liable for secondary infringement, because from this point on at least they will not be able to argue that they were innocent.

In *Bloomsbury Publishing Group Ltd and Another v News Group Newspapers Ltd and Others* [2003] EWHC 1205 (Ch), [2003] 3 All ER 736, the publisher and author of the 'Harry Potter' books obtained an injunction to restrain unauthorised publication of the fifth book in the series. A copy had been stolen from the printers and was being offered to some national newspapers, in advance of its official release date. The CDPA 1988, s 23 concerns 'possessing or dealing with an infringing copy'. In *Nouveau Fabrics Ltd v Voyage Decoration Ltd* [2004] EWHC 895 (Ch), the claimant's lawyers had written a letter before action informing the defendant of the claimant's copyright. The defendant was thus held to have had reason to believe that the fabrics it was importing were copies which infringed the claimant's copyright.

14.4.4 Defences – 'fair dealing'

In certain circumstances some use of a copyright work is allowed without the permission of the copyright owner. The approach usually followed by the courts is, first, to ascertain whether the defendant's act falls within the particular statutory purpose, and then, even if it is within that purpose, to see that the copying has not gone any further than necessary to comprise 'fair dealing' (*Hyde Park Residence Ltd v Yelland and Others* [2000] RPC 604). The important ones to be aware of are as follows.

14.4.4.1 Fair dealing for the purposes of research or private study (s 29)

This applies to LDMA works and to published editions. It basically allows the taking of copies of pages of books in the course of non-commercial studying or researching. It does not allow the librarian to take lots of copies, one for each student. In practice it must be read together with the provisions about librarians and archives and about schools, which are very complicated.

In *HM Stationery Office v Green Amps Ltd* [2007] EWHC 2755 (Ch), a private company, which had obtained unlicensed access to a mapping database which HMSO made available for licensed research, made use of the data for commercial purposes. The unlicensed infringement was not protected by s 29.

Implementation of Directive 2001/29/EC on copyright and related rights in the information society has inserted the words 'non-commercial' into this defence in relation to research, thus restricting it severely.

14.4.4.2 Fair dealing for the purpose of criticism and review (s 30(1))

If one wished to comment in an article on, say, the quality of a textbook on intellectual property, this fair dealing provision will permit copied extracts from the book to be used without the author's permission. The question whether this use is within the exception depends mainly on:

(a) the purpose of the use of the quote – if I copy what the textbook says in order to tell people about the law rather than in order to comment on the textbook then I am just letting the textbook do my work for me and this would not be within the exception; and

(b) how much I quote.

The Publishers' Association publishes guidelines on how much you can quote.

14.4.4.3 Fair dealing for the purpose of reporting current events (s 30(2))

This allows all works, other than photographs, to be used for reporting current events. If the report is in a newspaper or magazine there must be acknowledgement. If the report is on television, radio, etc then no acknowledgement is required (though in practice an acknowledgement is often given). Again, the question whether the dealing is fair depends on:

(a) the purpose; and

(b) how much is taken.

The purpose must truly be for reporting current events and not simply using something that has become of interest because of a particular current event. For example, the death of the Duchess of Windsor did not justify the publication of an exchange of letters between her and the Duke of Windsor without the permission of the copyright holder (*Associated Newspapers Group plc v News Group Newspapers Ltd* [1986] RPC 515). It also did not come under fair dealing for criticism and review (see **14.4.5.2**).

It will be very difficult to give any general rules about how much can be taken, as it will depend on the circumstances in each case.

In *HRH the Prince of Wales v Associated Newspapers Ltd* [2006] EWHC 522 (Ch), publication of passages from the Prince's personal journals could not be defended under s 30(2). The object of the articles was to reveal the existence and content of the articles, rather than any current event. The publishers knew, also, that the material had been obtained in breach of confidence. An appeal was dismissed by the Court of Appeal ([2006] EWCA Civ 1776).

In the case of *British Broadcasting Corporation v British Satellite Broadcasting Ltd* [1991] 3 WLR 174, the court held that the showing by BSB of BBC World Cup football clips lasting from 14–37 seconds, four times in 24 hours did amount to fair dealing. The use did not have to be in a general news programme. It was appropriate to use the extracts in a sports update programme.

In *Pro Sieben Media AG v Carlton UK Television Ltd and Another* [1999] 1 WLR 605, the case concerned the use by Carlton of a 30-second clip from an interview broadcast by a German satellite channel concerning Mandy Allwood, who was pregnant with eight embryos. The use was held to fall under 'the purposes of criticism or review'. The use by Carlton was in a programme looking at chequebook journalism, including the treatment of Ms Allwood by the media.

In *Newspaper Licensing Agency Ltd v Marks & Spencer plc*, it was held at first instance ([1999] RPC 536) that the copying and circulation within Marks & Spencer management of extracts from daily newspapers went beyond fair dealing for reporting current events. The making of between 80 and 120 copies of each article was held to be neither fair, nor for the purpose of reporting current events. On appeal, this aspect does not seem to have been disputed. The decision was overturned in the Court of Appeal ([2001] Ch 257) on the basis that any infringement of the copyright in the typographical arrangement must be that of a whole page of the newspaper, not of each article on the page, as had been held at first instance. So, copying an article, comprising a small part of a page, was not 'substantial taking' of the copyright in the page (see **14.4**). The House of Lords concurred ([2001] UKHL 38, [2003] 1 AC 551).

In *Hyde Park Residence Ltd v Yelland and Others*, the *Sun* newspaper published photographs taken from a security video of a property which had been visited by Diana Princess of Wales and Dodi al Fayed. It was held at first instance ([1999] RPC 655) that the use was fair dealing for reporting current events. The Court of Appeal reversed this decision ([2001] Ch 143). It held that the events were still 'current events' even a year after the deaths of the Princess and her companion, but that the use of the photographs was not fair. The newspaper had paid for dishonestly taken photographs, which were not essential to the story in the newspaper.

In *PCR Ltd v Dow Jones Telerate Ltd* [1998] FSR 170, an employee of the defendant wrote reports on the cocoa market. She used material from reports published by the claimant. It was held that a 'substantial part' of the claimant's material had been copied. Although the use was for reporting current events, the amount taken was too much to satisfy the test of fairness, so the claim for copyright infringement was upheld.

In *IPC Media v News Group Newspapers Ltd* [2005] EWHC 317 (Ch), the court held that the use in question was not fair dealing for the purpose of criticism or review. The 'Sun' newspaper had run a comparative advertisement showing its new television magazine, along with a reproduction of the claimant's magazine. The purpose had been to reduce sales of their competitor's magazine, not to review it.

In *Fraser-Woodward v British Broadcasting Corporation* [2005] EWHC 472 (Ch), the claimant failed in his claim for copyright infringement. The defendant television company had shown on air a copy of a newspaper containing the photographs in question, of David Beckham and his family. This use was held to be fair use for criticism or review of tabloid journalism.

14.4.4.4 Artistic works on public display (s 62)

Section 62 provides an important general provision that making graphic or photographic images, broadcasts or films of buildings, sculptures, models for buildings and works of artistic craftsmanship is not an infringement of any copyright in those things. This applies to things which can be seen, permanently sited, in public places or premises open to the public. This provision also protects any further publication or copying of images or representations of those things.

14.4.5 Other defences and licensing

In proceedings for infringement of an IP right, the defendant will often argue that the right in question is not valid and/or the claimant does not have the right to sue for infringement. Another defence is that the copying has been done with the consent of the copyright holder (ie, there is a licence). Such a licence could be express or implied from the circumstances of the case.

In *JHP Ltd v BBC Worldwide Ltd* [2008] EWHC 757 (Ch), the copyright material was the 'Dalek' characters, created by T (now deceased). The material had been published in three books by the claimant and in TV series by the defendants. From a series of agreements, the court concluded that the claimant had exclusive rights to publish the three books (but no more than that) and that the defendants had acquired a licence by estoppel from T's estate, the current owners of the copyright. That licence would extend to two new books proposed by the defendants.

You have already seen, at **14.2.5**, that the ownership of copyright, and the closely-connected question of the right to use it under a licence, are complex matters. No case illustrates these points better than the *Fisher v Brooker* litigation about the copyright interests in the well-known 1960s song, 'A Whiter Shade of Pale', by the band Procul Harum. The claimant had no part in the original version of the music and words, those parts of the copyright having first been owned by the authors, the first defendant and the band's manager; those rights were then assigned by them to Essex Music Ltd (E), just before the claimant joined the band as organist in 1967. After this date, the band quickly worked up the song, including the iconic 8-bar solo organ part of the arrangement, which was composed and played by the claimant on the first recording of the song, which became a huge and lasting success. The copyright dispute was very much about this final arrangement for the recording – you should be very clear on that point. This release was indisputably under E's licence; and at about the same time the band members entered into a recording contract with E, allowing E to exploit the band for a one-year period in return for royalties. In 1969, the claimant left the band, the other members agreeing to indemnify him against any claims from the band's creditors, in exchange for his waiving his rights to any royalties, except those in respect of the copyright in the major hit song. The other band members gained very large royalty payments over time from the song, but although the claimant knew of this and received nothing, he claimed nothing until April 2005. Shortly afterwards, he commenced proceedings.

The claimant's case, with which the judge agreed, was:

(a) the claimant was a co-author of the work, because of the distinctive part played by the organ solo;

(b) the claimant was a joint owner of the copyright, his share being assessed at 40%;

(c) the defendants had a licence to exploit the work, which had been revoked by the commencement of proceedings in May 2005. The judge was clear that this did not affect the claimant's copyright entitlement; it was simply a licence to exploit it.

The defendants appealed on the basis that even though the claimant had been declared to be the owner of part of the copyright (which point was not appealed), to allow him to assert such a right after such a period of time would be unconscionable, particularly as the real aim of the case was to determine rights for the future (ie from May 2005 for the remainder of the copyright period). The effect of that should be that the claimant should be declared to have lost his interest in the copyright by reason of the equitable remedies of estoppel, laches and acquiescence, by his failure to take action earlier. The Court of Appeal allowed the appeal.

On the claimant's appeal to the House of Lords – *Fisher v Brooker* [2009] UKHL 41, [2009] All ER (D) 338 (Jul) – their Lordships stressed the point that copyright is a fundamental property form throughout its full period; the judge had made an unassailable finding as to the claimant's property rights as co-author, and had made his directions as to those rights properly and carefully. The recording contract with E had not assigned the claimant's copyright but had simply created a licence to use it. The Court of Appeal had erroneously fallen into the trap of confusing declarations about property rights with the exercise of the court's discretion to allow relief on equitable grounds; there had been no detrimental reliance by the defendants sufficient to support any of the equitable reliefs that they had sought. Blackburne J's decision was affirmed.

This case gives probably one of clearest expositions of how the law on ownership and assertion of shared copyright works, as well as an explanation of the role of equitable, discretionary remedies in a copyright dispute. Students are urged to read the judgments for a better understanding of the whole area.

A licence might be implied, if it were necessary to give business efficacy to or to reflect the true intentions of parties to an agreement, but only to the minimum extent necessary. See *Meridian International Services Ltd v Richardson* [2007] EWHC 2539 (Ch). In *Fisher v Brooker* (above), the court was willing to find licensing terms by implication, but found that an outright assignment of the claimant's copyright was not necessary to give business efficacy to the agreement.

14.5 Remedies

By s 96(2) of the CDPA 1988, 'in an action for infringement of copyright all such relief by way of damages, injunctions, accounts or otherwise is available to the plaintiff as is available in respect of any other property right'. This range of remedies is open to the copyright owner and, to the extent that licensed material is infringed, it is also open to an exclusive licensee against third parties, concurrently with the copyright owner. A non-exclusive licensee of copyright may have that range of remedies if the licence is in writing and expressly grants the non-exclusive licensee a right of action (ss 101, 101A). Where the rights of action are held concurrently between the owner and the exclusive licensee, usually whichever one initiates the action will need to join the other as second claimant or as defendant, according to the circumstances (s 102).

Damages are available, usually based upon the tortious, compensatory measure, often (but not always) based upon what the infringer would have had to pay for a notional licence to achieve what he has attempted to do without permission. Damages are not available against an innocent infringer, or someone has no knowledge of or reason to believe in the existence of copyright in the material (s 97(1)), although that does not prejudice the availability of other remedies. Under s 97(2), there is a provision for 'additional damages' to be awarded according to the circumstances, particularly the flagrancy of the infringement and the likely benefit accruing to the defendant. This usually depends upon some seriously questionable behaviour by the defendant, over and beyond the simple question of copying (see *Cantor Fitzgerald International v Tradition (UK) Ltd* [2000] RPC 95).

Injunctions, particularly interim ones, are fairly widely used in copyright disputes, the courts deciding the matter upon the weight of the issues and consequences for each party. The test for the court, in interim matters, is usually one of whether there is a serious triable issue. If damages could fairly easily restore the position, without more, an injunction application is unlikely to succeed.

Account of profit is a broad alternative to damages in an appropriate case against any infringer, knowing or innocent. The usual problem applies, in that if the court orders an account to be taken and it turns out that little or no profit has accrued, it will not be possible to fall back upon a substantial damages claim; only nominal damages would be available. The claimant will need to think long and hard about his election.

Orders are available for delivery up of infringing copies or articles held in the reasonable knowledge or belief that they are used, or have been used, for infringement purposes, both in civil and in criminal proceedings (ss 99, 108). This is supported by forfeiture of such similar copies and articles as are found during criminal investigations or proceedings under s114A. There can also be orders to forfeit such articles to the copyright owner, for destruction or whatever the court may think fit as to disposal (s 114).

The CDPA 1988, s 100 allows a copyright owner to seize offending articles. However, the right is in fact very weak. It can be used only against market or street traders as the right excludes business premises. The police also have to be informed beforehand. Section 107 provides for criminal liability for making or dealing with infringing articles. Sections 108 and 114 allow for the delivery up or destruction of infringing copies. Section 111 allows for an order to prevent the importation of infringing copies.

14.6 Databases

The Copyright and Rights in Database Regulations 1997 implemented the Directive on the Legal Protection of Databases (Directive 96/9/EC) ('Database Directive') and introduced a new 'database right' which is not the same as copyright but which gives some safeguards which are similar to copyright (see **Chapter 15**).

The new right was introduced to protect the interests of database owners (eg, news agencies), though it applies both to electronic and paper databases. Under English law, many such databases would generally have qualified for copyright as compilations in the past, but in many European countries they might not have been protected by copyright (because they would not be regarded as sufficiently original – see **14.2.2.1**). Even where there was copyright protection, if somebody extracted just one or two pieces of information then this might not amount to substantial copying, so might not be an infringement. See how the database right deals with this at **15.6**.

The individual items from which the database was composed could each also get copyright as a literary work, if substantial enough to constitute a 'work'.

14.7 Copyright and information technology

An enormous practical problem in respect of information technology (IT) and the law is that technological advances constantly outstrip the law. For example, it was suggested at the time that the CDPA 1988 was going through Parliament that parts of it were already out of date.

Arguably, copyright is the most important of the 'general' IP rights in relation to IT matters. It is of more direct significance than either trade marks or patents (see also **Chapter 19**).

14.7.1 Computer programs

Perhaps the most important aspect of the application of copyright to IT is that computer programs are protected by literary copyright (see **14.4.1**). Unauthorised copying (including simple down-loading) of a program therefore amounts to breach of copyright (that is, basically, normal rules and remedies apply). So, the resulting anomaly is that something functional is protected by a literary right. It is also more likely that non-literal copying can be shown to infringe software copyright than other forms of literary copyright. This problem has been much considered under US copyright law.

The CDPA 1988, s 3(1), and the Copyright (Computer Programs) Regulations 1992 (SI 1992/3233) provide that software is protected as a literary work. (Note that there are also proposals to give patent protection to at least some computer programs; see **17.3.4**.)

14.7.2 The Internet

There seems to be a strongly held view in some quarters that the law cannot apply to or control the Internet at all. Nevertheless, the law undoubtedly does apply to the Internet. The fact is that copyright infringement is no less of an infringement simply because it involves the Internet. The only real issues concern the most effective method of dealing with jurisdictional and evidential problems that arise in pursuing large numbers of people in different countries.

Most Internet use, where the material is available to the public in the UK, will fall within s 20 of the CDPA 1988 as a 'communication to the public'; any unauthorised use of copyright material can, therefore, infringe. The section is expressed to apply to making works available by 'electronic transmission'. This sweeps up the former s 7 of the CDPA 1988, which dealt with 'cablecasts'. It does not matter where the host website is located.

There have already been cases which have decided that unauthorised use of material from the Internet can amount to breach of copyright (see, eg, *Shetland Times Ltd v Wills and Another* [1997] FSR 604, discussed at **19.6.2**). There is also the opposite situation where copyright material is used on the Internet without permission. For example, in January 1999, a considerable number of musicians and pop singers took out advertisements in newspapers to protest against the unauthorised Internet use of their material, and to demand tighter legal controls. You may be familiar with the litigation in the USA on the 'Napster' site, which various record companies sued for breach of copyright in their recordings. Napster has returned as a licensed site, where you have to pay money to download the recordings.

However, other sites have sprung up, such as Gnutella, Blubster, Newtella, MusicCity and KaZaA. These do not use a centralised server so it is harder to take action against them. They use P2P, software which enables one computer to communicate with another computer without going through a centralised server (P2P stands for 'peer to peer').

See the case of *Sony Music Entertainment (UK) Ltd and Others v Easyinternetcafé Ltd* at **14.4.2** for an instance of copyright infringement on the Internet. In the *Daily Telegraph*, 24 April 2003, it was reported that EMI is making 140,000 of its tracks available to customers via the Internet. It will charge customers, but less than they would have to pay to buy a CD version.

More recently, the Recording Industry Association of America (RIAA) has instituted proceedings against many people in the United States for allegedly using P2P copying, and this policy is now being actively pursued in the United Kingdom.

Despite these steps in defence of their rights, it does seem as if the emphasis is beginning to shift away from attempts to enforce IP rights against mass users of the Internet, towards a recognition by producers of mass media/entertainment that they will have to live with widespread publication of their products. The way forward is more likely to be by way of agreements between the entertainment providers and ISPs/advertisers.

14.8 Public performances – the collecting societies

It would be very difficult for the creators of music and songs, in particular, to enforce their rights acting individually, not least as their copyright could be infringed by a public performance anywhere in the country. To overcome this problem, the collecting societies have existed for many years. They operate either as licensees of the relevant copyrights, or as agents acting on behalf of the copyright holders. They employ staff to travel round the country to find places where public performances are taking place without a licence from one of the collecting societies. The typical problem locations are pubs and restaurants.

The Performing Rights Society (PRS) and the Mechanical Copyright Protection Society (MCPS) act for writers of music and lyrics and their publishers. The MCPS acts on behalf of its composer and publisher members. It negotiates agreements with those who wish to record the music of its members. It collects and distributes the 'mechanical' royalties which are generated from recording of the music on to many different formats. The PRS collects licence fees on behalf of composers, lyricists and music publishers for public performance or broadcast of their works. They co-operate closely under the name 'The Music Alliance'. Phonographic Performance Limited (PPL) acts for over 3,000 record companies, both large and small, and deals primarily with the copyright in sound recordings. Video Performance Limited (VPL) is responsible for music videos.

As well as their policing role, the collecting societies license performance of their works, including to broadcasters such as the BBC, ITV and Sky. All the societies cooperate closely to ensure that the copyright holders in each aspect of a work receive their fair share of a licence fee from a user. Disputes about the terms and other aspects of this system are heard by the Copyright Tribunal, formerly the Performing Right Tribunal. See *Phonographic Performance Ltd v Candy Rock Recording Ltd* [2000] EMLR 618, CA.

In the publishing world, the Copyright Licensing Agency Ltd (CLA) seeks to enforce its members' copyright in their works. It licenses businesses to copy protected works. The CLA is owned by the Authors Licensing and Collecting Society (ALCS) and the Publishers Licensing Society (PLS). The Newspaper Licensing Agency Ltd (NLA) was set up in 1996 to enforce newspaper proprietors' rights in their copyright. It licenses businesses to copy newspapers, and was involved in a high-profile case with Marks & Spencer (see **14.4** and **14.4.4.3**).

14.9 Developments in the law of copyright

Directive 2001/29/EC on Copyright and Related Rights in the Information Society ('Copyright Directive') deals with harmonisation of copyright through the EU. In particular, it addresses the issue of copyright protection on the Internet and satellite and cable broadcasts. It provides for an exemption from liability for an intermediary which carries out transient or incidental copying as part of a technological process. Articles 6 and 7 of the Directive are intended to outlaw the making and selling of devices which circumvent anti-copying technology. The Directive has now been implemented by the Copyright and Related Rights Regulations 2003 (SI 2003/2498), as of October 2003, and has amended the CDPA 1988 in this respect by the insertion of s 28A.

This important provision has been examined in detail by Kitchin J in *Football Association Premier League Ltd v QC Leisure* [2008] EWHC 1411 (Ch). The case concerns the use of foreign origin decoder cards for the purpose of allowing UK screening of Premier League matches in bars and similar places. The cards were necessary to allow UK access to broadcasts intended to be seen only in Greece, the Middle East and North Africa. The Premier League claimant controls the filming and the licensing of its matches; the use by the defendants of the cards was claimed to be an infringement of the copyrights involved, and as undermining the value of the licensing rights to licensor and licensees alike. In a very extensive preliminary examination of the law, the judge decided that the matter is so closely connected to European Community law, and that the issues are of such considerable significance to commercial and legal policies of the Community, that the only safe course was an adjournment to allow references on certain points to be made to the ECJ for a ruling.

This is a matter of very great importance to the whole question of cross-border satellite broadcasting and its reception; beyond this, it is likely to shed light on the larger question of the copyright implications of transient or incidental passage of copyright material within any computer operation which, as an operational part of a technological process, has no independent economic significance. It appears, from the preliminary analysis of the matter by Kitchin J, that he sees the question of independent economic significance as being of central importance to the need for the ECJ's view, both as to transient copies made within the cards themselves and also as to the transient copies produced on the TV screens. The ECJ ruling is expected shortly (late 2009).

Directive 2001/84/EC on the Resale Right for the Benefit of the Author of an Original Work of Art should have been implemented in Member States by 1 January 2006. This gives the creator of a copyright work a percentage of the sale price (the 'resale right' – reg 3) when the work is re-sold on the open market during the period of copyright protection (ie, up to 70 years after the author's death). There was some delay, following extensive consultation, but the Artist's Resale Rights Regulations 2006 (SI 2006/346) came into effect on 14 February 2006.

The resale right can be 'transmitted', under regs 9 and 16, to persons who become beneficially entitled, on the death of the author, either to the work itself or to the copyright in the work. The resale right will be exercisable on such 'transmitted rights' only for resale contracts after 1 January 2010. The resale right is capped at €12,500 per sale (max), and has already collected £5 million or so for living artists, which is unlikely to make much impact on a market worth several billion pounds each year.

14.10 International copyright protection

Internationally, there are two distinct levels of recognition and protection of copyright material. The first lies in the various measures taken by the European Community; the second is seen in international treaty obligations of the UK. It is only possible to give a brief outline of these matters here, but they can be summarised as follows.

Within the EC, the matter has been dealt with by directives, leading to national legislation, showing some degree of harmonisation. Examples are discussed at **14.9** above. Other examples are seen in computer programs (Directive 91/250/EEC), rental and lending rights in copyright (Directive 92/100/EEC), and database protection (Directive 96/9/EC). The general effect of all this legislation is that most national legislation within the EC is fairly consistent in its effect and application, but there are still anomalous situations, particularly with respect to performance and moral rights.

On the broader international stage, the UK is a signatory to two major treaties, the Berne Copyright Convention and the Universal Copyright Convention. Both treaties have a similar effect: they provide assurance, as between the signatory nations, that mutual recognition, availability of jurisdiction and national legal remedies will be given to the owners of copyright within the different signatory states. It is a sort of copyright club arrangement.

The Berne Convention was ratified by the UK in 1887 and has a wide international membership, including all EC members, the USA and China. It is administered by the World Intellectual Property Organisation. The broad effect of the Convention is that the qualification for protection part of the CDPA 1988, Chapter IX, extends the protection of the Act to citizens and bodies incorporated within the signatory nations of the Convention. The degree of protection may be limited in some cases where the courts of another signatory state would not give as much protection to a UK citizen as is available in the UK. Much depends upon the amount of protection available under national copyright law, which is not overridden by the Convention. Some rights suggested by the Convention are not generally available under English law; in some matters (notably, duration of protection), English law gives longer periods than the Convention and many other national laws. Very significantly, the Berne Convention is based upon the complete lack of formality that English law gives to the creation and recognition of copyright.

The Universal Copyright Convention ('UCC') is run by UNESCO and has a quite different membership to the Berne Convention, although the UK and the larger nations are signatories. The biggest difference from the Berne Convention lies in the UCC's requirement for quite a high degree of formality being required of the contracting states as well as the mandatory, prominent display upon the material of the copyright symbol, the owner's name and the date of first publication (even though that is not strictly required under English law).

There are other international agreements and organisations that can affect copyright matters, but these fall outside the remit of this work.

Chapter 15
The Database Right

15.1	Background and introduction	227
15.2	Definition of a database	227
15.3	Qualifications for the database right	228
15.4	Ownership of the database right	228
15.5	Duration of database protection	228
15.6	Infringement of the database right	228
15.7	Exceptions from the database right	229
15.8	Application of the database right	229

15.1 Background and introduction

There has been a difference of approach between English law and the Continental civil law systems on the protection of utilitarian information such as lists of customers' names and addresses, or entries in a phone directory. The English approach has been to grant copyright protection, but the Continental view was that such functional documents were not literary works and therefore could not be protected by copyright. This difference of approach was resolved by Directive 96/9/EC on the Legal Protection of Databases ('the Database Directive'). This was implemented by the Copyright and Rights in Databases Regulations 1997 ('the 1997 Regulations') (SI 1997/3032). These amended the CDPA 1988. The protection given by the 1997 Regulations is known as the 'database right'.

What is protected?	collections of information
What benefit is there?	protects against unauthorised copying
How is it obtained?	arises automatically (no registration)
How long does it last?	15 years from creation or substantial revision of the database

There remains, of course, a class of databases that is protected by copyright (see **14.2** and **15.2**). This class will, in almost all cases, be protected by both copyright and the database right under the 1997 Regulations. The problem that commonly arose for copyright database owners, prior to the 1997 Regulations, was that copying often took the form of repeated, low level use of the material, which usually failed to be a 'substantial' copying for infringement purposes. This gap has now been filled by reg 16(2) (see **15.6**).

15.2 Definition of a database

A database is defined in CDPA 1988, s 3A, as follows:

> **3A Databases**
>
> (1) In this Part 'database' means a collection of independent works, data or other materials which—
>
> (a) are arranged in a systematic or methodical way, and
>
> (b) are individually accessible by electronic or other means.
>
> (2) For the purposes of this Part a literary work consisting of a database is original if, and only if, by reason of the selection or arrangement of the contents of the database the database constitutes the author's own intellectual creation.

The definition of a 'database' covers information held in electronic form and also that held only as paper documents. This definition is also applied by the 1997 Regulations.

In practice, a database could, for example, be information on the daily price of stocks and shares, a telephone directory, Lexis or the CD-ROM law reports. Copyright protection may also be afforded to a database specifically as a literary work, although the standard is not only that of originality, but also that it is the 'author's own intellectual creation'. This seems to be a higher standard than for copyright in literary works in general, and so a database is unlikely to have copyright protection.

Whether or not it is protected by copyright, a database attracts the database right, which arises automatically. The database right runs for 15 years from the end of the year of completion. It prevents unauthorised use of the database or a substantial part of it.

Under reg 13 of the 1997 Regulations, the database right exists where there is 'substantial investment in obtaining, verifying or presenting the contents of the database.' Thus, data arrangements have the protection of the database right if there is a substantial investment (including any investment, whether of financial, human or technical resources):

(a) in quality or quantity; or
(b) in obtaining, verifying or presenting the data.

Further points to consider in relation to database right are discussed below.

15.3 Qualifications for the database right

There are copyright-style qualification requirements (1997 Regulations, reg 18) based on nationality, or corporate seat.

15.4 Ownership of the database right

The maker of a database protected by the database right is the person who takes the initiative in obtaining, verifying or presenting the contents of the database and who assumes the risk of investing in that obtaining (see 1997 Regulations, reg 14).

The maker is the first owner of the database right (reg 15).

Care is needed in asserting ownership of database rights. In *Google Inc v Copiepresse SCRL* [2007] ECDR 5, a database right infringement claim by a management company failed, simply because the company did not hold the database right but only managed copyright on behalf of various newspapers which were subjected to automatic searches by Google. Copyright infringements were upheld by the Belgian court.

15.5 Duration of database protection

The database right lasts for the longer of 15 years from the end of the calendar year:

(a) of completion of the database; or
(b) during which the database was first made available to the public (reg 17).

A 'substantial new investment', under s 17(3) will 'top up' the right so the period starts again. So, a telephone directory would in effect have a rolling 15-year protection, as a new edition is produced every year.

15.6 Infringement of the database right

Infringement is the extraction or re-utilisation of all or a substantial part of the contents of a database without the consent of the owner (reg 16).

'Extraction' means the permanent or temporary transfer of the contents of a database to another medium by any means, or in any form.

'Re-utilisation' means making those contents available to the public by any means.

'Substantial' is in terms of quality, or quantity or both.

'Substantial part' can include repeated extraction and/or re-utilisation of insubstantial parts (reg 16(2)). This is the most useful aspect of the right, in that it can prevent repeated, low-level use of the database by unauthorised persons.

15.7 Exceptions from the database right

Database rights are not infringed (regs 19 and 20):

(a) by fair dealing with a substantial part of a database made available to the public if:
    (i) such dealing is for illustration in teaching or research; and
    (ii) sufficient acknowledgement is given; or

(b) generally, by copying or use with the authority of the keeper of a database available for public inspection as a statutory record.

The database right can be licensed or assigned (as can the copyright in the database).

15.8 Application of the database right

The database right was introduced to give the database owner an action against people who extract information from the database without its permission, whether or not this would constitute copyright infringement. See the case below of *British Horseracing Board v William Hill Organisation Ltd* [2002] ECC 24 on the use of information on the runners and riders. The database right would also have applied to facts such as those in *Faccenda Chicken Ltd v Fowler* [1986] 1 All ER 617, where the unauthorised use was of a database which was a list of customers' names and addresses.

In *British Horseracing Board v William Hill,* the British Horseracing Board operated a computerised database containing the details of horse owners, trainers and jockeys, racing colours, horses and other information relating to races to be run in Great Britain. Information on the database was updated after each race. William Hill, a bookmaker with 1,500 licensed betting shops in the UK, legitimately used information from the British Horseracing Board service. In 2000, William Hill started an Internet betting service which used information from the British Horseracing Board service. This was outside the terms of William Hill's licence agreement. The British Horseracing Board therefore sued for breach of the database right.

It was held at first instance to be a breach and an injunction was granted. The Court of Appeal indicated that it was minded to uphold the judgment at first instance, but also referred some matters of interpretation of the underlying Directive to the ECJ. The defendants took out a conditional licence and the injunction was discharged for the time being.

In November 2004, the ECJ handed down its judgment, Case C-203/02. In essence, the ECJ held that there needed to be economic investment in resources used to create a database in order for the database right to arise. This was distinct from re-presenting existing materials, which was held to be the case here. The British Horseracing Board would have had to collect the information on runners and riders in any event for its own purposes as the supervisor of horseracing in the UK. The view of the ECJ was therefore that the database in question did not benefit from the database right, and so William Hill could not have infringed it. The Court of Appeal applied the ECJ judgment, [2005] EWCA Civ 863. There may prove to be repercussions from this case and implications for other databases which re-present existing materials, as distinct from reorganising or collating such materials. There could be a serious question about the protection available to such databases.

An interesting point was considered in *Cantor Gaming Ltd v Gameaccount Global Ltd* [2007] EWHC 1914 (Ch). The claimant had inserted a clause in its online game licence that if any use of its intellectual property were made by third party bookmakers, via the defendant, that would be a material breach of the licence. It was decided that the claimant's database, even though not used in a conventional way, had been stored, backed up, reproduced and accessed. That was sufficient to constitute an unlawful use of the database.

In *Cureton v Mark Insulations Ltd* [2006] EWHC 2279, an agent who had been given the task of selling insulation to his principal's customers began to collate more information about them for his own private purposes, unrelated to the agency function. In a termination dispute, the principal claimed ownership of the database. The court held that although the principal was justified in summarily dismissing the agent, the work in creating the database had been done by the agent and he was, therefore, the owner under reg 14 (see **15.4**).

Chapter 16
Design Rights

16.1	Introduction to design protection	231
16.2	Registered design right	234
16.3	Unregistered design right	239
16.4	Semiconductor topography design right	244
16.5	Registered and unregistered designs	245

16.1 Introduction to design protection

So far, in looking at IP rights, we have examined the protection of business reputation and creative expression through the trade mark, passing off and copyright, all areas which provide clear and obvious examples of matters that require and justify legal protection. The creator or owner of a business or a copyright work really does look like an owner of property in some form. In dealing with designs, however, somewhat different considerations come into play. Here, we are dealing with the way things look and with the shape and appearance of manufactured articles – often, the quite mundane objects that surround us in our everyday world. It is not so easy or practicable to accept that shapes and appearances of things should remain the monopoly of any particular person for any extensive length of time. Nevertheless, successful shapes and appearances cost money to design and are worth a great deal to their owner, commercially. In consequence, the law has had to develop to give a range of more limited rights to owners of designs, in terms both of period of protection and the scope of the protection offered, than those you have seen in the IP rights studied so far. There is a delicate balancing act here, between over-protection of design owners and the maintenance of general design freedom for other competing designers and manufacturers, who wish to use similar design features on the same, or even on different, types of article.

A simple example illustrates the point: a person buys an article, perhaps a motor cycle, and then decides it is so good that he wishes to keep it for a long time. If the manufacturer changes models after a short while and ceases to make spare parts for the earlier bike, can the enthusiastic owner go to someone else who is willing to make and sell a spare part to that design? It would be a great problem if the original manufacturer could exercise design rights to prevent such a thing permanently, or even stop other manufacturers, as competitors, from making the millions of genuine spare parts used in the everyday world. Design protection has to be able to deal with this practicality; the law has to recognise that where there is plenty of design freedom, an interesting design will merit protection for a period. Where there is little or no room to vary the design (such as with many spare parts, or in interfaces between component parts, or between scart, 3-pin or other cable connections, etc), the law will usually not provide protection for those design features.

The protections we look at below fall into two categories: the most protected category is achieved by initial registration of a design and maintenance of that registration up to a maximum of 25 years, this protection being limited to external shapes and appearances ('registered design right' or 'RDR'); a lesser, residual, unregistered design right will give a shorter period of protection to shapes and forms, but is capable of dealing with the often invisible internal shapes and forms of articles which cannot be protected by registration ('unregistered design right' or 'UDR'). It should be understood though, that it is not always the whole of an article that will be protected; the protection will apply only to those features which are capable of meeting the requirements of the relevant legislation, which tends to exclude many features as being unprotectable.

It is important to realise that RDR and UDR are not mutually exclusive; it is often the case that both rights may co-exist in the same design features or, alternatively, that the separate rights exist in separate features of the same article – eg, RDR protecting the surface decoration of it (to which UDR cannot apply, see **16.1.1** below), while UDR protects inner, unseen shapes and configurations (to which RDR cannot apply, see **16.1.2** below).

The law explained in the following paragraphs is discussed mainly by reference to the current English statutes and cases. Note, though, that this area has had to respond directly to the European Community interventions of the last 20 years or so. There have been, and continue to exist, some differences between the approaches to designs (and other IP rights) seen in national legal systems within the Community, but the current English design statutes are fairly closely aligned now with the law applicable throughout the Community, by virtue of the 'Design Directive' mentioned at **16.1.1** below. This alignment of Community and national laws has proceeded in parallel with the development of the 'Community Registered Design' ('CRD'), as well as the 'Community Unregistered Design' ('CUD'), administered by OHIM in Alicante (these are dealt with in outline at **16.2.11** and **16.3.9** respectively below). The strong similarities between domestic and Community law on these matters, particularly in registered designs, will become clear as the chapter proceeds. Consequently, little direct reference is made to the Community legislation, as much of our domestic legislation closely follows the EC form and drafting. It will be seen that several cases referred to, if examined in detail, have used Community Design terms and provisions, but detailed examination of the differences between domestic and Community law in this area is not necessary, or desirable, for the present purposes of this chapter. The English High Court, Court of Appeal and Patents County Court have jurisdiction to hear Community Design matters.

16.1.1 The RDR – origins and an overview

Registered designs have existed in England since at least the 1830s. They were bolstered at that time to protect the designs of fabrics from being copied by cheap imports. The RDR was strengthened in the CDPA 1988, with the aim of promoting its use for a wider range of articles. At the same time, copyright was pushed in the direction of artistic output, not least to resist the trend that had developed of trying to use copyright for industrial items such as, say, spare parts for cars, etc, to gain longer periods of protection. The interface between copyright and design protection is discussed at **16.3.7** below. Directive 98/71/EC on the Legal Protection of Design (the Design Directive), implemented by the Registered Design Regulations 2001 (SI 2001/3949), made further amendments to the legislation governing registered designs, the Registered Designs Act 1949 (RDA) 1949, effective from 9 December 2001. Regulation 6/2002 EC sets up the framework of the Community Design Scheme (see **16.2.11** and **16.3.9**).

The RDR now protects the visible, external appearance, during ordinary use, of all or part of a product, 'product' being very widely defined so as to include consumer or industrial products. The earlier scope of RDR was limited to items having eye appeal and aesthetic aspects; that limitation no longer applies. The effect of this is that most pre-2003 English case law on RDR offers little real guidance on the current situation. A much greater number of relevant cases are to be seen in the reports of the ECJ and CFI, but for present purposes, it will not be necessary to examine much case law.

A visit to the IPO website (www.ipo.gov.uk) and its registered designs search area, under 'products', will reveal designs for just about anything that can be manufactured, from the most artistically designed consumer articles to the most functional industrial items. The range is very wide, from tools, to clothes, to transport, so the protection has come a long way from fabric designs and purely consumer articles. The form of protection given is similar to other registered IP rights: the fact of registration gives notice to the world at large of the existence of the right, so that any commercial use or exploitation of the design, or of articles made to that design, with or without knowledge or intention, is within the scope of the protection (see infringements and remedies at **16.3.5** and **16.3.6**). In effect, RDR gives the owner of the design a monopoly period of up to 25 years (an initial five-year period, renewable in subsequent five-year periods) in which to use and exploit the design.

What is protected?	new designs for manufactured items
What benefit is there?	monopoly right
How is it obtained?	registration
How long does it last?	25 years from registration

16.1.2 The UDR – origins and an overview

The UDR is a relatively modern form of protection for designs, which has its origins in imaginative and ingenious attempts by manufacturers to obtain long-term protection for designs by the use of copyright techniques. One of the essential components of most replicable designs is some sort of design document. Such a document is almost sure to be protected by the law of copyright, potentially for a long period, and prior to the CDPA 1988, most industrial and manufacturer's design documents had artistic/graphic protection, capable of preventing unauthorised replication of the designs for the long periods associated with artistic copyright. More significantly, unauthorised reproduction of articles from those design documents also infringed the copyright, under the 2D to 3D transformation, as the law then stood. This was even more dangerous as, because of the informal nature of copyright creation and protection, no registration was required and a person could easily infringe copyright without knowing it.

What the 1988 Act did was to eradicate this long-term copyright protection of designs by the creation of the UDR, the effect being that to reproduce the design document, without permission, will certainly infringe any copyright in it (but the period of protection will typically be only for a maximum of 25 years); if the document is reproduced for the purpose of the unauthorised creation of articles to that design, that reproduction will also be an infringement of any UDR in the design (but protection is only for the maximum period of up to 15 years, more typically 10). The most significant change, though, is that any unauthorised making of articles from that infringing copy of the design document will not be an infringement of copyright but will be an infringement of any UDR in the design. The whole idea of this change was effectively to suppress the extensive copyright protection in favour of the much more limited UDR protection (the relationship between copyright and UDR, in a manufacturing, design or production context, is quite complex and more detail is given below, see **16.3.7**).

The scope of the protection given by UDR is quite wide, as it protects designs of any aspect of the shape or configuration, internal or external, of all or part of an article. It can be seen, at once, that this goes further than RDR in protecting internal shapes; but, as will be seen, it is more limited than RDR in that it cannot protect surface decoration.

What is protected?	3-dimensional shapes and configurations
What benefit is there?	prevents copying
How is it obtained?	arises automatically (no registration)
How long does it last?	10 years in most cases (15 years maximum)

16.2 Registered design right

16.2.1 Definitions – 'new' and 'individual character'

'Registered design' is defined in RDA 1949, s 1(2) as:

> ... the appearance of the whole or part of a product resulting from the features of, in particular, the lines, contours, shape, texture and/or materials of the product itself and/or its ornamentation.

'Product' is defined in s 1(3) as:

> any industrial or handicraft item other than a computer program; and in particular, includes packaging, get-up, graphic symbols, typographic type-faces and parts intended to be assembled into a complex product.

This definition now includes things that were not covered before (the amendments referred to at **16.1**), perhaps most notably the packaging and get-up (presentation) of goods. Thus, it would now be possible to register the appearance of packaging as a registered design. This would give such items the increased protection of a registered right.

A design must be 'new' and have 'individual character', which terms are defined as follows:

> **1B Requirement of novelty and individual character**
>
> (1) A design shall be protected by a right in a registered design to the extent that the design is new and has individual character.
>
> (2) For the purposes of subsection (1) above, a design is new if no identical design or no design whose features differ only in immaterial details has been made available to the public before the relevant date.
>
> (3) For the purposes of subsection (1) above, a design has individual character if the overall impression it produces on the informed user differs from the overall impression produced on such a user by any design which has been made available to the public before the relevant date.

As to the requirement for novelty, the test in s 1B(2) is clearly one of whether that design is available to the public, which raises further subordinate questions as to what is meant by 'available to the public' in terms of time, geographical scope and purpose of exposure of the design. The answers to these questions can be found in further examination of the rest of s 1B, particularly s 1B(5), (6) and (7). In broad terms, the time at which the novelty test must be met is when the application to register is first filed. The 'public' in question is probably now somewhat wider than the previous statutory test of the public within the UK. Section 1B(6)(a) indicates that the likely scope may well be as large as the purchasing public and the business community throughout the European Economic Area (EEA).

The question whether the design is new, at that date, is one of whether any largely identical design already exists in 'the prior art in the sector concerned'; that is the sort of designs which are already known of or in use at that date, both by buyers and by 'persons carrying on business . . . and specialising in the sector concerned' (s 1B(6)(a)). So, much depends upon what 'the sector' means. According to Lewison J, in *Green Lane Products Ltd v PMS International Group Ltd* [2007] EWHC 1712 (Pat), in dealing with a CRD, he felt that 'the sector concerned' was the sector in which the 'prior art' was located rather than the particular product sector for which the new registration was applied. That is an important finding, if it is right, in that it means that a design cannot be pirated simply by trying to use that design in a different product sector, as was being attempted in that case. This view has now been upheld by the Court of Appeal ([2008] EWCA Civ 358). This decision suggests that registration of a design for, say, a car, could prevent use of that design on a cake or a toy. The extent of 'the prior art' probably extends to almost any design, wherever located in the world, that is 'available' within the EEA. Registrations will not usually be invalidated by earlier designs in remote places, of which European industry would be unlikely to be aware. The Design Registry will not search prior art but will rely on third parties to object to the application when it is published.

The question of 'individual character' in s 1B(3) is also determined as at the date of first filing and really boils down to a question of evidence as to the overall impression made upon an 'informed user', presumably a person familiar with the designs used in the sector in question. In *J Choo (Jersey) Ltd v Towerstone Ltd* [2008] EWHC 346 (Ch), in a pirated handbag claim, the 'informed user' was said to be neither the woman in the street nor a handbag designer, but rather someone with knowledge of handbag design. The real question is usually whether the creator of the new design has taken advantage of any freedom of design that is available to him to make his new design different from what is already available; if he has not, it is likely that the new design will not have individual character. This is given statutory force in s 1B(4). It should be borne in mind that the different overall impression test might be passed by combining features from several different products to give a completely new amalgam of those features – see *In the Matter of Registered Design No 2044802 in the Name of Household Articles Ltd*, Ch D (Patents Ct) 22/1/98, [1998] FSR 676, a case under the old law, but one which would probably be decided the same way now. There are suggestions in the cases that evidence of both novelty and individual character should be limited to that of purchasers of or traders in the product in question. There is little room for any expert evidence and the court will not usually require it.

It appears, in many cases, that 'individual character' might not add much to the basic requirement that the design be new. Nevertheless, a different approach is now required by 'individual character' from the earlier test of 'eye appeal'. See *Oakley Inc v Animal Ltd* [2005] EWHC 210 (Ch), where the difference required a searching analysis of the changes arising from the Registered Design Regulations 2001.

Some helpful guidance on the 'overall different impression' test for individual character has now been given by the Court of Appeal in *Procter & Gamble Co v Reckitt Benckiser (UK) Ltd* [2007] EWCA Civ 936. In the context of a CRD infringement claim, concerning air freshener spray containers, the Court gave some general guidance as follows:

(a) The first point is that a different overall impression is sufficient and it does not need to be 'clearly' different.

(b) The notional informed user would be taken as being fairly familiar with design issues.

(c) Protection would be correspondingly greater for products which were novel, as compared to those only incrementally different from the prior art.

(d) The test for validity of the registered design remained 'Is the overall impression different?'.

(e) The court needed to identify the 'overall impression' with some care.

(f) The level of generality was very important and should be that of the notional informed user, rather than the casual customer.

(g) The court should than repeat this exercise with the alleged infringing design.

(h) The court should ask finally whether the overall impression of each design was different.

In the instant case, the judge had taken the similarities at too general a level and had come to a finding that there had been infringement. The Court of Appeal held that the informed user would have formed different overall impressions of the products and that therefore there was no infringement. Also, on the appeal, the claimant's original CRD registration was upheld.

16.2.2 'Grace period' of 12 months

The amended RDA 1949 now provides a grace period of 12 months during which a designer may disclose the design. This will not affect the design's novelty, or the assessment of its individual character in an application for registration by the end of the 12-month period (s 1B(5), (6)). There is no right to claim for infringement before the design has been granted registration (s 7A(6)). The very point was in issue in *Oakley Inc v Animal Ltd*, because the disclosure date created problems as to which law and tests applied. There are other provisions in s 1B(6) to protect against unauthorised or abusive disclosures of the design during the grace period.

It would still be important to keep evidence of the date of creation of the design (eg, by storing original drawings which should be dated and signed). Thus, if someone else claimed during the 12-month grace period that he had created the design in question, there would be evidence available to refute that claim. Once the design has been registered, any such disputes would be resolved by the registration, if it is valid.

16.2.3 Design features that cannot be protected

16.2.3.1 Technical function (s 1C)

There is an exclusion from registrability for features dictated 'solely by the product's technical function', but the feeling is that this will be construed less restrictively than was the case under the old law (which simply referred to 'function'). The requirement of 'solely' dictated raises the question of how much design freedom is available (see **16.2.3.2**); if there is some freedom to give a different appearance to the design, it is probably registrable, provided it is new and has individual character.

Section 1C(1) states: 'A right in a registered design shall not subsist in features of appearance of a product which are solely dictated by the product's technical function.' An example of such a feature would be the serrated blades of a dressmaker's crimping shears, which create a sawtooth edge on what is cut.

16.2.3.2 Interface features (s 1C(2))

Section 1C(2) excludes registration for any features of the design of a product which are compelled to be of a certain exact shape in order to be able to fit into, around or up against some other product so that either or both of the products can perform their proper function. The remaining features of either product may well be registrable, but the interface features are not.

One of the more pervasive features of modern designs has been the increasing use of modular ranges of products of all types – tools, furniture, utensils, household and vehicle fittings. By itself, s 1C(2) would create a problem for protecting the many ingenious designs for the interfaces between modular items. Section 1C(3) removes this problem by stating that s 1C(2) does not apply to features that allow for assembly or connection of mutually interchangeable products within a modular system; such features can now be registered and protected (although they would still need to be new and of individual character). That tends to cut back the rigour of both s 1C(2) and the earlier case law rule (seen in *Amp Inc v Utilux Pty Ltd* [1971] RPC 397) that such interface connections could never be registered.

16.2.4 Designs that can now be protected

Under the law pre-December 2001, it was not possible to have a design registration for a spare part (see *R v Registered Designs Appeal Tribunal, ex p Ford Motor Co* [1995] 1 WLR 18). However, it is now possible to have such a registration, provided the part is visible during the normal use of the whole product. For example, a new design of radio aerial for a car would be registrable as it would be visible, but a new design for an oil filter for a car would not, as it would be hidden during normal use. Thus, s 1B(8), (9) provide:

(8) For the purposes of this section, a design applied to or incorporated in a product which constitutes a component part of a complex product shall only be considered to be new and to have individual character—

(a) if the component part, once it has been incorporated into the complex product, remains visible during normal use of the complex product; and

(b) to the extent that those visible features of the component part are in themselves new and have individual character.

(9) In subsection (8) above "normal use" means use by the end user; but does not include any maintenance, servicing or repair work in relation to the product.

'Normal use' means that the visible parts of a wing mirror, in the *Ford* case, could now be registered as they are visible in the ordinary use of a car.

A design registration cannot be used against someone supplying a spare part for the repair of a complex product, 'so as to restore its original appearance' (eg, the car radio aerial mentioned above (s 7A(5)). So, while the registration can be used to stop another manufacturer from using that design for a car radio aerial on its make of car, it cannot be used to stop someone supplying spare aerials so as to restore the appearance of a car, made by the owner of the registered design. Care would be needed, of course, to avoid reproducing any logos or marks that had any separate rights, such as trade marks or passing off protection; licences would be needed to reproduce those.

16.2.5 The scope of the right

The proprietor has the exclusive right (subject to any compulsory licensing by the Crown under the RDA 1949, Sch 1) to use the design and 'any design which does not produce on the informed user a different overall impression' (s 7(1)). This in effect includes use of the design on any product. It will extend to manufacture, dealing in, importing, exporting, stocking and use of a product incorporating the design (see **16.2.9**).

Unlike the situation under the old law, designs no longer have to be registered in regard to certain types of product. So, use of a design intended for crockery on, say, tee shirts would be infringement of the design registration. That can be seen from an examination of the *Green Lane Products Ltd* case discussed at **16.2.1** above.

16.2.6 Duration of protection

The duration of protection is a maximum of 25 years (s 8). This is achieved by an initial registration of five years, renewable in five-year periods.

16.2.7 Ownership of registered designs (s 2)

The prima facie rule is that first ownership of the design rests in the 'author', ie the actual designer (s 2(1)). That is subject to the following points:

(a) If the design is created in the course of someone's employment, the ownership of the design belongs to the employer (s 2(1B)). This in effect is the same as copyright (see **14.2.5**).

(b) If the design is created as a result of a commission, then the ownership belongs to the commissioner, not to the designer (s 2(1A)). This is in contrast to the situation with copyright (see **14.2.5**).

Substantive validity of registration is completely dependent on the applicant having an objective basis for his claim to ownership of the design, at the date of application. This caused the failure of an infringement claim and a declaration of invalidity of a registered design in *Woodhouse UK plc v Architectural Lighting Systems* [2006] ECDR 11, [2006] RPC 1. It is probably the case that an exclusive licensee of RDR does not have the right to sue for infringement (cf patent licensees): see *Isaac Oren v Red Box Toy Factory Ltd*, Ch D (Patents Ct)

1/2/1999, [1999] FSR 785. It does seem that an exclusive licensee of CRD could sue for infringement with the holder's consent, or in circumstances where the right-holder refuses to cooperate.

16.2.8 Exhaustion of rights

Registered design right cannot be used to hinder parallel importing (s 7A(4)), where the product has been put on the market within the EEA by the registered proprietor, or with his consent.

16.2.9 Infringement of registered designs

There is no question of knowledge or intention about infringement. The fact of registration gives notice to all, regardless of knowledge. Knowledge becomes relevant only in considering what remedies are available (see **16.2.10**).

The registration of a design gives the registered proprietor the exclusive right to use the design and 'any design which does not produce on the informed user a different overall impression' (s 7(1)). Care is needed, here, to distinguish between an overall design concept and the particular features of the design that are protected by registration. These are quite different things, as can be seen in *Rowlawn Ltd v Turfmech Machinery Ltd* [2008] EWHC 989 (Pat). The defendant had clearly followed much of the broad concept of the claimant's registered design, but that was not what was protected by the registration. In the finer detail of the machinery (a type of mowing machine) the defendant's design differed and had been developed without copying.

'Using' the design is defined in s 7(2), including a reference to '… the making, offering, putting on the market, importing, exporting or using of a product in which the design is incorporated or to which it is applied'.

'Infringement' is defined in s 7A as doing anything that is the exclusive right of the proprietor without its consent. Exceptions in s 7A(2) include:

(a) an act which is done privately and for purposes which are not commercial;
(b) an act which is done for experimental purposes;
(c) an act of reproduction for teaching purposes …;
(d) …
(e) [these concern foreign ships and aircraft but which are temporarily in the UK]
(f) …

There are qualifications to the exceptions, in s 7A(3); if these are complied with, there is no infringement:

(a) the act of reproduction is compatible with fair trade practice and does not unduly prejudice the normal exploitation of the design, and
(b) mention is made of the source.

There can be no infringement before the date of the certificate of registration (s 7A(6)).

16.2.10 Remedies

Damages may not be awarded against an innocent infringer (s 24B). It is not enough to mark a design with the word 'registered' to overcome this; rather, the registration number of the design must also be marked on the product in question. Apart from this concession to a lack of awareness, the rest of the remedies are available without regard to knowledge of infringement. The position seems to be different where infringement of a CRD is concerned. In *J Choo (Jersey) Ltd v Towerstone Ltd* [2008] EWHC 346 (Ch), Floyd J held that s 24B, although effective in a claim under the RDA 1949, had no application to a claim based on a Community right such as the CRD.

Remedies can include:

(a) an injunction;
(b) damages;
(c) an account of profits; and
(d) an order for delivery up or destruction of the offending items.

The RDA 1949, s 26 provides for a remedy for groundless threats of infringement proceedings. This comprises a declaration, damages and an injunction. The reason for these types of provisions in the legislation governing IP rights is that the threat of infringement proceedings is a severe danger to a business.

There are also criminal offences of falsely representing a design as registered, both against individuals and against corporate bodies.

16.2.11 EU-registered design right – the CRD

Regulation 6/2002 set up an EU-registered design system, which deals with CRD registration. The system has been registering CRDs since 2003 under the Regulation. It is run by the EU Trade Marks Office (OHIM) in Alicante. For the purposes of this edition we are not dealing with this development in depth, but it will affect you when you are in practice, sooner or later. See **16.3.9** for the equivalent measure in unregistered designs.

Community registered designs are similar in many respects to the RDR examined at **16.2** above. The broad tests of novelty and individual character are very much the same, and a maximum 25-year term of protection is available. The big difference is that a CRD is effective throughout the Community, and is recognised by all Member States of the Community. There is no search mechanism before registration and it is for third parties, Member States or the Commission itself to appeal against registration to the OHIM, with an ultimate appeal to the ECJ.

16.3 Unregistered design right

This is referred to in the CDPA 1988 as 'design right'. 'Design' is defined in s 213(2) as 'any aspect of the shape or configuration (whether internal or external) of the whole or part of an article'. The design must be 'original' (s 213(1)), which is further explained as being 'not commonplace in the design field in question'.

No right subsists unless the design is recorded in a document, or an article has been made to the design (s 213(6)).

A further complication of the UDR regime is the necessity for the work to 'qualify' for protection within s 217. This depends upon the design having a qualifying connection to the UK via specified qualifying persons (including designers and commissioners), qualifying countries (in which trading or legal residence is established), or qualifying first marketing within the UK or the EC. This will often need to be addressed, once in practice.

16.3.1 Originality

The requirement of originality for UDR has two aspects:

(a) that it should be original, in the copyright sense of not itself being a copy; and
(b) that it should not be 'commonplace in the design field in question' (s 213(4)).

There have been some cases which have considered what it means to be 'commonplace'. The idea is that UDR protects a design against copying. For that concept to work, the design in question has to be distinguishable from all the other goods of that type in the marketplace. For example, see the following cases.

In *Farmers Build Ltd v Carrier Bulk Materials Handling Ltd* [1999] RPC 461, concerning a slurry separator, it was held that putting a number of different commonplace features together in a new way can result in a design that is not commonplace.

In *Jo-Y-Jo Ltd v Matalan Retail Ltd* [1999] EIPR 627, it was held that flowers embroidered on vests were commonplace.

In *Ocular Sciences Ltd and Another v Aspect Vision Care Ltd and Others; Galley v Ocular Sciences Ltd (No 2)* [1997] RPC 289, a design for contact lenses was held to be commonplace if trite, common-or-garden, or hackneyed. In that case, many features of the contact lenses were held to be commonplace, or subject to the 'must fit' exclusion (ie must fit the eye – see **16.3.2**).

In *Baby Dan v Brevi* [1999] FSR 377, the existence of UDR in a child safety barrier was upheld. It was also held that the right had been infringed.

In *Lambretta Clothing Company Ltd v Teddy Smith (UK) Ltd & Next Retail plc* [2003] EWHC (Ch), the subject matter was a 'retro-vintage' track top. On the existence of UDR, it was held that:

(a) the outline shape of the track top was not original as it had itself been copied from another garment;

(b) the Lambretta logos were surface decoration and therefore excluded from UDR (see **16.3.2.4**);

(c) mere juxtaposition of patches of colour on the garment did not fall within the meaning of 'configuration' in s 213(2), so did not attract UDR; and

(d) two-dimensional colour applied to the garment did not generate an original three-dimensional design.

Overall, there was no UDR existing in the garment.

In *A Fulton Co Ltd v Grant Barnett & Co Ltd* [2001] RPC 16, there was held to be UDR in the handle of an umbrella, which had been designed by a director of the claimant company. The designs were held to be original and not to be commonplace. They were also held to have been infringed by the defendant.

In *Guild v Eskandar Ltd* [2001] FSR 38, UDR was held to exist in garments based on Iranian ethnic clothing, that is, there was sufficient originality in the designs in question (see **14.2.2.3**).

In *Dyson Ltd v Qualtex (UK) Ltd* [2006] EWCA Civ 166, the Court of Appeal upheld a judge's approach of looking at originality by taking a short cut, considering, first, whether the whole of an article was original and, secondly, unless there was a special point about a particular aspect, taking the view that each and every aspect of the design of that article was original. That is very helpful to a designer, in that it is less likely that someone will be able to challenge his design by attempting to 'pick off' features, in a piecemeal way, as being commonplace, so as to challenge the originality of the whole. The Court also added the helpful observation that a very good design (the Dyson handle) did not lose its protection simply by becoming well known and recognised as a good design.

16.3.2 Exclusions

The CDPA 1988, s 213(3) sets out the exclusions from UDR.

16.3.2.1 Methods or principles of construction (s 213(3)(a))

These are excluded on the basis that methods of construction are the subject of patent law rather than design law. 'Method of construction' has been defined as a process or operation by which a shape is produced, as opposed to the design of the shape itself (*Kestos Ltd v Kempat Ltd* [1936] RPC 139). In *Landor & Hawa International Ltd v Azure Designs Ltd* [2006] EWCA

Civ 1285, this principle was applied to 'piping' arrangements, which cloaked the expanding joint in luggage when unexpanded. It was held not to be part of a method of construction and copying it was an infringement.

In *Christopher Tasker's Design Right References; Re Patent Office* [2001] RPC 3, various aspects of sliding doors for wardrobes were held to be subject to UDR, and therefore to come within s 213(2). However, the hiding from view of aluminium runners by the use of wooden mouldings was a method of construction, and excluded from UDR by s 213(3).

In *Bailey v Haynes*, PCC (Judge Fysh QC) LTL 20/10/2006, [2007] FSR 10, a warp-knitted micromesh freshwater fish bait bag was found to have no UDR protection in the 3D structure made by the thread stitching in the mesh. This was because the design used one of four basic warp-knit patterns, which had been known for centuries. It was, basically, a 'method or principle of construction', caught by the s 213(3)(a) exclusion. A claim to CUD in the design also failed.

16.3.2.2 Must fit (s 213(3)(b)(i))

This type of exclusion can be applied to both types of design right. See **16.2.3.2** for the equivalent in registered design. Functional designs are not excluded from UDR; indeed, one of the main purposes of this right is to protect more functional designs. There is, however, an exclusion for those aspects of the design which 'must fit' with other articles in order that either article may perform its function. It is only the 'interface' that is excluded from protection, ie the bits that have to fit into, up to or around the other object. Again, attention will focus on whether the designer truly has any freedom of design open to him. If there is some freedom to vary the design, the exclusion will not offer a defence to a copier of the design (see *Dyson v Qualtex* at **16.3.2.3**). If the spare part designer does have some latitude in designing replacement parts, he will be expected to use it or face infringement claims. The exclusion only applies to the interface connections between objects which are designed to be connected at some stage.

This exclusion would also apply to human spare parts (prostheses), or contact lenses (*Ocular Sciences Ltd and Another v Aspect Vision Care Ltd and Others; Galley v Ocular Sciences Ltd (No 2)* [1997] RPC 289). Another instance concerned a holder for a mobile phone, many features of which did not get UDR as its shape was dictated by the phone (*Parker v Tidball* [1997] FSR 680).

16.3.2.3 Must match (s 213(3)(b)(ii))

The UDR cannot apply to design features of an article if the appearance of those features is dependent on that of a larger article of which it is intended to form an integral part. There could, for example, be no UDR in spare parts (for cars or prostheses for people, eg artificial limbs).

The scope of the exclusion was considered in *Dyson Ltd v Qualtex (UK) Ltd* [2004] EWHC 2981 (Ch). Here, Dyson was seeking to prevent the sale of spare parts made by Qualtex to fit and match Dyson vacuum cleaners. The Qualtex spares in question were intended to resemble closely the Dyson spares, not least as they were visible in the normal use of the vacuum cleaners. It was held that the 'must match' exclusion will not apply if the design of the spare part could be itself be changed without radically changing the overall appearance of the whole article, ie a vacuum cleaner in this case. In other words, it was not necessary for the Qualtex spares to be identical in appearance to the Dyson ones, so the must match exclusion did not save Qualtex from infringement of Dyson's unregistered design right.

In *Dyson Ltd v Qualtex (UK) Ltd* [2006] EWCA Civ 166, the Court of Appeal broadly upheld the judge's approach and confirmed that it was for the spare parts dealer or manufacturer to show that, as a practical matter, there was a real need to copy some feature of shape or configuration (because the appearance of the entire article was dependent upon the relevant design feature of the spare part). If there was no such dependence, the consequence would be that any UDR subsisting in that feature of the original design and article could properly be protected; it would not be excluded by 'must match' and the spare part would constitute an infringing article.

16.3.2.4 Surface decoration (s 213(3)(c))

Surface decoration is excluded from UDR. This is really part of the definition, as UDR protects only the shape of a product (see the *Lambretta* case at **16.3.1**). There can be some difficulty in distinguishing surface decoration from 3-dimensional features of an article (see *A Fulton Co Ltd v Grant Burnett & Co Ltd* [2001] RPC 16).

An interesting case on this problem is *Helmet Integrated Systems Ltd v Mitchell Tunnard*, PCC 10/2/2006, LTL 15/12/2006, [2006] FSR 41. The dispute was about design features of a modular, state-of-the-art fire helmet and, in particular, scalloping features along the sides of the helmet. The evidence showed that scalloping had resulted in some advantages of strength, but the features had not been designed for anything other than appearance's sake. The feature was held to be surface decoration and fell within the exclusion.

16.3.3 Ownership of unregistered designs

If the design is created in the course of someone's employment, the ownership of the design belongs to the employer (s 215). This in effect is the same as copyright (see **14.2.5**).

In *Ultraframe (UK) Ltd v Clayton and Others; Ultraframe (UK) Ltd v Fielding and Others* [2002] EWHC 1964 (Ch), the claimant company was held to be the owner of unregistered designs created by the person who had been managing director and major shareholder. In *A Fulton Co Ltd v Grant Barnett & Co Ltd* [2001] RPC 16, the claimant company was also held to own an unregistered design created by a director, despite the lack of a service contract between company and director.

As with RDR, if the design is created as a result of a commission then the ownership belongs to the commissioner, not to the designer. This is in contrast to the situation with copyright (see **14.2.5** and **16.2.7**).

If the UDR arises by 'first marketing' qualifications (see **16.3**), the person who first markets the design will be the first owner of the UDR (s 215(4)).

Ownership is the same for both registered and unregistered designs. Why the difference from copyright? Primarily because design rights are thought of as commercial rights, so it makes sense that 'he who pays the piper calls the tune'. With copyright the position is more subtle. Although it covers other things as well, copyright is often considered to be the realm of the creative artist, so there the starting point is that the author should own his own creation.

16.3.4 Duration of protection

The UDR lasts for 15 years from the end of the calendar year in which the design was first created, or 10 years from being made available for sale or hire (s 216).

16.3.5 Infringement of unregistered designs

The UDR follows copyright in that there is primary and secondary infringement. Secondary infringement requires knowledge.

The owner of UDR has the exclusive right to reproduce the design for commercial purposes by making articles to that design, or by reproducing his design document for the purpose of making articles to that design (s 226(1)). The latter is seen in *Societa Esplosivi Industriali Spa v Ordnance Technologies (UK) Ltd* [2007] EWHC 2875 (Ch). Here, the defendant had used the designs for multiple warhead systems, which it had obtained in a collaborative enterprise with the claimant, for purposes different from those originally contemplated by the parties. The end result would have been that weapons would have been made to those designs by third parties. That did not protect the defendant. It did not need to make the weapons itself, to infringe the UDR.

Primary infringement is, therefore, for commercial purposes, directly or indirectly making articles to the design, or making a design document for the purpose of enabling such articles to be made, without the UDR owner's permission, or authorising anyone else to do so (s 226(3)).

Secondary infringement includes importation, possessing for commercial purposes, selling and hiring, but is relevant only if the person had knowledge or reason to believe that the items were infringing items (s 227).

16.3.6 Remedies

Remedies are damages, injunctions, accounts of profits (s 229(1)), order for delivery up of infringing articles (s 230), and an order for disposal of infringing articles (s 231). Damages are not available against an innocent primary infringer (s 233), although other remedies are available. Innocence requires an absence of knowledge of the existence of the UDR and no reason to believe in its existence.

There is a provision providing remedies against groundless threats of infringement proceedings (s 253). The remedies are a declaration, injunction and damages.

By contrast with RDR, exclusive licensees have the same remedies available, concurrently with the owner of the UDR.

16.3.7 Overlap with copyright

As we have seen in **Chapter 14**, a three-dimensional article cannot be protected by copyright unless it is itself an artistic object, typically either a sculpture or a 'work of artistic craftsmanship', or an engraving. The intention of the CDPA 1988 is to exclude from copyright protection any industrial or manufactured object that would itself not be protected by copyright. Thus, s 51 also excludes, from copyright protection, the use of any design *document* where an article has been made from that design. In other words, it is not possible to use copyright by the back door to protect the article in question by asserting the copyright in the design drawings (see **16.1.2**). It is simply not an infringement of any copyright that might exist in the design document (s 51(1)).

Instead, the creation of a three-dimensional article can only be protected by UDR, or by registered design right. It would, of course, have to meet the criteria for the design right in question. (Do not forget that if copyright does still apply to the article in question, the period of protection is shortened to 25 years from first production of the article if it is produced industrially – see s 52 and **14.2.4.2**.) The overall effect is that copyright protection is suppressed in favour of UDR protection.

Section 236 provides that any UDR that subsists in the article will be ignored if the article is protected by copyright. This would be the case if the article were, say, a sculpture. So, in this situation, copyright prevails (if in fact copyright does apply to the article – see s 51). The combined effect of s 51 and s 236 is to prevent overlap between copyright and design right protection.

By contrast, any registered design right can co-exist with the copyright in a three-dimensional article.

An interesting case that shows the working of s 51 is *Flashing Badge Co Ltd v Groves* [2007] EWHC 1372 (Ch). Here, the defendant had imported flat, flashing badges which were virtually identical to badges made by the claimant. The claimant owned copyright in the surface decoration on the badges. When this was asserted in infringement proceedings, the defendant raised s 51 as a defence, saying that the drawings on the face of the badges were designs for the creation of an article, the badge, and therefore protected by s 51(1). Rimer J held that the designs were surface decoration caught by s 51(3), which removed the disputed material outside the reach of being a 'design document' for the purposes of s 51(1). It was a straightforward copyright infringement.

16.3.8 Licences of right

In the last five years of the term of an unregistered design, anyone can apply for a licence to use the unregistered design (s 237). If terms cannot be agreed between the parties, then the terms are settled by the Designs Registry, which is part of the IPO.

16.3.9 Community unregistered design right – the CUD

Regulation 6/2002 introduced a Community unregistered design right. This right lasts for three years. However, it seems that the Community right is merely intended to protect registrable designs in the period before registration is applied for. In *Landor & Hawa International v Azure Designs* (see **16.3.2.1**), there was infringement of both design right and the Community unregistered design right.

In many respects, the CUD can be seen to be a short-term, interim form of protection with a dual purpose. It gives a short period of informal protection to many short-lived designs with commercial lives of not much more than three years. It also gives initial protection to many designs of longer commercial life, while consideration is given to obtaining more long-term protection by registration.

16.4 Semiconductor topography design right

It is no exaggeration to claim that the modern developed world is largely built around the computer. You will already realise that computer programs get literary copyright protection (see **14.2**). At the heart of computer operation is the integrated circuit or micro-chip, which is a tiny, complex pattern of hairsbreadth electrical circuits, formed by etching within a sandwich of insulating ('semiconducting') material. Under impetus from the USA, the European Community turned its attention to the necessity to offer some protection to the designs of the circuits within these vital components, resulting in a European Council Directive on the matter in 1987.

The designs of the chips and their functioning manner had largely been patent-protected, but once that stage was achieved, the precise patterns of etched circuits would not be suitable for patent protection, as there is no inventive step involved in simply using chips to make the computers carry out different operations. Copyright protection is also largely removed by the effect of s 51 of the CDPA 1988. Design protection was the obvious solution, and the result is that a specialised application of informal protection by UDR is given to these circuits, by protecting the topography (the 'map') of the circuits.

The solution eventually arrived at is found in the Design Right (Semiconductor Topographies) Regulations 1989 (SI 1989/1100). The way protection is achieved is to use the framework of the UDR provisions in the CDPA 1988 and to make such amendments as are necessary for precise application to microchips. The basis for protection is, as with UDR, originality, not being commonplace and a qualifying situation for protection. The infringing and permitted acts are, however, rather different from those applicable to UDR and resemble, in many ways, the 'fair dealing' provisions that apply to copyright material. This is clearly in contemplation of the need for a general freedom to use the technology to its limits by encouraging analysis and further development. Ownership and duration are very similar to UDR, and the doctrine of exhaustion applies to any articles using the protected material once they are sold, hired or imported into the EC by, or with the licence of, the topography right owner. Further discussion of this area is beyond the scope of this work.

16.5 Registered and unregistered designs

A summary of registered and unregistered designs is provided in the table below.

	RDR	UDR
Statute	RDA 1949 as amended by Registered Designs Regulations 2001	CDPA 1988
Definition	Appearance of whole or part of a product resulting from features of, in particular: (a) lines (b) contours (c) colours (d) shape (e) texture or materials (f) ornamentation 'Product' includes packaging, get up, graphic symbols, typographic type-faces and visible parts	Any aspect of: (a) shape, or (b) configuration of the whole or part of an article NB no right subsists unless the design is recorded in a document or an article has been made to the design
Originality	**New**: no identical design/design differing in only immaterial details has previously been made available to public, *and* **Individual character**: overall impression to informed user differs from that of any other design that has been made available to public, and **The design has not been made available to public:** ie not published, exhibited or used in the trade NB 12 months grace period	Must be **original**, ie must be: (a) **the result of independent effort** ie not copied, and (b) **not commonplace** in design field in question
Exclusions	(a) features solely dictated by technical function (b) interface (mechanical fittings only) (but modular designs are registrable)	(a) methods of construction (b) must fit (c) must match (d) surface decoration
Ownership	Commissioner; the employer; the designer, in that order	Commissioner; the employer; the designer, in that order
Duration	25 years in total (maximum)	The shorter of: (a) 15 years from the end of the year of creation/recording; or (b) 10 years from the end of the year of first sale/hire
Infringement	Making, offering, putting on market, importing or exporting any product incorporating the design or any design which does not produce a different overall impression. No need to prove copying NB private non-commercial acts are excluded	Primary: making articles to the design/ making document for purposes of making articles. Need to prove copying: substantial similarity is enough. Secondary: import, sell, hire, offer, possess with knowledge/reason to believe is an infringing article.

Chapter 17
Patents

17.1	Introduction	247
17.2	Obtaining a patent	247
17.3	Patentability	248
17.4	The patent specification	254
17.5	Who is entitled to grant of a patent?	256
17.6	Infringement	257
17.7	Infringers	260
17.8	Defences	260
17.9	Remedies	261

17.1 Introduction

Patents are monopoly rights granted by the Government to protect inventions under, today, the Patents Act 1977 (PA 1977). If a patent is granted, the inventor gets a monopoly over use of his invention for (generally) 20 years (ie, he can stop anybody else using it for this time). The quid pro quo of getting a patent so far as the inventor is concerned is that before the patent is granted, details of the invention go on a public register at the Patent Office which everyone may study. So, a patented invention cannot be kept secret. The idea is that others should be able to learn from the patent. It contributes to the general body of technological understanding. After the 20 years are up, the invention is available for anyone to use, but the general thinking behind the new invention will have been available to the rest of the world during that 20 years.

The main justification for patents is that if there were no patents, commercial organisations would not invest in the research needed to produce new inventions. They need to have a chance to recoup their expenditure on the invention that is a success, as well as the time spent on abortive projects. The estimated cost of putting a new pharmaceutical product on the market is £200 million, and it takes about 12 years. A business will need to recover this cost from its product, hence patent protection is very important in the business world.

What is protected?	new invention
What benefit is there?	monopoly right
How is it obtained?	registration
How long does it last?	20 years from application

17.2 Obtaining a patent

The patent system is a ‘first to file’, not a ‘first to invent’. In other words, the crucial step is the bureaucratic step of filing the application at the Patent Office. You may recall the tale of Elisha Gray, who filed his application for the telephone four hours later than Alexander Graham Bell. Bell therefore was awarded the patent by the US Supreme Court and became famous. Gray has been largely forgotten by history (but he in fact patented a telegraph system and founded the Western Electric Company, so do not feel too sorry for him).

A patent for the UK can be obtained:

(a) by applying to the UK Patent Office;

(b) by applying to the European Patent Office under the European Patent Convention (‘EPC’); or

(c) via an international application under the Patent Co-operation Treaty 1970 ('PCT').

The PCT would be used, for example, if the proprietor of a US or Japanese patent was also seeking to apply for a patent in the UK. It would then be assigned the priority date of the non-UK patent (see **17.4.1**), which is one big advantage of an application through either the PCT or EPC. There are more than 100 countries which are members of the PCT, including most major centres of technology.

The EPC does not provide a true European Patent (but see below for developments on this aspect). It awards a bundle of national patents for countries which are parties to the EPC. Not all EPC patent applications will specify all the countries of the EPC. It is a European system, not an EU one, and encompasses countries that are not EU Member States (eg, Switzerland), though all the EU Member States are individual members of the EPC.

The cost of a European patent (EPC) is high, being about £31,000, as opposed to perhaps £2,000 plus VAT for drafting and filing a UK patent. The headquarters of the European Patent Office (EPO) are in Munich and its search branch is in The Hague.

The PCT 1970 is administered by the WIPO in Geneva. It provides for a single application and preliminary search. The WIPO then sends the application on to national offices for them to decide whether to award a patent for their territory.

There have been discussions at EU level for several years aimed at setting up a Community patent system. The discussions have been dogged by disputes over which languages can be used, and the role of the national patent offices. On 3 March 2003, the Member States finally agreed on the approach to be taken. The key areas are:

(a) the existing framework of the EPC should be utilised;

(b) the EPO would run the Community patent system;

(c) it would grant a patent 'for the territory of the Community';

(d) the EU as such will need to ratify the EPC, though all current members of the EU are individual members of the EPC;

(e) the full patent specification could be filed in any one of English, French or German at the European Patent Office with the claims, only, translated into the other two languages; and

(f) a court to be called 'the Community Intellectual Property Court' will be established by Council Regulation (this proposal has now been overtaken by events and will be some years yet in becoming a reality).

Patents can be categorised as 'product' patents, which claim the end product of a manufacturing process (eg, a new drug, or a better vacuum cleaner), or as 'process' patents, which claim the manufacturing process itself (eg, the method for making 'Gore-Tex' waterproofing for outdoor clothing). It would of course be sensible to try to patent both the product and the method of making it. This would have to be done in separate patents. At present, the Community patent framework is still moving through an extensive consultation stage and there is no immediate sign of a clear timescale for implementation. There are some indications that some major decisions could be taken by 2009, but it is thought that implementation could take six to eight years. The process has now evolved into a plan to create a 'Unified Patent Litigation System'. This may achieve some tangible form by 2013, but at present many stages of consultation and negotiation remain to be dealt with.

17.3 Patentability

An invention will be patentable if it satisfies four conditions. It must:

(a) be new (PA 1977, s (1)(a));

(b) constitute an inventive step (s 1(1)(b));
(c) be capable of industrial application (s 1(1)(c)); and
(d) not be within any of the exclusions in s 1(2).

17.3.1 New

Novelty is judged by reference to the 'state of the art' at the 'priority date' (see **17.4.1**). Under Article 54(2) of the EPC:

> The state of the art shall be held to compromise everything made available to the public by means of a written or oral description, by use, or in any way, before the date of filing of the European patent application.

The information sources utilised would be:

(a) other granted patents or published applications, both UK and relevant foreign jurisdictions;
(b) published descriptions of relevant technology, eg in scientific journals or PhD theses; and
(c) existing products or processes that are in the public domain.

As a matter of practicality, these are matters known about within, or are accessible from, the jurisdiction. Third parties can bring material to the attention of the Patent Office when the application is published (see below).

So this involves a factual investigation (ie, has the invention been thought of before and has it been made public?). The investigation will be carried out by the Patent Office in its initial examination of the patent application. Third parties can also object after publication of the application by the Patent Office. The whole topic of novelty is also highly relevant in patent infringement actions, when the usual defence of the alleged infringer is to challenge the validity of the patent. This means that the topic of the prior art is examined again, but this time in retrospect, perhaps 20 years or more after the original patent application (see **17.8**). A common-form defence to infringement claims is that the patent should never have been granted in the first place and is invalid.

A problem that has arisen more significantly, since the EPC and the European patent system, is the uneasy relationship between the test for novelty and the exclusion, within s 1(2)(a) of the PA 1977, of the patentability of 'discoveries' (see **17.3.4**). Perhaps the greatest gain arising from (particularly) medical or pharmaceutical patents is that surprising and unexpected results can arise from their actual use; great progress can be achieved this way. Sometimes it is achieved by discoveries that radically different dosages bring about different effects. Is such a new development patentable? Is it an excluded 'discovery'? The EPC and the national courts have really taken the bull by the horns on this, and it is clear that many such developments are patentable, despite the prior disclosure of the drugs, etc in earlier patents. In *Actavis Ltd v Merck & Co Inc* [2008] EWCA Civ 444, the Court of Appeal held that novelty could be conferred by new dosage regimes or other forms of administration of a substance (known as 'Swiss-type' claims). This was in line with Article 52(4) of the EPC, and such claims were not simply excluded as discoveries or methods of treatment. Although this was a European patent matter, it is probably in line with the established English court approach, that a claim directed to the practical application of the technical effect of a discovery may well be patentable, as distinct from trying to patent the discovery itself.

The question is one of whether the invention has been 'disclosed' to the public before the date of filing of the application (or the priority date). It will only be treated as having been previously disclosed if there has been an 'enabling disclosure'. If there has been an enabling disclosure, the applicant will fail. As the term suggests, an enabling disclosure means a disclosure that would enable somebody to make the product, or work the process, as the case may be. The question the Patent Office asks is whether, at the priority date, a skilled worker could by observation or analysis reproduce the applicant's invention from the disclosure in question. So, if a newspaper reports that Professor X has created a new process for cloning sheep, this would not be an enabling disclosure. For it to be an enabling disclosure the report would have to describe the process in a way that would allow others to reproduce the invention. (A detailed scientific paper would undoubtedly give such information.)

In *Vericore Ltd v Vetrepharm Ltd and Another* [2003] EWHC 111 (Ch), a patent for a pesticide to attack sea lice infestation in farmed salmon was held to be invalid on the grounds of anticipation and obviousness. In other words, it was not 'new' and there was no 'inventive step' (see **17.3.2**). In particular, the patentee had failed to restrict his claims to synthetic pyrethroids and had impliedly claimed natural pyrethroids as well. The prior art already disclosed the use of natural pyrethroids for treatment of fish, so the patent claims were not 'new' as at the priority date of the patent (see **17.4.1**).

In what circumstances might an enabling disclosure arise? In the case of product patents, disclosure of the product will usually be an enabling disclosure, especially where the invention is a mechanical device. An obvious example is where there is already a product on the market which discloses the invention. For example, if the patent application is for a bagless vacuum cleaner and there is already a bagless vacuum cleaner on the market. This is clearly an enabling disclosure, because anyone taking the vacuum cleaner apart can see how the invention works. Similarly, if a vacuum cleaner embodying the invention had been exhibited at a trade fair then this would be an enabling disclosure (but some trade fairs are specifically excluded under PA 1977). The enabling disclosure could arise from a third-party product where the third party had thought of the idea first (eg, *Windsurfing International Inc v Tabur Marine* [1985] RPC 59). Alternatively, it could be the applicant for the patent marketing/exhibiting his invention before the filing date. This is called 'self-publication'.

In *Synthon BV v Smithklein Beecham plc* [2006] 1 All ER 685, HL, an interesting enabling disclosure was seen where the claimant had disclosed the nature of a chemical compound in an earlier initial patent application, which was not proceeded with. It was enough to have the defendant's later patent declared invalid.

In one case, the invention was a hay-raking machine in which the rake wheels were turned by contact with the ground rather than by an engine (*C Van der Lely NV v Bamfords Ltd* [1963] RPC 61). A photograph of the machine was printed in a newspaper. The question was whether the photograph was clear enough to show how the invention worked. If so, it was an enabling disclosure, and in this case it was held to be so.

In some cases the product may not disclose the invention. This would often be the case in relation to process patents. The end product of the patented process will not necessarily reveal the process itself. A consequence is that it may be possible to disclose the existence of a new product without showing how the process works. An example is *Quantel Ltd v Spaceward Microsystems Ltd* [1990] RPC 83, where the demonstration at an exhibition of a complex computer for creating visual effects on television would not have enabled someone to work out how it operated. Falconer J said in relation to this aspect:

> Demonstration of a prototype of the claimed invention at an exhibition where no-one was allowed near the actual machine and no engineering description was given, although individuals were allowed to use the stylus to draw a picture, could not possibly have been an enabling disclosure so as to anticipate any claim.

17.3.2 Inventive step

An invention might be new but it also needs to be a quantum leap over the existing technology. This second criterion for patentability is that the invention should involve an 'inventive step' (ie, it shows thinking which has not been seen before). The question asked here is whether the invention would be obvious to a somewhat unimaginative person skilled in the art, taking into account the state of the art at the priority date (see the *Vericore* case at **17.3.1**). The person skilled in the art here refers to the 'uninventive technician'. This is someone who is knowledgeable, but lacking that inventive spark. In the *Rockwater* case (see **17.6.3**), Jacobs LJ described the uninventive skilled man thus: 'It is settled that this man, if real, would be very boring – a nerd.'

In using the 'uninventive technician', the following limitation was referred to by Aldous LJ in *Amersham Pharmacia Biotech AB v Amicon Ltd and Others* [2001] EWCA Civ 1042:

> A fiction in patent law is that the notional uninventive skilled man in the art is deemed to have read and assimilated any piece of prior art pleaded by the party attacking the patent claim …
>
> The more distant a prior art document is from the field of technology covered by the patent, the greater the chance that an intelligent but uninventive person skilled in the art will fail to make the jump to the solution found by the patentee.

In other words, the prior art being used in an attempt to strike out a patent has to be highly relevant to the patent in question, rather than just anything, anywhere that just happens to cover the same matter but in a different application or use.

A widely-cited test is in *Windsurfing International Inc v Tabur Marine* [1985] RPC 59. Here, Oliver LJ described the test as having four stages:

(a) the court must identify the inventive concept embodied in the patent;

(b) it must assume the mantle of the normally skilled but unimaginative addressee in the art at the priority date and impute to him what was, at that date, common general knowledge in the art in question;

(c) it must identify what, if any, differences exist between the matters cited as being 'known or used' and the alleged invention; and

(d) it must ask itself whether, viewed without any knowledge of the alleged invention, those differences constituted steps which would have been obvious to the skilled man, or whether they required any degree of invention.

Put simply, what you have to do is, first, identify what the invention adds to the state of the art. If this new bit is not obvious to the uninventive technician then you have an inventive step.

Some useful guidance on this area is to be seen in *Generics (UK) Ltd v Lundbeck A/S* [2008] EWCA Civ 311, where a patentee brought infringement proceedings and the respondent generic drug manufacturer had raised defences of lack of novelty and inventive step. The Court of Appeal held that in ordinary product patents (as distinct from process patents), where the application satisfied the requirements of s 1, the product itself was the invention and the technical contribution to the world art is the product itself, rather than the process by which it was made. This was so, even if that process provided the only inventive step. In other words, the inventive step taken was in being able to make, for the first time, that new product. It did not matter if that manufacturing process had been used to make a thousand different earlier products; the first-instance judge had taken his eyes off the real invention, which was the new drug itself. The patentee's appeal succeeded.

The classic case was the 'sausage machine case' (*Williams v Nye* (1890) 7 RPC 62, CA). A patent was struck out for lack of inventive step because it was simply the combination of two known machines, a mincing machine and a sausage-filling machine. There were also arguments along these lines in the case of *Hickman v Andrews and Others* [1983] RPC 174, concerning infringement of the patent for the Black and Decker 'Workmate', invented by Ron Hickman. Clamping arrangements of this type were known before Ron Hickman invented the Workmate. However, the Court of Appeal upheld the patent.

In *IDA Ltd v Southampton University* [2006] EWCA Civ 145, the question of inventive step also decided the identity of the 'sole deviser' (and ownership) of a type of insect trap. Two fairly similar designs were only distinguishable because one inventor had used a new and different material. That was the inventive step.

Commercial success of the product is taken as being a good indicator of the patent having an inventive step. So is fulfilling a 'long felt want', that is, plugging a gap in the market. In other words, if it was such an obvious step from the existing technology, why had no one done it before the patentee had come up with his invention?

In *Biogen v Medeva* [1997] RPC 1, the House of Lords held:

> Anything inventive done for the first time was the result of adding a new idea to the existing stock of knowledge. If it was the idea of using established techniques to do something which no one had previously thought of doing, the inventive idea would be doing the new thing.

In other words, the inventive step could be a very small one and yet create a valid patent. For the record, the case concerned genetic engineering, and the patent was found to be invalid. The *Biogen* case involved a novel method of producing a vaccine for viral hepatitis B. Genetic engineering and computer programs are the big areas in patent practice at the moment (notwithstanding that computer programs are not patentable, strictly speaking; but see **17.3.4**). The first patent case after *Biogen* to go to the House of Lords was also on genetic engineering (*Kirin-Amgen Inc v Hoechst Marion Roussel Ltd* [2002] EWCA Civ 1096, [2003] RPC 3; see **17.6.3**).

The question of inventive step is, of course, a question of fact in each case, and if there is no inventive step, the application will fail for 'obviousness' (see *Pozzoli SpA v BDMO SA* [2007] EWCA Civ 588 – an application for a storage device for CDs which failed for obviousness). The judge in the *Generics (UK) Ltd* case, mentioned above, had been mistaken in considering the manufacture process as 'obvious'. He had ignored the point that an entirely new product was being made; it was not a 'process' patent.

17.3.3 Industrial application

It must be possible to make the product/carry out the process. Patents are not about abstract ideas. The invention must be able to be put into practice. In effect, this requirement is taken care of by the exclusions in PA 1977, s 1(2) and (3) (see **17.3.4**). There is a temptation to avoid disclosing too much detail about the invention, which may cause objections based upon insufficiency, as in *Rex v Arkwright* (1785) 1 WPC 64. There may also be objections that the device cannot be built or made to work at all. In *Duckett v Patent Office* [2005] EWHC 3140 (Pat), a perpetual motion device was rejected because its energy principle was contrary to all accepted views of physics. Its mechanical arrangement, linking a generator with a battery, failed for obviousness.

The desire to avoid too much information being disclosed at the early stage of a patent application often can cause problems of revocation applications, both on insufficiency (s 72(1)(c)), and on grounds of 'added material', (s 72(1)(d)). The latter happens where the matter disclosed in the specification extends beyond that disclosed in the filed application for the patent, ie 'drip-feeding' the information to the registry. That led to a confirmation by the Court of Appeal that a European patent should be revoked in *European Central Bank v Document Security Systems Inc* [2008] EWCA Civ 192 (see **17.6.3**).

17.3.4 Exclusions

The exclusions are listed in s 1(2) and (3) of the 1977 Act:

> (2) It is hereby declared that the following (among other things) are not inventions for the purposes of this Act, that is to say, anything which consists of—

(a) a discovery, scientific theory or mathematical method;

(b) a literary, dramatic, musical or artistic work or any other aesthetic creation whatsoever;

(c) a scheme, rule or method for performing a mental act, playing a game or doing business, or a program for a computer;

(d) the presentation of information;

but the foregoing provision shall prevent anything from being treated as an invention for the purposes of this Act only to the extent that a patent or application for a patent relates to that thing as such.

(3) A patent shall not be granted for an invention the commercial exploitation of which would be contrary to public policy or morality.

Section 1(2)(a) deals with discoveries of natural phenomena. These have not been invented by any human, so are not patentable. The paragraph also excludes methods of doing things. In *Citibank NA v Comptroller-General of Patents* (ChD, 9 June 2006), a computerised method for checking, statistically, the accuracy of data inputted into systems was not excluded as a 'business method' within s 1(2)(c). It was, however, excluded as a 'mathematical method' by s 1(2)(a). The rationale for excluding methodology is to prevent attempts at monopolising the thinking process itself.

Section 1(2)(b) deals with aesthetic creations which are protected by another IP right, that is copyright (see **Chapter 14**).

Section 1(2)(c) deals with mental acts, as explained above. How would you know if someone else was performing the mental act in question? Obviously, you could not, so making such matters patentable would be impractical as well as undesirable.

The borderline between a non-patentable method and a patentable technical contribution to the known art is hard to discern. In *Aerotel Ltd v Telco Holdings Ltd; Macrossan's Patent Application (No 0314464.9)* [2006] EWCA Civ 1371, in a conjoined appeal, the Court held that an automated method of assembling documents required to incorporate a company was excluded methodology. By contrast, the other appeal was successful because it involved a new physical combination of hardware items. That comprised a technical contribution and was patentable. It brought about the effect of making a computer run at a higher speed.

Computer programs are also in theory excluded (s 1(2)(c). However, this does not actually mean that computer programs can never be patented. The tendency in recent years has been to grant patents to more and more computer programs. Very broadly, the test is whether the program has a 'technical effect', that is, has it a practical application? One example is *Vicom's Application* [1987] OJ EPO 14, where a program for doing computer-aided design (CAD) of engineering products was held to be patentable. This case has greatly influenced the approach to computer program patents in both European and UK applications. This is a very complex area, but it might be summarised by saying that, for a computer program to form part of a patent, it must bring about some effect or consequence that, itself, as distinct from the computer program, is new and shows an inventive step. This was applied to exclude *Macrossan's Patent Application*, referred to above.

The approach of the EPO has been more inclined toward granting computer patents since its decisions in two cases – *IBM/Computer Programs* (Case T-935/97) [1999] EPOR 301 and *IBM/Computer Programs* (Case T-1173/97) [1999] EPOR 219. The EPO technical board of appeal held that the 'technical effect' requirement simply meant that to be patentable, the application had to go beyond the mere routine operation of a computer.

As matters presently stand, the UK Patent Office considers that the correct and definitive approach has been expressed by the Court of Appeal in the *Aerotel Ltd/Macrossan* appeals case discussed above, because the Court considered and evaluated all relevant UK and EPO authorities. The Court took the view that the EPO practice to exclusions had not stabilised sufficiently to be a firm guide in itself. Jacob LJ, after considering the decisions of the EPO boards of appeal, had suggested a four-step approach to dealing with the exclusions within s 1(2). The steps are:

(a) properly construe the claim;

(b) identify the actual contribution to the known art;

(c) ask whether it falls solely within the excluded subject matter (if it does, that would exclude the application);

(d) check whether the actual or alleged contribution is actually technical in nature (if it is not, that would exclude it).

The Patent Office considers this to replace all previous tests applied to exclusion issues under s 1(2); it has been used in many applications since and seems to work well. See *Kapur v Comptroller General of Patents Designs and Trade Marks* [2008] EWHC 649 (Pat) and *Symbian Ltd v Comptroller General of Patents* [2008] EWHC 518 (Pat).

Section 1(2)(d) deals with presentation of information. This could not constitute an 'invention' in itself, but a new mechanism or process of presentation could be patented.

Genetic engineering inventions are patentable, and indeed are a major area of activity for patent agents and lawyers (see **17.3.2**). Also, producing new varieties of plants is protectable under the Plant Varieties Act 1997, which is outside the scope of this book. In the US case on gene engineering (*Diamond v Chakrabarty* 65 Law Ed (2d) 144 (1980)), the Supreme Court held that 'anything under the sun', apart from a human being, should be regarded as patentable. Directive 98/44/EC on legal protection of biotechnological inventions led to changes to the PA 1977, by way of the Patent Regulations 2000 (SI 2000/2037), to take account of technical progress in this field.

17.4 The patent specification

The documents required for filing an application are a request for grant and the patent specification. A request for grant is what it says it is. The specification contains an abstract, the description and the claims. The abstract is a summary which is used for reference purposes. The description must disclose the invention sufficiently for it to be performed by a skilled person. The description and the claims must be a consistent match for each other. A case needs to be shown for the grant of a patent, in particular that there has been an inventive step above and beyond the existing technology (see the *Generics (UK)* case at **17.3.2**). The description also needs to provide support for the claims, especially the broadest ones. (Strictly speaking, the 'specification' is the term used for the descriptive part of the application or granted patent, but in common parlance amongst IP lawyers the term 'patent specification' is used to describe the whole document.)

A patent specification is a complex technical and legal document. A patent agent normally drafts it. This is someone with a scientific or engineering qualification, depending on the particular field they are working in. The costs of drafting a specification and dealing with the initial filing of the application are about £2,000 plus VAT. If there are queries from the patent examiner in the Patent Office then this will increase that cost.

If the patent is granted then it is the claims that define the scope of the monopoly granted to the inventor. The analogy of a fence is sometimes used. The idea is that the claims form a fence that surrounds the area which the inventor claims as his own. For someone to be liable for patent infringement, it is enough to infringe one claim in the patent specification (ie, to have crossed the fence in only one place).

In drafting the claims, the aim is to include all possible alternatives, whilst excluding those that already exist or are obvious. If an alternative is omitted, a competitor could claim that to be their own invention, or could use the gap to exploit the technology themselves. On the other hand, if too much is said in the claims, one danger is that improvements in the technology may not be patentable when they arise in the future. The reason is that a patent specification itself becomes part of the state of the art once it is published, so a new application would have to show that it has achieved an inventive step over the previous patent.

The first claim will be the widest. It will state the invention claimed in fairly general terms. Subsequent claims refine the first claim. Each claim usually narrows the invention down a bit. The final claims usually describe the commercial product that is going to be on the market.

The idea is that the wider the area of technology which is claimed, the further away the patent owner can keep rival inventors. In patent litigation, an inevitable area of dispute is that some of the patent claims are too wide and need to be narrowed, or struck out, as being unjustifiable.

The invention must be described in enough detail to allow a person with the requisite skills to carry out the invention. So, if the patent is for interleaving chocolate and ice-cream, the specification must describe the process in sufficient detail to allow a skilled ice cream maker to set up the process. See the cases on 'sufficiency' at **17.3.3** and also *Schering-Plough Ltd v Norbrook Laboratories Ltd* [2005] EWHC 2532 (Pat), where a patent was revoked because much more research was needed to make the invention work. A patent specification which is refused on this ground is said to lack 'sufficiency'. In *European Central Bank v Document Security Systems Inc* [2008] EWCA Civ 192, a European patent for producing security documents, such as shares or banknotes, that were copy-proof, was held to be invalid. It was only possible to work the invention by adding material not disclosed by the original application.

You should be aware of the difference between this and manufacturing 'know-how'. Manufacturing know-how is the extra tricks of the trade that help you make the process run with greatest efficiency. For example, it might be the speed of the production line to get the most cost-effective results, how much air to blow into the ice-cream, or the temperature at which the room should be maintained. So, even though the patent specification describes the basic invention, the know-how is often also needed for a licensee because it makes it economically feasible to set up and run the process.

17.4.1 The priority date

The 'first to file' basis of the patent system increases the pressure to be the first person to reach the Patent Office with an application.

Normally, the application or 'filing' date is the patent's priority date. The priority date is the date on which we judge whether the invention is new. The usual reason for the priority date being earlier than the date the papers were filed is that the proprietor is claiming priority from an earlier overseas patent under one of the international conventions (see **17.2**). (An alternative reason, which is much less common, is that PA 1977, s 15 allows the inventor to file an 'outline application' at an early stage in order to secure an early priority date. The outline application will be less detailed than a full application. A full application must be filed within 12 months.)

17.4.2 Timescale

The Patent Office takes about 18 months to do the initial examination. It is then published as an application and is on the public register (ie, the invention can no longer be kept secret). Third parties then have the opportunity to object to the grant of the patent. If there are no major problems then the patent will be granted six months or so after publication, that is two years after filing the papers. This period counts as part of the 20-year period for the life of the patent. If there is a major problem that delays grant of the patent, the useful life of the patent once granted could be severely reduced. However, the maximum period between publication and grant of the patent is now 36 months. In addition, there can be other regulatory problems which reduce the useful life of the patent, such as obtaining permission to market a new pharmaceutical product, or plant protection product. There are EU provisions which allow for an extension of up to five years to the life of a pharmaceutical patent (Regulation 1768/92), or to the life of a patent for a plant protection product (Regulation 1610/96). These are intended to compensate for the regulatory delays.

17.5 Who is entitled to grant of a patent?

The general rule is that the inventor is the first person entitled (s 7(2)). The inventor is the person who devised the invention. This can be more complicated than it seems, for example if there are multiple parties involved (eg, *Henry Bros (Magherafelt) Ltd v Ministry of Defence* [1999] RPC 442, where the Court of Appeal held that the test was to determine who had contributed to the main concept of the invention). This was applied in *IDA Ltd v Southampton University* [2006] EWCA Civ 145 (see **17.3.2**).

The principle of first entitlement resting with the inventor has recently been confirmed in *Rhone-Poulenc Rorer International Holdings Inc v Yeda Research and Development Co Ltd* [2007] UKHL 43.

17.5.1 Employees

Under PA 1977, s 39(1), if the inventor is an employee, the patent will belong to the employer if the invention is made in the course of the employee's normal duties, provided an invention might reasonably be expected to result from his duties. This is also the outcome if he owes the employer a special duty (eg, a director's duty to his company). In *Greater Glasgow Health Board's Application* [1996] RPC 207, it was held that a hospital doctor who had invented a new device for examining eyes owned the invention himself. He was employed to treat patients, not to invent, so the invention did not belong to his employer.

The rule is slightly different from the rule for ownership of copyright (see **14.2.5**) but the result is similar. Copyright also does not have any equivalent of the provision relating to employees with a special duty (PA 1977, s 39(1)(b)).

Another important difference is that PA 1977, s 42 does not allow contracting out of these provisions. With copyright there is nothing to stop the employer from putting a provision in the contract of employment that all copyright relevant to the employer's business will belong to the employer. With patents, any such provision would be void. However, there is nothing to stop the employer drafting the job description to emphasise that the employee is employed to make inventions. Also, the employer is still entitled to enforce contractual or common law confidentiality requirements (s 42(3)).

17.5.2 Compensation for employee inventors

Under PA 1977, s 40, an employee who invents something may be entitled to compensation where the patent belongs to the employer. This is the case if:

(a) having regard among other things to the size and nature of the employer's undertaking, the invention or the patent for it (or the combination of both) is of outstanding benefit to the employer; and

(b) it is just that compensation is awarded.

The statutory test is awkward to apply in practice because the criterion is the benefit of the patent or the invention, not the benefit the product which was sold in the marketplace. In the case of *Garrison's Patent* [1997] CIPA 297, an invention which provided 2%–3% of the turnover of a small company was held not to be of outstanding benefit, and therefore no compensation was awarded.

In determining the amount of compensation, s 41 gives guidance, including factors listed in s 41(3) (eg, the nature of the employee's duties and the amount of his remuneration).

Disputes of this type are often settled, and recorded cases are rare (but see **17.10**).

17.6 Infringement

17.6.1 Definition of infringment

Infringement arises where a third party engages in the acts prohibited under PA 1977, s 60. As patents are national rights, to infringe a UK patent the prohibited acts have to occur within the UK:

> **60 Meaning of infringement**
>
> (1) Subject to the provisions of this section, a person infringes a patent for an invention if, but only if, while the patent is in force, he does any of the following things in the United Kingdom in relation to the invention without the consent of the proprietor of the patent, that is to say—
>
> (a) where the invention is a product, he makes, disposes of, offers to dispose of, uses or imports the product or keeps it whether for disposal or otherwise;
>
> (b) where the invention is a process, he uses the process or he offers it for use in the United Kingdom when he knows, or it is obvious to a reasonable person in the circumstances, that its use there without the consent of the proprietor would be an infringement of the patent;
>
> (c) where the invention is a process, he disposes of, offers to dispose of, uses or imports any product obtained directly by means of that process or keeps any such product whether for disposal or otherwise.

You should note the distinction between infringing acts for a product patent and for a process patent; s 60(1)(b) requires actual or imputed knowledge of infringement, whereas s 60(1)(a) and (c) do not. However, even with a process patent, dealing with the products of that process will be infringement even though the products themselves are not patented.

Section 60(2) makes it an offence to supply or offer to supply 'any means … for putting the invention into effect'. So, in *Lacroix Duarib SA v Kwikform (UK) Ltd* [1998] FSR 493, the supply of a kit of parts would have infringed the claims in a patent for the completed article.

17.6.2 How do you judge if infringement has occurred?

The first thing to establish is whether the allegedly infringing product or process comes within one of the claims in the patent specification. That is, has the third party crossed the 'fence line' which is constituted by the claims and stepped on to the patentee's monopoly? It is enough for patent infringement if one of the patent claims is infringed.

Sometimes a supposed infringement is not what it seems to be. In *Novartis AG v Ivax Pharmaceuticals UK Ltd* [2007] EWCA Civ 971, the patentee had a patent for making a 'microemulsion' of a drug which was very resistant to solution in water. The defendant was not an infringer when it managed to achieve the same effect by dispersing tiny particles of the drug in a liquid which was not a microemulsion (ie there was no 'oil in water' carrier).

Patent specifications are drafted with conflicts in mind. Even in the context of patent licensing, the specification really becomes relevant only when the collaboration starts to fall apart.

The first claim is often the most important as it will be the broadest. So why bother with the other claims that narrow this down? The reason is that when you sue somebody for patent infringement, they will invariably counterclaim by saying that the patent is invalid. The patentee then has to defend his claims, particularly in relation to novelty and inventive step (see **17.3**). (The 'infringer' will go digging round in the prior art to try to find reasons why the patent should never have been granted in the first place.) The broader the claim, the more difficult it is to defend. So that is why you have the narrower claims too. If claim 1 falls by the wayside, you may still be able to defend one of the later claims. It is only necessary to show infringement of one claim to succeed against the infringer.

17.6.3 Interpreting the claims in the patent specification

How does the court approach the interpretation of the claims? The court takes a 'middle road' between interpreting the claims strictly, ie literally, and taking into account what the patentee must have intended. Although the courts are said to be taking the 'purposive' approach from *Catnic Components Ltd and Another v Hill & Smith Ltd* [1982] RPC 183, they tend to be a lot less generous to patentees than this might suggest. In effect, the courts tend to hold the view that if the patentee meant to cover a particular variation then he should have claimed it expressly. (It should be remembered that *Catnic* was decided under the PA 1949. It concerned a patent for steel lintels for use above doors and windows. The patent claimed a right angle in the cross-sectional shape of the lintel. The defendant's lintel was 4–5 degrees away from a right angle, but was still held to infringe.)

Improver Corporation and Others v Remington Consumer Products Ltd and Others [1990] FSR 181 was a case which reformulated the test. This was the case about the 'Epilady' device for removing hair. Here, the patented device featured a rotating spring mechanism. The defendant's device performed the same task, but a rubber tube mechanism with slits removed the hairs.

Hoffmann J restated the issues as two of fact and one of construction:

(a) Does the variant have a material effect upon the way the invention works? If so, the variant is outside the claim. If not . . .

(b) Would this (ie, that the variant had no material effect) have been obvious at the date of publication of the patent to a reader skilled in the art? If not, the variant is outside the claim. If so . . .

(c) Would the reader skilled in the art nevertheless have understood from the language of the claim that the patentee intended that strict compliance with the primary meaning was an essential requirement of the invention? If so, the variant is outside the claim.

There was held to be no infringement. It is regarded as an example of poor drafting by the patent agent, who apparently did not draft the first claim widely enough to catch the rubber tube variation but restricted it to a helical spring. This is a good illustration of how patent infringement litigation hinges on the precise wording of the claims in the patent specification (see also *Vericore* at **17.3.1**).

The distinctions made can be very fine indeed. In *Archibald Kenrick & Sons Ltd v Laird Security Hardware Ltd* [2006] EWHC 1675 (Ch), an amended claim showing the range and direction of movement of an internal bolt for sliding window panels was upheld. It had a material effect on how the system worked.

It is in the extension of the *Improver* questions away from the area of mechanical devices to chemical compounds that greatest difficulties have arisen (eg, *Pharmacia Corporation and Others v Merck & Co Inc and Another* [2001] EWCA Civ 1610). The Court of Appeal has re-affirmed the *Improver* approach in *Wheatley v Drillsafe Ltd* [2001] RPC 133, though the tests are now referred to as the 'Protocol questions', after the Protocol on the interpretation of Article 69 of the European Patent Convention (see **17.2**). This corresponds to PA 1977, s 125(1), on how to interpret the word 'invention'. In *Kirin-Amgen Inc v Hoechst Marion Roussel Ltd* [2004] UKHL 46, a case concerning genetic engineering, Lord Hoffmann said that it was important to distinguish between two matters. On the one hand, there were the guidelines set out in *Improver Corp* for deciding whether or not equivalent technology fell within the scope of the relevant patent claims. On the other hand, there was the principle of purposive construction established by *Catnic*. *Catnic* was expressed to be the bedrock of patent construction. It was important that the patentee be given the full extent, but no more than that, of the monopoly which the person skilled in the art would think he was intending to claim in the patent specification.

This question, of the precise range of monopoly claimed by the patentee, came up in the *Novartis AG* case mentioned in **17.6.2**. In *M-Systems Flash Disk Pioneers Ltd v Trek 2000 International Ltd* [2008] EWHC 102 (Pat), Kitchin J confirmed that the correct approach to interpretation of a patent specification is that it is to be read, as a whole, through the eyes of a skilled person, giving the words a purposive construction. See this case at **17.6.4** on revocation.

On the construction of the claims generally, in *Dyson Appliances Ltd v Hoover* [2001] EWCA Civ 1440, [2002] RPC 42, the Court of Appeal said that this was a matter for the judge. Evidence as to the factual situation was helpful, especially to explain the technology, but it was not acceptable to have expert witnesses who gave their own interpretation of the meaning of the claims.

It is also worth noting the words of the Court of Appeal in *Scanvaegt International AS v Pelcombe Ltd* [1998] FSR 786:

> lack of clarity … can result in the patentee being unable to establish infringement. If you cannot define the invention claimed, you cannot conclude that it is being used.

As an illustration of the detail into which patent litigation goes, in the case of *Rockwater v Technip France SA* [2004] EWCA 381 the dispute hinged on the meaning of the words 'last means for guiding the flexible conduit' in claim 3 of the patent in question. It was held that the defendant's ship did infringe the words in claim 3, and therefore the patent. (The patent concerned technology for laying pipes at sea.)

17.6.4 Amendments to the specification, invalidity and revocation

There is a very close connection between a patentee claiming infringement and the possibility of counterclaims that the patent is invalid for some reason and should be revoked. If the patent is invalid, it should not have been granted, and consequently there cannot have been an infringement. It does not follow that revocation proceedings cannot take place without infringement claims, but the two claims often go together; also, the Comptroller of Patents can revoke a patent on his own initiative, under s 73.

The only grounds for revocation are found s 72(1) and are:

(a) the invention is not a patentable invention (failure to comply with ss 1–4);

(b) the patent was granted to a person who was not entitled to that patent (failure to comply with s 7);

(c) the specification of the patent did not disclose the invention clearly enough and completely enough for it to be performed by a person skilled in the art (insufficiency);

(d) the matter disclosed in the specification extends beyond that disclosed in the patent application as filed ('added matter', forbidden by s 76);

(e) the protection conferred by the patent has been extended by an amendment which should not have been allowed (also forbidden by s 76).

These are the only grounds on which the validity of a patent may be 'put in issue' (s 74(3)), and the only proceedings in which validity can be raised are limited by s 74(1). It is not possible, for example, simply to seek only a declaration as to the validity or invalidity of a patent (s 74(2)). Validity can be put in issue in infringement cases (by way of defence), in proceedings for groundless threats of infringement or declarations of non-infringement, in revocation proceedings or in disputes as to Crown use under s 58. This greatly reduces the possibilities for unjustified claims or proceedings.

In infringement or revocation proceedings where validity is in issue, there is a limited power, under s 75, to allow the proprietor of the patent to amend the specification to try to bring the patent to a state of validity. In no circumstances can an amendment be permitted that results in the specification disclosing added matter, or which extends the protection conferred by the patent (s 76(3)). Many recent cases have involved disputes about material added on amendments (usually to try to overcome 'inventive step' or 'sufficency' problems), and some guidance can be found in the Court of Appeal cases of *Vector Corp v Glatt Air Techniques Ltd* [2007] EWCA Civ 805 and *European Central Bank v Document Security Systems Inc* [2008] EWCA Civ 192. The *M-Systems Flash Disk Pioneers* case, discussed at **17.6.3**, also contained an issue on this point and proposed amendments were held to be inadmissible.

17.7 Infringers

The acts listed in s 60 (see **17.6.1**) would cover those making a product, using a process or disposing of the product of a process. Section 60 covers disposing and keeping, so would cover all the parties in a supply chain, even including the ultimate customer. Do not forget that the acts have to take place in the UK for there to be infringement of a UK patent. In the case of *Stena Rederi Aktiebolag and Another v Irish Ferries Ltd* [2002] EWHC 737 (Ch), [2002] RPC 990; [2003] EWCA Civ 66, [2003] RPC 36, the infringing article, a high-speed passenger ship, came into UK waters for periods of only three hours at a time. The defendants were able to use the provisions in PA 1977, s 60(5)(d), which give exemptions for temporary entry into the UK of ships and aircraft.

17.8 Defences

The first possible defence is that the patentee has consented to the use by granting a licence.

The chief line of defence is an attack on the validity of the patent, in part or in total, as described at **17.6.4**. If the patent can be proved to be invalid, or at least some claims can be struck out, then the defendant could not be liable for having infringed an invalid claim.

Patent litigation can, however, become extremely complex and costly, and a very good example of this can be seen in *Edwards Lifesciences AG v Cook Biotech Incorporated* [2009] EWHC 1304 (Pat), and the subsequent costs hearing at [2009] EWHC 1443. This case illustrates how revocation proceedings and infringement claims interact, often at great expense to the parties, and also shows how easy it is for litigation to get somewhat out of control. Edwards ('E') initially sought revocation of a patent registered to Cook ('C'). C counterclaimed that E had infringed its patent by manufacturing a bio-prosthetic, implantable heart valve (C did not manufacture such things). A preliminary issue was ordered to be tried as to whether a product description, which accompanied the sold valves, could properly be described as confidential. The reason for this was that E was being asked to disclose this material for the purposes of the litigation to independent experts acting for C. The court gave its directions on this matter at [2008] All ER (D) 368 (Jul), broadly protecting the material. During the trial of the claim and counterclaim, C originally maintained that all 34 of its claims made in respect of the invention had independent validity; on being required to serve the details of these by the court, the number was reduced to 25. Eventually, just nine claims were considered by the court. The consequence of this was to greatly increase the costs incurred by E.

During the trial, C persisted in seeking disclosure of many documents, which the court subsequently held were irrelevant to the issues, further increasing the legal costs incurred by E. Subsequently, it was held that much of this disclosure was neither necessary nor proportionate. E won on its main points, that C's patent was not valid and that therefore E could not have infringed it, so C's counterclaim failed. Nevertheless, E was held to have failed on a number of the points that it had made, or had withdrawn them. The judge in the costs hearing ordered a reduction of 20% in the costs awarded to E, to reflect those points argued unsuccessfully by E.

A major use for trainees in an IP department is to have them spend weeks in the bowels of the libraries looking for documents on the topic in question which have been date stamped with a date earlier than the priority date. The patentee is fixed with such knowledge in any language, provided the document is within the jurisdiction. The documents may help to strike out some or all of the claims of the patent.

Another defence is that the alleged infringer is in fact a co-owner of the patent, and therefore is entitled to work the patent himself (PA 1977, s 36).

The use in question could be the subject of an implied licence under the patent (eg, *Betts v Wilmott* (1871) 6 Ch App 239). Likewise, repair of a patented product is not infringement of the patent. However, reconditioning the patented article may be regarded as going too far and be an infringing act (*Sirdar Rubber v Wallington, Weston & Co* (1907) 24 RPC 539).

Defences may be raised, relying on EC rules for free movement of goods. Goods sold on other markets by the patentee or its licensees may be parallel imported into the UK from other EU Member States, under Articles 28 and 30 of the Treaty of Amsterdam. The cases that arise usually concern pharmaceuticals, which are high value items and often have their price regulated by national governments (eg, *Centrafarm BV and Adrian de Peijper v Sterling Drug Inc* (Case 15/74) [1974] ECR 1147). The exercise of patent rights was held to be incompatible with the free movement of goods in that case. (Centrafarm bought a Sterling product in the UK and re-sold it in The Netherlands for twice the UK price.) In such circumstances, the patentee's rights are said to be exhausted. See generally **22.5** and **22.6**.

The PA 1977 provides for two general defences in s 60(5):

> An act which, apart from this subsection, would constitute an infringement of a patent for an invention shall not do so if—
>
> (a) it is done privately and for purposes which are not commercial;
>
> (b) it is done for experimental purposes relating to the subject matter of the invention.

The activities in s 60(5) are regarded as being for the public good, and therefore the patent system should not be a restraint. The type of activities covered include research by scientists in universities and research institutes.

Section 64 allows a defence of prior use where the defendant was using the relevant technology before the priority date. In practice, this is a very limited defence, as you cannot expand your use, only go on using the process or product exactly as you did before the priority date.

17.9 Remedies

Under s 61, the claimant may seek:

(a) an injunction restraining the defendant;

(b) an order for delivery up or destruction of the offending goods;

(c) damages;

(d) an account of profits (but not as well as damages); or

(e) a declaration that the patent is valid and has been infringed by the defendant.

Section 62 states that damages may not be awarded against an innocent infringer. See s 62(1) for the rules on notice to persons who claim innocent infringement.

Section 72 allows the court or the Patent Office to revoke a patent on the grounds of failing to meet the criteria for patentability in s 1(1). Section 75 allows for the amendment of patents under the control of the court or the Patent Office (see **17.6.4**).

You need to beware of a threats action under PA 1977, s 70. This is where the patentee can be held liable for a threat to sue someone for patent infringement if the threat turns out to be unjustified. The person threatened can sue for a declaration (that the threats are not justifiable), injunction and damages. An example of such an action is *Cintec International v Parkes* [2003] EWHC 2328. There, the patent proprietor alleged, without justification, that C's process infringed P's patents for water-filled bags for suppressing the effects of explosions. C was granted an order restraining P. Consequently, initial letters in patent disputes are very restrained! There is also a similar provision in relation to various IP rights (see **13.12**, **16.2.10** and **16.3.6**).

Chapter 18
Basics of the Law of Confidential Information

18.1	Introduction to the law of confidential information	263
18.2	The elements of confidentiality	264
18.3	Remedies and their availability	266
18.4	A right of privacy and the Human Rights Act 1998?	268

18.1 Introduction to the law of confidential information

Basically, the law will uphold a person's obligation to keep a secret, in certain circumstances. The law of confidence is not an IP right in a pure sense but is often classified with some of the mainstream rights. For example, maintaining confidentiality before submitting a patent application is vital to avoid destruction of the invention's novelty.

On the other hand, the law here can give protection in its own right. For example, the owner of confidential information relating to a product or process may decide to keep this 'know-how' secret, rather than formalise matters by seeking patent protection. The benefit of this is that a well-guarded secret may be protected indefinitely, rather than simply for the limited period afforded to IP rights (eg, 20 years for patents).

Case law rather than statute has governed and shaped the law of confidence and, as you would expect, the vast majority of cases relate to circumstances where express obligations of confidence are lacking and implied duties of confidentiality have to be considered. It is, however, important to remember that express obligations can (and often should) be imposed (eg, on key employees or independent contractors). See, for example, *Attorney-General v Observer Ltd and Others; Attorney-General v Times Newspapers Ltd and Another* [1990] AC 109, which concerned the book *Spycatcher* written by Peter Wright, an ex-employee of the security services. However, even an express confidentiality agreement may not be upheld by the court. For example, in *London Regional Transport v Mayor of London* [2003] EMLR 4, the Court of Appeal upheld the decision not to prevent publication of the report in question, as publication was held to be in the public interest. See *Norbrook Laboratories (GB) Ltd v Adair* [2008] EWHC 978 (QB) for an interesting case on protection of confidential information by the use of restrictive covenants in an employment contract.

So, what is the legal basis for giving such valuable protection? The principle arises from the equitable jurisdiction of the court to restrain unconscionable behaviour, where such behaviour may result in damage to a person. An early example is seen in the well-known case of *Prince Albert v Strange* (1849) 1 Mac & G 25, where an attempt was made by unscrupulous persons to show to the public some etchings, which were committed to a printer for the private purposes of Queen Victoria and the Prince Consort. This case set an early precedent by showing a readiness to injunct third-party recipients of confidential information or matter, within the court's discretion. The courts have been ready, ever since, to entertain such proceedings and to give a remedy, in appropriate cases.

Another factor that has supervened upon this area has been the way in which the European Convention on Human Rights has required English courts, via the Human Rights Act 1998, to deal with the Convention rights of respect for private life and freedom of expression (Articles 8 and 10). These matters have certainly made a subtle alteration to the way in which such applications to the court are dealt with, and pleaded, in the first place, but this chapter will attempt to give an overview of the way in which the courts deal with purely commercial-type disputes about confidentiality, rather than extending to a broad survey of the more rights-based claims (see **18.4** for these matters). The fairly consistent approach of the English courts in commercial/business confidence matters is somewhat easier to grasp and to explain than the more contentious interplay between individual rights and freedoms shown in the HRA 1998 claims.

The whole area has been given considerable publicity, in recent times, by the Michael Douglas and Catherine Zeta-Jones wedding photographs litigation, which raised the interesting point of whether there could be an analogous type of confidential material in photographs, intended for mass publication, but through only one intended publicity outlet (see **18.4** and *Douglas and Others v Hello! Ltd and Others (No 3)* [2007] 2 WLR 920). A person obtained surreptitiously taken photographs, knowing that this was in breach of all rules concerning the occasion. Aspects of this case will be mentioned at points where some of the basic elements of confidentiality are discussed below.

What is protected?	secret information
What benefit is there?	protects against unauthorised disclosure
How is it obtained?	arises automatically (no registration)
How long does it last?	indefinitely

18.2 The elements of confidentiality

The case of *De Maudsley v Palumbo and Others* [1996] FSR 447 demonstrates the difficulties faced by a claimant where no express obligation of confidentiality has been imposed. The facts related to the Ministry of Sound, the celebrated nightclub in Southeast London. The case report states:

> At a supper party held on November 1, 1989 between the plaintiff, the first defendant and the latter's girlfriend, the plaintiff communicated to the first defendant his idea for a night club which he claimed had five novel features:
>
> (1) it would be legally open all night long;
>
> (2) of large size with decor of a 'high tech industrial' warehouse style;
>
> (3) it would have separate areas for dancing, resting and socialising, and a VIP lounge;
>
> (4) an enclosed dance area of acoustic design ensuring excellent sound quality, light and atmosphere, with no leakage of those elements beyond its environment; and
>
> (5) it would employ top disc jockeys from the United Kingdom and around the world.

In the autumn of 1991 the defendants opened a nightclub called the Ministry of Sound, featuring some but not all of the plaintiff's ideas. The plaintiff was excluded from the project and subsequently sued for (inter alia) breach of confidence.

The judge (Knox J) relied on the three-point test from *Coco v AN Clark (Engineers) Ltd* [1969] RPC 41:

(a) Did the information have the necessary quality of confidence about it?

(b) Was the information imparted in circumstances importing an obligation of confidence?

(c) Was there any unauthorised use of the information?

18.2.1 Did the information have the necessary quality of confidence about it?

In the *De Maudsley* case, Knox J stated:

> Before the status of confidential information can be achieved by a concept or an idea, it is necessary to have gone far beyond identifying a desirable goal. A considerable degree of preliminary development of a definite product needs to be shown.

He found that the plaintiff's ideas were too vague to constitute confidential information.

He also found that, in order to merit protection, the idea must contain some element of originality. He took each element of the plaintiff's proposal, and criticised them for lack of novelty and/or vagueness.

Knox J accepted Hirst J's analysis in *Fraser and Others v Thames Television Ltd and Others* [1984] 1 QB 44 of the requirements for a literary, creative or entertainment idea to be protected as confidential information. This case concerned use of the law of confidential information to protect an idea for a television series about a female pop group. (Copyright will not protect a mere idea in these circumstances, see *Green v Broadcasting Corporation of New Zealand* [1989] 2 All ER 1086, which concerned the format for a game show.)

Hirst J said that the idea must:

(a) contain some element of originality;

(b) be clearly identifiable (as an idea of the confider);

(c) be of potential commercial attractiveness; and

(d) be sufficiently well developed to be capable of actual realisation.

In the *Douglas* case (see **18.1**), the highly valuable photographic rights to the wedding, and the resulting photographs, were held to be proper matters in which a quality of confidence would arise. This would extend to the wedding occasion itself having an obligation of confidence, so far as photography was concerned. All guests were under strict obligation in this respect, and this was enforced by security staff.

18.2.2 Was the information imparted in circumstances importing an obligation of confidence?

The problem here for the plaintiff in *De Maudsley* was that the relevant occasion on which he had imparted the information was a social one, not a business context. The plaintiff acknowledged in his evidence that he had deliberately refrained from explaining that the information was confidential, 'because [he] did not want to blow the deal there and then'. Lastly, there was no accepted trade practice in this area to substantiate the plaintiff's claim.

Failure to make confidentiality clear also caused the claimant's case to fail in *Shaw v API Group plc* (QBD District Registry (Manchester)), 10 April 2008, WL.

See *Vitof Ltd v Altoft* [2006] EWHC 1678, where computer source code, created in contemplation of the incorporation of a company which would exploit the code commercially, was held to have been imparted under an obligation of confidence.

This requirement can also extend to persons who obtain information in circumstances where they know or have reason to believe that they should not have it. This can be seen in cases such as the *Douglas* case and *Prince Albert v Strange* (see **18.1**). In the case of the photographer at the Douglas wedding, he knew at all times that what he was doing was a serious breach of trust.

In *Northern Rock plc v Financial Times Ltd* [2007] EWHC 2677 (QB), a highly confidential memorandum came into the hands of various publishing organisations. Financial Times Ltd published the whole memorandum, but others published only extracts. Northern Rock contended that the memorandum had been leaked by an employee in breach of his or her contract. An injunction was granted to prevent further publication of the full memorandum but not of the small, extracted parts that had already been widely circulated. There was detailed commercial information in the full document, and the public interest lay in enforcing the duties of confidence in the report.

employee = fiduciary duty
if not apply equitable duty

18.2.3 Was there any unauthorised use of the information?

Here, the judge in *De Maudsley* held that the plaintiff's ideas and the defendants' club did not overlap to a sufficient degree to constitute unauthorised use.

The plaintiff's action therefore failed on all three counts. However, the judge summarised the situation as follows:

> Mr de Maudsley was in my view rather shabbily treated in that he was encouraged to think that he would be part of the enterprise but was only told that this would not be so, long after Mr Palumbo and Mr Waterhouse had decided, almost certainly justifiably because of Mr de Maudsley's rather difficult character and limited abilities, that he would not be included in their project.

The moral of the story is not to rely upon an implied duty of confidence. It is far better to inject certainty into the situation with the use of a written confidentiality agreement.

In *Cray Valley Ltd v Deltech Europe Ltd and Others* [2003] EWHC 728 (Ch), an action for breach of confidence in relation to the manufacture of industrial resins failed. There were no express undertakings of confidence by the former employees in question. It was held that the information did not have the necessary quality of confidence, not least as much of it had been published already and was easy to reverse engineer. It was not imparted in circumstances importing an obligation of confidence, but merely in the normal running of a factory, without any express instructions to employees to treat it as confidential. A claim for breach of copyright did succeed. See also *HRH Prince of Wales v Associated Newspapers Ltd* [2006] EWCA Civ 1776, [2008] Ch 57.

18.3 Remedies and their availability

The most important measure will often be an injunction to prevent disclosure of the information, that is, a restraining order in advance. Once the information has been released it is usually too late to seek an injunction (but see *Northern Rock plc v Financial Times Ltd* at **18.2.2**). However, an injunction may be granted in regard to confidential information that is of commercial value where:

(a) there are two rival businesses and not to grant an injunction would give the wrong-doer an advantage (eg, *Speed Seal Products Ltd v Paddington and Another* [1986] 1 All ER 91); or

(b) the 'springboard' doctrine applies, ie where one business would gain an unfair advantage over its rivals because of unauthorised disclosure to it of commercial information (eg, *Terrapin Ltd v Builders' Supply Co (Hayes) Ltd* [1967] RPC 375; *Roger Bullivant v Ellis* [1987] FSR 172). The court will try to prevent such advantage, by injunction, where appropriate (see **18.3.1**).

Compensatory damages are available for breach of confidence (see *Seager v Copydex Ltd* [1967] 2 All ER 415).

An account of the defendant's profits is also possible (see *Peter Pan Manufacturing Corporation v Corsets Silhouette Ltd* [1964] 1 WLR 96).

An order for delivery up, or destruction under oath, of the offending document or articles made by use of the information is also possible (see *Industrial Furnaces Ltd v Reaves and Another* [1970] RPC 605).

18.3.1 Whether remedy is available

It will be clear, by now, that the law of confidential information rests upon the equitable jurisdiction to prevent unconscionable use of confidential information; any remedies or reliefs are available only as a matter of the court's discretion, not as of right. Nevertheless, the courts try to exercise their jurisdiction consistently, and a very helpful exposition of the principles involved is given by Arnold J in *Vestergaard Frandsen A/S v Bestnet Europe Ltd* [2009] EWHC 1456 (Ch), [2009] All ER (D) 57 (Oct).

The case arose out of the defendants' (former employees of the claimant) misuse of the claimant's trade secrets to develop a polytex mosquito net, which incorporated an insecticide in the material. The information came to them from their knowledge of the claimant's process for making a protective cattle net, also incorporating an insecticide. The court (at [2009] EWHC 657 (Ch)) held that the defendants had breached the confidentiality of the information, having applied the *Coco v AN Clark* three-point test discussed in **18.2**. The question then became one of how the court should exercise its discretion in granting the remedies sought. The following list is a summary of the valuable guidance given:

(a) *The general principles involved.* Where the claimant establishes that the defendant had acted in breach of confidence and that there was a sufficient risk of repetition, if there were no specific discretionary reasons to refuse an injunction, one would normally be granted, save in exceptional circumstances.

(b) *Where the 'springboard' doctrine was involved* (see **18.3** above). There was no sound authority that an injunction could be granted once the information had ceased to be confidential; publication of the confidential information, whether by confider, by confidant, or by stranger, ended the possibility of obtaining an injunction.

(c) *Where information had only a limited degree of confidence.* Here, as, for example, in circumstances where the information might be obtained by research in the public domain, an injunction could be ordered only for a limited period.

(d) *Whether an injunction could be granted to prevent a defendant from benefiting from a past misuse of confidential information.* In general, it was not clear that such an injunction could be granted, as the primary remedy should be financial. Great care should be exercised, in granting such an injunction, to ensure that the claimant was not thereby put in a position better than if there had been no misuse at all. The duration of such an injunction should not go beyond the period for which the defendant's illegitimate advantage could be expected to last.

(e) *Where a product derived from, or was manufactured using, confidential information.* An injunction could be granted to restrain the manufacture or sale of such product, where the manufacture represented a continued use of the information, always having regard to the extent and importance of the use of it. Otherwise, the appropriate remedy in respect of manufacture and sale of products derived from a past misuse of information was a financial one.

The resulting orders for the claimant were that the defendants should be restrained from using or disclosing the claimant's trade secrets (except any information which was now in the public domain). An injunction restrained any further production or sale of the first derived product, but did not extend to later developed products, where the derivation from the original information was not so clearly illustrated.

See also *First Conference Services Ltd v Bracchi* [2009] EWHC 2176 (Ch), where an employee, having decided that he would leave his job, e-mailed confidential information to a company that he himself had set up. He was held to have misappropriated the information; he had also involved himself in passing off. The court ordered injunctive relief.

18.3.2 The position of former employees

The majority of breach of confidence claims involve former employees as defendants, and it is important to realise that certain considerations should be added to those already examined where an employment situation is involved. The first point is that it is open to an employer to secure some protection for his secrets or other confidential information by requiring the employee to enter into a covenant in restraint of trade and confidentiality agreements. If the employer fails to do this, the court may take the view that some information, of an otherwise confidential nature, might not be viewed by either party as so significant as to be protected; it might blend in with information that the employee should feel free to use or to pass on, and the court may be unwilling to step in (see *AT Poeton (Gloucester Plating) Ltd v Horton* [2001] FSR 169, CA).

The second point is that there is considerable judicial guidance as to the different types of information that might come to an employee during his employment. The widely-cited analysis by Goulding J, at first instance, in *Faccenda Chicken v Fowler* [1985] 1 All ER 724, is instructive and helpful here. The judge categorised the types of information and consequent confidentiality status as falling into three groups:

(a) *Class 1* – mundane, easily obtained information (for all that it might be very technical) that is already in the public domain; such information is not confidential and cannot be protected.

(b) *Class 2* – confidential information that the employee knows, or ought to know, is confidential (perhaps something equivalent to a trade secret), but which enters the employee's mind as part of his own 'stock in trade' of skill and experience, to be used in his own future employment; this will normally remain confidential during the term of employment, but will not usually be protected after termination in the absence of an express covenant.

(c) *Class 3* – highly confidential information in the nature of trade secrets, customer information, etc; this type of information would be protected under an implied term of good faith between the parties, both during the employment and after termination, regardless of the absence of a restrictive covenant.

The Court of Appeal has repeatedly used this analysis in appeals and, despite some elaborations, the classification remains good guidance; judges have been criticised, on appeals, for not following this approach.

The main issue in such cases is often about whether the confidential information is easily isolated from other information that the employee is free to use; that will always depend upon the facts of the case (in the *AT Poeton* case, the claim was dismissed on appeal on this point). You should be clear, however, that the above guidance deals only with the nature of the confidential information and its consequent protectable status; it does not attempt to go further than that.

18.4 A right of privacy and the Human Rights Act 1998?

In the somewhat unusual case of *Douglas and Others v Hello! Ltd and Others* [2003] EWHC 786 (Ch), [2003] All ER (D) 209 (Apr); [2005] EWCA Civ 595, breach of confidence was used to prevent publication by a rival magazine of wedding coverage granted by two film stars to a magazine. It was held that the photographs of the event had the necessary quality of confidence about them, and deserved protection as a trade secret. The illicit photographer from the rival magazine (the defendant) had been under a duty of confidentiality when attending the wedding. The defendant knew of the arrangement between the couple and the other magazine, but had deliberately ignored it and took covert photographs. The law of confidence was held to have protected the claimants' right to respect for private life under the Human Rights Act 1998, Sch 1, Pt I, Art 8. It was therefore held that it was unnecessary to consider whether the Act had created a new right of privacy. The wedding and the party were private events held on private property. These were key factors in the Douglases succeeding. The Lords appeal concerned the nature and protectability of the obligation of confidence, rather than the privacy issue. In another case, the privacy of Princess Caroline of Monaco was protected by the European Convention on Human Rights under Article 8, even though the invasion of her privacy occurred in a public place (*von Hanover v Germany*, Application No 59320/00).

In *A v B (A Company) and Another* [2002] EWCA Civ 337, [2002] 2 All ER 545, the Court of Appeal refused to uphold an injunction under the 'respect for private life' provisions of the Act restraining two newspapers from publishing details of the extra-marital affairs of the claimant, a professional footballer.

In *Campbell v MGN Ltd* [2002] EWCA Civ 1373, [2003] QB 633, the Court of Appeal refused to uphold an injunction against a newspaper restraining publication of sensitive information about a well-known media personality, Naomi Campbell. She had been having treatment for drug addiction, having previously denied drug abuse. The Court held that the public interest in publishing the story overrode her privacy rights under the Human Rights Act 1998. However, the House of Lords overruled the Court of Appeal ([2004] 2 All ER 995). It held that the information about Ms Campbell seeking treatment for drug addiction and photographs of Ms Campbell attending treatment were unnecessary intrusions into her private life. Ms Campbell's right to respect for her private life under the Human Rights Act 1998, Sch 1, Pt I, Art 8, was held to outweigh M's freedom of expression under Article 10. A similar result followed in *HRH Prince of Wales v Associated Newspapers Ltd* [2007] EWHC 1685 (Ch), where the Prince of Wales was able to obtain summary judgment in his claims for breach of confidence and privacy, and infrigement of the copyright in his private journals.

Chapter 19
Information Technology

19.1	Introduction	271
19.2	Information technology and intellectual property rights	271
19.3	Semiconductor chip protection	272
19.4	Hardware contracts	273
19.5	Software	277
19.6	The Internet	283
19.7	Computer crime	285
19.8	Data protection	287
19.9	The database right	287

19.1 Introduction

The computer is a universal presence in offices, homes, schools and personal chattels throughout the developed world. The increase in computer use in the last 20 years or so has come about through the amazing reduction in the price of computing power. For comparison, if a new car had decreased in price to the same degree that computers have over the 20-year period, the car would now cost something less than a tankful of petrol, at current prices.

However, it should not be forgotten that a computer is basically a calculating machine with a very large memory. It needs to be told what to do. This chapter addresses some of the main legal and related issues which this raises:

(a) IP issues;

(b) semiconductor chip protection;

(c) hardware contracts;

(d) software contracts;

(e) the Internet;

(f) computer crime;

(g) data protection; and

(h) rights in databases.

Many of these issues are relevant to areas of law already covered elsewhere in this book, so, where appropriate, this chapter is cross-referenced to that material.

19.2 Information technology and intellectual property rights

All the major forms of legal protection of IP rights pre-date the electronic computer by a century or more. As they were not developed with the computer in mind, there have therefore been many problems in deciding whether a particular activity comes within the remit of the existing IP law. Indeed, there has been a considerable need to produce new forms of legal protection to deal with problems that have emerged. The following paragraphs summarise the way in which the various IP rights may be relevant to computer software and hardware.

19.2.1 Copyright

For the main points on the law of copyright itself, see **Chapter 14**. The relevance of copyright to computers is as protection for the software; in other words, the instructions required to enable the computer to perform the desired task. In order to be protected, the software would have to have been 'written down' on some medium at some stage of its existence, although of course when bought by the customer, the software will usually be on floppy disks or a CD. (For the avoidance of doubt, note that 'software' = 'computer programs'.)

A computer program is a series of written instructions telling a computer what to do. It will contain thousands of lines of instructions, each one of which relates to a simple step; but put together as a program, it enables the computer to be used, for example, for word processing. As already noted in **Chapter 14**, copyright exists in software as a literary work (CDPA 1988, s 3(1)); see further **19.5.2**.

Unauthorised use of a computer program (which includes simple down-loading) is therefore breach of copyright. The commercial arrangement for use of software is usually a licence, ie, a copyright licence.

(For the law on copyright in databases, and the relatively new 'database right', see **Chapter 15** and **19.9**.)

19.2.2 Patents

As noted in **Chapter 17**, PA 1977, s 1(2) excludes 'computer programs' from the remit of the patent system (although, as indicated in **17.3.4**, this does not necessarily mean that a program can never be patented).

The reality is that patents for computer programs are being granted in increasing numbers. The attitude of the UK Patent Office and the European Patent Office has become more relaxed over recent years, though not to the extent of the 'open doors' policy of the US Patent Office. The patent is really being granted for the technical effect brought about by the use of the program, as distinct from the program itself.

Patents do, of course, have relevance to protection of inventions in relation to computer hardware (ie, the electronics) if the necessary conditions for patentability are satisfied.

19.2.3 Trade marks

Trade marks are covered in **Chapter 13**. This becomes particularly relevant in the context of Internet 'domain' names, where trade mark infringement and passing off are the relevant causes of action (see further, **19.6**).

(Trade marks are, of course, also relevant in the usual context of being used in relation to goods and services, for example Microsoft, Dell, Compaq and so on will have various registered and unregistered marks which they use in connection with their businesses.)

19.2.4 Design rights

Registered and unregistered design rights (see **Chapter 16**) are intended to protect the outward appearance of items. The design rights are not often directly relevant to information technology (IT) (although they may be used to protect the outward appearance of a piece of hardware). However, note that the right which protects semiconductor chips is akin to a design right (see **19.3**).

19.3 Semiconductor chip protection

The chip is the brain of the computer. It is made up of millions of transistors and other electronic components, yet is only 2cm by 2cm or so in size. The 'Pentium' chip, made by Intel, is the commonest chip in desktop computers.

Obviously, such a marvel of miniaturisation could not be made by sitting at a work bench and soldering all the bits together. Rather, chips are made by a special type of photographic process, whereby the design of the circuit is etched on to the blank chip. As it is made by such a process, it can be copied in a similar manner.

The design of chips is protected in the EU by Directive 87/54/EEC. This has now been implemented in the UK by the Design Right (Semiconductor Topographies) Regulations 1989 (SI 1989/1100). Regulation 2(1) defines a semiconductor topography as a design within s 213 of the CDPA 1988 and which relates to a semiconductor product or component thereof. The design has to be recorded in a design document (see **16.4**).

Under the 1989 Regulations, there is prohibition on:

(a) unauthorised copying of a chip; and

(b) importation into, or sale in, the UK of unauthorised copy chips (but note that exhaustion of rights applies to sales within the EU; see further on this, **Chapter 23**).

Note that reverse engineering is not prohibited, so it is permissible for a third party to work out from the chip topography how it works, and then to produce a chip that performs the same function, without copying the topography or 'map' of the original.

The right lasts for 15 years from creation of the design, or 10 years from first sale of objects made to that design, whichever is the shorter (cf the period for UDR; see further **Chapter 16**).

19.4 Hardware contracts

The 'hardware' is the computer equipment. If you buy a computer, you are simply buying electrical equipment; therefore the contract for the purchase of computer hardware is a contract for sale of goods, and is in principle the same as, for example, buying a fridge from Comet. However, there is one important practical difference: it is fairly obvious when a fridge is not working properly, but it is more debatable whether or not a particular computer is doing all the things it is supposed to. Part of this problem is that it is the software which tells the hardware what to do (for more detail on software, see **19.5**).

Consequently, it is suggested that in producing a specification for a new computer system, it is better to specify the software first and then that the hardware to be supplied has to be able to run it (ie, make the buyer's particular purpose expressly known). Many of the contractual disputes in this area arise from a lack of clarity in specifying the performance requirements of the equipment.

Note that, in practice, it is possible either to buy or to lease hardware. With the decrease in the cost of hardware, buying has become more common in recent years. However, if the system is a major installation, leasing would still be encountered. In this case, the contract would be of a different type (see **19.4.2**).

The remainder of this section considers some of the legal issues which may arise in relation to computer hardware.

19.4.1 Pre-contract issues: negotiation

In *Mackenzie Patten & Co v British Olivetti Ltd* (1984) 1 CL&P 92, a firm of solicitors bought a computer system to run their accounts. The sales representative made various claims for the system. However, there was an exclusion clause in the contract in relation to his statements. The firm signed the contract. The system proved to be slow and hard to use. It was held that Olivetti were bound by the representative's claims, on the basis of a collateral contract. See *Watford Electronics Ltd v Sanderson* at **3.10.8.1**.

19.4.2 Leasing

With a lease of computer hardware, the lessee has the right to use the equipment but the lessor remains the owner of it. The SGSA 1982 is relevant here (the 1982 Act characterises a contract of this type as a contract of hire, but the term 'lease' is more commercially usual in practice).

Most computer leases will be 'finance leases'. This is a commercial term used to distinguish such a lease from an 'operating lease'. With an operating lease, the equipment is hired out to the user (the lessee) for a short period of time, returned to the lessor and then hired out to another user (this is, eg, how a tool-hire shop would normally operate). With a finance lease, the equipment is supplied to one user only, who retains possession of it for substantially the whole of its working life.

A finance lease basically works as follows. The finance company (lessor) acquires the computer hardware by buying it from a supplier. The finance company pays the supplier for the hardware. It then leases the hardware to the user, and the user pays the finance company a leasing payment, probably monthly. At the end of the lease, the hardware will have little residual value and will be sold off by the lessor. The lessor may credit the user with the sale proceeds (depending on the terms of the lease), but the user must not have the right to acquire title to the hardware, otherwise it will be a hire purchase contract, not a lease.

With a finance lease, note that there is no contractual relationship between the user and the supplier of the hardware. Therefore, it can be difficult for the user to obtain redress against the supplier. This problem can be solved by:

(a) *assignment of rights* by the finance company to the user, but the user's damages would be limited to those recoverable by the finance company, which could be nothing;

(b) *partial novation*, where the deal is structured as a sale to the user from the supplier, followed by novation of the financial terms between the finance company and the supplier, leaving the supplier liable to the user for, for example, the warranties on the system; and

(c) *a direct collateral contract*, where a collateral contract dealing with, for example, the warranties which cover the hardware is created between the user and the supplier.

Note that the lease should provide for the following matters where the user breaches the lease:

(a) the lessor to have the right to repossess the equipment (so the lease should include a right of entry on to the premises);

(b) a liquidated damages clause; this is more appropriate than unliquidated damages, which would be difficult to calculate, as the lessor has a duty to mitigate; or

(c) minimum payments, including accelerated payment of all future payments on default.

19.4.3 Sale

As noted at **19.4**, a contract for the sale of hardware is in principle the same as for the sale of any other electrical item. However, the following points will require particular care.

19.4.3.1 Delivery

Depending on the terms of a sale of goods contract, non-delivery or late delivery may entitle the buyer of goods to reject them (see **2.12.1**). Remember, however, that this is possible only if the time for delivery is of the essence (ie a condition of the contract: see **2.9.3**). Problems with hardware contracts can arise if the equipment is being specially produced or modified, or because the supplier is itself waiting for supplies of parts. In such cases, it may not be feasible for the parties to nominate a specific delivery date. It then has to be decided whether the goods have been delivered within a reasonable time. If the delay means that the intended use is no longer practicable then a reasonable time has elapsed. It is advisable for the buyer to inform the supplier at the outset of the intended uses of the equipment. However, it would be best also for the buyer to specify an end-stop date after which the equipment will not be accepted.

19.4.3.2 Payment and changes of specification

Terms on price and payment will need careful consideration.

In major hardware contracts, some changes of specification are likely (eg, it emerges in discussions between the supplier and the buyer that the buyer's future business plans make it advisable to increase the number of file servers, or the specification of the desktop computers). Changes should be categorised as those which are at the buyer's expense and those which are at the seller's expense.

A well-drafted contract will include express, detailed clauses containing the procedure for changing the specification as well as providing for timescales and some provision for dealing with failure to agree upon changes.

Payment under hardware contracts is commonly made in instalments as the various parts of the system are delivered. The buyer normally retains part of the total price until the complete system has been successfully tested.

Remember that SGA 1979, s 10(1) provides that time of payment is not of the essence in a sale of goods agreement unless otherwise agreed. Thus late payment does not entitle the seller to treat the contract as at an end unless the contract provides that the seller has this right (see **2.10.1.1**).

19.4.3.3 Passing of risk and property

The SGA 1979, s 20(1) provides that risk (of accidental loss or damage to the goods) passes at the same time as property (ie, ownership). Sections 16–19 dictate when the property in the goods passes. The issue is important in deciding which party should bear the risk, and therefore the cost of insurance, so remember that ss 16–20 can be ousted by contrary agreement. The parties should consider what is important to them, and provide accordingly.

19.4.3.4 Retention of title

A properly drafted retention of title clause provides added protection for the seller, particularly where standard, non-bespoke equipment is being supplied (see **2.14**).

19.4.3.5 Seller's obligations

Remember that in a sale of goods agreement, various conditions will be implied into the agreement by the SGA 1979:

(a) s 12 – that the seller will give good title and quiet possession (eg, the hardware will be free of third-party IP rights);

(b) s 13 – sale by description (the Misrepresentation Act 1967 could also be relevant);

(c) s 14(2) – satisfactory quality (it is, however, normally better to define 'quality' in the contract than to rely on the statutory implied condition); and

(d) s 14(3) – reasonable fitness for buyer's purpose (remember that the buyer has to make his purpose known to the seller).

Note that because the functioning of hardware is controlled by the software (ie, the program), it is often difficult to assess the hardware independently in relation to quality issues.

The implied terms in ss 13 and 14 can be excluded from the contract subject to UCTA 1977. This would often be done in computer supply contracts. In their place, the supplier would offer a warranty that the system complies with the specification agreed with the customer.

19.4.3.6 Buyer's remedies

Under SGA 1979, s 11(3), the buyer can reject the goods for breach of condition (see **2.12.1**).

Rejection of the goods is the buyer's primary remedy if the seller commits breach of condition. However, this may not be feasible commercially (eg, if the hardware is specially adapted, or made so that it would be difficult for the buyer to find an alternative supplier at short notice, or possibly at all).

In any event, the right to reject is lost if the goods have been accepted (see SGA 1979, s 35). Acceptance may arise in the following ways:

(a) Hardware contracts will contain acceptance-testing clauses, which would require that the hardware is able to perform certain defined tasks which demonstrate its capabilities. Passing the tests constitutes acceptance. Ordering more hardware from the same seller would normally also constitute acceptance.

(b) Using the goods beyond mere testing may also constitute acceptance.

(c) Retaining the goods beyond a reasonable time could also be acceptance. This could happen if the hardware is delivered in instalments.

Note that a buyer can elect not to reject the goods and can claim damages instead (SGA 1979, s 11(2)). A buyer could waive his right to reject, for example, where the hardware is not delivered on time and the buyer presses the seller to make delivery as soon as possible.

19.4.3.7 Seller's remedies

If the buyer refuses to accept the goods, the seller can sue for the price, but will have to mitigate by trying to re-sell the hardware. The question will then arise: is there a market for this particular hardware, and will the seller be able to get the same price? The seller could be awarded his lost profit under SGA 1979, s 50(2), if he can show that there are few alternative buyers.

19.4.3.8 Exclusion clauses

In many cases, UCTA 1977 will apply to a hardware contract. The most likely application is in relation to attempted exclusions of SGA 1979, ss 13–14 (ie, the implied conditions of description, satisfactory quality and reasonable fitness for purpose). In a commercial sale, the test will be one of 'reasonableness' (UCTA 1977, s 6).

The leading computer case on exclusion clauses is *St Albans City and District Council v ICL* [1996] 4 All ER 481. The loss suffered by St Albans District Council as a result of the computer system supplied by ICL failing to work properly was £1.3m, but the contract contained an exclusion of loss clause for losses over £100,000 (ie, compensation for loss caused was limited to this sum). This was held to be unreasonable because:

(a) ICL had more resources than the council did;

(b) ICL had product liability insurance of £50m worldwide;

(c) ICL could not justify the £100,000 limit;

(d) the contract was signed on superseded standard terms;

(e) local authorities are limited in what they can insure against;

(f) St Albans received no inducement to agree; and

(g) ICL had said that negotiation over terms would delay implementation of the deal.

After the *St Albans* case was decided, the restrictive interpretation of exclusion clauses was extended in *South West Water Services Ltd v International Computers Ltd* [1999] BLR 420. The defendant was held to be dealing on standard terms even though the terms had been varied by negotiation. The terms were therefore subject to the reasonableness test under UCTA 1977, s 3(1). (The terms also purported to exclude liability for fraudulent misrepresentation and were held unreasonable under s 3 of the Misrepresentation Act 1967.)

The tide has gone the other way to an extent with the case of *Watford Electronics Ltd v Sanderson CFL Ltd* [2001] EWCA Civ 317, [2001] 1 All ER (Comm) 696. An interesting point that went against the claimants is that they themselves used a similar limitation of liability clause in their own terms. They were therefore held to be aware of the commercial considerations and the effect on the price agreed for the job.

19.4.4 Maintenance agreements

Computer hardware will normally come with a guarantee (usually called a warranty) – an express promise from the supplier that it will do or provide certain things if the hardware goes wrong.

After the warranty expires, it makes sense for a buyer to set up a maintenance agreement for commercial hardware.

The key points for the owner of the hardware and the provider of the maintenance to consider when setting up such an agreement are:

(a) should it provide for repair on site, or return to base?

(b) the desired response time from the provider (the faster it is, the more expensive it is);

(c) is replacement equipment to be provided in the interim whilst repair is carried out?

(d) duration of the contract – the older the equipment, the more repairs it will need and the more it will cost to maintain; and

(e) is transfer of the agreement to a new owner of the hardware permitted, as this will increase the second-hand value of the hardware?

19.4.5 System supply contracts

A system supply contract is where the buyer receives some or all of the following:

(a) hardware;

(b) software;

(c) cabling, power supply;

(d) services (eg, installation, maintenance, support, systems integration).

Note that in a 'turnkey' contract (where the system is supplied ready to run, usually with all software and peripherals such as printers), the supplier may buy in various aspects of the goods or services, almost certainly including the software. This would be licensed direct to the user, rather than by licence to the supplier and sub-licence from him to the user. It is important that the user evaluates the terms of the licences to see if they are suitable for his purposes.

19.5 Software

'Software' means the computer program(s). It is the instructions which tell the hardware what to do.

Software can be 'off the peg' (ie, a standard package), or 'made to order'. Standard package software will be cheaper than made to order, but may not fulfil the user's requirements adequately. A middle way for the buyer of software to choose is to adapt standard software, in effect customising it. The trend is toward increased sales of standard software.

There is also a distinction between system software, which organises the way the hardware operates, and applications software, which performs the function required by the user (eg, 'Word' or 'Powerpoint' are applications software). System software is normally supplied by the maker of the hardware (eg, the BIOS – the Basic Input/Output System).

19.5.1 The functional specification

Before selecting (application) software, a user will write down his requirements in a detailed document. This is known as the functional specification, and is central to the tendering process (that is, when the user is seeking quotations for the work) and to the contract for the supply of the software itself.

In *Micron Computer Systems v Wang (UK) Ltd* (HC, 9 May 1990), the user failed in a claim against a supplier because it had not made known its requirement that 'transactional logging' (in effect, a sophisticated backup program) be included in the system.

In *St Albans City and District Council v ICL* [1996] 4 All ER 481 (see **19.4.3.7**), the invitation to tender was incorporated into the contract. The relevant requirements had been included, so the supplier was in breach of the contract.

19.5.2 What is software?

The problem is whether, legally speaking, software is classified as goods or services, and therefore which implied terms are relevant. This makes it necessary to consider the nature of software.

Software consists of many thousands of lines of written instructions, and is usually sold on floppy disks or CD-ROM disks. The disks themselves are clearly 'goods', but what about the instructions (the program)? In the *St Albans* case (see **19.5.1**), Glidewell LJ said that:

> A computer disk is within the definition of goods contained in s 61 of the Sale of Goods Act 1979 and s 18 of the Supply of Goods and Services Act 1982. A computer program, however, is not. Nevertheless, if a disk onto which a program designed and intended to instruct or enable a computer to achieve particular functions has been encoded is sold or hired but the program is defective, so that it will not instruct or enable the computer to achieve the intended purpose, the seller or hirer of the disk will be in breach of the terms as to quality and fitness for purpose implied by s 14 of the 1979 Act and s 9 of the 1982 Act.

(Remember that both SGA 1979, s 14 and SGSA 1982, s 9 deal with satisfactory quality and reasonable fitness for the buyer's purpose.)

On the other hand, if the software was regarded as services, the standard which the provider of the services would have to reach is that of providing those services with reasonable skill and care under SGSA 1982, s 13.

In practice, the legal status of software remains something of a grey area.

19.5.3 Software licensing

Software licensing came about with the appearance at the end of the 1960s of writers of software who were independent of the hardware manufacturers. Before then, the hardware manufacturers included the software with their systems. (Remember that, at that time, there were no desktop computers – the 1960s computers filled entire rooms, cost a fortune and did little more than a modern calculator would.)

It was not clear that copyright existed in software at that time, so licensing contracts treated software like confidential information (see **Chapter 18**) and therefore had restrictions on disclosure and copying. Today's software supply contracts are basically copyright licences (see **Chapter 14**), but also contain terms dealing with the supply of the physical manifestations of the software (eg, sometimes retaining title to the disks, or forbidding the possession of more than one set of back-up disks, or forbidding use other than on specified hardware).

As noted at **19.2.1,** there is specific legal provision on the IP position for software. Originally, the Copyright (Computer Software) Amendment Act 1985 provided that copyright existed in software as literary works. This was superseded by s 3(1) of the CDPA 1988, but the position remains the same. Under s 17(2) of CDPA 1988, unauthorised storage of a program in a computer is copyright infringement. EC Directive 91/250/EEC specifies further legal protection for software. It is implemented in the UK by the Copyright (Computer Programs) Regulations 1992 (SI 1992/3233).

Even where software is sold over the counter, licensing is still relevant. In this case, the software house tries to impose a licence on the user by specifying that opening the cellophane in which the software is wrapped constitutes acceptance of the terms of the standard-form licence visible through the wrapper (this is known as a 'shrink-wrap' licence, and is considered further at **19.5.6**).

(What will in practice happen in this sort of 'consumer' sale of software and shrink-wrap licence is that the software creator (eg, Microsoft) will sell the software to a retailer (eg, computer shop). The shop sells the software on to the customer; it is, however, Microsoft which imposes the shrink-wrap licence on the customer.)

19.5.4 Principal commercial terms in a software contract

19.5.4.1 Delivery

Software is usually delivered as 'object code'. In this form, it can be read by a computer and put into operation. However, software is actually written in source code (that is, the lines of instructions written by the programmer). In order to correct or update the software, access to the source code is needed. Hence the software supplier will supply only the object code to its customers, specifically so that the customer cannot alter the software (the contract usually provides (in effect) that the source code will not be supplied; in fact, what will most commonly happen is that it will provide expressly if the code *is* to be supplied). See *Saphena Computing Ltd v Allied Collection Agencies Ltd* [1995] FSR 616, for a case on unauthorised use of source code.

19.5.4.2 Acceptance

The software contract should specify the tests which the software has to pass in order to be accepted by the user. One important matter which will be dependent on acceptance is payment for the software. Acceptance will trigger payment of the whole fee, or the final instalment (as the case may be) of a lump sum fee or the start of payments in the case of a periodic fee (see **19.5.4.3** below).

After acceptance, the licensee's remedy will be for breach of warranty if problems arise with the software.

19.5.4.3 Payment

Obviously, under a commercial deal, the licensee will have to pay the licensor for the software. The contract could provide for a lump sum (which may be broken down into instalments), or a periodic fee.

With a lump sum, instalments may be payable on each of the following events: signature of contract; delivery of software; and software acceptance. Problems may arise because the parties' 'ideal' situations on payment are likely to differ considerably. Normally, for example, the licensor will be keen to be paid as soon as possible, but the licensee will not pay until it is happy with the software (in practice, what the contract actually provides on payment will depend on bargaining power; in other words, it is like any other commercial agreement).

With the periodic fee, there may be provisions to increase the fee (eg, once a year). There is often a provision for interest on overdue payments.

19.5.4.4 Term and termination

The licence will often be perpetual, subject to termination on reasonable notice.

19.5.4.5 Warranties

Note that contract terms in this context are often referred to as 'warranties', regardless of their statutory status as conditions.

Implied terms

When title to (ie, ownership of) the software is transferred, a sale of software is a sale of goods under SGA 1979. When title is not transferred, the deal is a hiring under the SGSA 1982. The relevant implied terms therefore apply:

(a) right to sell or grant possession – SGA 1979, s 12(1) and (2); SGSA 1982, s 7(1) and (2); and

(b) description, satisfactory quality and reasonable fitness for buyer's purpose – SGA 1979, ss 13(1) and 14(2) and (3); SGSA 1982, ss 8 and 9.

A problem with software is to what extent 'satisfactory quality' includes the 'bugs' (that is, the faults in the program).

In *Saphena Computing Ltd v Allied Collection Agencies Ltd* [1995] FSR 616, it was held that software should be reasonably fit for any purpose which the user has made known to the supplier.

Express terms

Most software licences will exclude the implied statutory terms (within the limits of UCTA 1977) and will substitute express terms ('warranties').

Express terms fall into two categories:

(a) that the software will comply with the functional specification or the user manual, or meet specified performance criteria; or

(b) that defects in the software will be corrected by the supplier.

However, a key problem is deciding what constitutes a defect. Is failure to perform a certain task a 'defect', or is a defect an operation that is outside the capabilities of this software?

Limitations on 'warranties'

Common limitations are:

(a) any warranty relating to quality will have a duration of 3–12 months. Thereafter, a maintenance contract applies;

(b) the licensor's only liability is to correct the defect (ie, it excludes the licensor's liability for damages); and

(c) warranties cease to apply if the licensee makes any additions or modifications to the software.

19.5.4.6 Exclusion of liability

Where a contract term purports to exclude liability in relation to the implied terms of description, satisfactory quality or reasonable fitness for the buyer's purpose, the reasonableness test will apply where the buyer does not deal as consumer (UCTA 1977, s 6 for sale contracts and s 7 for a hiring). Note that the exclusion in Sch 1 to UCTA 1977 (contracts to which UCTA 1977 does not apply) in relation to IP issues does not apply to UCTA 1977, ss 6 and 7.

Remember that the implied terms in relation to title, freedom from charges and encumbrances, and quiet possession cannot be excluded in a sale contract. However, with a hiring, the right to give possession and quiet possession can be excluded if reasonable.

The special nature of the computer software industry makes it practically a normal feature to include a very high level of exclusion of liability in non-consumer contracts. This tends towards the consequence that even very restrictive exclusion/limitation clauses can be upheld as reasonable (see *SAM Business Systems Ltd v Hedley & Co* [2002] EWHC 2733 (TCC)).

19.5.5 Source code escrow

If the licensor fails for some reason to provide agreed software maintenance to the licensee (eg, because the licensor goes out of business, or simply breaches its contractual duty to provide the maintenance), it will cause serious problems for the licensee, because the licensee will not normally be given the source code (see **19.5.4.1**).

A common way round the problem is to put the source code into escrow. Under the terms of the escrow agreement, the source code is released by the escrow agent (that is, a third party with whom the program is deposited) to the licensee on the occurrence of a specified event (eg, the appointment of a receiver over the assets of the licensor). The National Computing Centre and the Computer Services Association both provide escrow services. The arrangements work successfully. See *Cardbase Technologies Ltd v Valucard Nigeria* [2002] EWHC 991 (Ch).

However, there is the potential for an administrator or a liquidator to challenge release under an escrow agreement as a 'preference' under the Insolvency Act 1986, s 239, or to disclaim the agreement as an 'unprofitable contract' under s 178 of that Act. It could also be a breach of the *pari passu* principle under s 107 (that is, the principle that the company's assets are distributed equally subject to the claims of the preferential creditors). It is also arguable that release under escrow would require a court order under s 127 of the Insolvency Act 1986.

19.5.6 Shrink-wrap or click-wrap licensing

Most software today is bought off the shelf; that is, the software is a standard product, such as the 'Word' program used to create this document. As noted at **19.5.3** above, in order to create a licence between the software creator and the user, the device known as a 'shrink-wrap licence' is used (there would otherwise be a contractual link only between the user and the retailer). This means that terms of use can therefore be imposed by the software creator on the user.

The terms of the licence are set out on the outside of the packaging and are visible through the clear wrapping. The licence purportedly comes into being when the user opens the packaging, supposedly having read the terms and agreed to them (see **19.5.6.2** for potential problems of enforceability).

A licensing method which has become more common in recent years, both with software downloaded through the Internet and being downloaded from a CD ROM, is that of the 'click-wrap' licence. This is where customers are faced with the text of a licence agreement on screen. The customers have to click on the 'I agree' button before they are allowed access to the software.

19.5.6.1 Terms

Typical terms in a consumer licence include that:

(a) the licence is for use on one computer only;

(b) the software must not be copied (save for one back-up copy);

(c) the software must not be altered; and

(d) the licensor will replace defective disks and supply updates.

All other warranties or conditions are excluded (subject, of course, to the impact of UCTA 1977, or other provisions controlling exclusion or restriction of liability). As the licence will be a pure licence of the software creator's IP rights, the only heads of liability for the software creator are likely to be negligence or product liability. (Remember that exclusion of negligence will be subject to UCTA 1977, s 2; product liability cannot be excluded under s 7 of the Consumer Protection Act 1987.)

If the sale of software is a consumer sale, the Consumer Transactions (Restrictions on Statements) Order 1976 (SI 1976/1813) will apply. This requires there to be a statement that any warranty given does not affect the consumer's statutory rights. The Unfair Terms in Consumer Contracts Regulations 1999 (SI 1999/2083) may also be relevant in this situation (as noted in **Chapter 3**, these Regulations can only apply to consumer agreements).

19.5.6.2 Enforceability

The shrink-wrap or click-wrap licence purports to be a bilateral contract. However, remember that an offeror (in this situation, the licensor) cannot unilaterally decide that silence will constitute acceptance. In the absence of an act by the user (eg, signing a user registration card), the enforceability of the licence by the licensor is therefore dubious.

In the Scottish case of *Beta Computers (Europe) Ltd v Adobe Systems (Europe) Ltd* [1996] FSR 367, it was held that if the user had accepted the licence terms by opening the wrapping then the licensor must be able to rely on the licence as a third party beneficiary under Scots law.

Under English contract law, the doctrine of privity of contract caused problems in constructing valid contracts between the software creator and the retail customer. However, the Contracts (Rights of Third Parties) Act 1999 has solved many of the problems in this type of situation. Under the Act, the contract can impose only a benefit under the contract, not a burden, though there is nothing to stop a third party from voluntarily accepting a burden, for example an obligation to provide 'hotline' support to sort out problems with software on customers' computers. The Act only applies to contracts entered into after 11 May 2000.

19.5.7 Bespoke software

Bespoke software (ie, software 'tailored' to the precise needs of a particular user) is expensive, and will be the subject of a specific contract negotiated between the software house and the user, who in legal terms is the commissioner of the software (this is relevant to the ownership of the IP rights in the software; see below).

In this case, software is written to fulfil the functional specification put forward by the user. The software house will depend on the user supplying information on its business and how it is run in order to create a satisfactory program.

The specification may change during the design of the program, and the costs of such alterations need to be allocated between the parties.

Acceptance tests will need to be devised. The user will not accept the software until these have been passed.

A key problem will be that of ownership of the copyright in the program. As noted in **Chapter 14**, the copyright will (subject, of course, to any contrary agreement) vest in the creator (ie author) of the work, not in the person who commissions it. However, this may not fulfil the desires of the parties to the agreement here; the user might ideally want to have exclusive rights to the program which it paid the creator to devise, even if only to prevent third parties from benefiting from the program. The creator, on the other hand, would want to have the right to use at least some aspects of the program in future programs which it may write, not least because it regards it as part of its evolving expertise. In practice, this is another matter which will be determined by bargaining power; basically, users are unlikely to get exclusivity unless they are prepared to pay a substantial amount for it.

An example of the problems that can occur is *Cyprotex Discovery Ltd v University of Sheffield* [2004] EWCA Civ 380. There, the claimant company had employed a computer programmer to create some software, as part of an agreement with the university. Prima facie, the copyright in the programs belonged to the company as the programmer was its employee. However, the agreement with the university operated to vest copyright in the university and overrode the basic presumption of copyright vesting in the author.

Generally, the court will look for strong evidence before it will be prepared to find an equitable assignment of the copyright from the author to the user (*Saphena Computing Ltd v Allied Collection Agencies Ltd* [1995] FSR 616). Wherever possible, the matter should be dealt with expressly.

A contract for bespoke software will probably be construed as a contract for the supply of services and some ancillary goods. The SGSA 1982 will imply that the services be provided with reasonable skill and care, and that the materials must be reasonably fit for the user's purpose and of satisfactory quality. Specific warranties will often be included in the contract, for example that the software will meet the functional specification. As far as exclusion of terms is concerned, remember that UCTA 1977, s 2 provides that liability for negligence causing damage other than personal injury or death can be excluded only to the extent it is reasonable, but, as explained at **19.5.4.6**, such exclusion is very much the normal expectation in this type of contract.

19.5.8 Software maintenance

Software maintenance comprises:

(a) the correction of errors (so-called 'bugs') in the software; and

(b) providing enhancements and updates.

There will be a free warranty for the first 3–12 months after supply of the software. Thereafter, the user will need to take out a maintenance agreement if it wishes to ensure the continued running of that software.

As noted at **19.5.4.1**, users of software will not normally be able to undertake maintenance themselves, as they will not have been supplied with the 'source code' of the software (ie, the form in which the software is written and can be corrected). However, this is not always so. In *Andersen Consulting v CHP Consulting Ltd* (ChD, 26 July 1991), it was held that as the contract in that case provided for the supply of the source code to the user, there must have been the intent that the user was to be able to do the software maintenance. In the *Saphena Computing* case, discussed at **19.5.7**, the court was prepared to imply a similar term to use the source code for removing bugs. However, when the user used the source code to make improvements to the software, that was held to be an infringement of the author's copyright.

Usually, under the contract, the supplier will be obliged to provide only those updates which it is making generally available to its customers. On the other hand, the user will be obliged to utilise all the updates made available to it, so that the supplier's customer base will all be operating with the same versions of the software. This will make life easier for the supplier.

19.6 The Internet

The Internet is a system of linked computers throughout most of the world. It started off in the United States as a means of minimising the effects of a nuclear strike on the command system of the armed services, but has grown vastly since then, and is expected to continue to grow. It can be regarded as a sort of electronic post office and library.

19.6.1 Using a name

In order to send a message over the Internet, it has to have an address to go to. An Internet Protocol address has the form '130.132.59.234'. As the Internet Protocol addresses are essentially forgettable, the Domain Name System (DNS) was devised. 'Domain names' are names rather than numbers, and are translated into Internet Protocol addresses by some of the computers in the Internet. An example of a domain name is 'lawcol.co.uk'. So, for example, a message could be sent to Trevor.Adams@lawcol.co.uk.

Domain names have different 'levels'; for example, the top-level domain name in the above example is 'uk'. Obviously, this is the country where the relevant party is located. Other examples of top-level domain names are '.com', '.gov' or '.org'. There is little dispute about these. Rather, the problems which arise in relation to domain names usually concern the second-level names, especially where that name is the trade mark, registered or not, of a commercial product or organisation (eg, 'McDonalds.com'). Clearly, unauthorised use of that domain name would upset a certain chain of burger restaurants.

In the UK, the organisation known as Nominet allocates domain names and does so on the basis of first come, first served. It is located at www.nominet.org.uk.

In the United States, and in effect internationally as well, the body known as the Internet Corporation for Assigned Names and Numbers (ICANN) deals with many domain name issues also, and is located at www.icann.org. It has set up some new top-level domain names, for example '.pro' for lawyers and accountants. WIPO also has an input into domain name issues, especially from the trade mark perspective, and runs a dispute resolution procedure.

In England, in the case of *British Telecommunications plc and Others v One in a Million Ltd and Others* [1999] 1 WLR 903, the Court of Appeal held that the use of various business names as domain names without consent was passing off and infringement of the registered trade marks under the TMA 1994. The claimants were BT, Sainsbury's, Virgin, Ladbrokes and Marks & Spencer. Following this case, it seems clear that unauthorised use of a business name as a domain name will be taken by the English courts as constituting passing off and trade mark infringement (assuming that there is a valid trade mark registration). In *Bonnier Media Ltd v Greg Lloyd Smith* [2002] ETMR 86 (see **13.9**, it was held by the Scottish Court of Session that the intent of the infringer was a critical factor, ie were they intending to defraud the legitimate user of the trade mark?

If a domain name is a registered trade mark, the criteria used to decide if there is infringement are those under the TMA 1994. In particular, the criteria identified in the case of *British Sugar plc v James Robertson & Sons Ltd* [1996] RPC 281, concerning the use of the word 'Treat' in relation to sweet sauces and syrups, where it was held that it was not necessary for the infringing use to be use as a trade mark as such, provided it was use in the course of trade. See, at **13.9**, *Wilson v Yahoo! UK Ltd* [2008] EWHC 361 (Ch), on the non-infringing use of trade-marks in sponsored links in Internet search engines.

Even if the trade mark is not in use in the UK, it may be protected in the UK as a 'well known mark' under s 56 of the 1994 Act (see **13.10**).

19.6.2 Copyright issues

In the case of *Shetland Times Ltd v Wills and Another* [1997] FSR 604, the Shetland News Internet site had a link which enabled the reader to access pages from the *Shetland Times*, but without seeing the front page of the *Times*. Such unauthorised use of the *Times* pages was held to be breach of copyright. Unauthorised use of copyright material on the Internet now falls within s 20 of the CDPA 1988, which covers infringement by communication to the pubic within the UK, by electronic means.

The BBC has undertaken similar action with regard to infringement via the Internet of its copyright in the Teletubbies.

19.6.3 Intercepting communications

The Regulation of Investigatory Powers Act 2000 makes it illegal for a business to intercept communications without the consent of both the sender and recipient. Permitted interceptions may be allowed under the Telecommunications (Lawful Business Practice) (Interception of Communications) Regulations 2000 (SI 2000/2699). However, even permitted interceptions may fall foul of the Human Rights Act 1998, or the Data Protection Act 1998. See *Copland v United Kingdom*, Application No 62617/00, (2007) 45 EHRR 37.

See also the offences under the Computer Misuse Act 1990 at **19.7.**

19.7 Computer crime

There have been attempts in the past to use the law of theft and criminal damage in relation to problems related to computers (eg, problems caused by hackers, people who attempt to gain unauthorised access to computer systems). The problems in using the conventional law proved to be immense; what has been stolen, or what has been damaged? The Computer Misuse Act 1990 seeks to avoid such esoteric questions by creating offences that are specific to computers.

19.7.1 Section 1 – unauthorised access, hacking and like activities

Section 1 of the Computer Misuse Act 1990 makes it an offence to obtain unauthorised access to a computer system, as follows:

> (1) A person is guilty of an offence if—
>
> (a) he causes a computer to perform any function with intent to secure access to any program or data held in any computer;
>
> (b) the access he intends to secure is unauthorised; and
>
> (c) he knows at the time when he causes the computer to perform the function that that is the case.

The punishment is a maximum of six months' imprisonment and/or a fine.

In *R v Bow Street Metropolitan Stipendiary Magistrate, ex p United States (No 2); R v Governor of Brixton Prison, ex p Allison* [2000] 2 AC 216, the House of Lords held that the s 1 offence should not be construed as being restricted to hackers. The case concerned an employee of a credit card company who, with an accomplice, diverted very small amounts of money from a very large number of customer accounts. The problem was that she was 'authorised' to access some customer accounts as part of her job. However, it was held that she was not authorised to access all the accounts, and certainly not for the purposes of theft, so she would be liable for the s 1 offence.

In *Ellis v Director of Public Prosecutions* [2001] EWHC 362 (Admin), the appellant had been convicted of offences under s 1 of the 1990 Act, which were upheld on appeal. He was entitled as a graduate to use computers in the library, but only those designated as open access, which could not access the Internet. However, he had used non-open access computers in the university library, which he had found to be already logged on to the Internet. He used his unauthorised access to browse various Internet sites. Lord Woolf CJ held that s 1 was wide enough to cover the actions of the appellant and upheld the convictions.

Any evidence obtained by means of breaches of s 1 is likely to be held inadmissable. See *Morgans v DPP* [2001] 1 AC 315, HL.

19.7.2 Section 2 – the ulterior intent offence

This is committed by a person who secures unauthorised access to a computer system with the intent of using that access to facilitate the commission of a further serious criminal offence. Such offences are those where the sentence is fixed by law (eg, murder), or where a first offender aged over 18 years could be sentenced to five years in jail. For example, a case has been reported in France where access was sought to medical records in order to blackmail sufferers of AIDS. If such facts arose within the UK, they would be capable of giving rise to the s 2 offence.

The offence in s 2 is triable either way. The maximum sentence is five years' imprisonment.

In *R v Delamere* [2003] EWCA Crim 424, the appellant had pleaded guilty to two counts under s 2(1)(b). He was a bank employee and had provided details of two bank accounts to two people known to him. In the end, he was not paid for the information. The two acquaintances were convicted of attempting to obtain property by deception and given community punishment orders. The appellant's sentence was reduced on appeal from eight months in custody to four months. The court stressed that any disparity between the sentences of the two, who had committed other offences, and the sentence under appeal, was an irrelevance. The appellant had committed a serious breach of trust in addition to the ulterior intent offence.

19.7.3 Section 3 – modification of computer material

The act must be intended to impair the operation of a computer, or to prevent or hinder access to any programs or data, or to impair the operation of any program or reliability of the data. Sending out a computer virus would come within s 3, as would deleting or altering data, or indeed adding jocular comments to the Duke of Edinburgh's e-mail (*R v Gold* [1988] 2 WLR 984, where the prosecution failed under the then law).

The offence in s 3 is triable either way. The maximum sentence is five years' imprisonment.

In *R v Maxwell-King* [2000] 2 Cr App R (S) 136, the appellant had his sentence reduced to 150 hours' community service from four months' imprisonment. His company had had to pay £10,000 costs. He had engaged in the small-scale manufacture of 'multi-mode' boards for computers, which allowed access to television channels without paying the subscription. This was apparently the first case under s 3 of the 1990 Act. Wright J described the subject area as 'a field which makes up for in fascination what it loses in obscurity'.

In *R v Parr-Moore and Crumblehulme* [2003] 1 Cr App R (S), the Court of Appeal decreased the sentences of the appellants from seven months in custody to four months. They had manufactured and distributed devices known as cable cubes. These allowed people who subscribed to cable television services to view programmes they had not paid for. The appellants had made a total profit of about £6,000 from the sale of the cubes. They had both pleaded guilty.

In *R v Lindesay* [2001] EWCA Crim 1720, [2002] 1 Cr App R (S) 86, an appeal against of a sentence of nine months in custody was not allowed. The defendant was a computer consultant. He had been dismissed from his job with a computer company. In a fit of pique, he had accessed the Internet sites of three clients of the computer company and had deleted contents and images, but not done major harm. The total cost of the damage was estimated to be £9,000.

In *DPP v Lennon* [2006] EWHC 1201 (Admin), a prosecution appeal by way of case stated was allowed against a youth court decision that there was no case to answer on a 'mail-bombing' matter. The defendant had been dismissed from his employment and had put in place a program which resulted in his former employer receiving over 500,000 e-mails.

In *Zezev, Yarimaka v the Governor of HM Prison Brixton, the Government of the United States of America* [2002] EWHC 589 (Admin), [2002] Crim LR 648, it was held that the offence allegedly committed by the applicants was equivalent to the s 3 offence. They were also charged with four counts of blackmail and two of conspiracy. One of the applicants, Zezev, was employed by a company in Kazakstan, which used the services of Bloomberg LP. This is a business which provides news and financial information. Zezev and Yarimaka gained unauthorised access from Kazakstan to the Bloomberg system (which is located in New York). They were able to access the e-mail accounts of Mr Bloomberg himself and his head of security. They demanded $200,000 from Mr Bloomberg or they would reveal the breach of security to Bloomberg clients. Their extradition to the United States was being sought, and was granted.

19.7.4 Jurisdiction

The Computer Misuse Act 1990 introduced the concept of a 'significant link' with one of the UK jurisdictions. In the case of the s 1 or s 3 offences, it is enough that either the offender or the victim was located within the jurisdiction. For the s 2 offence, the court has jurisdiction only if the further act would be an offence in the country where it was intended that it should occur.

19.8 Data protection

The Data Protection Act 1998 has revised the law in this area. See **Chapter 21** for more detailed discussion.

The Act, which is complex, extends the principles of the Data Protection Act 1984. Broadly, it consists of provisions for:

(a) notification by those who use data;
(b) general data protection principles; and
(c) a supervisory body headed by the Information Commissioner.

The 1998 Act includes manual records, not just computer ones, as was the case under the 1984 Act.

Key definitions include:

(a) 'processing', which includes altering, retrieving, or disposing of data;
(b) 'data controller', who is the person who determines the purposes for which data are to be processed; and
(c) 'data processor', who is the person who processes data on behalf of the data controller. (Note that the data controller is responsible for the actions of the data processor.)

Common conditions that have to be met are:

(a) that the data subject (ie, the person to whom the data relate) has given his consent to processing; or
(b) that processing is necessary for the performance of a contract to which he is a party.

Data subjects have the right to:

(a) be informed that data are being processed;
(b) be informed of the nature of the data;
(c) require that data are not processed if it causes them damage or distress; and
(d) object to direct marketing.

For transfers of data outside the EEA, the countries of destination have to have an equivalent level of data protection. For example, Japan and the USA do *not* meet this requirement, though an agreement with the USA looks as if it will take shape around the European Commission's gradual acceptance of the US voluntary 'Safe Harbor' principle. See European Commission Decision of 27 July 2000.

19.9 The database right

As noted in **Chapter 15**, this is a relatively new right relating to the keeping of information. The Copyright and Rights in Databases Regulations 1997 (SI 1997/3032) implement Directive 96/9/EC on the Legal Protection of Databases by amending the Copyright Designs and Patents Act 1988 (CDPA 1988).

A 'database' is defined in CDPA 1988, s 3A(1) (see **15.2**). In practice, a database could, for example, be information on the daily price of stocks and shares, a telephone directory, 'Lexis', or the CD-ROM law reports. Copyright protection is also afforded to a database specifically as a literary work, although the standard is not only that of originality, but also that it is the 'author's intellectual creation'. To obtain 'database right' protection, only s 3A(1) needs to be met. For copyright protection, both s 3A(1) and (2) must be met.

Whether or not it is protected by copyright, a database also attracts a new database right, which arises automatically. The database right runs for 15 years from the end of the year of completion. It prevents unauthorised use of the database, or a substantial part of it.

As noted in **15.2,** data arrangements have the protection of database right if there is a substantial investment (including any investment, whether of financial, human or technical resources):

(a) in quality or quantity;
(b) in obtaining, verifying or presenting the data.

Further points to consider in relation to the database right are as follows.

19.9.1 Qualifications for the database right

There are copyright-style qualification requirements (Copyright and Rights in Databases Regulations 1997, reg 18) based on nationality or corporate seat.

19.9.2 Ownership of the database right

The maker of a database protected by the database right is the person who takes the initiative in obtaining, verifying or presenting the contents of the database and who assumes the risk of investing in that obtaining. (See Copyright and Rights in Databases Regulations 1997, reg 14.)

The maker is the first owner of the database right (reg 15).

19.9.3 Duration of lesser protection

The database right lasts for the longer of 15 years from the end of the calendar year:

(a) of completion of the database; or
(b) during which the database was first made available to the public (reg 17).

A 'substantial new investment' (see **19.9**) will 'top up' the right so the period starts again.

19.9.4 Infringement of the database right

Infringement is the extraction or re-utilisation of all or a substantial part of the contents of a database without the consent of the owner (reg 16).

'Extraction' means the permanent or temporary transfer of the contents of a database to another medium by any means, or in any form.

'Re-utilisation' means making those contents available to the public by any means.

'Substantial' is in terms of quality, or quantity or both.

'Substantial part' can include repeated extraction and/or re-utilisation of insubstantial parts (reg 16(2)). This is very important, as it means that copying of small extracts, which would not comprise a qualitatively sufficient copying for copyright infringement purposes, may still comprise a database right infringement, if done often enough.

19.9.5 Exceptions from the database right

Database rights are not infringed (regs 19 and 20):

(a) by fair dealing with a substantial part of a database made available to the public if:
   (i) such dealing is for illustration in teaching or research; and
   (ii) sufficient acknowledgement is given;

(b) generally, by copying or use with the authority of the keeper of a database available for public inspection as a statutory record.

The database right can be licensed or assigned (as can the copyright in the database).

Chapter 20
E-commerce

20.1	Introduction	291
20.2	The legal framework	291
20.3	Formation and proof of contract	292
20.4	Law and jurisdiction, choices and application	293
20.5	The application of intellectual property law to e-commerce	294
20.6	Business to business e-commerce	296
20.7	Business to consumer e-commerce	296
20.8	Payment aspects of e-commerce transactions	301
20.9	Liabilities of ISSPs and others	302
20.10	Conclusion	303

20.1 Introduction

The exponential growth in the commercial use of the World Wide Web in the last decade and a half, the developments in Internet shopping, and the general adaptation to online contracting by commercial parties and the consumer alike, arguably may be the most fundamental change to commercial activity in centuries. But is it such a change? At first sight one might think so, but the reality is that much of this, from the point of view of the lawyer, is a case of adapting existing, well-known principles to suit new fact situations. A good example of this is the way in which encryption and digital signatures have been introduced to give the legal certainty that would otherwise reside in a confidential agreement, signed by the parties, with a pen. That is not to say that this area of law is easy to understand and to apply; it is not, for the simple reason that the pace of technological and commercial developments has caused the courts and legislators to struggle to keep up. What follows is a summary of the main areas of legal issues and recent developments.

The term 'e-commerce' is used here to describe both contracts between business parties (B2B) and those between businesses and consumers (B2C). To arrive at a satisfactory definition of e-commerce, it is probably not necessary to go much further than to say that it covers business transactions in goods and services between remote parties, who communicate with each other by electronic means. Often, there will also be questions about the use of the Internet for advertising, and these are dealt with at **20.5** below. The aim of this chapter is to provide a preliminary understanding of some of the legal aspects of e-commerce for the budding commercial lawyer, and to highlight problem areas.

20.2 The legal framework

The very real difficulty with e-commerce is that parties can come to agreements without regard to national frontiers or distance; so can the parties simply forget about law and have a fine old time dealing together? Clearly that would never work, because there would be no legal way in which the parties could either enforce the contract or settle disputes. Consequently, all the major trading countries of the world have had to wrestle with the problem of applying legal systems to e-commerce, but there are still very wide differences in the approaches taken under different national legal systems. For the purposes of this chapter, the main focus will be on the harmonised laws of the EU and English domestic law; much of the law derives from the so-called E-commerce Directive, ie Council Directive 2000/31 EC. This is given effect in the UK by the Electronic Commerce (EC Directive) Regulations 2002 (SI 2002/2013) ('the 2002 Regulations')and is discussed in more depth at **20.7**.

While the Directive is generally about the provision of electronic services by Internet Service Providers (ISPs), it can extend out towards most types of commercial provision of electronic information. It can cover, in particular, website selling of goods and services, but the type of e-commerce that is concluded by parties using an exchange of e-mails is generally not affected by it. Nevertheless, by Article 9(1), Member States are required to ensure that national legal systems effectively facilitate the making of valid contracts by electronic means. The particular position of the consumer in a B2C contract is dealt with at **20.7**.

A distinction that should be raised at the outset is between the use of websites and the use of simple communication between parties by electronic means, such as e-mails. Most of the controlling legislation in this area is aimed at the former, by reference to 'information society services' (ISSs), which covers most of the business activity carried out by the use of websites. The general approach followed below is to deal with this distinction as and when required by the particular point being examined.

20.3 Formation and proof of contract

20.3.1 Offer and acceptance

Although the Internet is supra-national, every contract requires an applicable law before it can be legally analysed. The issues of law and jurisdiction of e-commerce contracts are dealt with at **20.4** below but, for the purposes of this chapter, it is assumed that the contract will be governed by English law. In essence, the law of offer and acceptance in contract, with which you are already familiar, works in exactly the same way in e-commerce; the point to remember is that the familiar steps and distinctions have to be looked at in the light of the particular way in which online transactional communications work. Thus:

(a) *Offer or invitation to treat*? This vital distinction applies just as much in e-commerce as when contracting elsewhere; the point of departure comes when one considers that e-commerce might be entered into either by a simple exchange of e-mails, or by using a website. If the matter is transacted by e-mail, the question will be dealt with exactly as with a traditional exchange of letters, ie whether the communication is an expression of willingness to contract on specified terms, made with the intention that it becomes binding as soon as it is accepted by the person to whom it is addressed. If it is anything less than this, it may be an invitation to treat but is not an offer.

    With a website, however, the details displayed by the supplier are much more likely to have been designed so as to constitute an invitation to treat. The reason for that is that the customer is required to make the offer, usually establishing his identity and payment assurance, before the seller will enter the contract by acceptance. The statutory assumption in the 2002 Regulations, reg 12, is that the customer's order will usually comprise the contractual offer, the supplier's acknowledgement being the acceptance.

(b) *Acceptance*. In e-commerce by exchanges of e-mail, the well-established rule of convenience and certainty analogous to the 'postal rule' is probably applicable. Under this, acceptance occurs when the offeree does the last act that is seen as contemplated by the parties: if that is acceptance by letter, the last act is posting the letter; if it is during an exchange of e-mails, the last act is the sending of the acceptance message. It remains possible, of course, for a 'battle of the forms' situation to arise even in this circumstance.

    Where the acceptance taking place is by the use of a website in a transaction to which the 2002 Regulations apply, the recipient of a service must have had explained to him by the provider, prior to placing an order, 'the different technical steps to follow to conclude the contract' (reg 9(1)(a)); additionally, 'the order and acknowledgement of receipt will be deemed to be received when the parties to whom they are addressed are able to access them' (reg 11(2)(a)), but note that parties who are non-consumers are free to agree other arrangements. That suggests that acceptance may take place at the earliest time at which the customer can access the supplier's acknowledgement of the order/

offer, regardless of whether the customer actually does so. There seems to be no particular reason why the special telex rule in *Entores Ltd v Miles Far East Corporation* [1955] 2 QB 327 should apply to e-commerce transactions.

(c) *Incorporation of terms*. In general, the same rules are likely to be applied to the incorporation of terms as in other contractual circumstances, including the court's jurisdiction to decide about the 'battle of forms' where standard-form contract terms are involved.

20.3.2 Electronic execution of documents, encryption and security

Most commercial transactions do not require formal execution by signature as a matter of law, but there are circumstances in which a signature may be required, either by the terms of the contract, or by the common law or by statute. The Electronic Signatures Regulations 2002 (SI 2002/318), made in response to Directive 1999/93 EC, constitute the United Kingdom's framework for providing for the supervision and liability of signature-certification service providers, related data protection measures and admissibility into evidence of electronic signatures (see also Pt II of the Electronic Communications Act 2000). Some statutory requirements for a 'signature' and 'writing' can, it seems, be met by e-mail exchanges (see *Mehta v J Pereira Fernandes SA* [2006] EWHC 813 (Ch), although on the facts of the case an e-mail address not contained in the body of the message did not comprise a 'signature' for the purpose of the Statute of Frauds 1677, s 4).

The security aspects of many online contractual arrangements and negotiations can be of extreme importance, and the problem may become even greater where bank details or the availability of a person's electronic signature are concerned. The ingenuity of fraudsters and computer hackers has no limit, and e-commerce would not be possible without the ability of encryption techniques to help safeguard the confidentiality of much of the material that is transmitted electronically. Such technical questions raise no particular legal problems, but you should be aware of the part that encryption plays in the role of certification providers, and in the use of card and bank details in commercial and consumer transactions.

20.4 Law and jurisdiction, choices and application

In many respects, the question of the system of law properly applicable to an e-commerce contract is very similar to what you have already looked at in **Chapter 8**, at **8.3** and **8.4**, on the Rome Convention and its replacement, Regulation (EC) No 593/2008. Primacy is given to the choice of law of the parties, subject only to the interposition of mandatory rules of law. Special provision is made to protect the positions of consumers and employees, and a most important provision is in place to deal with Internet selling to consumers; under Regulation (EC) 593/2008, Article 6.1(b), where any person exercising his trade or profession directs his activities by any means (including the Internet) at a Member State where the consumer has his habitual residence, the governing law of the contract will be that of the particular Member State.

As regards choice or determination of jurisdiction, this again is dealt with at **8.2;** and the special rules for determining the jurisdiction in consumer cases, particularly the rule on Internet selling to consumers in Member States under Regulation 44/2001 ('Brussels II'), Article 15, is explained at **8.2.4**.

In situations where, for whatever reason, none of the above provisions applies, the questions of jurisdiction and applicable law will be determined by the rules on jurisdiction and conflict of laws of the forum where the dispute is heard.

20.5 The application of intellectual property law to e-commerce

This is a highly complex and technical matter, some of which has already been been discussed, briefly, when looking at the separate types of IP rights in earlier chapters. A summary of the main areas relating to IP disputes is given below.

20.5.1 Domain name disputes

There have probably been more squabbles about the right to use domain names as such, or about IP-related claims that have a domain name angle to them, than about most other areas of e-commerce, so that a brief examination of the problem is called for. In respect of the right to the 'ownership' and use of any particular domain name, without any additional claim that someone's IP rights are infringed, this will sometimes involve a claimant who claims the right to use a domain name or stop others from using it; the defendants will often be the bodies concerned with the allocation or registration of such names, such as ICANN (US-based allocation system) and Nominet (the UK allocation body). These disputes are essentially contractual. Such a matter may be resolved by litigation, as in *Pitman Training Ltd v Nominet UK* [1997] FSR 797, but nowadays the issue will more usually be dealt with by recourse to the dispute resolution mechanism used by the particular allocation body.

Such disputes, often with an international aspect, can involve difficult constitutional law problems at times, as in *Pocket Kings Ltd v Safenames Ltd* [2009] EWHC 2529, [2009] All ER (D) 205 (Oct), where the High Court refused to enforce a penal forfeiture order against a domain name, made by the State of Kentucky, USA (the order was made on the basis that the activities promoted by the site were illegal in that state).

The other main problem area with domain names lies in the potential infringement of IP rights, where the domain name is the same as, or close to, a word trade mark which is owned by someone else. These issues are examined below.

20.5.2 Passing off

There are many cases where the use of a domain name allegedly passes off the user's products or services as those of another. The law on this is very much the same as with any other form of passing off. A very clear example is seen in *Phones 4u Ltd and Another v Phone4u.co.uk Internet Ltd* [2006] EWCA Civ 244, where the defendant, having registered the domain name 'Phone4u.co.uk' at a time when a chain of shops owned by the claimant had established a thriving business using the 'Phones 4u' mark, was held to have passed off its products as those of the claimant. From the date of acquisition of the domain name, there could not be any realistic use of the name without deception; to register and use the name of a well-known company as a domain name to draw in custom was fraudulent.

Beyond the mere use of the domain name, the way in which any e-commerce transmission, or website, uses or displays material may constitute a passing off of someone else's good or services, provided that the classic indicia of the tort – reputation, misrepresentation leading to confusion and damage – can be established. Indeed, the very width of the common law tort (relating to 'get up', display and promotional technique, etc, as well as marks) makes passing off a serious possibility in e-commerce.

20.5.3 Trade marks

Again, the potential infringement of a registered trade mark, either in the domain name or in the other transmitted material, arises in the same way as with any other circumstance, by coming within the statutory acts of infringement. You will have seen already (at **13.9**) that there are very many trade mark cases involving the use of websites, so it is not necessary to repeat that material here. Nevertheless, a case of huge importance to the use of trade marks on the Internet is presently on foot: in *Interflora Inc v Marks and Spencer plc* [2009] EWHC 1095

(Ch), [2009] All ER (D) 217 (May), Arnold J has agreed to refer to the ECJ for guidance certain questions that may have extensive repercussions. The case concerns the use by the defendant of Google's 'Adword' and sponsored link systems for allowing potential advertisers to purchase the use of keywords, many of which are the same as registered trade marks, urls and domain names (here, 'Interflora' signs and variations on them). Curiously, Google's current policy seems to be to accept notification by any affected mark owners and block the purchase of 'their' keywords by other would-be users in all the Member States of the EC, except for the UK and Ireland; this may, perhaps, be because Google feels that the last-named national courts would be more acquiescent to this policy.

This case and the ECJ reference should be watched with care, as the consequent guidance should be helpful to all persons interested in e-commerce, advertising and search engine design. The eventual result of the *L'Oréal SA v Bellure NV* litigation, in consequence of the ECJ reference, discussed at **13.9.2** above, should also help to clarify the limits of permissible use of trade marks in comparative advertising, both for the purposes of the UK law and for Community law.

Another very important case, in which guidance is being sought from the ECJ, is *L'Oréal SA v eBay International AG* [2009] EWHC 1094 (Ch). Here, the question is whether eBay can be held liable for the infringements of trade marks by the users of eBay, in arranging sales; Arnold J is, at the time of writing, in the process of referring several questions on this matter to the ECJ, and this is discussed, in the context of statutory defences available to 'information society service providers', ie websites, at **20.7.1** below.

20.5.4 Copyright

This is a vast topic, and a couple of paragraphs can do no more than skim over its surface; nevertheless, you should be aware of the enormous potential for problems from this direction. Almost everything that ever gets onto a website or into an electronic transmission has some sort of copyright in it, or would have were the material not out of its copyright period. The rules for the substantive existence and infringement of copyrights of different types have been explored in **Chapter 14**; in particular, you will have realised that the simple downloading of material by a computer will constitute a copying which, if it is not licensed by the owner of the right, may comprise an infringing act. You will also know that there are many defences to copying, such as 'fair use' for various purposes, as well as transient copying as part of a technological process under s 28A of CDPA 1988.

The most widespread defence available to the users of websites is that they use the site under the licence of the copyright owner, but that can avail them nothing where the person who put the material on the site did not own the copyright in it in the first place – he might have infringed the copyright and, theoretically, the person downloading it might become a secondary infringer (and, if he passes it on, a primary infringer). That has led to enormous problems involving 'framing' (placing material on a website so that it is displayed on a different site), 'deep linking' (linking one site to the inside pages on another site) and 'peer to peer/information/file sharing' sites.

All sorts of counter-measures have been tried to deal with unauthorised use of copyright material, but the one potent extension of legal powers in this area is probably the Copyright and Related Rights Regulations 2003 (SI 2003/2498), which aim to prevent the circumvention of technological measures which are in place to protect the copyright (and other IP rights such as the database right, etc), where copyright works are made available to the public by electronic means. This has led, inter alia, to the amendment of s 296 and the insertion of ss 296ZA–296ZG of CDPA 1988. Nevertheless, copyright issues are likely to provide the greatest IP challenge to the future development of the information society, the Internet and e-commerce; time alone will tell whether there is any achievable and practical answer. In the meantime, the courts and enforcement authorities wrestle with the problem using the tools currently available to them, on a case-by-case basis.

20.6 Business to business e-commerce

As explained at **20.1** above, most of the legislation in this area is aimed at the use of websites by consumers to obtain goods and services, not two businesses arranging a contract by e-mail, except in one crucial respect – almost all of this legislation is based upon the European Community requirement for a level playing field in respect of the conduct of business and commerce. Vital to that end are the requirements for fair consumer practice, for freedom of movement of goods and services, for rights of establishment and for fair competition practices. It would therefore be a great mistake to assume that the use of e-commerce would somehow release the parties from any of these requirements, if the contract could potentially generate any EC Member State effects at all. When one adds in the fact that electronic communications leave an indelible trail for the skilled investigator to follow (who may have impressive powers of investigation and enforcement where these EC or domestic matters are involved), it becomes clear that the apparent freedom from legislation is a dangerous trap for the unwary. The speed with which transactions can be entered into electronically only adds to the danger. The parties to a B2B arrangement, set up without the use of a public access website, should take very great care about the content and legal effect of all of their electronic communications.

Some of the likely risks for B2B arrangements come from competition law (dangers of 'concerted practices' arising out of frequent communications, even if there are no express agreements, for Article 81 EC Treaty purposes); from impermissible use of confidential information, or copyright or other protected material in e-mails or attachments; and from failing to deal with important points (such as law or jurisdiction points, or incorporation of terms) given the pressure, as regards pace and time, to enter a deal. If B2B contracts are entered into using a website, consideration has to be given to whether there is any way that one party (who must be a natural person) might be seen as acting as a 'consumer' in the transaction; although it will be a rare occurrence, that is not an impossibility, and it could make a great deal of difference as to statutory rules governing the contract (see **20.7** below).

20.7 Business to consumer e-commerce

Here, the emphasis moves to the consumer (in an extended sense) protection requirements of European and domestic law. This section is premised on the assumption that the consumer purchase of goods and/or services is via a website. The three main areas of statutory regulation that should be considered are set out in **20.7.1** to **20.7.3** below.

20.7.1 The Electronic Commerce (EC Directive) Regulations 2002

The 2002 Regulations were enacted, in response to the E-commerce Directive, to regulate the provision of goods, services and information to consumers (and others; see further below) by electronic means by 'information society service providers' (ISSPs). This is mainly aimed at the Internet, although it can extend to other means of electronic communication. The definition of an ISS, given in reg 2 (see the **Appendix** to this work), is

> any service normally provided for remuneration, at a distance, by means of electronic equipment for the processing … and storage of data, and at the individual request of the recipient of the service.

'Consumer' is defined as 'any natural person who is acting for purposes other than his trade, business or profession'. 'Recipient of the service' extends, by contrast, to 'any person who, *for professional ends or otherwise*, uses an information society service, in particular for the purposes of seeking information or making it accessible'(emphasis added). You will see, from this last definition, that the reach of the 2002 Regulations goes beyond mere consumer protection; care is needed in their application and interpretation, as many people may use such ISSs without necessarily intending to enter any consumer contracts. The E-commerce Directive makes clear in its Recitals that it is intended to cover economic activities, which comprise services providing on-line information and search facilities etc, regardless of the fact that those services may not be paid for by the immediate recipient of them.

Regulation 6 (see **Appendix**) governs the detailed information that must be provided by the ISSP. Regulation 6(1) deals with the requirement for transparency regarding the identity, location and contact details of the ISSP, and other professional and regulatory information, including the ISSP's VAT identification number (reg 6(1)(g)). Regulation 6(2) requires, vitally, that where an ISS refers to prices, they must be indicated clearly, unambiguously and indicate, in particular, whether they are inclusive of tax and delivery costs.

Regulation 7 deals with the required attributes and content of 'commercial communications'. A commercial communication is defined in reg 2 as:

> a communication, in any form, designed to promote, directly or indirectly, the goods, services or image of any person pursuing a commercial, industrial or craft activity or exercising a regulated profession ...

This is a very wide definition indeed, clearly extending to advertising. Where such a communication is made, it must be identifiable as such, it must identify the person on whose behalf it is made, it must clearly identify any promotional offer as such, and it must ensure that any conditions are made accessible and are clear and unambiguous (reg 7(a)–(d)). Remember that a commercial communication can arise simply in the provision of information services; it is not restricted to on-line contracting situations.

Regulations 9 and 11 are concerned with the provision of information and the placing of the order where a contract is to be concluded by electronic means (see **Appendix**). They have been considered briefly at **20.3.1** above, but the point to take from the wording of both regulations is that they do contemplate possible application to contracts where neither party deals as a consumer, in which case the parties may agree to arrangements different from those required by the Regulations. Where a consumer is involved, reg 9 requires that, *prior* to the placing of an order, certain information that is vital to the interests of the consumer must be provided in a clear and unambiguous form by the ISSP. Of fundamental importance, where the ISSP provides terms and conditions applicable to the contract, it must make these available to the service recipient in a way that allows for their storage and reproduction (reg 9(3)); this last provision is mandatory, even if the contract is concluded by individual e-mail exchange, whereas the other requirements of reg 9 do not apply in such non-website contracting situations. Regulation 11 deals with the requirements where an order is placed by 'technological means' (not defined); the ISSP must acknowledge receipt to the service recipient, without undue delay and by electronic means. The ISSP must also make available to the recipient satisfactory means of allowing him to identify and correct input errors, prior to the placing of the order (reg 11(1)(a), (b)). Regulation 11(1) is not applicable to contracts concluded by e-mail. Order and acknowledgement are deemed received when the addressees are able to access them (reg 11(2)).

Regulations 17–19 provide important defences to ISSPs, and it seems likely that these defences will enjoy even greater prominence with the increased sophistication of the types of Internet services becoming available. Each of these regulations provides that there shall not be any liability for damages or for any other pecuniary remedy, or for any criminal sanction as a result of certain types of transmission in a communication network (in respect of regs 17, 18), provision of access to an information network (reg 17 only), or storage of information, whether in a communication network or not (reg 19). These provisions are silent as to the court's injunctive powers, but reg 20 preserves such rights to apply to the court where regs 17–19 apply.

Regulation 17 deals with the situation where an ISSP acts as a 'mere conduit', ie where the ISSP did not initiate the transmission or select the receiver of it, and did not select or modify the information in the transmission (reg 17(1)). The 'mere conduit' aspect also applies where there is automatic, intermediate and transient storage of the information for the sole purpose of carrying out the transmission in the communication network, and the information is not stored for longer than reasonably necessary for the transmission (reg 17(2)).

Regulation 18 deals with 'caching', ie where the information in the transmission is stored for the sole purpose of making efficient onward transmission of the information to other recipients of the service upon their request. The defence will apply where the ISSP does not modify the information and complies with stringent requirements as to updating and access to the information, contained in reg 18(b).

Regulation 19 deals with 'hosting', ie where the ISSP stores information provided by the recipient of the service. The defence applies where the ISSP has no actual knowledge of unlawful activity or information and, where a damages claim is made, is not aware of facts or circumstances from which it would have been apparent to the ISSP that the activity or information was unlawful. It also applies where, upon obtaining such knowledge or awareness, the ISSP acts expeditiously to remove or disable access to the information. In either circumstance, it must be shown that the recipient of the service was not acting under the authority or control of the ISSP.

These are clearly valuable safeguards for the ISSP, but as yet there is little clear guidance on their application in practice. That may soon change, though, as a result of the forthcoming ECJ reference in *L'Oréal SA v eBay International AG* [2009] EWHC 1094 (Ch). In this case, Arnold J succinctly stated the issues as:

(a) whether eBay was responsible for trade mark infringements by users of its online marketplace; and

(b) whether eBay itself committed primary trade mark infringements in the same circumstance.

Certain of the defendants were held clearly to have infringed the claimant's marks, but on the basis of authorities on the procurement of torts by others and accessory liability, eBay was held not to be a joint tortfeasor with those defendants. The question was whether eBay had itself infringed various word trade marks, by its use and purchase of linkword and keyword methods of using sponsored links on major third-party search engines, eg Google etc. That allowed users of eBay to access many sites where counterfeit products, using infringing marks, were on offer. Linkmarks on eBay's site also brought about this result.

Among other contentions, there was a question as to whether eBay could raise a defence under Article 14 of the E-commerce Directive, upon which the statutory defences in regs 17-19 are based. It is very clear from the inconsistent case law discussed in the case report, and the decision to refer questions on the point to the ECJ, that there is a real lack of clarity about the true extent of these defences, particularly that of hosting (reg 19). It is probably not overstating the point to suggest that this guidance, along with at least three other ECJ references on allied points by other courts, when it becomes available, has the potential to cause some serious re-thinking of the responsibility and liability of ISSPs for whatever uses are made of their sites. It may also have considerable repercussions for the practice and consequences of keyword and linkword use and search design. We must await the guidance from the ECJ and its application by the English courts.

Non-compliance with the requirements of the 2002 Regulations is actionable at the instance of enforcement authorities (which may involve civil or criminal law proceedings) and at the instance of ISS recipients, whether parties to a contract covered by the 2002 Regulations or not. The principal statutory remedies are:

(a) a claim for damages for breach of statutory duty (reg 13);

(b) a court order to require the supply of contract terms or conditions to comply with reg 9(3) (reg 14);

(c) the right to apply to the court for rescission, if the ISSP does not provide the means for correcting input errors required by reg 11(1)(b) (reg 15);

(d) protection of the right of any person to seek court relief to stop infringement of any rights (reg 20).

20.7.2 The Consumer Protection (Distance Selling) Regulations 2000

The Consumer Protection (Distance Selling) Regulations 2000 (SI 2000/2334) ('the 2000 Regulations'), in contrast to the 2002 Regulations (see **20.7.1** above), really are a consumer protection measure, enacted in response to Council Directive 997/7/EC on Distance Selling. As this work is not primarily aimed at consumer protection law, only a brief explanation of the provisions is given below, to show the demands upon the suppliers of goods and services, mainly as regards the information requirements of 'distance communications' under contracts having a distance selling component ('distance contract'). It must be said that the 2000 Regulations came into being before today's white-knuckle ride into website selling really developed, and it is not always easy to apply the language of the Regulations to the modern retail situation. Nevertheless, the following points may be made:

(a) Under reg 3, a 'distance contract' means a consumer contract for goods or services under an organised distance sales or service provision scheme run by the supplier who, for the purpose of the contract, makes exclusive use of one or more means of distance communication, up to and including the moment when the contract is concluded. The definition of a 'means of distance communication' extends to any means, other than communication by the simultaneous physical presence of the parties; an indicative list in Sch 1 shows all sorts of paper and paperless communication as well as electronic mail, but clearly pre-dates the website age. Nevertheless, the 2000 Regulations would make little sense unless websites are included. That much is completely clear from the limited discussion of the Regulations in *L'Oréal SA v eBay International AG* [2009] EWHC 1094 (Ch).

(b) Regulations 5 and 6 concern 'excepted contracts' and contracts in which the Regulations apply only to parts. The main exceptions are land, building, financial services and auction contracts. Regulation 6(2) provides that the requirements imposed by regs 7–18 and 19(1) are not applicable to contracts for food, beverages or other everyday consumption articles delivered to a consumer's home or workplace by regular roundsmen (reg 6(2)(a)). Bearing in mind the massive increase in home deliveries of daily necessaries by the large general store groups, this raises a considerable question of applicability of the 2000 Regulations. Neither do those particular regulations apply to specific date/period provision of accommodation, transport, catering or leisure services (reg 6(2)(b)).

(c) Regulation 7 requires the provision, in good time prior to the conclusion of the contract, of details of the supplier and his commercial purpose; details of the goods or services; prices, including taxes and delivery costs; payment, delivery and performance details and requirements; notice of cancellation rights; period of validity of price or offer; details of substitutability of goods, etc and other matters. Regulation 8 deals with other written and additional information that may be required, according to circumstances, relating to rights of cancellation (reg 8(2)), obligations to return goods, complaints, after-sales service and guarantees, etc.

(d) Regulation 10(1) provides a powerful consumer protection measure, consisting of a right of cancellation by notice (as modified or excepted by regs 11–13). The effect of such notice, if properly given, is that the contract is treated as if it had never been made (reg 10(2)). The notice must be written or in other durable medium, available and accessible to the buyer; the available modes of giving the notice are prescribed (by reg 10(4)) as hand delivery, post, fax or e-mail.

Regulation 11 provides a withdrawal period (for the purposes of inspection, etc), so that the cancellation period for sales of goods begins on the day of conclusion (entry) of the contract and ends on the expiry of seven working days starting with the day of receipt of the goods (in circumstances where the supplier has complied with reg 8(2) – notice of the cancellation regime); where the supplier has not complied with his obligation under reg 8(2), the cancellation period can be much longer – up to three months and seven working days, beginning on the day after the day of receipt of the goods. Regulation 12 provides a very similar notice and cancellation regime for contracts for services.

There are a number of exceptions to the right to cancel to be seen in reg 13, the most important of which are: cases where performance of a contract to supply services had commenced, with the consumer's agreement; cases where there is the supply of goods or services, the price of which depended on financial market fluctuations beyond the supplier's control; contracts for the supply of customised goods or goods subject to rapid expiry or deterioration; situations where there is a supply of audio or video recordings or software that is unsealed by the consumer.

(e) Regulation 14 provides for the return, on a cancellation, of sums paid by the consumer as soon as possible, and in any case within 30 days starting with the day of notice of cancellation. Regulation 17 deals with the obligations of the consumer, on a cancellation, to retain and take care of the goods pending their return, and his duties in respect of their return. The consumer has no duty to deliver up the goods, except at his own premises and in pursuance of a written request given by the supplier to the consumer before or at the time of collection (reg 10(4)); the consumer can, however, send the goods back to the supplier at his own expense, so as to end his duties of safeguarding and retaining possession of them (reg 10(5)).

(f) Regulation 19(1) is important: unless the parties agree otherwise, the supplier shall perform the contract within a maximum of 30 days, beginning with the day after the day the consumer sent his order. A contract that has not been performed within that period (or whatever was otherwise agreed) is treated as if it had not been made, save for any rights that the consumer has under it for non-performance (reg 19(5)). Any security provided to the supplier for the contract performance must be returned in this circumstance.

(g) Regulation 24 deals with the situation of inertia selling, ie unsolicited goods sent to a person with a view to that person acquiring them, where there has been no agreement by the recipient to acquire or return them. The recipient is entitled to treat those goods (as between himself and the sender) as an unconditional gift.

Enforcement of the 2000 Regulations takes two main forms. First, the enforcement authorities may apply for injunctions to secure compliance under reg 27. The secondary form (but which is probably the most effective) is that there is no contracting out of the Regulations; any contract term that is inconsistent with the consumer protection provided by the Regulations is void to that extent (reg 25(1)).

The question of the applicability of the Regulations to some of the more novel methods of using e-commerce to sell things at a distance has not enjoyed a great deal of court time. In the recent case of *L'Oréal SA v eBay International AG* [2009] EWHC 1094 (Ch), the question arose as to the extent that the Regulations might apply to activities pursued on eBay. Arnold J was, at the time of writing (October 2009), in the process of hearing submissions on various issues, with the intention of making an ECJ reference on them; it is not clear whether these references will include anything on this point, but it seems unlikely as the point only arose at the hearing and was not expressly pleaded.

20.7.3 The Privacy and Electronic Communications (EC Directive) Regulations 2003

The Privacy and Electronic Communications (EC Directive) Regulations 2003 (SI 2003/2426) ('the 2003 Regulations') came into being as a result of Directive 2002/85 EC. They provide a specialised and focused regime of data protection in the realm of electronic communications, which are, of course, essential to the functioning of e-commerce. The 2003 Regulations have wider application than just to e-commerce, in that many of the provisions concern both Internet use and telephone network applications. The main provisions, for present purposes are regs 4–8 and 22–23.

Regulation 4 provides that nothing in the 2003 Regulations relieves a person of obligations under the Data Protection Act 1998 in respect of personal data. Really, the only concern, for present purposes, is with personal data, which is discussed at **21.2.1**. A good deal of the Act is concerned with the security and regulation of public electronic communications, which is beyond the direct relevance of this chapter.

Regulation 5 requires the provider of a public electronic communications service and the provider of any communications network by means of which that service is provided, between them to take appropriate measures to safeguard the security of that service. Notwithstanding this, if there remains a significant risk to the security of the system, the service provider must inform the subscriber, free of charge, about that risk and what might be done to safeguard against it, as well as the likely cost of such protective measures to the subscriber.

Regulation 6 deals with confidentiality of information, and prevents the accessing or storing of information from a subscriber's or user's computer terminal, except where that person is told about the purpose for the access or storage and is given the opportunity to refuse access or storage. This is the basis of the famous 'cookie' box on websites. Regulation 7 deals with the necessary limitations on 'traffic data', the normal electronic nuts and bolts that make the whole electronic communication transmission work. These data must be erased or modified so they cease to be 'personal' data, when no longer required for transmission purposes, unless the subscriber has given permission for their retention for the time necessary for specific marketing or 'value-adding' purposes. Regulation 8 further expands upon the scope of activities for which such permission may be sought, but provides the usual saving for provision of traffic data to competent authorities acting under statutory powers, or under any provision relating to the settlement of disputes (reg 8(4)).

Regulations 22 and 23 deal with transmission of unsolicited communications and for direct marketing, where the identity or address of the sender is concealed. They really are dealing with spam/junk. In both cases, the practices are forbidden by the Regulations, except that there is a provision in reg 22(3) which allows transmissions, for direct marketing purposes, of unsolicited communications where the recipient has 'opted in' to such communications.

Remedies for failure to comply with the 2003 Regulations are set out in reg 30 (proceedings for compensation for damage caused by failure to comply); reg 31 (enforcement of the requirements as under Data Protection Act 1998, Pt V, Schs 6, 9); reg 32 (requests to the Information Commissioner by OFCOM or aggrieved person to take enforcement action, or such steps by the Commissioner at his own instance).

20.8 Payment aspects of e-commerce transactions

You have already seen (at **Chapter 10**) how international sales of goods are facilitated by documentary methods, by the transfer of shipping and insurance documents, by documentary credits and by the use of bills of exchange. It should come as no surprise to you to find that all of these techniques are very easily adapted to e-commerce transactions and to other international and domestic contracts, for almost all purposes for which people enter contracts. With e-commerce, the entire process is greatly enhanced by the developments in the international banking world of Internet banking, of electronic transfer of funds and other documents between banks, and of the massive expansion of large-scale credit providers into credit/debit card provision. Again, it is necessary to draw distinctions between B2B e-commerce, using e-mails etc, and the use of website selling, the latter having far more B2C use. With B2B e-commerce, the risk of fraud (which is usually in obtaining something, without any intention of paying for it) can often be minimised where the supplier is in a strong enough bargaining position to obtain independent credit guarantees or money 'up front'. Where the supplier is not in such a strong position, there are considerable risks, but some of these might be reduced, at the supplier's expense, by credit insurance.

With B2C transactions, using websites, the situation can be better for the supplier, and particularly so for the consumer. A great deal of electronic selling involves credit card payment, and the supplier is largely safeguarded against fraudulent customers by the fact that the cost of any card fraud falls back on the credit supplier, the supplier's position being enhanced, in most cases, by the requirement that the credit/payment is available before any performance is made. The risk for a consumer of a fraudulent supplier trying to obtain either money or the customer's details is, nevertheless, quite high. A fair measure of protection for loss of money is provided by the Consumer Credit Act 1974 (CCA 1974), ss 83 and 84, to limit losses to £50 prior to notification to the bank that the card is lost, stolen or being misused. Further protection is given by the Consumer Protection (Distance Selling) Regulations 2000, reg 21, which provides that consumers can cancel a payment where fraudulent use is made of credit cards in contracts covered by the 2000 regulations; the consumer is then entitled to be re-credited, or to have money returned to him. The burden is on the card issuer to show that any use of the card was authorised by the card holder (reg 21(3)). Regulation 21 does not apply to any contract falling within s 83 of CCA 1974; these two mutually-exclusive provisions, between them, provide quite comprehensive protection to the consumer.

Protection for the consumer against poor performance of the contract by the supplier comes through the 'connected lender' liability imposed by s 75 of CCA 1974 for claims between £100 and £30,000 arising from a debtor/creditor/supplier arrangement (see *Office of Fair Trading v Lloyds TSB Bank plc and Others* [2006] EWCA Civ 268, [2007] QB 1). This is explained in more detail at **6.4.1.3**.

20.9 Liabilities of ISSPs and others

You will have already come across many instances of liability during your reading of this chapter, and it will perhaps help if a short summary of the position is offered. This is a rapidly developing field, and the courts will be likely to have to react to new techniques and novel legal questions with some rapidity over the coming years.

20.9.1 The position with contracts arranged by exchange of electronic mail

Normally, the situation here is as with any paper or oral contract: provided the parties have restricted their communications to what was necessary for the contract, the only liabilities to arise will usually be as between the parties. It would still be possible for liability to third parties to arise, under normal legal principles, if the arrangement created any tort (such as publishing defamatory statements, procuring breaches of contract or other economic torts, or breaches of trust, etc). Nevertheless, potential third-party liability is probably much less than where widely accessible websites are concerned.

20.9.2 The position with website e-commerce

Here, the situation is very different: the whole idea of a person being provided with virtually free access to a site from which links and connections may lead to an almost unlimited amount of data, belonging to and referring to all sorts of legal entities, is truly a modern Pandora's box.

The potential for legal liability to arise is, frankly, immense, particularly if one considers the further possibilities of defamation, IP infringements etc, associated with many sites.

The position of the ISSP's liability has been discussed already in various contexts; it might be summed up by saying that whatever it provides or facilitates is designed to be part of the information society, and there is no particular reason why it should not be responsible for whatever harms ensue to others, within the limits permissible under whatever laws are in place at the particular time. The material discussed at **20.7.1**, concerning the E-commerce Directive and the 2002 Regulations, shows that the liability of the ISSP can be very wide, but that we should be in a better position to understand the matter, and the position with regard to statutory hosting defences, once the ECJ has delivered rulings and guidance on the cases before it at the moment (late 2009). Probably the greatest immediate problems arise from the use of link/keyword practices, and from the questions concerning accessory liability for torts and other wrongs committed by service users using interactive sites.

The position between the ISSP and its own users is normally contractual, so that is probably easier to analyse than third-party liability; it will simply depend upon the terms of the contract between the parties, subject to the power of the governing legislation to affect or to invalidate those terms, including the effects of UCTA 1977.

20.10 Conclusion

As you will have seen, a body of law and practice has had to be created and applied with completely unprecedented rapidity, to deal with the growth of the information society and e-commerce. There are probably many more questions still to be asked and answered than have already been considered by the legislators and the courts, but the general framework of workable legal systems for e-commerce is discernible on both sides of the Atlantic. The real challenge will come as the giant nations of Asia begin to make their influence and impact felt – upon commerce generally, upon e-commerce in particular, and upon the world of the commercial lawyer. The emphasis is clearly becoming one of globalisation, so that the budding commercial lawyer is well advised to keep abreast of the information available from sources relevant to the growth in world trade. Some useful source locations are given below:

- International Chamber of Commerce – www.iccwbo.org
- ICANN (Internet Corporation for Assigned Names and Numbers) – www.icann.com
- Nominet UK – www.nominet.org.uk
- World Intellectual Property organisation – www.wipo.org
- World Trade Organisation – www.wto.org

Chapter 21
Data Protection and Freedom of Information

21.1	Introduction	305
21.2	Overview and scope of DPA 1998	306
21.3	The rights of the data subject and other persons under DPA 1998	311
21.4	The obligations of the data controller and disclosure restrictions	313
21.5	Exemptions	314
21.6	Requests from outside the EC	316
21.7	Enforcement, offences and civil damages	316
21.8	Conclusion on data protection	317
21.9	Freedom of information	318

21.1 Introduction

Data about persons or businesses have always been valuable and sensitive commodities, but in the last 30 years or so, the exponential growth and availability of computer systems to assemble, arrange and transfer data has posed a challenge for legal systems worldwide. The demand for such data is insatiable, and to allow unrestricted holding of, and access to them would rapidly lead to chaos and criminality. The only applicable English law, prior to the recent information explosion, worked on the basis of the protection of confidence (see **Chapter 18**), and there was little statutory control of data beyond that. That case law has the broad effect of treating certain confidential information as being within the reach and protection of the equitable jurisdiction. This was completely inadequate to deal with the huge proliferation of potentially accessible databases, containing mundane but highly valuable information. After major investigations and various government reports, coupled with the need to have legal protections compatible with those of the rest of the EC, the Data Protection Act 1984 was enacted. This Act was regulatory in effect and it could not cover paper-based systems; it set out certain guiding principles and its enforcement was largely in the hands of a Data Protection Registrar, with some compensation available for affected individuals. Its effect was to make the handling of personal information subject to controls which had not existed before.

21.1.1 Data Protection Act 1998

The 1984 Act proved a somewhat tentative start, but it was overtaken by a much more robust approach in the European Data Protection Directive of 1995 (95/46/EC). This was enacted as the Data Protection Act 1998 (DPA 1998), which is the current governing legislation. The main effects of the Act are to protect the right of individual privacy and to harmonise UK law with that of other Member States. At first glance, one might consider that this legislation is all about individual protection, but that would be a mistake. Directive 95/46/EC originated out of the highly protectionist attitudes, in some EC Member States, towards the national legal limitations that might be imposed upon the free flow of personal data between, and within, Member States. Data are a valuable source of commercial advantage, and it was certainly the case that, prior to the Directive, trade barriers effectively were being created by national rules on data protection and dissemination. The aim of the Directive is to give no more protection to data processing than is commensurate with a balance between the rights of natural persons and the maintenance of a free market within the EC, by harmonising national legal rules. This will be seen in some of the case law referred to below.

The scheme of the DPA 1998 is to require a 'data controller' to be registered (and to maintain registration) before he can lawfully 'process' any 'personal data' about a 'data subject' (see **21.2** for the meaning of these terms). In other words, before anyone can obtain or deal with any personal information about an identifiable individual, in a systematic way, that data controller must be on a publicly accessible register. Once on the register and in a position to deal with the data, the data controller may deal with the data only for the purposes and within the limits imposed by the Act; and even then, some 'sensitive personal data' will require further special treatment and protection.

The data subject is always in a position to require the data controller to give him basic rights of access to information about what data the controller holds and what is being done, or is likely to be done, with the data. There is a wide range of criminal sanctions available against persons who fail to comply with the requirements of the Act (see **21.7**). The enforcement of the Act is in the hands of the Information Commissioner (formerly known as the Data Protection Commissioner), who, along with his department, regulates, enforces and prosecutes on behalf of the public. The Commissioner is also involved in all aspects of data protection, including European cooperation, advice to the public and to individuals, and the encouragement of good practice, as well as the development and publication of codes of practice. There was formerly a Data Protection Tribunal, now known as the Information Tribunal ('the Tribunal'), which hears a variety of appeals against various regulatory steps taken under the DPA 1998 and the Freedom of Information Act 2000 (FOIA 2000).

21.1.2 Freedom of Information Act 2000

The emergence of data protection legislation has been mainly about protecting the individual's expectation to the privacy of personal data. Over the same period of time, another public expectation has arisen: that of open government and freedom of information about the acts of public authorities. Always a contentious matter, the 'right to know' was not particularly European in origin but has developed more in the common law nations of the world over the last half century. English public law and criminal law show many cases in which the relationship between public access to information and the privacy of the decision-making process is hard to discern with clarity. There was a clear public demand and need for more to be done. Following a period from 1994 during which the Government used a voluntary 'Code of Practice on Public Access to Government Information' (overseen by the Parliamentary Ombudsman), the FOIA 2000 was passed.

The big difference between the DPA 1998 and the FOIA 2000 is that the former deals with the private protection of personal data, whereas the latter is concerned with public access to government information. Nevertheless, there can be overlap, as public authorities, for FOIA 2000 purposes, may also be data controllers for the purpose of the DPA 1998. However, detailed discussion of that overlap is beyond the scope of this work. This chapter deals first with data protection and then with freedom of information.

21.2 Overview and scope of DPA 1998

The DPA 1998 improved upon the DPA 1984 in a number of ways:

(a) manual files are now included as well as automated data;

(b) new conditions for legal processing of data were laid down;

(c) a new category of personal data was created – 'sensitive data';

(d) transfer of personal data to countries outside the European Economic Area was prohibited, unless certain conditions were met;

(e) minimum security requirements for data were introduced; and

(f) more rights for individuals were introduced, including the right to compensation for damage or distress caused by unlawful processing.

The effects of the DPA 1998 fall into two categories. The first is to allow individuals access to information held about them, for example the information held about people by credit reference agencies. This may be inaccurate and a person would probably want to correct such inaccuracies. The second effect is to protect information about individuals from being disclosed improperly. So, if you give your bank or gas supplier certain information, you might not want them to disclose that information to another business, for example an insurance company, without your consent. Such information is very valuable commercially, and it should not be available for sale without your consent.

Nevertheless, protection of privacy has its limits; the DPA 1998 was given an unusual level of public attention following the murder of two young girls in the town of Soham in 2002. The killer would probably not have been given a job in proximity to children if background checks by two police forces had been carried out properly. In the resulting public inquiry conducted by Sir Michael Bichard, he rejected the suggestion that the DPA 1998 had prevented one police force adequately recording information about the man in question. To quote from the findings of the report:

> It is, as a member of the judiciary said recently, an 'inelegant and cumbersome' piece of legislation, but the legislation was not the problem. I suggest, however, that better guidance is needed on the collection, retention, deletion, use and sharing of information, so that police officers, social workers and other professionals can feel more confident in using information properly.

To understand the working of the Act, it is necessary first to look at some definitions which are closely interdependent (see **21.2.1**), then at some further interpretative measures (see **21.2.2**), and then to examine the principles of good practice and the preconditions for fair processing (see **21.2.3** and **21.2.4**).

21.2.1 The definitions of 'data controller', 'personal data', 'processing' and 'data subject'

These terms are defined in s 1(1) of the DPA 1998, by reference to each other, so that each and every definition and element must be satisfied in order to apply the law to the particular fact situation:

> 'data controller' means . . . a person who (either alone or jointly or in common with other persons) determines the purposes for which and the manner in which personal data are, or are to be, processed;
>
> 'personal data' means data which relate to a living individual who can be identified—
>
> (a) from those data, or
>
> (b) from those data and other information which is in the possession of, or is likely to come into the possession of, the data controller,
>
> and includes any expression of opinion about the individual and any indication of the intentions of the data controller or any other person in respect of the individual;
>
> 'processing', in relation to information or data, means obtaining, recording or holding the information or data or carrying out any operation or set of operations on the information or data, including—
>
> (a) organisation, adaptation or alteration of the information or data,
>
> (b) retrieval, consultation or use of the information or data,
>
> (c) disclosure of the information or data by transmission, dissemination or otherwise making available, or
>
> (d) alignment, combination, blocking, erasure or destruction of the information or data;
>
> 'data subject' means an individual who is the subject of personal data.

So, it is fairly easy to see the general scheme of the Act from the connection of these interpretative definitions; the data controller becomes responsible to the data subject from the first moment of dealing with any personal information that could identify the data subject as a living individual. At first sight, the DPA 1998 seems to have almost limitless scope, but that is deceptive because the Act has only limited application to the various processing methods by which data or information can be dealt with, as well as there being a wide range of exemptions provided for reasons of public policy; also, there have been some restrictive views of the courts as to how some parts of the Act are to be interpreted (see **21.2.2**).

In *Johnson v Medical Defence Union Ltd* [2007] EWCA Civ 262, the Court of Appeal, in a majority judgment, gave a restrictive view of the meaning of 'processing', after consideration of Directive 95/46/EC. The practice, at the defendant's business, whereby a risk manager summarised and made observations about selected files concerning the appellant, was held (Arden LJ dissenting) not to be 'processing' at all, for the purposes of the DPA 1998. The majority in the Court of Appeal took the view that the only matter complained about, which was the 'unfair' selecting of material by the risk manager, had been done by her own personal selection choice, there had been no automatic process at all at work. This seems to be an indication that the English courts view the purpose behind the Directive and the DPA 1998 to be that it is aimed at highly automated processing and retrieval schemes (see *Durant v FSA* at **21.2.2**).

21.2.2 'Personal data', 'data' and 'relevant filing systems'

We have already seen how the DPA 1998 works in a broad sense, but now it is necessary to see how far the provisions can reach. The definition of 'personal data' in s 1(1) is itself defined by reference to 'data'. The problem with that is that the s 1(1) definition of 'data' includes five, alternative classes of information, of which the most significant involves a 'relevant filing system', which term is then further defined in s 1(1).

The starting point is to find out what can comprise 'data' for these purposes:

> 'data' means information which—
>
> (a) is being processed by means of equipment operating automatically in response to instructions given for that purpose;
>
> (b) is recorded with the intention that it should be processed by means of such equipment;
>
> (c) is recorded as part of a relevant filing system or with the intention that it should form part of a relevant filing system;
>
> (d) does not fall within paragraph (a), (b) or (c) but forms part of an accessible record as defined by section 68; or
>
> (e) is recorded information held by a public authority and does not fall within any of paragraphs (a) to (d) ...

It is enough that the data fit within one class, although they may fit within more than one. Classes (a) and (b) are reasonably clear. Class (c) is very broad and can include paper-based systems. Class (d) can extend to health and education records that do not fit into other classes. Class (e) was added by the FOIA 2000.

Class (c) is likely to have much the most common application, and the definition of a 'relevant filing system' has caused, and will probably continue to cause, problems. That definition is as follows:

> 'relevant filing system' means any set of information relating to individuals to the extent that, although the information is not processed by means of equipment operating automatically in response to instructions given for that purpose, the set is structured, either by reference to individuals, or by reference to criteria relating to individuals, in such a way that specific information relating to a particular individual is readily accessible ...

In *Durant v Financial Services Authority* [2003] EWCA Civ 1746, the Court of Appeal restricted the meaning of a 'relevant filing system', and thus restricted the meaning of 'personal data'. Auld LJ held that the structure of a manual filing system would have to be 'on a par' with a computerised system for it to fall within the definition of a 'relevant filing system'. In other words, it would have to be highly organised. A mere collection of documents would not suffice. In the case in question, the effect was that the information did not have to be disclosed under the DPA 1998.

As regards the definition of 'personal data', the Court of Appeal held that data would 'relate to' an individual only if the data concerned a person's privacy. Two tests were suggested:

(a) Is the information *biographical* in a significant sense?

(b) Does the information have the *individual* as its focus, rather than other persons or matters?

The Information Commissioner has published guidance following the decision in *Durant*; see www.ico.gov.uk (search 'Durant'). Thus, it is suggested that the individual's name will be 'personal data' only where the name appears together with other information about the named individual such as address, telephone number or information regarding his hobbies. This comes from the decision of the ECJ in *Lindquist v Kammaraklagaren* (Case C-101/01) (ECJ, 6 November 2003). The Information Commissioner suggests that the following are also examples of personal data, provided the information in question can be linked to an identifiable individual:

(a) information about the medical history of an individual;

(b) an individual's salary details;

(c) information concerning an individual's tax liabilities;

(d) information comprising an individual's bank statements; and

(e) information about an individual's spending preferences.

In contrast, the Information Commissioner suggests that the following examples of information would not normally be personal data:

(a) mere reference to a person's name where the name is not associated with any other personal information;

(b) incidental mention in the minutes of a business meeting of an individual's attendance at that meeting in an official capacity; or

(c) where an individual's name appears on a document or e-mail indicating only that it has been sent or copied to that particular individual, the content of that document or e-mail does not amount to personal data about the individual unless there is other information about the individual within it.

Further, the Information Commissioner suggests that information which has as its focus something other than the individual will not constitute 'personal data'. For example, information which focuses on a property is not 'personal data'. The reason is that such information is not taken as something that will 'relate to' the individual. In contrast to this, there are circumstances where information about a house could be 'personal data'. For example, this could be a valuation of a house which was used in the context of divorce proceedings.

If an individual cannot be identified from the data in question then the data are not 'personal data', and therefore not subject to the DPA 1998. So, for example, if the information about patients taking part in a clinical experiment has the identifying information about individuals removed from the results, the results are not 'personal data'. The results are thus not subject to the access rights under the 1998 Act.

21.2.3 The eight principles of good practice

Anyone processing personal information must comply with eight enforceable principles of good information handling practice (DPA 1998, s 4(4)). These principles, contained in Sch 1, state that data must be:

1. fairly and lawfully processed;
2. processed for limited purposes;
3. adequate, relevant and not excessive;
4. accurate and up-to-date;
5. not kept longer than necessary;
6. processed in accordance with the individual's rights;
7. secure; and
8. not transferred to countries outside the European Economic Area unless the country has adequate protection for the individual.

To assist in facilitating good practice, s 51(3) of the DPA 1998 provides for the Information Commissioner and trade associations to be proactive in providing appropriate codes of practice to achieve industry/activity specific best practice in data protection. There are some widely used codes, including The Employment Practices Data Protection Code and The British Code of Advertising, Sales Promotion and Direct Marketing. This type of self-guidance and regulation is further supported by such measures as the Privacy and Electronic Communications (EC Directive) Regulations 2003 (SI 2003/2426), which generally apply to the area of electronic communication, including online marketing.

21.2.4 The six conditions for fair data processing and the obligation to register

At least one of the following conditions, seen in Sch 2 to the DPA 1998, must be met for personal information to be considered as having been processed fairly:

(a) the individual has consented to the processing;

(b) processing is necessary for the performance of a contract with the individual or for taking steps at the request of the individual with a view to entering into a contract;

(c) processing is required under a legal obligation (other than one imposed by the contract);

(d) processing is necessary to protect the vital interests of the individual;

(e) processing is necessary to carry out public functions, eg administration of justice; and

(f) processing is necessary in order to pursue the legitimate interests of the data controller or third parties (unless it could unjustifiably prejudice the interests of the individual).

In the *Johnson* case, discussed at **21.2.1**, it was said, obiter, in the Court of Appeal, that 'fairness' required consideration of both data subject and data user. The Court took the view that the defendant Medical Defence Union was running its business, as a mutual society for health professionals, for the benefit of all its members, as a whole. There was no suggestion of bad faith and it had adopted a clearly thought-out policy that was not, at its lowest, clearly unjustified. There were no grounds to interfere with the first instance finding that the processing was not unfair in any relevant respect. The defendant Union had acted as it did for the purpose of fulfilling its obligations to all its members; that can be seen to fit easily within, at the very least, conditions (c) and (f), above.

Where 'sensitive personal data' are to be processed (see **21.2.5**), one of the above conditions (at least) as well as at least one of a further set of conditions, found in Sch 3, must be met.

The requirement for data controllers to be on a public register stems from the 1995 Data Protection Directive, Article 18, which requires all Member States to provide that controllers notify supervisory authorities before carrying out any processing of personal data. This is put into effect by s 17 of the DPA 1998, which, in combination with s 21(1), makes it a criminal offence to process such data in the absence of registration of 'registrable particulars' and certain other matters concerning the data controller and its methods of achieving compliance with the seventh principle referred to in **21.2.3**: maintaining the security of the data. Currently, the registration period is 12 months, renewable in 12-month periods, for a fee of

£35 per data controller, regardless of the amount of processing involved. It must be stressed that s 17 must be complied with before any type of processing is commenced (including obtaining the data in the first place; see **21.2.1**); any unlawfulness cannot be cured retrospectively. See **21.7** for notification offences.

21.2.5 Sensitive personal data

Sensitive personal data are a sub-set of personal data. There are tighter controls on the processing of sensitive personal data. The relevant definition of 'sensitive personal data' is in s 2:

> In this Act 'sensitive personal data' means personal data consisting of information as to—
> (a) the racial or ethnic origin of the data subject,
> (b) his political opinions,
> (c) his religious beliefs or other beliefs of a similar nature,
> (d) whether he is a member of a trade union (within the meaning of the Trade Union and Labour Relations (Consolidation) Act 1992),
> (e) his physical or mental health or condition,
> (f) his sexual life,
> (g) the commission or alleged commission by him of any offence, or
> (h) any proceedings for any offence committed or alleged to have been committed by him, the disposal of such proceedings or the sentence of any court in such proceedings.

Sensitive personal data must be processed in accordance with the requirements of Sch 3, 'Conditions relevant for purposes of the first principle: processing of sensitive personal data'. For example:

> 1. The data subject has given his *explicit* [emphasis added] consent to the processing of the personal data.
> 2. (1) The processing is necessary for the purposes of exercising or performing any right or obligation which is conferred or imposed by law on the data controller in connection with employment.

There is a broad range of such conditions, based on public policy grounds. The conditions are alternatives and at least one must apply in any particular case.

21.2.6 Checklist to application of DPA 1998

At this point it is possible to see that some caution is needed in ascertaining whether the DPA 1998 applies to a situation in the first place. It is suggested that the following checklist order might be helpful:

(a) the data subject must be a living individual;
(b) data (within s 1(1)) must be in question; that may, but will not necessarily, involve consideration of whether a relevant filing system is involved;
(c) the data are personal data;
(d) some processing is involved;
(e) at least one precondition for processing within Sch 2 is met, and if sensitive personal data are involved, at least one from Sch 3 is met too;
(f) the data are processed in accordance with all the relevant data protection principles in Sch 1.

21.3 The rights of the data subject and other persons under DPA 1998

These matters are dealt with in Pt II of the Act. This Part recognises that personal data about one individual may well, if disclosed, identify other individuals and disclose information about those persons too. The rights, therefore, may extend to more than one individual in any particular case. The seven rights are as described at **21.3.1** to **21.3.7** below.

21.3.1 The right to subject access (s 7)

A data controller is not required to notify a data subject automatically about data held in respect of him. However, s 7 entitles a data subject to be informed by a data controller, upon request in writing, whether any personal data are being processed, what they comprise, the purposes for which they are being processed, and to whom the data are or may be disclosed. This is subject to some limits where multiple individuals might be identified and confidentiality is involved, but the right is enforceable by court order in difficult cases. Any request for information from a credit reference agency is deemed to be limited to personal data about financial standing, unless the contrary is clearly indicated in the request (s 9).

21.3.2 The right to prevent processing likely to cause damage or distress (s 10)

Any data subject is entitled to require, by written notice, that a data controller cease or not commence processing, or restrict processing, of his personal data, where the processing would otherwise be likely to cause unwarranted damage or distress to anyone at all. This right does not apply where any of the conditions in paras 1–4 of Sch 2 is fulfilled. These include where the data subject has already consented to processing, or the processing is necessary for the purposes of complying with contractual arrangements of the data subject, to meet legal or regulatory requirements upon the data holder or to protect the vital interests of the data subject. The data controller must reply to the notice within 21 days, stating just what he intends to do about the notice.

21.3.3 The right to prevent processing for purposes of direct marketing (s 11)

This is a very important right for any data subject to require, in writing, a data holder to cease, or not begin, any processing carried out for the purposes of allowing any person to direct advertising or marketing material towards particular individuals.

21.3.4 Rights in relation to automated decision taking (s 12)

This is a right that is likely to grow in significance. Any individual is allowed to object to decisions being taken that significantly affect that individual and which are based solely upon the automated processing of his or her personal data. Non-exclusive examples of such decision-making areas as work performance, creditworthiness, reliability and conduct are given in the section. The section provides that a data subject can require a data controller to ensure that such a decision is not to be made based solely on the automatic processing, or, if one has already been made, the data subject is to be notified that it was made on that basis, as soon as reasonably practicable. The data subject then has 21 days to require the data controller to reconsider the decision, or to take a fresh decision on a different basis. There are some categories of 'exempt decisions' in s 12(6) and (7), and these may be added to, in due course, by the Secretary of State; the existing exemptions mainly involve contractual matters of the data subject, or are based upon safeguarding the interests of the data subject.

21.3.5 The right to compensation (s 13)

Any individual, whether data subject or otherwise, can sue one or more data controllers as primarily or vicariously liable for breaches of the Act that lead to damage and/or distress. Distress claims seem to be limited to circumstances where the distress is accompanied by quantifiable damage, or where the personal data were processed for journalistic, artistic or literary purposes (see s 3). There is a defence against compensation claims if the data controller has taken reasonable care to comply with the Act (s 13(3)).

21.3.6 The right to rectification, blocking, erasure and destruction (s 14)

This gives the court, at the instance of a data subject, the power to order the data controller to rectify, block, erase or destroy any personal data, about the data subject or anyone else, which are inaccurate and personal data which contain expressions of opinion which appear to be based upon the inaccurate data. If the inaccurate data have been accurately recorded by the data holder, wherever they came from, the court may order that the data remain but be supplemented by an approved statement of correction.

21.3.7 The right to ask the Commissioner to assess whether the Act has been contravened (s 42)

This gives a discretion to the Commissioner as to the form and manner of making such an assessment, at the instance of any person who is, or who believes himself to be, directly affected by any processing. There is no discretion as to whether to assess; that is subject to the saving that the Commissioner must receive enough information from the complainant to be able to identify the complainant and to identify the particular processing. This remedy is used very widely, and the consequence is normally that the Commissioner serves an 'information notice' on the controller, stating how the notice came to be served and seeking information. This is backed up by criminal sanctions under s 47 if there is failure in compliance with the notice. A data controller has a right of appeal to the Tribunal against service of such notices.

21.4 The obligations of the data controller and disclosure restrictions

As we saw at **21.2.3**, data controllers must abide by the data protection principles. The two principles of most concern in regard to disclosure of personal data are the first two, namely that data must be fairly and lawfully processed, and processed for limited purposes. Let us now look at these two principles in further detail.

21.4.1 First principle of good practice: fair and lawful processing

As 'processing' is defined widely, the first principle has wide application to all use of personal data. It can be divided into four obligations:

(a) to process personal data fairly;

(b) to process such data lawfully;

(c) to comply with *at least one* of the Sch 2 conditions; and

(d) to comply additionally with *at least one* of the Sch 3 conditions if sensitive personal data are processed.

You will recall that the Sch 2 conditions include consent by the data subject, as well as such matters as being necessary for performance of contracts involving the data subject. It is not necessary for all of the Sch 2 conditions to be met, but clearly, if consent is safely to be relied upon as a precondition, that data subject would need to know, in advance, that consent is being given or strongly implied, and for what purposes any consent is given. 'Pushy' data controllers need to be careful about that. Where sensitive personal data are involved, consent must be 'explicit'.

In *British Gas Trading Ltd v Data Protection Registrar* [1998] Info TLR 393 (Data Protection Tribunal), British Gas were found to be processing customers' information unfairly. If a customer did not wish to receive information about other products and services, including from third parties, he had to return a form to British Gas. The tribunal found the processing of personal data was unfair unless done with the consent of the data subject, and that silence did not equate to acceptance. (The case was in fact decided under the 1984 Act, though the facts would still have breached the DPA 1998.) See also *Johnson v Medical Defence Union Ltd* [2007] EWCA Civ 262, discussed at **21.2.1** and **21.2.4**.

There are other conditions in Sch 2 which could be used to justify processing, depending on the circumstances. For example, condition 5(a), that the processing is necessary for the administration of justice. Condition 6(1) provides wide grounds for data processing:

> The processing is necessary for the purposes of legitimate interests pursued by the data controller or by the third party or parties to whom the data are disclosed, except where the processing is unwarranted in any particular case by reason of prejudice to the rights and freedoms or legitimate interests of the data subject.

In *Totalise plc v Motley Fool Ltd* [2001] EWCA Civ 1897, the defendants ran an Internet bulletin board. A third party posted defamatory statements about the claimants. The claimants sought information from the defendants as to the true identity of the third party, who used a pseudonym on the bulletin board. The defendants refused to supply the information, stating that release might breach the DPA 1998. The Court of Appeal held that a court would need to pay attention to condition 6 of Sch 2 before granting an order to reveal the third party's identity. In particular, the rights of the third party would need to be considered and to be balanced against those of the claimant. The right of the third party to respect for his or her private life under Article 8 of the European Convention on Human Rights would also need to be taken into account.

Processing of sensitive personal data is subject to the conditions in Sch 3. The conditions here are harder to satisfy than those in Sch 2. In practice, many instances of requests for the release of sensitive personal data are made in connection with a criminal investigation, or in regard to potential civil proceedings. Thus, under condition 6 in Sch 3, release of sensitive personal data can be justified if:

> the processing . . . is necessary for the purpose of, or in connection with, any legal proceedings (including prospective legal proceedings).

Under condition 10 of Sch 3, there is a power for the Secretary of State to make an order setting out the additional conditions where processing of sensitive personal data may take place on the grounds of substantial public interest. For example, the Data Protection (Processing of Sensitive Personal Data) Order 2000 (SI 2000/417) sets out a number of conditions concerning crime prevention or detection.

In many of the conditions in Schs 2 and 3, the processing of personal data must be 'necessary'. The Information Commissioner suggests that in judging whether processing is necessary, data controllers would need to consider whether:

(a) the purposes for which the data are being processed are valid;
(b) such purposes can be achieved only by the processing of personal data; and
(c) the processing is proportionate to the end pursued.

21.4.2 Second principle of good practice: processed for limited purposes

There is a lot of overlap between the first and second principles. The concept of processing for limited purposes means that the data should be processed only for the purposes to which the data subject has consented. The legal guidance from the Information Commissioner is in fact slightly wider and refers to different purposes which are not being 'envisaged' by the data subject at the time of the collection of the information. As we will see below, there are exceptions which may apply in various circumstances to this and other principles, for example in connection with crime prevention or legal proceedings.

21.5 Exemptions

Part IV of the DPA 1998 deals with the very wide range of exemptions to the provisions of the Act. These are seen in ss 27 to 39 and Schs 7 and 8. The reasons for most of the exempt situations are based on public policy. None of the matters provides absolute blanket exemption from all the effects of the Act, but instead work on the basis that certain disclosure and processing restrictions, normally required by the data protection principles, are removed in certain circumstances. Matters such as national security, crime, taxation, social work, examination marks, legal professional privilege, etc are included, and the range extends to almost all areas where there is a strong justification, based upon public interest, that the Act should not apply to its fullest extent. Because different heads of exemption receive different statutory treatment, consideration of the full range of matters is beyond the scope of this work, but two examples are given at **21.5.1**.

21.5.1 Exemptions for crime prevention and legal proceedings

Under s 29(3), personal data are exempt from the non-disclosure provisions and the right of subject access where the disclosure is for the purposes of preventing or detecting crime, apprehending or prosecuting offenders, or assessing or collecting tax, if the application of those provisions would prejudice any of those vital matters. It will still be necessary to show that at least one of the preconditions to processing is present. This exemption is further facilitated by the effect of the Data Protection (Processing of Sensitive Personal Data) Order 2000 (SI 2000/417; see **21.4.1**), which allows sensitive personal data to be processed without breaching the first principle, if processing is necessary for various purposes based upon 'the substantial public interest'. That provision covers police work as well as the other matters contained in s 29.

Under s 35(2):

> Personal data are exempt from the non-disclosure provisions where the disclosure is necessary—
>
> (a) for the purpose of, or in connection with, any legal proceedings (including prospective legal proceedings), or
>
> (b) for the purpose of obtaining legal advice,
>
> or is otherwise necessary for the purposes of establishing, exercising or defending legal rights.

So, a data controller might be required to disclose information to a third party in connection with legal proceedings, as indicated in the two subsections above. This could cover telecommunications companies who receive requests under the Regulation of Investigatory Powers Act 2000. It would also cover orders made under the Drug Trafficking Act 1994, or obligations to disclose information under the Money Laundering Regulations 2003 (SI 2003/3075). Less dramatically, it would also cover disclosure under the Civil Procedure Rules 1998. A court order would normally be required in this last instance (see the *Totalise* case at **21.4.1**).

Thus, it is clear that a data controller may be faced with a very wide range of matters, in which he may be required to disclose information that would normally be protected by the Act. On closer examination, it can be seen that the disclosure is usually going to be made to government agencies or to parties to legal proceedings; the obvious safeguard for the data controller is that, if necessary, the aid of the court may be sought to decide the matter.

In *Sayers v Smithkline Beecham Plc* [2007] EWHC 1346, the High Court was asked to authorise the supply of some copy documents of expert reports, which had been used in the English court in the MMR/MR vaccine litigation. These were required for use by the US Government, as it was a defendant in litigation in the US concerning alleged autism links to the MMR vaccine. This application was opposed by various claimants in the UK proceedings, on grounds that release of the documents would be contrary to the DPA 1998, as the data subjects had not given permission for this use in America. Keith J granted the US application on the basis that:

(a) the US courts could be trusted to use the documents only for the proper purpose of the litigation and on condition that anonymity could be preserved properly;

(b) the claimants would probably have consented to the use of the documents by the claimants in the US, so it was not in the interests of justice to deny their use to the defendants; and

(c) provided that the documents were properly anonymised, so as to prevent any link to identifiable persons, there could be no infringement of the DPA 1998 or of Article 8 of the European Convention on Human Rights (ECHR).

In *L v L* [2007] EWHC 140 (QB), the court was asked to order delivery up of all copies of the claimant husband's laptop hard drive that had been made or taken by his former wife, her solicitors and any of their agents. This was against a backdrop of financial proceedings, concerning the now-dissolved marriage, in the Swedish courts. The husband argued that the hard drive held much material, some protected by legal professional privilege, some confidential material that was not protected by privilege, and information about the personal and business affairs of identifiable friends and colleagues. He based his application on Article 8 of the ECHR, on the DPA 1998 and on the Computer Misuse Act 1990, s 1. The Court ordered delivery up into the hands of the husband's solicitors, subject to any subsequent requirement to give relevant disclosure in accordance with the rules of litigation.

It can be seen, from the above cases, that the courts take a balanced and principled view of the matter, and there seems to be no real problem in applying the current data protection law to litigation situations.

21.6 Requests from outside the EC

The eighth data protection principle prohibits the transfer of personal data to countries outside the European Economic Area, not just the EC, unless the country in question has an equivalent level of protection for personal data. A particular problem area is the United States. There are a number of exemptions to this prohibition which are broadly similar to those under s 35(2) (in effect that release is required or allowed by law; see **21.5.1**) but not identical to them. The Information Commissioner has stated that there is no blanket exemption allowing the transfer of information in regard to the law of another country. The transfer might be necessary for reasons of substantial public interest, or necessary in connection with legal proceedings, but a judgement has to be made in each case. Section 54 deals with international cooperation. The *Sayers v Smithkline Beecham plc* case gives a good illustration of the process in operation (see **21.5.1**).

An example of these difficulties has emerged with the increased requirements for security of aircraft. The US Bureau of Customs and Border Protection required EC airlines to disclose data comprising passenger lists. However, the European Commission considered that the release of these data would not be in compliance with the Directive on Data Protection from which the DPA 1998 stems. The problem was overcome by the adoption of a bilateral arrangement between the EC and the US in 2004. This contained assurances as to how the United States authorities would use and protect the data. Generally, the powers of the Commissioner are limited by the DPA 1998, and any further steps usually require government intervention. In summary, the prevailing ECJ view is that passenger name records, dealt with for security purposes, fall within the exemptions for public safety and crime prevention.

21.7 Enforcement, offences and civil damages

We have already seen how the Commissioner might assist the data subject by assessing what a data controller is doing, or is likely to be doing, with personal data and what steps the controller is taking to comply with the DPA 1998. Now it is necessary to see how these statutory requirements are enforced. The Act creates a wide range of criminal offences, but these fall, generally, within one of three classes: notification offences, enforcement offences, and disclosure offences. Most are 'either way' offences, punishable by fine.

Notification offences are those matters arising out of Pt III of the Act, which deals with the obligations of the data controller to notify the Commissioner of 'registrable particulars', to ask to be put on the register and to notify the Commissioner of any changes to the particulars. Processing without registration and failure to notify changes are offences under s 21.

Enforcement offences are found in Pt V of the Act and arise where there is a failure by the data controller to comply with the enforcement mechanisms employed by the Commissioner. If the Commissioner becomes involved in assessment of any particular processing by a data holder, the first step taken will be service of an information notice (see **21.3.6**). Then, if the Commissioner becomes satisfied that the data controller is, or will become, in contravention of any of the data protection principles, an 'enforcement notice' will be served, requiring the data controller to remedy the situation (subject to appeal against the notice to the Tribunal). Under s 47, failure to comply with any of these notices is a criminal offence.

Disclosure offences can arise in various ways. The definition of 'processing' is wide enough to cover improper disclosure, which can thus fall within the offences under s 21 discussed above (eg, simply handling data without being registered). Section 55 creates a wide-ranging offence where personal data (or information contained within the personal data) are obtained or disclosed without the consent of the data controller (usually catching errant employees or others in league with them). This can catch persons who procure the disclosure in such circumstances and anyone who sells, or offers to sell, personal data obtained in that way. This is very useful to prevent further dissemination or use of the data, after an initial illegal disclosure. For this purpose, advertising the sale is treated as offering to sell the data (s 55(6)). Interestingly, s 59 creates an offence of wrongful disclosure by the Commission itself (Commissioner, staff or agents).

Most claims for damages are likely to be brought, unreported, in the county court, because of the level of damages involved. Nevertheless, if injunctive relief is sought, some may get into the High Court. Two reported cases where the court awarded damages for breach of the DPA 1998 are *Campbell v MGN Ltd* [2002] EWCA Civ 1373 and *Douglas and Others v Hello! Ltd and Others* [2003] EWHC 786 (Ch) (see **18.4**). It may be that more claims might be brought for distress arising from breach of the Act, but the principles of assessment for distress are not clear yet.

21.8 Conclusion on data protection

There have been valuable and practical benefits to the general public being able to prevent, for example, utility providers – or anyone else with vast amounts of commercially valuable personal data – simply selling that data to the highest bidder. It has also been of the greatest importance that individuals have been able to find out just what personal data are held by data controllers, and to what end.

The legal framework seems to be reasonably applicable and workable, considering the exceptional difficulties in regulating the holding and processing of data in an information-based society. There are, currently, some signs that the commercial pressure to make the fullest use and exploitation of data is creating some unease for many people; the Information Commissioner and Parliament are beginning to respond to public concerns about this. Nevertheless, that should not be seen as any failure of the basic data protection legislative structure. A more difficult problem is the purely technical aspect of keeping data processing systems secure against fraudsters, theft and negligence. There have recently been some massive failures of security around data held by government departments and other large organisations; data protection law can do little to prevent such failures and the matter is not discussed further.

Overall, the practical problems have been more about organisations failing to disclose information, rather than organisations disclosing information too readily. As we have said, the tendency is for bureaucrats to treat the DPA 1998 as a charter to keep things secret. The obvious examples are the Soham murder case, resulting in the Bichard Report, mentioned at **21.2** above, and the reported failure by British Gas to disclose information to social services about vulnerable pensioners who might have problems surviving in cold weather. This is really a question of the interface problems between data protection, freedom of information and human rights law. This area must, necessarily, be left to the courts to examine as and when it becomes necessary to do so.

21.9 Freedom of information

Freedom of information appears, at first glance, to be quite the opposite of data protection, but there is no fundamental reason for the two concepts to be incompatible. All that is necessary is for public authority users and holders of information to be aware of the difference between duties owed to the general public and those duties owed to the private individual. The Information Commissioner is responsible for both data protection and freedom of information; a very wide range of further information can be found at ico.gov.uk.

The basic approach of British bureaucracy, up until the last 20 years or so, was to deal with most information on a strict 'need to know' basis, usually claiming that it was covered by the Official Secrets Act and therefore protected from disclosure. Even very mundane information was treated in a similar way. This became an ever-more pressing problem with the growth in number and powers of public agencies and local government authorities. There were many piecemeal initiatives and steps taken to widen access in various areas, such as access to medical records, housing records, meetings of local authorities, etc; but much a more general advance was demanded, so the FOIA 2000 was enacted, coming fully into force on 1 January 2005. The Act has enhanced many of the existing statutory access rights, but many of those earlier rights still remain and, where this is the case, the FOIA 2000 is not applicable (FOIA 2000, s 21). The philosophy of the Act is to allow much wider citizen participation in the development of public policy and the decision-making process. It also has the merit of increasing the public awareness and accountability of public bodies.

An important limitation on public access under the Act is that it applies only to recorded information held by a public body. So, matters which are not so recorded, but which may well be known to public servants, are beyond the reach of the Act; other methods will need to be employed to find out about those matters. Another considerable limitation is that any request by the data subject which involves any of his personal data can be made only under the DPA 1998. Such a matter is exempted under s 40(1) of the FOIA 2000. It is possible to obtain data concerning individuals other than the applicant in very restricted circumstances set out in s 40(2)–(4)

21.9.1 Application of the Freedom of Information Act 2000

The 2000 Act applies only to information held by 'public authorities', as defined in s 3(1). These include:

(a) central government departments and agencies;
(b) local government;
(c) the police;
(d) the NHS;
(e) State schools, colleges and universities; and
(f) publicly-owned companies such as the Royal Mail.

The Secretary of State is empowered under s 5 to designate an entity as a public authority. The above list can therefore be added to by that means. This could apply, for example, to a contractor providing services on behalf of a government department. The Act also provides that certain public authorities come within it only in respect of information of a specified description (s 7). See *BBC v Sugar* [2008] EWCA Civ 191.

21.9.2 Accessible information

Section 1 of the 2000 Act defines the right to information. Section 1(1) deals with the basic right:

> (1) Any person making a request for information to a public authority is entitled:
>
> (a) to be informed in writing by the public authority whether it holds information of the description specified in the request, and
>
> (b) if that is the case, to have that information communicated to him.

The provisions of para (a) are referred to as the 'duty to confirm or deny'. 'Awareness Guidance No 21' from the Information Commissioner deals with this matter. In essence, the thinking behind these provisions is quite straightforward. If information has been requested but is not held by the authority in question, it would normally be reasonable to inform the applicant of that fact. However, there may be some exceptional cases where it would not even be right to confirm or deny that information requested is held. An obvious example is the area of policing, where it would not make sense to allow criminals to discover whether they were under suspicion or not.

Basically, all information held by a public authority is available to an individual under the provisions of the Act, but there are seven absolute exemptions and 16 qualified exemptions from the general right (see **21.9.5**). The right is to 'information', not to documents or to a file. The public authority can therefore edit documents or files, where they also contain information that would be subject to an exemption. The public authority should not refuse a request for access on the basis that there is exempt information as well as accessible information in the document or file. Considerable editing may result, in practice.

The Act has given rise to a very wide range and complexity of requests, and there is some concern in public bodies about the cost of compliance. There is a discretion, where the cost of compliance would exceed a statutory limit, to require the applicant to agree to pay the actual cost, or part of it, in advance. The response time allowed is normally a maximum of 20 days, but this may be extended by notice to the applicant, where reasonable to do so.

The accessible information is that 'held' by the public authority, not that 'created' by the authority. Thus, information from or about businesses which is held by a public authority is accessible to the public, if it is not subject to an exemption. This could cover, for example, details of a bid made for government work under the Public Private Partnership. This aspect of the Act is a key concern to businesses and their lawyers.

The Act applies to information obtained by a public authority before the Act came into force (s 1(4)). In other words, information is not exempted from disclosure because it was obtained before the implementation date of the Act.

21.9.3 Publication schemes

A voluntary code of practice on access to government information was introduced in 1994. Government departments, their agencies and some other public bodies followed this code. It promoted the disclosure of information by public bodies, subject to some exemptions. It was sufficiently flexible that the departments in question could operate either a relatively open or a restrictive regime and still come within the code. The code ceased to have effect from 1 January 2005.

All public authorities which are subject to the FOIA 2000 have been obliged to operate approved publication schemes since 30 June 2004, under s 19. These schemes have to be approved by the Information Commissioner. The schemes must have regard to the public interest in, for example, the publication of reasons for decisions which have been made by a public authority. There is a wide range of schemes under the 2000 Act, including, for example, a number for the NHS. A publication scheme will usually comprise four sections:

(a) information about the public authority, its responsibilities and the scheme;
(b) classes of information published or to be published;
(c) the manner in which the information is to be published;
(d) whether the publication is to be free of charge or not.

The presence of a publication scheme does not, of itself, prevent successful applications for further, more detailed information under the Act. In *Corporate Officer of the House of Commons v Information Commissioner* [2008] EWHC 1084 (Admin), the decisions of the Information Commissioner and Information Tribunal, to order the provision of detailed breakdowns of claims for accommodation allowances by 14 Members of Parliament, were upheld by the Divisional Court. The consideration of the publication of private addresses had been properly dealt with and had been found to be outweighed by the deeply flawed allowances system; public scrutiny was justified.

21.9.4 Codes for access to information and for management of information

Under s 45 of the 2000 Act, the Secretary of State is required to issue a code of practice giving guidance to public authorities. The Information Commissioner has to be consulted, and the code must be approved by Parliament. This code gives guidance relating to the following:

(a) the provision of advice by public authorities to applicants – public authorities must provide advice and assistance;
(b) the transfer of requests by a public authority to another authority which may be the holder of the information;
(c) consultation with persons to whom the information relates, or whose interests are likely to be affected;
(d) the inclusion in contracts entered into by public authorities of terms relating to the disclosure of information;
(e) the provision by public authorities of procedures for dealing with complaints about requests for information.

This code is available at www.dca.gov.uk/foi/reference/imprep/codepafunc.htm.

Under s 46, the Lord Chancellor is obliged to issue a code for public authorities relating to the keeping, management and destruction of their records. This is available at www.dca.gov.uk/foi/reference/imprep/codemanrec.htm. Once a record has been destroyed, there is no access to the information that was contained within it. In some other jurisdictions, the recollections of civil servants are treated as accessible information, but this is not the case in the UK system under the FOIA 2000.

21.9.5 Absolute and qualified exemptions

Section 2 of the FOIA 2000 sets out the circumstances in which a public authority may refuse a request for information. These fall into two categories, namely, absolute exemptions and qualified exemptions. If an absolute exemption applies there is no legal right of access at all, for example information relating to public security matters. If a qualified exemption applies, a public authority must consider whether there is a greater public interest in, first, confirming or denying the existence of the information requested and, secondly, providing the information to the applicant or not.

The *absolute exemptions* are:

(a) information accessible by other means (s 21);

(b) information supplied by, or relating to, bodies dealing with security matters (s 23);
(c) court records (s 32);
(d) parliamentary privilege (s 34);
(e) personal information (s 40);
(f) information provided in confidence (s 41); and
(g) information the disclosure of which is prohibited by law (s 44).

An example of (d) above is seen in *Office of Government Commerce v Information Commissioner* [2008] EWHC 737 (Admin). Here, Parliamentary privilege was held to apply to review documents prepared for the use of Parliament in connection with the Government's identity card programme. The court allowed an appeal against the Information Commissioner's decision to order disclosure.

Examples of (f) are seen in *Secretary of State for the Home Office v British Union for the Abolition of Vivisection* [2008] EWHC 892 (QB) and *Bluck v Information Commissioner*, Information Tribunal (2007) 98 BMLR. In the first case, the High Court allowed an appeal against a decision of the Information Tribunal that information held by the Home Office should be disclosed. The information that had been obtained by the Home Office was commercially sensitive and had been obtained under statutory powers, with a very strong implication of confidentiality; the Tribunal's approach had been wrong in law. In the *Bluck* case, a father lost his appeal against a decision of the Information Commissioner that medical records concerning his daughter should not be disclosed without the consent of her husband. The daughter had died in hospital, the hospital had admitted liability and a settlement had been reached with the husband. The Tribunal held that the public interest, that patients retained trust in the confidentiality of their records, greatly outweighed any public interest in their disclosure. Interestingly, the Tribunal took the view that the right to enforce and protect confidentiality, relating to medical records, probably passed to personal representatives, despite earlier authorities to the contrary.

Note that much personal information is exempted from the FOIA 2000, and can only be accessed via the DPA 1998.

The *qualified exemptions* are:

(a) information intended for future publication (s 22);
(b) national security (ss 23–24);
(c) defence (s 26);
(d) international relations (s 27);
(e) relations within the UK (s 28);
(f) the economy (s 29);
(g) investigations and proceedings (s 30);
(h) law enforcement (s 31);
(i) audit functions (s 33);
(j) formulation of government policy (s 35);
(k) prejudice to effective conduct of public affairs (s 36);
(l) communications with Her Majesty (s 37);
(m) health and safety (s 38);
(n) some personal information (s 40);
(o) legal professional privilege (s 42); and
(p) commercial interests (s 43).

Qualified exemptions may be class-based, or not. Class exemptions under the Act are intended to give protection to *all* information falling within a particular category, for example legal professional privilege.

On the other hand, a qualified exemption could be prejudice-based. Such exemptions come into force only if a disclosure of particular information would cause prejudice to that category of activity, for example prejudice to international relations. If it does not then the information must be disclosed. This applies in relation to the following qualified exemptions:

(a) defence;

(b) international relations;

(c) relations within the UK;

(d) the economy;

(e) law enforcement;

(f) audit functions; and

(g) commercial interests.

In addition, two sections use alternative words for 'prejudice'. These are:

(a) prejudice to effective conduct of public affairs (s 36), where 'inhibit' is used in s 36(2)(b); and

(b) health and safety (s 38).

Both class- and prejudice-based exemptions are subject to the public interest test, unless the Act states that they are absolute exemptions.

21.9.6 Policing the Act

The Information Commissioner enforces the 2000 Act and is required to promote good practice (s 18). He was previously the Data Protection Commissioner, but now combines that role with his role under the FOIA 2000. He is also responsible for enforcement of the Environmental Information Regulations 2004, which operate separately from the FOIA 2000.

Under s 50, a dissatisfied applicant can apply to the Information Commissioner for a decision. The applicant must have exhausted any complaints procedure which is provided by the public authority. (Such a procedure is required by the access code – see **21.9.4**.)

If the Information Commissioner believes that the public authority has failed to abide by the Act, he can issue an enforcement notice. Under s 54, if the public authority fails to comply with the notice, the Information Commissioner may apply to the court. If the court agrees with the notice, failure to comply is contempt of court. There is an appeal from the decision of the Commissioner to the Information Tribunal under s 57 by either the complainant or the public authority, or both. These appeals apply to decision notices, information notices and enforcement notices. This is a complex area, and in some circumstances it can appear that the Commissioner has reached a decision whereas the reality is that what he has decided is that the matter complained of is beyond his jurisdiction under the Act. That happened in the *BBC v Sugar* case, discussed at **21.9.1**. In this circumstance, the appropriate recourse would be to seek judicial review of the Commissioner's decision, rather than to appeal under the Act.

21.9.7 Interface with the Human Rights Act 1998

Under s 6 of the Human Rights Act 1998, it is unlawful for a public authority to act in a way which is incompatible with a Convention right. Under s 12, the right to free speech is upheld. So, suppose that a business wished to obtain an injunction to stop a public authority from releasing confidential information which had originally been obtained from that business, eg a tender for a contract. The business would have to show, in effect, that it was likely to succeed at the full trial. This is a very heavy evidential burden. The court must in any event consider whether it would be in the public interest for the information to be disclosed. (For a case on the public interest in disclosing information, see *London Regional Transport v Mayor of London* [2001] EWCA Civ 1491.)

A more recent case which involved consideration of the situation where data protection, freedom of information and human rights are engaged is *Michael Stone v South East Coast Strategic Health Authority and Others* [2006] EWHC 1668 (Admin). Here, the decision to publish a report following an independent inquiry into the care, treatment and supervision of Michael Stone prior to his committing two murders and attempting another was upheld. The public interest justified the decision, and the publication was not in breach of the claimant's human rights or his rights under the DPA 1998.

There are hints in the *Corporate Officer of the House of Commons v Information Commissioner* case, discussed at **21.9.3**, that the privacy of private addresses would need to be of a very pressing nature to defeat the public interest in freedom of information in matters which disclose serious shortfalls in the conduct of public bodies. See also *L v L* at **21.5.1**.

Part III Summary
Intellectual Property

Topic	*Summary*
Passing off	This is a common law tort, in which a person misrepresents his goods or services as being those of some other person, or one of numerous variations on that theme. For a person to succeed in proving passing off, he must show that he has some discernible goodwill in some particular aspect of his own goods or services, that the defendant is misrepresenting that aspect, in some way, so that customers are likely to be confused as to the trade origin of the goods or services that they are purchasing, and that there is some identifiable damage to the claimant's business.
Trade mark	This is a sign, capable of graphic representation, that is capable of distinguishing the goods and services of one undertaking from those of another. It must be capable of performing its feature of providing distinctiveness if it is to be registered. Without registration, the mark will not get the statutory protection and the right to a potentially permanent monopoly over that mark in the form in which it is registered.
Descriptive marks	Trade marks which only serve to describe aspects of the type, origin, quality or quantity of the goods are not usually registrable. Often, combining these aspects with other non-excluded matters, such as a logo or different wording, will get around the problem, as can distinctiveness acquired through use of the mark.
Shape marks	There is a limited possibility for registration of trade marks which comprise shapes, but, in general, it is quite difficult to obtain long-term protection by trade mark for shape marks.
Generic marks	These are trade marks which, over time, have lost their ability to distinguish the objects bearing them from similar objects emanating from different trade sources. If a registered trade mark becomes generic, the registration may be revoked. The term simply becomes part of general trade usage.
Community Trade Mark	This is trade mark registration system that applies right across the EC and which is available provided there is no ground of objection arising in any one of the Member States. The system is administered by OHIM.
Registered Design Right	This is available to protect aspects of the visible external appearance of objects for a limited period of up to 25 years. The main limitation is that the design feature requiring protection must be new (not available before) and of individual character (creating a different overall impression to what had previously been available to the public).

Topic	*Summary*
Unregistered Design Right	This is a residual form of protection that applies to features of the shape or configuration of manufactured articles, internally or externally. The protection is available for up to a maximum of 15 years, more usually 10. To get protection, the feature must be original, in the sense of not being copied, and not commonplace in the design field in question.
Exhaustion of rights	This term describes the process by which the owner of intellectual property rights such as trade marks, patents or design rights loses the power to prevent the further marketing of objects within the EC, once the first dealing in or importation into the EC of the object has taken place, with the right owner's express or implied permission. His rights are said to be exhausted.
Copyright	This is a property right comprising the right to prevent a person copying, for other than a very limited group of 'fair dealing' purposes, an original work of literature, drama, music or art. The right comes into being upon the creation of the work itself and, in most cases, lasts for 70 years from the year in which the creator dies.
Moral rights	These are statutory rights which exist in parallel with the original copyright in most literary, dramatic, musical and artistic works and films. They are designed to remain to the advantage, use and protection of the creator of the work, in the event that he assigns his copyright to someone else.
Entrepreneurial copyright	This is a class of rights that arise out of the exploitation and commercialisation of original copyright works. In the main, they arise as a second generation of rights and are more limited in duration than the original copyright works from which they come. Matters such as films, broadcasts and sound recordings can fall within this category.
Database right	This is a statutory protection that can arise on the creation of databases, that is collections of data or other material that are arranged in a systematic way and which are individually accessible. It applies to both copyright-protected databases as well as non-copyright protected databases. The difference is that, to be copyright protected, the database must have had some human intellectual input in arranging and selecting the material; this is not necessary for non-copyright databases and could be computer created. The right arises automatically on creation and does not need registration. It lasts for 15 years from creation or substantial revision.

Topic	*Summary*
Patent	The grant of a patent is the giving of a monopoly right to use and exploit an invention of some sort. The right is given in exchange for the invention being made public, so that whatever inventive step is comprised within the idea can enter the 'world art' and become known to all. The effect is that the inventor has a 'lead time' of 20 years in which to exploit his invention to the full, but the rest of the world is able to see, throughout that period, what he has developed and is free to build upon the inventor's thinking, for further developments and inventions. The invention, to be patentable, must be new, comprise some inventive step, be capable of industrial application and not be caught by any statutory exclusion.
Inventive step	This means some new aspect of an invention that, at the time of applying for a patent for it, would not be obvious to a person reasonably skilled in the relevant field of invention and development, but who was not of a particularly imaginative or intuitive mind.
Patent claims	These are a part of the patent specification that must be provided by applicants for grant of patent. They comprise a series of numbered paragraphs, in which the inventor describes features of his invention which are, arguably, things or ways of doing things that no person has done or thought about before. The approach is normally to claim, as the first claim, the widest and most general feature of the invention and then, progressively, to narrow and refine the features and qualities claimed as being new to the world art. A person only needs to infringe any one of the claims to infringe a patent.
Confidential information	Some types of confidential information can be protected from disclosure, even though the information is not intellectual property in itself. Material that has been disclosed to someone else, under circumstances where that other person has reason to believe that he has received it under an obligation of confidentiality, can sometimes be the subject of restraining injunctions as well as compensatory damages for unauthorised disclosure. The legal principles involved are trust and fiduciary in nature. Often, the matter is expressly covered in contractual non-disclosure clauses, but where these are not present or applicable the court must be approached.

Topic	*Summary*
Data protection	This is a statutory form of protection which applies where persons obtain or deal with information about individuals, identifiable from the data, in a systematic way. Where this is the case, the persons who are creating, holding or dealing with the information, become liable to registration on a publicly-accessible register. They also become subject to eight statutory principles of good practice and must meet, at least, one of six preconditions before they can be seen as having processed any personal information fairly and lawfully. The individual who is the data subject has a number of statutory rights available, with respect to the processing of the data relating to him.

Part IV

COMPETITION LAW

Chapter 22
Competition Law and Commercial Agreements

22.1	Introduction	331
22.2	English competition law	333
22.3	EC competition law	336
22.4	Selective distribution	346

22.1 Introduction

The topic of EC competition law is introduced in ***Legal Foundations*** and ***Business Law and Practice***.

This chapter aims to place it into context by considering the ways in which it may affect the drafting and operation of commercial agreements. In addition, the chapter briefly considers English competition law and its impact on commercial agreements. Before looking at these two areas of competition law, however, it may be useful to consider some of the general points which arise when advising on competition law in the context of commercial agreements.

22.1.1 Advice to clients

It is important for the solicitor to appreciate the different ways in which competition law may be relevant to a client's business, and to be able to advise accordingly. For example, a client who is expanding his business into continental Europe may realise that there could be competition law difficulties and seek advice specifically on this point, but what about the client who is simply expanding within the UK? What if a client intends to make a deal with another company in the UK which will effectively keep competitors based in other EC Member States out of the UK market in a particular product?

It is also important for the solicitor to keep the client's documentation under review. For example, it may be necessary to advise a client that a particular commercial agreement can be used for deals which have no connection at all with the EC, but must not be used for deals which may affect trade and competition within the EC, or even for deals outside the EC which could have some impact within the EC. The EC and the ECJ have increasingly become ready to interfere with business arrangements external to the EC but which may have consequences within Member States. The solicitor may wish to 'audit' the client's documentation from time to time, checking that each document is still suitable for the client's purposes and is being used by the client in the correct way (and, of course, that it still complies with EC law).

22.1.2 Which law applies?

A commercial agreement between two parties based in the UK might, of course, be affected by English competition law (see **22.2**). However, because the relevant Articles of the European Community Treaty (often still referred to as the 'Treaty of Rome') have direct effect in each Member State, these may apply to the agreement as well. It is important to remember that it is not necessary for the parties to be based in different Member States for EC competition law to apply; broadly speaking, as long as the agreement may affect the natural flow of trade between Member States, EC competition law is potentially relevant. Thus, even where both parties are based in the same Member State, the solicitor must be aware of its possible impact on trade between that State and other Member States. EC competition law could also apply to an agreement made between a business based within the EU and one based outside if there is a strong trading interaction between the markets involved. Although the Commission may have practical problems in enforcing EC competition law in these circumstances, this will not stop it becoming involved. In addition, it should be noted that parts of the EC Treaty, including its competition law rules, (in effect) formally apply to the non-EC countries which are Member States of the European Economic Area (EEA: see **22.1.3**). Note that, at the time of writing (September 2009), it is looking likely that the Treaty of Rome will be superseded by the Treaty of Lisbon as planned. If this does happen, some changes will be made to EC competition law (see **22.3.1**).

Now that the Competition Act 1998 (CA 1998) (see **22.2**) has been in force for some time, the English and EC competition authorities are working out how to draw the dividing line between the ambit of EC competition law and English competition law (important now that the Office of Fair Trading can apply both CA 1998 and Articles 81 and 82 EC). It is, however, still likely to take some time for this to become really clear.

22.1.3 The European Economic Area

Broadly speaking, the EEA Agreement extends many of the basic legal rules of the EC to all nations within the EEA, including the principles of free movement of goods, persons, services and capital, and competition law. As far as competition law is concerned, Articles 53 and 54 of the EEA Agreement are similar to Articles 81 EC and 82 EC, except that they apply where an agreement may affect trade between the countries of the EEA.

The EEA consists of the Member States of the European Union, plus Iceland, Liechtenstein and Norway. There are 27 Member States of the EU (and European Community). They are, in alphabetical order: Austria, Belgium, Bulgaria, Cyprus, Czech Republic, Denmark, Estonia, Finland, France, Germany, Greece, Hungary, Ireland, Italy, Latvia, Lithuania, Luxembourg, Malta, the Netherlands, Poland, Portugal, Romania, Slovakia, Slovenia, Spain, Sweden and the United Kingdom.

22.1.4 Drafting and competition law

The solicitor should always consider how competition law problems can be minimised by appropriate drafting. If an agreement is likely to be affected by EC competition law, the solicitor should at least be able to avoid obvious drafting pitfalls (such as drafting export bans and price-fixing clauses), and should also consider taking advantage of any relevant block exemption (see **22.3.6**). However, both solicitor and client must appreciate that with many agreements, it is difficult to be certain that problems with EC competition law will not arise. This is also true of the system of English competition law introduced by the CA 1998: see **22.2.1**.

22.1.5 Types of agreement

This chapter is largely concerned with individual vertical commercial agreements (those between parties at different levels of supply, such as manufacturer and wholesaler, supplier and distributor, principal and agent). It does not consider horizontal agreements in detail (those between parties at the same level of supply, such as manufacturers). The reason for this is that horizontal agreements, such as cartels, have a far greater potential to cause competition law problems and therefore occur much less frequently than vertical agreements; in most circumstances, such agreements will be illegal. There is no better example of this than *Competition Authority v Beef Industry Development Society Ltd* (Case C-209/107) [2009] All ER 367 (EC), ECJ, where the Irish beef producers association formulated an agreement between producers, under which some producers would leave the industry to reduce over-production. The ECJ held the agreement to be unenforceable. The aim of Article 81(1) was to prohibit any form of co-ordination which deliberately substituted practical co-operation between undertakings for the risks of competition. This chapter concentrates on the distribution agreement (in particular, the exclusive distribution agreement, where the supplier agrees that the distributor will be the only authorised reseller of the supplier's goods within a defined territory).

It is worth noting that although solicitors in practice are still much more likely to encounter issues relating to individual vertical agreements at a transactional level (hence the focus of this chapter), competition law authorities are increasingly turning their attention to the pursuit of horizontal agreements (eg cartels which fix prices and share markets).

22.1.6 The relevant competition law

22.1.6.1 English law

This chapter is concerned primarily with the system of competition law introduced in 2000 by the CA 1998 (see further **22.2**). There are other competition law provisions (concerning, eg, control of mergers), but these are outside the scope of this book.

22.1.6.2 EC law

In relation to EC law, this chapter is concerned primarily with Article 81 EC. It is the Article most likely to apply to individual commercial agreements, as it applies to agreements and other business arrangements which may affect trade between Member States and which have as their object or effect the prevention, restriction or distortion of competition within the common market (see further **22.3**). Articles 81 and 82 EC are reproduced in the **Appendix** to this book.

22.2 English competition law

22.2.1 The Competition Act 1998

The CA 1998 (subject to transitional provisions) repealed much of the UK's existing competition law, including the Restrictive Trade Practices Acts 1976 and 1977, the Resale Prices Act 1976 (RPA 1976) and most of the Competition Act 1980. Its main provisions are modelled very closely on EC competition law in the form of Articles 81 EC and 82 EC. These provisions are known as the Chapter I and Chapter II Prohibitions. The Chapter I Prohibition (contained in s 2) is the equivalent of Article 81 EC, and the Chapter II Prohibition (contained in s 18) is the equivalent of Article 82 EC.

The CA 1998 came into force on 1 March 2000.

The UK authorities must deal with cases under the Act in a way that ensures consistency with EC competition law (CA 1998, s 60, often known as the 'governing principles' section), both in interpreting and in applying the Act.

The Office of Fair Trading (OFT) is responsible for administering the CA 1998; there is a Competition Commission to hear appeals from its decisions.

22.2.2 The Chapter I prohibition

The Chapter I prohibition, contained in s 2(1) of CA 1998, is similar in its wording to Article 81 EC; the main difference is that the Act refers to effects upon trade and competition within 'the United Kingdom', where Article 81 EC refers to 'the common market' or 'Member States'. In other words, this Act and prohibition are purely domestic, national measures; they run in parallel with the EC competition law rather than as alternatives to it. Like Article 81 EC, the prohibition applies to both informal and formal arrangements, whether or not they are in writing. Also, like Article 81(1) EC, s 2(2) of CA 1988 lists specific types of arrangement which are caught by the prohibition (eg, agreeing to fix purchase or selling prices or other trading conditions).

However, as with Article 81 EC, the list merely provides guidance; the important thing is whether the arrangement between the parties falls within the prohibition.

An agreement, decision or concerted practice prohibited by s 2(1) is void (s 2(4)).

22.2.3 The Chapter II prohibition

This prohibition, contained in s 18 of CA 1998, is similar in its wording to Article 82 EC. It covers the abuse by one or more undertakings of a dominant position within the UK in a 'market' (in Article 82 EC, 'market' covers both the relevant product market and the relevant geographical market: the position will be the same under the Chapter II prohibition) if it may affect trade within the UK.

Dominance will be assessed in the same way as it is under Article 82 EC, and market share will often be the most significant factor. Generally, an undertaking is unlikely to be considered dominant if it has a market share of less than 40%. However, as in EC law, other factors will also be relevant when assessing dominance. For example, an undertaking with a lower market share may be considered dominant if it structures the market in such a way to enable it to act independently of its competitors. Like Article 82 EC, s 18(2) of CA 1998 gives specific examples of types of conduct that are likely to be considered an abuse (eg, imposing unfair purchase or selling prices).

However, as with the Chapter I prohibition, this provides guidance only; it is whether or not the prohibition itself actually applies which is important.

22.2.4 Investigative powers

The OFT has wide-ranging investigative powers under the CA 1998 (ss 25–31 of Chapter III cover these powers). These include the power to enter premises and to require the production of documents that are considered relevant to the investigation (cf the Commission's powers of investigation under Articles 81 EC and 82 EC). These investigative powers have been further enhanced by the Enterprise Act 2002.

22.2.5 Consequences of infringement

22.2.5.1 Enforcement

The rules on enforcement are in ss 32–40 of Chapter III of CA 1998, and give the OFT substantial powers. For example, an offending agreement may have to be terminated or amended by order of the OFT. Any offending conduct may also be ordered to cease.

The OFT has the power to order interim measures which require an undertaking to refrain from engaging in suspected illegal activity while the matter is investigated. This power will be exercised only when the OFT considers it necessary to take urgent action to protect third parties from suffering serious irreparable damage, or to protect the wider public interest.

22.2.5.2 Financial penalties

Infringing undertakings may be fined up to 10% of their worldwide turnover for infringement of either the Chapter I or the Chapter II prohibitions (CA 1998, s 36, and Competition Act 1998 (Determination of Turnover for Penalties) Order 2000 (SI 2000/309, as amended by SI 2004/1259)).

22.2.6 Methods of avoiding infringement

There are various ways in which an agreement may avoid infringement (primarily infringement of the Chapter I prohibition, but in one case, the Chapter II prohibition).

22.2.6.1 Parallel exemption

Under s 10 of CA 1998, an agreement, decision or practice is exempt from the Chapter I prohibition if it is exempt from 'the Community prohibition' (ie, Article 81 EC) for one of the following reasons:

(a) It falls within an EC block exemption (eg, Regulation 2790/99: see **22.3.7**).

(b) It has been exempted by a decision of the Commission under Article 10 of Regulation 1/2003 (for more on this Regulation, see **22.3.4**).

Thus a vertical agreement which has the benefit of Regulation 2790/99 will not fall within the Chapter I prohibition.

Section 10(2) further provides that an agreement is exempt from the Chapter I prohibition if it does not affect trade between Member States but otherwise falls within a category of agreement which is exempt from Article 81 EC by virtue of a Regulation. So, for example, an agreement that, if it affected trade between Member States, would be saved by the Vertical Agreements Block Exemption, but which is purely domestic in its effect, is contemplated by s 10(2). Parallel exemption can therefore be given even where there has been no breach of EC law on competition.

It is not necessary to apply for a parallel exemption.

22.2.6.2 Appreciability

In administering CA 1998, the OFT and the courts will also respect an 'appreciable effect' test, which applies the thresholds which are relevant under the Notice on Agreements of Minor Importance (see **22.3.5.4**). This means that an agreement will not infringe the Chapter I prohibition where the parties' joint market share does not exceed 10% in the case of competitors, and 15% for each party in the case of non-competitors

You should be clear that 'appreciability' in this context refers to appreciable effects on competition. Care must be taken to distinguish that from the test for 'appreciability' of effects on trade between Member States of the EC, as explained in NAAT (see **22.3.5.5** below).

22.2.6.3 Limited immunity

Section 39 of CA 1998 provides a 'limited immunity' from the Chapter I prohibition for what it refers to as 'small agreements'. This means that the agreement is immune from penalties (ie, fines) under s 36. A 'small agreement' is one where the parties' joint turnover does not exceed £20 million (s 39(1)(a) and the Competition Act (Small Agreements and Conduct of Minor Significance) Regulations 2000, SI 2000/262). It is very important to note, however, that a 'price-fixing agreement' cannot be a small agreement (s 39(1)(b)). A 'price-fixing agreement' is defined by s 39(9) as:

> an agreement which has as its object or effect, or one of its objects or effects, restricting the freedom of a party to the agreement to determine the price to be charged (otherwise than as between that party and another party to the agreement) for the product, service or other matter to which the agreement relates.

Even where the agreement qualifies as a small agreement, the OFT has power to withdraw the immunity if, as a result of an investigation, it considers that the agreement is likely to infringe the Chapter I prohibition (s 39(3), (4)).

Section 40 provides a limited immunity from the Chapter II prohibition where there is 'conduct of minor significance'; this applies where an undertaking's turnover is less than £50 million (s 40(2) and Competition Act 1998 (Small Agreements and Conduct of Minor Significance) Regulations 2000, see above). As with s 39, the immunity given is immunity from fines, and can be withdrawn if, following an investigation, the OFT considers that conduct of minor significance is nevertheless likely to infringe the Chapter II prohibition (s 40(3) and (4)).

22.2.6.4 Block exemption

Exemption for particular categories of agreement can be given by the Secretary of State for Trade and Industry on the recommendation of the OFT (s 6(1), (2)), based on the OFT's opinion that agreements within that category are likely to be exempt agreements under s 9. The conditions under which an agreement is exempt under s 9 are the same as those set out in Article 81(3) EC. An agreement which falls within a category specified in a block exemption order is exempt from the Chapter I prohibition (s 6(3)). In practice, it is likely that parallel exemption (see **22.2.6.1**) will be more significant than block exemption under the CA 1998. An example of block exemption made under the CA 1998 is that granted for public transport ticketing schemes, which came into force on 1 March 2001.

22.2.7 Transitional provisions

For a year after the coming into force of the CA 1998, transitional provisions applied to 'old' agreements (very broadly, agreements which were already in existence before the Act came into force). Although problems relating to these provisions may still be relevant in practice for some time after their expiry, consideration of these provisions is outside the scope of this book.

22.2.8 The Enterprise Act 2002

This Act contains a number of significant competition law provisions. Much of the Act is concerned with instituting a new merger control regime within the UK, and is therefore outside the scope of this course. However, it is important to note that the Act created (for the first time in the UK) a criminal offence in relation to certain types of anti-competitive arrangement.

By s 188, it is a criminal offence (the 'cartel offence') for an individual dishonestly to agree with one or more other persons to make or implement certain types of cartel arrangements. These include agreements which directly or indirectly fix prices for the supply of goods or services in the UK, and agreements to share markets or customers in certain circumstances.

The offence can be committed only where those participating in the arrangements are at the same level of the supply chain (ie, it applies only to horizontal agreements).

By s 190(4), the OFT can issue a notice to prevent proceedings (known as a 'no action letter') against a person who would otherwise be liable to prosecution for the offence; the idea is to encourage 'whistleblowers' who have been participating in a cartel to come forward and give details about the cartel to the OFT. The OFT is given extensive powers to investigate persons suspected of committing the offence, and has produced a guidance note indicating how it will exercise those powers.

22.3 EC competition law

22.3.1 The relevant competition law

This chapter concentrates on Article 81 EC; as indicated previously, it is the Article which is most likely to be relevant when drafting a commercial agreement. However, when considering the general impact of EC competition law, the solicitor should also be aware of the following Articles:

(a) Article 3(1)(g) EC, which provides that the activities of the EC shall include a system ensuring that competition in the internal market is not distorted (but see below).

(b) Articles 28–30 EC (formerly Articles 30–36 of the EC Treaty), which prohibit restrictions imposed by import and export controls (and measures having equivalent effect) on the free movement of goods around the common market. These Articles will be only indirectly relevant to most individual commercial agreements, but can be significant where the licensing of IP rights is concerned. This topic is considered further in **Chapter 23**.

(c) Article 82 EC, which prohibits the abuse by one or more undertakings of a dominant position within the common market or a substantial part of it, in so far as it may affect trade between Member States. This Article, which is covered more fully in ***Legal Foundations*** and ***Business Law and Practice***, is not considered further in this chapter, because it will usually apply to the activities of one undertaking rather than to an agreement between undertakings. The solicitor should always be aware, however, that even the most careful drafting of an agreement cannot prevent Article 82 EC from applying if one of the parties is dominant within a particular product and geographical market, and the Commission finds that there is abuse of that dominant position.

Note that, in June 2007, the European Council agreed the basis of a Reform Treaty, designed to replace the former (and never ratified) Constitutional Treaty as an instrument for reforming the governance of the EU and the EC. It was widely reported at the time that President Sarkozy of France had succeeded in getting agreement to remove Article 3(1)(g) EC, ie the provision which covers the EC's general commitment to undistorted competition. The final text of the Reform Treaty (now officially the Treaty of Lisbon) has been agreed but not yet ratified; Article 3(1)(g) has been removed. There is, however, to be no change to Articles 81 and 82 EC if and when the Reform Treaty comes into force, other than the fact that they will be renumbered as part of the Treaty on the Functioning of the EU.

22.3.2 Article 81 EC – a brief reminder

The basic principles of EC competition law are considered in ***Legal Foundations*** and ***Business Law and Practice***. However, a brief reminder of Article 81 EC may be useful.

Article 81(1) EC prohibits as incompatible with the common market any agreements, decisions by associations of undertakings and concerted practices which may affect trade between Member States, and which have as their object or effect the prevention, restriction or distortion of competition within the common market. The Article contains a non-exhaustive list of the types of business practice which are likely to infringe this prohibition. Agreements need not be formal or legally binding for Article 81 EC to apply, and both actual and potential effects on trade can be considered. It is also important to remember that the Article can apply to agreements confined to one Member State (or where one or more parties are based outside the EU altogether).

It is not always easy to predict when Article 81 EC will apply to vertical agreements, but, for example, distribution agreements which contain territorial restrictions are potentially at risk. For example, a distribution agreement between an English supplier and a French distributor, which gives the distributor 'exclusive territory' (ie, the distributor is the only authorised seller of the supplier's goods in France), is potentially likely to infringe Article 81(1) EC. The agreement may affect trade and competition within the common market if, for example, it makes it more difficult for other businesses to break into the French market for the product in question, or it cuts down on the sources of supply for French customers. However, note that this potential infringement of Article 81 EC may in appropriate circumstances be sanctioned by block exemption: see **22.3.7**.

22.3.3 Effect of infringing Article 81 EC – a brief reminder

It may be possible to sever from an agreement terms which infringe Article 81 EC without invalidating the rest of the agreement. Whether this can be done is a matter of national law, not EC law: it will therefore depend on what the governing law of the agreement provides about severance. If the offending terms cannot be severed, however, the whole agreement will be void: Article 81(2) EC provides that anything prohibited by Article 81(1) EC will be void. Note that it may be impossible to sever offending provisions from a distribution agreement if they are 'exclusive territory' provisions as described at **22.3.2**, because they will normally be part of the consideration for the agreement.

There may also be other consequences of infringement. For example, the Commission can impose fines on the parties for infringement of Article 81 EC, and undertakings which have been affected by an infringement may be able to take proceedings in their national courts to obtain damages and/or an injunction.

22.3.4 The Commission's powers

The Commission (strictly speaking, the Competition Directorate-General, formerly known as DG IV) has wide powers to enforce EC competition law, including the power to obtain information about undertakings and their agreements and business practices. These powers are set out in Regulation 1/2003, which is sometimes referred to as the 'modernisation regulation'.

It is worth being aware in outline that enforcement of EC competition law changed substantially on 1 May 2004, when Regulation 1/2003 came into force. Under the former enforcement regime, the Commission (and only the Commission) had power to grant individual exemption under Article 81(3) EC to an agreement which infringed Article 81(1) EC. To gain this individual exemption, which would prevent the parties being liable for infringement of Article 81(1), an agreement had to satisfy the conditions laid down in Article 81(3) EC; broadly speaking, this meant the parties notifying the agreement to the Commission, and the Commission being satisfied that the operation of the agreement benefited consumers without unduly restricting competition.

In practice, the former enforcement regime was unsatisfactory in a number of respects, in particular, those relating to individual exemption and the notification system. The Commission could not cope with all the requests for individual exemption, very few were actually granted, and the Commission usually responded to requests with a comfort letter (a non-binding but persuasive statement of the Commission's opinion about the status of an agreement in relation to Article 81 EC).

Under the regime introduced by Regulation 1/2003, the former system of notification to the Commission and grant of individual exemption by the Commission ceased to exist. Instead, the Regulation introduced a process of what is in effect self-assessment by the parties to an agreement to gain exception from the provisions of Article 81(1) EC. Undertakings now have to assess for themselves whether their agreement satisfies the conditions set out in Article 81(3) EC (note that the conditions themselves are not in any way altered by the 2003 Regulation). If disputes arise as to whether an agreement fulfils the Article 81(3) EC conditions, these are settled by national competition authorities ('NCAs': in the United Kingdom, the NCA is the OFT) and, ultimately, by the national courts. The Commission retains a residual power under Article 10 of the Regulation to declare that Article 81 EC is inapplicable to agreements in cases where the Community public interest requires it, but this power has been designed to be used only rarely. For further discussion of the important exemption provided by Article 81(3), see **22.3.6** below.

The Commission has issued further guidance on a number of important aspects of the Regulation's operation and how enforcement policy will be co-ordinated between Member States. It is also inevitable that, with the greater emphasis on the role of national authorities and courts in enforcing EC law, some overlaps will arise between EC and national competition law which will need to be resolved, and further guidance is likely to be forthcoming.

Although Regulation 1/2003 puts much greater emphasis on the role of NCAs, national courts and even the parties to an agreement themselves, the Commission is still prepared to give informal guidance to undertakings about novel and difficult situations which arise under Articles 81 and 82 EC. It has issued a Notice ([2004] OJ C101/6) setting out the circumstances in which it is prepared to issue 'guidance letters' to businesses in such situations.

22.3.5 Avoiding the impact of Article 81 EC

Because the operation of Article 81 EC is effects-based rather than form-based, it is difficult to be sure of avoiding infringement simply by drafting an agreement in a particular way. However, depending on the circumstances and the type of agreement, there are various ways in which the solicitor can minimise the risks of infringement. This section considers the most important ways in the context of the Wood Magic distribution agreement example from **Chapter 5**. (It is worth noting that the following principles will apply equally to UK agreements under the CA 1998.)

Example

Assume that before seeking advice on their proposed distribution agreement, Wood Magic and Bois Massif had in principle agreed the following terms:

(1) Wood Magic agreed that Bois Massif would get France as its exclusive territory.

(2) In return, Bois Massif agreed that:

- (i) it would not export the goods from France;
- (ii) it would not solicit orders from outside France;
- (iii) it would not meet unsolicited orders from outside France;
- (iv) it would not sell below the prices set by Wood Magic.

Would an agreement on these terms run into difficulties with Article 81(1) EC, and, if so, would it be possible to avoid this happening?

22.3.5.1 Article 81(1) EC problems

Although it may seem obvious to say so, the solicitor first needs to assess whether Article 81(1) EC would apply to the proposed agreement before looking for ways round it. In particular, it is important to remember that Article 81(1) EC will not apply to a distribution agreement simply because it *is* a distribution agreement. The question is whether, given the commercial context in which it operates, the agreement and its terms may affect trade and competition within the common market. The proposed agreement here certainly has the capacity to do so, because its terms amount to territorial restrictions, export bans, (direct and indirect) customer restrictions and price-fixing. How (if at all) could Wood Magic and Bois Massif contract on those terms without infringing Article 81(1) EC? This requires consideration of the various ways of avoiding the impact of Article 81 EC.

22.3.5.2 Parent and subsidiary companies

An agency or distribution agreement made between a parent and a subsidiary company will normally fall outside Article 81 EC. In most cases, the companies will be taken to be one undertaking, and so the Article cannot apply; there is no 'agreement between undertakings'. This is a potentially useful way of avoiding the impact of Article 81 EC, but is clearly irrelevant to Wood Magic and Bois Massif.

22.3.5.3 Agency agreements

As already noted in **Chapter 5**, many agency agreements will fall outside Article 81 EC because they are covered by paras 12–20 of the Commission's Notice of May 2000, which provides guidelines on vertical restraints. It may be possible, therefore, to avoid problems by drafting an agreement to be a 'genuine' agency agreement if this is commercially appropriate. Again, however, this will not be of use to Wood Magic and Bois Massif, who have chosen to enter into a distribution agreement.

22.3.5.4 The '*de minimis*' provision – effects upon competition

The agreement may be covered by the Notice on Agreements of Minor Importance (NAOMI). The Commission adopted its most recent version of this Notice ([2001] OJ C368/7) in December 2001. As a basic proposition, if NAOMI applies to an agreement, the Commission will not take proceedings against the parties for infringement of Article 81 EC (but the matter is still within the scope of Article 81; cf NATT, discussed at **22.3.5.5**).

Under Point 7 of NAOMI, the Commission accepts that, in certain circumstances, agreements between undertakings which may affect trade between Member States nevertheless do not appreciably restrict competition within the meaning of Article 81(1) EC (note that the emphasis and thrust of this provision are concerned with the effects upon competition not trade; cf NATT, discussed at **22.3.5.5**). These circumstances are as follows:

(a) Where the agreement is made between undertakings which are actual or potential competitors (known as 'agreements between competitors') the agreement does not appreciably restrict competition if the aggregate market share of the parties does not exceed 10% on any of the relevant markets affected by the agreement.

(b) Where the agreement is made between undertakings which are not actual or potential competitors (known as 'agreements between non-competitors'), the agreement does not appreciably restrict competition if the market share held by each of the parties to the agreement does not exceed 15% on any of the relevant markets affected by the agreement.

A footnote to Point 7 of the Notice indicates that guidance on whether businesses are actual or potential competitors can be found in a set of Commission guidelines on the applicability of Article 81 EC to horizontal co-operation agreements ([2001] OJ C3). However, broadly speaking, horizontal agreements are likely to be 'agreements between competitors', and vertical agreements are likely to be 'agreements between non-competitors'.

If an agreement is difficult to classify, the 10% threshold is applicable.

Point 4 of NAOMI clearly states that in cases covered by the Notice, 'the Commission will not institute proceedings' (ie, for infringement of Article 81 EC). Although, strictly speaking, the Notice does not bind the Commission, Point 4 is so clearly expressed that it is likely to be difficult in practice for the Commission to go back on it. The Notice will not, however, automatically bind national courts, nor will it prevent third parties from making a claim based on infringement of Article 81.

To benefit from NAOMI, the agreement must not contain any hardcore restrictions: Point 11(2) of the Notice makes it clear that for agreements between non-competitors, these hardcore restrictions are the same as those in Article 4 of the vertical agreements block exemption (see **22.3.7**), which include price fixing and certain customer/territorial restrictions. In addition, Point 8 seems to reserve a certain amount of discretion to the Commission where certain market conditions ('cumulative foreclosure effect') apply.

Could Wood Magic and Bois Massif benefit from NAOMI? It seems likely that this is an agreement between non-competitors; however, we do not currently know the market share each of them enjoys in the relevant market. (Point 10 of the Notice gives some guidance on the calculation of market share: in particular, the Commission's Notice on market definition ([1997] OJ C372/5) is relevant.) However, even if the shares are within the 15% threshold, there is a problem as the proposed agreement contains hardcore terms (eg, fixed minimum prices, export ban). As long as the hardcore terms remain in the agreement, the Notice will not apply.

22.3.5.5 NAAT – effects upon trade between Member States

In **22.3.5.4**, the *de minimis* provision in NAOMI was examined, as a means of saving an agreement or a practice that fell within the scope of Article 81 but nevertheless had minimal effects upon competition. Applying the 'non-appreciable affectation of trade' (NAAT) rule, by contrast, may mean that the agreement never falls within the scope of Article 81 in the first place, because it does not 'affect trade between Member States'. The Guidelines as to whether an agreement may have this effect or not are given in Commission Notice [2004] OJ C101/7. The Guidelines (para 4) make very clear that they have no relevance to the question of whether an agreement has appreciable effects upon competition; that remains firmly within the NAOMI/*de minimis* rule. Nevertheless, if an agreement can be brought within the NAAT rule, NAOMI will never be needed, nor any other exemption under EC law (but of course domestic, national law may still need to be considered)

The Guidelines give a generalised approach, from which the following conclusions may be drawn:

(a) In principle (para 52), agreements are presumed not to be capable of having an appreciable effect upon trade between Member States where the aggregate market share of the parties, on any relevant market within the EC affected by the agreement, is less than 5% and, additionally, the parties do not exceed certain turnover figures. With a horizontal agreement, this is a combined annual Community turnover of undertakings concerned in the production covered by the agreement not exceeding €40 million (eg two competitor manufacturers of skis, each turning over €15 million per year in the EC, would fit within this). If the agreement is vertical, the aggregate annual Community turnover in the products is that of the supplier of the products only, the same limit of €40 million applying.

(b) There is a rebuttable positive presumption of an appreciable effect upon trade where the aggregate market share or turnover limits seen in (a) above are exceeded, but that presumption is not applied where the agreement covers only part of a single Member State (para 53). The best indicator of the capacity of an agreement appreciably to affect trade between Member States, where the agreement covers only part of a single Member State, is considered to be the share of the national market, by volume, in that State; it must be a significant share to establish Community jurisdiction (para 90).

(c) Primary distinctions are drawn between agreements/practices that are confined to single Member States (or parts of one) and those which cover more than one such State, or those which involve third countries outside the EC (para 60).

(d) In cases where the NAAT rule is considered to apply to an agreement/practice, the Commission will normally not institute proceedings upon its own initiative, or on application by others, irrespective of the nature of the restrictions being imposed (including 'hardcore' restrictions such as price fixing, etc) (para 50).

22.3.6 Block exemptions and other exemptions arising from Article 81(3)

It is central to an understanding of the Article 81(1) prohibition to consider properly the effect and application of Article 81(3). You have already seen (at **22.3.4**) that it is possible to 'self-assess' whether any particular agreement would benefit from the wide and useful exemption given by Article 81(3). To gain the benefit of the exemption, the agreement must display each and all of four distinct aspects:

(a) It must 'improve the production or distribution of goods, or promote technical or economic progress'. The use of 'or' shows that any one or more of these four grouped effects may be relied upon to help show entitlement to the exception. That may not be too hard to demonstrate in many cases.

(b) It must achieve (a) above while 'allowing consumers a fair share of the resulting benefit'. This may not always be so easy to demonstrate, particularly with agreements made by, or originating from, trade associations, which tend to be protectionist in nature.

(c) At the same time as satisfying (a) and (b) above, the agreement must 'not impose upon the undertaking restrictions which are not indispensable to' achieving (a) and (b). That shows that the arrangement cannot be used restrictively, purely and solely for the purpose of benefiting one or more parties by making it harder for others to trade in competition.

(d) The final cumulative requirement is that the agreement must not 'afford such undertakings the possibility of eliminating competition in respect of a substantial part of the production in question'. Thus, anything that has the potential to get rid of most of the competition cannot possibly benefit from the exemption, no matter what positive aspects it might display; that is the unforgivable sin, just having the potential to get rid of serious competition.

Article 81(3) has its widest application, by far, in allowing the introduction of the 'block exemption', ie a general framework of exemption aimed at particular forms and areas of widespread contractual and/or consensual agreement or practice. Some of the best known of these relate to vertical (distribution type) agreements (Regulation 2790/99 EC, see **22.3.7**), motor vehicle sale and distribution (Regulation 1400/2002), and technology transfer (Regulation 772/2004, see **23.4.2**).

The general principle behind block exemption is to ensure that the Commission does not have to investigate agreements which may at first sight appear to infringe Article 81(1) EC but do not in practice impose serious restrictions on competition (and which may in fact stimulate trade and benefit consumers), thereby satisfying the conditions under Article 81(3) EC. Block exemption is given in the form of Commission Regulations. Traditionally, block exemptions provided quite detailed guidance on which terms were acceptable and which were unacceptable in particular agreements. However, a rather different approach has been taken by more recent block exemptions, including that given by Regulation 2790/99 (see **22.3.7**), which is to allow general freedom to parties falling within the Regulation, except where a matter is expressly forbidden by the Regulation itself.

Block exemption was unaffected by the enforcement regime introduced by Regulation 1/2003 (see **22.3.4**). It remains the case that if an agreement falls squarely within the terms of a block exemption, it will fall outside Article 81(1) EC and the Commission will take no interest in it (unless circumstances change). It is therefore advantageous for the parties to draft an agreement to fall within any relevant block exemption; the existing block exemption Regulations all give relatively clear guidance (albeit in a variety of ways) as to when they will (and will not) apply, and, at least while the operation of the Regulation 1/2003 regime is still being worked out in practice, modifying the agreement to fit within a block exemption is likely to be easier and safer in most cases than relying on 'self-assessment' as introduced by Regulation 1/2003.

22.3.7 Block exemption and vertical agreements

The position in relation to how Article 81(1) EC applies to vertical agreements changed substantially in 2000 with the introduction of a new style of block exemption.

This block exemption, contained in Regulation 2790/99, was adopted on 22 December 1999 and is expressed to expire on 31 May 2010. At the time of writing, the precise form of the replacement is not clear.

Strictly speaking, the block exemption came into force on 1 January 2000. However, it did not begin to apply to agreements until 1 June 2000.

As previously noted in relation to agency agreements (see **22.3.5.3**), the Commission has produced a Notice giving guidelines on vertical restraints generally; the bulk of these guidelines relate to this block exemption and its application. These guidelines are likely to be helpful in practice as an indication of the Commission's thinking, but cannot be a substitute for study and application of the text of the Regulation itself.

Two features of Regulation 2790/99 are particularly significant:

(a) By Article 3, the block exemption does not apply where the market share of the relevant party (usually the seller: see the discussion of Article 3 at **22.3.7.1**) exceeds 30%.

(b) Unlike its predecessors (and some other existing block exemptions), this block exemption has no list of permissible terms (a so-called 'white list'). Instead, it proceeds on the basis that a term is acceptable unless specifically forbidden (see the discussion of Articles 4 and 5 at **22.3.7.1**). This is confirmed by para 21 of the guidelines, which actually state that the Regulation 'creates a presumption of legality for vertical agreements, depending on the market share of the supplier or buyer' (referred to as the 'safe harbour' created by the Regulation).

22.3.7.1 The block exemption in outline

Preamble

As is customary with block exemptions, the initial recitals explain the Commission's reasons for granting block exemption in the way in which this Regulation has done (eg, Recitals 8 and 9 explain the policy behind the market share threshold in Article 3). It is therefore helpful to study the preamble carefully before going on to the Articles themselves.

Broadly speaking, the block exemption applies to vertical agreements for the sale of goods/ supply of services where the relevant party has a market share of no more than 30%.

Article 1

This is the block exemption's 'definitions section'. Note, in particular, the definitions of 'non-compete obligation' (see the note on Article 5 below), 'exclusive supply obligation' (important for the application of Article 3: see below) and 'selective distribution system' (important for the application of Article 4: see below).

However, note also that the vital definition of 'vertical agreement' does not appear here; it is found in the next Article.

Article 2

This Article states the scope of the exemption provided by the block exemption. Article 2(1) in effect provides that Article 81(1) EC will not apply to:

(a) agreements or concerted practices;

(b) entered into between two or more undertakings;

(c) where the undertakings operate in such a way that the agreement or practice satisfies the definition of a 'vertical agreement'.

For an agreement to be a vertical agreement within the meaning of Article 2(1), the parties must operate at different levels of the production or distribution chain, and the agreement or practice must relate to the conditions under which the parties may 'purchase, sell or resell certain goods or services'. This will cover, for example, all types of distribution agreements, franchising agreements and agency agreements.

Note that Regulation 2790/99 is capable of applying to a situation where more than two undertakings are involved, and that it extends to the provision of services.

Article 2(2) allows the block exemption to apply (subject to certain conditions) to vertical agreements between, for example, a trade association and its members or suppliers.

Article 2(3) allows the block exemption to cover vertical agreements under which IP rights are licensed or assigned, as long as the IP provisions of the agreement do not constitute the 'primary object' of the agreement.

Article 2(4) provides specific rules for vertical agreements between competing undertakings. Article 2(5) means that this block exemption cannot apply where the subject-matter of the agreement is dealt with under another block exemption (eg, technology transfer under Regulation (EC) No 772/2004: see **23.4.2**).

Article 3

This is a crucial element of the block exemption – using market share to determine its applicability.

In most cases, the block exemption applies only if the *supplier's* share of the relevant market does not exceed 30% (Article 3(1)). However, where the agreement contains 'exclusive supply obligations' (see definition in Article 1; broadly, a situation where the seller is selling to one buyer only), it is the market share of the *buyer* which must not exceed 30% for the block exemption to apply.

Note that Article 9 sets out how to calculate market share (see below).

Article 4

This is the list of forbidden restrictions (referred to in the guidelines, although not in the Regulation itself, as 'hardcore restrictions'). If the vertical agreement has as its object any of the matters listed here, the block exemption will not apply to the agreement as a whole.

Article 4(a) outlaws price-fixing (although note that the possibility of imposing a maximum sale price, or recommending a sale price, still remains).

Article 4(b) outlaws restrictions on the buyer in relation to the territory into which the buyer can sell, or the customers to which the buyer can sell (so, eg, straightforward export bans are outlawed). However, note that there are some exceptions (ie, certain restrictions can legitimately be imposed on the buyer, notably the restriction of certain types of active sale).

Article 4(c) and (d) relate only to selective distribution systems (see definition in Article 1): restrictions on active and passive sales to end users, and cross-supplies between members of the system are outlawed. Selective distribution is discussed in more detail at **21.4**.

Article 4(e) also relates to a specific situation: a restriction agreed between a supplier and buyer of components limiting the supplier's freedom in relation to sales of spare parts to repairers or service providers.

Article 5

Note the wording of the first two lines of Article 5: if any of the three obligations listed in Article 5 is included in the agreement, then *that obligation* will not have the benefit of the block exemption; the rest of the agreement can still benefit (as long as there are no hardcore restrictions, of course).

Article 5 is generally concerned with restrictions of competition. Note that under Article 5(a), a non-compete obligation (see definition in Article 1: it need not be total) therefore loses the benefit of the block exemption if it is for an indefinite period, or a period exceeding five years (subject to an exception where the supplier provides the buyer with premises – eg, a 'tied' pub).

Article 6

All block exemptions have the equivalent of this provision, giving the Commission power to withdraw the exemption from a particular agreement if necessary. The power is, however, rarely used.

Article 7

This provision, however, was novel at the time the block exemption was made – granting power to Member States to withdraw the block exemption from a particular agreement if necessary. The power is used sparingly.

Article 8

This gives the Commission the power to withdraw the block exemption from a particular sector of business. Again, the power is used sparingly.

Article 9

As noted above, this indicates how to calculate market share for the purposes of Article 3. Note that the test in Article 9(1) is based on substitutability (ie, the test used for defining markets under Article 82 EC). Rules for the actual calculation of the figure are in Article 9(2).

Article 10

This indicates how to calculate 'total annual turnover' for the purposes of Article 2(2) and (4).

Article 11

This indicates that when the Regulation uses the terms 'undertaking', 'supplier' and 'buyer', connected undertakings (as defined in Article 11) are included.

Articles 12 and 13

These articles provide for the commencement of the Regulation and set out transitional provisions relating to the block exemptions which this Regulation replaced.

22.3.7.2 A block exemption checklist

The following checklist may be useful in applying the block exemption. It is still vital, however, to apply Article 81 EC to determine whether there is a problem with EC competition law in the first place; there may also be other relevant ways of avoiding infringement of Article 81 EC which should be investigated on any given set of facts.

(a) Are you dealing with a 'vertical agreement' as defined in Article 2(1) of the block exemption (eg, a distribution agreement (sole or exclusive), an exclusive purchasing agreement, a franchising agreement)?

(b) If so, check the market share threshold in Article 3 (usually the supplier's share of the relevant market; but if the agreement is an exclusive supply agreement, it will be the buyer's market share).

(c) If the relevant market share does not exceed 30%, the block exemption is potentially applicable.

(d) Does the agreement have as its object any of the restrictions listed in Article 4 (eg, price-fixing, export ban)?

(e) If so, the block exemption does not apply.

(f) If not, the agreement benefits from the block exemption. (NB: be careful of Article 5; the obligations in that Article are not themselves exempted, although their inclusion does not stop the block exemption applying to the agreement as a whole.)

22.4 Selective distribution

22.4.1 What is a selective distribution agreement?

This name is given to the type of distribution agreement in which the supplier specifies the persons to whom the distributor can supply the goods. This type of distribution agreement is often considered to be essential by manufacturers of specialist and luxury goods (eg, cameras, perfume) in order to maintain the brand image and reputation of the goods, ensuring that the goods are sold only through outlets which the manufacturer deems suitable. A classic selective distribution arrangement would operate as follows. A manufacturer enters into distribution agreements with a number of different wholesalers (in other words, there is usually a 'network' of agreements), appointing them as distributors for its products. In each agreement, the manufacturer specifies the retail outlets which the wholesalers can supply; this is usually done by the manufacturer laying down conditions which the retail outlets must satisfy before the wholesaler is permitted to sell to them. Depending on how these conditions are expressed (see **22.4.2**), competition law problems may result, especially if the manufacturer is using the agreement simply to stop certain outlets selling its products. An extensive network of similar distribution agreements can effectively close off a particular market to potential resellers.

22.4.2 The attitude of the Commission and the courts

The Commission has not been particularly consistent in its attitude towards selective distribution agreements. It has, for example, sometimes been prepared to agree that Article 81 EC does not apply at all to a particular selective distribution agreement (or network). However, this will be the case only if the supplier's criteria for selecting the persons to whom the distributor can sell are purely qualitative (ie, based on those persons' suitability to sell the product, taking into account such matters as the standard of their premises, their qualifications, and the expertise and training of their staff) rather than quantitative (ie, simply based on restricting the number of outlets for the supplier's product in a particular area). In addition, the selection criteria must be applied without discriminating against particular outlets. In other cases, however, the Commission has concluded that Article 81(1) EC does apply and that it has been infringed.

It is interesting to note that both the Court of First Instance and the ECJ appear, in certain circumstances, to accept the principle that selective distribution arrangements are not only acceptable but also necessary in respect of certain types of goods. For example, this was borne out in the *Galec* case (*Groupement d'Achat Edouard Leclerc (Galec) v Commission of the European Communities* (Case T-19/92) [1996] ECR II-1851). The case was, in fact, about the grant of individual exemption (under the competition law enforcement system which was then in force) to a selective distribution system for Yves Saint Laurent perfumes. However, it is interesting to note that, as part of its ruling, the court accepted that most of YSL's selection criteria for outlets were necessary and in the interests of the consumer; it commented that these were products in respect of which maintaining 'an aura of luxury and exclusivity' was vitally important.

As noted at **22.3.7**, Regulation 2790/99 is capable of applying to selective distribution as long as the agreement satisfies the relevant conditions.

Chapter 23
EC Law and Intellectual Property Rights

23.1	Introduction	347
23.2	Attempting to resolve the conflict	348
23.3	Article 81 EC and the exploitation of intellectual property rights	348
23.4	Licensing agreements and competition law	349
23.5	Article 82 EC and intellectual property rights	351
23.6	Articles 28–30 EC and intellectual property rights	352
23.7	Article 28 EC and Articles 81–82 EC: relationship	354
23.8	EC competition law and franchising agreements	354

23.1 Introduction

This chapter looks at the relationship between EC law and IP rights. It concentrates on the competition law problems which may arise in relation to the exploitation of IP rights (with particular reference to the licensing of patents), but also briefly considers the ways in which IP rights may come into conflict with the provisions of the European Community Treaty relating to the free movement of goods (Articles 28–30 EC).

23.1.1 Exploiting intellectual property rights

Assume that Frodsby Engineering Ltd, a small company, has developed a revolutionary new machine, in respect of which it has obtained patents in the UK and other Member States, including France. Frodsby's directors are now looking for ways to make money out of the 20-year monopoly right which English law has conferred on the company (not least so that it gets a return on the time and money spent on developing the machine; the directors see this as a just reward for the company's creativity and effort).

Their two main options are:

(a) make money by Frodsby manufacturing and selling the machine itself;

(b) make money by licensing the right to other businesses to manufacture and sell the machine (ie, allowing other businesses to make use of the patent).

The advantages of licensing are covered briefly in **Chapter 34** of ***Business Law and Practice***. It is possible here that Frodsby may choose to license the patent because it is not geared up to manufacture the machine in sufficient quantities, or in other ways lacks the resources to exploit the patent fully, or because it finds a licensee with a better knowledge of the machine's target market.

23.1.2 How might the patent holder's actions cause competition law problems?

English law gives Frodsby as patent holder a right which arguably in itself could restrict trade and competition. Frodsby can rely on the patent to stop anyone else making or selling the machine, or even developing a similar machine which comes too close to the patent. Even if Frodsby allows other businesses to use the patent (by licensing it out), it could directly or indirectly restrict trade and competition by the terms which it includes in the licence; for example, it could grant a licensee exclusive territory, or stop a licensee exporting the machine from that territory.

23.1.3 The response of EC law

EC law has a balancing act to perform in this situation. It must try to deal fairly with two potentially conflicting situations: on the one hand, the desire of the patent holder to be rewarded for its creativity (failure to permit this could stifle innovation and the development of new markets); and on the other hand, the need to stop IP rights granted under national law interfering with trade and competition within the common market.

The EC Treaty does not try to stop Member States passing laws which grant IP rights (although, increasingly, attempts are being made to harmonise national systems: see **Part III**). Article 295 EC (formerly Article 222 of the EC Treaty) provides that the Treaty 'shall in no way prejudice the rules in Member States governing the system of property ownership', which has led the EC competition authorities to take the view that EC law should not seek to control the mere existence of IP rights. What the law does seek to control, however, is the exploitation (or, as it is more commonly expressed, the 'exercise') of rights (see further **23.2**).

23.1.4 Which rights may cause problems?

Many of the points covered by this chapter are relevant to all types of IP right. However, problems arise most often in relation to three of the rights because of their particular characteristics. Patents (on which the chapter concentrates) are particularly likely to pose problems because of their monopoly aspect. Trade marks can, if regularly re-registered, last for an indefinite period of time. Copyright cannot last indefinitely but has the longest periods of guaranteed validity of any IP right (ie, 70 years from the end of the year of the author's death in the case of most LDMA works).

23.2 Attempting to resolve the conflict

The distinction mentioned in **23.1.3** between the existence of an IP right and its exercise was developed by the ECJ as an attempt to reconcile Article 295 EC with other, possibly conflicting, Treaty provisions. Briefly, the ECJ's interpretation is that Article 295 EC is concerned with safeguarding the existence of national IP rights; other Articles (such as Articles 28–30 EC and Articles 81–82 EC) with controlling their exercise. As a basic rule, if the exercise of an IP right interferes with a Treaty provision (other than Article 295 EC), that right will be compromised; its exercise will be forbidden or restricted.

23.3 Article 81 EC and the exploitation of intellectual property rights

If the holder of an IP right licenses it out, as Frodsby is contemplating doing in the example in **23.1.1**, this will involve an agreement between the holder and the licensee (a licensing agreement, sometimes simply called a 'licence'). Broadly speaking, any IP right can be licensed in this way. In Frodsby's case, the right happens to be a patent, and the agreement would be referred to as a patent licensing agreement, or patent licence. Because there is an agreement, Article 81 EC may apply (depending, of course, on the terms of the agreement). The existence of the IP rights which are being licensed will not, as such, infringe Article 81(1) EC. However, the licence agreement itself could, if it might affect trade and competition within the common market. In addition, the bringing of proceedings to stop infringement of an IP right may infringe Article 81(1) EC if the proceedings may affect trade within the common market, and are brought as a result of an agreement. In other words, exercise of the right may be restricted if there is evidence that the exercise infringes Article 81(1) EC. (Note that if Article 81 EC applies to an agreement and the Commission suspects a breach, the Commission can take action because of its duty to enforce Article 81 EC. However, the Commission has no similar power to intervene where Articles 28–30 EC are at issue: see **23.6**.) Depending on the circumstances and the terms of the agreement, the licensing of any IP right may give rise to competition law problems. However, it is convenient to concentrate on patent licensing, in the light of the Frodsby example.

Assume that Frodsby is contemplating licensing the patent for the machine to Megaco, a French company. Megaco will use the patent to manufacture the machine. The parties have agreed the following licence terms in principle:

(a) Frodsby has agreed that it will not appoint any licensees in France other than Megaco.

(b) Megaco has agreed that it will pay royalties to Frodsby on the use of the patent of a minimum of £10,000 per month.

(c) Megaco will sell the machines at a price which Frodsby will determine.

Would an agreement on these terms run into difficulties with Article 81(1) EC; and if so, would it be possible to avoid this happening?

23.4 Licensing agreements and competition law

23.4.1 Likely competition law problems

As explained in **23.3,** if a proposed licensing agreement may affect trade and competition within the common market, it may infringe Article 81(1) EC. If so (assuming that the agreement does not fall within the Notice on Agreements of Minor Importance), the parties will normally have two main ways of trying to resolve this problem. Either they can assess their agreement to see if it is likely to get the benefit of Article 81(3) EC, or, if the agreement is of a certain type (eg, a patent licensing agreement), they can try to redraft the agreement in order to get the benefit of the relevant block exemption (see **23.4.2**).

Licensing agreements are capable of giving rise to many of the competition law problems associated with distribution agreements, in particular if there is the grant of territorial protection to the licensee. This could therefore be a problem for Frodsby and Megaco. However, the parties often regard having some sort of territorial protection as an essential term of the agreement; the licensee in particular may not be prepared to get involved on any other basis because of the financial risks of exploiting the licence. It is also important to realise that, in some circumstances, the grant of protection may actually stimulate trade and competition despite its restrictive appearance; in the case of Frodsby and Megaco, it may lead to more efficient exploitation of the patent and better marketing of the patented item, with benefits for consumers (who might not get the item at all if the protection were not permitted).

Generally, in deciding whether or not an agreement (or any given term, such as exclusive territory) does infringe Article 81(1) EC, the Commission recognises the distinction drawn by the ECJ between the existence and the exercise of rights. There are cases (eg, *Nungesser (LC) AG and Kurt Eisle v Commission for the European Communities* (Case 258/78) [1982] ECR 2015) where the Court appears to have decided that the terms of a particular licence agreement did not infringe Article 81(1) EC at all. However, the case law can be difficult to interpret, and it can also be difficult to decide which terms in an agreement relate to the existence of the right and which to its exercise. Broadly, the former are terms which are necessary for protecting the very essence, or 'specific subject-matter' (see **23.6.3** for further discussion of this concept) of the rights, and will not infringe Article 81(1) EC. The latter are terms relating to exploitation of the right rather than the right itself, and are capable of infringing Article 81(1) EC. In practice, most terms in a licensing agreement (particularly a patent licensing agreement like that between Frodsby and Megaco) are likely to fall into the second category, which means that it is very important to consider ways of avoiding infringement of Article 81 EC.

Frodsby and Megaco are proposing to enter an agreement containing terms which will restrict each party's commercial freedom, and which could, because of their nature, cause competition law problems (a type of territorial restriction, fixed minimum payment by one party to the other, and price-fixing). The solicitor must therefore now consider ways of avoiding infringement of Article 81(1) EC. It will be worth checking whether the parties satisfy the conditions for the Notice on Agreements of Minor Importance to apply; the other line worth proceeding with is drafting the agreement to fall within the relevant block exemption.

23.4.2 Block exemption

The current block exemption relating to IP licensing is Commission Regulation (EC) No 772/2004 of 27 April 2004. It repeals and replaces the former block exemption in this area (Regulation 240/96) and came into force on 1 May 2004. Its title indicates that it covers 'categories of technology transfer agreements'; for an indication of the scope of this area, see below.

The Commission has also published guidelines on the application of EC competition law to technology transfer agreements; these can be accessed via the EU's Europa server (www.europa.eu) in the competition section.

Regulation 772/2004 adopts a broadly similar approach to that taken by Regulation 2790/99 on vertical agreements (see **22.3.6** and **22.3.7**); in doing so, it departs radically from the approach taken by the old Regulation 240/96. As the Preamble to Regulation 772/2004 explains, certain types of technology transfer agreement (defined in Article 1, para 1(b) as patent licensing agreements, know-how licensing agreements, software copyright licensing agreements, or a combination of any of these) can improve economic efficiency and be pro-competitive because they can (amongst other things) reduce the need for duplication of research and development, and can make it easier for new technologies to reach the market, thus increasing competition.

As with vertical agreements, the presumption under Regulation 772/2004 is broadly that technology transfer agreements will qualify for exemption from the prohibition in Article 81(1) EC where the parties' market shares do not exceed specified thresholds, and where the agreements do not contain certain severely anti-competitive ('hard-core') terms.

The structure and content of the new block exemption is set out below in outline. However, although it has much in common with the vertical agreements block exemption, Regulation 2790/99, it is by no means identical; there are many differences of detail, and one major difference of substance (see **23.4.2.1**). Thus, when drafting or reviewing an agreement which might benefit from Regulation 772/2004, the solicitor should check the individual provisions of this block exemption very carefully, and not simply assume that they will work in the same way as Regulation 2790/99.

23.4.2.1 Competitors and non-competitors

There is one major difference between the operation of the new technology transfer block exemption and that of the vertical agreements block exemption. The difference arises because the Commission is concerned that IP licences can be used by businesses which would normally compete with one another, as a means of dividing markets up between themselves. The classic situation arises where competitors license technologies to each other, and in return agree not to compete with each other in other fields. What looks like a licence, designed to make technology more widely available, is therefore in fact little more than a cover for an agreement not to compete. The technology covered by the licences may even be relatively unimportant to the parties; what really matters to them is the non-compete agreement.

Because of this danger, the new Regulation applies different rules to agreements between competitors and agreements between non-competitors. The market share thresholds are different, as are the lists of 'hardcore' anti-competitive terms. The new Regulation makes a further distinction between two types of agreement between competitors. On the one hand there is the 'reciprocal' agreement, where each licenses technology to the other. This is seen as open to the sort of abuse described above. The other type of agreement between competitors is the 'non-reciprocal' agreement, where one competitor licenses technology to another. This is more likely to be a genuine licence and less likely to be used as a cover for an agreement dividing markets between the parties, and so is subject to fewer restrictions.

23.4.2.2 The structure of the new Regulation

Like the vertical agreements block exemption Regulation, the new technology transfer block exemption Regulation begins in Article 1 with a list of definitions. The exemption itself is contained in Article 2. Article 3 sets the market share thresholds.

Article 4 contains the 'hardcore' restrictions (unlike Regulation 2790/99, Regulation 772/2004 actually uses this term!). Here, there are two lists. Article 4, para 1 deals with restrictions in agreements between competitors; Article 4, para 2 deals with agreements between non-competitors.

Article 5 lists restrictions which are not in themselves exempt but the inclusion of which will not stop the block exemption from applying to the remainder of the licence agreement. It therefore works in the same way as Article 5 of Regulation 2790/99.

Article 6 allows the Commission and the national competition authorities of the Member States to withdraw the block exemption from any given agreement if they find that the agreement is anti-competitive and so does not qualify for exemption under Article 81(3) EC. One of the situations in which they can do this is where the parties do not exploit the licensed technology; this may be a 'sham' licence agreement of the sort mentioned at **23.4.2.1**. Article 7 allows the Commission to disapply the block exemption from entire markets which are dominated by parallel networks of similar technology transfer agreements. Article 8 sets out detailed rules for the calculation of market share for the purposes of Article 3.

23.4.2.3 Does the Frodsby–Megaco agreement fall within Regulation 772/2004?

The proposed agreement appears to fall within Article 2, in that it is a 'technology transfer agreement' (a patent licensing agreement) which contemplates the production of products made with the licensed technology, and which is between two undertakings, Frodsby and Megaco (agreements between more than two undertakings are not covered). We do not know whether Frodsby and Megaco are competing or non-competing undertakings, and we do not know whether the market shares of the undertakings fall within Article 3. However, there is definitely a hardcore restriction, in that Megaco cannot determine its prices when selling the machines to third parties. This is a hardcore restriction regardless of whether the parties to the agreement are competing or non-competing (Article 4(1)(a) and 4(2(a)), and so even if the market shares do fall within Article 3, the presence of this hardcore restriction will prevent the block exemption from applying.

23.4.3 Drafting a patent licensing agreement

Both *Practical Commercial Precedents* (Section G), and the *Encyclopaedia of Forms and Precedents* (Volume 21 on Intellectual Property, updated by Service Volume B) provide complete precedents for patent licensing agreements, and indicate how an agreement can be tailored to gain the benefit of the existing block exemption.

23.5 Article 82 EC and intellectual property rights

The ownership of IP rights may confer a dominant position on an undertaking within a particular geographic or product market. For example, a business may become dominant in a relevant product market by acquiring a patent; the patented item may form a market by itself if its novelty and inventiveness mean that consumers do not regard any other product as a substitute for it. However, this of itself (ie, the existence of the IP right) will not infringe Article 82 EC. Infringement requires abuse of a dominant position, which would mean improper exercise of the right in question. Not all exercises will be improper and, therefore, 'abusive'; it will depend on the circumstances, and in particular the effect on competition in the markets concerned. These general principles were confirmed by the ECJ in *Radio Telefis Eireann and Another v Commission of the European Communities and Another* (Cases C-241/91P and C-242/91P) [1995] ECR 1-801 (the 'Magill' case). However, some uncertainty still remains about the relationship between Article 82 EC and the exercise of IP rights; notably, exactly how far a right-holder's refusal to license its right to others amounts to abusive behaviour. For a more recent ECJ ruling on the matter, see *IMS Health GmbH and Co OHG v NDC Health GmbH and Co KG* (Case C-418/01) [2004] ECR I-5039.

23.6 Articles 28–30 EC and intellectual property rights

23.6.1 Introduction

The competition authorities of the EC cannot resolve all the problems which arise from the existence and exercise of IP rights by using the specific competition law Articles of the European Community Treaty (Articles 81 and 82 EC). For example, in many cases, Article 81 EC does not apply because the situation does not involve a business arrangement of the type to which it can apply. It will then be necessary for the authorities to control the exercise of IP rights by relying on the principles of free movement of goods (Articles 28–30 EC).

23.6.2 How Articles 28–30 EC may be relevant

Assume that Frodsby Engineering Ltd puts its patented machine on the market in Germany as well as in the UK. Market conditions in Germany mean that Frodsby can afford to sell the machine more cheaply there than it can in the UK. Fred, a businessman, realises that he can make money by (lawfully) buying the machine in Germany and reselling it in the UK at a price which still undercuts Frodsby's UK price. What if Frodsby were to try to rely on its patent rights under English law to prevent Fred from importing the machines into the UK, claiming that those rights give it absolute control over what happens to the machines at all times?

Fred may try to argue that English patent law is a 'measure having equivalent effect' to a quantitative restriction on imports under Article 28 EC, as the patent holder is attempting to use the law to stop imports of patented goods into the UK. Article 28 EC prohibits such measures, so use of the UK patent rights to stop the imports may not be justified, being incompatible with the free movement of goods around the common market.

However, Article 28 EC must be read subject to Article 30 EC. This permits derogations from Article 28 EC in certain circumstances, such as where the measure is necessary for 'the protection of industrial or commercial property rights', an expression which will cover IP rights such as patents. Thus, under Article 30 EC, the national measure (ie, the law on patents) may be justified if it protects something about the patent which needs protection.

There are, in turn, however, limits on the use of Article 30 EC. The Article itself provides that it cannot be invoked to justify a measure which amounts to 'arbitrary discrimination' or 'a disguised restriction on trade', and the ECJ has used this to ensure that any derogations from Article 28 EC do not go too far (the Court has also indicated that the measure must be proportionate). In particular, the Court has developed the doctrine that Article 30 EC can be invoked by the holder of an IP right only if the infringement action is necessary to protect the 'specific subject-matter' of the right. In other words, although EC law recognises that national IP rights need protection in certain circumstances, it also attempts to ensure that they do not interfere too much with trade within the common market.

23.6.3 Specific subject-matter

What constitutes the specific subject-matter of an IP right will vary according to the right concerned. The ECJ has held that the specific subject-matter of a patent is 'the guarantee that the patentee, to reward the creative effort of the inventor, has the exclusive right to use an invention with a view to manufacturing industrial products and putting them into circulation for the first time, either directly or by the grant of licences to third parties, as well as the right to oppose infringement' (*Centrafarm BV and Adrian de Peijper v Sterling Drug Inc* (Case 15/74) [1974] ECR 1147). For a trade mark, however, the specific subject-matter is 'the guarantee that the owner of the trade mark has the exclusive right to use that trade mark, for the purpose of putting products protected by the mark into circulation for the first time, and is, therefore, intended to protect him against competitors wishing to take advantage of the status and reputation of the trade mark by selling products illegally bearing that trade mark' (*Centrafarm BV and Adrian de Peijper v Winthrop BV* (Case 16/74) [1974] ECR 1183). The position in relation to copyright is less clear; this is at least partly because national systems of copyright law within the EU still vary quite considerably.

The specific subject-matter of an IP right may, therefore, be seen as a limit on the use of the principles relating to free movement of goods. The Court recognises that there is something central to each IP right which needs protection, but is reluctant to allow the right to be exercised in an uncontrolled manner; the Court will always be prepared to stop the use of IP rights if they are being used to restrict trade and competition within the common market.

23.6.4 Exhaustion of rights

This is further illustrated by the concept of 'exhaustion of rights', which the ECJ has applied to most IP rights, including patents, copyright and trade marks. Its effect is that when goods which are subject to an IP right are lawfully put on the market for the first time in the EEA (either by the right holder, or with its consent), this 'exhausts' the right holder's opportunities to control what subsequently happens to the goods. In particular, the right holder cannot use the right to prevent the goods being imported into another Member State. However, note that this only applies to attempts by the right holder to control the movement of the goods around the EEA; it does not take away the holder's right to take action if the right has actually been infringed.

The case of *Silhouette International Schmied GmbH and Co KG v Hartlauer Handelsgesellschaft mbH* (Case C-355/96) [2000] All ER (EC) 769 showed the doctrine at work in relation to trade marks. The ECJ interpreted Article 7 of the Trade Marks Directive (89/140/EEC) to mean that exhaustion occurred only in the circumstances described above (lawful marketing in the EEA by the owner, or with the owner's consent). Thus, the owner of a trade mark would be entitled to stop products bearing the mark being imported into the EEA from outside that area (in this case, spectacle frames bearing Silhouette's mark being imported from Bulgaria into Austria). However, even after the *Silhouette* case, this area continued to prove problematic, particularly on the issue of the trade mark owner's consent. For example, how far could the owner's consent to imports of its goods into the EEA be implied when the owner had put its goods on the market outside the EEA without express restrictions as to where they could be re-sold?

The questions relating to consent now appear to have been answered by the ECJ's ruling in the joined cases of *Zino Davidoff SA v A & G Imports Ltd; Levi Strauss & Co and Another v Tesco Stores Ltd and Another; Levi Strauss & Co and Another v Costco Wholesale UK* (Joined Cases C-414/99, C-415/99 and C-416/99) [2002] All ER (EC) 55. The Court in effect ruled that there had to be some positive expression of consent by the trade mark owner to its goods being imported into the EEA from outside. Consent cannot be implied from silence; there would have to be some unequivocal demonstration from the circumstances that the trade mark owner had given up its right to control the import into and marketing of the goods within the EEA. This ruling appears greatly to have strengthened the hand of trade mark owners: for example, it appears that there is now no need to state expressly in an agreement for goods which are to be sold outside the EEA that they must not be imported into and sold in the EEA.

23.7 Article 28 EC and Articles 81–82 EC: relationship

It seems clear that some attempts to use IP rights to prevent the import of goods from one Member State into another may be capable of infringing both Article 28 EC and Article 81 EC (or Article 82 EC) (*Nungesser (LC) and Kurt Eisle v Commission for the European Communities* (Case 258/78) [1982] ECR 2015: the 'Maize Seeds' case). Application of the rules on free movement of goods to a case does not necessarily preclude the application of the competition rules, although in practice it is comparatively rare for both to be argued actively in the same case.

23.8 EC competition law and franchising agreements

Like the other types of agreement considered in **Chapters 22** and **23**, franchising agreements have the potential to infringe Article 81(1) EC. They will frequently contain terms restricting the parties' commercial freedom (eg, territorial restrictions, restrictions on the use that can be made of the IP rights which are part of the franchise package). If the agreement is capable of affecting trade and competition within the common market, then the parties will need to consider how to avoid infringing Article 81(1) EC.

All the normal methods of avoidance are available, including block exemption. Prior to 1 June 2000, franchising agreements were covered by a specific block exemption, granted by Regulation 4087/88. This has, however, now been replaced by the vertical agreements block exemption, Regulation 2790/99, so franchising agreements can enjoy block exemption on the terms of that Regulation (see **22.3.7**).

Part IV Summary
Competition Law

Topic	*Summary*
Competition law	This might, broadly speaking, be defined as the area of law which seeks to regulate the way in which businesses are allowed to operate when seeking custom and trying to gain market share for themselves.
Scope	Many jurisdictions have competition laws; the two with which we are concerned here are UK competition law and EC competition law.
Competition Act 1998	The UK's own national competition law is chiefly to be found in the Competition Act 1998. The provisions of the Act are heavily based on EC competition law, including the Chapter I prohibition on anti-competitive agreements (based on Article 81 EC) and the Chapter II prohibition of abuse of a dominant position (based on Article 82 EC).
Chapter I prohibition	This applies to arrangements between two or more businesses which may affect trade within the UK, and which have as their object or effect the prevention, restriction or distortion of competition within the UK.
Avoiding the impact of the Chapter I prohibition	The Act outlines a number of ways in which businesses can avoid the impact of the Chapter I prohibition. In particular, any arrangement which is exempt from the provisions of Article 81 EC is also exempt from the Chapter I prohibition.
Chapter II prohibition	This prohibits abuse of a dominant position which may affect trade within the UK. Like its EC law counterpart (see below), it most commonly applies to the activities of a single business (eg, predatory pricing, refusal to supply).
Enforcement	As well as the possibility of private enforcement, a business which infringes either prohibition should be aware that it can be investigated and fined by the UK Competition Authority (the OFT).
EC Treaty	Articles 81 and 82 of the EC Treaty contain the main EC competition law provisions which apply purely to private businesses (Article 87 EC covers State aid to businesses).
Article 81 EC	This applies to arrangements which may affect trade between Member States, and which have as their object or effect the prevention, restriction or distortion of competition within the common market.
Avoiding the impact of Article 81 EC	There are a number of methods of avoiding infringement, notably block exemption and individual assessment under Article 81(3) EC.
Article 82 EC	This prohibits abuse of a dominant position which may affect trade between Member States, and most commonly applies to the activities of just one business (rather than businesses acting collectively, as is the case with Article 81 EC).

Topic	*Summary*
Avoiding the impact of Article 82 EC	The only way to do this is to avoid abusing a dominant position in the first place; unlike Article 81 EC, no exemptions are available.
Enforcement	As well as private enforcement (by other businesses which are harmed by breach of EC competition law), businesses committing infringement can be investigated and fined by the EC competition authorities (the Commission). In addition, an agreement entered into in breach of Article 81 EC is void.
Relationship with other areas of EC law	In some cases, Articles 28–30 EC are also relevant; where a factual scenario concerns national law which imposes hindrances on the free flow of goods between Member States. In addition, where the scenario involves the existence or exercise of intellectual property rights, Article 295 EC (on property ownership) and/or specific EC intellectual property law (such as Regulation 772/2004 on licensing patents and other IP rights) may come into play.

Appendix

Legislation

Registered Designs Act 1949
1949 c. 88

An Act to consolidate certain enactments relating to registered designs

[16th December 1949]

Registrable designs and proceedings for registration

1. Registration of designs

(1) A design may, subject to the following provisions of this Act, be registered under this Act on the making of an application for registration.

(2) In this Act "design" means the appearance of the whole or a part of a product resulting from the features of, in particular, the lines, contours, colours, shape, texture or materials of the product or its ornamentation.

(3) In this Act—

"complex product" means a product which is composed of at least two replaceable component parts permitting disassembly and reassembly of the product; and

"product" means any industrial or handicraft item other than a computer program; and, in particular, includes packaging, get-up, graphic symbols, typographic type-faces and parts intended to be assembled into a complex product.

1B. Requirement of novelty and individual character

(1) A design shall be protected by a right in a registered design to the extent that the design is new and has individual character.

(2) For the purposes of subsection (1) above, a design is new if no identical design or no design whose features differ only in immaterial details has been made available to the public before the relevant date.

(3) For the purposes of subsection (1) above, a design has individual character if the overall impression it produces on the informed user differs from the overall impression produced on such a user by any design which has been made available to the public before the relevant date.

(4) In determining the extent to which a design has individual character, the degree of freedom of the author in creating the design shall be taken into consideration.

(5) For the purposes of this section, a design has been made available to the public before the relevant date if—

(a) it has been published (whether following registration or otherwise), exhibited, used in trade or otherwise disclosed before that date; and

(b) the disclosure does not fall within subsection (6) below.

(6) A disclosure falls within this subsection if—

(a) it could not reasonably have become known before the relevant date in the normal course of business to persons carrying on business in the European Economic Area and specialising in the sector concerned;

(b) it was made to a person other than the designer, or any successor in title of his, under conditions of confidentiality (whether express or implied);

(c) it was made by the designer, or any successor in title of his, during the period of 12 months immediately preceding the relevant date;

(d) it was made by a person other than the designer, or any successor in title of his, during the period of 12 months immediately preceding the relevant date in consequence of information provided or other action taken by the designer or any successor in title of his; or

(e) it was made during the period of 12 months immediately preceding the relevant date as a consequence of an abuse in relation to the designer or any successor in title of his.

(7) In subsections (2), (3), (5) and (6) above "the relevant date" means the date on which the application for the registration of the design was made or is treated by virtue of section 3B(2), (3) or (5) or 14(2) of this Act as having been made.

(8) For the purposes of this section, a design applied to or incorporated in a product which constitutes a component part of a complex product shall only be considered to be new and to have individual character—

(a) if the component part, once it has been incorporated into the complex product, remains visible during normal use of the complex product; and

(b) to the extent that those visible features of the component part are in themselves new and have individual character.

(9) In subsection (8) above "normal use" means use by the end user; but does not include any maintenance, servicing or repair work in relation to the product.

1C. Designs dictated by their technical function

(1) A right in a registered design shall not subsist in features of appearance of a product which are solely dictated by the product's technical function.

(2) A right in a registered design shall not subsist in features of appearance of a product which must necessarily be reproduced in their exact form and dimensions so as to permit the product in which the design is incorporated or to which it is applied to be mechanically connected to, or placed in, around or against, another product so that either product may perform its function.

(3) Subsection (2) above does not prevent a right in a registered design subsisting in a design serving the purpose of allowing multiple assembly or connection of mutually interchangeable products within a modular system.

2. Proprietorship of designs

(1) The author of a design shall be treated for the purposes of this Act as the original proprietor of the design, subject to the following provisions.

(1A) Where a design is created in pursuance of a commission for money or money's worth, the person commissioning the design shall be treated as the original proprietor of the design.

(1B) Where, in a case not falling within subsection (1A), a design is created by an employee in the course of his employment, his employer shall be treated as the original proprietor of the design.

(2) Where a design becomes vested, whether by assignment, transmission or operation of law, in any person other than the original proprietor, either alone or jointly with the original proprietor, that other person, or as the case may be the original proprietor and that other person, shall be treated for the purposes of this Act as the proprietor of the design.

(3) In this Act the "author" of a design means the person who creates it.

(4) In the case of a design generated by computer in circumstances such that there is no human author, the person by whom the arrangements necessary for the creation of the design are made shall be taken to be the author.

7. Right given by registration

(1) The registration of a design under this Act gives the registered proprietor the exclusive right to use the design and any design which does not produce on the informed user a different overall impression.

(2) For the purposes of subsection (1) above and section 7A of this Act any reference to the use of a design includes a reference to—

(a) the making, offering, putting on the market, importing, exporting or using of a product in which the design is incorporated or to which it is applied; or

(b) stocking such a product for those purposes.

(3) In determining for the purposes of subsection (1) above whether a design produces a different overall impression on the informed user, the degree of freedom of the author in creating his design shall be taken into consideration.

(4) The right conferred by subsection (1) above is subject to any limitation attaching to the registration in question (including, in particular, any partial disclaimer or any declaration by the registrar or a court of partial invalidity).

7A. Infringements of rights in registered designs

(1) Subject as follows, the right in a registered design is infringed by a person who, without the consent of the registered proprietor, does anything which by virtue of section 7 of this Act is the exclusive right of the registered proprietor.

(2) The right in a registered design is not infringed by—

(a) an act which is done privately and for purposes which are not commercial;

(b) an act which is done for experimental purposes;

(c) an act of reproduction for teaching purposes or for the purpose of making citations provided that the conditions mentioned in subsection (3) below are satisfied;

(d) the use of equipment on ships or aircraft which are registered in another country but which are temporarily in the United Kingdom;

(e) the importation into the United Kingdom of spare parts or accessories for the purpose of repairing such ships or aircraft; or

(f) the carrying out of repairs on such ships or aircraft.

(3) The conditions mentioned in this subsection are—

(a) the act of reproduction is compatible with fair trade practice and does not unduly prejudice the normal exploitation of the design; and

(b) mention is made of the source.

(4) The right in a registered design is not infringed by an act which relates to a product in which any design protected by the registration is incorporated or to which it is applied if the product has been put on the market in the European Economic Area by the registered proprietor or with his consent.

(5) The right in a registered design of a component part which may be used for the purpose of the repair of a complex product so as to restore its original appearance is not infringed by the use for that purpose of any design protected by the registration.

(6) No proceedings shall be taken in respect of an infringement of the right in a registered design committed before the date on which the certificate of registration of the design under this Act is granted.

8. Duration of right in registered design

(1) The right in a registered design subsists in the first instance for a period of five years from the date of the registration of the design.

(2) The period for which the right subsists may be extended for a second, third, fourth and fifth period of five years, by applying to the registrar for an extension and paying the prescribed renewal fee.

(3) If the first, second, third or fourth period expires without such application and payment being made, the right shall cease to have effect; and the registrar shall, in accordance with rules made by the Secretary of State, notify the proprietor of that fact.

(4) If during the period of six months immediately following the end of that period an application for extension is made and the prescribed renewal fee and any prescribed additional fee is paid, the right shall be treated as if it had never expired, with the result that—

(a) anything done under or in relation to the right during that further period shall be treated as valid,

(b) an act which would have constituted an infringement of the right if it had not expired shall be treated as an infringement, and

(c) an act which would have constituted use of the design for the services of the Crown if the right had not expired shall be treated as such use.

8A. Restoration of lapsed right in design

(1) Where the right in a registered design has expired by reason of a failure to extend, in accordance with section 8(2) or (4), the period for which the right subsists, an application for the restoration of the right in the design may be made to the registrar within the prescribed period.

(2) The application may be made by the person who was the registered proprietor of the design or by any other person who would have been entitled to the right in the design if it had not expired; and where the design was held by two or more persons jointly, the application may, with the leave of the registrar, be made by one or more of them without joining the others.

(3) Notice of the application shall be published by the registrar in the prescribed manner.

(4) If the registrar is satisfied that the failure of the proprietor to see that the period for which the right subsisted was extended in accordance with section 8(2) or (4) was unintentional, he shall, on payment of any unpaid renewal fee and any prescribed additional fee, order the restoration of the right in the design.

(5) The order may be made subject to such conditions as the registrar thinks fit, and if the proprietor of the design does not comply with any condition the registrar may revoke the order and give such consequential directions as he thinks fit.

(6) Rules altering the period prescribed for the purposes of subsection (1) may contain such transitional provisions and savings as appear to the Secretary of State to be necessary or expedient.

8B. Effect of order for restoration of right

(1) The effect of an order under section 8A for the restoration of the right in a registered design is as follows.

(2) Anything done under or in relation to the right during the period between expiry and restoration shall be treated as valid.

(3) Anything done during that period which would have constituted an infringement if the right had not expired shall be treated as an infringement—

(a) if done at a time when it was possible for an application for extension to be made under section 8(4); or

(b) if it was a continuation or repetition of an earlier infringing act.

(4) If, after it was no longer possible for such an application for extension to be made and before publication of notice of the application for restoration, a person—

(a) began in good faith to do an act which would have constituted an infringement of the right in the design if it had not expired, or

(b) made in good faith effective and serious preparations to do such an act,

he has the right to continue to do the act or, as the case may be, to do the act, notwithstanding the restoration of the right in the design; but this does not extend to granting a licence to another person to do the act.

(5) If the act was done, or the preparations were made, in the course of a business, the person entitled to the right conferred by subsection (4) may—

(a) authorise the doing of that act by any partners of his for the time being in that business, and

(b) assign that right, or transmit it on death (or in the case of a body corporate on its dissolution), to any person who acquires that part of the business in the course of which the act was done or the preparations were made.

(6) Where a product is disposed of to another in exercise of the rights conferred by subsection (4) or subsection (5), that other and any person claiming through him may deal with the product in the same way as if it had been disposed of by the registered proprietor of the design.

(7) The above provisions apply in relation to the use of a registered design for the services of the Crown as they apply in relation to infringement of the right in the design.

Property in and dealing with registered designs and applications

15B. Assignment, &c of registered designs and applications for registered designs

(1) A registered design or an application for a registered design is transmissible by assignment, testamentary disposition or operation of law in the same way as other personal or moveable property, subject to the following provisions of this section.

(2) Any transmission of a registered design or an application for a registered design is subject to any rights vested in any other person of which notice is entered in the register of designs, or in the case of applications, notice is given to the registrar.

(3) An assignment of, or an assent relating to, a registered design or application for a registered design is not effective unless it is in writing signed by or on behalf of the assignor or, as the case may be, a personal representative.

(4) Except in Scotland, the requirement in subsection (3) may be satisfied in a case where the assignor or personal representative is a body corporate by the affixing of its seal.

(5) Subsections (3) and (4) apply to assignment by way of security as in relation to any other assignment.

(6) A registered design or application for a registered design may be the subject of a charge (in Scotland, security) in the same way as other personal or moveable property.

(7) The proprietor of a registered design may grant a licence to use that registered design.

(8) Any equities (in Scotland, rights) in respect of a registered design or an application for a registered design may be enforced in like manner as in respect of any other personal or moveable property.

15C. Exclusive licences

(1) In this Act an "exclusive licence" means a licence in writing signed by or on behalf of the proprietor of the registered design authorising the licensee to the exclusion of all other persons, including the person granting the licence, to exercise a right which would otherwise be exercisable exclusively by the proprietor of the registered design.

(2) The licensee under an exclusive licence has the same rights against any successor in title who is bound by the licence as he has against the person granting the licence.

Register of designs, etc.

19. Registration of assignments, etc.

(1) Where any person becomes entitled by assignment, transmission or operation of law to a registered design or to a share in a registered design, or becomes entitled as mortgagee, licensee or otherwise to any other interest in a registered design, he shall apply to the registrar in the prescribed manner for the registration of his title as proprietor or co-proprietor or, as the case may be, of notice of his interest, in the register of designs.

(2) Without prejudice to the provisions of the foregoing subsection, an application for the registration of the title of any person becoming entitled by assignment to a registered design or a share in a registered design, or becoming entitled by virtue of a mortgage, licence or other instrument to any other interest in a registered design, may be made in the prescribed manner by the assign or, mortgagor, licensor or other party to that instrument, as the case may be.

(3) Where application is made under this section for the registration of the title of any person, the registrar shall, upon proof of title to his satisfaction—

(a) where that person is entitled to a registered design or a share in a registered design, register him in the register of designs as proprietor or co-proprietor of the design, and enter in that register particulars of the instrument or event by which he derives title; or

(b) where that person is entitled to any other interest in the registered design, enter in that register notice of his interest, with particulars of the instrument (if any) creating it.

(3A) Where national unregistered design right subsists in a registered design, the registrar shall not register an interest under subsection (3) unless he is satisfied that the person entitled to that interest is also entitled to a corresponding interest in the national unregistered design right.

(3B) Where national unregistered design right subsists in a registered design and the proprietor of the registered design is also the design right owner, an assignment of the national unregistered design right shall be taken to be also an assignment of the right in the registered design, unless a contrary intention appears.

(4) ...

(5) Except for the purposes of an application to rectify the register under the following provisions of this Act, a document in respect of which no entry has been made in the register of designs under subsection (3) of this section shall not be admitted in any court as evidence of the title of any person to a registered design or share of or interest in a registered design unless the court otherwise directs.

24A. Action for infringement

(1) An infringement of the right in a registered design is actionable by the registered proprietor.

(2) In an action for infringement all such relief by way of damages, injunctions, accounts or otherwise is available to him as is available in respect of the infringement of any other property right.

(3) This section has effect subject to section 24B of this Act (exemption of innocent infringer from liability).

24B. Exemption of innocent infringer from liability

(1) In proceedings for the infringement of the right in a registered design damages shall not be awarded, and no order shall be made for an account of profits, against a defendant who proves that at the date of the infringement he was not aware, and had no reasonable ground for supposing, that the design was registered.

(2) For the purposes of subsection (1), a person shall not be deemed to have been aware or to have had reasonable grounds for supposing that the design was registered by reason only of the marking of a product with—

(a) the word 'registered' or any abbreviation thereof, or

(b) any word or words expressing or implying that the design applied to, or incorporated in, the product has been registered,

unless the number of the design accompanied the word or words or the abbreviation in question.

(3) Nothing in this section shall affect the power of the court to grant an injunction in any proceedings for infringement of the right in a registered design.

24C. Order for delivery up

(1) Where a person—

(a) has in his possession, custody or control for commercial purposes an infringing article, or

(b) has in his possession, custody or control anything specifically designed or adapted for making articles to a particular design which is a registered design, knowing or having reason to believe that it has been or is to be used to make an infringing article,

the registered proprietor in question may apply to the court for an order that the infringing article or other thing be delivered up to him or to such other person as the court may direct.

(2) An application shall not be made after the end of the period specified in the following provisions of this section; and no order shall be made unless the court also makes, or it appears to the court that there are grounds for making, an order under section 24D of this Act (order as to disposal of infringing article, &c).

(3) An application for an order under this section may not be made after the end of the period of six years from the date on which the article or thing in question was made, subject to subsection (4).

(4) If during the whole or any part of that period the registered proprietor—

(a) is under a disability, or

(b) is prevented by fraud or concealment from discovering the facts entitling him to apply for an order,

an application may be made at any time before the end of the period of six years from the date on which he ceased to be under a disability or, as the case may be, could with reasonable diligence have discovered those facts.

(5) In subsection (4) 'disability'—

(a) in England and Wales, has the same meaning as in the Limitation Act 1980;

(b) in Scotland, means legal disability within the meaning of the Prescription and Limitation (Scotland) Act 1973;

(c) in Northern Ireland, has the same meaning as in the Statute of Limitations (Northern Ireland) 1958.

(6) A person to whom an infringing article or other thing is delivered up in pursuance of an order under this section shall, if an order under section 24D of this Act is not made, retain it pending the making of an order, or the decision not to make an order, under that section.

(7) The reference in subsection (1) to an act being done in relation to an article for 'commercial purposes' are to its being done with a view to the article in question being sold or hired in the course of a business.

(8) Nothing in this section affects any other power of the court.

24D. Order as to disposal of infringing articles, &c

(1) An application may be made to the court for an order that an infringing article or other thing delivered up in pursuance of an order under section 24C of this Act shall be—

(a) forfeited to the registered proprietor, or

(b) destroyed or otherwise dealt with as the court may think fit,

or for a decision that no such order should be made.

(2) In considering what order (if any) should be made, the court shall consider whether other remedies available in an action for infringement of the right in a registered design would be adequate to compensate the registered proprietor and to protect his interests.

(3) Where there is more than one person interested in an article or other thing, the court shall make such order as it thinks just and may (in particular) direct that the thing be sold, or otherwise dealt with, and the proceeds divided.

(4) If the court decides that no order should be made under this section, the person in whose possession, custody or control the article or other thing was before being delivered up is entitled to its return.

(5) References in this section to a person having an interest in an article or other thing include any person in whose favour an order could be made in respect of it—

(a) under this section;

(b) under section 19 of Trade Marks Act 1994 (including that section as applied by regulation 4 of the Community Trade Mark Regulations 2006 (SI 2006/1027));

(c) under section 114, 204 or 231 of the Copyright, Designs and Patents Act 1988; or

(d) under regulation 1C of the Community Design Regulations 2005 (SI 2005/2339).

24E. Jurisdiction of county court and sheriff court

(1) In Northern Ireland a county court may entertain proceedings under the following provisions of this Act—

section 24C (order for delivery up of infringing article, &c),

section 24D (order as to disposal of infringing article, &c), or

section 24F(8) (application by exclusive licensee having concurrent rights),

where the value of the infringing articles and other things in question does not exceed the county court limit for actions in tort.

(2) In Scotland proceedings for an order under any of those provisions may be brought in the sheriff court.

(3) Nothing in this section shall be construed as affecting the jurisdiction of the Court of Session or the High Court in Northern Ireland.

Legal proceedings and appeals

24F. Rights and remedies of exclusive licensee

(1) In relation to a registered design, an exclusive licensee has, except against the registered proprietor, the same rights and remedies in respect of matters occurring after the grant of the licence as if the licence had been an assignment.

(2) His rights and remedies are concurrent with those of the registered proprietor; and references to the registered proprietor in the provisions of this Act relating to infringement shall be construed accordingly.

(3) In an action brought by an exclusive licensee by virtue of this section a defendant may avail himself of any defence which would have been available to him if the action had been brought by the registered proprietor.

(4) Where an action for infringement of the right in a registered design brought by the registered proprietor or an exclusive licensee relates (wholly or partly) to an infringement in respect of which they have concurrent rights of action, the proprietor

or, as the case may be, the exclusive licensee may not, without the leave of the court, proceed with the action unless the other is either joined as a claimant or added as a defendant.

(5) A registered proprietor or exclusive licensee who is added as a defendant in pursuance of subsection (4) is not liable for any costs in the action unless he takes part in the proceedings.

(6) Subsections (4) and (5) do not affect the granting of interlocutory relief on the application of the registered proprietor or an exclusive licensee.

(7) Where an action for infringement of the right in a registered design is brought which relates (wholly or partly) to an infringement in respect of which the registered proprietor and an exclusive licensee have concurrent rights of action—

(a) the court shall, in assessing damages, take into account—

(i) the terms of the licence, and

(ii) any pecuniary remedy already awarded or available to either of them in respect of the infringement;

(b) no account of profits shall be directed if an award of damages has been made, or an account of profits has been directed, in favour of the other of them in respect of the infringement; and

(c) the court shall if an account of profits is directed apportion the profits between them as the court considers just, subject to any agreement between them;

and these provisions apply whether or not the proprietor and the exclusive licensee are both parties to the action.

(8) The registered proprietor shall notify any exclusive licensee having concurrent rights before applying for an order under section 24C this Act (order for delivery up of infringing article, &c); and the court may on the application of the licensee make such order under that section as it thinks fit having regard to the terms of the licence.

24G. Meaning of 'infringing article'

(1) In this Act 'infringing article', in relation to a design, shall be construed in accordance with this section.

(2) An article is an infringing article if its making to that design was an infringement of the right in a registered design.

(3) An article is also an infringing article if—

(a) it has been or is proposed to be imported into the United Kingdom, and

(b) its making to that design in the United Kingdom would have been an infringement of the right in a registered design or a breach of an exclusive licensing agreement relating to that registered design.

(4) Where it is shown that an article is made to a design which is or has been a registered design, it shall be presumed until the contrary is proved that the article was made at a time when the right in the registered design subsisted.

(5) Nothing in subsection (3) shall be construed as applying to an article which may be lawfully imported into the United Kingdom by virtue of an enforceable Community right within the meaning of section 2(1) of the European Communities Act 1972.

26. Remedy for groundless threats of infringement proceedings

(1) Where any person (whether entitled to or interested in a registered design or an application for registration of a design or not) by circulars, advertisements or otherwise threatens any other person with proceedings for infringement of the right in a registered design, any person aggrieved thereby may bring an action against him for any such relief as is mentioned in the next following subsection.

(2) Unless in any action brought by virtue of this section the defendant proves that the acts in respect of which proceedings were threatened constitute or, if done, would constitute, an infringement of the right in a registered design the registration of which is not shown by the claimant to be invalid, the claimant shall be entitled to the following relief, that is to say:—

(a) a declaration to the effect that the threats are unjustifiable;

(b) an injunction against the continuance of the threats; and

(c) such damages, if any, as he has sustained thereby.

(2A) Proceedings may not be brought under this section in respect of a threat to bring proceedings for an infringement alleged to consist of the making or importing of anything.

(3) For the avoidance of doubt it is hereby declared that a mere notification that a design is registered does not constitute a threat of proceedings within the meaning of this section.

Patents Act 1977
1977 c. 37

An Act to establish a new law of patents applicable to future patents and applications for patents; to amend the law of patents applicable to existing patents and applications for patents; to give effect to certain international conventions on patents; and for connected purposes [29th July 1977]

Part I
New Domestic Law

Patentability

1. Patentable inventions

(1) A patent may be granted only for an invention in respect of which the following conditions are satisfied, that is to say—

(a) the invention is new;

(b) it involves an inventive step;

(c) it is capable of industrial application;

(d) the grant of a patent for it is not excluded by subsections (2) and (3) or section 4A below;

and references in this Act to a patentable invention shall be construed accordingly.

(2) It is hereby declared that the following (among other things) are not inventions for the purposes of this Act, that is to say, anything which consists of—

(a) a discovery, scientific theory or mathematical method;

(b) a literary, dramatic, musical or artistic work or any other aesthetic creation whatsoever;

(c) a scheme, rule or method for performing a mental act, playing a game or doing business, or a program for a computer;

(d) the presentation of information;

but the foregoing provision shall prevent anything from being treated as an invention for the purposes of this Act only to the extent that a patent or application for a patent relates to that thing as such.

(3) A patent shall not be granted for an invention the commercial exploitation of which would be contrary to public policy or morality.

(4) For the purposes of subsection (3) above exploitation shall not be regarded as contrary to public policy or morality only because it is prohibited by any law in force in the United Kingdom or any part of it.

(5) The Secretary of State may by order vary the provisions of subsection (2) above for the purpose of maintaining them in conformity with developments in science and technology; and no such order shall be made unless a draft of the order has been laid before, and approved by resolution of, each House of Parliament.

2. Novelty

(1) An invention shall be taken to be new if it does not form part of the state of the art.

(2) The state of the art in the case of an invention shall be taken to comprise all matter (whether a product, a process, information about either, or anything else) which has at any time before the priority date of that invention been made available to the public (whether in the United Kingdom or elsewhere) by written or oral description, by use or in any other way.

(3) The state of the art in the case of an invention to which an application for a patent or a patent relates shall be taken also to comprise matter contained in an application for

another patent which was published on or after the priority date of that invention, if the following conditions are satisfied, that is to say—

(a) that matter was contained in the application for that other patent both as filed and as published; and

(b) the priority date of that matter is earlier than that of the invention.

(4) For the purposes of this section the disclosure of matter constituting an invention shall be disregarded in the case of a patent or an application for a patent if occurring later than the beginning of the period of six months immediately preceding the date of filing the application for the patent and either—

(a) the disclosure was due to, or made in consequence of, the matter having been obtained unlawfully or in breach of confidence by any person—

(i) from the inventor or from any other person to whom the matter was made available in confidence by the inventor or who obtained it from the inventor because he or the inventor believed that he was entitled to obtain it; or

(ii) from any other person to whom the matter was made available in confidence by any person mentioned in sub-paragraph (i) above or in this sub-paragraph or who obtained it from any person so mentioned because he or the person from whom he obtained it believed that he was entitled to obtain it;

(b) the disclosure was made in breach of confidence by any person who obtained the matter in confidence from the inventor or from any other person to whom it was made available, or who obtained it, from the inventor; or

(c) the disclosure was due to, or made in consequence of the inventor displaying the invention at an international exhibition and the applicant states, on filing the application, that the invention has been so displayed and also, within the prescribed period, files written evidence in support of the statement complying with any prescribed conditions.

(5) In this section references to the inventor include references to any proprietor of the invention for the time being.

3. Inventive step

An invention shall be taken to involve an inventive step if it is not obvious to a person skilled in the art, having regard to any matter which forms part of the state of the art by virtue only of section 2(2) above (and disregarding section 2(3) above).

4. Industrial application

(1) An invention shall be taken to be capable of industrial application if it can be made or used in any kind of industry, including agriculture.

4A. Methods of treatment or diagnosis

(1) A patent shall not be granted for the invention of—

(a) a method of treatment of the human or animal body by surgery or therapy, or

(b) a method of diagnosis practised on the human or animal body.

(2) Subsection (1) above does not apply to an invention consisting of a substance or composition for use in any such method.

(3) In the case of an invention consisting of a substance or composition for use in any such method, the fact that the substance or composition forms part of the state of the art shall not prevent the invention from being taken to be new if the use of the substance or composition in any such method does not form part of the state of the art.

(4) In the case of an invention consisting of a substance or composition for a specific use in any such method, the fact that the substance or composition forms part of the state of

the art shall not prevent the invention from being taken to be new if that specific use does not form part of the state of the art.

Property in patents and applications, and registration

30. Nature of, and transactions in, patents and applications for patents

(1) Any patent or application for a patent is personal property (without being a thing in action), and any patent or any such application and rights in or under it may be transferred, created or granted in accordance with subsections (2) to (7) below.

(2) Subject to section 36(3) below, any patent or any such application, or any right in it, may be assigned or mortgaged.

(3) Any patent or any such application or right shall vest by operation of law in the same way as any other personal property and may be vested by an assent of personal representatives.

(4) Subject to section 36(3) below, a licence may be granted under any patent or any such application for working the invention which is the subject of the patent or the application; and—

(a) to the extent that the licence so provides, a sub-licence may be granted under any such licence and any such licence or sub-licence may be assigned or mortgaged; and

(b) any such licence or sub-licence shall vest by operation of law in the same way as any other personal property and may be vested by an assent of personal representatives.

(5) Subsections (2) to (4) above shall have effect subject to the following provisions of this Act.

(6) Any of the following transactions, that is to say—

(a) any assignment or mortgage of a patent or any such application, or any right in a patent or any such application;

(b) any assent relating to any patent or any such application or right;

shall be void unless it is in writing and is signed by or on behalf of the assignor or mortgagor (or, in the case of an assent or other transaction by a personal representative, by or on behalf of the personal representative).

(6A) If a transaction mentioned in subsection (6) above is by a body corporate, references in that subsection to such a transaction being signed by or on behalf of the assignor or mortgagor shall be taken to include references to its being under the seal of the body corporate.

(7) An assignment of a patent or any such application or a share in it, and an exclusive licence granted under any patent or any such application, may confer on the assignee or licensee the right of the assignor or licensor to bring proceedings by virtue of section 61 or 69 below for a previous infringement or to bring proceedings under section 58 below for a previous act.

33. Effect of registration, etc., on rights in patents

(1) Any person who claims to have acquired the property in a patent or application for a patent by virtue of any transaction, instrument or event to which this section applies shall be entitled as against any other person who claims to have acquired that property by virtue of an earlier transaction, instrument or event to which this section applies if, at the time of the later transaction, instrument or event—

(a) the earlier transaction, instrument or event was not registered, or

(b) in the case of any application which has not been published, notice of the earlier transaction, instrument or event had not been given to the comptroller, and

(c) in any case, the person claiming under the later transaction, instrument or event, did not know of the earlier transaction, instrument or event.

(2) Subsection (1) above shall apply equally to the case where any person claims to have acquired any right in or under a patent or application for a patent, by virtue of a transaction, instrument or event to which this section applies, and that right is incompatible with any such right acquired by virtue of an earlier transaction, instrument or event to which this section applies.

(3) This section applies to the following transactions, instruments and events—

(a) the assignment or assignation of a patent or application for a patent, or a right in it;

(b) the mortgage of a patent or application or the granting of security over it;

(c) the grant, assignment or assignation of a licence or sub-licence, or mortgage of a licence or sub-licence, under a patent or application;

(d) the death of the proprietor or one of the proprietors of any such patent or application or any person having a right in or under a patent or application and the vesting by an assent of personal representatives of a patent, application or any such right; and

(e) any order or directions of a court or other competent authority—

(i) transferring a patent or application or any right in or under it to any person; or

(ii) that an application should proceed in the name of any person;

and in either case the event by virtue of which the court or authority had power to make any such order or give any such directions.

(4) Where an application for the registration of a transaction, instrument or event has been made, but the transaction, instrument or event has not been registered, then, for the purposes of subsection (1)(a) above, registration of the application shall be treated as registration of the transaction, instrument or event.

Employees' inventions

39. Right to employees' inventions

(1) Notwithstanding anything in any rule of law, an invention made by an employee shall, as between him and his employer, be taken to belong to his employer for the purposes of this Act and all other purposes if—

(a) it was made in the course of the normal duties of the employee or in the course of duties falling outside his normal duties, but specifically assigned to him, and the circumstances in either case were such that an invention might reasonably be expected to result from the carrying out of his duties; or

(b) the invention was made in the course of the duties of the employee and, at the time of making the invention, because of the nature of his duties and the particular responsibilities arising from the nature of his duties he had a special obligation to further the interests of the employer's undertaking.

(2) Any other invention made by an employee shall, as between him and his employer, be taken for those purposes to belong to the employee.

(3) Where by virtue of this section an invention belongs, as between him and his employer, to an employee, nothing done—

(a) by or on behalf of the employee or any person claiming under him for the purposes of pursuing an application for a patent, or

(b) by any person for the purpose of performing or working the invention,

shall be taken to infringe any copyright or design right to which, as between him and his employer, his employer is entitled in any model or document relating to the invention.

40. Compensation of employees for certain inventions

(1) Where it appears to the court or the comptroller on an application made by an employee within the prescribed period that—

(a) the employee has made an invention belonging to the employer for which a patent has been granted,

(b) having regard among other things to the size and nature of the employer's undertaking, the invention or the patent for it (or the combination of both) is of outstanding benefit to the employer, and

(c) by reason of those facts it is just that the employee should be awarded compensation to be paid by the employer,

the court or the comptroller may award him such compensation of an amount determined under section 41 below.

(2) Where it appears to the court or the comptroller on an application made by an employee within the prescribed period that—

(a) a patent has been granted for an invention made by and belonging to the employee;

(b) his rights in the invention, or in any patent or application for a patent for the invention, have since the appointed day been assigned to the employer or an exclusive licence under the patent or application has since the appointed day been granted to the employer;

(c) the benefit derived by the employee from the contract of assignment, assignation or grant or any ancillary contract ("the relevant contract") is inadequate in relation to the benefit derived by the employer from the invention or the patent for it (or both); and

(d) by reason of those facts it is just that the employee should be awarded compensation to be paid by the employer in addition to the benefit derived from the relevant contract;

the court or the comptroller may award him such compensation of an amount determined under section 41 below.

(3) Subsections (1) and (2) above shall not apply to the invention of an employee where a relevant collective agreement provides for the payment of compensation in respect of inventions of the same description as that invention to employees of the same description as that employee.

(4) Subsection (2) above shall have effect notwithstanding anything in the relevant contract or any agreement applicable to the invention (other than any such collective agreement).

(5) If it appears to the comptroller on an application under this section that the application involves matters which would more properly be determined by the court, he may decline to deal with it.

(6) In this section—

"the prescribed period", in relation to proceedings before the court, means the period prescribed by rules of court, and

"relevant collective agreement" means a collective agreement within the meaning of the Trade Union and Labour Relations (Consolidation) Act 1992, made by or on behalf of a trade union to which the employee belongs, and by the employer or an employers' association to which the employer belongs which is in force at the time of the making of the invention.

(7) References in this section to an invention belonging to an employer or employee are references to it so belonging as between the employer and the employee.

41. Amount of compensation

(1) An award of compensation to an employee under section 40(1) or (2) above shall be such as will secure for the employee a fair share (having regard to all the circumstances) of the benefit which the employer has derived, or may reasonably be expected to derive, from any of the following—

(a) the invention in question;

(b) the patent for the invention;

(c) the assignment, assignation or grant of—

(i) the property or any right in the invention, or

(ii) the property in, or any right in or under, an application for the patent,

to a person connected with the employer.

(2) For the purposes of subsection (1) above the amount of any benefit derived or expected to be derived by an employer from the assignment, assignation or grant of—

(a) the property in, or any right in or under, a patent for the invention or an application for such a patent; or

(b) the property or any right in the invention;

to a person connected with him shall be taken to be the amount which could reasonably be expected to be so derived by the employer if that person had not been connected with him.

(3) Where the Crown or a Research Council in its capacity as employer assigns or grants the property in, or any right in or under, an invention, patent or application for a patent to a body having among its functions that of developing or exploiting inventions resulting from public research and does so for no consideration or only a nominal consideration, any benefit derived from the invention, patent or application by that body shall be treated for the purposes of the foregoing provisions of this section as so derived by the Crown or, as the case may be, Research Council.

In this subsection "Research Council" means a body which is a Research Council for the purposes of the Science and Technology Act 1965 or the Arts and Humanities Research Council (as defined by section 1 of the Higher Education Act 2004).

(4) In determining the fair share of the benefit to be secured for an employee in respect of an invention which has always belonged to an employer, the court or the comptroller shall, among other things, take the following matters into account, that is to say—

(a) the nature of the employee's duties, his remuneration and the other advantages he derives or has derived from his employment or has derived in relation to the invention under this Act;

(b) the effort and skill which the employee has devoted to making the invention;

(c) the effort and skill which any other person has devoted to making the invention jointly with the employee concerned, and the advice and other assistance contributed by any other employee who is not a joint inventor of the invention; and

(d) the contribution made by the employer to the making, developing and working of the invention by the provision of advice, facilities and other assistance, by the provision of opportunities and by his managerial and commercial skill and activities.

(5) In determining the fair share of the benefit to be secured for an employee in respect of an invention which originally belonged to him, the court or the comptroller shall, among other things, take the following matters into account, that is to say—

(a) any conditions in a licence or licences granted under this Act or otherwise in respect of the invention or the patent for it;

(b) the extent to which the invention was made jointly by the employee with any other person; and

(c) the contribution made by the employer to the making, developing and working of the invention as mentioned in subsection (4)(d) above.

(6) Any order for the payment of compensation under section 40 above may be an order for the payment of a lump sum or for periodical payment, or both.

(7) Without prejudice to section 32 of the Interpretation Act 1889 (which provides that a statutory power may in general be exercised from time to time), the refusal of the court or the comptroller to make any such order on an application made by an employee under section 40 above shall not prevent a further application being made under that section by him or any successor in title of his.

(8) Where the court or the comptroller has made any such order, the court or he may on the application of either the employer or the employee vary or discharge it or suspend any provision of the order and revive any provision so suspended, and section 40(5) above shall apply to the application as it applies to an application under that section.

(9) In England and Wales any sums awarded by the comptroller under section 40 above shall, if a county court so orders, be recoverable *by execution issued from the county court* or otherwise as if they were payable under an order of that court.

(10) In Scotland an order made under section 40 above by the comptroller for the payment of any sums may be enforced in like manner as an extract registered decree arbitral bearing a warrant for execution issued by the sheriff court of any sheriffdom in Scotland.

(11) In Northern Ireland an order made under section 40 above by the comptroller for the payment of any sums may be enforced as if it were a money judgment.

Note. The italicized words in subsection (9) are substituted by the words 'under section 85 of the County Courts Act 1984' by the Tribunals, Courts and Enforcement Act 2007, s. 62(3), Sch. 13, paras. 39, 40, as from a day to be appointed.

42. Enforceability of contracts relating to employees' inventions

(1) This section applies to any contract (whenever made) relating to inventions made by an employee, being a contract entered into by him—

(a) with the employer (alone or with another); or

(b) with some other person at the request of the employer or in pursuance of the employee's contract of employment.

(2) Any term in a contract to which this section applies which diminishes the employee's rights in inventions of any description made by him after the appointed day and the date of the contract, or in or under patents for those inventions or applications for such patents, shall be unenforceable against him to the extent that it diminishes his rights in an invention of that description so made, or in or under a patent for such an invention or an application for any such patent.

(3) Subsection (2) above shall not be construed as derogating from any duty of confidentiality owed to his employer by an employee by virtue of any rule of law of otherwise.

(4) This section applies to any arrangement made with a Crown employee by or on behalf of the Crown as his employer as it applies to any contract made between an employee and an employer other than the Crown, and for the purposes of this section "Crown employee" means a person employed under or for the purposes of a government department or any officer or body exercising on behalf of the Crown functions conferred by any enactment or a person serving in the naval, military or air forces of the Crown.

Infringement

60. Meaning of infringement

(1) Subject to the provisions of this section, a person infringes a patent for an invention if, but only if, while the patent is in force, he does any of the following things in the United Kingdom in relation to the invention without the consent of the proprietor of the patent, that is to say—

(a) where the invention is a product, he makes, disposes of, offers to dispose of, uses or imports the product or keeps it whether for disposal or otherwise;

(b) where the invention is a process, he uses the process or he offers it for use in the United Kingdom when he knows, or it is obvious to a reasonable person in the circumstances, that its use there without the consent of the proprietor would be an infringement of the patent;

(c) where the invention is a process, he disposes of, offers to dispose of, uses or imports any product obtained directly by means of that process or keeps any such product whether for disposal or otherwise.

(2) Subject to the following provisions of this section, a person (other than the proprietor of the patent) also infringes a patent for an invention if, while the patent is in force and without the consent of the proprietor, he supplies or offers to supply in the United Kingdom a person other than a licensee or other person entitled to work the invention with any of the means, relating to an essential element of the invention, for putting the invention into effect when he knows, or it is obvious to a reasonable person in the circumstances, that those means are suitable for putting, and are intended to put, the invention into effect in the United Kingdom.

(3) Subsection (2) above shall not apply to the supply or offer of a staple commercial product unless the supply or the offer is made for the purpose of inducing the person supplied or, as the case may be, the person to whom the offer is made to do an act which constitutes an infringement of the patent by virtue of subsection (1) above.

(5) An act which, apart from this subsection, would constitute an infringement of a patent for an invention shall not do so if—

(a) it is done privately and for purposes which are not commercial;

(b) it is done for experimental purposes relating to the subject-matter of the invention;

(c) it consists of the extemporaneous preparation in a pharmacy of a medicine for an individual in accordance with a prescription given by a registered medical or dental practitioner or consists of dealing with a medicine so prepared;

(d) it consists of the use, exclusively for the needs of a relevant ship, of a product or process in the body of such a ship or in its machinery, tackle, apparatus or other accessories, in a case where the ship has temporarily or accidentally entered the internal or territorial waters of the United Kingdom;

(e) it consists of the use of a product or process in the body or operation of a relevant aircraft, hovercraft or vehicle which has temporarily or accidentally entered or is crossing the United Kingdom (including the air space above it and its territorial waters) or the use of accessories for such a relevant aircraft, hovercraft or vehicle;

(f) it consists of the use of an exempted aircraft which has lawfully entered or is lawfully crossing the United Kingdom as aforesaid or of the importation into the United Kingdom, or the use or storage there, of any part or accessory for such an aircraft;

(g) it consists of the use by a farmer of the product of his harvest for propagation or multiplication by him on his own holding, where there has been a sale of plant propagating material to the farmer by the proprietor of the patent or with his consent for agricultural use;

(h) it consists of the use of an animal or animal reproductive material by a farmer for an agricultural purpose following a sale to the farmer, by the proprietor of the patent or with his consent, of breeding stock or other animal reproductive material which constitutes or contains the patented invention.

(i) it consists of—

(i) an act done in conducting a study, test or trial which is necessary for and is conducted with a view to the application of paragraphs 1 to 5 of article 13 of Directive 2001/82/EC or paragraphs 1 to 4 of article 10 of Directive 2001/83/EC, or

(ii) any other act which is required for the purpose of the application of those paragraphs.

(6) For the purposes of subsection (2) above a person who does an act in relation to an invention which is prevented only by virtue of paragraph (a), (b) or (c) of subsection (5) above from constituting an infringement of a patent for the invention shall not be treated as a person entitled to work the invention, but—

(a) the reference in that subsection to a person entitled to work an invention includes a reference to a person so entitled by virtue of section 55 above, and

(b) a person who by virtue of section 20B(4) or (5) above or section 28A(4) or (5) above or section 64 below or section 117A(4) or (5) below is entitled to do an act in relation to the invention without it constituting such an infringement shall, so far as concerns that act, be treated as a person entitled to work the invention.

(6A) Schedule A1 contains—

(a) provisions restricting the circumstances in which subsection (5)(g) applies; and

(b) provisions which apply where an act would constitute an infringement of a patent but for subsection (5)(g).

(6B) For the purposes of subsection (5)(h), use for an agricultural purpose—

(a) includes making an animal or animal reproductive material available for the purposes of pursuing the farmer's agricultural activity; but

(b) does not include sale within the framework, or for the purposes, of a commercial reproduction activity.

(6C) In paragraphs (g) and (h) of subsection (5) "sale" includes any other form of commercialisation.

(7) In this section—

"relevant ship" and "relevant aircraft, hovercraft or vehicle" mean respectively a ship and an aircraft, hovercraft or vehicle registered in, or belonging to, any country, other than the United Kingdom, which is a party to the Convention for the Protection of Industrial Property signed at Paris on 20th March 1883 or which is a member of the World Trade Organisation; and

"exempted aircraft" means an aircraft to which section 89 of the Civil Aviation Act 1982 (aircraft exempted from seizure in respect of patent claims) applies.

"Directive 2001/82/EC" means Directive 2001/82/EC of the European Parliament and of the Council on the Community code relating to veterinary medicinal products as amended by Directive 2004/28 of the European Parliament and of the Council;

"Directive 2001/83/EC" means Directive 2001/83/EC of the European Parliament and of the Council on the Community code relating to medicinal products for human use, as amended by Directive 2002/98/EC of the European Parliament and of the Council, by Commission Directive 2003/63/EC and by Directives 2004/24/EC and 2004/27/EC of the European Parliament and of the Council.

61. Proceedings for infringement of patent

(1) Subject to the following provisions of this Part of this Act, civil proceedings may be brought in the court by the proprietor of a patent in respect of any act alleged to infringe the patent and (without prejudice to any other jurisdiction of the court) in those proceedings a claim may be made—

(a) for an injunction or interdict restraining the defendant or defender from any apprehended act of infringement;

(b) for an order for him to deliver up or destroy any patented product in relation to which the patent is infringed or any article in which that product is inextricably comprised;

(c) for damages in respect of the infringement;

(d) for an account of the profits derived by him from the infringement;

(e) for a declaration or declarator that the patent is valid and has been infringed by him.

(2) The court shall not, in respect of the same infringement, both award the proprietor of a patent damages and order that he shall be given an account of the profits.

(3) The proprietor of a patent and any other person may by agreement with each other refer to the comptroller the question whether that other person has infringed the patent and on the reference the proprietor of the patent may make any claim mentioned in subsection (1)(c) or (e) above.

(4) Except so far as the context requires, in the following provisions of this Act—

(a) any reference to proceedings for infringement and the bringing of such proceedings includes a reference to a reference under subsection (3) above and the making of such a reference;

(b) any reference to a claimant or pursuer includes a reference to the proprietor of the patent; and

(c) any reference to a defendant or defender includes a reference to any other party to the reference.

(5) If it appears to the comptroller on a reference under subsection (3) above that the question referred to him would more properly be determined by the court, he may decline to deal with it and the court shall have jurisdiction to determine the question as if the reference were proceedings brought in the court.

(6) Subject to the following provisions of this Part of this Act, in determining whether or not to grant any kind of relief claimed under this section and the extent of the relief granted the court or the comptroller shall apply the principles applied by the court in relation to that kind of relief immediately before the appointed day.

(7) If the comptroller awards any sum by way of damages on a reference under subsection (3) above, then—

(a) in England and Wales, the sum shall be recoverable, if a county court so orders, *by execution issued from the county court* or otherwise as if it were payable under an order of that court;

(b) in Scotland, payment of the sum may be enforced in like manner as an extract registered decree arbitral bearing a warrant for execution issued by the sheriff court of any sheriffdom in Scotland;

(c) in Northern Ireland, payment of the sum may be enforced as if it were a money judgment.

Note. The italicized words in subsection (7)(a) are substituted by the words 'under section 85 of the County Courts Act 1984' by the Tribunals, Courts and Enforcement Act 2007, s. 62(3), Sch. 13, paras. 39, 41, as from a day to be appointed.

62. Restrictions on recovery of damages for infringement

(1) In proceedings for infringement of a patent damages shall not be awarded, and no order shall be made for an account of profits, against a defendant or defender who proves that at the date of the infringement he was not aware, and had no reasonable grounds for supposing, that the patent existed; and a person shall not be taken to have been so aware or to have had reasonable grounds for so supposing by reason only of the application to a product of the word "patent" or "patented", or any word or words expressing or implying that a patent has been obtained for the product, unless the number of the patent accompanied the word or words in question.

(2) In proceedings for infringement of a patent the court or the comptroller may, if it or he thinks fit, refuse to award any damages or make any such order in respect of an infringement committed during the further period specified in section 25(4) above, but before the payment of the renewal fee and any additional fee prescribed for the purposes of that subsection.

(3) Where an amendment of the specification of a patent has been allowed under any of the provisions of this Act, the court or the comptroller shall, when awarding damages or making an order for an account of profits in proceedings for an infringement of the patent committed before the decision to allow the amendment, take into account the following—

(a) whether at the date of infringement the defendant or defender knew, or had reasonable grounds to know, that he was infringing the patent;

(b) whether the specification of the patent as published was framed in good faith and with reasonable skill and knowledge;

(c) whether the proceedings are brought in good faith.

Infringement

67. Proceedings for infringement by exclusive licensee

(1) Subject to the provisions of this section, the holder of an exclusive licence under a patent shall have the same right as the proprietor of the patent to bring proceedings in respect of any infringement of the patent committed after the date of the licence; and references to the proprietor of the patent in the provisions of this Act relating to infringement shall be construed accordingly.

(2) In awarding damages or granting any other relief in any such proceedings the court or the comptroller shall take into consideration any loss suffered or likely to be suffered by the exclusive licensee as such as a result of the infringement, or, as the case may be, the profits derived from the infringement, so far as it constitutes an infringement of the rights of the exclusive licensee as such.

(3) In any proceedings taken by an exclusive licensee by virtue of this section the proprietor of the patent shall be made a party to the proceedings, but if made a defendant or defender shall not be liable for any costs or expenses unless he enters an appearance and takes part in the proceedings.

70. Remedy for groundless threats of infringement proceedings

(1) Where a person (whether or not the proprietor of, or entitled to any right in, a patent) by circulars, advertisements or otherwise threatens another person with proceedings for any infringement of a patent, a person aggrieved by the threats (whether or not he is the person to whom the threats are made) may, subject to subsection (4) below, bring proceedings in the court against the person making the threats, claiming any relief mentioned in subsection (3) below.

(2) In any such proceedings the claimant or pursuer shall, subject to subsection (2A) below, be entitled to the relief claimed if he proves that the threats were so made and satisfies the court that he is a person aggrieved by them.

(2A) If the defendant or defender proves that the acts in respect of which proceedings were threatened constitute or, if done, would constitute an infringement of a patent—

(a) the claimant or pursuer shall be entitled to the relief claimed only if he shows that the patent alleged to be infringed is invalid in a relevant respect;

(b) even if the claimant or pursuer does show that the patent is invalid in a relevant respect, he shall not be entitled to the relief claimed if the defendant or defender proves that at the time of making the threats he did not know, and had no reason to suspect, that the patent was invalid in that respect.

(3) The said relief is—

(a) a declaration or declarator to the effect that the threats are unjustifiable;

(b) an injunction or interdict against the continuance of the threats; and

(c) damages in respect of any loss which the claimant or pursuer has sustained by the threats.

72. Power to revoke patents on application

(1) Subject to the following provisions of this Act, the court or the comptroller may by order revoke a patent for an invention on the application of any person (including the proprietor of the patent) on (but only on) any of the following grounds, that is to say—

(a) the invention is not a patentable invention;

(b) that the patent was granted to a person who was not entitled to be granted that patent;

(c) the specification of the patent does not disclose the invention clearly enough and completely enough for it to be performed by a person skilled in the art;

(d) the matter disclosed in the specification of the patent extends beyond that disclosed in the application for the patent, as filed, or, if the patent was granted on a new application filed under section 8(3), 12 or 37(4) above or as mentioned in section 15(9) above, in the earlier application, as filed;

(e) the protection conferred by the patent has been extended by an amendment which should not have been allowed.

74. Proceedings in which validity of patent may be put in issue

(1) Subject to the following provisions of this section, the validity of a patent may be put in issue—

(a) by way of defence, in proceedings for infringement of the patent under section 61 above or proceedings under section 69 above for infringement of rights conferred by the publication of an application;

(b) in proceedings under section 70 above;

(c) in proceedings in which a declaration in relation to the patent is sought under section 71 above;

(d) in proceedings before the court or the comptroller under section 72 above for the revocation of the patent;

(e) in proceedings under section 58 above.

(2) The validity of a patent may not be put in issue in any other proceedings and, in particular, no proceedings may be instituted (whether under this Act or otherwise) seeking only a declaration as to the validity or invalidity of a patent.

(3) The only grounds on which the validity of a patent may be put in issue (whether in proceedings for revocation under section 72 above or otherwise) are the grounds on which the patent may be revoked under that section.

125. Extent of invention

(1) For the purposes of this Act an invention for a patent for which an application has been made or for which a patent has been granted shall, unless the context otherwise requires, be taken to be that specified in a claim of the specification of the application or patent, as the case may be, as interpreted by the description and any drawings contained in that specification, and the extent of the protection conferred by a patent or application for a patent shall be determined accordingly.

(2) It is hereby declared for the avoidance of doubt that where more than one invention is specified in any such claim, each invention may have a different priority date under section 5 above.

(3) The Protocol on the Interpretation of Article 69 of the European Patent Convention (which Article contains a provision corresponding to subsection (1) above) shall, as for the time being in force, apply for the purposes of subsection (1) above as it applies for the purposes of that Article.

Copyright, Designs and Patents Act 1988
1988 c. 48

An Act to restate the law of copyright, with amendments; to make fresh provision as to the rights of performers and others in performances; to confer a design right in original designs; to amend the Registered Designs Act 1949; to make provision with respect to patent agents and trade mark agents; to confer patents and designs jurisdiction on certain county courts; to amend the law of patents; to make provision with respect to devices designed to circumvent copy-protection of works in electronic form; to make fresh provision penalising the fraudulent reception of transmissions; to make the fraudulent application or use of a trade mark an offence; to make provision for the benefit of the Hospital for Sick Children, Great Ormond Street, London; to enable financial assistance to be given to certain international bodies; and for connected purposes [15th November 1988]

Part I
Copyright

Chapter I
Subsistence, ownership and duration of copyright

Introductory

1. Copyright and copyright works

(1) Copyright is a property right which subsists in accordance with this Part in the following descriptions of work—

(a) original literary, dramatic, musical or artistic works,

(b) sound recordings, films or broadcasts, and

(c) the typographical arrangement of published editions.

(2) In this Part "copyright work" means a work of any of those descriptions in which copyright subsists.

(3) Copyright does not subsist in a work unless the requirements of this Part with respect to qualification for copyright protection are met (see section 153 and the provisions referred to there).

2. Rights subsisting in copyright works

(1) The owner of the copyright in a work of any description has the exclusive right to do the acts specified in Chapter II as the acts restricted by the copyright in a work of that description.

(2) In relation to certain descriptions of copyright work the following rights conferred by Chapter IV (moral rights) subsist in favour of the author, director or commissioner of the work, whether or not he is the owner of the copyright—

(a) section 77 (right to be identified as author or director),

(b) section 80 (right to object to derogatory treatment of work), and

(c) section 85 (right to privacy of certain photographs and films).

Descriptions of work and related provisions

3. Literary, dramatic and musical works

(1) In this Part—

"literary work" means any work, other than a dramatic or musical work, which is written, spoken or sung, and accordingly includes—

(a) a table or compilation other than a database,

(b) a computer program,

(c) preparatory design material for a computer program and

(d) a database;

"dramatic work" includes a work of dance or mime; and

"musical work" means a work consisting of music, exclusive of any words or action intended to be sung, spoken or performed with the music.

(2) Copyright does not subsist in a literary, dramatic or musical work unless and until it is recorded, in writing or otherwise; and references in this Part to the time at which such a work is made are to the time at which it is so recorded.

(3) It is immaterial for the purposes of subsection (2) whether the work is recorded by or with the permission of the author; and where it is not recorded by the author, nothing in that subsection affects the question whether copyright subsists in the record as distinct from the work recorded.

3A. Databases

(1) In this Part "database" means a collection of independent works, data or other materials which—

(a) are arranged in a systematic or methodical way, and

(b) are individually accessible by electronic or other means.

(2) For the purposes of this Part a literary work consisting of a database is original if, and only if, by reason of the selection or arrangement of the contents of the database the database constitutes the author's own intellectual creation.

4. Artistic works

(1) In this Part "artistic work" means—

(a) a graphic work, photograph, sculpture or collage, irrespective of artistic quality,

(b) a work of architecture being a building or a model for a building, or

(c) a work of artistic craftsmanship.

(2) In this Part—

"building" includes any fixed structure, and a part of a building or fixed structure;

"graphic work" includes—

(a) any painting, drawing, diagram, map, chart or plan, and

(b) any engraving, etching, lithograph, woodcut or similar work;

"photograph" means a recording of light or other radiation on any medium on which an image is produced or from which an image may by any means be produced, and which is not part of a film;

"sculpture" includes a cast or model made for purposes of sculpture.

5A. Sound recordings

(1) In this Part "sound recording" means—

(a) a recording of sounds, from which the sounds may be reproduced, or

(b) a recording of the whole or any part of a literary, dramatic or musical work, from which sounds reproducing the work or part may be produced,

regardless of the medium on which the recording is made or the method by which the sounds are reproduced or produced.

(2) Copyright does not subsist in a sound recording which is, or to the extent that it is, a copy taken from a previous sound recording.

5B. Films

(1) In this Part "film" means a recording on any medium from which a moving image may by any means be produced.

(2) The sound track accompanying a film shall be treated as part of the film for the purposes of this Part.

(3) Without prejudice to the generality of subsection (2), where that subsection applies—

(a) references in this Part to showing a film include playing the film sound track to accompany the film,

(b) references in this Part to playing a sound recording, or to communicating a sound recording to the public, do not include playing or communicating the film sound track to accompany the film,

(c) references in this Part to copying a work, so far as they apply to a sound recording, do not include copying the film sound track to accompany the film, and

(d) references in this Part to the issuing, rental or lending of copies of a work, so far as they apply to a sound recording, do not include the issuing, rental or lending of copies of the sound track to accompany the film.

(4) Copyright does not subsist in a film which is, or to the extent that it is, a copy taken from a previous film.

(5) Nothing in this section affects any copyright subsisting in a film sound track as a sound recording.

6. Broadcasts

(1) In this Part a "broadcast" means an electronic transmission of visual images, sounds or other information which—

(a) is transmitted for simultaneous reception by members of the public and is capable of being lawfully received by them, or

(b) is transmitted at a time determined solely by the person making the transmission for presentation to members of the public,

and which is not excepted by subsection (1A); and references to broadcasting shall be construed accordingly.

(1A) Excepted from the definition of "broadcast" is any internet transmission unless it is—

(a) a transmission taking place simultaneously on the internet and by other means,

(b) a concurrent transmission of a live event, or

(c) a transmission of recorded moving images or sounds forming part of a programme service offered by the person responsible for making the transmission, being a service in which programmes are transmitted at scheduled times determined by that person.

(2) An encrypted transmission shall be regarded as capable of being lawfully received by members of the public only if decoding equipment has been made available to members of the public by or with the authority of the person making the transmission or the person providing the contents of the transmission.

(3) References in this Part to the person making a broadcast or a transmission which is a broadcast are—

(a) to the person transmitting the programme, if he has responsibility to any extent for its contents, and

(b) to any person providing the programme who makes with the person transmitting it the arrangements necessary for its transmission;

and references in this Part to a programme, in the context of broadcasting, are to any item included in a broadcast.

(4) For the purposes of this Part, the place from which a wireless broadcast is made is the place where, under the control and responsibility of the person making the broadcast, the programme-carrying signals are introduced into an uninterrupted chain of communication (including, in the case of a satellite transmission, the chain leading to the satellite and down towards the earth).

(4A) Subsections (3) and (4) have effect subject to section 6A (safeguards in case of certain satellite broadcasts).

(5) References in this Part to the reception of a broadcast include reception of a broadcast relayed by means of a telecommunications system.

(5A) The relaying of a broadcast by reception and immediate re-transmission shall be regarded for the purposes of this Part as a separate act of broadcasting from the making of the broadcast which is so re-transmitted.

(6) Copyright does not subsist in a broadcast which infringes, or to the extent that it infringes, the copyright in another broadcast.

8. Published editions

(1) In this Part "published edition", in the context of copyright in the typographical arrangement of a published edition, means a published edition of the whole or any part of one or more literary, dramatic or musical works.

(2) Copyright does not subsist in the typographical arrangement of a published edition if, or to the extent that, it reproduces the typographical arrangement of a previous edition.

Authorship and ownership of copyright

9. Authorship of work

(1) In this Part "author", in relation to a work, means the person who creates it.

(2) That person shall be taken to be—

(aa) in the case of a sound recording, the producer;

(ab) in the case of a film, the producer and the principal director;

(b) in the case of a broadcast, the person making the broadcast (see section 6(3)) or, in the case of a broadcast which relays another broadcast by reception and immediate re-transmission, the person making that other broadcast;

(d) in the case of the typographical arrangement of a published edition, the publisher.

(3) In the case of a literary, dramatic, musical or artistic work which is computer-generated, the author shall be taken to be the person by whom the arrangements necessary for the creation of the work are undertaken.

(4) For the purposes of this Part a work is of "unknown authorship" if the identity of the author is unknown or, in the case of a work of joint authorship, if the identity of none of the authors is known.

(5) For the purposes of this Part the identity of an author shall be regarded as unknown if it is not possible for a person to ascertain his identity by reasonable inquiry; but if his identity is once known it shall not subsequently be regarded as unknown.

11. First ownership of copyright

(1) The author of a work is the first owner of any copyright in it, subject to the following provisions.

(2) Where a literary, dramatic, musical or artistic work, or a film, is made by an employee in the course of his employment, his employer is the first owner of any copyright in the work subject to any agreement to the contrary.

(3) This section does not apply to Crown copyright or Parliamentary copyright (see sections 163 and 165) or to copyright which subsists by virtue of section 168 (copyright of certain international organisations).

Duration of copyright

12. Duration of copyright in literary, dramatic, musical or artistic works

(1) The following provisions have effect with respect to the duration of copyright in a literary, dramatic, musical or artistic work.

(2) Copyright expires at the end of the period of 70 years from the end of the calendar year in which the author dies, subject as follows.

(3) If the work is of unknown authorship, copyright expires—

(a) at the end of the period of 70 years from the end of the calendar year in which the work was made, or

(b) if during that period the work is made available to the public, at the end of the period of 70 years from the end of the calendar year in which it is first so made available,

subject as follows.

(4) Subsection (2) applies if the identity of the author becomes known before the end of the period specified in paragraph (a) or (b) of subsection (3).

(5) For the purposes of subsection (3) making available to the public includes—

(a) in the case of a literary, dramatic or musical work—

(i) performance in public, or

(ii) communication to the public;

(b) in the case of an artistic work—

(i) exhibition in public,

(ii) a film including the work being shown in public, or

(iii) communication to the public;

but in determining generally for the purposes of that subsection whether a work has been made available to the public no account shall be taken of any unauthorised act.

(6) Where the country of origin of the work is not an EEA state and the author of the work is not a national of an EEA state, the duration of copyright is that to which the work is entitled in the country of origin, provided that does not exceed the period which would apply under subsections (2) to (5).

(7) If the work is computer-generated the above provisions do not apply and copyright expires at the end of the period of 50 years from the end of the calendar year in which the work was made.

(8) The provisions of this section are adapted as follows in relation to a work of joint authorship—

(a) the reference in subsection (2) to the death of the author shall be construed—

(i) if the identity of all the authors is known, as a reference to the death of the last of them to die, and

(ii) if the identity of one or more of the authors is known and the identity of one or more others is not, as a reference to the death of the last whose identity is known;

(b) the reference in subsection (4) to the identity of the author becoming known shall be construed as a reference to the identity of any of the authors becoming known;

(c) the reference in subsection (6) to the author not being a national of an EEA state shall be construed as a reference to none of the authors being a national of an EEA state.

(9) This section does not apply to Crown copyright or Parliamentary copyright (see sections 163 to 166D) or to copyright which subsists by virtue of section 168 (copyright of certain international organisations).

Chapter II
Rights of Copyright Owner

The acts restricted by copyright

16. The acts restricted by copyright in a work

(1) The owner of the copyright in a work has, in accordance with the following provisions of this Chapter, the exclusive right to do the following acts in the United Kingdom—

(a) to copy the work (see section 17);

(b) to issue copies of the work to the public (see section 18);

(ba) to rent or lend the work to the public (see section 18A);

(c) to perform, show or play the work in public (see section 19);

(d) to communicate the work to the public (see section 20);

(e) to make an adaptation of the work or do any of the above in relation to an adaptation (see section 21);

and those acts are referred to in this Part as the "acts restricted by the copyright".

(2) Copyright in a work is infringed by a person who without the licence of the copyright owner does, or authorises another to do, any of the acts restricted by the copyright.

(3) References in this Part to the doing of an act restricted by the copyright in a work are to the doing of it—

(a) in relation to the work as a whole or any substantial part of it, and

(b) either directly or indirectly;

and it is immaterial whether any intervening acts themselves infringe copyright.

(4) This Chapter has effect subject to—

(a) the provisions of Chapter III (acts permitted in relation to copyright works), and

(b) the provisions of Chapter VII (provisions with respect to copyright licensing).

17. Infringement of copyright by copying

(1) The copying of the work is an act restricted by the copyright in every description of copyright work; and references in this Part to copying and copies shall be construed as follows.

(2) Copying in relation to a literary, dramatic, musical or artistic work means reproducing the work in any material form.

This includes storing the work in any medium by electronic means.

(3) In relation to an artistic work copying includes the making of a copy in three dimensions of a two-dimensional work and the making of a copy in two dimensions of a three-dimensional work.

(4) Copying in relation to a film or broadcast includes making a photograph of the whole or any substantial part of any image forming part of the film or broadcast.

(5) Copying in relation to the typographical arrangement of a published edition means making a facsimile copy of the arrangement.

(6) Copying in relation to any description of work includes the making of copies which are transient or are incidental to some other use of the work.

18. Infringement by issue of copies to the public

(1) The issue to the public of copies of the work is an act restricted by the copyright in every description of copyright work.

(2) References in this Part to the issue to the public of copies of a work are to—

(a) the act of putting into circulation in the EEA copies not previously put into circulation in the EEA by or with the consent of the copyright owner, or

(b) the act of putting into circulation outside the EEA copies not previously put into circulation in the EEA or elsewhere.

(3) References in this Part to the issue to the public of copies of a work do not include—

(a) any subsequent distribution, sale, hiring or loan of copies previously put into circulation (but see section 18A: infringement by rental or lending), or

(b) any subsequent importation of such copies into the United Kingdom or another EEA state,

except so far as paragraph (a) of subsection (2) applies to putting into circulation in the EEA copies previously put into circulation outside the EEA.

(4) References in this Part to the issue of copies of a work include the issue of the original.

18A. Infringement by rental or lending of work to the public

(1) The rental or lending of copies of the work to the public is an act restricted by the copyright in—

(a) a literary, dramatic or musical work,

(b) an artistic work, other than—

(i) a work of architecture in the form of a building or a model for a building, or

(ii) a work of applied art, or

(c) a film or a sound recording.

(2) In this Part, subject to the following provisions of this section—

(a) "rental" means making a copy of the work available for use, on terms that it will or may be returned, for direct or indirect economic or commercial advantage, and

(b) "lending" means making a copy of the work available for use, on terms that it will or may be returned, otherwise than for direct or indirect economic or commercial advantage, through an establishment which is accessible to the public.

(3) The expressions "rental" and "lending" do not include—

(a) making available for the purpose of public performance, playing or showing in public or communication to the public;

(b) making available for the purpose of exhibition in public; or

(c) making available for on-the-spot reference use.

(4) The expression "lending" does not include making available between establishments which are accessible to the public.

(5) Where lending by an establishment accessible to the public gives rise to a payment the amount of which does not go beyond what is necessary to cover the operating costs of the establishment, there is no direct or indirect economic or commercial advantage for the purposes of this section.

(6) References in this Part to the rental or lending of copies of a work include the rental or lending of the original.

19. Infringement by performance, showing or playing of work in public

(1) The performance of the work in public is an act restricted by the copyright in a literary, dramatic or musical work.

(2) In this Part "performance", in relation to a work—

(a) includes delivery in the case of lectures, addresses, speeches and sermons, and

(b) in general, includes any mode of visual or acoustic presentation, including presentation by means of a sound recording, film or broadcast of the work.

(3) The playing or showing of the work in public is an act restricted by the copyright in a sound recording, film or broadcast.

(4) Where copyright in a work is infringed by its being performed, played or shown in public by means of apparatus for receiving visual images or sounds conveyed by

electronic means, the person by whom the visual images or sounds are sent, and in the case of a performance the performers, shall not be regarded as responsible for the infringement.

20. Infringement by communication to the public

(1) The communication to the public of the work is an act restricted by the copyright in—

(a) a literary, dramatic, musical or artistic work,

(b) a sound recording or film, or

(c) a broadcast.

(2) References in this Part to communication to the public are to communication to the public by electronic transmission, and in relation to a work include—

(a) the broadcasting of the work;

(b) the making available to the public of the work by electronic transmission in such a way that members of the public may access it from a place and at a time individually chosen by them.

21. Infringement by making adaptation or act done in relation to adaptation

(1) The making of an adaptation of the work is an act restricted by the copyright in a literary, dramatic or musical work.

For this purpose an adaptation is made when it is recorded, in writing or otherwise.

(2) The doing of any of the acts specified in sections 17 to 20, or subsection (1) above, in relation to an adaptation of the work is also an act restricted by the copyright in a literary, dramatic or musical work.

For this purpose it is immaterial whether the adaptation has been recorded, in writing or otherwise, at the time the act is done.

(3) In this Part "adaptation"—

(a) in relation to a literary work, other than a computer program or a database, or in relation to a dramatic work, means—

(i) a translation of the work;

(ii) a version of a dramatic work in which it is converted into a non-dramatic work or, as the case may be, of a non-dramatic work in which it is converted into a dramatic work;

(iii) a version of the work in which the story or action is conveyed wholly or mainly by means of pictures in a form suitable for reproduction in a book, or in a newspaper, magazine or similar periodical;

(ab) in relation to a computer program, means an arrangement or altered version of the program or a translation of it;

(ac) in relation to a database, means an arrangement or altered version of the database or a translation of it;

(b) in relation to a musical work, means an arrangement or transcription of the work.

(4) In relation to a computer program a "translation" includes a version of the program in which it is converted into or out of a computer language or code or into a different computer language or code.

(5) No inference shall be drawn from this section as to what does or does not amount to copying a work.

Secondary infringement of copyright

22. Secondary infringement: importing infringing copy

The copyright in a work is infringed by a person who, without the licence of the copyright owner, imports into the United Kingdom, otherwise than for his private and domestic use, an article which is, and which he knows or has reason to believe is, an infringing copy of the work.

23. Secondary infringement: possessing or dealing with infringing copy

The copyright in a work is infringed by a person who, without the licence of the copyright owner—

(a) possesses in the course of a business,

(b) sells or lets for hire, or offers or exposes for sale or hire,

(c) in the course of a business exhibits in public or distributes, or

(d) distributes otherwise than in the course of a business to such an extent as to affect prejudicially the owner of the copyright,

an article which is, and which he knows or has reason to believe is, an infringing copy of the work.

24. Secondary infringement: providing means for making infringing copies

(1) Copyright in a work is infringed by a person who, without the licence of the copyright owner—

(a) makes,

(b) imports into the United Kingdom,

(c) possesses in the course of a business, or

(d) sells or lets for hire, or offers or exposes for sale or hire,

an article specifically designed or adapted for making copies of that work, knowing or having reason to believe that it is to be used to make infringing copies.

(2) Copyright in a work is infringed by a person who without the licence of the copyright owner transmits the work by means of a telecommunications system (otherwise than by communication to the public), knowing or having reason to believe that infringing copies of the work will be made by means of the reception of the transmission in the United Kingdom or elsewhere.

25. Secondary infringement: permitting use of premises for infringing performance

(1) Where the copyright in a literary, dramatic or musical work is infringed by a performance at a place of public entertainment, any person who gave permission for that place to be used for the performance is also liable for the infringement unless when he gave permission he believed on reasonable grounds that the performance would not infringe copyright.

(2) In this section "place of public entertainment" includes premises which are occupied mainly for other purposes but are from time to time made available for hire for the purposes of public entertainment.

26. Secondary infringement: provision of apparatus for infringing performance, &c.

(1) Where copyright in a work is infringed by a public performance of the work, or by the playing or showing of the work in public, by means of apparatus for—

(a) playing sound recordings,

(b) showing films, or

(c) receiving visual images or sounds conveyed by electronic means,

the following persons are also liable for the infringement.

(2) A person who supplied the apparatus, or any substantial part of it, is liable for the infringement if when he supplied the apparatus or part—

(a) he knew or had reason to believe that the apparatus was likely to be so used as to infringe copyright, or

(b) in the case of apparatus whose normal use involves a public performance, playing or showing, he did not believe on reasonable grounds that it would not be so used as to infringe copyright.

(3) An occupier of premises who gave permission for the apparatus to be brought onto the premises is liable for the infringement if when he gave permission he knew or had reason to believe that the apparatus was likely to be so used as to infringe copyright.

(4) A person who supplied a copy of a sound recording or film used to infringe copyright is liable for the infringement if when he supplied it he knew or had reason to believe that what he supplied, or a copy made directly or indirectly from it, was likely to be so used as to infringe copyright.

Designs

51. Design documents and models

(1) It is not an infringement of any copyright in a design document or model recording or embodying a design for anything other than an artistic work or a typeface to make an article to the design or to copy an article made to the design.

(2) Nor is it an infringement of the copyright to issue to the public, or include in a film or communicate to the public, anything the making of which was, by virtue of subsection (1), not an infringement of that copyright.

(3) In this section—

"design" means the design of any aspect of the shape or configuration (whether internal or external) of the whole or part of an article, other than surface decoration; and

"design document" means any record of a design, whether in the form of a drawing, a written description, a photograph, data stored in a computer or otherwise.

52. Effect of exploitation of design derived from artistic work

(1) This section applies where an artistic work has been exploited, by or with the licence of the copyright owner, by—

(a) making by an industrial process articles falling to be treated for the purposes of this Part as copies of the work, and

(b) marketing such articles, in the United Kingdom or elsewhere.

(2) After the end of the period of 25 years from the end of the calendar year in which such articles are first marketed, the work may be copied by making articles of any description, or doing anything for the purpose of making articles of any description, and anything may be done in relation to articles so made, without infringing copyright in the work.

(3) Where only part of an artistic work is exploited as mentioned in subsection (1), subsection (2) applies only in relation to that part.

(4) The Secretary of State may by order make provision—

(a) as to the circumstances in which an article, or any description of article, is to be regarded for the purposes of this section as made by an industrial process;

(b) excluding from the operation of this section such articles of a primarily literary or artistic character as he thinks fit.

(5) An order shall be made by statutory instrument which shall be subject to annulment in pursuance of a resolution of either House of Parliament.

(6) In this section—

(a) references to articles do not include films; and

(b) references to the marketing of an article are to its being sold or let for hire or offered or exposed for sale or hire.

Chapter IV
Moral Rights

Right to be identified as author or director

77. Right to be identified as author or director

(1) The author of a copyright literary, dramatic, musical or artistic work, and the director of a copyright film, has the right to be identified as the author or director of the work in the circumstances mentioned in this section; but the right is not infringed unless it has been asserted in accordance with section 78.

(2) The author of a literary work (other than words intended to be sung or spoken with music) or a dramatic work has the right to be identified whenever—

(a) the work is published commercially, performed in public or communicated to the public; or

(b) copies of a film or sound recording including the work are issued to the public;

and that right includes the right to be identified whenever any of those events occur in relation to an adaptation of the work as the author of the work from which the adaptation was made.

(3) The author of a musical work, or a literary work consisting of words intended to be sung or spoken with music, has the right to be identified whenever—

(a) the work is published commercially;

(b) copies of a sound recording of the work are issued to the public; or

(c) a film of which the sound-track includes the work is shown in public or copies of such a film are issued to the public;

and that right includes the right to be identified whenever any of those events occur in relation to an adaptation of the work as the author of the work from which the adaptation was made.

(4) The author of an artistic work has the right to be identified whenever—

(a) the work is published commercially or exhibited in public, or a visual image of it is communicated to the public;

(b) a film including a visual image of the work is shown in public or copies of such a film are issued to the public; or

(c) in the case of a work of architecture in the form of a building or a model for a building, a sculpture or a work of artistic craftsmanship, copies of a graphic work representing it, or of a photograph of it, are issued to the public.

(5) The author of a work of architecture in the form of a building also has the right to be identified on the building as constructed or, where more than one building is constructed to the design, on the first to be constructed.

(6) The director of a film has the right to be identified whenever the film is shown in public or communicated to the public or copies of the film are issued to the public.

(7) The right of the author or director under this section is—

(a) in the case of commercial publication or the issue to the public of copies of a film or sound recording, to be identified in or on each copy or, if that is not appropriate, in some other manner likely to bring his identity to the notice of a person acquiring a copy,

(b) in the case of identification on a building, to be identified by appropriate means visible to persons entering or approaching the building, and

(c) in any other case, to be identified in a manner likely to bring his identity to the attention of a person seeing or hearing the performance, exhibition, showing or communication to the public in question;

and the identification must in each case be clear and reasonably prominent.

(8) If the author or director in asserting his right to be identified specifies a pseudonym, initials or some other particular form of identification, that form shall be used; otherwise any reasonable form of identification may be used.

(9) This section has effect subject to section 79 (exceptions to right).

Right to object to derogatory treatment of work

80. Right to object to derogatory treatment of work

(1) The author of a copyright literary, dramatic, musical or artistic work, and the director of a copyright film, has the right in the circumstances mentioned in this section not to have his work subjected to derogatory treatment.

(2) For the purposes of this section—

(a) "treatment" of a work means any addition to, deletion from or alteration to or adaptation of the work, other than—

(i) a translation of a literary or dramatic work, or

(ii) an arrangement or transcription of a musical work involving no more than a change of key or register; and

(b) the treatment of a work is derogatory if it amounts to distortion or mutilation of the work or is otherwise prejudicial to the honour or reputation of the author or director;

and in the following provisions of this section references to a derogatory treatment of a work shall be construed accordingly.

(3) In the case of a literary, dramatic or musical work the right is infringed by a person who—

(a) publishes commercially, performs in public or communicates to the public a derogatory treatment of the work; or

(b) issues to the public copies of a film or sound recording of, or including, a derogatory treatment of the work.

(4) In the case of an artistic work the right is infringed by a person who—

(a) publishes commercially or exhibits in public a derogatory treatment of the work, or communicates to the public a visual image of a derogatory treatment of the work,

(b) shows in public a film including a visual image of a derogatory treatment of the work or issues to the public copies of such a film, or

(c) in the case of—

(i) a work of architecture in the form of a model for a building,

(ii) a sculpture, or

(iii) a work of artistic craftsmanship,

issues to the public copies of a graphic work representing, or of a photograph of, a derogatory treatment of the work.

(5) Subsection (4) does not apply to a work of architecture in the form of a building; but where the author of such a work is identified on the building and it is the subject of derogatory treatment he has the right to require the identification to be removed.

(6) In the case of a film, the right is infringed by a person who—

(a) shows in public or communicates to the public a derogatory treatment of the film; or

(b) issues to the public copies of a derogatory treatment of the film,

(7) The right conferred by this section extends to the treatment of parts of a work resulting from a previous treatment by a person other than the author or director, if those parts are attributed to, or are likely to be regarded as the work of, the author or director.

(8) This section has effect subject to sections 81 and 82 (exceptions to and qualifications of right).

False attribution of work

84. False attribution of work

(1) A person has the right in the circumstances mentioned in this section—

(a) not to have a literary, dramatic, musical or artistic work falsely attributed to him as author, and

(b) not to have a film falsely attributed to him as director;

and in this section an "attribution", in relation to such a work, means a statement (express or implied) as to who is the author or director.

(2) The right is infringed by a person who—

(a) issues to the public copies of a work of any of those descriptions in or on which there is a false attribution, or

(b) exhibits in public an artistic work, or a copy of an artistic work, in or on which there is a false attribution.

(3) The right is also infringed by a person who—

(a) in the case of a literary, dramatic or musical work, performs the work in public or communicates it to the public as being the work of a person, or

(b) in the case of a film, shows it in public or communicates it to the public as being directed by a person,

knowing or having reason to believe that the attribution is false.

(4) The right is also infringed by the issue to the public or public display of material containing a false attribution in connection with any of the acts mentioned in subsection (2) or (3).

(5) The right is also infringed by a person who in the course of a business—

(a) possesses or deals with a copy of a work of any of the descriptions mentioned in subsection (1) in or on which there is a false attribution, or

(b) in the case of an artistic work, possesses or deals with the work itself when there is a false attribution in or on it,

knowing or having reason to believe that there is such an attribution and that it is false.

(6) In the case of an artistic work the right is also infringed by a person who in the course of a business—

(a) deals with a work which has been altered after the author parted with possession of it as being the unaltered work of the author, or

(b) deals with a copy of such a work as being a copy of the unaltered work of the author,

knowing or having reason to believe that that is not the case.

(7) References in this section to dealing are to selling or letting for hire, offering or exposing for sale or hire, exhibiting in public, or distributing.

(8) This section applies where, contrary to the fact—

(a) a literary, dramatic or musical work is falsely represented as being an adaptation of the work of a person, or

(b) a copy of an artistic work is falsely represented as being a copy made by the author of the artistic work,

as it applies where the work is falsely attributed to a person as author.

Right to privacy of certain photographs and films

85. Right to privacy of certain photographs and films

(1) A person who for private and domestic purposes commissions the taking of a photograph or the making of a film has, where copyright subsists in the resulting work, the right not to have—

(a) copies of the work issued to the public,

(b) the work exhibited or shown in public, or

(c) the work communicated to the public;

and, except as mentioned in subsection (2), a person who does or authorises the doing of any of those acts infringes that right.

(2) The right is not infringed by an act which by virtue of any of the following provisions would not infringe copyright in the work—

(a) section 31 (incidental inclusion of work in an artistic work, film or broadcast);

(b) section 45 (parliamentary and judicial proceedings);

(c) section 46 (Royal Commissions and statutory inquiries);

(d) section 50 (acts done under statutory authority);

(e) section 57 or 66A (acts permitted on assumptions as to expiry of copyright, &c.).

Chapter V
Dealings with Rights in Copyright Works

Copyright

90. Assignment and licences

(1) Copyright is transmissible by assignment, by testamentary disposition or by operation of law, as personal or moveable property.

(2) An assignment or other transmission of copyright may be partial, that is, limited so as to apply—

(a) to one or more, but not all, of the things the copyright owner has the exclusive right to do;

(b) to part, but not the whole, of the period for which the copyright is to subsist.

(3) An assignment of copyright is not effective unless it is in writing signed by or on behalf of the assignor.

(4) A licence granted by a copyright owner is binding on every successor in title to his interest in the copyright, except a purchaser in good faith for valuable consideration and without notice (actual or constructive) of the licence or a person deriving title from such a purchaser; and references in this Part to doing anything with, or without, the licence of the copyright owner shall be construed accordingly.

92. Exclusive licences

(1) In this Part an "exclusive licence" means a licence in writing signed by or on behalf of the copyright owner authorising the licensee to the exclusion of all other persons, including the person granting the licence, to exercise a right which would otherwise be exercisable exclusively by the copyright owner.

(2) The licensee under an exclusive licence has the same rights against a successor in title who is bound by the licence as he has against the person granting the licence.

Moral rights

94. Moral rights not assignable

The rights conferred by Chapter IV (moral rights) are not assignable.

Chapter VI
Remedies for Infringement

Rights and remedies of copyright owner

96. Infringement actionable by copyright owner

(1) An infringement of copyright is actionable by the copyright owner.

(2) In an action for infringement of copyright all such relief by way of damages, injunctions, accounts or otherwise is available to the plaintiff as is available in respect of the infringement of any other property right.

(3) This section has effect subject to the following provisions of this Chapter.

97. Provisions as to damages in infringement action

(1) Where in an action for infringement of copyright it is shown that at the time of the infringement the defendant did not know, and had no reason to believe, that copyright subsisted in the work to which the action relates, the plaintiff is not entitled to damages against him, but without prejudice to any other remedy.

(2) The court may in an action for infringement of copyright having regard to all the circumstances, and in particular to—

(a) the flagrancy of the infringement, and

(b) any benefit accruing to the defendant by reason of the infringement,

award such additional damages as the justice of the case may require.

99. Order for delivery up

(1) Where a person—

(a) has an infringing copy of a work in his possession, custody or control in the course of a business, or

(b) has in his possession, custody or control an article specifically designed or adapted for making copies of a particular copyright work, knowing or having reason to believe that it has been or is to be used to make infringing copies,

the owner of the copyright in the work may apply to the court for an order that the infringing copy or article be delivered up to him or to such other person as the court may direct.

(2) An application shall not be made after the end of the period specified in section 113 (period after which remedy of delivery up not available); and no order shall be made unless the court also makes, or it appears to the court that there are grounds for making, an order under section 114 (order as to disposal of infringing copy or other article).

(3) A person to whom an infringing copy or other article is delivered up in pursuance of an order under this section shall, if an order under section 114 is not made, retain it pending the making of an order, or the decision not to make an order, under that section.

(4) Nothing in this section affects any other power of the court.

100. Right to seize infringing copies and other articles

(1) An infringing copy of a work which is found exposed or otherwise immediately available for sale or hire, and in respect of which the copyright owner would be entitled to apply for an order under section 99, may be seized and detained by him or a person authorised by him.

The right to seize and detain is exercisable subject to the following conditions and is subject to any decision of the court under section 114.

(2) Before anything is seized under this section notice of the time and place of the proposed seizure must be given to a local police station.

(3) A person may for the purpose of exercising the right conferred by this section enter premises to which the public have access but may not seize anything in the possession, custody or control of a person at a permanent or regular place of business of his, and may not use any force.

(4) At the time when anything is seized under this section there shall be left at the place where it was seized a notice in the prescribed form containing the prescribed particulars as to the person by whom or on whose authority the seizure is made and the grounds on which it is made.

(5) In this section—

"premises" includes land, buildings, moveable structures, vehicles, vessels, aircraft and hovercraft; and

"prescribed" means prescribed by order of the Secretary of State.

(6) An order of the Secretary of State under this section shall be made by statutory instrument which shall be subject to annulment in pursuance of a resolution of either House of Parliament.

Rights and remedies of exclusive licensee

101. Rights and remedies of exclusive licensee

(1) An exclusive licensee has, except against the copyright owner, the same rights and remedies in respect of matters occurring after the grant of the licence as if the licence had been an assignment.

(2) His rights and remedies are concurrent with those of the copyright owner; and references in the relevant provisions of this Part to the copyright owner shall be construed accordingly.

(3) In an action brought by an exclusive licensee by virtue of this section a defendant may avail himself of any defence which would have been available to him if the action had been brought by the copyright owner.

101A. Certain infringements actionable by a non-exclusive licensee

(1) A non-exclusive licensee may bring an action for infringement of copyright if—

(a) the infringing act was directly connected to a prior licensed act of the licensee; and

(b) the licence—

(i) is in writing and is signed by or on behalf of the copyright owner; and

(ii) expressly grants the non-exclusive licensee a right of action under this section.

(2) In an action brought under this section, the non-exclusive licensee shall have the same rights and remedies available to him as the copyright owner would have had if he had brought the action.

(3) The rights granted under this section are concurrent with those of the copyright owner and references in the relevant provisions of this Part to the copyright owner shall be construed accordingly.

(4) In an action brought by a non-exclusive licensee by virtue of this section a defendant may avail himself of any defence which would have been available to him if the action had been brought by the copyright owner.

(5) Subsections (1) to (4) of section 102 shall apply to a non-exclusive licensee who has a right of action by virtue of this section as it applies to an exclusive licensee.

(6) In this section a "non-exclusive licensee" means the holder of a licence authorising the licensee to exercise a right which remains exercisable by the copyright owner.

102. Exercise of concurrent rights

(1) Where an action for infringement of copyright brought by the copyright owner or an exclusive licensee relates (wholly or partly) to an infringement in respect of which they have concurrent rights of action, the copyright owner or, as the case may be, the exclusive licensee may not, without the leave of the court, proceed with the action unless the other is either joined as a plaintiff or added as a defendant.

(2) A copyright owner or exclusive licensee who is added as a defendant in pursuance of subsection (1) is not liable for any costs in the action unless he takes part in the proceedings.

(3) The above provisions do not affect the granting of interlocutory relief on an application by a copyright owner or exclusive licensee alone.

(4) Where an action for infringement of copyright is brought which relates (wholly or partly) to an infringement in respect of which the copyright owner and an exclusive licensee have or had concurrent rights of action—

(a) the court shall in assessing damages take into account—

(i) the terms of the licence, and

(ii) any pecuniary remedy already awarded or available to either of them in respect of the infringement;

(b) no account of profits shall be directed if an award of damages has been made, or an account of profits has been directed, in favour of the other of them in respect of the infringement; and

(c) the court shall if an account of profits is directed apportion the profits between them as the court considers just, subject to any agreement between them;

and these provisions apply whether or not the copyright owner and the exclusive licensee are both parties to the action.

(5) The copyright owner shall notify any exclusive licensee having concurrent rights before applying for an order under section 99 (order for delivery up) or exercising the right conferred by section 100 (right of seizure); and the court may on the application of the licensee make such order under section 99 or, as the case may be, prohibiting or permitting the exercise by the copyright owner of the right conferred by section 100, as it thinks fit having regard to the terms of the licence.

Offences

107. Criminal liability for making or dealing with infringing articles, &c.

(1) A person commits an offence who, without the licence of the copyright owner—

(a) makes for sale or hire, or

(b) imports into the United Kingdom otherwise than for his private and domestic use, or

(c) possesses in the course of a business with a view to committing any act infringing the copyright, or

(d) in the course of a business—

(i) sells or lets for hire, or

(ii) offers or exposes for sale or hire, or

(iii) exhibits in public, or

(iv) distributes, or

(e) distributes otherwise than in the course of a business to such an extent as to affect prejudicially the owner of the copyright,

an article which is, and which he knows or has reason to believe is, an infringing copy of a copyright work.

(2) A person commits an offence who—

(a) makes an article specifically designed or adapted for making copies of a particular copyright work, or

(b) has such an article in his possession,

knowing or having reason to believe that it is to be used to make infringing copies for sale or hire or for use in the course of a business.

(2A) A person who infringes copyright in a work by communicating the work to the public—

(a) in the course of a business, or

(b) otherwise than in the course of a business to such an extent as to affect prejudicially the owner of the copyright,

commits an offence if he knows or has reason to believe that, by doing so, he is infringing copyright in that work.

(3) Where copyright is infringed (otherwise than by reception of a communication to the public)—

(a) by the public performance of a literary, dramatic or musical work, or

(b) by the playing or showing in public of a sound recording or film,

any person who caused the work to be so performed, played or shown is guilty of an offence if he knew or had reason to believe that copyright would be infringed.

(4) A person guilty of an offence under subsection (1)(a), (b), (d)(iv) or (e) is liable—

(a) on summary conviction to imprisonment for a term not exceeding six months or a fine not exceeding the statutory maximum, or both;

(b) on conviction on indictment to a fine or imprisonment for a term not exceeding ten years, or both.

(4A) A person guilty of an offence under subsection (2A) is liable—

(a) on summary conviction to imprisonment for a term not exceeding three months or a fine not exceeding the statutory maximum, or both;

(b) on conviction on indictment to a fine or imprisonment for a term not exceeding two years, or both.

(5) A person guilty of any other offence under this section is liable on summary conviction to imprisonment for a term not exceeding six months or a fine not exceeding level 5 on the standard scale, or both.

(6) Sections 104 to 106 (presumptions as to various matters connected with copyright) do not apply to proceedings for an offence under this section; but without prejudice to their application in proceedings for an order under section 108 below.

107A. Enforcement by local weights and measures authority

(1) It is the duty of every local weights and measures authority to enforce within their area the provisions of section 107.

(2) The following provisions of the Trade Descriptions Act 1968 apply in relation to the enforcement of that section by such an authority as in relation to the enforcement of that Act—

section 27 (power to make test purchases),

section 28 (power to enter premises and inspect and seize goods and documents),

section 29 (obstruction of authorised officers), and

section 33 (compensation for loss, &c of goods seized).

(3) Subsection (1) above does not apply in relation to the enforcement of section 107 in Northern Ireland, but it is the duty of the Department of Economic Development to enforce that section in Northern Ireland.

For that purpose the provisions of the Trade Descriptions Act 1968 specified in subsection (2) apply as if for the references to a local weights and measures authority and any officer of such an authority there were substituted references to that Department and any of its officers.

(4) Any enactment which authorises the disclosure of information for the purpose of facilitating the enforcement of the Trade Descriptions Act 1968 shall apply as if section 107 were contained in that Act and as if the functions of any person in relation to the enforcement of that section were functions under that Act.

(5) Nothing in this section shall be construed as authorising a local weights and measures authority to bring proceedings in Scotland for an offence.

108. Order for delivery up in criminal proceedings

(1) The court before which proceedings are brought against a person for an offence under section 107 may, if satisfied that at the time of his arrest or charge—

(a) he had in his possession, custody or control in the course of a business an infringing copy of a copyright work, or

(b) he had in his possession, custody or control an article specifically designed or adapted for making copies of a particular copyright work, knowing or having reason to believe that it had been or was to be used to make infringing copies,

order that the infringing copy or article be delivered up to the copyright owner or to such other person as the court may direct.

(2) For this purpose a person shall be treated as charged with an offence—

(a) in England, Wales and Northern Ireland, when he is orally charged or is served with a summons or indictment;

(b) in Scotland, when he is cautioned, charged or served with a complaint or indictment.

(3) An order may be made by the court of its own motion or on the application of the prosecutor (or, in Scotland, the Lord Advocate or procurator-fiscal), and may be made whether or not the person is convicted of the offence, but shall not be made—

(a) after the end of the period specified in section 113 (period after which remedy of delivery up not available), or

(b) if it appears to the court unlikely that any order will be made under section 114 (order as to disposal of infringing copy or other article).

(4) An appeal lies from an order made under this section by a magistrates' court—

(a) in England and Wales, to the Crown Court, and

(b) in Northern Ireland, to the county court;

and in Scotland, where an order has been made under this section, the person from whose possession, custody or control the infringing copy or article has been removed may, without prejudice to any other form of appeal under any rule of law, appeal against that order in the same manner as against sentence.

(5) A person to whom an infringing copy or other article is delivered up in pursuance of an order under this section shall retain it pending the making of an order, or the decision not to make an order, under section 114.

(6) Nothing in this section affects the powers of the court under section 143 of the Powers of Criminal Courts (Sentencing) Act 2000, Part II of the Proceeds of Crime (Scotland) Act 1995 or Article 11 of the Criminal Justice (Northern Ireland) Order 1994 (general provisions as to forfeiture in criminal proceedings).

114. Order as to disposal of infringing copy or other article

(1) An application may be made to the court for an order that an infringing copy or other article delivered up in pursuance of an order under section 99 or 108, or seized and detained in pursuance of the right conferred by section 100, shall be—

(a) forfeited to the copyright owner, or

(b) destroyed or otherwise dealt with as the court may think fit,

or for a decision that no such order should be made.

(2) In considering what order (if any) should be made, the court shall consider whether other remedies available in an action for infringement of copyright would be adequate to compensate the copyright owner and to protect his interests.

(3) Provision shall be made by rules of court as to the service of notice on persons having an interest in the copy or other articles, and any such person is entitled—

(a) to appear in proceedings for an order under this section, whether or not he was served with notice, and

(b) to appeal against any order made, whether or not he appeared;

and an order shall not take effect until the end of the period within which notice of an appeal may be given or, if before the end of that period notice of appeal is duly given, until the final determination or abandonment of the proceedings on the appeal.

(4) Where there is more than one person interested in a copy or other article, the court shall make such order as it thinks just and may (in particular) direct that the article be sold, or otherwise dealt with, and the proceeds divided.

(5) If the court decides that no order should be made under this section, the person in whose possession, custody or control the copy or other article was before being delivered up or seized is entitled to its return.

(6) References in this section to a person having an interest in a copy or other article include any person in whose favour an order could be made in respect of it—

(a) under this section or under section 204 or 231 of this Act;

(b) under section 24D of the Registered Designs Act 1949;

(c) under section 19 of Trade Marks Act 1994 (including that section as applied by regulation 4 of the Community Trade Mark Regulations 2006 (SI 2006/1027)); or

(d) under regulation 1C of the Community Design Regulations 2005 (SI 2005/2339).

Part III
Design Right

Chapter I
Design Right in Original Designs

Introductory

213. Design right

(1) Design right is a property right which subsists in accordance with this Part in an original design.

(2) In this Part "design" means the design of any aspect of the shape or configuration (whether internal or external) of the whole or part of an article.

(3) Design right does not subsist in—

(a) a method or principle of construction,

(b) features of shape or configuration of an article which—

(i) enable the article to be connected to, or placed in, around or against, another article so that either article may perform its function, or

(ii) are dependent upon the appearance of another article of which the article is intended by the designer to form an integral part, or

(c) surface decoration.

(4) A design is not "original" for the purposes of this Part if it is commonplace in the design field in question at the time of its creation.

(5) Design right subsists in a design only if the design qualifies for design right protection by reference to—

(a) the designer or the person by whom the design was commissioned or the designer employed (see sections 218 and 219), or

(b) the person by whom and country in which articles made to the design were first marketed (see section 220),

or in accordance with any Order under section 221 (power to make further provision with respect to qualification).

(5A) Design right does not subsist in a design which consists of or contains a controlled representation within the meaning of the Olympic Symbol etc. (Protection) Act 1995.

(6) Design right does not subsist unless and until the design has been recorded in a design document or an article has been made to the design.

(7) Design right does not subsist in a design which was so recorded, or to which an article was made, before the commencement of this Part.

214. The designer

(1) In this Part the "designer", in relation to a design, means the person who creates it.

(2) In the case of a computer-generated design the person by whom the arrangements necessary for the creation of the design are undertaken shall be taken to be the designer.

215. Ownership of design right

(1) The designer is the first owner of any design right in a design which is not created in pursuance of a commission or in the course of employment.

(2) Where a design is created in pursuance of a commission, the person commissioning the design is the first owner of any design right in it.

(3) Where, in a case not falling within subsection (2) a design is created by an employee in the course of his employment, his employer is the first owner of any design right in the design.

(4) If a design qualifies for design right protection by virtue of section 220 (qualification by reference to first marketing of articles made to the design), the above rules do not apply and the person by whom the articles in question are marketed is the first owner of the design right.

216. Duration of design right

(1) Design right expires—

(a) fifteen years from the end of the calendar year in which the design was first recorded in a design document or an article was first made to the design, whichever first occurred, or

(b) if articles made to the design are made available for sale or hire within five years from the end of that calendar year, ten years from the end of the calendar year in which that first occurred.

(2) The reference in subsection (1) to articles being made available for sale or hire is to their being made so available anywhere in the world by or with the licence of the design right owner.

Chapter II
Rights of Design Right Owner and Remedies

Infringement of design right

226. Primary infringement of design right

(1) The owner of design right in a design has the exclusive right to reproduce the design for commercial purposes—

(a) by making articles to that design, or

(b) by making a design document recording the design for the purpose of enabling such articles to be made.

(2) Reproduction of a design by making articles to the design means copying the design so as to produce articles exactly or substantially to that design, and references in this Part to making articles to a design shall be construed accordingly.

(3) Design right is infringed by a person who without the licence of the design right owner does, or authorises another to do, anything which by virtue of this section is the exclusive right of the design right owner.

(4) For the purposes of this section reproduction may be direct or indirect, and it is immaterial whether any intervening acts themselves infringe the design right.

(5) This section has effect subject to the provisions of Chapter III (exceptions to rights of design right owner).

227. Secondary infringement: importing or dealing with infringing article

(1) Design right is infringed by a person who, without the licence of the design right owner—

(a) imports into the United Kingdom for commercial purposes, or

(b) has in his possession for commercial purposes, or

(c) sells, lets for hire, or offers or exposes for sale or hire, in the course of a business,

an article which is, and which he knows or has reason to believe is, an infringing article.

(2) This section has effect subject to the provisions of Chapter III (exceptions to rights of design right owner).

Remedies for infringement

229. Rights and remedies of design right owner

(1) An infringement of design right is actionable by the design right owner.

(2) In an action for infringement of design right all such relief by way of damages, injunctions, accounts or otherwise is available to the plaintiff as is available in respect of the infringement of any other property right.

(3) The court may in an action for infringement of design right, having regard to all the circumstances and in particular to—

(a) the flagrancy of the infringement, and

(b) any benefit accruing to the defendant by reason of the infringement,

award such additional damages as the justice of the case may require.

(4) This section has effect subject to section 233 (innocent infringement).

230. Order for delivery up

(1) Where a person—

(a) has in his possession, custody or control for commercial purposes an infringing article, or

(b) has in his possession, custody or control anything specifically designed or adapted for making articles to a particular design, knowing or having reason to believe that it has been or is to be used to make an infringing article,

the owner of the design right in the design in question may apply to the court for an order that the infringing article or other thing be delivered up to him or to such other person as the court may direct.

(2) An application shall not be made after the end of the period specified in the following provisions of this section; and no order shall be made unless the court also makes, or it appears to the court that there are grounds for making, an order under section 231 (order as to disposal of infringing article, &c.).

(3) An application for an order under this section may not be made after the end of the period of six years from the date on which the article or thing in question was made, subject to subsection (4).

(4) If during the whole or any part of that period the design right owner—

(a) is under a disability, or

(b) is prevented by fraud or concealment from discovering the facts entitling him to apply for an order,

an application may be made at any time before the end of the period of six years from the date on which he ceased to be under a disability or, as the case may be, could with reasonable diligence have discovered those facts.

(5) In subsection (4) "disability"—

(a) in England and Wales, has the same meaning as in the Limitation Act 1980;

(b) in Scotland, means legal disability within the meaning of the Prescription and Limitation (Scotland) Act 1973;

(c) in Northern Ireland, has the same meaning as in the Statute of Limitations (Northern Ireland) 1958.

(6) A person to whom an infringing article or other thing is delivered up in pursuance of an order under this section shall, if an order under section 231 is not made, retain it pending the making of an order, or the decision not to make an order, under that section.

(7) Nothing in this section affects any other power of the court.

231. Order as to disposal of infringing articles, &c.

(1) An application may be made to the court for an order that an infringing article or other thing delivered up in pursuance of an order under section 230 shall be—

(a) forfeited to the design right owner, or

(b) destroyed or otherwise dealt with as the court may think fit,

or for a decision that no such order should be made.

(2) In considering what order (if any) should be made, the court shall consider whether other remedies available in an action for infringement of design right would be adequate to compensate the design right owner and to protect his interests.

(3) Provision shall be made by rules of court as to the service of notice on persons having an interest in the article or other thing, and any such person is entitled—

(a) to appear in proceedings for an order under this section, whether or not he was served with notice, and

(b) to appeal against any order made, whether or not he appeared;

and an order shall not take effect until the end of the period within which notice of an appeal may be given or, if before the end of that period notice of appeal is duly given, until the final determination or abandonment of the proceedings on the appeal.

(4) Where there is more than one person interested in an article or other thing, the court shall make such order as it thinks just and may (in particular) direct that the thing be sold, or otherwise dealt with, and the proceeds divided.

(5) If the court decides that no order should be made under this section, the person in whose possession, custody or control the article or other thing was before being delivered up is entitled to its return.

(6) References in this section to a person having an interest in an article or other thing include any person in whose favour an order could be made in respect of it—

(a) under this section or under section 114 or 204 of this Act;

(b) under section 24D of the Registered Designs Act 1949;

(c) under section 19 of Trade Marks Act 1994 (including that section as applied by regulation 4 of the Community Trade Mark Regulations 2006 (SI 2006/1027)); or

(d) under regulation 1C of the Community Design Regulations 2005 (SI 2005/2339).

233. Innocent infringement

(1) Where in an action for infringement of design right brought by virtue of section 226 (primary infringement) it is shown that at the time of the infringement the defendant did not know, and had no reason to believe, that design right subsisted in the design to which the action relates, the plaintiff is not entitled to damages against him, but without prejudice to any other remedy.

(2) Where in an action for infringement of design right brought by virtue of section 227 (secondary infringement) a defendant shows that the infringing article was innocently acquired by him or a predecessor in title of his, the only remedy available against him in respect of the infringement is damages not exceeding a reasonable royalty in respect of the act complained of.

(3) In subsection (2) "innocently acquired" means that the person acquiring the article did not know and had no reason to believe that it was an infringing article.

Chapter III
Exceptions to Rights of Design Right Owners

Infringement of copyright

236. Infringement of copyright

Where copyright subsists in a work which consists of or includes a design in which design right subsists, it is not an infringement of design right in the design to do anything which is an infringement of the copyright in that work.

Trade Marks Act 1994
1994 c. 26

An Act to make new provision for registered trade marks, implementing Council Directive No. 89/104/EEC of 21st December 1988 to approximate the laws of the Member States relating to trade marks; to make provision in connection with Council Regulation (EC) No. 40/94 of 20th December 1993 on the Community trade mark; to give effect to the Madrid Protocol Relating to the International Registration of Marks of 27th June 1989, and to certain provisions of the Paris Convention for the Protection of Industrial Property of 20th March 1883, as revised and amended; and for connected purposes [21st July 1994]

Part I
Registered Trade Marks

Introductory

1. Trade Marks

(1) In this Act a "trade mark" means any sign capable of being represented graphically which is capable of distinguishing goods or services of one undertaking from those of other undertakings.

A trade mark may, in particular, consist of words (including personal names), designs, letters, numerals or the shape of goods or their packaging.

(2) References in this Act to a trade mark include, unless the context otherwise requires, references to a collective mark (see section 49) or certification mark (see section 50).

Grounds for refusal of registration

3. Absolute grounds for refusal of registration

(1) The following shall not be registered—

(a) signs which do not satisfy the requirements of section 1(1),

(b) trade marks which are devoid of any distinctive character,

(c) trade marks which consist exclusively of signs or indications which may serve, in trade, to designate the kind, quality, quantity, intended purpose, value, geographical origin, the time of production of goods or of rendering of services, or other characteristics of goods or services,

(d) trade marks which consist exclusively of signs or indications which have become customary in the current language or in the bona fide and established practices of the trade:

Provided that, a trade mark shall not be refused registration by virtue of paragraph (b), (c) or (d) above if, before the date of application for registration, it has in fact acquired a distinctive character as a result of the use made of it.

(2) A sign shall not be registered as a trade mark if it consists exclusively of—

(a) the shape which results from the nature of the goods themselves,

(b) the shape of goods which is necessary to obtain a technical result, or

(c) the shape which gives substantial value to the goods.

(3) A trade mark shall not be registered if it is—

(a) contrary to public policy or to accepted principles of morality, or

(b) of such a nature as to deceive the public (for instance as to the nature, quality or geographical origin of the goods or service).

(4) A trade mark shall not be registered if or to the extent that its use is prohibited in the United Kingdom by any enactment or rule of law or by any provision of Community law.

(5) A trade mark shall not be registered in the cases specified, or referred to, in section 4 (specially protected emblems).

(6) A trade mark shall not be registered if or to the extent that the application is made in bad faith.

5. Relative grounds for refusal of registration

(1) A trade mark shall not be registered if it is identical with an earlier trade mark and the goods or services for which the trade mark is applied for are identical with the goods or services for which the earlier trade mark is protected.

(2) A trade mark shall not be registered if because—

(a) it is identical with an earlier trade mark and is to be registered for goods or services similar to those for which the earlier trade mark is protected, or

(b) it is similar to an earlier trade mark and is to be registered for goods or services identical with or similar to those for which the earlier trade mark is protected,

there exists a likelihood of confusion on the part of the public, which includes the likelihood of association with the earlier trade mark.

(3) A trade mark which—

(a) is identical with or similar to an earlier trade mark,

shall not be registered if, or to the extent that, the earlier trade mark has a reputation in the United Kingdom (or, in the case of a Community trade mark or international trade mark (EC), in the European Community) and the use of the later mark without due cause would take unfair advantage of, or be detrimental to, the distinctive character or the repute of the earlier trade mark.

(4) A trade mark shall not be registered if, or to the extent that, its use in the United Kingdom is liable to be prevented—

(a) by virtue of any rule of law (in particular, the law of passing off) protecting an unregistered trade mark or other sign used in the course of trade, or

(b) by virtue of an earlier right other than those referred to in subsections (1) to (3) or paragraph (a) above, in particular by virtue of the law of copyright, design right or registered designs.

A person thus entitled to prevent the use of a trade mark is referred to in this Act as the proprietor of an "earlier right" in relation to the trade mark.

(5) Nothing in this section prevents the registration of a trade mark where the proprietor of the earlier trade mark or other earlier right consents to the registration.

Effects of registered trade mark

9. Rights conferred by registered trade mark

(1) The proprietor of a registered trade mark has exclusive rights in the trade mark which are infringed by use of the trade mark in the United Kingdom without his consent.

The acts amounting to infringement, if done without the consent of the proprietor, are specified in section 10.

(2) References in this Act to the infringement of a registered trade mark are to any such infringement of the rights of the proprietor.

(3) The rights of the proprietor have effect from the date of registration (which in accordance with section 40(3) is the date of filing of the application for registration):

Provided that—

(a) no infringement proceedings may be begun before the date on which the trade mark is in fact registered; and

(b) no offence under section 92 (unauthorised use of trade mark, &c in relation to goods) is committed by anything done before the date of publication of the registration.

10. Infringement of registered trade mark

(1) A person infringes a registered trade mark if he uses in the course of trade a sign which is identical with the trade mark in relation to goods or services which are identical with those for which it is registered.

(2) A person infringes a registered trade mark if he uses in the course of trade a sign where because—

(a) the sign is identical with the trade mark and is used in relation to goods or services similar to those for which the trade mark is registered, or

(b) the sign is similar to the trade mark and is used in relation to goods or services identical with or similar to those for which the trade mark is registered,

there exists a likelihood of confusion on the part of the public, which includes the likelihood of association with the trade mark.

(3) A person infringes a registered trade mark if he uses in the course of trade, in relation to goods or services, a sign which—

(a) is identical with or similar to the trade mark,

where the trade mark has a reputation in the United Kingdom and the use of the sign, being without due cause, takes unfair advantage of, or is detrimental to, the distinctive character or the repute of the trade mark.

(4) For the purposes of this section a person uses a sign if, in particular, he—

(a) affixes it to goods or the packaging thereof;

(b) offers or exposes goods for sale, puts them on the market or stocks them for those purposes under the sign, or offers or supplies services under the sign;

(c) imports or exports goods under the sign; or

(d) uses the sign on business papers or in advertising.

(5) A person who applies a registered trade mark to material intended to be used for labelling or packaging goods, as a business paper, or for advertising goods or services, shall be treated as a party to any use of the material which infringes the registered trade mark if when he applied the mark he knew or had reason to believe that the application of the mark was not duly authorised by the proprietor or a licensee.

(6) Nothing in the preceding provisions of this section shall be construed as preventing the use of a registered trade mark by any person for the purpose of identifying goods or services as those of the proprietor or a licensee.

But any such use otherwise than in accordance with honest practices in industrial or commercial matters shall be treated as infringing the registered trade mark if the use without due cause takes unfair advantage of, or is detrimental to, the distinctive character or repute of the trade mark.

11. Limits on effect of registered trade mark

(1) A registered trade mark is not infringed by the use of another registered trade mark in relation to goods or services for which the latter is registered (but see section 47(6) (effect of declaration of invalidity of registration)).

(2) A registered trade mark is not infringed by—

(a) the use by a person of his own name or address,

(b) the use of indications concerning the kind, quality, quantity, intended purpose, value, geographical origin, the time of production of goods or of rendering of services, or other characteristics of goods or services, or

(c) the use of the trade mark where it is necessary to indicate the intended purpose of a product or service (in particular, as accessories or spare parts),

provided the use is in accordance with honest practices in industrial or commercial matters.

(3) A registered trade mark is not infringed by the use in the course of trade in a particular locality of an earlier right which applies only in that locality.

For this purpose an "earlier right" means an unregistered trade mark or other sign continuously used in relation to goods or services by a person or a predecessor in title of his from a date prior to whichever is the earlier of—

(a) the use of the first-mentioned trade mark in relation to those goods or services by the proprietor or a predecessor in title of his, or

(b) the registration of the first-mentioned trade mark in respect of those goods or services in the name of the proprietor or a predecessor in title of his;

and an earlier right shall be regarded as applying in a locality if, or to the extent that, its use in that locality is protected by virtue of any rule of law (in particular, the law of passing off).

12. Exhaustion of rights conferred by registered trade mark

(1) A registered trade mark is not infringed by the use of the trade mark in relation to goods which have been put on the market in the European Economic Area under that trade mark by the proprietor or with his consent.

(2) Subsection (1) does not apply where there exist legitimate reasons for the proprietor to oppose further dealings in the goods (in particular, where the condition of the goods has been changed or impaired after they have been put on the market).

Infringement proceedings

14. Action for infringement

(1) An infringement of a registered trade mark is actionable by the proprietor of the trade mark.

(2) In an action for infringement all such relief by way of damages, injunctions, accounts or otherwise is available to him as is available in respect of the infringement of any other property right.

15. Order for erasure, &c. of offending sign

(1) Where a person is found to have infringed a registered trade mark, the court may make an order requiring him—

(a) to cause the offending sign to be erased, removed or obliterated from any infringing goods, material or articles in his possession, custody or control, or

(b) if it is not reasonably practicable for the offending sign to be erased, removed or obliterated, to secure the destruction of the infringing goods, material or articles in question.

(2) If an order under subsection (1) is not complied with, or it appears to the court likely that such an order would not be complied with, the court may order that the infringing goods, material or articles be delivered to such person as the court may direct for erasure, removal or obliteration of the sign, or for destruction, as the case may be.

16. Order for delivery up of infringing goods, material or articles

(1) The proprietor of a registered trade mark may apply to the court for an order for the delivery up to him, or such other person as the court may direct, of any infringing goods, material or articles which a person has in his possession, custody or control in the course of a business.

(2) An application shall not be made after the end of the period specified in section 18 (period after which remedy of delivery up not available); and no order shall be made unless the court also makes, or it appears to the court that there are grounds for making, an order under section 19 (order as to disposal of infringing goods, &c.).

(3) A person to whom any infringing goods, material or articles are delivered up in pursuance of an order under this section shall, if an order under section 19 is not made, retain them pending the making of an order, or the decision not to make an order, under that section.

(4) Nothing in this section affects any other power of the court.

19. Order as to disposal of infringing goods, material or articles

(1) Where infringing goods, material or articles have been delivered up in pursuance of an order under section 16, an application may be made to the court—

(a) for an order that they be destroyed or forfeited to such person as the court may think fit, or

(b) for a decision that no such order should be made.

(2) In considering what order (if any) should be made, the court shall consider whether other remedies available in an action for infringement of the registered trade mark would be adequate to compensate the proprietor and any licensee and protect their interests.

(3) Provision shall be made by rules of court as to the service of notice on persons having an interest in the goods, material or articles, and any such person is entitled—

(a) to appear in proceedings for an order under this section, whether or not he was served with notice, and

(b) to appeal against any order made, whether or not he appeared;

and an order shall not take effect until the end of the period within which notice of an appeal may be given or, if before the end of that period notice of appeal is duly given, until the final determination or abandonment of the proceedings on the appeal.

(4) Where there is more than one person interested in the goods, material or articles, the court shall make such order as it thinks just.

(5) If the court decides that no order should be made under this section, the person in whose possession, custody or control the goods, material or articles were before being delivered up is entitled to their return.

(6) References in this section to a person having an interest in goods, material or articles include any person in whose favour an order could be made —

(a) under this section (including that section as applied by regulation 4 of the Community Trade Mark Regulations 2006 (SI 2006/1027));

(b) under section 24D of the Registered Designs Act 1949;

(c) under section 114, 204 or 231 of the Copyright, Designs and Patents Act 1988; or

(d) under regulation 1C of the Community Design Regulations 2005 (SI 2005/2339).

21. Remedy for groundless threats of infringement proceedings

(1) Where a person threatens another with proceedings for infringement of a registered trade mark other than—

(a) the application of the mark to goods or their packaging,

(b) the importation of goods to which, or to the packaging of which, the mark has been applied, or

(c) the supply of services under the mark,

any person aggrieved may bring proceedings for relief under this section.

(2) The relief which may be applied for is any of the following—

(a) a declaration that the threats are unjustifiable,

(b) an injunction against the continuance of the threats,

(c) damages in respect of any loss he has sustained by the threats;

and the plaintiff is entitled to such relief unless the defendant shows that the acts in respect of which proceedings were threatened constitute (or if done would constitute) an infringement of the registered trade mark concerned.

(3) If that is shown by the defendant, the plaintiff is nevertheless entitled to relief if he shows that the registration of the trade mark is invalid or liable to be revoked in a relevant respect.

(4) The mere notification that a trade mark is registered, or that an application for registration has been made, does not constitute a threat of proceedings for the purposes of this section.

Registered trade mark as object of property

24. Assignment, &c. of registered trade mark

(1) A registered trade mark is transmissible by assignment, testamentary disposition or operation of law in the same way as other personal or moveable property.

It is so transmissible either in connection with the goodwill of a business or independently.

(2) An assignment or other transmission of a registered trade mark may be partial, that is, limited so as to apply—

(a) in relation to some but not all of the goods or services for which the trade mark is registered, or

(b) in relation to use of the trade mark in a particular manner or a particular locality.

(3) An assignment of a registered trade mark, or an assent relating to a registered trade mark, is not effective unless it is in writing signed by or on behalf of the assignor or, as the case may be, a personal representative.

Except in Scotland, this requirement may be satisfied in a case where the assignor or personal representative is a body corporate by the affixing of its seal.

(4) The above provisions apply to assignment by way of security as in relation to any other assignment.

(5) A registered trade mark may be the subject of a charge (in Scotland, security) in the same way as other personal or moveable property.

(6) Nothing in this Act shall be construed as affecting the assignment or other transmission of an unregistered trade mark as part of the goodwill of a business.

25. Registration of transactions affecting registered trade mark

(1) On application being made to the registrar by—

(a) a person claiming to be entitled to an interest in or under a registered trade mark by virtue of a registrable transaction, or

(b) any other person claiming to be affected by such a transaction,

the prescribed particulars of the transaction shall be entered in the register.

(2) The following are registrable transactions—

(a) an assignment of a registered trade mark or any right in it;

(b) the grant of a licence under a registered trade mark;

(c) the granting of any security interest (whether fixed or floating) over a registered trade mark or any right in or under it;

(d) the making by personal representatives of an assent in relation to a registered trade mark or any right in or under it;

(e) an order of a court or other competent authority transferring a registered trade mark or any right in or under it.

(3) Until an application has been made for registration of the prescribed particulars of a registrable transaction—

(a) the transaction is ineffective as against a person acquiring a conflicting interest in or under the registered trade mark in ignorance of it, and

(b) a person claiming to be a licensee by virtue of the transaction does not have the protection of section 30 or 31 (rights and remedies of licensee in relation to infringement).

(4) Where a person becomes the proprietor or a licensee of a registered trade mark by virtue of a registrable transaction and the mark is infringed before the prescribed particulars of the transaction are registered, in proceedings for such an infringement, the court shall not award him costs unless—

(a) an application for registration of the prescribed particulars of the transaction is made before the end of the period of six months beginning with its date, or

(b) the court is satisfied that it was not practicable for such an application to be made before the end of that period and that an application was made as soon as practicable thereafter.

(5) Provision may be made by rules as to—

(a) the amendment of registered particulars relating to a licence so as to reflect any alteration of the terms of the licence, and

(b) the removal of such particulars from the register—

(i) where it appears from the registered particulars that the licence was granted for a fixed period and that period has expired, or

(ii) where no such period is indicated and, after such period as may be prescribed, the registrar has notified the parties of his intention to remove the particulars from the register.

(6) Provision may also be made by rules as to the amendment or removal from the register of particulars relating to a security interest on the application of, or with the consent of, the person entitled to the benefit of that interest.

Licensing

28. Licensing of registered trade mark

(1) A licence to use a registered trade mark may be general or limited.

A limited licence may, in particular, apply—

(a) in relation to some but not all of the goods or services for which the trade mark is registered, or

(b) in relation to use of the trade mark in a particular manner or a particular locality.

(2) A licence is not effective unless it is in writing signed by or on behalf of the grantor.

Except in Scotland, this requirement may be satisfied in a case where the grantor is a body corporate by the affixing of its seal.

(3) Unless the licence provides otherwise, it is binding on a successor in title to the grantor's interest.

References in this Act to doing anything with, or without, the consent of the proprietor of a registered trade mark shall be construed accordingly.

(4) Where the licence so provides, a sub-licence may be granted by the licensee; and references in this Act to a licence or licensee include a sub-licence or sub-licensee.

30. General provisions as to rights of licensees in case of infringement

(1) This section has effect with respect to the rights of a licensee in relation to infringement of a registered trade mark.

The provisions of this section do not apply where or to the extent that, by virtue of section 31(1) below (exclusive licensee having rights and remedies of assignee), the licensee has a right to bring proceedings in his own name.

(2) A licensee is entitled, unless his licence, or any licence through which his interest is derived, provides otherwise, to call on the proprietor of the registered trade mark to take infringement proceedings in respect of any matter which affects his interests.

(3) If the proprietor—

(a) refuses to do so, or

(b) fails to do so within two months after being called upon.

the licensee may bring the proceedings in his own name as if he were the proprietor.

(4) Where infringement proceedings are brought by a licensee by virtue of this section the licensee may not, without the leave of the court, proceed with the action unless the proprietor is either joined as a plaintiff or added as a defendant.

This does not affect the granting of interlocutory relief on an application by a licensee alone.

(5) A proprietor who is added as a defendant as mentioned in subsection (4) shall not be made liable for any costs in the action unless he takes part in the proceedings.

(6) In infringement proceedings brought by the proprietor of a registered trade mark any loss suffered or likely to be suffered by licensees shall be taken into account; and the court may give such directions as it thinks fit as to the extent to which the plaintiff is to hold the proceeds of any pecuniary remedy on behalf of licensees.

(7) The provisions of this section apply in relation to an exclusive licensee if or to the extent that he has, by virtue of section 31(1), the rights and remedies of an assignee as if he were the proprietor of the registered trade mark.

31. Exclusive licensee having rights and remedies of assignee

(1) An exclusive licence may provide that the licensee shall have, to such extent as may be provided by the licence, the same rights and remedies in respect of matters occurring after the grant of the licence as if the licence had been an assignment.

Where or to the extent that such provision is made, the licensee is entitled, subject to the provisions of the licence and to the following provisions of this section, to bring infringement proceedings, against any person other than the proprietor, in his own name.

(2) Any such rights and remedies of an exclusive licensee are concurrent with those of the proprietor of the registered trade mark, and references to the proprietor of a registered trade mark in the provisions of this Act relating to infringement shall be construed accordingly.

(3) In an action brought by an exclusive licensee by virtue of this section a defendant may avail himself of any defence which would have been available to him if the action had been brought by the proprietor of the registered trade mark.

(4) Where proceedings for infringement of a registered trade mark brought by the proprietor or an exclusive licensee relate wholly or partly to an infringement in respect of which they have concurrent rights of action, the proprietor or, as the case may be, the exclusive licensee may not, without the leave of the court, proceed with the action unless the other is either joined as a plaintiff or added as a defendant.

This does not affect the granting of interlocutory relief on an application by a proprietor or exclusive licensee alone.

(5) A person who is added as a defendant as mentioned in subsection (4) shall not be made liable for any costs in the action unless he takes part in the proceedings.

(6) Where an action for infringement of a registered trade mark is brought which relates holly or partly to an infringement in respect of which the proprietor and an exclusive licensee have or had concurrent rights of action—

(a) the court shall in assessing damages take into account—

(i) the terms of the licence, and

(ii) any pecuniary remedy already awarded or available to either of them in respect of the infringement;

(b) no account of profits shall be directed if an award of damages has been made, or an account of profits has been directed, in favour of the other of them in respect of the infringement; and

(c) the court shall if an account of profits is directed apportion the profits between them as the court considers just, subject to any agreement between them.

The provisions of this subsection apply whether or not the proprietor and the exclusive licensee are both parties to the action, and if they are not both parties the court may give such directions as it thinks fit as to the extent to which the party to the proceedings is to hold the proceeds of any pecuniary remedy on behalf of the other.

(7) The proprietor of a registered trade mark shall notify any exclusive licensee who has a concurrent right of action before applying for an order under section 16 (order for delivery up), and the court may on the application of the licensee make such order under that section as it thinks fit having regard to the terms of the licence.

(8) The provisions of subsections (4) to (7) above have effect subject to any agreement to the contrary between the exclusive licensee and the proprietor.

Duration, renewal and alteration of registered trade mark

42. Duration of registration

(1) A trade mark shall be registered for a period of ten years from the date of registration.

(2) Registration may be renewed in accordance with section 43 for further periods of ten years.

46. Revocation of registration

(1) The registration of a trade mark may be revoked on any of the following grounds—

(a) that within the period of five years following the date of completion of the registration procedure it has not been put to genuine use in the United Kingdom, by the proprietor or with his consent, in relation to the goods or services for which it is registered, and there are no proper reasons for non-use;

(b) that such use has been suspended for an uninterrupted period of five years, and there are no proper reasons for non-use;

(c) that, in consequence of acts or inactivity of the proprietor, it has become the common name in the trade for a product or service for which it is registered;

(d) that in consequence of the use made of it by the proprietor or with his consent in relation to the goods or services for which it is registered, it is liable to mislead the public, particularly as to the nature, quality or geographical origin of those goods or services.

(2) For the purposes of subsection (1) use of a trade mark includes use in a form differing in elements which do not alter the distinctive character of the mark in the form in which it was registered, and use in the United Kingdom includes affixing the trade mark to goods or to the packaging of goods in the United Kingdom solely for export purposes.

(3) The registration of a trade mark shall not be revoked on the ground mentioned in subsection (1)(a) or (b) if such use as is referred to in that paragraph is commenced or

resumed after the expiry of the five year period and before the application for revocation is made:

Provided that, any such commencement or resumption of use after the expiry of the five year period but within the period of three months before the making of the application shall be disregarded unless preparations for the commencement or resumption began before the proprietor became aware that the application might be made.

(4) An application for revocation may be made by any person, and may be made either to the registrar or to the court, except that—

(a) if proceedings concerning the trade mark in question are pending in the court, the application must be made to the court; and

(b) if in any other case the application is made to the registrar, he may at any stage of the proceedings refer the application to the court.

(5) Where grounds for revocation exist in respect of only some of the goods or services for which the trade mark is registered, revocation shall relate to those goods or services only.

(6) Where the registration of a trade mark is revoked to any extent, the rights of the proprietor shall be deemed to have ceased to that extent as from—

(a) the date of the application for revocation, or

(b) if the registrar or court is satisfied that the grounds for revocation existed at an earlier date, that date.

47. Grounds for invalidity of registration

(1) The registration of a trade mark may be declared invalid on he ground that the trade mark was registered in breach of section 3 or any of the provisions referred to in that section (absolute grounds for refusal of registration).

Where the trade mark was registered in breach of subsection (1)(b), (c) or (d) of that section, it shall not be declared invalid if, in consequence of the use which has been made of it, it has after registration acquired a distinctive character in relation to the goods or services for which it is registered.

(2) The registration of a trade mark may be declared invalid on the ground—

(a) that there is an earlier trade mark in relation to which the conditions set out in section 5(1), (2) or (3) obtain, or

(b) that there is an earlier right in relation to which the condition set out in section 5(4) is satisfied,

unless the proprietor of that earlier trade mark or other earlier right has consented to the registration.

(2A) But the registration of a trade mark may not be declared invalid on the ground that there is an earlier trade mark unless—

(a) the registration procedure for the earlier trade mark was completed within the period of five years ending with the date of the application for the declaration,

(b) the registration procedure for the earlier trade mark was not completed before that date, or

(c) the use conditions are met.

(2B) The use conditions are met if—

(a) within the period of five years ending with the date of the application for the declaration the earlier trade mark has been put to genuine use in the United Kingdom by the proprietor or with his consent in relation to the goods or services for which it is registered, or

(b) it has not been so used, but there are proper reasons for non-use.

(2C) For these purposes—

(a) use of a trade mark includes use in a form differing in elements which do not alter the distinctive character of the mark in the form in which it was registered, and

(b) use in the United Kingdom includes affixing the trade mark to goods or to the packaging of goods in the United Kingdom solely for export purposes.

(2D) In relation to a Community trade mark or international trade mark (EC), any reference in subsection (2B) or (2C) to the United Kingdom shall be construed as a reference to the European Community.

(2E) Where an earlier trade mark satisfies the use conditions in respect of some only of the goods or services for which it is registered, it shall be treated for the purposes of this section as if it were registered only in respect of those goods or services.

(2F) Subsection (2A) does not apply where the earlier trade mark is a trade mark within section 6(1)(c).

(3) An application for a declaration of invalidity may be made by any person, and may be made either to the registrar or to the court, except that—

(a) if proceedings concerning the trade mark in question are pending in the court, the application must be made to the court; and

(b) if in any other case the application is made to the registrar, he may at any stage of the proceedings refer the application to the court.

(4) In the case of bad faith in the registration of a trade mark, the registrar himself may apply to the court for a declaration of the invalidity of the registration.

(5) Where the grounds of invalidity exist in respect of only some of the goods or services for which the trade mark is registered, the trade mark shall be declared invalid as regards those goods or services only.

(6) Where the registration of a trade mark is declared invalid to any extent, the registration shall to that extent be deemed never to have been made:

Provided that this shall not affect transactions past and closed.

56. Protection of well-known trade marks: Article 6bis

(1) References in this Act to a trade mark which is entitled to protection under the Paris Convention or the WTO agreement as a well known trade mark are to a mark which is well-known in the United Kingdom as being the mark of a person who—

(a) is a national of a Convention country, or

(b) is domiciled in, or has a real and effective industrial or commercial establishment in, a Convention country,

whether or not that person carries on business, or has any goodwill, in the United Kingdom.

References to the proprietor of such a mark shall be construed accordingly.

(2) The proprietor of a trade mark which is entitled to protection under the Paris Convention or the WTO agreement as a well known trade mark is entitled to restrain by injunction the use in the United Kingdom of a trade mark which, or the essential part of which, is identical or similar to his mark, in relation to identical or similar goods or services, where the use is likely to cause confusion.

This right is subject to section 48 (effect of acquiescence by proprietor of earlier trade mark).

(3) Nothing in subsection (2) affects the continuation of any bona fide use of a trade mark begun before the commencement of this section.

Competition Act 1998
1998 c. 41

An Act to make provision about competition and the abuse of a dominant position in the market; to confer powers in relation to investigations conducted in connection with Article 85 or 86 of the treaty establishing the European Community; to amend the Fair Trading Act 1973 in relation to information which may be required in connection with investigations under that Act; to make provision with respect to the meaning of "supply of services" in the Fair Trading Act 1973; and for connected purposes.

[9th November 1998]

The prohibition

2. Agreements etc preventing, restricting or distorting competition

(1) Subject to section 3, agreements between undertakings, decisions by associations of undertakings or concerted practices which—

(a) may affect trade within the United Kingdom, and

(b) have as their object or effect the prevention, restriction or distortion of competition within the United Kingdom,

are prohibited unless they are exempt in accordance with the provisions of this Part.

(2) Subsection (1) applies, in particular, to agreements, decisions or practices which—

(a) directly or indirectly fix purchase or selling prices or any other trading conditions;

(b) limit or control production, markets, technical development or investment;

(c) share markets or sources of supply;

(d) apply dissimilar conditions to equivalent transactions with other trading parties, thereby placing them at a competitive disadvantage;

(e) make the conclusion of contracts subject to acceptance by the other parties of supplementary obligations which, by their nature or according to commercial usage, have no connection with the subject of such contracts.

(3) Subsection (1) applies only if the agreement, decision or practice is, or is intended to be, implemented in the United Kingdom.

(4) Any agreement or decision which is prohibited by subsection (1) is void.

(5) A provision of this Part which is expressed to apply to, or in relation to, an agreement is to be read as applying equally to, or in relation to, a decision by an association of undertakings or a concerted practice (but with any necessary modifications).

(6) Subsection (5) does not apply where the context otherwise requires.

(7) In this section "the United Kingdom" means, in relation to an agreement which operates or is intended to operate only in a part of the United Kingdom, that part.

(8) The prohibition imposed by subsection (1) is referred to in this Act as "the Chapter I prohibition".

9. Exempt agreements

(1) An agreement is exempt from the Chapter I prohibition if it—

(a) contributes to—

(i) improving production or distribution, or

(ii) promoting technical or economic progress,

while allowing consumers a fair share of the resulting benefit; and

(b) does not—

(i) impose on the undertakings concerned restrictions which are not indispensable to the attainment of those objectives; or

(ii) afford the undertakings concerned the possibility of eliminating competition in respect of a substantial part of the products in question.

(2) In any proceedings in which it is alleged that the Chapter I prohibition is being or has been infringed by an agreement, any undertaking or association of undertakings claiming the benefit of subsection (1) shall bear the burden of proving that the conditions of that subsection are satisfied.

10. Parallel exemptions

(1) An agreement is exempt from the Chapter I prohibition if it is exempt from the Community prohibition—

(a) by virtue of a Regulation, or

(b) because of a decision of the Commission under Article 10 of the EC Competition Regulation.

(2) An agreement is exempt from the Chapter I prohibition if it does not affect trade between Member States but otherwise falls within a category of agreement which is exempt from the Community prohibition by virtue of a Regulation.

(3) An exemption from the Chapter I prohibition under this section is referred to in this Part as a parallel exemption.

(4) A parallel exemption—

(a) takes effect on the date on which the relevant exemption from the Community prohibition takes effect or, in the case of a parallel exemption under subsection (2), would take effect if the agreement in question affected trade between Member States; and

(b) ceases to have effect—

(i) if the relevant exemption from the Community prohibition ceases to have effect; or

(ii) on being cancelled by virtue of subsection (5) or (7).

(5) In such circumstances and manner as may be specified in rules made under section 51, the OFT may—

(a) impose conditions or obligations subject to which a parallel exemption is to have effect;

(b) vary or remove any such condition or obligation;

(c) impose one or more additional conditions or obligations;

(d) cancel the exemption.

(6) In such circumstances as may be specified in rules made under section 51, the date from which cancellation of an exemption is to take effect may be earlier than the date on which notice of cancellation is given.

(7) Breach of a condition imposed by the OFT has the effect of cancelling the exemption.

(8) In exercising its powers under this section, the OFT may require any person who is a party to the agreement in question to give it such information as it may require.

(9) For the purpose of this section references to an agreement being exempt from the Community prohibition are to be read as including references to the prohibition being inapplicable to the agreement by virtue of a Regulation other than the EC Competition Regulation or a decision by the Commission.

(10) In this section—

"the Community prohibition" means the prohibition contained in—

(a) Article 81(1);

(b) any corresponding provision replacing, or otherwise derived from, that provision;

(c) such other Regulation as the Secretary of State may by order specify; and

"Regulation" means a Regulation adopted by the Commission or by the Council.

(11) This section has effect in relation to the prohibition contained in paragraph 1 of Article 53 of the EEA Agreement (and the EFTA Surveillance Authority) as it has effect in relation to the Community prohibition (and the Commission) subject to any modifications which the Secretary of State may by order prescribe.

39. Limited immunity in relation to the Chapter I prohibition

(1) In this section "small agreement" means an agreement—

(a) which falls within a category prescribed for the purposes of this section; but

(b) is not a price fixing agreement.

(2) The criteria by reference to which a category of agreement is prescribed may, in particular, include—

(a) the combined turnover of the parties to the agreement (determined in accordance with prescribed provisions);

(b) the share of the market affected by the agreement (determined in that way).

(3) A party to a small agreement is immune from the effect of section 36(1) so far as that provision relates to decisions about infringement of the Chapter I prohibition; but the OFT may withdraw that immunity under subsection (4).

(4) If the OFT has investigated a small agreement, it may make a decision withdrawing the immunity given by subsection (3) if, as a result of its investigation, it considers that the agreement is likely to infringe the Chapter I prohibition.

(5) The OFT must give each of the parties in respect of which immunity is withdrawn written notice of its decision to withdraw the immunity.

(6) A decision under subsection (4) takes effect on such date ("the withdrawal date") as may be specified in the decision.

(7) The withdrawal date must be a date after the date on which the decision is made.

(8) In determining the withdrawal date, the OFT must have regard to the amount of time which the parties are likely to require in order to secure that there is no further infringement of the Chapter I prohibition with respect to the agreement.

(9) In subsection (1) "price fixing agreement" means an agreement which has as its object or effect, or one of its objects or effects, restricting the freedom of a party to the agreement to determine the price to be charged (otherwise than as between that party and another party to the agreement) for the product, service or other matter to which the agreement relates.

Enterprise Act 2002
(2002 c. 40)

An act to . . . to create an offence for those entering into certain anti-competitive agreements . . .

[7th November 2002]

Part 6
Cartel Offence

Cartel offence

188. Cartel offence

(1) An individual is guilty of an offence if he dishonestly agrees with one or more other persons to make or implement, or to cause to be made or implemented, arrangements of the following kind relating to at least two undertakings (A and B).

(2) The arrangements must be ones which, if operating as the parties to the agreement intend, would—

(a) directly or indirectly fix a price for the supply by A in the United Kingdom (otherwise than to B) of a product or service,

(b) limit or prevent supply by A in the United Kingdom of a product or service,

(c) limit or prevent production by A in the United Kingdom of a product,

(d) divide between A and B the supply in the United Kingdom of a product or service to a customer or customers,

(e) divide between A and B customers for the supply in the United Kingdom of a product or service, or

(f) be bid-rigging arrangements.

(3) Unless subsection (2)(d), (e) or (f) applies, the arrangements must also be ones which, if operating as the parties to the agreement intend, would—

(a) directly or indirectly fix a price for the supply by B in the United Kingdom (otherwise than to A) of a product or service,

(b) limit or prevent supply by B in the United Kingdom of a product or service, or

(c) limit or prevent production by B in the United Kingdom of a product.

(4) In subsections (2)(a) to (d) and (3), references to supply or production are to supply or production in the appropriate circumstances (for which see section 189).

(5) 'Bid-rigging arrangements' are arrangements under which, in response to a request for bids for the supply of a product or service in the United Kingdom, or for the production of a product in the United Kingdom—

(a) A but not B may make a bid, or

(b) A and B may each make a bid but, in one case or both, only a bid arrived at in accordance with the arrangements.

(6) But arrangements are not bid-rigging arrangements if, under them, the person requesting bids would be informed of them at or before the time when a bid is made.

(7) 'Undertaking' has the same meaning as in Part 1 of the 1998 Act.

189. Cartel offence: supplementary

(1) For section 188(2)(a), the appropriate circumstances are that A's supply of the product or service would be at a level in the supply chain at which the product or service would at the same time be supplied by B in the United Kingdom.

(2) For section 188(2)(b), the appropriate circumstances are that A's supply of the product or service would be at a level in the supply chain—

(a) at which the product or service would at the same time be supplied by B in the United Kingdom, or

(b) at which supply by B in the United Kingdom of the product or service would be limited or prevented by the arrangements.

(3) For section 188(2)(c), the appropriate circumstances are that A's production of the product would be at a level in the production chain—

(a) at which the product would at the same time be produced by B in the United Kingdom, or

(b) at which production by B in the United Kingdom of the product would be limited or prevented by the arrangements.

(4) For section 188(2)(d), the appropriate circumstances are that A's supply of the product or service would be at the same level in the supply chain as B's.

(5) For section 188(3)(a), the appropriate circumstances are that B's supply of the product or service would be at a level in the supply chain at which the product or service would at the same time be supplied by A in the United Kingdom.

(6) For section 188(3)(b), the appropriate circumstances are that B's supply of the product or service would be at a level in the supply chain—

(a) at which the product or service would at the same time be supplied by A in the United Kingdom, or

(b) at which supply by A in the United Kingdom of the product or service would be limited or prevented by the arrangements.

(7) For section 188(3)(c), the appropriate circumstances are that B's production of the product would be at a level in the production chain—

(a) at which the product would at the same time be produced by A in the United Kingdom, or

(b) at which production by A in the United Kingdom of the product would be limited or prevented by the arrangements.

190. Cartel offence: penalty and prosecution

(1) A person guilty of an offence under section 188 is liable—

(a) on conviction on indictment, to imprisonment for a term not exceeding five years or to a fine, or to both;

(b) on summary conviction, to imprisonment for a term not exceeding six months or to a fine not exceeding the statutory maximum, or to both.

(2) In England and Wales and Northern Ireland, proceedings for an offence under section 188 may be instituted only—

(a) by the Director of the Serious Fraud Office, or

(b) by or with the consent of the OFT.

(3) No proceedings may be brought for an offence under section 188 in respect of an agreement outside the United Kingdom, unless it has been implemented in whole or in part in the United Kingdom.

(4) Where, for the purpose of the investigation or prosecution of offences under section 188, the OFT gives a person written notice under this subsection, no proceedings for an offence under section 188 that falls within a description specified in the notice may be brought against that person in England and Wales or Northern Ireland except in circumstances specified in the notice.

Commercial Agents (Council Directive) Regulations 1993 (S.I. 1993 No. 3053)

Part I
General

1. Citation, commencement and applicable law

(1) These Regulations may be cited as the Commercial Agents (Council Directive) Regulations 1993 and shall come into force on 1st January 1994.

(2) These Regulations govern the relations between commercial agents and their principals and, subject to paragraph (3), apply in relation to the activities of commercial agents in Great Britain. ← There is similar legislation, based on the same directive in all other EU MS.

(3) A court or tribunal shall:

(a) apply the law of the other member State concerned in place of regulations 3 to 22 where the parties have agreed that the agency contract is to be governed by the law of that member State;

(b) (whether or not it would otherwise be required to do so) apply these regulations where the law of another member State corresponding to these regulations enables the parties to agree that the agency contract is to be governed by the law of a different member State and the parties have agreed that it is to be governed by the law of England and Wales or Scotland.

2. Interpretation, application and extent

(1) In these Regulations—

"commercial agent" means a self-employed intermediary who has continuing authority to negotiate the sale or purchase of goods on behalf of another person (the "principal"), or to negotiate and conclude the sale or purchase of goods on behalf of and in the name of that principal; but shall be understood as not including in particular:

It seems that the Reg. apply to sales agents and to marketing agents who have authority to negotiate some terms of the sale with the customer. However, in the 1st instance decision of PJ Pipe and Valve Co Ltd v Audco India Ltd, the judge held that the word 'negotiate' should be given a broad meaning, so that the reg. would cover any agent who expended time, money + his own resources to develop the market. The higher courts have yet to consider the point.

(i) a person who, in his capacity as an officer of a company or association, is empowered to enter into commitments binding on that company or association;

(ii) a partner who is lawfully authorised to enter into commitments binding on his partners;

(iii) a person who acts as an insolvency practitioner (as that expression is defined in section 388 of the Insolvency Act 1986) or the equivalent in any other jurisdiction;

"commission" means any part of the remuneration of a commercial agent which varies with the number or value of business transactions;

"EEA Agreement" means the Agreement on the European Economic Area signed at Oporto on 2nd May 1992 as adjusted by the Protocol signed at Brussels on 17th March 1993;

"member State" includes a State which is a contracting party to the EEA Agreement;

"restraint of trade clause" means an agreement restricting the business activities of a commercial agent following termination of the agency contract.

(2) These Regulations do not apply to—

(a) commercial agents whose activities are unpaid;

(b) commercial agents when they operate on commodity exchanges or in the commodity market;

(c) the Crown Agents for Overseas Governments and Administrations, as set up under the Crown Agents Act 1979, or its subsidiaries.

(3) The provisions of the Schedule to these Regulations have effect for the purpose of determining the persons whose activities as commercial agents are to be considered secondary.

It seems to be intended in particular to exclude individuals who have another job as well as working as agents, but it raises other issues too.

(4) These Regulations shall not apply to the persons referred to in paragraph (3) above.

(5) These Regulations do not extend to Northern Ireland.

Part II
Rights and Obligations

3. Duties of a commercial agent to his principal

(1) In performing his activities a commercial agent must look after the interests of his principal and act dutifully and in good faith.

(2) In particular, a commercial agent must—

- (a) make proper efforts to negotiate and, where appropriate, conclude the transactions he is instructed to take care of;
- (b) communicate to his principal all the necessary information available to him;
- (c) comply with reasonable instructions given by his principal.

4. Duties of a principal to his commercial agent

(1) In his relations with his commercial agent a principal must act dutifully and in good faith.

(2) In particular, a principal must—

- (a) provide his commercial agent with the necessary documentation relating to the goods concerned;
- (b) obtain for his commercial agent the information necessary for the performance of the agency contract, and in particular notify his commercial agent within a reasonable period once he anticipates that the volume of commercial transactions will be significantly lower than that which the commercial agent could normally have expected.

(3) A principal shall, in addition, inform his commercial agent within a reasonable period of his acceptance or refusal of, and of any non-execution by him of, a commercial transaction which the commercial agent has procured for him.

5. Prohibition on derogation from regulations 3 and 4 and consequence of breach

(1) The parties may not derogate from regulations 3 and 4 above.

(2) The law applicable to the contract shall govern the consequence of breach of the rights and obligations under regulations 3 and 4 above.

Part III
Remuneration

6. Form and amount of remuneration in absence of agreement

(1) In the absence of any agreement as to remuneration between the parties, a commercial agent shall be entitled to the remuneration that commercial agents appointed for the goods forming the subject of his agency contract are customarily allowed in the place where he carries on his activities and, if there is no such customary practice, a commercial agent shall be entitled to reasonable remuneration taking into account all the aspects of the transaction.

(2) This regulation is without prejudice to the application of any enactment or rule of law concerning the level of remuneration.

(3) Where a commercial agent is not remunerated (wholly or in part) by commission, regulations 7 to 12 below shall not apply.

7. Entitlement to commission on transactions concluded during agency contract

(1) A commercial agent shall be entitled to commission on commercial transactions concluded during the period covered by the agency contract—

(a) where the transaction has been concluded as a result of his action; or

(b) where the transaction is concluded with a third party whom he has previously acquired as a customer for transactions of the same kind.

(2) A commercial agent shall also be entitled to commission on transactions concluded during the period covered by the agency contract where he has an exclusive right to a specific geographical area or to a specific group of customers and where the transaction has been entered into with a customer belonging to that area or group.

8. Entitlement to commission on transactions concluded after agency contract has terminated

Subject to regulation 9 below, a commercial agent shall be entitled to commission on commercial transactions concluded after the agency contract has terminated if—

(a) the transaction is mainly attributable to his efforts during the period covered by the agency contract and if the transaction was entered into within a reasonable period after that contract terminated; or

(b) in accordance with the conditions mentioned in regulation 7 above, the order of the third party reached the principal or the commercial agent before the agency contract terminated.

9. Apportionment of commission between new and previous commercial agents

(1) A commercial agent shall not be entitled to the commission referred to in regulation 7 above if that commission is payable, by virtue of regulation 8 above, to the previous commercial agent, unless it is equitable because of the circumstances for the commission to be shared between the commercial agents.

(2) The principal shall be liable for any sum due under paragraph (1) above to the person entitled to it in accordance with that paragraph, and any sum which the other commercial agent receives to which he is not entitled shall be refunded to the principal.

10. When commission due and date for payment

(1) Commission shall become due as soon as, and to the extent that, one of the following circumstances occurs:

(a) the principal has executed the transaction; or

(b) the principal should, according to his agreement with the third party, have executed the transaction; or

(c) the third party has executed the transaction.

(2) Commission shall become due at the latest when the third party has executed his part of the transaction or should have done so if the principal had executed his part of the transaction, as he should have.

(3) The commission shall be paid not later than on the last day of the month following the quarter in which it became due, and, for the purposes of these Regulations, unless otherwise agreed between the parties, the first quarter period shall run from the date the agency contract takes effect, and subsequent periods shall run from that date in the third month thereafter or the beginning of the fourth month, whichever is the sooner.

(4) Any agreement to derogate from paragraphs (2) and (3) above to the detriment of the commercial agent shall be void.

11. Extinction of right to commission

(1) The right to commission can be extinguished only if and to the extent that—

(a) it is established that the contract between the third party and the principal will not be executed; and

(b) that fact is due to a reason for which the principal is not to blame.

(2) Any commission which the commercial agent has already received shall be refunded if the right to it is extinguished.

(3) Any agreement to derogate from paragraph (1) above to the detriment of the commercial agent shall be void.

12. Periodic supply of information as to commission due and right of inspection of principal's books

(1) The principal shall supply his commercial agent with a statement of the commission due, not later than the last day of the month following the quarter in which the commission has become due, and such statement shall set out the main components used in calculating the amount of the commission.

(2) A commercial agent shall be entitled to demand that he be provided with all the information (and in particular an extract from the books) which is available to his principal and which he needs in order to check the amount of the commission due to him.

(3) Any agreement to derogate from paragraphs (1) and (2) above shall be void.

(4) Nothing in this regulation shall remove or restrict the effect of, or prevent reliance upon, any enactment or rule of law which recognises the right of an agent to inspect the books of a principal.

Part IV
Conclusion and Termination of the Agency Contract

13. Right to signed written statement of terms of agency contract

(1) The commercial agent and principal shall each be entitled to receive from the other, on request, a signed written document setting out the terms of the agency contract including any terms subsequently agreed.

(2) Any purported waiver of the right referred to in paragraph (1) above shall be void.

14. Conversion of agency contract after expiry of fixed period

An agency contract for a fixed period which continues to be performed by both parties after that period has expired shall be deemed to be converted into an agency contract for an indefinite period.

15. Minimum periods of notice for termination of agency contract

(1) Where an agency contract is concluded for an indefinite period either party may terminate it by notice.

(2) The period of notice shall be—

(a) 1 month for the first year of the contract;

(b) 2 months for the second year commenced;

(c) 3 months for the third year commenced and for the subsequent years;

and the parties may not agree on any shorter periods of notice.

(3) If the parties agree on longer periods than those laid down in paragraph (2) above, the period of notice to be observed by the principal must not be shorter than that to be observed by the commercial agent.

(4) Unless otherwise agreed by the parties, the end of the period of notice must coincide with the end of a calendar month.

(5) The provisions of this regulation shall also apply to an agency contract for a fixed period where it is converted under regulation 14 above into an agency contract for an indefinite period subject to the proviso that the earlier fixed period must be taken into account in the calculation of the period of notice.

16. Savings with regard to immediate termination

These Regulations shall not affect the application of any enactment or rule of law which provides for the immediate termination of the agency contract—

(a) because of the failure of one party to carry out all or part of his obligations under that contract; or

(b) where exceptional circumstances arise.

17. Entitlement of commercial agent to indemnity or compensation on termination of agency contract

(1) This regulation has effect for the purpose of ensuring that the commercial agent is, after termination of the agency contract, indemnified in accordance with paragraphs (3) to (5) below or compensated for damage in accordance with paragraphs (6) and (7) below.

(2) Except where the agency contract otherwise provides, the commercial agent shall be entitled to be compensated rather than indemnified.

(3) Subject to paragraph (9) and to regulation 18 below, the commercial agent shall be entitled to an indemnity if and to the extent that—

- (a) he has brought the principal new customers or has significantly increased the volume of business with existing customers and the principal continues to derive substantial benefits from the business with such customers; and
- (b) the payment of this indemnity is equitable having regard to all the circumstances and, in particular, the commission lost by the commercial agent on the business transacted with such customers.

(4) The amount of the indemnity shall not exceed a figure equivalent to an indemnity for one year calculated from the commercial agent's average annual remuneration over the preceding five years and if the contract goes back less than five years the indemnity shall be calculated on the average for the period in question.

(5) The grant of an indemnity as mentioned above shall not prevent the commercial agent from seeking damages.

(6) Subject to paragraph (9) and to regulation 18 below, the commercial agent shall be entitled to compensation for the damage he suffers as a result of the termination of his relations with his principal.

(7) For the purpose of these Regulations such damage shall be deemed to occur particularly when the termination takes place in either or both of the following circumstances, namely circumstances which—

- (a) deprive the commercial agent of the commission which proper performance of the agency contract would have procured for him whilst providing his principal with substantial benefits linked to the activities of the commercial agent; or
- (b) have not enabled the commercial agent to amortize the costs and expenses that he had incurred in the performance of the agency contract on the advice of his principal.

(8) Entitlement to the indemnity or compensation for damage as provided for under paragraphs (2) to (7) above shall also arise where the agency contract is terminated as a result of the death of the commercial agent.

(9) The commercial agent shall lose his entitlement to the indemnity or compensation for damage in the instances provided for in paragraphs (2) to (8) above if within one year following termination of his agency contract he has not notified his principal that he intends pursuing his entitlement.

18. Grounds for excluding payment of indemnity or compensation under regulation 17

The indemnity or compensation referred to in regulation 17 above shall not be payable to the commercial agent where—

(a) the principal has terminated the agency contract because of default attributable to the commercial agent which would justify immediate termination of the agency contract pursuant to regulation 16 above; or

(b) the commercial agent has himself terminated the agency contract, unless such termination is justified—

(i) by circumstances attributable to the principal, or

(ii) on grounds of the age, infirmity or illness of the commercial agent in consequence of which he cannot reasonably be required to continue his activities; or

(c) the commercial agent, with the agreement of his principal, assigns his rights and duties under the agency contract to another person.

19. Prohibition on derogation from regulations 17 and 18

The parties may not derogate from regulations 17 and 18 to the detriment of the commercial agent before the agency contract expires.

20. Restraint of trade clauses

(1) A restraint of trade clause shall be valid only if and to the extent that—

(a) it is concluded in writing; and

(b) it relates to the geographical area or the group of customers and the geographical area entrusted to the commercial agent and to the kind of goods covered by his agency under the contract.

(2) A restraint of trade clause shall be valid for not more than two years after termination of the agency contract.

(3) Nothing in this regulation shall affect any enactment or rule of law which imposes other restrictions on the validity or enforceability of restraint of trade clauses or which enables a court to reduce the obligations on the parties resulting from such clauses.

Part V
Miscellaneous and Supplemental

21. Disclosure of information

Nothing in these Regulations shall require information to be given where such disclosure would be contrary to public policy.

22. Service of notice etc.

(1) Any notice, statement or other document to be given or supplied to a commercial agent or to be given or supplied to the principal under these Regulations may be so given or supplied:

(a) by delivering it to him;

(b) by leaving it at his proper address addressed to him by name;

(c) by sending it by post to him addressed either to his registered address or to the address of his registered or principal office;

or by any other means provided for in the agency contract.

(2) Any such notice, statement or document may—

(a) in the case of a body corporate, be given or served on the secretary or clerk of that body;

(b) in the case of a partnership, be given to or served on any partner or on any person having the control or management of the partnership business.

23. Transitional provisions

(1) Notwithstanding any provision in an agency contract made before 1st January 1994, these Regulations shall apply to that contract after that date and, accordingly any provision which is inconsistent with these Regulations shall have effect subject to them.

(2) Nothing in these Regulations shall affect the rights and liabilities of a commercial agent or a principal which have accrued before 1st January 1994.

Copyright and Rights in Databases Regulations 1997 (S.I. 1997 No. 3032)

Part III
Database Right

12. Interpretation

(1) In this Part—

'database' has the meaning given by section 3A(1) of the 1988 Act (as inserted by Regulation 6);

'extraction', in relation to any contents of a database, means the permanent or temporary transfer of those contents to another medium by any means or in any form;

'insubstantial', in relation to part of the contents of a database, shall be construed subject to Regulation 16(2);

'investment' includes any investment, whether of financial, human or technical resources;

'jointly', in relation to the making of a database, shall be construed in accordance with Regulation 14(6);

'lawful user', in relation to a database, means any person who (whether under a licence to do any of the acts restricted by any database right in the database or otherwise) has a right to use the database;

'maker', in relation to a database, shall be construed in accordance with Regulation 14;

're-utilisation', in relation to any contents of a database, means making those contents available to the public by any means;

'substantial', in relation to any investment, extraction or re-utilisation, means substantial in terms of quantity or quality or a combination of both.

(2) The making of a copy of a database available for use, on terms that it will or may be returned, otherwise than for direct or indirect economic or commercial advantage, through an establishment which is accessible to the public shall not be taken for the purposes of this Part to constitute extraction or re-utilisation of the contents of the database.

(3) Where the making of a copy of a database available through an establishment which is accessible to the public gives rise to a payment the amount of which does not go beyond what is necessary to cover the costs of the establishment, there is no direct or indirect economic or commercial advantage for the purposes of paragraph (2).

(4) Paragraph (2) does not apply to the making of a copy of a database available for on-the-spot reference use.

(5) Where a copy of a database has been sold within the EEA or the Isle of Man by, or with the consent of, the owner of the database right in the database, the further sale within the EEA or the Isle of Man of that copy shall not be taken for the purposes of this Part to constitute extraction or re-utilisation of the contents of the database.

13. Database right

(1) A property right ("database right") subsists, in accordance with this Part, in a database if there has been a substantial investment in obtaining, verifying or presenting the contents of the database.

(2) For the purposes of paragraph (1) it is immaterial whether or not the database or any of its contents is a copyright work, within the meaning of Part I of the 1988 Act.

(3) This Regulation has effect subject to Regulation 18.

14. The maker of a database

(1) Subject to paragraphs (2) to (4), the person who takes the initiative in obtaining, verifying or presenting the contents of a database and assumes the risk of investing in that obtaining, verification or presentation shall be regarded as the maker of, and as having made, the database.

(2) Where a database is made by an employee in the course of his employment, his employer shall be regarded as the maker of the database, subject to any agreement to the contrary.

(3) Subject to paragraph (4), where a database is made by Her Majesty or by an officer or servant of the Crown in the course of his duties, Her Majesty shall be regarded as the maker of the database.

(4) Where a database is made by or under the direction or control of the House of Commons or the House of Lords—

(a) the House by whom, or under whose direction or control, the database is made shall be regarded as the maker of the database, and

(b) if the database is made by or under the direction or control of both Houses, the two Houses shall be regarded as the joint makers of the database.

(4A) Where a database is made by or under the direction or control of the Scottish Parliament, the Scottish Parliamentary Corporate Body shall be regarded as the maker of the database.

(5) For the purposes of this Part a database is made jointly if two or more persons acting together in collaboration take the initiative in obtaining, verifying or presenting the contents of the database and assume the risk of investing in that obtaining, verification or presentation.

(6) References in this Part to the maker of a database shall, except as otherwise provided, be construed, in relation to a database which is made jointly, as references to all the makers of the database.

15. First ownership of database right

The maker of a database is the first owner of database right in it.

16. Acts infringing database right

(1) Subject to the provisions of this Part, a person infringes database right in a database if, without the consent of the owner of the right, he extracts or re-utilises all or a substantial part of the contents of the database.

(2) For the purposes of this Part, the repeated and systematic extraction or re-utilisation of insubstantial parts of the contents of a database may amount to the extraction or re-utilisation of a substantial part of those contents.

17. Term of protection

(1) Database right in a database expires at the end of the period of fifteen years from the end of the calendar year in which the making of the database was completed.

(2) Where a database is made available to the public before the end of the period referred to in paragraph (1), database right in the database shall expire fifteen years from the end of the calendar year in which the database was first made available to the public.

(3) Any substantial change to the contents of a database, including a substantial change resulting from the accumulation of successive additions, deletions or alterations, which would result in the database being considered to be a substantial new investment shall qualify the database resulting from that investment for its own term of protection.

(4) This Regulation has effect subject to Regulation 30.

18. Qualification for database right

(1) Database right does not subsist in a database unless, at the material time, its maker, or if it was made jointly, one or more of its makers, was—

(a) an individual who was a national of an EEA state or habitually resident within the EEA,

(b) a body which was incorporated under the law of an EEA state and which, at that time, satisfied one of the conditions in paragraph (2),

(c) a partnership or other unincorporated body which was formed under the law of an EEA state and which, at that time, satisfied the condition in paragraph (2)(a),

(d) an individual who was habitually resident within the Isle of Man,

(e) a body which was incorporated under the law of the Isle of Man and which, at that time, satisfied one of the conditions in paragraph (2A), or

(f) a partnership or other unincorporated body which was formed under the law of the Isle of Man and which, at that time, satisfied the condition in paragraph (2A)(a).

(2) The conditions mentioned in paragraphs (1)(b) and (c) are—

(a) that the body has its central administration or principal place of business within the EEA, or

(b) that the body has its registered office within the EEA and the body's operations are linked on an ongoing basis with the economy of an EEA state.

(2A) The conditions mentioned in paragraphs (1)(e) and (f) are—

(a) that the body has its central administration or principal place of business within the Isle of Man, or

(b) that the body has its registered office within the Isle of Man and the body's operations are linked on an ongoing basis with the economy of the Isle of Man.

(3) Paragraph (1) does not apply in any case falling within Regulation 14(4).

(4) In this Regulation—

(a) "EEA" and "EEA state" have the meaning given by section 172A of the 1988 Act;

(b) "the material time" means the time when the database was made, or if the making extended over a period, a substantial part of that period.

19. Avoidance of certain terms affecting lawful users

(1) A lawful user of a database which has been made available to the public in any manner shall be entitled to extract or re-utilise insubstantial parts of the contents of the database for any purpose.

(2) Where under an agreement a person has a right to use a database, or part of a database, which has been made available to the public in any manner, any term or condition in the agreement shall be void in so far as it purports to prevent that person from extracting or re-utilising insubstantial parts of the contents of the database, or of that part of the database, for any purpose.

20. Exceptions to database right

(1) Database right in a database which has been made available to the public in any manner is not infringed by fair dealing with a substantial part of its contents if—

(a) that part is extracted from the database by a person who is apart from this paragraph a lawful user of the database,

(b) it is extracted for the purpose of illustration for teaching or research and not for any commercial purpose, and

(c) the source is indicated.

(2) The provisions of Schedule 1 specify other acts which may be done in relation to a database notwithstanding the existence of database right.

23. Application of copyright provisions to database right

The following provisions of the 1988 Act apply in relation to database right and databases in which that right subsists as they apply in relation to copyright and copyright works—

sections 90 to 93 (dealing with rights in copyright works)
sections 96 to 102 (rights and remedies of copyright owner and exclusive licensee)
sections 113 and 114 (supplementary provisions relating to delivery up)
section 115 (jurisdiction of county court and sheriff court).

Consumer Protection (Distance Selling) Regulations 2000 (S.I. 2000 No. 2334)

3. Interpretation

(1) In these Regulations—

"the 2000 Act" means the Financial Services and Markets Act 2000;

"appointed representative" has the same meaning as in section 39(2) of the 2000 Act;

"authorised person" has the same meaning as in section 31(2) of the 2000 Act;

"breach" means contravention by a supplier of a prohibition in, or failure to comply with a requirement of, these Regulations;

"business" includes a trade or profession;

"consumer" means any natural person who, in contracts to which these Regulations apply, is acting for purposes which are outside his business;

"court" in relation to England and Wales and Northern Ireland means a county court or the High Court, and in relation to Scotland means the Sheriff Court or the Court of Session;

"credit" includes a cash loan and any other form of financial accommodation, and for this purpose "cash" includes money in any form;

"OFT" means the Office of Fair Trading;

"distance contract" means any contract concerning goods or services concluded between a supplier and a consumer under an organised distance sales or service provision scheme run by the supplier who, for the purpose of the contract, makes exclusive use of one or more means of distance communication up to and including the moment at which the contract is concluded;

"EEA Agreement" means the Agreement on the European Economic Area signed at Oporto on 2 May 1992 as adjusted by the Protocol signed at Brussels on 17 March 1993;

"enactment" includes an enactment comprised in, or in an instrument made under, an Act of the Scottish Parliament;

"enforcement authority" means the OFT, every weights and measures authority in Great Britain, and the Department of Enterprise, Trade and Investment in Northern Ireland;

"excepted contract" means a contract such as is mentioned in regulation 5(1);

"financial service" means any service of a banking, credit, insurance, personal pension, investment or payment nature;

"means of distance communication" means any means which, without the simultaneous physical presence of the supplier and the consumer, may be used for the conclusion of a contract between those parties; and an indicative list of such means is contained in Schedule 1;

"Member State" means a State which is a contracting party to the EEA Agreement;

"operator of a means of communication" means any public or private person whose business involves making one or more means of distance communication available to suppliers;

"period for performance" has the meaning given by regulation 19(2);

"personal credit agreement" has the meaning given by regulation 14(8);

"regulated activity" has the same meaning as in section 22 of the 2000 Act;

"related credit agreement" has the meaning given by regulation 15(5);

"supplier" means any person who, in contracts to which these Regulations apply, is acting in his commercial or professional capacity; and

"working days" means all days other than Saturdays, Sundays and public holidays.

(2) In the application of these Regulations to Scotland, for references to an "injunction" or an "interim injunction" there shall be substituted references to an "interdict" or an "interim interdict" respectively.

5. Excepted contracts

(1) The following are excepted contracts, namely any contract—

(a) for the sale or other disposition of an interest in land except for a rental agreement;

(b) for the construction of a building where the contract also provides for a sale or other disposition of an interest in land on which the building is constructed, except for a rental agreement;

(c) relating to financial services, a non-exhaustive list of which is contained in Schedule 2;

(d) concluded by means of an automated vending machine or automated commercial premises;

(e) concluded with a telecommunications operator through the use of a public pay-phone;

(f) concluded at an auction.

(2) References in paragraph (1) to a rental agreement—

(a) if the land is situated in England and Wales, are references to any agreement which does not have to be made in writing (whether or not in fact made in writing) because of section 2(5)(a) of the Law of Property (Miscellaneous Provisions) Act 1989;

(b) if the land is situated in Scotland, are references to any agreement for the creation, transfer, variation or extinction of an interest in land, which does not have to be made in writing (whether or not in fact made in writing) as provided for in section 1(2) and (7) of the Requirements of Writing (Scotland) Act 1995; and

(c) if the land is situated in Northern Ireland, are references to any agreement which is not one to which section II of the Statute of Frauds, (Ireland) 1695 applies.

(3) Paragraph (2) shall not be taken to mean that a rental agreement in respect of land situated outside the United Kingdom is not capable of being a distance contract to which these Regulations apply.

6. Contracts to which only part of these Regulations apply

(1) Regulations 7 to 20 shall not apply to a contract which is a "timeshare agreement" within the meaning of the Timeshare Act 1992 and to which that Act applies.

(2) Regulations 7 to 19(1) shall not apply to—

(a) contracts for the supply of food, beverages or other goods intended for everyday consumption supplied to the consumer's residence or to his workplace by regular roundsmen; or

(b) contracts for the provision of accommodation, transport, catering or leisure services, where the supplier undertakes, when the contract is concluded, to provide these services on a specific date or within a specific period.

(3) Regulations 19(2) to (8) and 20 do not apply to a contract for a "package" within the meaning of the Package Travel, Package Holidays and Package Tours Regulations 1992 which is sold or offered for sale in the territory of the Member States.

(4) Regulations 7 to 14, 17 to 20 and 25 do not apply to any contract which is made, and regulation 24 does not apply to any unsolicited services which are supplied, by an authorised person where the making or performance of that contract or the supply of those services, as the case may be, constitutes or is part of a regulated activity carried on by him.

(5) Regulations 7 to 9, 17 to 20 and 25 do not apply to any contract which is made, and regulation 24 does not apply to any unsolicited services which are supplied, by an appointed representative where the making or performance of that contract or the supply of those services, as the case may be, constitutes or is part of a regulated activity carried on by him.

7. Information required prior to the conclusion of the contract

(1) Subject to paragraph (4), in good time prior to the conclusion of the contract the supplier shall—

(a) provide to the consumer the following information—

(i) the identity of the supplier and, where the contract requires payment in advance, the supplier's address;

(ii) a description of the main characteristics of the goods or services;

(iii) the price of the goods or services including all taxes;

(iv) delivery costs where appropriate;

(v) the arrangements for payment, delivery or performance;

(vi) the existence of a right of cancellation except in the cases referred to in regulation 13;

(vii) the cost of using the means of distance communication where it is calculated other than at the basic rate;

(viii) the period for which the offer or the price remains valid; and

(ix) where appropriate, the minimum duration of the contract, in the case of contracts for the supply of goods or services to be performed permanently or recurrently;

(b) inform the consumer if he proposes, in the event of the goods or services ordered by the consumer being unavailable, to provide substitute goods or services (as the case may be) of equivalent quality and price; and

(c) inform the consumer that the cost of returning any such substitute goods to the supplier in the event of cancellation by the consumer would be met by the supplier.

(2) The supplier shall ensure that the information required by paragraph (1) is provided in a clear and comprehensible manner appropriate to the means of distance communication used, with due regard in particular to the principles of good faith in commercial transactions and the principles governing the protection of those who are unable to give their consent such as minors.

(3) Subject to paragraph (4), the supplier shall ensure that his commercial purpose is made clear when providing the information required by paragraph (1).

(4) In the case of a telephone communication, the identity of the supplier and the commercial purpose of the call shall be made clear at the beginning of the conversation with the consumer.

8. Written and additional information

(1) Subject to regulation 9, the supplier shall provide to the consumer in writing, or in another durable medium which is available and accessible to the consumer, the information referred to in paragraph (2), either—

(a) prior to the conclusion of the contract, or

(b) thereafter, in good time and in any event—

(i) during the performance of the contract, in the case of services; and

(ii) at the latest at the time of delivery where goods not for delivery to third parties are concerned.

(2) The information required to be provided by paragraph (1) is—

(a) the information set out in paragraphs (i) to (vi) of Regulation 7(1)(a);

(b) information about the conditions and procedures for exercising the right to cancel under regulation 10, including—

(i) where a term of the contract requires (or the supplier intends that it will require) that the consumer shall return the goods to the supplier in the event of cancellation, notification of that requirement; . . .

(ii) information as to whether the consumer or the supplier would be responsible under these Regulations for the cost of returning any goods to the supplier, or the cost of his recovering them, if the consumer cancels the contract under regulation 10;

(iii) in the case of a contract for the supply of services, information as to how the right to cancel may be affected by the consumer agreeing to performance of the services beginning before the end of the seven working day period referred to in regulation 12;

(c) the geographical address of the place of business of the supplier to which the consumer may address any complaints;

(d) information about any after-sales services and guarantees; and

(e) the conditions for exercising any contractual right to cancel the contract, where the contract is of an unspecified duration or a duration exceeding one year.

10. Right to cancel

(1) Subject to regulation 13, if within the cancellation period set out in regulations 11 and 12, the consumer gives a notice of cancellation to the supplier, or any other person previously notified by the supplier to the consumer as a person to whom notice of cancellation may be given, the notice of cancellation shall operate to cancel the contract.

(2) Except as otherwise provided by these Regulations, the effect of a notice of cancellation is that the contract shall be treated as if it had not been made.

(3) For the purposes of these Regulations, a notice of cancellation is a notice in writing or in another durable medium available and accessible to the supplier (or to the other person to whom it is given) which, however expressed, indicates the intention of the consumer to cancel the contract.

(4) A notice of cancellation given under this regulation by a consumer to a supplier or other person is to be treated as having been properly given if the consumer—

(a) leaves it at the address last known to the consumer and addressed to the supplier or other person by name (in which case it is to be taken to have been given on the day on which it was left);

(b) sends it by post to the address last known to the consumer and addressed to the supplier or other person by name (in which case, it is to be taken to have been given on the day on which it was posted);

(c) sends it by facsimile to the business facsimile number last known to the consumer (in which case it is to be taken to have been given on the day on which it is sent); or

(d) sends it by electronic mail, to the business electronic mail address last known to the consumer (in which case it is to be taken to have been given on the day on which it is sent).

(5) Where a consumer gives a notice in accordance with paragraph (4)(a) or (b) to a supplier who is a body corporate or a partnership, the notice is to be treated as having been properly given if—

(a) in the case of a body corporate, it is left at the address of, or sent to, the secretary or clerk of that body; or

(b) in the case of a partnership, it is left with or sent to a partner or a person having control or management of the partnership business.

11. Cancellation period in the case of contracts for the supply of goods

(1) For the purposes of regulation 10, the cancellation period in the case of contracts for the supply of goods begins with the day on which the contract is concluded and ends as provided in paragraphs (2) to (5).

(2) Where the supplier complies with regulation 8, the cancellation period ends on the expiry of the period of seven working days beginning with the day after the day on which the consumer receives the goods.

(3) Where a supplier who has not complied with regulation 8 provides to the consumer the information referred to in regulation 8(2), and does so in writing or in another durable medium available and accessible to the consumer, within the period of three months beginning with the day after the day on which the consumer receives the goods, the cancellation period ends on the expiry of the period of seven working days beginning with the day after the day on which the consumer receives the information.

(4) Where neither paragraph (2) nor (3) applies, the cancellation period ends on the expiry of the period of three months and seven working days beginning with the day after the day on which the consumer receives the goods.

(5) In the case of contracts for goods for delivery to third parties, paragraphs (2) to (4) shall apply as if the consumer had received the goods on the day on which they were received by the third party.

12. Cancellation period in the case of contracts for the supply of services

(1) For the purposes of regulation 10, the cancellation period in the case of contracts for the supply of services begins with the day on which the contract is concluded and ends as provided in paragraphs (2) to (4).

(2) Where the supplier complies with regulation 8 on or before the day on which the contract is concluded, the cancellation period ends on the expiry of the period of seven working days beginning with the day after the day on which the contract is concluded.

(3) Where a supplier who has not complied with regulation 8 on or before the day on which the contract is concluded provides to the consumer the information referred to in regulation 8(2) and (3), and does so in writing or in another durable medium available and accessible to the consumer, within the period of three months beginning with the day after the day on which the contract is concluded, the cancellation period ends on the expiry of the period of seven working days beginning with the day after the day on which the consumer receives the information.

(4) Where neither paragraph (2) nor (3) applies, the cancellation period ends on the expiry of the period of three months and seven working days beginning with the day after the day on which the contract is concluded.

13. Exceptions to the right to cancel

(1) Unless the parties have agreed otherwise, the consumer will not have the right to cancel the contract by giving notice of cancellation pursuant to regulation 10 in respect of contracts—

(a) for the supply of services if the performance of the contract has begun with the consumer's agreement—

(i) before the end of the cancellation period applicable under regulation 12(2); and

(ii) after the supplier has provided the information referred to in regulation 8(2);

(b) for the supply of goods or services the price of which is dependent on fluctuations in the financial market which cannot be controlled by the supplier;

(c) for the supply of goods made to the consumer's specifications or clearly personalised or which by reason of their nature cannot be returned or are liable to deteriorate or expire rapidly;

(d) for the supply of audio or video recordings or computer software if they are unsealed by the consumer;

(e) for the supply of newspapers, periodicals or magazines; or

(f) for gaming, betting or lottery services.

14. Recovery of sums paid by or on behalf of the consumer on cancellation, and return of security

(1) On the cancellation of a contract under regulation 10, the supplier shall reimburse any sum paid by or on behalf of the consumer under or in relation to the contract to the person by whom it was made free of any charge, less any charge made in accordance with paragraph (5).

(2) The reference in paragraph (1) to any sum paid on behalf of the consumer includes any sum paid by a creditor who is not the same person as the supplier under a personal credit agreement with the consumer.

(3) The supplier shall make the reimbursement referred to in paragraph (1) as soon as possible and in any case within a period not exceeding 30 days beginning with the day on which the notice of cancellation was given.

(4) Where any security has been provided in relation to the contract, the security (so far as it is so provided) shall, on cancellation under regulation 10, be treated as never having had effect and any property lodged with the supplier solely for the purposes of the security as so provided shall be returned by him forthwith.

(5) Subject to paragraphs (6) and (7), the supplier may make a charge, not exceeding the direct costs of recovering any goods supplied under the contract, where a term of the contract provides that the consumer must return any goods supplied if he cancels the contract under regulation 10 but the consumer does not comply with this provision or returns the goods at the expense of the supplier.

(6) Paragraph (5) shall not apply where—

(a) the consumer cancels in circumstances where he has the right to reject the goods under a term of the contract, including a term implied by virtue of any enactment, or

(b) the term requiring the consumer to return any goods supplied if he cancels the contract is an "unfair term" within the meaning of the Unfair Terms in Consumer Contracts Regulations 1999.

(7) Paragraph (5) shall not apply to the cost of recovering any goods which were supplied as substitutes for the goods ordered by the consumer.

(8) For the purposes of these Regulations, a personal credit agreement is an agreement between the consumer and any other person ("the creditor") by which the creditor provides the consumer with credit of any amount.

15. Automatic cancellation of a related credit agreement

(1) Where a notice of cancellation is given under regulation 10 which has the effect of cancelling the contract, the giving of the notice shall also have the effect of cancelling any related credit agreement.

(2) Where a related credit agreement is cancelled by virtue of paragraph (1), the supplier shall, if he is not the same person as the creditor under that agreement, forthwith on receipt of the notice of cancellation inform the creditor that the notice has been given.

(3) Where a related credit agreement is cancelled by virtue of paragraph (1)—

(a) any sum paid by or on behalf of the consumer under, or in relation to, the credit agreement which the supplier is not obliged to reimburse under regulation 14(1) shall be reimbursed, except for any sum which, if it had not already been paid, would have to be paid under subparagraph (b);

(b) the agreement shall continue in force so far as it relates to repayment of the credit and payment of interest, subject to regulation 16; and

(c) subject to subparagraph (b), the agreement shall cease to be enforceable.

(4) Where any security has been provided under a related credit agreement, the security, so far as it is so provided, shall be treated as never having had effect and any property lodged with the creditor solely for the purposes of the security as so provided shall be returned by him forthwith.

(5) For the purposes of this regulation and regulation 16, a "related credit agreement" means an agreement under which fixed sum credit which fully or partly covers the price under a contract cancelled under regulation 10 is granted—

(a) by the supplier, or

(b) by another person, under an arrangement between that person and the supplier.

(6) For the purposes of this regulation and regulation 16—

(a) "creditor" is a person who grants credit under a related credit agreement;

(b) "fixed sum credit" has the same meaning as in section 10 of the Consumer Credit Act 1974;

(c) "repayment" in relation to credit means repayment of money received by the consumer, and cognate expressions shall be construed accordingly; and

(d) "interest" means interest on money so received.

17. Restoration of goods by consumer after cancellation

(1) This regulation applies where a contract is cancelled under regulation 10 after the consumer has acquired possession of any goods under the contract other than any goods mentioned in regulation 13(1)(b) to (e).

(2) The consumer shall be treated as having been under a duty throughout the period prior to cancellation—

(a) to retain possession of the goods, and

(b) to take reasonable care of them.

(3) On cancellation, the consumer shall be under a duty to restore the goods to the supplier in accordance with this regulation, and in the meanwhile to retain possession of the goods and take reasonable care of them.

(4) The consumer shall not be under any duty to deliver the goods except at his own premises and in pursuance of a request in writing, or in another durable medium available and accessible to the consumer, from the supplier and given to the consumer either before, or at the time when, the goods are collected from those premises.

(5) If the consumer—

(a) delivers the goods (whether at his own premises or elsewhere) to any person to whom, under regulation 10(1), a notice of cancellation could have been given; or

(b) sends the goods at his own expense to such a person,

he shall be discharged from any duty to retain possession of the goods or restore them to the supplier.

(6) Where the consumer delivers the goods in accordance with paragraph (5)(a), his obligation to take care of the goods shall cease; and if he sends the goods in accordance with paragraph (5)(b), he shall be under a duty to take reasonable care to see that they are received by the supplier and not damaged in transit, but in other respects his duty to take care of the goods shall cease when he sends them.

(7) Where, at any time during the period of 21 days beginning with the day notice of cancellation was given, the consumer receives such a request as is mentioned in paragraph (4), and unreasonably refuses or unreasonably fails to comply with it, his duty to retain possession and take reasonable care of the goods shall continue until he delivers or sends the goods as mentioned in paragraph (5), but if within that period he does not receive such a request his duty to take reasonable care of the goods shall cease at the end of that period.

(8) Where—

(a) a term of the contract provides that if the consumer cancels the contract, he must return the goods to the supplier, and

(b) the consumer is not otherwise entitled to reject the goods under the terms of the contract or by virtue of any enactment,

paragraph (7) shall apply as if for the period of 21 days there were substituted the period of 6 months.

(9) Where any security has been provided in relation to the cancelled contract, the duty to restore goods imposed on the consumer by this regulation shall not be enforceable before the supplier has discharged any duty imposed on him by regulation 14(4) to return any property lodged with him as security on cancellation.

(10) Breach of a duty imposed by this regulation on a consumer is actionable as a breach of statutory duty.

19. Performance

(1) Unless the parties agree otherwise, the supplier shall perform the contract within a maximum of 30 days beginning with the day after the day the consumer sent his order to the supplier.

(2) Subject to paragraphs (7) and (8), where the supplier is unable to perform the contract because the goods or services ordered are not available, within the period for performance referred to in paragraph (1) or such other period as the parties agree ("the period for performance"), he shall—

(a) inform the consumer; and

(b) reimburse any sum paid by or on behalf of the consumer under or in relation to the contract to the person by whom it was made.

(3) The reference in paragraph (2)(b) to any sum paid on behalf of the consumer includes any sum paid by a creditor who is not the same person as the supplier under a personal credit agreement with the consumer.

(4) The supplier shall make the reimbursement referred to in paragraph (2)(b) as soon as possible and in any event within a period of 30 days beginning with the day after the day on which the period for performance expired.

(5) A contract which has not been performed within the period for performance shall be treated as if it had not been made, save for any rights or remedies which the consumer has under it as a result of the non-performance.

(6) Where any security has been provided in relation to the contract, the security (so far as it is so provided) shall, where the supplier is unable to perform the contract within the period for performance, be treated as never having had any effect and any property lodged with the supplier solely for the purposes of the security as so provided shall be returned by him forthwith.

(7) Where the supplier is unable to supply the goods or services ordered by the consumer, the supplier may perform the contract for the purposes of these Regulations by providing substitute goods or services (as the case may be) of equivalent quality and price provided that—

(a) this possibility was provided for in the contract;

(b) prior to the conclusion of the contract the supplier gave the consumer the information required by regulation 7(1)(b) and (c) in the manner required by regulation 7(2).

(8) In the case of outdoor leisure events which by their nature cannot be rescheduled, paragraph 2(b) shall not apply where the consumer and the supplier so agree.

25. No contracting-out

(1) A term contained in any contract to which these Regulations apply is void if, and to the extent that, it is inconsistent with a provision for the protection of the consumer contained in these Regulations.

(2) Where a provision of these Regulations specifies a duty or liability of the consumer in certain circumstances, a term contained in a contract to which these Regulations apply, other than a term to which paragraph (3) applies, is inconsistent with that provision if it purports to impose, directly or indirectly, an additional duty or liability on him in those circumstances.

(3) This paragraph applies to a term which requires the consumer to return any goods supplied to him under the contract if he cancels it under regulation 10.

(4) A term to which paragraph (3) applies shall, in the event of cancellation by the consumer under regulation 10, have effect only for the purposes of regulation 14(5) and 17(8).

(5) These Regulations shall apply notwithstanding any contract term which applies or purports to apply the law of a non-Member State if the contract has a close connection with the territory of a Member State.

Electronic Commerce (EC Directive) Regulations 2002 (S.I. 2002 No. 2013)

2. Interpretation

(1) In these Regulations and in the Schedule—

"commercial communication" means a communication, in any form, designed to promote, directly or indirectly, the goods, services or image of any person pursuing a commercial, industrial or craft activity or exercising a regulated profession, other than a communication—

(a) consisting only of information allowing direct access to the activity of that person including a geographic address, a domain name or an electronic mail address; or

(b) relating to the goods, services or image of that person provided that the communication has been prepared independently of the person making it (and for this purpose, a communication prepared without financial consideration is to be taken to have been prepared independently unless the contrary is shown);

"the Commission" means the Commission of the European Communities;

"consumer" means any natural person who is acting for purposes other than those of his trade, business or profession;

"coordinated field" means requirements applicable to information society service providers or information society services, regardless of whether they are of a general nature or specifically designed for them, and covers requirements with which the service provider has to comply in respect of—

(a) the taking up of the activity of an information society service, such as requirements concerning qualifications, authorisation or notification, and

(b) the pursuit of the activity of an information society service, such as requirements concerning the behaviour of the service provider, requirements regarding the quality or content of the service including those applicable to advertising and contracts, or requirements concerning the liability of the service provider, but does not cover requirements such as those applicable to goods as such, to the delivery of goods or to services not provided by electronic means;

"the Directive" means Directive 2000/31/EC of the European Parliament and of the Council of 8 June 2000 on certain legal aspects of information society services, in particular electronic commerce, in the Internal Market (Directive on electronic commerce);

"EEA Agreement" means the Agreement on the European Economic Area signed at Oporto on 2 May 1992 as adjusted by the Protocol signed at Brussels on 17 March 1993;

"enactment" includes an enactment comprised in Northern Ireland legislation and comprised in, or an instrument made under, an Act of the Scottish Parliament;

"enforcement action" means any form of enforcement action including, in particular—

(a) in relation to any legal requirement imposed by or under any enactment, any action taken with a view to or in connection with imposing any sanction (whether criminal or otherwise) for failure to observe or comply with it; and

(b) in relation to a permission or authorisation, anything done with a view to removing or restricting that permission or authorisation;

"enforcement authority" does not include courts but, subject to that, means any person who is authorised, whether by or under an enactment or otherwise, to take enforcement action;

"established service provider" means a service provider who is a national of a member State or a company or firm as mentioned in Article 48 of the Treaty and who effectively pursues an economic activity by virtue of which he is a service provider using a fixed establishment in a member State for an indefinite period, but the presence and use of the technical means and technologies required to provide the information society service do not, in themselves, constitute an establishment of the provider; in cases where it cannot be determined from which of a number of places of establishment a given service is provided, that service is to be regarded as provided from the place of establishment where the provider has the centre of his activities relating to that service; references to a service provider being established or to the establishment of a service provider shall be construed accordingly;

"information society services" (which is summarised in recital 17 of the Directive as covering "any service normally provided for remuneration, at a distance, by means of electronic equipment for the processing (including digital compression) and storage of data, and at the individual request of a recipient of a service") has the meaning set out in Article 2(a) of the Directive, (which refers to Article 1(2) of Directive 98/34/EC of the European Parliament and of the Council of 22 June 1998 laying down a procedure for the provision of information in the field of technical standards and regulations, as amended by Directive 98/48/EC of 20 July 1998);

"member State" includes a State which is a contracting party to the EEA Agreement;

"recipient of the service" means any person who, for professional ends or otherwise, uses an information society service, in particular for the purposes of seeking information or making it accessible;

"regulated profession" means any profession within the meaning of either Article 1(d) of Council Directive 89/48/EEC of 21 December 1988 on a general system for the recognition of higher-education diplomas awarded on completion of professional education and training of at least three years' duration or of Article 1(f) of Council Directive 92/51/EEC of 18 June 1992 on a second general system for the recognition of professional education and training to supplement Directive 89/48/EEC;

"service provider" means any person providing an information society service;

"the Treaty" means the treaty establishing the European Community.

(2) In regulation 4 and 5, "requirement" means any legal requirement under the law of the United Kingdom, or any part of it, imposed by or under any enactment or otherwise.

(3) Terms used in the Directive other than those in paragraph (1) above shall have the same meaning as in the Directive.

6. General information to be provided by a person providing an information society service

(1) A person providing an information society service shall make available to the recipient of the service and any relevant enforcement authority, in a form and manner which is easily, directly and permanently accessible, the following information—

(a) the name of the service provider;

(b) the geographic address at which the service provider is established;

(c) the details of the service provider, including his electronic mail address, which make it possible to contact him rapidly and communicate with him in a direct and effective manner;

(d) where the service provider is registered in a trade or similar register available to the public, details of the register in which the service provider is entered and his registration number, or equivalent means of identification in that register;

(e) where the provision of the service is subject to an authorisation scheme, the particulars of the relevant supervisory authority;

(f) where the service provider exercises a regulated profession—

(i) the details of any professional body or similar institution with which the service provider is registered;

(ii) his professional title and the member State where that title has been granted;

(iii) a reference to the professional rules applicable to the service provider in the member State of establishment and the means to access them; and

(g) where the service provider undertakes an activity that is subject to value added tax, the identification number referred to in Article 22(1) of the sixth Council Directive 77/388/EEC of 17 May 1977 on the harmonisation of the laws of the member States relating to turnover taxes—Common system of value added tax: uniform basis of assessment.

(2) Where a person providing an information society service refers to prices, these shall be indicated clearly and unambiguously and, in particular, shall indicate whether they are inclusive of tax and delivery costs.

7. Commercial communications

A service provider shall ensure that any commercial communication provided by him and which constitutes or forms part of an information society service shall—

(a) be clearly identifiable as a commercial communication;

(b) clearly identify the person on whose behalf the commercial communication is made;

(c) clearly identify as such any promotional offer (including any discount, premium or gift) and ensure that any conditions which must be met to qualify for it are easily accessible, and presented clearly and unambiguously; and

(d) clearly identify as such any promotional competition or game and ensure that any conditions for participation are easily accessible and presented clearly and unambiguously.

9. Information to be provided where contracts are concluded by electronic means

(1) Unless parties who are not consumers have agreed otherwise, where a contract is to be concluded by electronic means a service provider shall, prior to an order being placed by the recipient of a service, provide to that recipient in a clear, comprehensible and unambiguous manner the information set out in (a) to (d) below—

(a) the different technical steps to follow to conclude the contract;

(b) whether or not the concluded contract will be filed by the service provider and whether it will be accessible;

(c) the technical means for identifying and correcting input errors prior to the placing of the order; and

(d) the languages offered for the conclusion of the contract.

(2) Unless parties who are not consumers have agreed otherwise, a service provider shall indicate which relevant codes of conduct he subscribes to and give information on how those codes can be consulted electronically.

(3) Where the service provider provides terms and conditions applicable to the contract to the recipient, the service provider shall make them available to him in a way that allows him to store and reproduce them.

(4) The requirements of paragraphs (1) and (2) above shall not apply to contracts concluded exclusively by exchange of electronic mail or by equivalent individual communications.

11. Placing of the order

(1) Unless parties who are not consumers have agreed otherwise, where the recipient of the service places his order through technological means, a service provider shall—

(a) acknowledge receipt of the order to the recipient of the service without undue delay and by electronic means; and

(b) make available to the recipient of the service appropriate, effective and accessible technical means allowing him to identify and correct input errors prior to the placing of the order.

(2) For the purposes of paragraph (1)(a) above—

(a) the order and the acknowledgement of receipt will be deemed to be received when the parties to whom they are addressed are able to access them; and

(b) the acknowledgement of receipt may take the form of the provision of the service paid for where that service is an information society service.

(3) The requirements of paragraph (1) above shall not apply to contracts concluded exclusively by exchange of electronic mail or by equivalent individual communications.

17. Mere conduit

(1) Where an information society service is provided which consists of the transmission in a communication network of information provided by a recipient of the service or the provision of access to a communication network, the service provider (if he otherwise would) shall not be liable for damages or for any other pecuniary remedy or for any criminal sanction as a result of that transmission where the service provider—

(a) did not initiate the transmission;

(b) did not select the receiver of the transmission; and

(c) did not select or modify the information contained in the transmission.

(2) The acts of transmission and of provision of access referred to in paragraph (1) include the automatic, intermediate and transient storage of the information transmitted where:

(a) this takes place for the sole purpose of carrying out the transmission in the communication network, and

(b) the information is not stored for any period longer than is reasonably necessary for the transmission.

18. Caching

Where an information society service is provided which consists of the transmission in a communication network of information provided by a recipient of the service, the service provider (if he otherwise would) shall not be liable for damages or for any other pecuniary remedy or for any criminal sanction as a result of that transmission where—

(a) the information is the subject of automatic, intermediate and temporary storage where that storage is for the sole purpose of making more efficient onward transmission of the information to other recipients of the service upon their request, and

(b) the service provider—

(i) does not modify the information;

(ii) complies with conditions on access to the information;

(iii) complies with any rules regarding the updating of the information, specified in a manner widely recognised and used by industry;

(iv) does not interfere with the lawful use of technology, widely recognised and used by industry, to obtain data on the use of the information; and

(v) acts expeditiously to remove or to disable access to the information he has stored upon obtaining actual knowledge of the fact that the information at the initial source of the transmission has been removed from the network, or access to it has been disabled, or that a court or an administrative authority has ordered such removal or disablement.

19. Hosting

Where an information society service is provided which consists of the storage of information provided by a recipient of the service, the service provider (if he otherwise would) shall not be liable for damages or for any other pecuniary remedy or for any criminal sanction as a result of that storage where—

(a) the service provider—

 (i) does not have actual knowledge of unlawful activity or information and, where a claim for damages is made, is not aware of facts or circumstances from which it would have been apparent to the service provider that the activity or information was unlawful; or

 (ii) upon obtaining such knowledge or awareness, acts expeditiously to remove or to disable access to the information, and

(b) the recipient of the service was not acting under the authority or the control of the service provider.

Privacy and Electronic Communications (EC Directive) Regulations 2003 (S.I. 2003 No. 2426)

2. Interpretation

(1) In these Regulations—

"bill" includes an invoice, account, statement or other document of similar character and "billing" shall be construed accordingly;

"call" means a connection established by means of a telephone service available to the public allowing two-way communication in real time;

"communication" means any information exchanged or conveyed between a finite number of parties by means of a public electronic communications service, but does not include information conveyed as part of a programme service, except to the extent that such information can be related to the identifiable subscriber or user receiving the information;

"communications provider" has the meaning given by section 405 of the Communications Act 2003;

"corporate subscriber" means a subscriber who is—

(a) a company within the meaning of section 735(1) of the Companies Act 1985;

(b) a company incorporated in pursuance of a royal charter or letters patent;

(c) a partnership in Scotland;

(d) a corporation sole; or

(e) any other body corporate or entity which is a legal person distinct from its members;

"the Directive" means Directive 2002/58/EC of the European Parliament and of the Council of 12 July 2002 concerning the processing of personal data and the protection of privacy in the electronic communications sector (Directive on privacy and electronic communications);

"electronic communications network" has the meaning given by section 32 of the Communications Act 2003;

"electronic communications service" has the meaning given by section 32 of the Communications Act 2003;

"electronic mail" means any text, voice, sound or image message sent over a public electronic communications network which can be stored in the network or in the recipient's terminal equipment until it is collected by the recipient and includes messages sent using a short message service;

"enactment" includes an enactment comprised in, or in an instrument made under, an Act of the Scottish Parliament;

"individual" means a living individual and includes an unincorporated body of such individuals;

"the Information Commissioner" and "the Commissioner" both mean the Commissioner appointed under section 6 of the Data Protection Act 1998;

"information society service" has the meaning given in regulation 2(1) of the Electronic Commerce (EC Directive) Regulations 2002;

"location data" means any data processed in an electronic communications network indicating the geographical position of the terminal equipment of a user of a public electronic communications service, including data relating to—

(f) the latitude, longitude or altitude of the terminal equipment;

(g) the direction of travel of the user; or

(h) the time the location information was recorded;

"OFCOM" means the Office of Communications as established by section 1 of the Office of Communications Act 2002;

"programme service" has the meaning given in section 201 of the Broadcasting Act 1990;

"public communications provider" means a provider of a public electronic communications network or a public electronic communications service;

"public electronic communications network" has the meaning given in section 151 of the Communications Act 2003;

"public electronic communications service" has the meaning given in section 151 of the Communications Act 2003;

"subscriber" means a person who is a party to a contract with a provider of public electronic communications services for the supply of such services;

"traffic data" means any data processed for the purpose of the conveyance of a communication on an electronic communications network or for the billing in respect of that communication and includes data relating to the routing, duration or time of a communication;

"user" means any individual using a public electronic communications service; and

"value added service" means any service which requires the processing of traffic data or location data beyond that which is necessary for the transmission of a communication or the billing in respect of that communication.

(2) Expressions used in these Regulations that are not defined in paragraph (1) and are defined in the Data Protection Act 1998 shall have the same meaning as in that Act.

(3) Expressions used in these Regulations that are not defined in paragraph (1) or the Data Protection Act 1998 and are defined in the Directive shall have the same meaning as in the Directive.

(4) Any reference in these Regulations to a line shall, without prejudice to paragraph (3), be construed as including a reference to anything that performs the function of a line, and "connected", in relation to a line, is to be construed accordingly.

6. Confidentiality of communications

(1) Subject to paragraph (4), a person shall not use an electronic communications network to store information, or to gain access to information stored, in the terminal equipment of a subscriber or user unless the requirements of paragraph (2) are met.

(2) The requirements are that the subscriber or user of that terminal equipment—

(a) is provided with clear and comprehensive information about the purposes of the storage of, or access to, that information; and

(b) is given the opportunity to refuse the storage of or access to that information.

(3) Where an electronic communications network is used by the same person to store or access information in the terminal equipment of a subscriber or user on more than one occasion, it is sufficient for the purposes of this regulation that the requirements of paragraph (2) are met in respect of the initial use.

(4) Paragraph (1) shall not apply to the technical storage of, or access to, information—

(a) for the sole purpose of carrying out or facilitating the transmission of a communication over an electronic communications network; or

(b) where such storage or access is strictly necessary for the provision of an information society service requested by the subscriber or user.

22. Use of electronic mail for direct marketing purposes

(1) This regulation applies to the transmission of unsolicited communications by means of electronic mail to individual subscribers.

(2) Except in the circumstances referred to in paragraph (3), a person shall neither transmit, nor instigate the transmission of, unsolicited communications for the purposes of direct marketing by means of electronic mail unless the recipient of the electronic mail has previously notified the sender that he consents for the time being to such communications being sent by, or at the instigation of, the sender.

(3) A person may send or instigate the sending of electronic mail for the purposes of direct marketing where—

- (a) that person has obtained the contact details of the recipient of that electronic mail in the course of the sale or negotiations for the sale of a product or service to that recipient;
- (b) the direct marketing is in respect of that person's similar products and services only; and
- (c) the recipient has been given a simple means of refusing (free of charge except for the costs of the transmission of the refusal) the use of his contact details for the purposes of such direct marketing, at the time that the details were initially collected, and, where he did not initially refuse the use of the details, at the time of each subsequent communication.

(4) A subscriber shall not permit his line to be used in contravention of paragraph (2).

23. Use of electronic mail for direct marketing purposes where the identity or address of the sender is concealed

A person shall neither transmit, nor instigate the transmission of, a communication for the purposes of direct marketing by means of electronic mail—

(a) where the identity of the person on whose behalf the communication has been sent has been disguised or concealed; or

(b) where a valid address to which the recipient of the communication may send a request that such communications cease has not been provided.

EC Treaty

Article 81

1. The following shall be prohibited as incompatible with the internal market: all agreements between undertakings, decisions by associations of undertakings and concerted practices which may affect trade between Member States and which have as their object or effect the prevention, restriction or distortion of competition within the internal market, and in particular those which:

   (a) directly or indirectly fix purchase or selling prices or any other trading conditions;

   (b) limit or control production, markets, technical development, or investment;

   (c) share markets or sources of supply;

   (d) apply dissimilar conditions to equivalent transactions with other trading parties, thereby placing them at a competitive disadvantage;

   (e) make the conclusion of contracts subject to acceptance by the other parties of supplementary obligations which, by their nature or according to commercial usage, have no connection with the subject of such contracts.

2. Any agreements or decisions prohibited pursuant to this Article shall be automatically void.

3. The provisions of paragraph 1 may, however, be declared inapplicable in the case of:

   – any agreement or category of agreements between undertakings,

   – any decision or category of decisions by associations of undertakings,

   – any concerted practice or category of concerted practices,

   which contributes to improving the production or distribution of goods or to promoting technical or economic progress, while allowing consumers a fair share of the resulting benefit, and which does not:

   (a) impose on the undertakings concerned restrictions which are not indispensable to the attainment of these objectives;

   (b) afford such undertakings the possibility of eliminating competition in respect of a substantial part of the products in question.

Article 82

Any abuse by one or more undertakings of a dominant position within the internal market or in a substantial part of it shall be prohibited as incompatible with the internal market in so far as it may affect trade between Member States.

Such abuse may, in particular, consist in:

(a) directly or indirectly imposing unfair purchase or selling prices or other unfair trading conditions;

(b) limiting production, markets or technical development to the prejudice of consumers;

(c) applying dissimilar conditions to equivalent transactions with other trading parties, thereby placing them at a competitive disadvantage;

(d) making the conclusion of contracts subject to acceptance by the other parties of supplementary obligations which, by their nature or according to commercial usage, have no connection with the subject of such contracts.

Index

abuse of dominant position 351–2, 448
acceptance by buyer 21–2
 IT software 279
 non-acceptance 23–4
acceptance of offer 10–11
acceptor 151
accounting
 agency and 85
action for damages 25
action for the price 23
advertising
 consumer credit business 98
 duties of distributor 92
advising banks 151
agency 73, 74–88
 accounting arrangements 85
 appointment 80, 88
 authority of agent 80
 commission 84–5
 competition law and 75–6, 339
 del credere agency 80
 distribution agreements compared 90
 drafting agency agreements 75–88
  statutory restrictions 77–8
 duration of agreement 80
 financial provisions 84–5
 initial advice 74–5
 interpretation of agency agreements 79
 introduction to agency agreements 79–80
 no authority clauses and 6–7
 operations of agent 80
 particular points to consider 88
 precedents for agency agreements 78
 preliminary considerations 75–9
 reference to principles of agency law 76–7
 rights and duties of agent 81–3
 rights and duties of principal 83–4
 structure of agreements 94
 termination of agreement 80, 85–8
agreement
 agreement to agree 14
 failure to agree 11
 price 14
all moneys clauses 29
anti-competitive agreements 75–6
appointment
 agents 80, 88
 distributor 90–1
artistic works, copyright 204–11
 level of effort 205–7
 originality 205
assignment
 no assignment clauses 8

bailment 71
banks
 bank notes 140
banks – *continued*
 bankers' drafts 140
 international sales 151–3
 liabilities 151–3
 overdrafts 104
 responsibilities 151–3
barter 57
battle of the forms 10
 prevail clauses and 6, 10
Berne Copyright Convention 225
bills of exchange 137–9, 141–4
 claused bills 143
 documentary bills 143–4
 example 145
 holder in due course 143
 liability on 143
 parties 141
 term bills and sight bills 141–2
 underlying sales contract and 142–3
 use 142
bills of lading 126–7
boiler-plate clauses 6–8
BOLERO system 135
breach of contract 12
 remedies 12
  see also individual remedies
buyers
 age and experience of 45
 checks on 32–3
 duties 20–2
 insolvency 7, 24
 knowledge and understanding of exclusion clauses 48–9
 rejection of goods 24–5
 rights 24–6

care and skill, reasonable *see* reasonable care and skill
carriage and insurance paid to (CIP) 134
carriage paid to (CPT) 134
certification trade marks 179
charge cards 104
charges
 retention of title clauses and 32
cheques 140, 141
 guarantee cards 104
choice of jurisdiction and law
 contracting out 115
 e-commerce 293
 EU regulation 113–16, 118–19
 first to file 115–16
 habitual residence 119
 local mandatory rules 117
 Rome Convention 116–19
collateral contracts 10
collecting banks 151, 152
collective trade marks 179

Commercial Agents (Council Directive) Regulations 1993
text 420–6
commercial law 3
principles 3–4
sources 4
commission
agency and 84–5
Commission's powers 338–9
common law
exclusion clauses and 41
Community Trade Mark 195
compensation
for employees as inventors 256–7
termination of agency agreement and 86–8
Competition Act 1998
text 415–17
competition law
advice to clients 331
agency agreements and 75–6
distribution agreements and 90
drafting and 332
English
appreciability 335
avoiding infringement 334–6
block exemptions 336
Chapter I prohibition 333–4
Chapter II prohibition 334
consequences of infringement 334
enforcement 334
Enterprise Act 2002 336
financial penalties 334
investigative powers 334
limited immunity 335–6
parallel exemptions 335
transitional provisions 336
vertical agreements 335
European Economic Area (EEA) 332
European Union (EU) 75–6, 333, 336–8
avoiding impact of Art 81 EC 339–41
block exemption 341–5, 350–1
Commission's powers 338–9
de minimis provision 340
effect of infringement 337–8
franchising agreements 354
guidelines 341
non-appreciable affectation of trade 341
parent and subsidiary companies 339
selective distribution agreements 346
vertical agreements 342–5
licensing agreements and 348, 349–52
drafting 351
patents and 347
types of agreement and 332–3
which law applies 331–2
computer crime
hacking/unauthorised access 285
jurisdiction 287
modification of computer material 286–7
ulterior intent offence 285–6
see also **software**
computer systems
finance leases 68–9
conditional sale agreements 58
conditional sales 63–4, 104
hire purchase compared 66–7
confidentiality 263–4
agency and 82
distributors and 93
elements 264–6
intellectual property 164, 166
privacy right 268–9
remedies 266–8
confirming banks 151, 152, 153
consequential loss 12
consideration 10
construction of exclusion clauses 39–40
consumer contracts 28
choice of jurisdiction and law and 115, 117–18
consumers 34
credit 34, 97–8
classification of agreements 105–6
commercial work and 98
conditional sale 104
consumer credit agreements 99–103
credit cards 20, 104, 302
credit sale 104
extortionate bargains 102–3
hire purchase 58, 103
loans 103–4
outline of legislation 98–9
overdrafts 104
types of credit 105
distance selling 299–300
e-commerce 296–301
extortionate bargains 102–3
unfair relationships 102–3
unfair terms 42–3
Consumer Protection (Distance Selling) Regulations 2000 299–300
text 431–9
container transport 128
***contra proferentem* 39**
contracts
basics 10–12
drafting 4–5
limitation of liability 8, 49–50
see also individual topics
copyright 163, 165
artistic works 204–11
level of effort 205–7
originality 205
databases *see* **database right**
developments in law 224
duration 207–8, 214
e-commerce 295–6
entrepreneurial 211–14
information technology and
computer software 216, 222, 271–2
internet 222–3, 224, 284, 295–6
infringement 214–20
computer software 216
defences 217–19
fair dealing 217–19
primary 216
remedies 221

copyright – *continued*
secondary 217
international protection 224–5
meaning 203–4
moral rights 210–11
overlap with design right 243–4
ownership 208–10, 213–14
public performance collecting societies 223
recorded works 207
Copyright, Designs and Patents Act 1988
text 380–403
Copyright and Rights in Databases Regulations 1997
text 427–30
cost and freight (CFR) 133–4
cost insurance freight (CIF) 133
course of dealing 4
exclusion clauses and 38
courts
exclusion clauses and 46
credit 15, 34, 97–8
back to back credits 150
classification of agreements 105–6
commercial work and 98
conditional sale 104
Consumer Credit Act 2006 97, 101, 102
consumer credit agreements 99–103
control 32–3
credit cards 20, 104, 302
credit risk insurance 33
credit sale 104
DC agreement 105
determining 106
documentary *see* **documentary credits**
extortionate bargains 102–3
hire purchase 58, 103
loans 103–4
negotiation 150
outline of legislation 98–9
overdrafts 104
revolving 150
standby 150
straight 150
three-party DCS agreement 106
two-party DCS agreement 105
types of activity 106
types of credit 105
unfair relationships 102–3
custom and usage 4
quality and 20

damage
passing off and 171–2
damages 12
action for 25
late payment 21
misrepresentation 26
non-acceptance of goods 23–4
data protection 287
automated decision taking 312
blocking 313
civil damages 316–17
compensation 312
data protection – *continued*
criminal offences 316–17
data controller 307
disclosure restrictions 313–14
data processing conditions 310–11
Data Protection Act 1998 305–6
checklist for application 311
overview 306–7
destruction 313
direct marketing 312
enforcement 316–17
erasure 313
exemptions 314–15
crime prevention 315–16
legal proceedings 315–16
Information Commissioner 309, 313, 322
discretion of 313
legislation 305–6
penalties 316–17
personal data 307–9
processing *see* processing of personal data
sensitive 311
principle of good practice 309–10
privacy 301, 305
processing of personal data 307
damage or distress 312
direct marketing 312
fair and lawful 313–14
likely to cause damage or distress 312
limited purposes 314
rectification 313
requests from outside EC 316
restrictions on disclosure
fair and lawful processing 313–14
processed for limited purposes 314
sensitive personal data 311
subject access 312
subjects, rights of 311–13
see also **freedom of information**
database right 165, 221–2, 287–9
application 229–30
Copyright and Rights in Databases Regulations 1997 text 427–30
definition of database 227–8
duration 228, 288
exceptions 229, 288–9
infringement 228–9, 288
ownership 228, 288
qualifications for 228, 288
DC agreement 105
DCS agreement
three-party 106
two-party 105
debit cards 104
debt factoring 33
deception
refusal of trade mark registration and 181–2
defences
copyright infringement 217–20
patent infringement 260–1
trade mark infringement 193–4
definitions clauses 5
del credere agency 80

delivered at frontier (DAF) 135
delivered duty paid/unpaid (DDP/DDU) 135
delivered ex quay (DEQ) 134–5
delivered ex ship (DES) 134
delivery
definition 14–15
duty to take 21–2
international sales 124, 128–35
IT hardware 274
IT software 279
methods 15
payment for 17–18
place 17
right quantity 18
seller's duty 16
stoppage in transit 23
time 16–17
description, sale by 18
design right 163
definition 231, 234–5
designs that can be protected 236–7
duration 237, 242
EU and 244
exclusions 236, 240–2
exhaustion 238
grace period 235–6
information technology 272
infringement 238, 242–3
innocent infringement 243
licences of right 244
originality 239–40
overlap with copyright 243–4
ownership 237–8, 242
registered 165, 232–3, 234–9, 245
remedies 238–9, 243
scope 237
semiconductor chip protection 244, 272–3
unregistered 166, 233, 239–44, 245
detachable goods 32
discharge of contracts 11–12
distance selling
consumer protection 299–300
Consumer Protection (Distance Selling) Regulations 2000 431–9
distribution agreements 73
advantages and disadvantages 74
agency agreements compared 90
appointment of distributor 90–1
competition 90, 93
confidentiality 93
distributor's duties 91–3
drafting 89–94
initial advice 89
intellectual property 93
interpretation 90
introduction 90–1
minimum target obligations 91–2
miscellaneous provisions 94
sale of goods terms 93
selective distribution agreements 346
stock 92
structure 94
supplier's duties 93
distribution agreements – *continued*
termination 93–4
documentary credits 137–8, 144–50
assignment 150
autonomy 147
back to back credits 150
definition 147
duration 153
example 146
expiry 153
issuing bank 149
negotiation credit 150
opening 153
payment 150
period of validity 149–50
practical matters 149–50
revolving credit 150
standby credit 150
straight credit 150
strict compliance 148, 150
fraud exception 148–9
transfer 150
Uniform Customs and Practice 147
duty defining clauses 36

e-commerce 4
business to business 296, 301
business to consumer 296–301, 302
choice of jurisdiction and law and 115, 293
Consumer Protection (Distance Selling) Regulations 2000 299–300
contract formation 292–3
acceptance 292–3
electronic execution 293
offer 292
security 293
copyright 295–6
definition 291
domain names 294
Electronic Commerce (EC Directive) Regulations 2002 296–9
intellectual property and 294–6
jurisdiction 293
legal framework 291–2
legislation 296–301
liability of ISSPs 302–3
passing off 294
payment 301–2
Privacy and Electronic Communications (EC Directive) Regulations 2003 301
trade marks 294–5
e-mail
contracts and 292, 293, 302
see also **information technology**
***ejusdem generis* 39**
Electronic Commerce (EC Directive) Regulations 2002 296–9
text 440–4
employees
patents and 256–7
employment contracts
choice of jurisdiction and law and 115, 117–18
enforcement 4

Enterprise Act 2002
cartel offences, text 418–19
entire agreement clauses 6, 10
entry rights
retention of title and 30
European Economic Area (EEA) 332
European Union (EU)
abuse of dominant position 351–2, 448
agency agreements and 77
choice of jurisdiction regulation 113–16, 118–19
Community Trade Mark 195
competition law 75–6, 333, 336–8, 448
avoiding impact of Art 81 EC 339–41
block exemption 341–5, 350–1
de minimis provision 340
effect of infringement 337–8
franchising agreements 354
guidelines 341
non-appreciable affectation of trade 341
parent and subsidiary companies 339
selective distribution agreements 346
vertical agreements 342–5
copyright and 208, 224
design right and 232, 239
distributors and 92
e-commerce 291–2, 296–301
exhaustion of rights 353
intellectual property rights and 347–54
trade marks and 179–80, 183
ex works (EXW) 130–1
exchange and barter contracts 57
exclusion clauses 12
advice 37
attempt to exclude everything 52
basic rules 35–6
common law principles 41
consequential loss 55
construction 39–40
definition 36
drafting 48, 51–6
effectiveness 37–8
exclusion or limitation 49–50
incorporation 38–9, 49
indirect loss 55
instructions 37
IT hardware contracts 276
IT software 280
loss of profits 55
positive 51
preparation 36–7
printing and layout 48
reasonableness 41–2
allocation of risk and insurance 47
buyer's knowledge and understanding 48–9
choice 46
clauses subject to test 51
general principles 43–4
price 47
relationship between parties and 44–6
trade associations and 47–8
tactics 48–9, 50
testing 37
exclusion clauses – *continued*
unfair terms legislation 56
unfair terms legislation and 40–2, 53–4
void 41, 50–1
***expressio unius est exclusio alterius* 39**
extortionate credit bargains 102–3

factoring
debt factoring 33
failure to agree 11
finance leases 68–9
computer systems 68–9
financial pressure 45
financing
against receivables 71–2
against stock 70–1
bailment 71
international sale agreements 137–50
security over stock 71
wholesale finance 70–1
fitness for purpose
goods 19
services 63
fixed-sum credit 105
force majeure clauses 7–8, 17, 27–8, 51–3
drafting 53
frustration of contract 52–3
meaning of 'force majeure' 52
franchising agreements 95
EU competition law and 354
fraud
documentary credits and 148–9
e-commerce 302
free alongside ship (FAS) 131
free on board (FOB) 131–2
free carrier (FCA) 131
freedom of information 318
absolute exemptions 320–2
accessible information 319
code of practice 320
Freedom of Information Act 2000 306
application of 318–19
policing 322
human rights and 322–3
Information Commissioner 322
publication schemes 319–20
qualified exemptions 320–2
right to information 319
see also **data protection**
frustration 12
definition 52
effect 52
force majeure clauses and 52–3
future goods 13

goods 45
definition 13
repair 28
replacement 28
sale *see* **sale of goods**
goodwill
passing off and 168–9

hardware contracts 273
leasing 68–9, 273–4
negotiation 273
sale 274–6
hire agreements 58
hire purchase 58, 63–4, 103
arrangements 64–6
block discounting 65
conditional sale and 66–7
development of 64
direct collection 65
human rights
freedom of information and 322–3

incorporation
exclusion clauses 38–9, 49
Incoterms 128–35
C group 132–4
D group 134–5
ex works (EXW) 130–1
F group 131–2
information
agency and 82
confidential *see* **confidentiality**
see also **data protection; freedom of information**
Information Commissioner
data protection 309, 313
discretion of 313
freedom of information 322
information technology
computer crime
hacking/unauthorised access 285
jurisdiction 287
modification of computer material 286–7
ulterior intent offence 285–6
data protection 287
e-commerce 4
business to business 296
business to consumer 296–301
choice of jurisdiction and law and 115, 293
contract formation 292–3
definition 291
intellectual property and 294–6
jurisdiction 293
legal framework 291–2
legislation 296–301
liability of ISSPs 302–3
payment 301–2
hardware contracts 273
leasing 68–9, 273–4
maintenance 277
negotiation 273
sale 274–6
intellectual property and 271
copyright 222–3, 271–2, 295–6
database right 165, 221–2, 227–30, 287–9
design rights 272
domain names 294
e-commerce 294–6
patents 253, 272
semiconductor chip protection 244, 272–3
trade marks 272, 294–5
information technology – *continued*
internet 283
copyright and 222–3, 224, 284, 295–6
domain names 283–4, 294
intercepting communications 284–5
software
acceptance 279
bespoke 282–3
definition 278
delivery 279
exclusion clauses 280
functional specification 277–8
as goods 13
licensing 278–9, 281–2
maintenance 283
payment 279
source code escrow 281
warranties 279–80
injunctions 12
insolvency of buyer 7, 24
instalments
delivery in 18
insurance
choice of jurisdiction and law and 115
credit risk insurance 33
exclusion clauses and 47
international sale agreements 111, 127
intellectual property 161–6
abuse of dominant position 351–2
administration 164
agency and 82–3
confidential information 164, 166
copyright 163, 165
artistic works 204–11
computer software 216, 222, 271–2
developments in law 224
duration 207–8, 214
e-commerce 295–6
entrepreneurial 211–14
information technology and 222–3
infringement 214–20
meaning 203–4
moral rights 210–11
overlap with design right 243–4
ownership 208–10, 213–14
public performance collecting societies 223
recorded works 207
database right 165, 221–2, 287–9
application 229–30
definition of database 227–8
duration 228, 288
exceptions 229, 288–9
infringement 228–9, 288
ownership 228, 288
qualifications for 228, 288
design right 163
definition 231, 234–5
designs that can be protected 236–7
designs that cannot be protected 236, 240–2
duration 237, 242
EU and 232, 239, 244
exhaustion 238
grace period 235–6

intellectual property – *continued*
- infringement 238, 242–3
- innocent infringement 243
- licences of right 244
- originality 239–40
- overlap with copyright 243–4
- ownership 237–8, 242
- registered 165, 232–3, 234–9, 245
- remedies 238–9, 243
- scope 237
- unregistered 166, 233, 239–44, 245

distributors and 93
e-commerce 294–6
European Union (EU) 347–54
- block exemptions 350–1
- exhaustion of rights 353
- franchising agreements 354
- licensing agreements 348, 349–52
- specific subject matter 352–3

exploitation 347, 348–9
information technology and 271
- copyright 222–3, 271–2, 295–6
- design rights 272
- domain names 294
- e-commerce 294–6
- patents 272
- semiconductor chip protection 244, 272–3
- trade marks 272, 294–5

licensing agreements 94–5
meaning 161–2
passing off *see* **passing off**
patents 163–4, 166
- competition law and 347
- computer software 253, 272
- defences to infringement 260–1
- drafting licensing agreement 351
- EU and 248
- exclusions 252–4
- infringement 257–60
- obtaining patent 247–8
- patentability 248–54
- process 248
- product 248
- remedies 261–2
- specification 254–5, 258–9
- who is entitled to grant 256

public registration 164
summary of rights 165–6
trade marks 162, 165
- becoming generic 188
- classes used in Register 195–201
- collective and certification trade marks 179
- Community Trade Mark 195
- e-commerce 294–5
- foreign 193
- functions 173
- information technology 272
- infringement 188–93
- international 194–5
- Madrid Protocol 195
- misleading 188
- non-use 187–8
- protection after registration 187–8

intellectual property – *continued*
- publication of application 186–7
- reasons to register 173–4
- refusal 176–82, 183–7
- registration process 174–5
- searches 184
- *see also* **passing off**

types 162–4

interest
- extortionate credit bargains 102
- for late payment 21, 33–4

international sale agreements 111, 121–2
- BOLERO system 135
- choice of jurisdiction and law
  - contracting out 115
  - EU regulation 113–16, 118–19
  - first to file 115–16
  - local mandatory rules 117
  - Rome Convention 116–19
- delivery 124
- developments 135
- documents
  - bill of lading 126–7
  - commercial invoices 127
  - container transport 128
  - effect of transfer 127–8
  - insurance policies 111, 127
  - multimodal transport 128
  - road, rail or air transport 128
  - waybills 127
- financing 137–50
  - bills of exchange 138–9, 141–4
  - collection arrangements 138–9
  - documentary credits 144–50
  - example 139–40
  - negotiable instruments 140–1
  - payment methods 138–9
- Incoterms 128–35
  - C group 132–4
  - D group 134–5
  - ex works (EXW) 130–1
  - F group 131–2
- information provision 125
- passing of property 124–5
- passing of risk 125
- responsibilities of parties 124, 125
- stages 122–3
- UNCITRAL 136

international trade marks 194–5

internet 283
- copyright and 222–3, 224, 284, 295–6
- domain names 283–4, 294
- intercepting communications 284–5
- ISSPs
  - business to consumer e-commerce 297–8
  - liability 302–3
- trade marks 192, 294–5
- *see also* **e-commerce**

interpretation 11
- distribution agreements 90
- interpretation clauses 5

invitations to treat 10

invoices
international sale agreements 127
issuing banks 151, 152, 153

joint ventures 95
jurisdiction
choice of
clauses in contract 7
e-commerce 293
EU regulation 113–16, 118–19
habitual residence 119
Rome Convention 116–19
computer crime 287

late payment 21
interest 33–4
lease purchase 67
leases of goods 67
accounts 69
contract 69–70
finance leases 68–9
hardware contracts 68–9, 273–4
operating leases 69
sale of goods contract 70
legal advice
agency agreements 74–5
competition law 331
distribution agreements 89
effect of 45
letters of credit *see* documentary credits
licences
agency and 81
competition law and 349–52
consumer credit business 98
design right 244
drafting agreement 351
IT software 278–9, 281–2
licensing agreements 94–5
lien
seller's 23
limitation of liability 8, 49–50
limitation periods
time bar clauses 53–4
loans
consumer contracts 103–4
loose terminology
avoidance 40

maintenance
IT hardware agreements 277
IT software 283
marketing agreements
agency agreements 73, 74–88
advantages and disadvantages 74
competition law and 75–6
definitions and interpretation 79
distribution agreements compared 90
drafting 75–88
financial provisions 84–5
initial advice 74–5
introduction 79–80
particular points to consider 88
precedents 78
marketing agreements – *continued*
preliminary considerations 75–9
reference to principles of agency law 76–7
rights and duties of agent 81–3
rights and duties of principal 83–4
statutory restrictions 77–8
structure 94
termination 80, 85–8
distribution agreements 73
advantages and disadvantages 74
agency agreements compared 90
appointment of distributor 90–1
competition 90, 93
confidentiality 93
distributor's duties 91–3
drafting 89–94
initial advice 89
intellectual property 93
interpretation 90
introduction 90–1
minimum target obligations 91–2
miscellaneous provisions 94
sale of goods terms 93
stock 92
structure 94
supplier's duties 93
termination 93–4
franchising 95
joint ventures 95
licensing 94–5
markets 4, 45
misrepresentation 11
damages for 26
entire agreement clauses and 6
passing off and 169–71
rescission for 26
mistake 11
mitigation of loss 12
mixed goods
claiming ownership 31–2
moral rights 210–11
morality
refusal of trade mark registration and 182
multimodal transport 128

negotiable instruments 140–1
negotiation 4, 44
hardware contracts 273
no assignment/subcontracting clauses 8
no authority clauses 6–7
no partnership clauses 8
nominated banks 151, 152, 153
non-acceptance of goods 23–4
non-rejection clauses 54
notice
service 7
time of delivery 16–17

offer
acceptance and 10–11
overdrafts 104
ownership
copyright 208–10, 213–14

ownership – *continued*
database right 228, 288
design right 237–8, 242
hire purchase 58
transfer 26–7

Paris Convention 195
parol evidence rule 6
parties to contracts 5
agency agreements 79
bills of exchange 141
distribution agreements 90
relationship between 44–6
partnership
no partnership clauses 8
passing off 162, 165, 167–8, 173, 184
confusion 170–1
damage 171–2
defences 172
e-commerce 294
elements 168–72
goodwill 168–9
international aspects 172
misrepresentation 169–71
remedies 172
passing of property
international sales 124–5
passing of risk *see* risk
patents 163–4, 166
competition law and 347
drafting licensing agreement 351
computer software 253, 272
EU and 248
infringement
defences 260–1
definition 257
infringers 260
interpretation of claims 258–9
judging if infringement has occurred 257–8
remedies 261–2
invalidity 259
obtaining patent 247–8
patentability
exclusions 252–4
industrial application 252
inventive step 250–2
novelty 249–50
process 248
product 248
revocation 259
specification 254–5, 258–9
priority date 255
timescale 255–6
who is entitled to grant 256
Patents Act 1977
text 367–79
payment 15, 27
delivery 17–18
documentary credits 150
duty to pay 20
e-commerce 301–2
IT hardware contracts 274–5
IT software 279

payment – *continued*
late 21, 33–4
time for 20–1
performance of contract 11
perishing of goods 13
permits
agency and 81
pre-payment cards 104
precedents
agency agreements 78
exclusion clauses 37
presenting banks 151
prevail clauses 6, 10
price
action for 23
agreement 14
definition 13–14
exclusion clauses reasonableness and 47
two-tier pricing 46
VAT and 14
see also **payment**
printing 48–9
Privacy and Electronic Communications (EC Directive) Regulations 2003 301
text 445–7
privacy right 268–9
promotion and marketing
agency and 81–2
consumer credit business 98
duties of distributor 92
public interest
refusal of trade mark registration and 182
public performance collecting societies 223

quality
fitness for purpose 19
sale by description 18
sale by sample 20
satisfactory 18–19
trade usage 20

rail transport
international 128
re-sale by seller 23
retention of title and 30
reasonable care and skill
application of 60–1
contract and tort 62
exclusion of liability for 62
implied term 60–2
meaning 60–1
provision of services 60–2
remedies for breach 62
subcontracting and 61–2
reasonableness
allocation of risk and insurance 47
buyer's knowledge and understanding 48–9
choice 46
exclusion clauses 41–2, 43–50
general principles 43–4
price 47
relationship between parties and 44–6
trade associations and 47–8

receivables financing 71–2
Registered Designs Act 1949
text 357–66
rejection of goods 24–5
remedies
breach of contract 12
confidential information 266–8
copyright infringement 221
design right infringement 238–9, 243
infringement of trade marks 194
IT hardware contracts 275–6
passing off 172
patent infringement 261–2
trade mark infringement 194
remitting banks 151, 152
repair of goods 28
replacement of goods 28
repudiation of contract 24
rescission for misrepresentation 26
restricted-use credit 105
retention of title 24, 28–9
backing up 32–4
creation of charges and 32
detachable goods 32
drafting of clause 29–32
entry, seizure and sale rights 30
insolvency of buyer and 7
IT hardware contracts 275
mixed goods 31–2
passing of risk 30
reserving title 29–30
storage of goods 30
tracing proceeds of sale 30–1
risk
allocation of 47
credit risk insurance 33
passing 15, 27, 30, 125, 275
road transport
international 128
Romalpa clauses ***see*** **retention of title**
running-account credit 105

sale of goods
basics of contracts 10–12
buyer's duties 20–2
buyer's rights 24–6
definition 13
delivery 14–15, 274, 279
distribution agreements and 93
effects of contract 26–8
formation of contract 9–10
international *see* **international sale agreements**
IT hardware contracts 274–6
legislation 12
price 13–14
seller's duties 16–20, 275
seller's rights 22–4
sample, sale by 20
satisfactory quality 18–19
seizure rights
retention of title and 30
selective distribution agreements 346
sellers
duties 16–20, 275
not in possession of goods 24
rights 22–4
unpaid 22–3
seller's lien 23
semiconductor chip protection 244, 272–3
services
contracts for provision of 58–63
financial services 59
fitness for purpose 63
reasonable care and skill
application of 60–1
contract and tort 62
exclusion of liability for 62
implied term 60–2
meaning 60–1
remedies for breach 62
subcontracting and 61–2
reasonable price 63
satisfactory quality 63
statutory control 59
subcontracting 61–2
Supply of Goods and Services Act 1982 59–60
time for performance 62
trade marks and 178–9
sight bills 141–2
signature on contracts 10
e-commerce 293
exclusion clauses and 38
software
acceptance 279
bespoke 282–3
definition 278
delivery 279
exclusion clauses 280
functional specification 277–8
as goods 13
licensing 278–9, 281–2
maintenance 283
payment 279
source code escrow 281
warranties 279–80
see also **computer crime**
specific performance 12, 25–6
standard-form contracts 44
stock
agency and 82
distributors and 92
stoppage in transit 23
storage
seller's goods in buyer's possession 30
subcontracting
no subcontracting clauses 8
reasonable care and skill 61–2
subsidiary companies
competition law and 339
system supply contracts 277

term bills 141–2
termination
agency 80, 85–8
consumer credit agreements 102

termination – *continued*
distribution agreements 93–4
third parties
contracts and 11
time bar clauses 53–4
title
passing 16, 275
retention *see* **retention of title**
tracing proceeds of sale 30–1
trade associations
reasonableness of exclusion clauses and 47–8
trade marks 162, 165
becoming generic 188
classes used in Register 195–201
collective and certification trade marks 179
Community Trade Mark 195
distinguishing nature 176
e-commerce 294–5
foreign 193
functions 173
graphic representation 175–6
honest and fair use 193
information technology 192, 272, 294–5
infringement 188–93
defences 193–4
remedies 194
see also **passing off**
international 194–5
Madrid Protocol 195
misleading 188
non-use 187–8
protection after registration 187–8
publication of application 186–7
reasons to register 173–4
refusal 176–82
bad faith 182

trade marks – *continued*
characteristics of the goods 178–9
evidence of use to overcome 182–3
geographical names 179–80
names 177–8
public interest 182
relative grounds 183–7
shape of goods or packaging 180–1
registration process 174–5
searches 184
Trade Marks Act 1994
text 404–14
TRIPS 195

uncertainty in contracts 11
UNCITRAL 136
Universal Copyright Convention 225
unrestricted-use credit 105

value added tax (VAT)
price and 14
vertical agreements
competition law and 342–5

warranties 25
IT software 279–80
waybills 127
websites
acceptance of contract 292
business to consumer e-commerce 296–301
copyright 295–6
e-commerce 292–3, 302–3
trade marks 192, 294–5
see also **information technology**
wholesale finance 70–1
work and materials contracts 58–9
written contracts 11